THE ROUTLEDGE EDUCATION STUDIES READER

The Routledge Education Studies Reader provides an authoritative overview of the key aspects of education for students beyond the introductory stages of a degree programme in Education Studies, enabling students to deepen their understanding.

The *Reader* provides a blend of classic and contemporary readings, based on a combination of empirical research and established theory, and covers the following issues:

- globalisation and the impact of new technologies
- educational policies and society
- curriculum and pedagogy
- assessment
- professional learning
- learning beyond schools.

In order to encourage engagement with the literature, each reading is introduced by the editors. Key questions accompany every reading, enabling the student to reflect on the piece, and suggestions for further reading are made and explained throughout.

The Routledge Education Studies Reader is an essential resource for students of Education Studies, especially during years 2 and 3 of the undergraduate degree. It will prove useful to other students and professionals interested in the study of education.

A companion volume, *The Routledge Education Studies Textbook* by the same editors is an academically wide-ranging and appropriately challenging textbook that has been designed to be used alongside this *Reader*.

James Arthur is Professor of Education and Civic Engagement at the University of Birmingham, UK.

Ian Davies is Professor in Educational Studies at the University of York, UK.

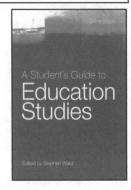

THE ROUTLEDGE EDUCATION STUDIES READER

Edited by
James Arthur and Ian Davies

Routledge
Taylor & Francis Group

LONDON AND NEW YORK

First published 2010
by Routledge
2 Park Square, Milton Park, Abingdon, Oxon OX14 4RN

Simultaneously published in the USA and Canada
by Routledge
270 Madison Ave, New York, NY 10016

Routledge is an imprint of the Taylor & Francis Group, an informa business

© 2010 James Arthur and Ian Davies for editorial material and selection.

Typeset in Times New Roman by Swales & Willis Ltd, Exeter, Devon
Printed and bound in Great Britain by the MPG Books Group

British Library Cataloguing in Publication Data
A catalogue record for this book is available from the British Library

Library of Congress Cataloging-in-Publication Data
The Routledge education studies reader / edited by James Arthur and Ian Davies.
    p. cm.
    Includes bibliographical references and index.
    1. Education—Study and teaching (Higher)—Textbooks. I. Arthur, James, 1957-
    II. Davies, Ian, 1957-
LB17.R674 2009
370.71'1—dc22
2009021907

ISBN10: 0–415–48235–6 (hbk)
ISBN10: 0–415–48236–4 (pbk)

ISBN13: 978–0–415–48235–6 (hbk)
ISBN13: 978–0–415–48236–3 (pbk)

CONTENTS

CONTENTS ■ ■ ■

ACKNOWLEDGEMENTS

1. Disciplines contributing to education? Educational studies and the disciplines *Gary McCulloch* (Disciplines contributing to education? Educational studies and the disciplines, McCulloch, G. Copyright © 2002 Society for Educational Studies (SES). Reproduced with permission of Blackwell Publishing Ltd.)

2. What is an educational process? *R. S. Peters* (From: *The Concept of Education*, R.S. Peters (ed), Copyright 1967, Routledge. Reproduced by permission of Taylor & Francis Books UK.)

3. Learning: Meaning, language and culture *David Carr* (*Making Sense of Education*, D. Carr, Copyright 2003, Routledge. Reproduced by permission of Taylor & Francis Books UK.)

4. Who decides what children learn and how they should learn it? The recent historical experience of the United Kingdom *Roy Lowe* (R. Lowe, 'Who decides what children learn and how they should learn it? The recent historical experience of the United Kingdom' is a chapter taken from *History, Politics and Policy-making in Education: a festschrift presented to Richard Aldrich* by David Crook and Gary McCulloch (eds) (Institute of Education, University of London: 2007) and reproduced with the kind permission of the publisher, Institute of Education Publications www.ioe.ac.uk/publications)).

5. The history of education: Its importance for understanding *Brian Simon* ('The history of education: Its importance for understanding' by Brian Simon in *The State and Educational Change: essays in the history of education and pedagogy*, Brian Simon - Lawrence and Wishart, London 1994, pp. 3–23).

6. Culture, mind and education *Jerome Bruner* ('Culture, mind and education', reprinted by permission of the publisher from *The Culture Of Education* by Jerome Bruner, pp. 1–44, Cambridge, Mass.: Harvard University Press, Copyright © 1996 by the President and Fellows of Harvard College).

7. Explaining socioeconomic inequalities in student achievement: The role of home and school factors *Gary N. Marks, John Cresswell and John Ainley* (Explaining socioeconomic inequalities in student achievement, Gary N. Marks, John Cresswell and John Ainley, *Educational Research and Evaluation*, 2006, Taylor & Francis Ltd, http://www.informaworld.com, reprinted by permission of the publisher.)

8. The effect of childhood segregation on minority academic performance at selective colleges *Douglas S. Massey and Mary J. Fischer* (The effect of childhood segregation on minority academic performance at selective colleges, Douglas S. Massey and Mary J. Fischer, *Ethnic and Racial Studies*, 2006, Taylor & Francis Ltd, http://www.informaworld.com, reprinted by permission of the publisher.)

9. Reclassifying upward mobility: Femininity and the neo-liberal subject *Valerie Walkerdine* (Reclassifying upward mobility: Femininity and the neo-liberal subject, Valerie Walkerdine, *Gender and Education*, 2003, Taylor & Francis Ltd, http://www.informaworld.com, reprinted by permission of the publisher.)

10. Certifying the workforce: Economic imperative or failed social policy? *Alison Wolf, Andrew Jenkins and Anna Vignoles* (Certifying the workforce: Economic imperative or failed social policy?, Alison Wolf, Andrew Jenkins and Anna Vignoles, *Journal of Education Policy*, 2006, Taylor & Francis Ltd, http://www.informaworld.com, reprinted by permission of the publisher.)

11. Education as a social function *John Dewey* (Reprinted with the permission of Scribner, a Division of Simon & Schuster, Inc., from *Democracy and Education* by John Dewey. Copyright © 1916 by The Macmillan Company. Copyright renewed © 1944 by John Dewey. All rights reserved.)

12. Curriculum reform and curriculum theory: A case of historical amnesia *Ivor F. Goodson* (Goodson, I., *Studying Curriculum*, © 1994, Reproduced with the kind permission of Open University Press. All rights reserved.)

13. The common strands of pedagogy and their implications *Judith Ireson, Peter Mortimore and Susan Hallam* (Reproduced by permission of SAGE Publications, London, Los Angeles, New Delhi and Singapore, from P. Mortimore (ed), *Understanding Pedagogy and Its Impact on Learning*, Copyright (© Sage Publications, 1999))

14. Beyond testing: Towards a theory of educational assessment *Caroline Gipps* (*Beyond testing: towards a theory of educational assessment*, C. V. Gipps, Copyright 1994, Routledge. Reproduced by permission of Taylor & Francis Books UK.)

15. From technical rationality to reflection-in-action *Donald A. Schön* (From *The Reflective Practitioner* by Donald Schön (Copyright © 1983 by Basic Books, Inc.) Reprinted by permission of BASIC BOOKS, a member of Perseus Books Group).

16. Why we must disestablish school *Ivan D. Illich* (Marion Boyars Publishers 1971 (London and New York))

17. Social networking as an educational tool *Robin Mason and Frank Rennie* (From: *e-Learning and Social Networking Handbook*, Robin Mason and Frank Rennie, Copyright 2008, Routledge. Reproduced by permission of Taylor & Francis Books UK.)

18. Rethinking education *James Tooley* (James Tooley, *Reclaiming Education*, Continuum, 2000. By kind permission of Continuum International Publishing Group.)

19. Measuring Catholic school performance *James Arthur* (*Faith Schools: consensus or conflict?*, Roy Gardner, Jo Cairns and Denis Lawton (eds), Copyright 2005, Routledge. Reproduced by permission of Taylor & Francis Books UK.)

20. How children fail *John Holt* (*How Children Fail* by John Holt (Copyright © John Holt, 1964) Reprinted by permission of A.M. Heath & Co Ltd.)

21. What is evidence-based education? *Philip Davies* (What is evidence-based education?, Davies, P. Copyright © 1999 Society for Educational Studies (SES). Reproduced with permission of Blackwell Publishing Ltd.)

22. Towards a judgement-based statistical analysis *Stephen Gorard* (Towards a judgement-based statistical analysis, Stephen Gorard, *British Journal of Sociology of Education*, 2006, Taylor & Francis Ltd, http://www.informaworld.com, reprinted by permission of the publisher.)

23. The obviousness of social and educational research results *N. L. Gage* (N. L. Gage, *Educational Researcher* (20, 1), pp. 10–16, copyright © 1991 by Sage, Publications, Reprinted by Permission of SAGE Publications.)

ACKNOWLEDGEMENTS ■ ■ ■

We gratefully acknowledge the contributions of very many colleagues in the UK and elsewhere who have suggested material to include in this Reader. There are too many people who have contributed suggestions for this publication for individual names to be highlighted. But all those people deserve our thanks. Many made suggestions directly and immediately in relation to this publication and, even more, offered advice more circuitously over a very long period of time about what topics and what specific articles, books and other material really matter.

We are grateful to Anna Clarkson who supported the project throughout. We are particularly indebted to Emma Joyes who collaborated with us very positively and made very many essential contributions.

We also acknowledge a great deal of personal support from very many people. Ian Davies would particularly like to thank Lynn, Hannah, Rachael and Matthew Davies.

INTRODUCTION

James Arthur and Ian Davies

This *Reader* contains material that will help develop understandings of:

- The key concepts that are centrally relevant to an understanding of education
- Significant contexts within which education is enacted
- The ways in which education is investigated.

The *Reader* complements *The Routledge Education Studies Textbook*. As it contains a wide variety of material published at different times, covering many different topics and written from numerous perspectives it will be of interest to many readers. We hope that teachers, academics, policy-makers and others will have some interest in reading or re-reading the material that is presented here. But our principal audience is those students, primarily in years 2 and 3 of their 3-year programme, who are reading Education under-graduate degrees. We have chosen material that is accessible, but is not obviously intro-ductory. Of course, we accept that material can be – and should be – read by people at many different points in an academic programme and we would not wish to be exclusive. In making our selection, however, we had in mind an undergraduate who is already familiar with some of the ideas and issues about education and who wants to move on to the next stage.

We have already, in *The Routledge Education Studies Textbook*, made some com-ments about the nature and purpose of undergraduate degrees in education and will not repeat that here. Nevertheless, the growth of those programmes, the significance of the issues that they raise and the many individual career outcomes that are experienced by grad-uates led us to avoid a narrow selection of articles and chapters. We wanted something that would stimulate this varied group of students to continue asking questions and developing provisional answers about some of the major issues that affect and characterise education.

The following are some of the ideas behind our selection of material:

- The three-part structure of the *Reader*: fundamental educational ideas; educational contexts; and educational research.

It is probably impossible to define or characterise education in a simple and final manner and this means that any attempt to include material that covers all aspects of education is unlikely to succeed. That said, there is, of course, a benchmark statement for education studies (see http://www.qaa.ac.uk/academicinfrastructure/benchmark/honours/Educa-tion07.asp, accessed 23 February 2009) which is a vital point of reference for staff and stu-dents at many universities and other higher education institutions in the UK. Beyond this sort of official characterisation (that may be used thoughtfully and usefully to explore the meaning of education, or narrowly in rather mechanistic ways to consider what must be included to satisfy inspectors and examiners), there are very many individual and group perspectives that are put forward. We have not simply inserted into this *Reader* what would have been a rather personal and idiosyncratic selection of our favourite pieces – that would have been too self-indulgent. But although we consulted widely with colleagues about what sort of material should be included, this particular selection is distinct and we recognise that it would have been possible to make other choices.

Our selection of material is based on the idea that there is a need to consider three broad areas: the fundamental ideas that tell us what education is; the contexts or places in which education takes place; and the ways in which education may be explored through research. Of course, these three dimensions overlap. Educational researchers, for example, are exploring fundamental ideas in specific contexts. But for the purposes of managing the material and organising our ideas we wanted in the first section of the *Reader* to have some pieces of writing about the nature of education studies and then to encourage readers to explore these from the perspective of the traditional four disciplines: history, philosophy, psychology and sociology. It seemed convenient to finish Section 1 with a consideration of class, 'race', and sex, almost as if this material would provide a bridge to Section 2 that deals with contexts within which education takes place.

Those contexts that are explored in Section 2 are deliberately rather eclectic. We want to recognise the broad issues to do with enacting education in society and so we begin with something about policy and move through matters to do with curriculum and pedagogy, assessment, professional learning in schools and elsewhere. Importantly, we did not want to suggest that a focus on context could indicate that we were dealing with rather simple issues of implementation. Throughout we have chosen pieces in which the authors are making an argument for a particular way of looking at the world and this is perhaps most explicitly noticeable in the case of the material on private education, faith-based education and freedom and education. Context in this sense is not a location, but a perspective.

Section 3 includes material that explains and, perhaps, provokes. Research is not conducted in tranquil settings by intellectuals who seek some sort of lofty disinterestedness. Rather, it is fiercely argued about. Conflicting ideas about the purpose and nature of 'good' research are partly a simple and rather unedifying spectacle of academics competing for funding or for promoting their own particular view of the world for their own ends. But for the majority, research is understood as one way better to understand and improve the world. The varied reasons for doing research, the ways in which it could and should be conducted and the relationship between it and what actually happens to students and teachers within and beyond educational institutions is vitally important.

■ The inclusion of different types of material.

Within the three-section structure referred to above we have included many different types of material. We thought for a long time about including extracts from classic education texts – Plato's *Republic*, Rousseau's *Emile* and so on. There are many benefits from developing a familiarity with – and understanding of – such work and, in arguing about whether or not they deserve to be regarded as 'classic'. We eventually decided that it would be very difficult to include a sufficiency of this material to give a proper sense of the meaning of the text. We wished to avoid a simplistic series of supposedly key quotations from the 'great' books. To some extent, this attempt to allow readers to develop an in-depth understanding of the work of our authors led us to include many journal articles and book chapters. We have tried not to meddle too much with what was published although, almost inevitably, we have excised some material. Within the material that has been included we have tried to include a range in which most of the pieces are fairly recent (education is a contemporary business). We have included work by Bruner, Dewey, and Holt as well as a reasonable weight of material from the 21st century. As such, we have gone some way towards what a colleague of ours used to advise when teaching students of undergraduate education studies: "draw their attention to the 'classic' and the 'hot' and make sure you avoid the merely out of date". The blend that we have provided is intended to engage students in what is hugely significant contemporary matter with at least an opportunity for achieving some critical distance on current passions.

■   The encouragement of critical reading.

We have shaped the Readings that we have selected in ways that are intended to encourage critical reading. We would not be at all pleased if students saw this *Reader* as containing material that they had to remember, as if it has some sort of magical significance. We do not pretend that we agree with everything that our authors have written, but we do respect their work and feel that they have something of value for educational communities. What they have to offer can be best achieved through careful consideration and reflection, rather than simple acceptance.

We wanted to provide the basis for a proper understanding of the readings and so have given brief introductory statements about the work of the authors. We hope that we have not written these statements in a way that is inaccurate or otherwise inappropriate. There are many dangers in providing such external descriptions and, of course, many of the authors themselves would be much better placed to say who they are and what they have done. More widely, there is the potential problem that attempts to describe and summarise in such ways are simply inappropriate. We certainly wish to avoid simple descriptions that inappropriately imply links between the work of authors and their biographies or their imagined ideological commitments. We have tried to avoid those excesses in the interests of 'locating' the work of our chosen authors. We have also provided suggestions for Further Reading and posed a number of questions. In this way, we want to encourage the readers' engagement and further thinking and work. The material included here will work well if it is seen as a springboard to further exploration, greater understandings and intelligent participation in the development of education.

DISCIPLINES CONTRIBUTING TO EDUCATION?

Educational studies and the disciplines

Gary McCulloch

INTRODUCTION

Gary McCulloch is Brian Simon Professor of the History of Education at the Institute of Education, University of London and is widely regarded as one of Britain's most important historians of education. He has written widely and extensively in the field and in this article, he examines the contribution that different disciplinary approaches have made to educational studies in the last 50 years. We feel that the article is important because it places the establishment of the so-called 'foundation disciplines' of education within their historical context and traces their development. The article also offers an analysis and assessment of educational studies in this period which helps us to understand and attempt to address the changing nature of studying education today. Not all educationalists would agree with McCulloch's conclusion that the 'foundation disciplines' of history, philosophy, psychology and sociology within educational studies have survived in difficult times and remain as entrenched communities of knowledge. The article introduces the background to an important debate about the future content and methodologies of educational studies.

KEY QUESTIONS

1. The so-called 'foundation disciplines' of history, philosophy, psychology and sociology are often perceived as being remote from educational practice so are they still relevant to the study of education?
2. McCulloch refers to 'a pluralistic and eclectic approach' to the study of education – what does this mean in practice for the student of education?

FURTHER READING

One of the best readings on this theme is contained within the special edition of the *British Journal of Educational Studies* (Vol. 50 No. 1, March 2002) entitled 'Educational studies in Britain

1952–2002'. McCulloch's own article is drawn from this collection of seven articles which address the evolution of educational studies as a field of enquiry in Britain and raises a series of questions for contemporary consideration. Another issue of the same journal (Vol. 30 No. 1) from 1982 specifically addresses and surveys the foundation disciplines of educational studies and is therefore worth reading as background to the current debate in which McCulloch situates his article.

This Reading links with Chapters 1, 2, 3, 4, 5, 7 and 11 of *The Routledge Education Studies Textbook.*

INTRODUCTION

In his inaugural lecture as professor of the philosophy of education at the Institute of Education, London, in 1963, Richard Peters insisted that 'education is not an autonomous discipline, but a field, like politics, where the disciplines of history, philosophy, psychology, and sociology have application' (Peters, 1963/1980, p. 273). This conviction reflected a conscious reaction against what Peters described as the 'undifferentiated mush' of educational theory, which in his view had 'contributed so much to the low standing of the study of education in this country'. The current article will explore some of the approaches that were developed by exponents of each of these four key disciplines, history, philosophy, psychology and sociology, in terms of the characteristic content, interests and methodologies that they involved. It will also trace the attempts that have been made on behalf of the disciplines from the 1970s onwards to maintain a central and distinct role in educational studies, notwithstanding the many challenges to their position that emerged over this period. It will conclude with an assessment of the general significance of such 'differentiated' work for the development of educational studies over the past 50 years and in the future.

The developing role of disciplinary perspectives on education has had a vital bearing on the nature of educational studies in Britain over the past 50 years. In particular, it tended to suggest that educational studies should be regarded principally as the application of a range of approaches borrowed from the disciplines, rather than as a single discipline. The rise of a more unitary notion described as 'educational research' from the 1970s onwards, on the other hand, promoted the view that education was a distinctive and specialised area of study in its own right, and therefore challenged the primacy of the disciplines of philosophy, history, sociology and psychology. For example, Michael Bassey, executive secretary of the British Educational Research Association (BERA), sought to distinguish between educational research, which he defined as 'critical enquiry aimed at informing educational judgements and decisions in order to improve educational action', and disciplinary research conducted in educational settings, which 'aims critically to inform understandings of phenomena pertinent to the discipline in educational settings' (Bassey, 1999, p. 39). On this somewhat rigid distinction, a dependence on the disciplines could be seen not only as unduly theoretical and tenuous in its connections with educational concerns, but as restrictive in holding back the growth of an independent field of inquiry. This article will assess the contrary claims put forward on behalf of disciplinary studies over this period, that a grounding in the disciplines was essential as a means of understanding educational theories and practices.

In some ways, as Peters suggested in his inaugural address of 1963, an especially instructive parallel can be drawn with the field of politics. Here, too, there has been a continuing debate between those who have perceived the field as a single discipline, and those who have emphasised the way in which it borrows from a range of different disciplines (see for example Almond, 1991; Goodin and Klingemann, 1996). Gamble points out that on the one hand there are proponents of a political science that involves acceptance of a single core of evidence, theories and methods, one that will refine itself and become cumulative over time. On the other hand, according to Gamble:

> The alternative view places the subject before the methodology. The study of politics is eclectic because it draws on different disciplines – philosophy, history, economics, law and sociology. The choice is dictated by what is most appropriate to understand the subject matter. Such a study is necessarily pluralist and fragmented rather than unified around a single methodological or theoretical core. (Gamble, 2001)

As Gamble also points out, moreover, 'Ultimately, these are not simply intellectual questions but questions of power . . . the attempt to define the discipline in such a way that other approaches are excluded, which affects who gets published, who gets appointed and who gets promoted' (Gamble, 2001). The debate over disciplinary studies in education may be addressed in a similar fashion, in terms of a conflict between a pluralist, eclectic outlook conveyed as 'educational studies' in which the disciplines are pre-eminent, and a quasi-scientific approach expressed as 'educational research' in which the disciplines are relegated to the margins.

Another framework for addressing the issues involved relates to the notion of a 'discipline' itself. This may be defined, following King and Brownell (1966, p. 68), not simply as an area of study or of knowledge, but as a community of scholars who share a domain of intellectual inquiry or discourse. This commonly involves a shared heritage and tradition, a specialised language or other system of shared symbols, a set of shared concepts, an infrastructure of books, articles and research reports, a system of communication among the membership, and a means of instruction and initiation. It is therefore concerned with teaching as well as research, and with a specific audience or constituency. It is also a dynamic as opposed to a static group, often a coalition of contested views and priorities (see also for example Goodson, 1983, on 'subject coalitions'). On this general basis, in beginning to trace and assess the disciplinary studies of education, we may emphasise the nature of the books, articles and reports that have been published in each area. Nevertheless, it is also fundamental to such a study to note the kinds of community that each of the disciplines has generated, especially in the form of societies, journals and conferences. Such institutions have often been the most prominent manifestations of the educational disciplines, as well as the natural home of their adherents. They are the discipline rendered tangible and visible; they represent thought and ideas turned into personal and collegial interaction. They thus make it possible to discuss the history of educational studies not simply in terms of intellectual history, but also as a form of social history.

Conceived in these terms, the general argument of this article is that the history of disciplinary studies in education over the past half-century should not be read in simple terms as one of a rise to prominence followed by a fall from grace. There is a subtly different story to be told than of a straightforward 'rise and fall', first about the establishment of the disciplines in educational studies over the first half of the period, and then about their consolidation, survival and adaptation in a rapidly changing educational and political context.

ESTABLISHING THE DISCIPLINES, 1952–77

The educational disciplines became established in Britain in two principal ways during the first quarter-century of our period. In one sense, they were established separately, as distinct and discrete disciplinary communities, each with their own endeavours and priorities, and each with their own bases in research and teaching. To be more accurate, it was the disciplines of philosophy and history that were especially prominent in their development in the 1950s and 1960s, since psychology was already a dominant influence before the 1950s, and sociology was less clearly formed as a distinct community until the 1970s and 1980s. Nevertheless, in broad terms these 'four disciplines' all staked a claim to be the key to understanding educational theory and practice during this time. They all involved specialisation in a particular mode of analysis, demanded a specific form of expertise, and claimed their own unique inheritance of a tradition of knowledge and values. Equally, they were dedicated to following the intellectual currents of their 'parent' disciplines practised broadly across the universities, often to the extent of being subordinated to them. At various times there were other specialisms that emerged to make similar claims, such as comparative education and the economics of education, but it was these four disciplines in particular that became entrenched in tangible and institutional form.

In another sense, the disciplines were established together, as complementary approaches to the study of education. It was the combination of their different forms of expertise that was taken to be the most effective means of addressing the problems and processes of education. The disciplines thereby signalled a pluralist vision of educational studies that sought to draw on a wide range of human knowledge and experience. This vision was especially evident in educational discourse from the creation of the *British Journal of Educational Studies* (*BJES*), in 1952, until the launching of the self-styled 'Great Debate' on education by the Labour Prime Minister James Callaghan in October 1976.

The *BJES* originated from a conference held on 19 December 1951, attended by professors of education and directors of institutes of education from England, Scotland, Wales and Northern Ireland. The aim of the conference was to discuss the 'problems raised by the growth of educational research' over the previous few decades (*BJES*, 1952, p. 67). As was noted in the first issue of the *BJES*, 'It is generally felt that British studies in the various fields of education – philosophical, historical, social, psychological and pedagogic – need to be better organised and better known.' (*BJES*, 1952, p. 67). This rationale, rooted in an awareness of the separate disciplines of study, underlay the formation of new institutions designed to further the cause of educational studies. To this end, the Standing Conference on Studies in Education was formed, chaired by Professor W.R. Niblett of the University of Leeds, and with Professor J.W. Tibble of University College, Leicester, as its first secretary. There were 74 members of the Standing Conference, 55 representing English institutions, 11 Scottish, 5 Welsh, one from Northern Ireland, and two from elsewhere (*BJES*, 1952, pp. 191–2). The *Journal* itself, to be edited by A.C.F. Beales of Kings College, London, was conceived as a means of communicating new research in a range of areas. It was suggested that since psychology was already well catered for in the journals of the British Psychological Society, the *BJES* would be mainly concerned with other aspects of the study of education. On the other hand, it would not be 'narrowly specialist', but was 'concerned to serve the needs and interests of everyone concerned with education whom the implications of specialised research affect'. Its 'broad objects' would be 'to explain the significance of new thought, to provide philosophical discussion at a high level, and to deepen existing interest in the purposes and problems of current educational policy' (*BJES*, 1952, p. 67). These objects were to be approached through specialised study rooted in the separate disciplines.

The contents of the first issue in the initial volume of the *BJES* vividly reflect these disciplinary aims. It included detailed studies based in philosophy, history and sociology. The author of the first article in the inaugural issue of the *Journal*, most fittingly, was Louis Arnaud Reid, who held the chair in the philosophy of education at the Institute of Education, University of London, which had been established in 1947. The establishment of this chair was itself a significant development in the disciplinary study of education. Chairs had already been established at the Institute of Education in educational psychology, history of education, and comparative education and, under G.B. Jeffrey as director of the Institute, separate chairs in the philosophy of education and in sociology of education were also created. Reid was himself a widely respected philosopher who had published work on ethics, the philosophy of religion, and aesthetics (Hirst, 1998, p. 3). In his *BJES* article, entitled 'Education and the map of knowledge', Reid engaged in a scholarly discussion of the nature of knowledge, albeit with little reference to education. In the final paragraph of the paper, he confessed that he would not attempt to work out the implications of the tangled complex of knowledge for lifelong education, but insisted nevertheless that 'our view of the "size" of knowledge will affect much, perhaps all, of what we do and think in education' (Reid, 1952, p. 16). A further notable characteristic of his paper was that it included no references at all, despite drawing on ideas and direct quotations from a wide range of sources including Basil Willey, Bertrand Russell, and Wordsworth. Other quotations are given without any clear attribution. The implication is that even the most esoteric sources will already be well known to readers, and therefore require no elaboration. While discussing very broad issues, therefore, the paper is addressed principally to a smaller disciplinary community.

The second paper included in the first issue of the *BJES* was a specialised historical survey of the origins of mechanics' institutes by Thomas Kelly, director of extra-mural studies at the University of Liverpool. According to Kelly, the origins of the mechanics' institute movement had continuing significance because although they generally failed in their principal objective to provide manual workers with instruction in scientific principles, they were influential among a broader range of social groups, and 'in its disintegration it laid the foundations of our modern system of technical education and, in no small degree, of our public library system' (Kelly, 1952, p. 17). Thus Kelly's concern was to rescue the heritage of contemporary education from its prevailing obscurity. His paper investigated the underlying social factors in the spread of the institutes, their local manifestations and the contribution of the pioneers of the movement such as John Anderson and George Birkbeck. Again, then, there was both a general and a particular intent involved in the publication of this paper. In general, it sought to help establish a historical foundation for the continuing work of educators, not only in schools but also in many other kinds of educational institution. At the same time, it asserted a role for detailed analysis of historical documents in the understanding of education, based in the study of published and unpublished primary source material.

A further contribution to this first issue of the *BJES,* by W.A.C. Stewart, professor of education at the University College of North Staffordshire, was a study of the role of Karl Mannheim in the sociology of education. Mannheim had been appointed to the newly created chair in the sociology of education at the Institute of Education, London, in 1946, but died the following year. Stewart set out to explain the nature of Mannheim's thought as it was expressed in his published work, and the significance of his approach for the development of the sociology of education. Stewart emphasised Mannheim's concern to understand education in terms of 'sociological analysis of what is being and ought to be done now in a democratic society at a stage of crisis in its existence' (Stewart, 1952, p. 107). Furthermore, according to Stewart, Mannheim's notion of the study of education was one of a social science that involved 'a synoptic study for pursuing which data could be collected and collated from many different fields' (Stewart, 1952, p. 112). To these ends, Stewart proposed:

> Just as the Modern Greats School at Oxford had to work out the content and relationship of the studies involved, so too Education, from the sociological point of view, would have to show how aspects of history, philosophy, anthropology,

> economics, political theory, aesthetics and pedagogy could be brought into some synthesis, or, in another fashionable word, could form some discipline. (Stewart, 1952, p. 112)

Stewart's paper therefore culminated in a celebration of the role of the disciplines in the study of education, a role in which sociology would play a leading part. Nor, surely, was it an accident that Stewart enlisted Karl Mannheim to this cause. Mannheim's published work established a disciplinary heritage, an inspiration and source for continued sociological work. In the same way, his briefly attained position at the Institute of Education signalled the success of the sociology of education in establishing itself at the highest levels. Mannheim was henceforward revered as a totemic figure, a symbol for those who related to sociology not only as a key approach to the study of education, but as the basis for a disciplinary community in its own right.

Over the following decade, the disciplinary approach was successfully established as the dominant mode of educational study, forming the basis of a range of new research and also of teaching in many institutions of higher education around the UK. History and philosophy were the most active of the disciplines, and thus established an opposite pole based in the humanities to the quasi-scientific approach that was already established in educational psychology. W.H.G. Armytage, professor of education at the University of Sheffield, went so far as to suggest in his inaugural address that university education departments should be a unique focus for the reconciliation of the arts and sciences; as a historian himself, he was at pains to add that such a synoptic study was most effectively achieved through the study of history (Armytage, 1954/1980). A decade later, another leading historian, Brian Simon, also perceived a new purpose for university schools of education in the cultivation of the disciplines, partly for their separate contributions but also for what they could achieve collectively. According to Simon:

> Disciplines, as they come into being and develop, do not merely lay claim to territory and fence it around. Each may cultivate a particular field in a particular way, but there remains an essential interdependence, and as all continue to develop these interrelationships become more complex. (Simon, 1966/1980, p. 90)

In developing this interdependence or 'fruitful cooperation', in which 'no one lays down the laws but everyone rubs off corners' (p. 91), Simon suggested that the disciplines would come to have different concerns in their application to education than they did in their natural habitats. For example, history and philosophy should not be regarded as mutually exclusive, but should join together in the common cause of addressing the problems of education. This in turn would involve 'a conscious cultivation of interrelations and at all levels', akin to the historical process through which 'an Anglo-Saxon country, invaded in turn by Danes and Normans, triumphantly emerged from the process as English' (p. 91).

The challenge of establishing disciplines that would be both distinctive in their approaches yet also interdependent in their contributions to educational studies yielded fruit in the 1960s and early 1970s in a number of tangible ways. Their interdependence was fostered in a number of published works intended for students of education, and also in the rise of the new area of curriculum studies. At the same time, stimulated by a rapid expansion in initial teacher education and the teaching opportunities that this presented, separate and distinct disciplinary communities became consolidated. This process was marked by the creation of new journals, conferences and associations dedicated to the promotion of teaching and research in these specific domains.

Probably the best known published work of the period to promote a disciplinary approach to educational studies was *The Study of Education,* edited by the former secretary of the Standing Conference, J.W. Tibble. It was produced as an introduction to an ambitious venture entitled the Students Library of Education, published by Routledge and Kegan Paul. Tibble's edited collection was intended to explore the nature of education as a subject of study, and the nature of its contributory disciplines (Tibble, 1966). The Students Library of Education itself was an imposing monument to disciplinary studies. The editorial board, chaired by Tibble, was composed of representatives of the four disciplines: Ben Morris of the University of Bristol for psychology, Richard Peters of the Institute of Education in London for philosophy, Brian Simon for history, and William Taylor of the University of Bristol for sociology. It was intended that the Library should consist of a series of basic books, each of 25,000 to 30,000 words in length, and available for students in paperbacked editions. Some, as Tibble noted, would illustrate the separate contributions of the different disciplines to the study of education, while others would deal with a major educational topic in an interdisciplinary way, 'showing the contributions which different forms of thought can make to it' (Tibble, 1966, p. vii). The early contributions to the series, moreover, were categorised for ease of reference into disciplinary sections. Works by Armytage, Bernbaum, Eaglesham, Lawson and Seaborne, for example, were included in the historical section; Dearden, Peters and Wilson contributed books in the philosophy section; Pidgeon and Yates, Richardson and Beard produced works for the psychology section; while Eggleston, Bantock and Hoyle each produced books for the sociology section.

Tibble repeated his winning formula with a further edited collection introducing the study of education based on the disciplines, specifically addressed to intending teachers (Tibble, 1971a). He was confident as to the value of this chosen approach in terms of understanding education, and insisted:

> It is clear that 'education' is a field subject, not a basic discipline; there is no distinctively 'educational' way of thinking; in studying education one is using psychological or historical or sociological or philosophical ways of thinking to throw light on some problem in the field of human learning. (Tibble, 1971b, p. 16)

In this volume, D.G. Watts, senior counsellor at the Open University, was responsible for a survey of educational psychology, while Anne Dufton of Ulster College, Belfast, reviewed the sociology of education, Malcolm Seaborne of the University of Leicester explored the history of education, and R.F. Dearden of the Institute of Education discussed the philosophy of education. Each of these papers again emphasised the distinctive values and traditions of the specific discipline being treated, no less than the complementary nature of their collective contribution to the study of education.

This dominant set of assumptions was strengthened further in the late 1960s and early 1970s through the rise of 'curriculum studies' as an approach to educational studies. This area was stimulated by the development of curriculum initiatives and especially the activities of the new Schools Council for the Curriculum and Examinations, which were expected to transform the character of the school curriculum. Curriculum studies was a means of evaluating the success of these new initiatives and of understanding them in their broader context. The *Journal of Curriculum Studies*, first published in 1968, was concerned with issues such as 'How does the curriculum change? What is the nature of curriculum evaluation? How is the curriculum related to teaching and what kind of statements give an inner consistency to discussion about the curriculum?' (*Journal of Curriculum Studies*, 1969).

Curriculum studies as an area was deeply imbued with a disciplinary outlook, reflected for example in the ideas of John F. Kerr, professor of education at the University of Leicester. In his inaugural lecture, 'The problem of curriculum reform', presented in January 1967, Kerr sought to encourage broader attention to issues of curriculum change. He was confident (unduly so in retrospect) as to the prospects of the new curriculum initiatives: 'At the practical and organisational levels, the new curricula promise to revolutionise English education' (Kerr, 1968a, p. 15). Nevertheless, he was concerned that those involved in such initiatives were basing their decisions principally upon experience and personal judgements, and called for more research and evaluation in order to build into the process a more coherent theoretical framework. Kerr argued that philosophy, psychology, sociology and history, in cooperation with each other, could make a major contribution towards this end. He also proposed that practising educationists should be able to consult specialists in the disciplines for advice about particular problems 'in the same way as the medical profession calls upon physiologists, biochemists, bacteriologists and so on' (Kerr, 1968a, p. 36). This view suggested the promotion of a closer affinity between 'practice' in the training and everyday work of teachers, and the 'theory' embodied in the disciplines.

Kerr pursued this theme further through a series of public lectures arranged during spring 1967 at the University of Leicester. These were intended to draw attention to the contribution that the separate disciplines might make to curriculum planning and development. The lectures dealt respectively with the contribution of philosophy to the study of the curriculum (by Paul Hirst of King's College, London), the contribution of history (by Kenneth Charlton of the University of Birmingham), the contribution of psychology (by Philip Taylor of the University of Birmingham), and the contribution of sociology (by Frank Musgrove of the University of Bradford). In published form (Kerr, 1968b), this set of essays is markedly similar in its organisation to Tibble's edited collections. Hirst's paper emphasised the ways in which philosophy of education could have a beneficial influence on 'what goes on in the classroom', although he noted that further 'hard analytical work' was needed for this to be achieved properly or fully (Hirst, 1968, p. 61). He acknowledged that it would be difficult for most teachers and educationists to understand philosophical issues, but concluded rather condescendingly, *de haul en bas*, 'I hope I have succeeded in making you just a little more aware than you were of the distinctive and important role philosophers have to play in this matter' (Hirst, 1968, p. 61). Hirst thus made an explicit distinction between two types of audience: members of the disciplinary community of the philosophy of education, and teachers and educationists in general. Charlton's paper on the contribution of history also emphasised distinctive disciplinary claims, first in terms of the structural disciplines of historical investigation, and second in terms of drawing on the content of history, 'not to provide particular and concrete answers or solutions to current problems, but to make us aware of the possibility of change, of the complexity of change, and of the carry over of the past into our present situation and future aspirations' (Charlton, 1968, p. 77). Similarly, Taylor pointed out that psychological theories and constructs could be useful for studying the curriculum, but should still be regarded as belonging to psychology, rather than to education (Taylor, 1968, p. 92). Musgrove, for his part, was at pains to show that the evaluation of curricula from the point of view of social objectives should be guided by 'sophisticated sociological theory' (Musgrove, 1968, p. 109). Each of these contributions, then, was anxious to avow its theoretical base in the parent discipline at the same time that it asserted its practical relevance to education.

The role of curriculum studies in sustaining the disciplines was carried further by Denis Lawton of the Institute of Education in London. As he noted in his inaugural lecture, delivered in 1978, the Institute of Education established a Department of Curriculum Studies in 1972 partly because it was felt that 'curriculum, perhaps even more than other educational issues, needed to be studied simultaneously from the viewpoints of several educational disciplines' (Lawton, 1978/1980, p. 306). In his own work, Lawton was highly effective in channelling a combination of these disciplinary viewpoints towards the study of the curriculum. For example, Lawton's first major work, published in 1973, set out the contribution of philosophical, sociological, psychological, and historical issues in defining the curriculum as a 'selection from the culture of a society' (Lawton, 1973, p. 9), in a way that was designed to be helpful for teachers.

Lawrence Stenhouse, director of the Schools Council Humanities Curriculum Project and then of the Centre for Applied Research in Education (CARE) at the University of East Anglia, expressed similar concerns. According to Stenhouse, the teaching of education as an undifferentiated field had been 'largely supplanted' by the teaching of constituent disciplines, especially in his view philosophy, psychology and sociology. This change, he argued, had increased the 'rigour' and the 'intellectual tone' of education courses, but had done little for 'their relevance to the problem of improving the practice of teaching'. He proposed the further development of curriculum studies as a means of building on the disciplines to foster a close study of curriculum and teaching that would be relevant to practice in the schools (Stenhouse, 1975, p. vii).

Nevertheless, while the disciplines were continuing to establish their complementary claims in relation to the general study of education, they were also entrenching their separate disciplinary identities. This was reflected especially in the philosophy of education and in the history of education in terms of collegial activities that led to the formation of new journals and societies in these areas. In 1965, the philosophy of education consolidated an avowedly analytical approach, derived especially from the so-called 'London school' led by Hirst and Peters, through the creation of the Philosophy of Education Society of Great Britain. This soon generated its own published proceedings, which in turn became the *Journal of Philosophy of Education.* Meanwhile, the history of education was represented formally through the establishment of the History of Education Society in 1967, leading again to regular newsletters and conferences as distinguishing marks of the disciplinary community. A new journal, the *Journal of Educational Administration and History*, was formed in 1968, based at the University of Leeds. The new Society established its own journal, entitled simply *History of Education*, from 1972. In common with philosophers of education, historians of education tended in the main to style themselves according to current trends in their parent discipline. It was notable that the leading social historian Asa Briggs was invited to contribute the first article in *History of Education,* and the paramount intention was evident from his very first sentence which ran thus: 'The study of the history of education is best considered as part of the wider study of the history of society, social history with the politics, economics and, it is necessary to add, the religion put in' (Briggs, 1972, p. 160; see also Richardson (1999) for a detailed discussion of the formation of the History of Education Society, and McCulloch and Richardson (2000) on long-term trends in the history of education).

By the mid-1970s, then, the disciplines were well established, both in terms of their general rationale for contributing to the study of education as a whole, and also increasingly as clearly defined and discrete disciplinary communities in their own right. They aligned themselves closely in a theoretical sense to a 'mainstream' disciplinary culture. Nevertheless they were concerned to assert and foster their relevance to practical issues in teaching and curriculum, with particular success in the emergence of curriculum studies.

SURVIVAL OF THE DISCIPLINES, 1977–2002

If the disciplines became established in the period 1952–77, it has become commonplace to emphasise their decline since that time. Simon, for example, notes that their 'hegemony' was 'certainly broken in the fields of teaching, research and published scholarly studies' (Simon, 1994, p. 144). From the Great Debate onwards, education came under increasing scrutiny to be more accountable to current social and economic demands, leading to a growing emphasis on 'practical' approaches at the expense of 'theory'. This general trend was reflected both in courses in education, for teacher training and continuing professional development, and in research. At the same time, 'educational research' was increasingly advanced as a unitary and autonomous kind of study in its own right. In 1974, the British Educational Research Association was founded as a major initiative to unite educational-ists of all backgrounds around a common cause, and a single organisation. BERA's flag-ship journal the *British Educational Research Journal*, founded in the same year, pursued the goal of forging a single body of knowledge from the disparate traditions that had hith-erto held sway.

In these circumstances, it is perhaps remarkable that the disciplines survived at all. Yet survive they did, not only with their claims for a general contribution to education but also as discrete disciplinary communities. Indeed, although contemporary pressures undermined their overall standing, they became entrenched still further in their separate disciplinary bases as a result of external challenge. Further disciplinary activity leading to conferences and new journals was also evident in this period, now stemming especially from the sociology of education.

The continuing strength of the disciplines in educational studies was evidenced, appropriately enough, in the 30th anniversary issue of the *BJES,* published in 1982. This included separate papers on all four of the major disciplines, alongside a personal account of the past three decades by Alan Blyth of the University of Liverpool, and other contribu-tions on educational administration, comparative education, the economics of education, and changes in the education systems of England and Wales, Scotland, and Northern Ire-land. The editorial of this anniversary issue celebrated the importance of the various disci-plines and defended specialisation, but it also expressed unease that 'uncoordinated digging at the chalkface' (*BJES,* 1982, p. 6) might achieve little, and that too few special-ists were able or willing to generalise. Blyth's contribution was also significant for its observation that over the past three decades, studies in education had evolved from being a series of responses to problems, to becoming a predominantly autonomous study (Blyth, 1982).

A further edited collection published the following year (Hirst, 1983a) also expressed continuity in terms of the cultivation of the disciplines, now dignified by the title of 'foundation disciplines'. Edited by Paul Hirst, the format of this volume was highly reminiscent of Tibble's earlier influential collections. Hirst himself introduced the collec-tion with an essay on educational theory that signalled some retreat from the abrasive con-fidence that he had shown on behalf of the disciplines during the 1960s. In particular, he now suggested that although educational theory drew upon the disciplines in order to develop rational principles for educational practice, the disciplines in themselves did not constitute principles for practice. He continued:

> The disciplines cannot tackle any given practical questions as such for each tackles questions which are peculiar to itself, those that can be raised only within its own distinctive conceptual apparatus. Psychologists, sociologists or philosophers faced with any matter of practical policy on, say, the grouping of pupils in schools or the use of punishment, can legitimately comment only on different psychological, soci-ological or philosophical issues that may be at stake. (Hirst, 1983b, p. 6)

The other contributions to the volume provided a review of how the different disciplines had developed in their content and methods over the previous 20 years. Each of these noted a struggle to adapt to changing and threatening conditions, but they were also able to detect promising signs of survival. Thus Richard Peters, examining the philosophy of education, noted the onset of 'a period of consolidation – some would say a struggle for survival' (Peters, 1983, p. 35), but observed nevertheless that the Philosophy of Education Society of Great Britain now had over 500 members, while the *Journal of Philosophy of Education* sold over 1,000 copies per issue. He was critical of what he saw as the piecemeal, *ad hoc* approach of much philosophy of education, and hoped for the emergence of a fresh stand-point from which to explore uncharted areas of education, but remained confident that there would be further work and new challenges to overcome in the future.

Brian Simon, re-evaluating the history of education, adopted a similar position. He emphasised the continuing importance of the work of the History of Education Society and of its journal, and insisted upon the unique contribution of the history of education towards an understanding of education: 'The drive to historical investigation is the drive to under-standing. Not all need such an understanding, but I suggest that all those professionally engaged in education do' (Simon, 1983, p. 65). Simon was also able to map out a number of areas in which historians of education could bring significant insights to bear. John Nis-bet of the University of Aberdeen, on behalf of educational psychology, acknowledged evidence that this disciplinary area had been in retreat for the past 20 years, but remained convinced that 'rumours of the death of educational psychology are premature, and that in recent times psychology has made significant advances which offer a promise of a basis for a theory of education, at least in its cognitive aspects' (Nisbet, 1983, p. 85). Similarly, Brian Davies of Chelsea College, University of London accepted that the sociology of education had suffered from new pressures, especially what he called 'the constricting pressure upon theory, pressed into the service of practice' (Davies, 1983, p. 105). On the other hand, he too could point to a continuing and broadening agenda for further study, made more urgent by a renewed awareness of the social and political conditions within which education operated.

In the case of sociology of education, indeed, there were particular grounds for a vigorous assertion of relevance. In the 1970s and 1980s, new institutional forms arose that were specifically related to sociology of education as a disciplinary community. In some respects these originated from a self-styled 'new' sociology of education that put empha-sis on the social basis of 'what counts as knowledge' in schools and particular societies; the manifesto of this approach was a collection of papers edited by Michael Young under the heading *Knowledge and Control* (Young, 1971). A renewed awareness of the need to relate to the problems experienced by schools and teachers was also an underlying dimen-sion of the strengthening role of sociology of education during the 1970s, with the aim of providing sociological perspectives 'to give as full a diagnosis of the problems of teaching as possible alongside the current insights of psychology, history and philosophy' (Meighan, 1973, p. 173). This was strongly influenced by Marxist perspectives on what was often characterised as a crisis of schooling in the broader context of industrial and eco-nomic decline, social dislocation, and political turbulence, culminating in 1979 in the elec-tion of a Conservative government under Margaret Thatcher. A new Open University course, 'School and Society' (followed by 'Schooling and Society'), reflected a general concern to apply the sociology of education to the needs of teachers in training and in the classroom (Barton and Walker, 1978, p. 275). This led in turn to a debate over how to develop a radical reappraisal of education and schooling, 'be it in terms of changing the system, of raising the consciousness of teachers or of attempting to show education as reflecting and contributing to the contradictions of the social, political and economic order' (Barton and Walker, 1978, p. 280).

One major forum for the development of this debate was the Westhill Sociology of Education conference, held annually at Westhill College, Birmingham. The inaugural conference was held in January 1978 'in order to examine the prevailing condition of the subject in the light of its application to issues relating to schooling and classrooms' (Bar-ton and Meighan, 1978a, p. 1). It was intended to use the device of a regular conference to raise and discuss ideas, present current research, and establish contacts; in other words, to develop an informal network that would become a disciplinary community. The papers presented at the 1978 conference were revised and published as an edited collection around the theme of 'Sociological interpretations of schooling and classrooms: a reappraisal' (Barton and Meighan, 1978b). This was the first of many such collaborative works to be published over the following decade as outcomes of the Westhill Conference (see for example Barton and Meighan, 1979; Barton, Meighan and Walker, 1980; Barton and Ball, 1981; Barton and Walker, 1983; Walker and Barton, 1983). These conferences were significant in terms of providing an organisational focus and a regular meeting place for sociologists of education in the absence of a formal society. Meanwhile, another set of workshops held on a regular basis at Whitelands College in London began to develop a closely related discussion around qualitative methodology in education which was again dominated by sociological concerns (for example Burgess, 1984, 1985).

Another product of this disciplinary activity was a new journal, the *British Journal of Sociology of Education* (*BJSE*), launched in 1980 and edited by Len Barton. This was envisaged explicitly as 'a forum for the consolidation and development of debate' (*BJSE*, 1980, p. 3), which would 'try to initiate themes and discussions and ventilate controversies, all to the benefit of the discipline' (*BJSE*, 1980, p. 4). The editorial board of the new Journal included representatives of a range of theoretical perspectives and methods. In terms of the readership, meanwhile, the Journal hoped to 'consider the needs of both education and sociologists [sic]', since although the needs of these two interests might not always diverge, 'it would be foolish to pretend that they are always identical' (*BJSE*, 1980, p. 5). Thus, in common with the *British Journal of Educational Studies* and with other disciplinary-based journals in education, there were to be basically two audiences: a disciplinary priesthood and a broader educational laity. At the same time, the Journal saw no contradiction in defining as its cardinal objective 'to contribute to a better understanding of schools and education systems' (*BJSE*, 1980, p. 5). Another journal, *International Studies in Sociology of Education*, was launched in 1991, again emerging from the Westhill network which had now relocated to the University of Sheffield.

No separate association or society was formed for sociologists of education, which in itself was significant. Although a disciplinary community had emerged, it remained a loose and informal affiliation with disparate interests that resisted a more formal structure. Nevertheless, activities around the sociology of education in the 1980s and 1990s reflected continued support for disciplinary endeavour in educational studies. Like the other 'foundation disciplines', the sociology of education was able to survive and adapt in rapidly changing conditions alongside the growing presence of BERA, and it was more effective than the other disciplines in influencing the developing field of educational research as a whole (see for example Demaine, 2001; McCulloch, 2000).

By the turn of the century, significant new challenges were emerging to the unrivalled status of the so-called 'foundation disciplines'. One major American symposium published in 2000, for example, emphasised, 'among the many disciplines influencing the study of education', those of anthropology, pedagogy, linguistics, psychology, and sociology (Stewart and Brizella, 2000, p. 22). History and philosophy, so prominent in the 1960s, were not included in this list. Nevertheless, there were signs that the four disciplines of history, philosophy, psychology and sociology retained a particular appeal. BERA for example welcomed new members with the message that it represented a 'broad church', with 'psychologists, sociologists, historians and philosophers among the discipline-minded members and a strong contingent of educationists with special interests in curriculum, pedagogy, assessment, or management and taking either a theoretical, or evaluative or action-research perspective on education' (Bassey, 2000). Here was at least a grudging endorsement of the continued role of the foundation disciplines associated with 'educational studies', in the context of 'educational research'. Another indication was the set of criteria expressed in the Research Assessment Exercise of 2001 for Education as a unit of assessment, which included *'Disciplines contributing to education: History, psychology, philosophy, sociology and other disciplines of education'* (RAE, 1999, paragraph 3.59.4.d).

CONCLUSIONS

Over the past 50 years, the disciplines, separately and together, have made a significant contribution to the study of education. Throughout this period, they have stimulated a pluralist approach to the study of education, one that has drawn opportunistically from the humanities and social sciences to seek to understand and address the changing problems of education. In this respect, exponents of educational studies have been akin to those of political studies as a loose coalition of disparate factions, as opposed to a single homogeneous group. In many cases, disciplinary based studies were aligned more clearly to the parent discipline than to the study of education, and they could often be remote from educational practice. A core disciplinary audience, attuned to particular issues and codes, tended to be given precedence over a general educational audience that was seeking applications to broader problems. Against this, links between theory and practice did not go entirely unremarked. Interesting and significant attempts were made to establish useful connections between them, especially through combining the insights of the disciplines, for example in curriculum studies and the Students Library of Education. Having successfully established themselves and survived in difficult conditions, they remain as entrenched communities of knowledge. Undaunted, if not unscathed, the disciplines continue in the 21st century to represent central pillars of educational studies and research.

REFERENCES

Almond, G. (1991) *A Discipline Divided: Schools and Sects in Political Science.* London: Sage.

Armytage, W.H.G. (1954/1980) The role of an education department in a modern university. In P. Gordon (ed.), *The Study of Education*, 1. London: Woburn, 160–79.

Barton, L. and Ball, S. (eds) (1981) *Schools, Teachers and Teaching.* London: Falmer.

Barton, L. and Meighan, R. (1978a) Introduction. In L. Barton and R. Meighan (eds), *Sociological Interpretations of Schooling and Classrooms*, 1–5.

Barton, L. and Meighan, R. (eds) (1978b) *Sociological Interpretations of Schooling and Classrooms: A Re-appraisal.* Driffield: Nafferton.

Barton, L. and Meighan, R. (eds) (1979) *Schools, Pupils and Deviance.* Driffield: Nafferton.

Barton, L., Meighan, R. and Walker, S. (eds) (1980) *Schooling Ideology and the Curriculum.* London: Falmer.

Barton, L. and Walker, S. (1978) Sociology of education at the crossroads, *Educational Review*, 30(3), 269–83.

Barton, L. and Walker, S. (eds) (1983) *Gender, Class and Education.* London: Falmer.

Bassey, M. (1999) *Case Study Research in Educational Settings.* Buckingham, Open University Press.

Bassey, M. (2000) Internet notes for newcomers to BERA, March, http://www.bera.ac.uk/newcomers.html

Blyth, A. (1982) Response and autonomy in the study of education: a personal account of three decades, *BJES*, 30(1), 7–17.

Briggs, A. (1972) The study of the history of education, *History of Education*, 1(1), 5–16.

British Journal of Educational Studies (BJES) (1952) Notes and news, 1(1), p. 67.

BJES (1982) Editorial, 30(1), 5–6.

British Journal of Sociology of Education (BJSE) (1980) Editorial, 1(1), 3–5.

Burgess, R. (ed.) (1984) *The Research Process in Educational Settings: Ten Case Studies.* London: Falmer.

Burgess, R. (ed.) (1985) *Field Methods in the Study of Education.* London: Falmer.

Charlton, K. (1968) The contribution of history to the study of the curriculum. In Kerr (ed.), *Changing the Curriculum*, 63–78.

Davies, B. (1983) The sociology of education. In Hirst (ed.), *Educational Theory and its Foundation Disciplines*, 100–45.

Demaine, J. (ed.) (2001) *Sociology of Education Today.* London: Routledge Falmer.

Gamble, A. (2001) Every voice of dissent adds to unity, *The Times Higher Education Supplement*, 16 February, 28.

Goodin, R.E. and Klingemann, H.-D. (1996) Political science: the discipline. In R.E. Goodin and H.-D. Klingemann (eds), *A New Handbook of Political Science*. Oxford: Oxford University Press, 3–26.

Goodson, I. (1983) *School Subjects and Curriculum Change*. London: Croom Helm.

Hirst, P. (1968) The contribution of philosophy to the study of the curriculum. In J.F. Kerr (ed.), *Changing The Curriculum*, 39–62.

Hirst, P. (ed.) (1983a) *Educational Theory and its Foundation Disciplines*. London: Routledge and Kegan Paul.

Hirst, P. (1983b) Educational theory. In P. Hirst (ed.), *Educational Theory and its Foundation Disciplines*, 3–29.

Hirst, P. (1998) Philosophy of education: the evolution of a discipline. In G. Haydon (ed.), *50 Years of Philosophy of Education: Progress and Prospects*. London: Institute of Education, 1–22.

Journal of Curriculum Studies (1969) 1(2), Editorial.

Kelly, T. (1952) The origin of mechanics' institutes, *BJES*, 1(1), 17–27.

Kerr, J.F. (1968a) The problem of curriculum reform. In J.F. Kerr (ed.) *Changing the Curriculum*, 13–38.

Kerr, J.F. (ed.) (1968b) *Changing the Curriculum*. London: University of London Press.

King, A.R. and Brownell, J.A. (1966) *The Curriculum and the Disciplines of Knowledge: a Theory of Curriculum Practice*. London: John Wiley and Sons.

Lawton, D. (1973) *Social Change, Educational Theory and Curriculum Planning*. London: University of London Press.

Lawton, D. (1978/1980) The end of the secret garden? In P. Gordon (ed.), *The Study of Education* 2. London: Woburn, 305–25.

McCulloch, G. (2000) Publicising the educational past. In D. Crook and R. Aldrich (eds), *History of Education for the 21st Century*. London: Institute of Education, 1–16.

McCulloch, G. and Richardson, W. (2000) *Historical Research in Educational Settings*. Buckingham: Open University Press.

Meighan, R. (1973) Sociology and teaching: a reappraisal in the light of current trends in the sociology of education, *Educational Review*, 25(3), 163–74.

Musgrove, F. (1968) The contribution of sociology to the study of the curriculum. In Kerr (ed.), *Changing The Curriculum*, 96–109.

Nisbet, J. (1983) Educational psychology. In P. Hirst (ed.), *Educational Theory and its Foundation Disciplines*, 84–99.

Peters, R. (1963/1980) Education as initiation. In P. Gordon (ed.), *The Study of Education*, 1. London: Woburn, 273–99.

Peters, R. (1983) Philosophy of education. In P. Hirst (ed.), *Educational Theory and its Foundation Disciplines*, 30–61.

Reid, L.A. (1952) Education and the map of knowledge, *BJES*, 1(1), 3–16.

Research Assessment Exercise (RAE) (1999) *Research Assessment Exercise 2001: Assessment Panels' Criteria and Working Methods*, circular 5/99. Bristol: Higher Education Funding Councils.

Richardson, W. (1999) Historians and educationists: the history of education as a field of study in post-war England, Part I: 1945–72, *History of Education*, 28(1), 1–30.

Simon, B. (1966/1980) Education: the new perspective. In P. Gordon (ed.), *The Study of Education*, 2. London: Woburn, 71–94.

Simon, B. (1983) History of education. In P. Hirst (ed.), *Educational Theory and its Foundation Disciplines*, 62–83.

Simon, B. (1994) The study of education as a university subject in Britain. In B. Simon, *The State and Educational Change: Essays in the History of Education and Pedagogy.* London: Lawrence and Wishart, 127–46.

Simon, B. (1998) *A Life in Education.* London: Lawrence and Wishart.

Stenhouse, L. (1975) *An Introduction to Curriculum Research and Development.* London: Heinemann.

Stewart, J. and Brizuela, B. (2000) 'Habits of thought and work' – the disciplines and qualitative research: an introduction, *Harvard Educational Review*, 70(1), 22.

Stewart, W.A.C. (1952) Karl Mannheim and the sociology of education, *BJES*, 1(1), 99–113.

Taylor, W. (1978) The contribution of psychology to the study of the curriculum, in Kerr (ed.), *Changing the Curriculum*, 79–95.

Tibble, J.W. (ed.) (1966) *The Study of Education.* London: Routledge and Kegan Paul.

Tibble, J.W. (ed.) (1971a) *An Introduction to the Study of Education: An Outline for the Student.* London, Routledge and Kegan Paul.

Tibble, J.W. (1971b) The development of the study of education. In J.W. Tibble (ed.), *An Introduction to the Study of Education*, 5–17.

Walker, S. and Barton, L. (eds) (1983) *Race, Class and Education.* London: Croom Helm.

Young, M.F.D. (ed.) (1971) *Knowledge and Control: New Directions in the Sociology of Education.* London: Collier-Macmillan.

2

WHAT IS AN EDUCATIONAL PROCESS?

R. S. Peters

INTRODUCTION

Richard Stanley Peters was a professional philosopher who effectively founded modern British approaches to the philosophy of education. He became Professor of philosophy of education at the Institute of Education, University of London and transformed philosophy of education into an influential new sub-discipline of philosophy. He produced a great number of influential articles and books. This chapter is taken from his third major book, first published in 1967 with the title *The Concept of Education*. This first chapter in the book was Peter's attempt to map out the concept of education, which had not previously been done. His conceptual analysis of education was hugely influential, as was his definition of an educated person: one who has acquired (a) a considerable body of knowledge, (b) a breadth of understanding, and (c) a non-instrumental attitude towards the major activities that are pursued.

KEY QUESTIONS

1. What is the importance of philosophy in educational debate and as a preparation for understanding any practical activity in education, such as teaching?
2. What is involved in the idea of educating a person or the idea of educational success?

FURTHER READING

Two articles are worth reading to recognise the historical significance of R. S. Peters. First, Wilfred Carr's article on 'R S Peters' philosophy of education', Review article in the *British Journal of Educational Studies* (Vol. 32 No. 1, 1986) and John Earwaker's article 'R S Peters and the concept of education', in the *Journal of Philosophy of Education* (Vol. 7 No. 2, 2006).

This Reading links with Chapters 1, 2, 8 and 12 and Debate 5 of *The Routledge Education Studies Textbook.*

INTRODUCTION

In exploring the concept of education a territory is being entered where there are few sign-posts. To use Ryle's phrase, the 'logical geography' of concepts in the area of education has not yet been mapped. This feature of the field of education was vividly brought home to me in the autumn of 1963 when I was working on my Inaugural Lecture on *Education as Initiation*, and was unable to unearth any previous explicit attempt to demarcate the concept of 'education'. It is not surprising, therefore, that in presenting at the start what amounts to a bird's eye view of the contours of this territory, I have to rely mainly on my own previous attempt to map it.

THE TASK-ACHIEVEMENT ANALYSIS OF 'EDUCATION'

Any such survey must start with the observation that 'education' is a concept which is not very close to the ground. By this I mean that it is not a concept like 'red' which picks out a simple quality, like 'horse' which picks out an object, or like 'running' or 'smiling' which pick out observable occurrences. We do not ask 'Are you instructing him in algebra or are you educating him in algebra?' as if these were two alternative processes. But we might ask 'Are you educating him by instructing him in algebra?' 'Education', in other words, refers to no particular process; rather it encapsulates criteria to which any one of a family of processes must conform. In this respect it is rather like 'reform'. 'Reform' picks out no particular process. People can be reformed, perhaps, by preventive detention, by reading the Bible, or by the devotion of a loving wife. In a similar way people can be educated by reading books, by exploring their environment, by travel and conversation – even by talk and chalk in a classroom. The concepts of 'reform' and 'education' have proper application if these processes satisfy certain criteria. 'Education' and 'reform' are not part of the furniture of the earth or mind; they are more like stamps of approval issued by 'Good Housekeeping' proclaiming that furniture has come up to certain standards.

How then are we to conceive of processes by means of which such standards are to be achieved? In my Inaugural Lecture I attacked misleading models which provide pictures of what goes on in terms of shaping material according to a specification, or of allowing children to 'grow'. I mentioned in a footnote, which I did not have time to develop, that a much more adequate way of conceiving of what goes on, which provides a rationale for my notion of education as initiation, is to regard processes of education as tasks relative to achievements. This accounts for the feature of education, which I rather laboured, that its standards are intrinsic not extrinsic to it. This task-achievement analysis I now propose to explain.

Aristotle made the point long ago in relation to performances such as 'learning' and 'inferring', that the end is built into the concepts. Ryle has made it more recently in relation to activities such as 'looking' and 'running'. When a man finds something that he has lost or wins a race, he does not indulge in something different from looking or running, neither does he produce something or reach an end which is extrinsic to the activity in which he is engaged. He merely succeeds in it. He achieves the standard or attains the end which is internal to the activity and which gives it point. In a similar way a man who is educated is a man who has succeeded in relation to certain tasks on which he and his teacher have been engaged for a considerable period of time. Just as 'finding' is the achievement relative to 'looking', so 'being educated' is the achievement relative to a family of tasks which we call processes of education.

'Education' is, of course, different in certain respects from the examples of achievements that Ryle gives. To start with 'education' like 'teaching' can be used as both a task and an achievement verb.[1] Teachers can work away at teaching without success, and still be teaching; but there is a sense, also, in which teaching someone something implies success. 'I taught the boy the ablative absolute construction' implies that I was successful in my task. But I can also say 'I taught him Latin for years, but he learnt nothing.' Similarly I can work away at educating people, without the implication that I or they achieve success in the various tasks which are engaged in; but if I talk of them as 'educated' there is an implication of success.

But whose success are we talking about? That of the teacher or of the learner? This is tantamount to asking to whose tasks the achievements which constitute 'being educated' are relative, those of the teacher or those of the learner. Obviously both are usually involved, but it is important to realize that the tasks of the teacher could not be characterized unless we had a notion of the tasks of the learner. For whereas 'learning' could be characterized without introducing the notion of 'teaching', 'teaching' could not be characterized without the notion of 'learning'. The tasks of the teacher consist in the employment of various methods to get learning processes going. These processes of learning in their turn cannot be characterized without reference to the achievements in which they culminate. For to learn something is to come up to some standard, to succeed in some respect. So the achievement must be that of the learner in the end. The teacher's success, in other words, can only be defined in terms of that of the learner. This presumably is the logical truth dormant in the saying that all education is self-education. This is what makes the notion of 'initiation' an appropriate one to characterize an educational situation; for a learner is 'initiated' by another into something which he has to master, know, or remember. 'Education' picks out processes by means of which people get started on the road to such achievements.

THE MORAL REQUIREMENTS OF 'EDUCATION'

The second way in which 'education' is different from ordinary cases of tasks and achievements is that it is inseparable from judgements of value. It is, as I have pointed out, a logical truth that any method of education employed by a teacher must put the pupil in a situation where he is learning, where some sort of task is presented to him. But a teacher might try to condition children to 'pick up' certain things without their realizing that they were picking anything up. In saying that this is not a process of education we would be implying that this was morally bad, because conditions of wittingness and voluntariness on the part of the pupil were missing; for we regard it as morally unjustifiable to treat others in this way. To say that we are educating people commits us, in other words, to morally legitimate procedures. Often such minimal moral demands, which are connected with respect for persons, are further extended to exclude procedures such as giving children orders, which is thought by some to involve some sort of moral indignity. Discouragement of individual choice would be another procedure which many might condemn as being morally reprehensible. They might express their disapproval by saying that this was not 'education'.

The way in which moral considerations enter into the achievement aspects of education is clearer than the way in which they enter into the task aspect. For it is obvious enough that the achievements or states of mind that give content to the notion of an educated man must be regarded as valuable. Finding a thimble that has been hidden is a Rylean type of achievement: but it is a trivial one. The achievements involved in education cannot be of this type. For if something is to count as 'education', what is learnt must be regarded as worth-while just as the manner in which it is learnt must be regarded as morally unobjectionable; for not all learning is 'educational' in relation to the content of what is learnt. If it were we might have periods on the time-table devoted to astrology and to Bingo and homilies by headmasters on the art of torture.

In this respect, also, 'education' is like 'reform'; for it would be as much of a contradiction to say 'My son has been educated but has learnt nothing of value' as it would be to say 'My son has been reformed but has changed in no way for the better.' This, by the way, is a purely conceptual point. The connexion between 'education' and what is valuable can be made explicit without commitment to content. It is a *further question* what the particular standards are in virtue of which achievements are thought to be of value and what grounds there might be for claiming that these are the correct ones. It may well be that arguments can be produced to show why rational men should value some standards rather than others; but at the moment there is no such established harmony. So when people speak of 'education' it is essential to know what their standards of valuation are in order to ascertain the aspect under which some process or state of mind is being commended.

This connexion with commendation does not, of course, prevent us from speaking of 'poor' education when a worth-while job has been botched or of 'bad education' when we think that much of what people are working at is not worth-while, though it is a nice question to determine at what point we pass from saying that something is 'bad education' to saying that it is not education at all. Neither does it prevent us from using the word in a purely external descriptive way when we speak of an 'educational system' just as we can use the term 'moral' of someone else's code without committing ourselves to the judgements of value of those whose code it is. Anthropologists can talk of the moral system of a tribe; so also can we talk as sociologists or economists of the educational system of a community. In employing the concept in this derivative sense we need not think that what is going on is worth-while, but members of the society, whose system it is, must think it is.

Talk of 'education', then, from the inside of a form of life, is inseparable from talk of what is worth-while, but with the additional notion written into it that what is worth-while has been or is being transmitted in a morally unobjectionable manner. But under this general ægis of desirability 'education' picks out no one type of task or achievement. People differ in their estimates of desirability. They therefore differ in the emphasis which they place on achievement and states of mind that can be thought of as desirable. This diversity is what makes talk of 'aims of education' apposite; for people who talk in this way are not suggesting aims extrinsic to education: They are enunciating their priorities in giving content to the notion of an 'educated man'.

To take a parallel: it might be said that the aim of reform was to make men better. This is harmless enough provided that it is realized that 'making men better' is built into the concept of 'reform'. But something more specific might be said such as the aim of reform is to encourage a sense of responsibility. This might be countered by saying that the aim of reform is to get people to have respect for persons. Such a dispute would be an attempt to give precise content to the general notion of 'making a man better'. Similarly discussions about the aims of education are attempts to give more precise content to the notion of the 'educated man' or of a man who has achieved some desirable state of mind. Is moral education more important, for instance, than the development of scientific understanding? This might have particular point when talking about some of the children referred to in the Newsom Report. Or perhaps we talk about 'wholeness' in order to emphasize all-round excellence and sensitivity. Or we may want to stress the importance of cutting the coat of what is worth-while according to the cloth of individual aptitude. Talk of developing the potentialities of the individual is then appropriate. Such 'aims' point out specific achievements and states of mind which give content to the formal notion of 'the educated man' which is a short-hand for summarizing our notion of a form of life which is worth-while enough to deserve being handed on from generation to generation.[2]

So much, then, for the moral aspect of 'education' as a family of tasks and achievements which make it rather different from the simpler cases used by Ryle to illustrate this way of conceiving of certain classes of intentional activities. I want now to consider other criteria of 'being educated' as an achievement which have to do with knowledge and understanding. I shall then deal with the tasks which lead up to achievements falling under these criteria.

THE ACHIEVEMENT ASPECT OF 'EDUCATION'

We do not call a person educated who has simply mastered a skill even though the skill may be very worth-while, like that of moulding clay. For a man to be educated it is insufficient that he should possess a 'know-how' or knack. He must also know that certain things are the case. He must have developed some sort of conceptual scheme at least in the area in which he is skilled and must have organized a fair amount of information by means of it.

But even this is not enough; for we would be disinclined to call a man who was merely well-informed an educated man. To be educated requires also some understanding of principles, of the 'reason why' of things. The Spartans, for instance, were military and morally trained. They knew how to fight; they knew what was right and wrong; they were possessed of a certain kind of lore, which stood them in good stead in stock situations. They were thus able to comb their hair with aplomb when the Persians were approaching at Thermopylae. But we could not say that they had received a military or moral education; for they had never been encouraged to understand the principles underlying their code. They had mastered the content of forms of thought and behaviour without ever grasping or being able to operate with the principles that could enable them to manage on their own. They were notorious for falling victims to potentates, priests, and profligates on leaving their natural habitat where their code was part of the order of things. Failure to grasp underlying principles leads to unintelligent rule of thumb application of rules, to the inability to make exceptions on relevant grounds and to bewilderment when confronted with novel situations.

Given, then, that being educated implies the possession of knowledge, but rules out *mere* knowledge, in that it also requires understanding of principles, could a man be educated whose knowledge and understanding is confined to one sphere – mathematics, for instance ? There is a strong inclination to deny that we could call a man 'educated' who had only developed his awareness and understanding in such a limited way; for our notion of an educated man suggests a more all-round type of development. When we say that people go to a university to become educated and not just to become scientists, from what does this antithesis derive? Does it derive from the concept of 'education' or from our underlying valuations about the constituents of the good life which ought to be passed on which includes e.g. aesthetic and moral awareness as well as scientific understanding? Certainly 'training' always suggests confinement. People are trained *for* jobs, *as* mechanics, and *in* science. No one can be trained in a general sort of way. But this lack of specificity is just what is suggested by 'education'. It is not clear to me whether this is due to the concept of 'education' itself or to our refusal to grant that what is worth-while could be confined to one form of awareness. To pose the problem succinctly: Is the saying 'Education is of the whole man' a conceptual truth in that 'education' rules out one-sided development? Or is it an expression of our moral valuations about what is worth-while?

There is no necessity, for the purposes of this article, to decide between these two alternatives, as it has no particular implications for what is to count as an educational process. There is, however, another aspect of the knowledge requirement built into 'education' which has implications. This is its attitudinal aspect. By this I mean that the knowledge which a man must possess to qualify as being educated must be built into his way of looking at things. It cannot be merely inert. It is possible for a man to know a lot of history, in the sense that he can give correct answers to questions in classrooms and in examinations, without ever developing a historical sense. For instance he might fail to connect his knowledge of the Industrial Revolution with what he sees when visiting Manchester or the Welsh Valleys. We might describe such a man as 'knowledgeable' but we would never describe him as 'educated'; for 'education' implies that a man's outlook is transformed by what he knows.

It is this requirement built into 'education' that makes the usual contrast between 'education' and 'life' rather ridiculous. Those who make it usually have in mind a contrast between the activities that go on in classrooms and studies and those that go on in industry, politics, agriculture, and rearing a family. The curriculum of schools and universities is then criticized because, as the knowledge passed on is not instrumental in any obvious sense to 'living', it is assumed that is is 'academic' or relevant only to the classroom, cloister, study, and library. What is forgotten is that activities like history, literary appreciation, and philosophy, unlike Bingo and billiards, involve forms of thought and awareness that can and should spill over into things that go on outside and transform them. For they are concerned with the explanation, evaluation and imaginative exploration of forms of life. As a result of them what is called 'life' develops different dimensions. In schools and universities there is concentration on the development of this determinant of our form of life. The problem of the educator is to pass on this knowledge and understanding in such a way that they develop a life of their own in the minds of others and transform how they see the world, and hence how they feel about it.

There is another element in what I have called the 'attitudinal aspect' of the sort of knowledge which is built into the concept of 'being educated' which was first stressed by Socrates and Plato in their doctrine that 'virtue is knowledge'. Such knowledge must not be 'inert' in another sense; it must involve the kind of commitment which comes through being on the inside of a form of thought and awareness. A man cannot really understand what it is to think scientifically unless he not only knows that evidence must be found for assumptions, but cares that it should be found; in forms of thought where proof is possible, cogency, simplicity, and elegance must be felt to matter. And what would historical or philosophical thought amount to if there was no concern about relevance or coherence? All forms of thought and awareness have their own internal standards of appraisal. To be on the inside of them is both to understand this and to care. Indeed the understanding is difficult to distinguish from the caring; for without such care the activities lose their point. I do not think that we would call a person 'educated' whose knowledge of such forms of thought and awareness was purely external and 'inert' in this way. There can be no End of the Affair where The Heart of the Matter is lacking. And, of course, there never *is* an End of the Affair. For to be educated is not to have arrived; it is to travel with a different view.

The achievement aspect of 'education' connected with knowledge has now been sketched. Before passing to the task aspect, under which educational processes have to be considered, it will be as well to pause and summarize the main criteria of 'education' under this aspect which are to be satisfied by an 'educated' man.

(i) An educated man is one whose form of life, as exhibited in his conduct, the activities to which he is committed, his judgements, and feelings, is thought to be desirable.

(ii) Whatever he is trained to do he must have knowledge, not just knack, and an understanding of principles. His form of life must also exhibit some mastery of forms of thought and awareness, which are not harnessed purely to utilitarian or vocational purposes or completely confined to one mode.

(iii) His knowledge and understanding must not be inert either in the sense that they make no difference to his general view of the world, his actions within it and reactions to it *or* in the sense that they involve no concern for the standards immanent in forms of thought and awareness, as well as the ability to attain them.

CRITERIA INVOLVED IN THE TASK ASPECT OF 'EDUCATION'

Educational processes are related to these various activities and modes of thought and conduct characterizing an 'educated man' as task is related to achievement. They are those in which people are initiated into or got going on activities and forms of thought and conduct which they eventually come to master. I have argued already that, apart from the requirement that processes belonging to this family be morally unobjectionable, they must also be considered from the point of view of the learner whose achievements give content to the concept of an 'educated man'. They must therefore approximate to tasks in which the learner knows what he is doing and gradually develops towards those standards of excellence which constitute the relevant achievement. In this family obviously are included processes such as training, instruction, learning by experience, teaching, and so on.

If we look at such processes from the teacher's point of view he is intentionally trying to get learning processes going by exhibiting, drawing attention to, emphasizing, or explicating some feature of what has to be learnt and putting the learner in a position where his experience is likely to become structured along desirable lines. From the learner's point of view such processes must be ones in which he knows what he is doing. Things may happen to him while asleep or under hypnosis which bring about modifications of his consciousness; but we would not call them processes of education. The learner must know what he is doing, must be conscious of something that he is trying to master, understand, or remember. Such processes, therefore, must involve attention on his part and some type of action, activity, or performance by means of which he begins to structure his movements and consciousness according to the public standards immanent in what has to be learnt.

It is necessary, however, to distinguish educational processes proper from other processes bordering on them which do not satisfy one or other of these criteria. There are first of all what I will call extrinsic aids and secondly what I will call rather loosely processes of 'picking things up'. Let us consider them briefly in this order.

Extrinsic aids

There are all sorts of things done by teachers in classrooms which help children to learn things which are really aids to education rather than processes of education. I mean conditions such as praise and reward which help children to learn things. These are not processes of education; for their connexion with what is learnt is purely extrinsic. They may facilitate the learning of anything; but what is involved in learning anything can be explicated without reference to them. To take a parallel; it is an empirical fact that children learn things better if they are nice and warm rather than shivering with cold. So a sensible teacher will make sure that the radiators in the classroom are turned on. It may also be the case that children learn things better if the teacher smiles approvingly when the child gets things right. This is, perhaps, another empirical fact which is relevant to education. But neither turning on the radiators nor smiling at children are educational processes, whatever their status as aids to education.

The appeal to children's interests occupies a more twilight sort of status because of ambiguities in the notion of 'interests'. Such interests can be intrinsic or extrinsic to what has to be learnt. Children are naturally curious at certain ages and have a desire to master things and get them right. They may also be interested in finding out about and mastering the specific things that have to be learnt. As an interest in such worth-while things is part of what is meant by 'an educated man' the job in this case is that of fostering such intrinsic interests and superimposing on them the precision and standards of achievement which are necessary. Having such intrinsic interests is not part of what is meant by an educational process; it is built into the achievement, and this aspect of the achievement can be present at the start.

Unfortunately few children are motivated in this way all the time and many children scarcely at all. Therefore extrinsic interests have to be used, as well as other forms of pressure. For children do not have to be interested in something in order to learn it; it is often sufficient that they attend to it, for whatever reason. If they attend long enough, and if the teacher is skilled and imaginative, they may become interested. The ability to *stimulate* interest is one of the greatest gifts of a teacher. The danger of too much reliance on extrinsic interests is that a child may pick up something that the teacher does not intend, namely to become a thorough instrumentalist, the prisoner of an attitude which always looks to what things lead to rather than what they are in themselves. A child may be interested in outstripping his fellows and may be willing to learn almost anything that is geared to this end. This may be educationally very bad if what is 'picked up' is the conviction that effort should only be made if gain results. Using these sorts of interests may not be in the interests of the child. So we pass to processes of 'picking things up'.

Picking things up

I used the word 'picked up' rather than 'learnt' advisedly to characterize a way of acquiring an attitude that borders on education, without being a process of education in a strict sense.[3] Obviously enough this attitude is implicit in the practice of the teacher who employs such a method and is passed on partly by identification. All sorts of things are picked up in this way – desirable things such as a passion for poetry, nuances of style and argument, objectivity towards facts, respect for persons; undesirable things such as partisan allegiances, contempt for people of different persuasions, bad manners, and class-consciousness; and trivial things such as mannerisms, a tone of voice, gestures.

My reluctance to call such goings-on processes of education is not just due to the fact that what is passed on may be trivial or undesirable, but to the difficulty of conceiving of them as tasks either on the part of the teacher or of the learner. From the teacher's point of view he is explicitly trying to get children on the inside of a form of thought or awareness; to do this he uses certain methods. Yet the fact is that so much is caught rather than explicitly taught. The best teachers are not necessarily those who are au fait with all the latest methods or very knowledgeable about their subject. They are those whose genuine concern for what they are passing on is manifest in the manner in which they do it. Education, like most meetings between human beings, is a very chancy business. The wind of the spirit bloweth where it listeth. Some catch on; others don't. It depends so much whether the learners are drawn to the teacher or not. And what is more chancy than human attractions? If the learners are so drawn, then identification, suggestion, and other such indeterminate transactions may occur. These are not 'learning' processes in a full sense; for they are different from explicit imitation or copying, where something is explicitly attended to for assimilation. They happen to people; they are not achievements. Nevertheless this kind of contagion only actually spreads if both teacher and learner are actively engaged on something. It does not happen if the teacher is just fiddling about or the children are staring out of the window. The attention of both has to be focussed on some task; then these subsidiary processes may get going. If the teacher gets too self-conscious about them, the business gets blurred. He has to have his mind on what Lawrence called 'the holy ground' between teacher and taught. His dedication to it may then become incorporated in the consciousness of his pupils, and many other nuances may be imparted.

Conditioning

Cases where children pick up things without being aware of them are not confined to processes such as identification and suggestion; there are also those falling under the concept of 'conditioning'. Classical conditioning is, of course, completely irrelevant as it was concerned only with involuntary behaviour such as salivation and eye-blinks which could never be thought of as achievements. In operant conditioning what has to be learnt is not grasped by the learner to start with, if ever, as being instrumentally related to what counts as a reinforcement. Some movement is made, often of a random sort, which brings about acute pain or something attractive like food or a mate. This is not like rewarding children or punishing them when we do at least explain to them what will happen if they do something, and when what has to be learnt is presented as a means to the reward and can come to be thought of as such. Nothing like this happens in strict conditioning. Secondly there is no consciousness in conditioning of what has to be learnt as a *task*. A movement or series of movements is made and miraculously something like a pellet of food appears. It is really something of an anthropomorphism to say that the animal learns to press the lever. All that has happened is that some movement has been stamped in which we regard as an achievement. But it is more an achievement on the part of the experimenter than on the part of the animal.

It is very questionable, as a matter of fact, how much of animal learning, outside the narrow confines of laboratories, takes place according to principles of conditioning. For how often are animals in a position where their random responses are systematically reinforced ? How often, too, are the situations in which they learn things such that there is no discernible relationship between obtaining something like food and movements which have to be learnt as means to this? Looked at objectively animals are 'conditioned' to do such incredibly trivial and non-functional things – pressing bars, running mazes, leaping grids, begging for biscuits, and balancing balls on their noses. The situations in which they 'learn' things by 'conditioning' are those in which opportunities for the use of intelligence are cut down to a minimum. So even at the animal level a certain amount of scepticism is necessary about the applicability of 'conditioning', in any strict sense, to the learning of animals. This perhaps should be extended to some of the things allegedly learnt in this way in laboratories.

At the human level, a fortiori, the applicability of conditioning is even more questionable. Presumably certain positive and negative reactions are picked up in this way and simple sequences of movements are stamped in before the consciousness of a child has been sufficiently differentiated to pick out objects in a public world which he wants and means that can be taken to get them. But once he can distinguish himself from others and can copy others and understand instructions, once he begins to develop a grasp of causal and means–end connexions, it is very difficult to conceive of what could be learnt by strict conditioning. For how can we be sure that what is to be learnt presents itself in no way as an intelligible means to a desired end or as something to be mastered or copied? How do we know that it is not picked up by imitation or suggestion? Certainly it is difficult to call such forms of 'learning' educational processes on the account here given of 'education'. For, apart from the moral objections to treating other human beings in this way, which do not derive solely from what is learnt, these goings-on cannot possibly be regarded as tasks culminating in achievements. When things happen to us, which occasion the development of phobias or of stereotyped patterns of reaction, is seems odd to call such goings-on processes of 'education'. For 'education' does suggest some kind of intentionality on the part of the learner, however embryonic.

EDUCATIONAL PROCESSES

I have now, as it were, got out of the way what I called aids to education and processes of picking things up, both of which border on being processes of education. I want now to pass on to processes of education proper which can be viewed as a family of tasks leading up to the achievement of being educated. The achievement of being 'educated', as I have set it out, is complex. It involves mastery of some skills, knowledge, and understanding of principles. For such an ideal to be realized many different sorts of things have to be learnt.

In view of this it is improbable that there can be just one educational process. Too many educational theories are extrapolations from one type of learning situation which is taken as a paradigm for all. I propose therefore to isolate the different aspects of 'being educated' and consider briefly which educational processes are of particular relevance to each of them.

Training

Consider, first of all, the learning of skills. This presents itself preeminently as a task to the learner. He is usually presented with a paradigm of a skilled performance and, by a mixture of constant practice and imitation, he may eventually come to master it. A skill is not by its very nature something that could be learnt for all time in a flash of insight. Neither can it be learnt by reading books or by instruction alone. This helps of course, but only because it provides a guide for practice. Constant practice is absolutely essential, especially under the eye of a skilled performer who both corrects and provides a paradigm of the performance. Skills are difficult to master; so extrinsic forms of motivation usually have to supplement the intrinsic motivation provided by the desire to achieve or get something right.

To a teacher 'skills' usually denote reading, writing, and computation which have to be mastered before education can proceed very far. Because of the difficulties they present to a child, all kinds of attempts are made to harness the learning of these skills to other things that the child wants to do. But this is merely an intelligent way of providing an incentive to learning; it is nothing to do with the type of learning process required to master the skill. A child may be brought to the task of reading by the incentive of advertisements or by the necessity of reading instructions if he wants to cook. But when the actual reading begins there is no escape from practice, instruction, correction and example.

The general name we have for this type of learning process is 'training'. The concept of 'training' has application when (i) there is some specifiable type of performance that has to be mastered, (ii) practice is required for the mastery of it, (iii) little emphasis is placed on the underlying rationale. Example and instruction by another are a great help in the realm of skill, but they are not absolutely essential. A person might learn to type, for instance, without either, though it would be a lengthy business. But he could never learn to do this without practice. 'Training' has application, however, in a wider realm than that of skill; for roughly speaking the concept of 'training' also has application whenever anything coming up to a clear-cut specification has to be learnt. Military training includes not only arms drill and training skills such as shooting; it also includes the inculcation of habits such as punctuality and tidiness. Such habits cannot be learnt by practice and imitations alone as might a skill like swimming or swinging a golf club, because of the lack of close connexion with bodily movements. It is conceivable that something like swimming could be just picked up or 'caught' by practice and imitation without a word being said. But a habit like that of honesty, which is not just a kind of 'know-how' or knack, could never be picked up just like this.

Consider, for instance, what a child has got to know before he can develop a habit like that of stealing. He must be able to distinguish between himself and others and must have developed the notion of property; he must also grasp that people have a right to things and that these things must not be appropriated without permission. A child, strictly speaking, cannot 'steal' who has not a range of concepts such as these. He cannot learn what 'stealing' is just by watching others. For he cannot tell what an action is just from the outside; he has also to know how the agent conceives what he is doing. To realize that something is a case of theft he must, therefore, have developed the conceptual scheme without which 'theft' is an unintelligible notion. The notion of theft cannot be tied down, either, to any specifiable range of bodily movements. For all sorts of things can count as property and there are infinite number of ways of appropriating them. A child cannot therefore learn to steal or not to steal without instruction and correction as well as practice and imitation. The notion of 'moral training' as distinct from that of 'moral education' suggests the learning of a moral code which is tied down to specifiable rules such as 'Thou shalt not steal'. Moral education suggests, in addition, the passing on of the underlying rationale, the understanding of principles. But even training in this sphere, as well as in many others, involves much more than the mere mastery of a 'know-how' or 'knack'. The child has also to know that certain classes of action are wrong. Such knowledge could never just be 'caught'. The learning of skills is thus only one particular case of 'training'.

Instruction and learning by experience

Knowing what things are and that certain things are the case is a matter of developing a conceptual scheme that has to be fitted to phenomena. This can only be learnt by a process which involves the meaningful use of language by a teacher to structure relevant experience by the learner. In acquiring a body of knowledge of this sort instruction and explanation are as essential as first-hand experience. There is prevalent at the moment a widespread horror of instruction because this is associated with sitting children down in rows and telling them things which may be beyond their ken and which they may not be interested in learning about anyway. It is argued in reaction to this that children have at certain ages spontaneous curiosity in what things are and why they happen; they also have a natural desire to master things, provided they are not too difficult. A wise teacher will therefore be thoroughly cognizant of the stage of conceptual development which each child has reached. She will often take the children out of the classroom where the children can be confronted with the relevant experiences and will fill the classroom itself with things which are carefully related to these stages of conceptual development. She will be at hand always when the child's natural curiosity impels him to ask questions which are almost inevitable, given the confrontation between intriguing objects and a conceptual scheme which is ripe for the next increment. In this way there can be no danger of knowledge being inert. For what is learnt is always what the child is ready to absorb and eager to discover. In this way information from adults and from books can be built firmly into the developing cognitive structure of the child in relation to first-hand experience.

This is admirable provided that the teachers attempting to practise such a method are intelligent enough to understand what they are meant to be doing and skilful enough to make provision for children to whom they cannot be attending,[4] and provided that classroom conditions and the teacher-pupil ratio do not make it a pipe-dream. But it should be realized that it is really just a more intelligent method of instruction. Rather a lot of nonsense is talked in this context about children 'discovering' things which is rather reminiscent of Socrates' demonstration in *The Meno* that even a slave can make a geometrical 'discovery' if he is given the chance. The point is that a child may find out what others know, but he does not, if he is not asked the right sort of questions at the appropriate time, and if his experience is not guided in certain directions. A certain amount of practice is required for the child to learn to use the necessary concepts; but nothing like the same amount as in the case of skills. For once the rule has been grasped governing the use of the concept further instances are easily recognized. Of course knowledge acquired in this or any other way must be used fairly often or else it may be forgotten. But the supposition is that if it is required spontaneously in relation to first-hand experience forgetting is less likely.

Teaching and the learning of principles

If the knowledge of the human race had ended with Aristotle this account of knowledge and of the methods necessary to acquire it might be sufficient. It is indeed significant that those who advocate educational methods which stress the importance of first-hand experience have in mind mainly children of 7–12 who are at what Piaget calls the stage of concrete operational thought when the world of things presented through the senses is being ordered and structured. What is required at this stage is plenty of experience together with classificatory schemes to structure it. The classroom thus becomes a Lyceum in miniature.

But what of the grasp of principles necessary for understanding rather than low-level knowledge? What of the 'rape of the senses' necessary for principles like the law of inertia to emerge? What of the reliance on one typical and crucial instance so central to the hypothetico-deductive method of Galileo which Piaget postulates as developing almost naturally from the previous stage? Of what importance at this stage is all this dashing around and first-hand experience? As Hobbes put it, under the spell of Galileo: 'For when we calculate the magnitude and motions of heaven or earth, we do not ascend into heaven that we may divide it into parts, or measure the motions thereof, but we do it sitting still in our closets, or in the dark.'[5] Understanding of principles does not depend upon the accumulation of extra items of knowledge. Rather it requires reflection on what we already know, so that a principle can be found to illuminate the facts. This often involves the postulation of what is unobservable to explain what is observed. So it could never be lighted upon by 'experience'.

What then is there to be said about the learning of principles? The basic requisite is that people should first acquire in some way or other the low-level rules or assumptions which the principles illuminate. It is both logically absurd and educationally unsound to suppose that people could attain the necessary understanding of principles without first having acquired quite a lot of knowledge; for principles provide backing to rules or assumptions at a lower level of generality. In science, for instance, there could be no appeal to principles unless there were a mass of empirical generalizations which could be seen to fall under them; in morals there could be no appeal to principles without rules to justify by means of them. The grasp of principles, therefore, is inseparable from the acquisition of knowledge of a more mundane sort. This logical truth is often neglected by rationalistic educators who think that people can grasp scientific concepts, or pass them on to children, without knowing any science, or who believe that moral principles can be grasped by children who have not had a basic training in moral rules.

There is, of course, nothing absolute about what constitutes a principle. It is merely a higher-level assumption or rule that can be appealed to in order to substantiate and give unity to lower order ones. The one is thus immanent in the many. Evidence that the principles has been grasped is provided if a person knows how to go on and deal with new situations in the light of it. People are brought to a grasp of principles by a mixture of explanation and a selective survey of the many. Words like 'insight' are used in connexion with the grasp of principles. It is difficult to state precisely what is meant by such words, but once people have it very little in the way of further practice is necessary as in the case of skills. Neither are principles quickly forgotten like the lower-level information which they unify. The typical term for the educational process by means of which people are brought to understand principles is 'teaching'; for 'teach' unlike 'train' or 'instruct', suggests that a rationale is to be grasped behind the skill or body of knowledge.

The transmission of critical thought

Societies can persist in which bodies of knowledge with principles immanent in them can be handed on without any systematic attempt to explain and justify them or to deal honestly with phenomena that do not fit. Fixed beliefs are thus perpetuated. When this is done we are presumably confronted with what is called indoctrination rather than teaching; for indoctrination is incompatible with the development of critical thought. Critical thought, however, is a rationalistic abstraction without a body of knowledge to be critical about. The problem of the teacher is to pass on a body of knowledge in such a way that a critical attitude towards it can also develop. If too much emphasis is placed on critical thought the danger is that all processes of education will be conceived too much in terms of what is necessary for a critical attitude to emerge. This is one of the dangers immanent in Dewey's system in which the concept of being 'educated' is more or less co-extensive with that of being critical.

There is no innate tendency to think critically, neither is it easy to acquire. Indeed as Bacon argued, it goes against the inveterate tendency of the human race which is to believe what we want to believe and to accept things that we are told on trust. The clue to how such an inveterate tendency can be overcome was provided by Plato when he described thought as the soul's dialogue with itself. It is a pity that this clue was not followed up. For the notion might not then have developed that reason is a sort of mental gadget that can be used by the individual if it is not too clogged up with passion or, as Hume described it, 'a wonderful and unintelligible instinct in our souls'. Given that critical thought about the assumptions in which we are nurtured rather goes against the grain, it will only develop if we keep critical company so that a critic is incorporated within our own consciousness. The dialogue within is a reflection of the dialogue without. This is a paradigm of an educational situation; for educational processes are those by means of which public modes of thought and awareness, which are mainly enshrined in language, take root in the consciousness of the individual and provide avenues of access to a public world.

The best way of making sure of such a living organic structure of thought is probably to employ the *ad hominem* method of question and answer used by Socrates. This brings the learner very quickly to probe into his presuppositions and to make explicit principles which were previously only dimly apprehended. If the learner is constantly prodded into doing this he gradually begins to think in a more clear, coherent, and structured way; for there is a sense in which we do not really know what we think about anything until we have had to state it explicitly and defend it. If this process continues for quite a time the learner gradually takes the questioner into his own mind and begins to develop the form of thought himself. He can come to formulate objections to his assumptions himself and keep on reformulating what he thinks or proposes to do until he hits on something to which he can find no objections.

It is important to realize that such a critical clarification of principles as a very different exercise from applying them in concrete circumstances. This seems to be the burden of Oakeshott's attack on rationalism and the starting point of his conception of political education.[6] He is not much interested in the discussion and justification of principles. What fascinates him is the judgement required to apply them in particular circumstances. He sees clearly that such judgement cannot be acquired in salons, studies, or seminars. It comes through practical experience in the presence of those who already have it.

It does not follow either that a person who has mastered a form of thought such as history, or one of the sciences, is skilled in testing the hypothesis that may emerge from reflection or discussion. He must, of course, be familiar from the inside with how experiments can be designed, or how records and manuscripts are interpreted. But many of the great theoretical scientists have been poor experimentalists just as some of the great historians have arranged the facts in a new pattern rather than discovered a lot of new ones by ingenious techniques of research. From the point of view of education what is essential is the grasp of a conceptual scheme for ordering facts rather than skill in research.[7] The various forms of thought – historical, moral, scientific, aesthetic – all have their own such schemes and thus provide different perspectives for the interpretation of experience. They can, however, only have such a transforming effect on a person's outlook if they are passed on in the right way at the right time and if they are informed by that passion for truth which lies at the heart of all of them. Without this critical discussion can degenerate into verbal leger-de-main and a parade of principles can be equivalent to name-dropping. Whether such a passion is due to fostering the natural curiosity of the child, whether it is caught from those who are already possessed by it, or whether it develops because an individual is confronted by conflicting opinions, is difficult to determine.

Conversation and 'the whole man'

What then of the processes which lead to the development of an educated man in the full sense of a man whose knowledge and understanding is not confined to one form of thought or awareness ? Nowadays all sorts of educational experiments are being contrived to 'liberalize' vocational training and to ensure that premature specialization does not distort a man's view of the world. No doubt formalized correctives to specialization are necessary, though it is arguable that the proper place for them is at school rather than at university. But the question is whether explicit learning situations are sufficient to bring about this integrated outlook. The classical way of ensuring this, surely, has been not courses but conversation.

Conversation is not structured like a discussion group in terms of one form of thought, or towards the solution of a problem. In a conversation lecturing to others is bad form; so is using the remarks of others as springboards for self-display. The point is to create a common world to which all bring their distinctive contributions. By participating in such a shared experience much is learnt, though no one sets out to teach anyone anything. And one of the things that is learnt is to see the world from the viewpoint of another whose perspective is very different. To be able to take an active part in a real conversation is, of course, an achievement. It is not possible without knowledge, understanding, objectivity, and sensitivity to others. But it is also a learning situation of an informal sort. A vast amount of learning all through life takes place in such informal situations. Are we losing faith in the likelihood of anything emerging if it is not carefully contrived? Or are we just the victims of shortage of space, pressure of numbers, and the bureaucratization of our educational system?

This is the point of mentioning conversation at the culmination of a lecture on educational processes which has been concerned mainly with what goes on in formal situations. For just as educational processes are not confined to classrooms, so also for an educated man the distinction between formal and informal situations of learning is only one of degree. His experience is not only transformed by all that he has mastered, learnt, and understood, but is always exemplifying the processes by means of which such mastery, knowledge, and understanding has been acquired. The achievements constantly generate new tasks. Even in his middle age he can really listen to what people say irrespective of the use he can make of it or them. This is a considerable achievement. But then as Spinoza said of the state of human blessedness: 'all excellent things are as difficult as they are rare'.

NOTES

1. Sec Scheffler, I., *The Language of Education* (Thomas, Springfield, 1960), Ch. IV.
2. It should be stressed that what has been said relates only to thinking of something as a form of *education*. It is only under this aspect that we are implying that there is something worth-while immanent in scientific activity, for instance, and that there is no discontinuity between the tasks and the achievements. But we can train people to do 'science' for purely utilitarian or vocational purposes if we wish. The same applies to carpentry or cooking. We *can* look at such activities in

a purely instrumental way. Whether we should do so or not is a further question. In discussing this we are not engaged in a debate about the aims of education, but in a debate about whether we ought to educate people rather than train them, or whether something like science or carpentry has the intrinsic value which many would ascribe to it. It may well be too that there are many tasks and achievements engaged in at school, such as reading and computation, which, like boarding a bus or doing five-finger exercises, have a value which is almost entirely instrumental in relation to our educational aims. This may well be so. It does not contradict my thesis; rather it draws attention to the necessity of looking at what goes on in schools in a wider context. Schools are obviously concerned with things other than education – with health, for instance, with selection, and with vocational training.

3. The concept of education, could, perhaps, be extended to include such borderline processes. What exactly one calls 'education' in this twilight area does not much matter provided that the similarities and differences are recognised.

4. See Sarason, S. B., Davidson, K. S., and Blatt, B., *The Preparation of Teachers* (John Wiley, N.Y., 1962).

5. Hobbes, T., *De Corpore* (Molesworth Ed., 1839), English Works 1, Ch. 7.

6. See Oakeshott, M., *Rationalism in Politics* (Methuen, London, 1962).

7. It is important to make this point at a time when there is a growing demand that universities should fulfil two functions which are not altogether compatible – develop research not so much for its own sake but in order to solve *the* practical problems of the nation, and provide a 'liberal' education for a larger percentage of the population than heretofore.

3 LEARNING
Meaning, language and culture

David Carr

INTRODUCTION

David Carr is Professor of Education at Edinburgh University. His research interests include philosophy of education, ethics, virtues and moral education. He is well known for his work on 'The Nature of Professionalism and Professional Ethics'; 'Knowledge, Education and Curriculum Theory' and 'Virtue Ethics and the Influence of Aristotle in Philosophical and Psychological Perspectives on Moral Development and Education'. This chapter is taken from Carr's book *Making Sense of Education: An Introduction to the Philosophy and Theory of Education*, in which Carr explores major past and present conceptions of education, teaching and learning. The chapter will take some serious study, as it is an exploration of the concept of understanding within the thought of Frege and Wittgenstein. Carr argues that 'processes' in education cannot be separated from so-called 'products' or 'behavioural outcomes' and he criticises educational techniques that encourage children to be happy or attempt to raise their self-esteem without teaching them anything.

KEY QUESTIONS

1. What is the connection between 'process' and 'product' in the concept of understanding?
2. What relation is there between a behavioural experiment in educational research and the concept of learning?
3. Is there confusion present about definition of terms?

FURTHER READING

We recommend you look at P. T. Geach in *Mental Acts* (Routledge, London, 1957), which offers some important modern arguments against abstractionist accounts of concept-formations. Above all, we would recommend David Carr's 'Education, learning and understanding: the process and the product', in the *Journal of Philosophy of Education* (Vol. 26, 1992) pp. 215–225.

This Reading links with Chapters 1, 2 and 8 of *The Routledge Education Studies Textbook.*

INTRODUCTION

We have seen that the behavioural experiments of learning theorists are hard put to account for the *semantic* or meaning-implicated aspects of learning: insofar as the kind of learning presupposed to human education entails some *understanding* of what is learned, and understanding is a matter of a grasp of its *meaning*, behavioural psychology seems of questionable utility in accounting for any such educational understanding. Gestaltists and cognitive structuralists argue that human meaning-making cannot be entirely explained in terms of behavioural processes, because understanding (a dance or a picture) is a matter of active imposition of meaning-constitutive rules and principles on the brute data of sensory perception: this is the basic Kantian insight that 'intuitions without concepts are blind'.[1] However, the question now arises of the *source* from which these principles of construction might be derived. It is at this point that cognitivist or related constructivist accounts seem to face something of a dilemma. On the one hand, if they adopt Kant's position of maintaining that the principles by which psychology organises experience are logically *a priori* and/or necessary, they appear vulnerable to some kind of irreconcilable Cartesian or other dualism of mind and body, or reason and sense-experience, which also carries the burden of explaining the origin of such principles. On the other hand, however, there are serious objections to what may seem to be the only alternative of supposing, like Piaget and other modern cognitivists, that such organising principles are abstracted from sensible experience. First, there are well-rehearsed difficulties about understanding concept formation in terms of abstraction, which go back to Plato.[2] For one thing, given that the particulars we are inclined to include under this or that concept are often fairly disparate (consider, even in the case of concepts of direct sense-experience, the wide variety of colour shades to which we apply the term 'red'), it is hard to see how they might be regarded as having some *common* abstractable feature – apart, that is, from being the particulars we have *chosen* to refer to by this or that label (which is basically the philosophical position known as *nominalism*). For another, it is highly implausible to suppose that *some* concepts might be formed by abstraction from *any* feature of sensible experience: consider, for example, the difficulty of abstracting the logical sign for negation ('not') from common experiences of negativity (whatever that might mean).[3]

A related problem about any cognitivist view that the principles of experiential organisation are abstractions from experience is that of how we could *know* this to be so. Much here seems to turn on the cognitivist claim that this might be determined *empirically*: it may appear plausible to suppose from repeated observation that children develop (in perhaps culturally invariant ways) certain principles of experiential organisation. But how could *empirical* inquiry support any such claim? In order to be a strictly empirical generalisation, any such claim must rest on *induction*: repeated experience serves to support a general rule to the effect that learners (here and everywhere) organise their experience according to such and such principles – because all hitherto observed learners have been observed to do so. But such inductive generalisation is always open to *disconfirmation* in the light of further experience, and (as Hume showed)[4] cannot conclusively establish that things will always continue as previous experience has led us to expect. In short, it may be that further research shows that hitherto unobserved learners do not make sense of experience (as, say, organised in terms of cause and effect) in the same way as those previously observed. Thus, on the one hand, if cognitive structuralists argue that organising principles are discovered on the basis of empirical scientific investigation, then the claim that such principles have a key role in the meaningful organisation of human experience cannot be shown to have more than *provisional* or contingent status. On the other hand, if (closer to Kant) they argue that such organisational principles are *necessary* features of any meaningful human experience – that any learners anywhere would *have* to organise their experience in this or that way – it is not clear how any such claim might be grounded in empirical scientific investigation, as distinct from the kind of metaphysical considerations that precisely support an *a priori* rationalist dualism of reason and experience.

To be sure, there is another way in which cognitive and other conceptual structuralists may be inclined to maintain that certain *a priori* principles of rational organisation are necessarily presupposed to making sense of features of human experience. We have already observed that Gestalt psychologists sometimes sought to account for such organisational principles as 'closure' in neurophysiological terms, and such later cognitivists as Chomsky have opposed associationist views of language learning on the grounds that any such learning requires the grasp of a *grammar* that could not itself be acquired through experience, and which we might therefore suppose to be innately encoded or biologically 'hard-wired' into the neurophysiology of potential language users.[5] However, the same general difficulty that we observed in the case of behaviourist theories of learning concerning the potential gap between meaning and (any empirical) process also arises here. Indeed, in criticising behaviourism, we noted a crucial connection between the failure of learning theory to give an account of meaning, and behaviourist blurring of the distinction between the processes we undergo and the actions we undertake. It is precisely insofar as the notion of human agency requires some reference to intention or purpose – to the capacity of human agents to plan their actions and invest them with sense and significance – that human action cannot be reduced to mere sequences of 'colourless' behavioural or physical events. In this light, however, it is not much clearer why the causal operation of hard-wired grammatical programmes would guarantee the meaning of human experience or activity, than it is how such meaning might be generated by the acquisition of environmentally conditioned sequences of behaviour. Moreover, we have lately observed that no scientific story in terms of neural wiring could be sufficient to explain such Gestaltist phenomena of experiential organisation as 'closure' – since it is quite conceivable that someone might possess the hardware apt for the identification of a given ambiguous figure as a rabbit rather than a duck, but yet be unable to recognise the rabbit aspect insofar as they are culturally or environmentally denied (as was once true of Australian Aborigines) any direct access to rabbits. In short, possession of a rabbit concept would appear to require more than just the presence and/or operation of some internal biological mechanism. What, however, might this be?

RECOGNISING THE WORLD 'OUT THERE': HUME AND KANT

The most obvious temptation now, perhaps, is to suppose that some direct personal acquaintance with rabbits would be enough to supply the conceptual deficit: in short, that what the agent would need to acquire a concept of 'rabbit' is some kind of experiential access to rabbits. Surprisingly, however, it is not obvious that this is so – at any rate, if such acquaintance means only the entry of creatures we refer to by this term into our experiential field. The fact is that agents may *not* recognise rabbits – or, at least, those creatures under that name that we (in our culture) give to them – even though they are within their experiential reach. Of course, what agents do not see as rabbits they might well see as something else – as members of a larger, less differentiated category of rodentine creatures, or as a kind of walking foodstuff;[6] but it is also just possible that they might not even see rabbits at all – even though they are (or would appear to us to be) directly under their noses. Moreover, if this possibility seems hard to grasp, it may only be because we are in the grip of a powerful picture of concept-acquisition of long and distinguished philosophical pedigree. This picture is a central feature of the philosophical tradition known as (British) *empiricism* – although it can also be found in non-empiricist philosophical perspectives, and it probably survives vestigially even in Kant's ingenious reconstruction and synthesis of rationalism and empiricism. The basic idea behind this view of concept-formation is that concepts are effects of the unmediated impact of experience on the human senses. According to Locke, the main founding father of British empiricism, any knowledge of the world expressed in true judgements involves the exercise of *ideas* (his term for concepts), such knowledge is acquired via the senses, and therefore the ideas presupposed to such knowledge are best construed as causally engendered mental representations of an external order of things.[7] In short, the concept of rabbit is engendered in us by the causal impact on our senses of a particular object in the world 'out there': without that impact we could not have the idea of rabbit, and given the presence of the source of that impact in our perceptual field, it is difficult (on the face of it) to see how we might *avoid* having that idea. Notoriously, however, the high priest of empiricism, David Hume, was more sceptical about the very existence of any such Lockean external objective order. Hume argued there can be no certain knowledge of anything beyond the flux of fleeting impressions (sounds, textures, colours, and so on) that constitutes our immediate experience – and which, as they pass or subside, leave behind traces in the form of ideas: on this view, concepts or ideas are no more than faded (faintly recollected) sensory impressions, and no idea could have genuine sense unless it can be shown to correspond to some actual (past or present) impression.[8] Hence, for Hume, only two kinds of statement or judgement can have genuine meaning. On the one hand, there are what he calls *statements of fact* – in which the constituent terms of such propositions correspond to impressions: statements such as 'the cat sat on the mat' or 'bachelors are less prone to heart attacks' would fall into this category. On the other hand, there are what he calls *relations of ideas* – which are merely definitions of terms or rules for the uses of words: statements such as 'a bachelor is an unmarried man' and 'a square is an equilateral rectangle' fall into this second category. The empiricist view is essentially that concepts or ideas acquire sense by *referring* to items of experience: in short, in 'the cat sat on the mat', the terms 'cat', 'mat' and 'sat' function logically or grammatically rather like *names* or descriptions of things, properties or relations. Moreover, this basic empiricist view of concept acquisition as a matter of direct reference to experience survives well into twentieth-century philosophy: it resurfaces in one well-known form, for example, in the 'picture theory of meaning' of Wittgenstein's early *Tractatus-Logico-Philosophicus*.[9]

Still, whatever the initial plausibility of this basic theory of concept-formation, it has been the concern of many modern philosophers – particularly of the last two centuries – to call it into question. In this connection, a major source of criticism undoubtedly hails from the direction of what we may call post-Kantian *idealism*. There are different, more and less plausible, forms of idealism. What might be called 'subjective idealism' is just the radical (empiricist) sceptical view that we can have no knowledge of the world beyond our 'inner', mental or subjective impressions of it: for all we know, what we take to be experience of an objective order of things and other people is just a dream or hallucination to which no stable reality actually corresponds. The Irish philosopher, George Berkeley[10], seems to have held some such view (expressed in the slogan '*esse est percipi*': to be is to be perceived) – and, as we have seen, Hume also sailed perilously close to it. It is doubtful, however, whether subjective idealism is at all coherent. Most notably, Kant criticises the explicit idealism of Berkeley and the more implicit idealism of Hume on the grounds that it only makes sense to claim that all experience is subjective given that very distinction between the subjective and the objective that idealists deny we can make: if all experience is subjective, then we might just as well say that *none* of it is – for we can make sense of the subjective only by contrast with what is objective.[11] How, for example, can Hume draw the distinction between fact and falsehood if all impressions are on the same experiential level, and there is no basis upon which to draw the distinction between veridical (true) and non-veridical (illusory) sense-perceptions? Hence, Kant's attempt to reclaim the distinction between objective reality and subjective experience from subjective idealist scepticism has two main foundations. First, he argues that the objectivity of genuine perception is given precisely by the conformity of our experience of reality to certain rational principles of causal order, identity and difference, and so on: for example, objective things and real events are distinguished by (respectively) their *stability* and *regularity* from the protean nature of subjective dreams, delusions and hallucinations. Hume held that causal laws were rationally contentious or dubious inferences from experience. Kant argues that such Humean doubts about the rational basis of causal order could only be raised by someone who already understands the world as ordered in certain specifiably rational ways: to that extent, rational principles of identity and difference, cause and effect, and so on, are logical preconditions of any intelligible human experience, and if things were as Hume suggests they might be, he would not even be in a position to describe this circumstance. Again, all this is summed up in Kant's famous dictum that 'intuitions without concepts are blind'.

But Kant also held (the other half of the above dictum) that 'thoughts without content are empty'. He agrees essentially with empiricists that experience marks the bounds of what may be intelligibly thought and said: what we can know of the world in any substantial sense of the term 'know' (that is, excluding definitions or other logically true statements) must ultimately be based on experiences we have reason to suppose objectively grounded. Thus, one reason why 'tritons eat mermaids' is hardly intelligible, let alone true, is that it cannot correspond to any objective experience – precisely because there is nothing in sensible experience to which the terms 'triton' and 'mermaid' could correspond. In this regard, despite Kant's insistence that sense-experience needs conceptualisation in order to be meaningful, it is not clear that he greatly questions the empiricist idea that meaningfulness is significantly a function of reference to objective experience. Moreover, Kant is at pains to insist that one principal condition of the truth of our knowledge claims consists in their relationship or correspondence to those objective states, events and particulars that he expresses through the idea of 'things-in-themselves'. Indeed, it is because Kant fails to question the empiricist idea that all perception is of the *appearances* of things – their observable properties of size, shape, colour, odour, texture, and so on – that he feels compelled to say that something 'behind' appearances is needed to secure the complete objectivity of accurate perceptions. On this view, 'things-in-themselves' are not *themselves* sensible or perceivable – for if they were, they would only be further sense-impressions; rather they are the utterly imperceptible and pre-conceptual (and therefore purely hypothetical) objective substrates of such properties and qualities. Thus, for Kant, it seems to be a general condition of the meaningfulness of a knowledge claim – and therefore of our understanding of it – that it refers or corresponds to ordered sense-impressions that are themselves grounded in the objective extra-sensible reality of 'things-in-themselves'.

CONCEPTUAL IDEALISM: THE SOCIAL PROVENANCE OF CONCEPTS

Kant's epistemology represents a kind of crossroads in modern philosophy: his work is a necessary reference point for all subsequent philosophical attempts to understand knowledge and concept-acquisition – and, with regard to his educational relevance, we have already observed Kant's decisive influence on modern cognitive psychology. However, the most immediate response and challenge to Kant's work was to come from a new nineteenth-century brand of idealism. Although such post-Kantian idealism[12] is mainly sympathetic to Kant's critique of the subjectivist tendencies of much empiricism – particularly to the idea that unconceptualised sensations or impressions could not in and of themselves give rise to knowledge – it also raises the most obvious difficulty for Kant's account: the role in his epistemology of 'things-in-themselves'. For what possible explanatory role could be played by things or objects about which absolutely nothing can be said because they underlie all appearances – and are, by that token, themselves beyond conceptualisation? The short answer given by post-Kantian idealists to this question is that insofar as it cannot play any intelligible role, we might as well abandon the 'thing-in-itself'. On the new idealist view, Kant is right to claim that there can be no coherent conception of the world on the basis of unconceptualised sensations alone – and that meaning is therefore a function of the imposition of concepts and categories on the impressions of sense – but he is mistaken in holding that the intelligibility of concepts and/or the validity of knowledge claims rests upon their correspondence to an objective reality lying 'out there' beyond or 'behind' our concepts of it. In a nutshell, the world or reality as we experience and understand it is comprised not so much of objects or things as of *ideas*.

It is extremely important to distinguish this kind of idealism – which we shall here call *conceptual idealism* – from the subjective idealism of such empiricists as Berkeley. Unlike subjective idealism, conceptual idealism does not take our knowledge of the world to be just a dubious personal construction from individual sense-impressions, but agrees with Kant that it involves the rational ordering of experience – recognising significant distinctions, for example, between more and less credible or trustworthy experiences. Where it effectively departs from Kant is in denying that what gives meaning, coherence and validity to our best epistemic claims is not any external order of unconceptualised 'things-in-themselves' – for there can be no such external order (or none that we could talk about): in short, the world is made or 'constructed' according to our conceptions, and has no order in and of itself. But if our picture of the world is not determined by the independent order of things as they are in themselves, from whence could it derive, other than from (as subjective idealism maintains) individual personal experience? In a nutshell, conceptual idealism holds that the concepts and categories by means of which human agents seek to make some sort of non-subjective sense of their experience are *interpersonal* or *social* in origin, and are constructed in the course of human cultural evolution. The new idealist insight is that both Kant's epistemology and the empiricism of which it is critical are prey to the common error of supposing that knowledge is a matter of personal confrontation with experience, and that the problem of objectivity is essentially that of accounting for the way in which the individual can break through the veil of appearance to make contact with the hard reality lying 'behind' that appearance. For conceptual idealists there is no such reality, and human meaning-making is less an individual than a *collective* matter: knowledge is in a significant sense conventional – as, indeed, historically changing conceptions of what counts as human knowledge might seem to confirm – and human groups construct their knowledge perspectives in response to evolutionarily encountered problems of survival. Nineteenth-century idealism is therefore a prime source of the widespread contemporary philosophical thesis of the *social character of meaning* – the view that human meaning-making is interpersonal rather than individual, and that human interaction and community are necessarily presupposed to any sort of conceptualisation.

The obvious problem for conceptual idealism, however, is that if our perspectives on the world are not to be judged true or false, credible or incredible, by virtue of their correspondence or otherwise to an objective order of 'things-in-themselves', how might they be validated? Broadly speaking, idealism replaces correspondence (to things-in-themselves) with *coherence* as the key criterion of meaning and truth. Although there can (by definition) be no concept-independent assessment of how things-in-themselves are, there can be evaluation of different conceptual perspectives in terms of logical coherence or consistency: thus, it will be more reasonable to believe some things than others on the grounds that we are well advised to avoid (practical as well as theoretical) inconsistency, and even within the terms of our local conceptual conventions there will be better sense-dependent grounds for some propositions than others. Hence, it would seem sensible from any *rational* point of view to deny the statement 'tritons eat mermaids' on the grounds that this proposition cannot be both true and false, and that there is hardly any empirical evidence for supposing that either tritons (as fish-men) or mermaids (as fish-women) exist. Indeed, on a highly rationalist view of conceptual idealism associated with the great

German idealist G. W. F. Hegel, the application of such rational criteria to the plethora of socially constructed human perspectives may be expected (in the literal fullness of time) to lead to a conception of the world that is *absolutely* true rather than just locally credible. Thus, according to what may be called *absolute idealism*, human inquiry advances by the systematic rational sifting of often contradictory human perspectives in the interests of an ultimately incontrovertible 'God's-eye' grasp of ultimate truth – and Hegel seems to have conceived human history as a matter of conceptual or 'spiritual' evolution towards some such absolute vision. On this view, different sociocultural constituencies have developed different and conflicting conceptions of the world in the course of their evolution, but since these perspectives are often far from logically consistent, they are not simultaneously credible. Thus, since these perspectives are as finite and limited as the human minds that construct them, they stand in need of correction and completion through an historically embedded process of so-called *dialectic*. The dialectical comparison and/or contrast of one perspective with another, of what Hegel calls 'thesis' with 'antithesis', is therefore held (ultimately) to yield an intellectual 'synthesis' that resolves all contradictions in the interests of a more comprehensive error-free vision of reality.

Several educationally significant philosophers of some stature are more or less directly indebted to Hegel and nineteenth-century idealism – and later, we shall consider the views of Karl Marx and John Dewey, who may (in their different ways) be regarded as key exponents of the thesis of social character of meaning. Both of these philosophers repudiate empiricist and 'realist' epistemology in favour of a social constructivist conception of meaning-making, and regard human knowledge and inquiry as subject to evolutionary development and change – although Dewey is ultimately unsympathetic to the absolute idealist tendencies of both German philosophers. For the purposes of this chapter, however, it may be more illuminating to explore the implications for understanding learning and concept-acquisition of a body of philosophical work that might seem somewhat remote from either Hegel, Marx or Dewey. All the same, it is arguably in the twentieth-century work of the philosopher Ludwig Wittgenstein that we come nearest to an account of concept-formation that most clearly identifies the difficulties of representational theories of meaning: in particular, Wittgenstein's seminal *Philosophical Investigations*[13] represents perhaps the most sustained modern attack on the idea that concepts are internal mental ideas or inner impressions that take on meaning by referring to aspects of experience. Despite this, Wittgenstein seems more obviously indebted to such pioneers of modern logical analysis as the German mathematician Gottlob Frege and the British logician Bertrand Russell than to any philosophers in the idealist tradition. Indeed, the notorious picture theory of meaning he defended in his early *Tractatus* was deeply influenced by the representationalism of Russell's own empiricist epistemology of 'logical atomism'.[14] All the same, Wittgenstein's later posthumously published work, which is expressly intended to demolish the picture theory of meaning, is arguably more continuous with some of the key anti-representational insights of Frege – as well as with a Deweyan instrumental construal of the nature of ideas and concepts as more like *tools* of public commerce than inner sensible representations. However, it is probably best to introduce Wittgenstein by way of some observations on the work of Frege.

FREGE'S REVOLUTIONARY SEMANTIC INSIGHTS

Frege was primarily a mathematical logician, and his pioneering formalisation of an important segment of natural language was largely a by-product of his even more ambitious project to derive mathematics from logic.[15] However, his inquiries into the nature of reason and inference begin with an examination of the basic notion of a thought.[16] From the outset, he clearly distinguishes thoughts as the *content* of psychological states from their conscious experiential or subjective embodiments or expressions: a thought is a *logical* rather than a psychological entity. From this viewpoint, the thought that (say) 'the boss was in a foul mood' is what is common to some such range of psychological states as 'he believed the boss was in a foul mood', 'he expected the boss was in a foul mood', 'he feared the boss was in a foul mood', and so on. This 'de-psychologisation' of thought is a key move in the development of Frege's logical grammar: whatever empiricists and others may have believed, Frege argues that thoughts are *not* empirical impressions, sensations, conscious states or other 'internal' psychological events. In support of this insight, he introduces a range of other important distinctions between concept and object, function and concept, and sense and reference.[17] Frege's logical distinction between concept and object reflects (roughly) the ordinary grammatical distinction between subject and predicate, and is primarily concerned to distinguish between terms that *refer* to objects in the world and terms which do not: thus, in 'the boss was in a foul mood', the subject term functions like a *name* and refers (presumably) to an objectively existing person, whereas Frege regards the predicate ' – was in a foul mood' as a concept expression that does not refer (ignoring the rather technical sense in which Frege held that concepts rather than objects are the referents of predicates[18]) in the sense of picking out experienced particulars. We might be tempted to judge otherwise, since we could at least feel drawn to say that in the sentence 'the bus is red', ' – is red' refers to a colour. But it may help here to distinguish reference from *description*: insofar as ' – is red' and ' – was in a foul mood' are *adjectives*, they describe things, but as adjectives they are grammatically incomplete apart from the objects they describe and should not therefore be held to refer as names do. Indeed, perhaps Frege's key insight rests on his recognition of an analogy between grammatical predicates and algebraic functions. In algebraic expressions of the form '2 $(x)^2 + (x)$' mathematicians distinguish between what they call the *argument* 'x' and the *function* '2 $(\ )^2 + (\ )$' – which is what remains after the removal of 'x': whereas the argument – whatever 'x' refers to or stands for – has significance apart from the function, functions are 'unsaturated' expressions having no determinate sense apart from arguments. For Frege, in 'the boss was in a foul mood', 'the boss' functions (with other name-like expressions) like a mathematical argument, whereas the concept expression '– was in a foul mood' behaves logically like an algebraic function.

However, the distinction of concept from object and the analysis of concept in terms of function interlock with another key Fregean distinction between sense and reference. Irrespective of their referential functions, according to Frege, all linguistic signs have a *sense*. Crucially, indeed, it is the possession of a sense by both concept expressions and the sentences to which they contribute that enables us to understand – grasp the *meaning* of – such false statements as 'Tony Blair is the king of Siam': contrary to those empiricist theories according to which any sentences that do not correspond to facts or definitions must be *meaningless*, we can clearly *understand* 'Tony Blair is the king of Siam' (for example, we can imagine what it would be like for it to be true) even though there is no experience to which it corresponds. Thus, although such 'unsaturated' concept expressions as '–is the king of Siam' do not have reference, they have a sense. But it is also clear from the analogy with mathematical functions that we cannot be sure precisely what the sense of a predicate expression is in advance of its application to a subject term: just as a mathematical operation such as 'the square root of …' has no clear meaning in advance of its application to particular arguments – and, of course, such application is liable to give rather different values for different arguments – so it cannot be very clear what ' – is the king of Siam' means in advance of its true or false predication of some object term. In the case of many predicates, indeed, it would seem that we could hardly know what is being said of an object until we know just what object it is being said of.[19] Consider, for example, what it means to predicate the most general term of evaluation '– is good' of something. If we ask what this *means*, it soon becomes clear that it means nothing *in general*. Rules or criteria for the application of ' – is good' to 'this knife' will be quite different from those we utilise in applying it to 'this doctor' or 'this woman': in short, a knife is good in quite a *different* sense from a professional role or a human being – and it is crucial for proper understanding to distinguish between these diverse senses of goodness. But just as predicates need subject terms in order to make determinate sense, so objects can be definitely identified only in terms of the properties expressed in predicates: I can know who Tony Blair is only via a set of descriptions that are presumably logically exclusive of his being the king of Siam. At all events, meaning appears to be a function of the grammatical cooperation or interplay of reference and predication: the one cannot make much sense without the other. Frege expresses all of this in his well-known aphorism that we should 'never ask for the meaning of a word in isolation, but only in the context of a proposition'.[20]

WITTGENSTEIN'S DEVELOPMENT OF FREGE

Wittgenstein's influential exploration of meaning and understanding in his *Philosophical Investigations* and other posthumously published works can be taken (in contrast with his earlier, more Russellian *Tractatus*) as an extension or ampification of these key insights of Frege. By way of ground-clearing, however, Wittgenstein sets out to show – via what has come to be known as the *private-language* argument[21] – that any empiricist or other account which takes concept-formation to be a matter of individual abstraction from the deliverances of sense-experience is bound to be incoherent. Just as Frege's work on the foundations of arithmetic had shown that one could not possibly derive simple or complex mathematical concepts of '2', 'minus 9', 'the square root of', and so on, from empirical experience, Wittgenstein sets out to show that concepts (Fregean 'senses') could not *generally* be derived via individual discrimination of aspects of inner or outer sense. Indeed, both Frege's anti-empiricist conception of number and Wittgenstein's private-language argument belong to a time-honoured tradition of philosophical concern about the nature of concept-formation reaching at least as far back as (and most obviously to) Plato. Plato's notorious theory of forms – the idea that since sense-experience cannot be considered a reliable source of genuine knowledge of the world, the concepts that guarantee such knowledge must hail from an intelligible realm of pure ideas that lie outside any sensible order – is clearly driven by a very real concern about how the concepts through which we understand the world of experience might have causal or other origins in that experience.[22] In philosophical contemplation of a cricket ball, for example, we might ask how we acquire the concepts of round and red – and the empiricist's reply is essentially that we derive them from repeated experiences of red and round things. Plato's point, however, is that since our concepts of red and round are ideal types to which nothing in particular experience corresponds, this hardly seems possible: the cricket ball is not perfectly (mathematically) round and is only one of the shades of red (which may be significantly *different* from other shades) to which we regularly apply the term 'red'. From this viewpoint, we may seem compelled to say (in the manner of one well-known contemporary judgement on this precise issue) that concepts are *mind-made*, and *applied* to human experience rather than abstracted from it.[23]

Wittgenstein's arguments against empiricist ideas of concept-formation are not at all far removed from such Platonic considerations. If the grasp of meaning is modelled on the idea of confrontation between the individual and *unconceptualised* sense-experience, how indeed might the individual succeed in abstracting the concept of 'red' from any such experience? Could this perhaps be achieved by some kind of inner *pointing* (ostension) to the items of experience to which he or she wished to draw attention? But how would the subject know what to point to, or which features of a given experience to identify as salient: how should he or she decide that these impressions count as red, whereas those are orange or purple? Even in the case of public rather than 'inner' experiential pointing there would need to be some grasp on the part of those for whom the pointing is intended that it is this rather than that feature that is in question – something, in short, to give meaningful contextualisation to such pointing. All the same, someone might say, there would have to be at least some cases of concept-formation by 'inner pointing'. For example, insofar as psychological experiences are *private* more or less *by definition* – just as I can only experience my pain, so you can experience only yours – how could I acquire concepts of such essentially 'private' experiences as being anxious or in pain other than by inner or 'private' ostension. Wittgenstein's repudiation of the empiricist account of concept-formation, however, is best appreciated in relation to his more surprising claim that even our concepts of psychological experience could not be acquired by any process of private reference to intrinsically internal states.

For one thing, Wittgenstein denies that it does follow from my inability to experience other people's pain that I cannot *know* that they are in pain – for such a conclusion would only follow from the assumption that the concept of pain, and any knowledge of the other's pain, is primarily a matter of 'inner' or private experience. Without denying that such experiences do enter into our avowals and ascriptions of pain, Wittgenstein holds that even insofar as the concept of pain is descriptive, it is not descriptive of an (indicated) experience. Certainly, in teaching children the concept of pain, parents will use the term descriptively in connection with people falling into nettles, fracturing limbs, receiving first aid, and so on. But, according to Wittgenstein, when people give vent to the first-person utterances 'I'm hurting' or 'it's painful', they are not at all describing or referring to experiences, but *expressing* how they feel: first-person pain utterances are *themselves* forms of pain behaviour. (This is the point behind Wittgenstein's rather paradoxical claim that it does not make sense to say 'I know that I'm in pain': knowledge claims are normally made on the basis of evidence – but I do not need *evidence* that I am in pain.) Thus, far from resting on private reference and/or abstraction, acquiring the concept of pain (as just one case of 'inner' experience) is as public a matter as acquiring any other concept: the descriptive content of the concept is taught by parents to children in relation to perfectly observable (and verifiable) circumstances of hurt and injury, and the expressive uses are encouraged in circumstances where parents want and need to know if their children are unwell. A central concern of Wittgenstein's here, again very much in the spirit of Frege's important insights into the nature of concepts and predication, is to dislodge the (empiricist and other philosophical) assumption or prejudice that the concepts expressed by grammatical predicates are invariably *descriptive* of (sensory or other) experience: thus, although we may also teach children that an adjective is a describing word, it appears that this need not always be so. If, for example, I observe that 'Helen is a beautiful girl' or 'the sorbet is delicious', it may not be that I am here *describing* Helen or the dessert, but rather that I am *evaluating* them as more pleasing or attractive (to my taste) than other girls or desserts. Likewise, if I say 'I'm over the moon', I am not obviously describing anything (not least my spatial position), but expressing how I feel.

Indeed, Wittgenstein argues that the surface grammar of linguistic usage is often quite misleading – so that, for example, what might seem to function like an adjective may not actually do so. We have already indicated that even with respect to genuine adjectival uses of the tricky term 'good', we may need to apply different criteria or rules of evaluation in relation to 'good girl' from those we utilise with respect to 'good knife': indeed, some philosophers of meaning-as-use have (contentiously) argued that to call persons 'good' in a moral sense is not to describe them at all, but to *commend* or express personal admiration for them.[24] Be that as it may, if someone says 'Good morning' on a very rainy day, one would clearly have got hold of the wrong end of the stick to say: 'No it isn't, stop telling lies'. Here, it is a plain error to construe the term 'good' as functioning *either* descriptively *or* adjectivally: what someone clearly intends by saying 'Good morning' is not to describe the weather, but to *wish* me well in my business of the day. (In this respect, the American idiom 'have a nice day', though more irritating, is less grammatically misleading.) Wittgenstein insists that such mistakes are endemic in past philosophical treatments of the problems of knowledge, mind, morality, religion, aesthetics, and so on, and that a great many philosophical puzzles rest ultimately on a failure to appreciate that language has many practical uses other than to describe or report on the world. Wittgenstein is fond of an analogy between language and a box of tools: just as the tool box contains diverse implements for different uses, so language contains the resources for promising, complaining, commending, approving, commanding, questioning, explaining, and so on, as well as for describing. In this connection, Wittgenstein is also sceptical of the received philosophical method of trying to *define* the meanings of words in terms of *necessary* and *sufficient* conditions – holding that this also encourages the idea that a term like 'good' has a fixed or once-and-for-always sense, which might be determined by ascertaining what or how it describes. Wittgenstein therefore insists that we should look not for the meaning of a term but to its *use* – by which, of course, he means to say that a grasp of the use is the key to a proper appreciation of the meaning.

However, if understanding or the grasp of meaning is not a function of reference to aspects of inner experience, but a matter of mastery of the grammar of usage in different contexts of human agency, endeavour and association, it cannot be an *individual* or 'private' psychological achievement. As we have seen, even the conceptualisation of aspects of personal experience is something to which contexts of interpersonal and public communication are presupposed: a pre-linguistic Robinson Crusoe raised by animals on a desert island could certainly feel and suffer pain, but he could not meaningfully be said to have a *concept* of pain in the absence of a language in which the term 'pain' could acquire a determinate context of use. For Wittgenstein, then, concept possession is essentially a function of the capacity to grasp the complexities of linguistic usage, and the grasp of such complexities depends in turn upon initiation into the inevitably cooperative and interpersonal practices that give point to such usage: hence meaning and understanding are quite incompatible with the idea of a 'private language'. It is in this connection that Wittgenstein insists – again somewhat perplexingly – that 'understanding is not a mental process'. The common temptation here – which too many past philosophers have not resisted – is to suppose that understanding is a *psychological* phenomenon, and that it must therefore go on 'in the head'. Wittgenstein's rather surprising claim is that understanding goes on not in the head, but in perfectly public contexts of teaching and learning. In fact, on this view, what 'goes on in the head' – the inner experiences that a learner has in the course of learning something – may be quite irrelevant to the business of learning this or that. It may help here to bear in mind that we speak of people understanding things even when they are asleep or unconscious: a person who is unconscious will have no experiences, and someone who is asleep may be dreaming, but neither of these circumstances is of relevance to the fact that he or she (right now) understands quantum theory or knows how to play 'Tiger Rag' on the clarinet. Understanding is not a mental experience but a capacity or a *disposition*: a person understands when he or she has now grasped 'how to go on' with respect to some public procedure or (mental or physical) skill. We need to get into our heads the point that, as a later philosopher has put it, 'meanings ain't in the head'.[25]

CONCEPTS AS SOCIAL, INTERPERSONAL AND PRACTICAL RULES

For Wittgenstein, in sum, a concept is not an inner experience, but a kind of *rule* that has a primarily practical (though not necessarily instrumental) use within some context of human life. It is also a rule that requires public criteria for its correct application: a learner has understood or grasped a concept when he or she can execute a procedure or follow a rule according to standard practice or common convention. From this viewpoint, concept-acquisition could never be a matter of the private labelling of internal impressions, for how could we know from this that we had got something right? But this shows that the rule-following presupposed to concept-acquisition is more a *sociocultural* matter than a natural-developmental process: meaning and understanding are essentially products of active participation and engagement in interpersonal and cooperative human institutions and practices. Moreover, the distinctive character of human meaning and understanding is given primarily through that form of public communication familiar to us as language: language-acquisition is thus the most potent – if not the only – source of human concepts and conceptualisation. All of this, if true, has immense implications for understanding human conceptual development, and for issues about the contribution of scientific or experimental psychology to our understanding of such development. For example, we have already noted the general tendency of some empirical psychologists to construe the conceptual development of children in terms of the quasi-biological development of age-related cognitive structures. In this respect, there can be no doubt that cognitive psychologists have made rather heavy weather of explaining the conceptual transitions that are said to occur from pre-concrete to concrete learning on the basis of Piaget's conservation experiments. What, psychologists have asked, can explain how a child moves from a mistaken judgement that the same amount of water is more in the tall thin beaker than it is in the short fat one, to saying that the amount is the same? Whereas some notable cognitivists have offered some rather far-fetched epistemological explanations to explain such transitions, they are in fact quite inexplicable in empiricist terms, but very much less mysterious on a normative Wittgensteinian view of concept-formation. For, on a Wittgensteinian view, we have only to recognise that an infant's mastery of language is less advanced than a primary child's: that whereas the younger child may use a term like 'more' to mean either 'heavier' or 'taller', the older child may more easily discriminate. In short, although conceptual growth is a matter of the progress of principled understanding, such progress follows not from the biological development of cognitive *processes*, but from enhanced grasp of practice and usage.[26]

There can also be little doubt that the language of 'process' has come to play a very suspect role in modern theorising about learning and the curriculum – probably under the direct influence of modern cognitive psychology. Indeed, it would appear that a certain preference for the expression of educational objectives in terms of the cultivation of *processes*, rather than the production of so-called 'products' or 'outcomes', seems to have gone hand in hand with the cognitive psychological rejection of behavioural objectives analyses of learning and curriculum. The fair complaint of cognitive psychologists against such analyses is that such objectives can often be achieved in the absence of real understanding: indeed, it has been the time-honoured complaint of progressive educationalists that the rote and mechanical learning of skills and information of bygone schooling has all too often been meaningless, and has made little or no lasting or significant impact on young minds or lives. So it is not hard to agree that there is more to learning and education than the promotion of blind behavioural outcomes. But latter-day educational sloganising to the effect that the process is more important than the product, or worse, that we should seek to promote processes *rather than* products, is liable to serious and debilitating educational ambiguity and confusion.[27] On the one hand, it precisely suggests a dualistic conception of processes as entirely separate from, or only contingently related to, products or behavioural outcomes. For whilst in the course of learning children may well experience valuable psychological states or processes – of, say, enjoyment, satisfaction, and so on – that are only contingently related to learning outcomes, it is not at all clear how these might constitute *educational* aims of teaching. Although we may well agree that it is a good thing for children to experience confidence, satisfaction and enjoyment in the course of their learning, and recognise that good teachers are those who try to ensure this, we should also recognise that this could not possibly be an *intended* aim of teaching: that, indeed, parents would have cause to complain about any teacher who had made his or her pupils happy or confident without teaching them anything. It would appear, all the same, that careless talk about the importance of process over product has encouraged some recent tendency to regard the promotion of such inner states of well-being as actual aims of education – which (however desirable they may be) they are not.[28]

On the other hand, however, if processes are construed as the operations of thought or understanding, or the grasp of principles and reasons, it should by now be clear that they cannot be conceptually separated from so-called 'products' or 'behavioural outcomes'. In short, if the slogan that the process is more important than the product comes down to the claim that there can be no real knowledge without *understanding*, then – insofar as understanding is the mastery of public and interpersonal rules, practices and procedures – it can make little real sense to say that process matters *more than* product. Indeed, any idea that one might have understanding of an activity or skill apart from the procedures and practices that embody such understanding could only rest on the dualist mistake about mind that seeks to account for meaning in terms of private experience. Thus, Wittgenstein's observation in *Philosophical Investigations* that understanding is *not* a mental process gets straight to the heart of what is wrong with empirical psychological analyses of conceptual learning in terms of the growth of cognitive processes or structures – and, hence, to a proper appreciation of the confusion inherent in any educational talk of process rather than product. Indeed, Wittgenstein went so far as to question the value of modern experimental psychology as a coherent theoretical enterprise. At the very end of the *Investigations*, he declares that the problems of empirical psychology are not to be excused on the grounds that it is a young science in need of further refinement: the trouble is, he said, that psychology is all 'experimental methods and conceptual confusion'.[29] In view of the enormous and often less than helpful influence of empirical psychology on educational theory from the beginning of the twentieth century to the present day, educationalists might often have done well to take these very famous philosophical sentiments more closely to their hearts.[30]

POSSIBLE TASKS

1. Bearing in mind the potentially misleading nature of simple definitions, consider how you would set about teaching a young person to appreciate what is meant by the words 'tragic', 'absurd' or 'ironic' as applied to this or that human situation or work of art.
2. Consider how you might go about assisting a child to appreciate the metaphorical or analogical character of a passage of poetry.

NOTES

1. For Kant on thoughts, content, intuitions and concepts, see: I. Kant, *The Critique of Pure Reason*, trans. N. Kemp Smith, London, Macmillan, 1968, p. 93.
2. For some of Plato's difficulties over explaining the nature of concept-formation, see: Plato's *Republic* and *Parmenides*, in E. Hamilton and H. Cairns (eds), *Plato: The Collected Dialogues*, Princeton, Princeton University Press, 1961.
3. For some important modern arguments against abstractionist accounts of concept-formation, see: P.T. Geach, *Mental Acts*, London, Routledge and Kegan Paul, 1957.
4. For David Hume on problems of induction, see: D. Hume, *A Treatise of Human Nature*, Harmondsworth, Penguin, 1969.
5. For the linguistic theorist Noam Chomsky's innatism, see: N. Chomsky, *Language and Mind*, Harcourt, Brace and World, 1968.

6. For some interesting related points, see: D.E. Cooper, 'Grammar and the possession of concepts', *Proceedings of the Philosophy of Education Society of Great Britain*, vol. 7, 1973, pp. 204–22.

7. For John Locke's account of concept-formation, see: J. Locke, *An Essay Concerning Human Understanding*, Oxford, Oxford University Press, 1934.

8. For David Hume on impressions and ideas, see: Hume, *A Treatise of Human Nature*.

9. See: L.Wittgenstein, *Tractatus-Logico-Philosophicus*, trans. D.F. Pears and B. McGuinness, London, Routledge and Kegan Paul, 1961.

10. See: G. Berkeley, *A Treatise Concerning the Principles of Human Knowledge*, La Salle, Ill., Open Court, 1915.

11. For Kant's criticism of subjective idealism, see: Kant, *The Critique of Pure Reason*. Kant's argument against subjective idealism clearly pioneers the argument from polar opposites that is also explored by modern philosophers in, for example: G. Ryle, *Dilemmas*, Cambridge, Cambridge University Press, 1960, chapter 7; and J. Passmore, *Philosophical Reasoning*, London: Duckworth, 1970, chapter 6.

12. The German philosophers J.G. Fichte and G.W.F. Hegel may be considered key figures in the development of post-Kantian idealism. See, for example: J.G. Fichte, *The Vocation of Man*, trans. W. Smith, La Salle, Ill., Open Court, 1965; and G.W.F. Hegel, *The Phenomenology of Mind*, trans. J.B. Baillie, London, George Allen and Unwin, 1971. See also: C. Friedrich, *The Philosophy of Hegel*, New York, Random House, 1953.

13. See: L. Wittgenstein, *Philosophical Investigations*, trans. G.E.M. Anscombe, Oxford, Blackwell, 1953.

14. For Russell's philosophy of logical atomism, see: B. Russell, *Logic and Knowledge: Essays 1901–1950*, London, George Allen and Unwin, 1956.

15. For Frege's attempt to logicise mathematics, see: G. Frege, *The Foundations of Arithmetic: A Logico-Mathematical Enquiry into the Concept of Number*, trans. J.L. Austin, Oxford, Blackwell, 1978.

16. See: G. Frege, 'The thought', in P. Strawson (ed.), *Philosophical Logic*, Oxford, Oxford University Press, 1967.

17. See various essays in: P.T. Geach and M. Black (eds), *Translations from the Philosophical Writings of Gottlob Frege*, Oxford, Blackwell, 1966.

18. For a helpful discussion of some of the labyrinthine complexities of Frege's view of the referential status of concepts, see: A. Kenny, *Frege: An Introduction to the Founder of Modern Analytical Philosophy*, Harmondsworth, Penguin, 1995, especially chapters 6 and 7.

19. These ideas are also helpfully discusssed in: M. Luntley, *Contemporary Philosophy of Thought: Truth, World, Content*, Oxford, Blackwell, 1999.

20. For Frege's contextual criterion of meaning, see: Frege, *The Foundations of Arithmetic*, Introduction, p. xe.

21. For a very clear account of Wittgenstein's private-language argument, see: A. Kenny, *Wittgenstein*, London, Allen Lane: The Penguin Press, 1973.

22. For Plato's theory of forms, see: Plato's *Republic*.

23. See: Geach, *Mental Acts*.

24. However, for some trenchant criticism of so-called 'ascriptivist' accounts of meaning, see: P.T. Geach, *Logic Matters*, Oxford, Blackwell, 1972, section 8.

25. This point is made by Hilary Putnam. See H. Putnam: 'The meaning of meaning', in *Mind, Language and Reality*, Cambridge, Cambridge University Press, 1975; and *Reason, Truth and History*, Cambridge, Cambridge University Press, 1981.

26. For criticism of Piaget and Bruner in this connection, see: D. Carr, 'Knowledge and curriculum: four dogmas of child-centred education', *Journal of Philosophy of Education*, vol. 22, 1988, pp. 151–62.

27. On process and product, see: D. Carr, 'Education, learning and understanding: the process and the product', *Journal of Philosophy of Education*, vol. 26, 1992, pp. 215–25.

28. For suggestions that self-esteem and other processes might be regarded as aims of education, see: Scottish Office Education Department: *Personal and Social Education 5–14*, Edinburgh, SOED, 1993; and J. MacBeath, *Personal and Social Education*, Edinburgh, Scottish Academic Press, 1988. For some strong criticism of this idea, see: D. Carr, 'Emotional

intelligence, PSE and self-esteem: a cautionary note', *Pastoral Care in Education*, vol. 18, 2000, pp. 27–33.

29. For Wittgenstein's condemnation of empirical psychology, see: Wittgenstein, *Philosophical Investigations*, part II, p. 232.
30. On this issue, see: D. Carr, 'Educational enquiry and professional knowledge', *Educational Studies*, vol. 20, 1994, pp. 33–52.

4 WHO DECIDES WHAT CHILDREN LEARN AND HOW THEY SHOULD LEARN IT?

The recent historical experience of the United Kingdom

Roy Lowe

INTRODUCTION

Professor Roy Lowe is an expert in the education policies of the post-war British governments with publications that include *Education in the Post-War Years: A Social History* (1988) and *Schooling & Social Change 1964–1990* (1997) (both books published by Routledge). Lowe suggests that there are broadly two visions for schooling: one that is limiting, hierarchical and exclusive; the other which is more open, and underpinned by a view of the shared qualities of humankind. The way in which the article is written suggests that Lowe is clearly more in favour of the latter and suspicious of attention paid to precise intended learning outcomes which may lead to the sort of bureaucracy that will emphasise performance portrayed in the form of league tables. But Lowe avoids simplistic conclusions and suggests, explicitly, that it is important for people to think about these things and to decide what should be taught, how it should be learned and who should decide.

KEY QUESTIONS

1. Does popular education as provided by the State represents an attempt by those in power to establish through schooling a form of social control?

2. Should all children learn the same things?
3. How should they be taught?

FURTHER READING

Ross, A. (2000) *Curriculum: Construction and Critique* (Routledge, London). This provides an overview and intelligent discussion of different ways of approaching curriculum. We also recommend Fielding, M. (2007) 'The human cost and intellectual poverty of high performance schooling: radical philosophy, John Macmurray and the remaking of person-centred education' in *Journal of Education Policy* (Vol. 22 No. 4) pp. 383–409. Fielding argues against simplistic utilitarian approaches to education.

This Reading links with Chapter 3 and Debate 1 of *The Routledge Education Studies Textbook.*

INTRODUCTION

The work of historians of education sometimes involves posing basic questions about the nature and workings of modern society. Much of the work initiated and conducted by Richard Aldrich has involved asking fundamental questions about the recent development of schooling, and demonstrating the significance of educational change for social development. In the introduction to *Education for the Nation*, he stressed that his 'substantial purpose' was to 'provide a basis for the restoration of informed discussion and decision-making in education . . . to increase the understanding of education in this country' (Aldrich 1996: 2). This chapter in Richard's honour is written in that spirit and towards that end.

Richard Aldrich's work stands alongside that of Brian Simon, who in a lengthy career raised the possibility that popular education, as provided by the State, was not popular at all but in reality represented an attempt by those in power to establish through schooling a form of social control which ensured the ongoing separation of social groups and social classes (Simon 1960, 1965, 1974, 1991). Similarly, Fritz Ringer's work (1979) identified schooling as a device whose key function was to impose forms of social stratification right across the industrialising world. Although Ringer's work focuses on northwest Europe during the period of industrialisation, it has implications for current developments in countries such as China and India. Many historians have focused on gender issues, and in particular on the ways in which schools and higher education have been devices for the establishment and maintenance of distinctions between the sexes and for the promotion of different social routes and lifestyles for boys and girls (e.g. contributors to Lowe 2000, vol. 1, part V). Each of these debates impinges on, and needs to be kept in mind, whilst approaching the issues in this chapter.

In two public statements (Lowe 2002, 2005), I have argued for a new history of education which addresses the pressing issues confronting humankind at the present time, in particular global warming and the stark contrasts between rich and poor countries. It is time for historians to focus on, and go some way to explain, the role of schooling in establishing and maintaining these contrasts. Whilst the present chapter falls short of these major issues, it does address what must surely be seen as a central question for all educators. What should children be taught in schools and who should be making the decisions? How should they learn it? Another question necessarily arises, too: should all children be taught the same things or are differing curricula and teaching methods preferable for different groups of children? These questions are of significance not just for historians, but for all involved in education. The chapter argument will be founded in historical research but will necessarily involve some speculation and some claims which go beyond that narrow brief. Issues are raised which no one individual can hope to answer fully, but which none the less demand a response from anyone involved in the act of 'educating' children.

TWO STRANDS IN THE DEBATE ON SCHOOLING

Since the coming of popular education it has been possible to identify those who would set strict limits on what should constitute an education (particularly that of the common people) and those who held more lofty ambitions. Bernard de Mandeville in the eighteenth century, Bell, Lancaster, Davies Giddy and Bishop Fraser of Manchester in the nineteenth, each, in their own way, held to a very limited view of what was possible in school. Their pronouncements are well known and stand as an indictment of many who, through popular schooling, sought to keep the lower orders in their proper place (see Sylvester 1970: 176–82, 286–7; Simon 1960: 132; Maclure 1965: 79–80).

Their views have been echoed in some of the arguments of the emerging radical right in the period since the Second World War. Geoffrey Bantock, Professor of Education at the University of Leicester, argued publicly, in 1961, that

> syllabuses can only be built up as a result of honest admission of radical differences of ability. . . . We seem to be committed to the attempt, doomed to failure from the start, to bring all elements of the population to a similar level of consciousness. . . . in the school for the average child, the domestic life will concern the girls . . . for the boys an interest in the machine will play a major part. . . . What goes out? Formal history and geography should disappear. . . . Much waste matter could be removed from the mathematics syllabus. No second language should be studied. . . . What a school CAN accomplish is always sadly limited.
>
> (*The Times Educational Supplement*, 6 January 1961: 11)

The grounds on which such arguments were based may have changed beyond recognition, particularly given the input of the growing army of professional psychometricians during the twentieth century, but the central claim, that the education of the majority must remain strictly limited, appears remarkably familiar. In 1980, Roger Scruton observed that

> the attempt to provide equality of opportunity . . . is simply a confused stumble in the dark. . . . It is simply not possible to provide universal education. Nor, indeed, is it desirable. . . . The appetite for learning points people in only a certain direction: it siphons them away from those places where they might have been contented.
>
> (Scruton 1980: 75)

The determination to set limits on the schooling of the bulk of the population has been evident more recently in claims for the primacy of the so-called 'core curriculum'. Thatcherite and post-Thatcherite arguments that schooling must be 'useful' in terms of its relationship to employment and must be shown through inspection and public accounting to be both effective and efficient all bear marks of this nineteenth-century legacy.

This observation is equally true of the second major strand in educational discourse, namely the appeal to the nature, the needs and the interests of the child. Set against the arguments that the extent of education should be strictly limited, there have, for over two centuries, been those who took a radically different view of the potential of humankind.

The high priests of this movement are also extremely familiar to us. Jean-Jacques Rousseau, starting from what was seen at the time as the extremely controversial proposition that 'there is no original sin' in the human heart, spelt out an educational regime which was essentially libertarian and heuristic. Based on an attempt to explain the nature of childhood and to devise the educational regime which best suited that, Rousseau told the teacher:

> it is rarely your business to suggest what he ought to learn. . . . You should put it within his reach, should skilfully awaken the desire and supply him with the means for its satisfaction. . . . Let all the lessons of young people take the form of doing rather than talking; let them learn nothing from books that they can learn from experience.
>
> (Rousseau 1911: 142, 214)

These ideas, linked to the Pestalozzian view that all education was derived from sense impressions, became the basis of Robert Owen's claims that all humankind were rational beings and that it was the responsibility of the educator to 'either give the poor a rational or useful training, or mock not their ignorance, their poverty and their misery by merely instructing them to become conscious of the degradation under which they exist' (Silver 1965: 108). This underlying theme of the improvability of humankind underpinned the thinking of all those who pressed the claims of so-called 'progressive' education through the nineteenth and twentieth centuries. A host of figures such as Maria Montessori and Homer Lane, as well as those involved in the turn-of-the-century child-study movement, took a radically different view of both human potential and of educational methods from those who would set strict limits to what was possible in the classroom.

This became very evident in the period immediately following the Second World War. Advocates of child-centred education, of the 'play way' and of discovery methods seemed, briefly at least, to be in control of the rhetoric around popular education. John Newsom, the chief education officer of Hertfordshire, believed 'that the child was educated by the whole environment in which he or she was taught . . . he wanted schools that elevated the spirit and ennobled the mind' (Maclure 1984: 37–60). Newsom, with Alec Clegg in the West Riding and Stewart Mason in Leicestershire, were among the leading administrators advocating a progressive approach at this time.

The popularity of these ideas extended beyond teacher educators and primary school specialists. Indeed, *The New Secondary Education* reported the official government view that

> the majority of children learn most easily by dealing with things following a course rooted in their own day-to-day experience. . . . The majority will do best . . . in an atmosphere which enables them to develop freely along their own lines.
>
> (Ministry of Education 1947: 22–3)

The influence of this lobby was so powerful that, in the years following 1945, child-centred education, the 'play way', activity methods, de-streaming and the use of projects became almost universal rallying cries within education and were widely promulgated to the growing army of teacher training students.

Thus, for over two centuries, it has been possible to discern two conflicting themes in the debate on schooling: the one limiting, hierarchical and involving exclusivity; the other more open, underpinned by a view of the shared qualities of humankind rather than what differentiates them, and more ready to place responsibility on the shoulders of the learner. What can we learn from this dichotomy? What can it tell us about the central questions of what children should be taught, how they should be taught and who should decide on these issues?

THE CURRICULUM: WHAT SHOULD CHILDREN BE TAUGHT?

It is not oversimplifying to claim that the origins of popular schooling during the early industrial revolution were driven by several interlinked motives. Acceptance of the national religion, obedience, the training of a docile and cooperative labour force which was not over-educated and (particularly in view of events in France) the avoidance of revolution: these were the main concerns. All of this was brilliantly summarised by Richard Johnson (1970) as the imposition of social control. He saw the introduction of the schools' Inspectorate in the 1840s as the visible token of the imposition of that control, which remains important today. Any society that publicly funds an activity such as teaching understandably seeks to maintain some degree of control over how those monies are spent. Recently, in the United States of America, for example, the teaching of evolution has been banned in several states (see *Guardian*, 25 October 2005: 17). A list of topics and themes that are either proscribed or discouraged in schools in different parts of the globe could quickly be compiled.

Two themes are especially apposite when we consider the school curriculum in industrial Britain. The first has to do with elite education. Not only did the 'establishment' seek to put strict limits on the education of the working poor, the need to devise an appropriate form of schooling for their own children also led to the development of a powerful system of nineteenth-century private schools in which the curriculum approach was entirely different. The 1864 Parliamentary Report on the public schools commented that it is not easy to estimate

> the degree to which the English people are indebted to these schools . . . or their capacity to govern others and control themselves. . . their aptitude for combining freedom with order. . . . These schools have been the chief nurseries of our statesmen. They have perhaps the largest share in moulding the character of an English gentleman.
>
> (Chandos 1984: 328)

This distinctiveness of the public schools was founded on a curriculum which wove the teaching of modern subjects around a core of classical studies and which depended also on particular approaches to curriculum and teaching so as to encourage qualities such as self-assurance, independence of mind and leadership, all of which were thought to be important for the future lives of the pupils and for the British Empire. In brief, a differing career route required a quite different school curriculum. It is interesting, and significant, too, that although these schools have become subject to inspection by the State, they remain largely outside and aloof from political debates on the school curriculum and they continue to thrive. They have educated roughly 7 per cent of the population throughout the period since the Second World War, and they continue to do so.

Second, it is clear that swift economic change, particularly the development of what is best described as the second industrial revolution at the end of the nineteenth century, led to a growing need for curriculum change. On the one hand, industrialists were determined that the schools should not become places where trade secrets were communicated to young people who might end up working for their rivals. But, at the same time, it was vital that a more highly trained and an essentially literate labour force was generated to staff the growing electrical, chemical and engineering businesses which were very different from the earlier textile, mining and ironworking industries where a literate workforce would have been almost a distraction. Thus, economic change has been another constant in the debate on the school curriculum. Whether it is the white blouse revolution and the rise of the female secretary during the Edwardian era, or the rise of the service industries and the tertiary sector after the Second World War, or the computer revolution and the globalisation of knowledge most recently, whatever the impulse, there has been a succession of new strands in the debate on the curriculum during the past 150 years. These strands have always demanded that schools should offer their pupils 'useful' experiences, though understandings of what was most useful at any particular time changed.

Curriculum differentiation

If the distinction of the public schools from those of the common people was underpinned by a belief that differing curricula were needed for rich and poor, the evolving economic and social context was to lead to its own dynamic of curriculum differentiation within the fast-growing state sector. The rise of specialisation and of examinations supported the argument that some children would have to follow different curricular routes from others. By the mid-nineteenth century, this was becoming an element in public policy. The 1868 Schools Inquiry Commission, chaired by Henry Baron Taunton, assumed that the expansion of secondary education would necessarily cater separately for those whose parents wished them to stay in school to 18 years of age, those wishing to leave at 16 and those who saw no need of an education beyond 14. This meant three grades of secondary school with different curricula. Significantly, it was the parents whose wishes were to be paramount. And, significantly, during the following 30 years, when over 1,000 secondary schools were reconstituted by the Schools Commissioners appointed in 1869, although a major effort was made to impose three differing curricula (classical, modern and basic skills), with every school being designated first, second or third grade, in reality, teachers defeated the plan by simply adding those subjects which were not prescribed for their own school as additional subjects available after normal school hours at a fee. The distinctions became increasingly those of wealth and class, while curricula became increasingly similar across all schools of whatever type.

This proved to be almost an exact model for developments during the following century. A succession of government initiatives set out to impose different kinds of specialisation on the secondary schools. In the 1890s it was the higher grade schools set up to teach the sciences, while central schools were expected to prepare their pupils for particular kinds of employment in the early twentieth century. After the Second World War, new arguments (that children had differing kinds of mind and so needed different curricula) were advanced, but the attempt to distinguish between grammar, modern and technical schools bore all the hallmarks of the nineteenth-century planners. More recently, city technology colleges, specialist schools and academies have sought to differentiate curricula, with the interests and aspirations of the pupils ostensibly justifying the differentiation. Finally, in the autumn of 2005, the Labour government announced, in its twelfth Education White Paper, the introduction of 'self-governing' schools, which would enable parents to control a school's 'ethos and individualism' (DfES 2005). Over a century and a half the grounds have constantly shifted, but the central intention, to offer differing curricula to different pupils, has remained amazingly intact.

A few historical moments stand out as bucking this trend. The first was the publication of Robert Morant's 1904 *Regulations for Secondary Schools* (Board of Education 1904), which imposed a common curriculum for all schools in receipt of state support. These were in force for three years but had a massive long-term impact. Similarly, the shift towards comprehensive secondary schooling during the 1960s and 1970s was based in part on a belief in communality, which necessarily meant a shared experience of schooling and common curricula. It is clear, too, that the National Curriculum introduced by Margaret Thatcher as part of the 1988 Education Reform Act involved some kind of reaffirmation of a common experience of schooling, despite her efforts to establish schools that were distinctive. But, in reality, at any moment since the mid-nineteenth century, any visitor to England would have been struck more by what was common to schools than by how much they differed in curriculum. Certainly, those using the schools had a distinct sense of social class, of which schools were most effective in delivering a 'good' curriculum, and this view determined local property prices and much of the nature of suburban development in Britain. That sense of competitiveness is also an enduring feature. But it is worth remembering that in order to be seen as 'successful', any school would inevitably seek to mirror best practice, not least in matters of the curriculum. In brief, it is this social competitiveness which has made lasting curriculum distinctions a complete impossibility.

TEACHING METHOD

For many years, questions of teaching method were the great unspoken assumption of English education. Certainly during the late nineteenth and early twentieth centuries there were debates on teaching method involving such leading educationalists as Quick (1898) and Adams (1936), but conducted in private. In this field, as in many others, it was widely accepted that the professionals knew best. Indeed, the 1944 Education Act did not use the word 'curriculum' but was focused entirely on the structure of the system, which was seen as the proper arena for political differences.

So why, following the reforms of the period immediately after the Second World War, involving the introduction of novel methods of teaching and the complete restructuring of secondary education, did society become increasingly unwilling to acquiesce in whatever settlement the teaching profession imposed upon it? One explanation is that society was becoming more consumerist. Individuals became accustomed to exercising choice in areas in which people had previously been told what was best for them. Changes in the media facilitated the politicisation of education policy in a way that had been impossible before 1939. Education was likely to become more politicised anyway as it demanded a steadily increasing percentage of national spending. Parents, meanwhile, became anxious when they saw their children undergoing experiences that were in stark contrast to their own classroom memories. These are all necessary elements in explaining the rise of a 'new right' in education and the imposition of a new educational order under Margaret Thatcher, John Major and Tony Blair. At another level, however, many of the ingredients for increased parental concern about their children's schooling and for a sharper political interest in the details of educational practice had been in place for some time. The social functions of schooling had not changed and we know from well-established research that good schools have impacted on house prices in their immediate locality since before the end of the nineteenth century (see e.g. Marsden 1987; Goodenow and Marsden 1992).

Another element in the recent debate on teaching method is the subtle tension between the interests of parents and those of the government of the day. It is usual for governments to invoke parental power in educational reform programmes. But, in reality, what government appears to give with one hand it often takes away with the other. Margaret Thatcher's appeal to parental involvement, for example, was underpinned by the claim that the maintenance of educational standards was a government responsibility.

To summarise, the subtle shifts in the control of classroom practices since the Second World War are intimately related to questions of teaching method. For more than 30 years after the 1944 Education Act, the teaching profession itself held sway. Politicians and parents were loath to question classroom practice, notwithstanding the unprecedented advocacy of 'child-centred' approaches, of discovery methods, the use of projects and of more informal classroom arrangements. Although the ORACLE project at the University of Leicester was to throw doubt on how widespread in practice were these approaches (Galton 1987), the vast majority of public pronouncements, from teacher educators and others, called for one or other version of a more progressive approach. During the 1960s and 1970s, some more extreme versions of this advocacy called for pupils themselves to become the arbiters of their own learning. Lawrence Stenhouse's Humanities Curriculum Project saw the role of the teacher as overseer rather than didact and gave pupils control of their own curriculum (Schools Council 1969). The belief that the pupil should take control in this way never became widespread, and was dealt a heavy blow by publicity surrounding Islington's William Tyndale Primary School in 1975. Here, parents objected to the teachers opting for an extreme version of child-centred education, many moving their children to neighbouring schools. The Auld Report into what had gone on (Auld 1976) seemed to link progressivism to left-wing politics and did untold harm to the cause of those advocating more liberal approaches in the classroom. In the same year, the Bennett Report (Bennett 1976) was used by the press to claim that pupils did better in primary schools that were formally organised and heavily didactic. The issue was becoming politicised.

These developments, together with the impact of the Black Papers, published between 1969 and 1977, were the cue for government to become more involved. James Callaghan's widely publicised Ruskin speech in the autumn of 1976 insisted that there was a limit to the amount the state could afford to spend on education, and, equally, that schools should be more accountable. After this came the curbing of local authority powers, the closer regulation and scrutiny of teachers, the introduction of a national curriculum that curtailed possibilities for experiment in the classroom and the strengthening of inspectorial arrangements.

The post-1945 era has seen, at different moments and in different contexts, teachers, pupils, local authorities, central government, the Inspectorate, school governors and parents being thought of as the best arbiters of classroom practice. The period after the Second World War, in which the teachers themselves, and to a lesser extent the pupils, called the tune can be seen as a high point for child-centred approaches. Equally, the imposition of greater control by central government has meant less freedom to experiment, a greater focus on the core curriculum and basic skills, and more answerability through external checks and controls. Much of this has focused on the structure of the school day rather than on the details of classroom method and pedagogy, the introduction in 1998 of the 'literacy hour' in all primary schools being one example. There is much in this that bears an uncanny resemblance to nineteenth-century contests over schooling.

FURTHER CONSIDERATIONS AND CONCLUSIONS

The reasons why these changes took place when they did are complex, but those from the 1970s and 1980s coincided with new, and significant, approaches to educational research. Much of the reform of education during the post-war years was underpinned by research at the macro-level, social surveys which took a wide sweep and were heavily focused on issues of access and social class. Under the influence of intellectuals such as Tawney and Beveridge, researchers, not least Jackson and Marsden, Douglas, Mays, Halsey and Floud (Lowe 1988: 146) provided the intellectual ammunition for those seeking to work towards a more egalitarian provision of education. For many, this meant more open approaches in the classroom.

Elsewhere, other strategies, which were to increasingly dominate educational discourses of the 1970s and 1980s, were being devised. First, two Americans, Dan Flanders and E.J. Amidon, in what they later claimed was no more than a casual conversation in Wellington, New Zealand, in 1957, determined to establish the criteria for a closer analysis of what actually went on in the classroom. Their collaboration with J.B. Hough resulted in a voluminous 'classroom analysis' or, more precisely, 'interaction analysis' literature. Flanders explained in one book that their aim was to 'explain the variability of teacher influence' (Flanders 1967). British researchers such as Paul Croll, Neville Bennett, Michael Bassey and Maurice Galton can all be seen as working in the shadow of this pioneering American work. Their influence on the focus of policy was to be very significant during the 1970s and 1980s.

Second, two other American researchers, Bloom and Krathwohl, were setting out at about the same time to construe their own account of the teaching process. Their focus was less on the classroom exchange and more on the identification of teacher objectives. Their most important work, *A Taxonomy of Educational Objectives* (Bloom and Krathwohl 1964), laboriously drew up a list – or taxonomy – of educational goals. It is hard to understate the significance of these initiatives for the debate on schooling in Britain. They not only played a large part in the collapse of macro-theoretical approaches to the sociology of education, but they enabled teachers and educationalists to think in terms of objectives, as never before. It was not long before these 'objectives' were reworked as 'outcomes', and a whole new slant to educational policy and planning became possible. If the aims of the teacher could now be more precisely articulated, what was more natural than the setting of 'targets' by politicians to identify how well they had been met in practice? The devices for a gradual increase in the checks and controls operating on the teaching profession were almost imperceptibly coming into place.

A number of recent initiatives have resurrected the time-honoured tradition of governments seeking to ensure diversity in school curricula. First, the city technology colleges, announced at the 1986 Conservative Party conference, were set up to provide a strong emphasis on technological, scientific and practical work which would be part-sponsored by private business. The City Technology Colleges Trust was set up in 1987 and, one year later, Kingshurst School in Solihull, West Midlands, became the first such college. In 1994, all secondary schools were invited to take on a specialist role and, thus far, over 2,000 schools have responded as the incentives have been increased and the range of acceptable specialisms widened. On taking power in 1997, Tony Blair promised continuity in this policy of encouraging specialism at secondary level and in 2003 the Trust was redesignated the Specialist Schools Trust. Meanwhile, the city academies, which had been introduced in 2000 to raise standards in the most disadvantaged areas, again with financial support from the private sector, were in 2005 rolled into this scheme through a further redesignation as the Specialist Schools and Academies Trust. Finally, in the October 2005 White Paper, *Higher Standards, Better Schools for All*, the government proposed that all schools should be run by 'a self-governing trust. . . with independence and freedom to innovate . . . to determine its own admissions policy, to determine curriculum and to choose specialisms and expansion plans'. The role of local authorities is to be changed from being 'a provider of education' to 'a more strategic commissioning role . . . a champion for the needs of parents' with 'a focus on driving up standards rather than the day to day running of individual schools' (DfES 2005: 7–12). Behind this welter of changes there is a striking parallel with what went on in the nineteenth and early twentieth centuries.

It is important to step back from this account of a whirlwind of political activity to reflect on the underlying and persistent controversies around the education system. In our context these include, over the whole period during which the State has taken an interest in schooling, issues around where power and decision-making should lie: at central or local government level or with one or other of the interested local parties? They include persistent questions about whether the focus should be on a core curriculum, on basic skills or on a wider educational experience. They include questions around how far the curriculum should be common for all pupils or to what extent, at what ages and in which directions should children specialise. They include the question of how far it is the proper job of the schools to service the immediate needs of the economy. And they include, too, the vexed question of who should take prime responsibility for determining the day-by-day curriculum and teaching methods. All these issues are as relevant and as fiercely contested now as they have been for the past two centuries.

Understanding these power struggles requires consideration of the deeper social functions of schooling. Beyond simply instructing their pupils, inculcating appropriate attitudes and skills, and working towards social cohesion (all immediately apparent functions of an education system), one other key function of schools over the last two centuries has been the inter-generational defence of social or economic advantage. Either wittingly or unwittingly, parents have used the formal education of their children as a way of ensuring that their life chances are enhanced. This means ensuring, to the best of any parent's ability, that their child goes to what is seen to be a 'good' school, 'good' being defined by its ability to provide the appropriate skills, habits or accent for whatever career and lifestyle is thought to await the child. In many cases, this has involved the relocation of parents to an address which will give access to a desirable school. This indirect price rationing of education through the housing market, which has gone on, in Britain at least, for more than a century, makes irrelevant much discussion of the rights and wrongs of private, as against state, education, since significant parts of the public provision are effectively privatised through house prices. I have addressed this issue in greater length elsewhere (Lowe 2005), but it is necessary to refer to it here to offer any meaningful explanation of the ways in which the content of the curriculum, the provision of specialist schools and the control of school curricula are contested in an industrial or post-industrial society. To offer two rhetorical questions which highlight this dilemma: What would happen if every parent in a particular city or region wanted their children all to go to the same specialist school? And what would happen if all parents had the same power to influence which schools their children attended? It is the inability to provide any meaningful answer to these paradoxes that points towards an answer to the issues addressed in this chapter.

It follows that there is no simple, or single or straightforward answer to the questions posed at the outset. For each individual, the answers lie in their own particular understandings of the social functions of formal schooling. Depending on their political persuasion or their view of society, people will take quite different views of whether or not all children should follow the same curriculum, of how far they should specialise and at what points in their education, of exactly what that curriculum should be and of who should be the major influences on what goes on in school. Similarly, the question of where power should lie in the making of these decisions has been contested from the time of the first industrial revolution and is likely to remain so. But anyone with a serious interest in schooling, whether as parent, provider or observer, should have some understanding of their own position on these issues and be able to answer the questions 'what should children be taught?', 'how should they learn?' and 'who should decide?'. And it would be easier to defend their answers if they were also able to clarify which of the social functions of schooling they see as most significant and what is their concept of the model society. An understanding of history can help us towards a better set of responses to these questions, and the history of schooling, in its social context, can help us understand why certain views of these issues seem to be in the ascendant at particular times.

REFERENCES

Adams, J. (1936) *Modern Developments in Educational Practice.* London: University of London Press.

Aldrich, R. (1996) *Education for the Nation.* London: Cassell.

Amidon, E.J. and Hough, J.B. (eds) (1967) *Interaction Analysis: Theory, research and application.* Reading, MA: Addison-Wesley.

Auld, R.E. (1976) *The William Tyndale Junior and Infant Schools: Report of the public inquiry.* London: ILEA.

Bennett, N. (1976) *Teaching Styles and Pupil Progress*. London: Open Books.

Bloom, B.S. and Krathwohl, D.A. (1964) *A Taxonomy of Educational Objectives: The classification of educational goals*. London: Longman.

Board of Education (1904) *Regulations for Secondary Schools, 1904–5*. London: HMSO.

Chandos, J. (1984) *Boys Together: English public schools, 1800–1864*. London: Hutchinson.

Department for Education and Skids (DfES) (2005) *Higher Standards, Better Schools for All. More choice for parents and pupils* (White Paper, Cm 6677). London: The Stationery Office.

Flanders, N.A. (1967) 'Introduction'. In E.J. Amidon and J.B. Hough (eds) *Interaction Analysis: Theory, research and application*. Reading, MA: Addison-Wesley.

Galton, M. (1987) 'Change and continuity in the primary school: the research evidence'. *Oxford Review of Education*, 13(1), 81–93.

Goodenow, R.K. and Marsden, W. (eds) (1992) *The City and Education in Four Nations*. Cambridge: Cambridge University Press.

Johnson, R. (1970) 'Educational policy and social control in early Victorian Britain'. *Past and Present*, 49, 96–119.

Lowe, R. (1988) *Education in the Post-war Years: A social history*. London: Routledge.

Lowe, R. (ed.) (2000) *History of Education: Major themes* (5 volumes). London: Routledge-Falmer.

Lowe, R. (2002) 'Presidential address. Do we still need history of education: is it central or peripheral?' *History of Education*, 31(6), 491–504.

Lowe, R. (2005) *Whatever Happened to Progressivism? The demise of child-centred education in modern Britain*. London: Institute of Education.

Maclure, J.S. (1965) *Educational Documents, England and Wales 1816–1963*. London: Methuen.

Maclure, J.S. (1984) *Educational Development and School Building: Aspects of public policy, 1945–73*. Harlow: Longman.

Marsden, W. (1987) *Unequal Educational Provision in England and Wales*. London: Woburn Press.

Ministry of Education (1947) *The New Secondary Education* (Pamphlet 9). London: HMSO.

Quick, R.H. (1898) *Essays on Educational Reformers*. London: Longmans Green.

Ringer, F. (1979) *Education and Society in Modern Europe*. Bloomington: Indiana University Press.

Rousseau, J.J. (1911) *Emile*. London: Dent (originally published in 1780).

Schools Council (1969) *Humanities for the Young School Leaver: An approach through history*. London: Evans and Methuen.

Scruton, R. (1980) *The Meaning of Conservatism*. London: Penguin.

Silver, H. (1965) *The Concept of Popular Education*. London: MacGibbon and Kee.

Simon, B. (1960) *The Two Nations and the Educational Structure, 1780–1870*. London: Lawrence and Wishart.

Simon, B. (1965) *Education and the Labour Movement, 1870–1920*. London: Lawrence and Wishart.

Simon, B. (1974) *The Two Nations and the Educational Structure, 1780–1870*. London: Lawrence and Wishart.

Simon, B. (1991) *Education and the Social Order, 1940–1990*. London: Lawrence and Wishart.

Sylvester, D. (1970) *Educational Documents 800–1816*. London: Methuen.

5

THE HISTORY OF EDUCATION

Its importance for understanding*

Brian Simon

INTRODUCTION

Brian Simon (1915–2002) was a communist, an historian (his four-volume history of education is a classic work), an educationalist who researched and wrote about many topics and a campaigner for comprehensive schools. In this article, Simon manages both to provide a history of education and to give an argument for the historical study of education. He suggests that history can help us to understand change, to realise that education is a site of struggle, to get a sense of perspective on contemporary and other events and issues and, by so doing, develop critical awareness. He argues that teachers should be educated historically and so this article has important connections to notions of professional development.

KEY QUESTIONS

1. Is knowledge and understanding of the history of education useful to teachers?
2. Is it useful for educationalists who are not teachers?
3. Are there any differences between your answers to questions 1 and 2? Justify your point of view.
4. Do you think that comprehensive schools are useful for developing a just society and in raising academic standards?

FURTHER READING

The four volumes of *Studies in the History of Education* by Simon are still useful. Work on comprehensive education relates directly to Simon's concerns, e.g. Kerckhoff, A., Fogelman, K., Crook, D. and Reeder, D. (eds) (1996) *Going Comprehensive in England and Wales: A Study of Uneven Change* (The Woburn Press, London).

This Reading links with Chapters 3, 11 and 15 of *The Routledge Education Studies Textbook.*

* From Kadriya Salimova and Erwin V. Johanningmeier, *Why Should We Teach History of Education?*, The Library of International Academy of Self-Improvement, Moscow, 1993.

ADVANCES AND RETREATS

Education is about the empowerment of individuals. It is about discovering, and providing the conditions which encourage the fuller development of abilities and skills in every sphere of human activity – artistic, scientific, social and spiritual. But, more generally, education has been strikingly described as the *mode of development of human beings in society*,[1] and, seen in this light, the *process* of education involves all those formative influences, including the family, peer groups, the churches, apprenticeship, neighbourhood and civic relations with which all are involved from the earliest times; relationships growing in complexity, of course, as society itself becomes more complex. Within these sets of interrelations, organized schooling, which until recently only affected a small proportion of the population, now plays a central role. Together with the family it is the chief means by which new generations are inducted into the future.

It is of crucial importance, therefore, to attempt to penetrate the relations between education and society, between educational and social change. If schools, colleges, universities and teaching and learning institutions of all kinds are to flourish, and so realize their purpose of empowerment, we need to understand what circumstances hinder or encourage such a situation. This involves historical analysis. Such analysis indicates that there are no simple answers to these questions; that the whole issue is a great deal more complex than might, at first, be realized. There have been times, for instance, in most countries, when everything in the world of education seems to be advancing tumultuously; when the whole field seems animated by a positive spirit; when all seem to be working to the same end; when generous funding is made available, and when it seems that a new breakthrough is about to be made which will result in more widespread, more genuine opportunities for all, even given the continued existence of powerful forces resistant to change.

Most countries have experienced such a movement at least once during this century. If I may take Britain as an example, then I would argue that, in recent years, the 1960s saw precisely such a movement, one having national significance. This period saw, first, a rapid, planned expansion of higher education involving the establishment of many new universities (and the polytechnics), underpinned by the formulation of a twenty year plan of development right across the board – a plan that was fully accepted, supported and resourced, by government. Second, this period saw the start of a locally based grass roots swing to 'comprehensive' secondary education, again (from 1965) officially supported by government, a movement that sought to bring to an end, in formal terms at least, the divided, fractured, selective system of the past. Nor was this all. This period also saw the first serious recognition, historically, of primary education as a phase of crucial significance; the abandonment of long-established divisive practices (streaming), and the establishment of humane pedagogic means within these schools. Finally, this period also saw a significant decline in the importance (and number) of the private, or 'independent' schools, together with a growing questioning of their legitimacy. This resulted from increased acceptance of the primacy of the publicly provided (state-maintained) system, and so the emergence of a truly national system of education, locally, and democratically, controlled.

There have been other such periods in Britain, but none where the advances appeared so sweeping. In the late nineteenth century (1880–1900), for instance, a system of elementary education having finally been established, the outlines of an 'alternative system' to that inherited from the past (class-based, hierarchic) began to emerge, particularly in the great industrial cities of the Midlands and North. This (unexpected) upthrust embodied new forms of 'higher grade' schools, 'higher tops' in elementary schools, the so-called 'organized science schools', and so on, all emerging from within the elementary system itself. At the same time new institutions were now being created – technical schools and colleges, art colleges, and other such forms, including local universities only now being founded. So there began to emerge, sometimes rapidly, the lineaments of locally controlled, cohesive systems embracing educational facilities from the primary school to the new universities. In this development, local, directly elected School Boards played a crucial role. Women could be elected to these, as were also representatives of the local labour movement. 'Citadels of radicalism' was how the French historian, Elie Halevy, described these Boards and their work, which marked a definite and very positive phase in the evolution of the educational system.[2]

So there have been periods of advance – including, in Britain, other times when hopes were high, for instance, the few years after World War I and World War II. During both these wars progressive acts of parliament were passed embodying consensus views as to desirable advance – in 1918 and again 1944. But study of the history of education, as well as our own experience today, teaches us that, at least under a capitalist social order, educational advance does not take place in a simple linear fashion. Advances at one time are not necessarily followed by yet further positive developments; nor does history indicate any support for the so-called 'Whig' interpretation of economic, social and political affairs generally – that everything gradually, but regularly, consistently and evenly, improves over time.

On the contrary, periods of advance are often followed by a reaction against all that has been achieved; indeed that reaction may be building up just when the advances are most far-reaching and tempestuous. If circumstances (economic, social, political) are then propitious to these 'new' views, the advances previously experienced may be reversed. There can now be a move, more or less rapidly, towards new forms of control, towards overall constraint, the imposition of new divisions, a reversion to once rejected practices within systems, within schools and colleges, accompanied by the ideological transformations necessary once again to legitimize discarded approaches and practices.

In the case of the two examples just given, this was the English experience. The thrust forward of the 1880s and 1890s was deliberately halted by a conservative government with a large majority in Parliament through the passage of the Education Act of 1902. This *abolished* the school boards under whose auspices the advance had taken place, disallowed and, in effect, abolished the higher grade schools, established a selective elitist system of secondary education and removed education from directly elected popular control. In much the same way the thrust forward of the 1960s has been followed by similar measures, embodied in the 1988 Education Act passed again by a large Conservative parliamentary majority. These latter measures were designed to circumvent, and so to weaken, comprehensive secondary education; to marginalize, or thrust aside, the role of local education authorities in controlling local school systems; to develop a competitive, hierarchic structure of schooling through establishment of a market system in education, and to strengthen privatization of the system.

So historical study highlights the variability of educational change: 'the best of times, the worst of times', as Charles Dickens once put it. The cases just described indicate the complexity of the relations between education and society. Even though it is clear that education, and educational institutions, do at certain periods achieve a degree of autonomy (which varies by country and over time), and even though it is this which gives it its power, yet relationships generally in this field are clearly directly subject to wider, more all-embracing economic, social and political developments within society as a whole. Some of these are confined to a single country; others seemingly influence and affect the world as a whole (the 1960s expansion appears to have been a world-wide phenomenon).

THEORY AND PRACTICE

One of the outstanding characteristics of periods of advance in education appears to be a close link (or bondage) between educational theory and practice, though, paradoxically perhaps, this may also be a characteristic of a period of reaction – and when this is the case it presents particular problems.

For example, the educational theory which was dominant in the 1880s and 1890s in England, when the 'alternative system', just described, was thrusting energetically forward, was directly based on the classic materialist theory of human development, and specifically on its implications for teaching and learning. This tradition, or outlook, was derived from John Locke (particularly his *Essay Concerning Human Understanding*, 1690), but as developed by David Hartley into the form of associationism and then taken further, particularly as regards its educational implications, by Joseph Priestley, James Mill and many others culminating, perhaps, in Alexander Bain's *Education as a Science* published, significantly, in 1879 – just at the moment when the democratic thrust forward, led by the advanced School Boards, was about to take place. Fundamentally it was this theory which underlay the concept of human perfectibility as enunciated by Condorcet, Helvetius and others during the Enlightenment. This led to the view that all were educable – that, as Joseph Priestley argued, the teacher's action must have a necessary effect; and that to achieve positive outcomes the child's surroundings and all the influences to which he or she was subject must be carefully designed and structured to achieve the desired objectives in terms of human development.[3]

It was this theory, if sometimes crudely enunciated, which underlay and indeed legitimized the thrust forward of the late nineteenth century in Britain. It empowered teachers and underpinned their work as educators. In a different, but related form, such theories were also powerful at this time in Germany, particularly Prussia, the Mecca of educationists in the late nineteenth century, where Herbart's ideas, also based on associationist theory, were widely popular among teachers and educators. Indeed Herbartian theories played a very important role also in England and in the western world generally (including the United States) at this time.

It is a striking fact, however, that *the hegemony of these ideas and theories was broken in the early years of this century in England and also elsewhere (for instance, the United States), by the thrust of eugenics and biological thinking* generally which now accorded the greatest power over individual human development to heredity. We now enter the period of mass elementary education and of what has been described as 'the great 'psychological capture'' of the school.[4] The new theories found their psychological embodiment in the 'science' of psychometry, or mental measurement, and, using these tools, were applied to the schools where they were used for purposes of categorization or selection.

These theories, in contrast to those of Locke, Condorcet and Bain, stressed the limitation of human powers, the narrow function of education which could not enhance that which was 'given' through heredity, and so down-graded the functions of the schools and teachers. Psychometricians (or mental testers) claimed to be able accurately to measure inborn intellectual abilities. Class and other social differences crystallized within hierarchical school systems simply reflected, in this view, the *natural* differences between individuals. All was for the best in the best of all possible worlds.

This ideology, embodied in the theories of mental testing, and developed in Britain by psychologists working within the field of education (for instance, Cyril Burt), precisely reflected, in the sphere of ideas, the economic, social and so the educational stagnation of the inter-war years (1920–1940). Selection, segregation, categorization became the order of the day as everything slowed down. Educational failure on the part of the great majority of the population was explained (and legitimated) as the direct result of inborn limitations – of psychological failure, incapacity of the human mind. So, once again there was a new bonding between theory and practice; but acting, this time, as a powerful force underpinning educational stagnation.

It is significant that this theory, which achieved hegemony over the whole period from the early 1920s, had to be broken – in the sense of critically analysed and rejected – before the advances of the 1960s, described earlier, could be achieved. And indeed, for the historian, it is crucial to understand that there was, in fact, a deliberate, reasoned, conscious rejection of the fatalistic ideas of the inter-war period at the very start of this decade of advance – a clear rejection that was officially accepted and formed the ideological basis for the famous Robbins Report of 1963 which set out the programme of massive, planned expansion in higher education referred to earlier.[5] The rationale for the rejection of the ideas embodied in what may be called the classic standpoint of psychometry was articulated in 'evidence' given to the Robbins Committee by P. E. Vernon and Jean Floud, a leading academic psychologist and sociologist respectively. The former denied the classic theories of psychometry which held that the proportion of any age group capable of profiting from higher education is 'fixed by some immutable distribution of intelligence', while the latter dismissed the concept of a fixed 'pool of ability' as 'scientifically virtually valueless'. The supply of potential students, Floud argued, is a function of 'social change and social policy' and can be altered by changes in that policy. 'What only the few could do yesterday the many can do today.' Nor is there any 'iron law of the national intellect' imposing 'an upper limit on the educational potential of the population'.[6]

This critique heralded a complete and rapid transformation in the leading ideas relating to education. Now the work of psychologists like A. R. Luria and especially L. S. Vygotsky began to penetrate the West, while in the United States, Jerome Bruner and others advocated similar ideas, as also their counterparts in Britain. In the fields of both primary and secondary education the stress was once again laid on the educability of the normal child, but now on a new level of scientific understanding. It was this transformation in ideas and thinking which provided the theoretical underpinning for the thrust forward of the 1960s. Streaming was now rapidly abolished in primary schools, as also the system of selection at eleven into different, but parallel, types of secondary school. The swing to comprehensive secondary education now really got underway, powered by a new understanding of the extent of human educability. One lesson of history, then, concerns the central importance of ideas in the determination of development.

EDUCATION AND SOCIAL CHANGE

A crucial issue to which historical study can and should make a direct contribution, is that of the relation between educational and social change. This affects teachers and all involved in education which, as argued at the start, is essentially about human empowerment. If this is accepted as a major objective, then those working in this field must look to a society in which fuller scope is in fact given to human activity, since it is through activity in a social setting that human powers are realized. And this necessarily involves social change. Further it may be argued, human energy is likely to be more effective the more people believe in their power to effect change – to bend society more nearly to their aspirations. To subscribe to the belief in the mechanistic determination of educational or social change by structural forces outside human control is, on the other hand, a passport to fatalism – and so to inactivity and, finally, despair.

Can education change society? Or, to put it sharply, is the role of education, as it exists in institutionalized form in most advanced countries today, simply to reflect and perpetuate existing social relations? This is a difficult issue about which there has been much controversy. These opposite standpoints are often presented as stark alternatives – as if the answer must be one or the other. The fact that the role of education may differ in different circumstances is not taken into account. This is a possibility which we will return to later.

The view that educational change is crucial to social change has a long history, and has been expressed at different times in different forms. The great humanist educators of the sixteenth century, such as Erasmus and Melanchthon, certainly held this view. For this reason both exerted themselves throughout their lives to effect educational change. The great Moravian educator, Comenius, whose influence was widespread throughout Europe both in his own lifetime and later, fully accepted this standpoint, as did (as already mentioned) the *philosophies* of the Enlightenment (particularly the French, Helvetius and Condorcet). Rousseau in his own way expressed the same view as John Locke, Joseph Priestley and many others in England including, incidentally, Robert Owen who saw education as central to social change, and whose co-operative communities were seen as its vehicle. From Owen this tradition transferred into the modern socialist movement generally in the nineteenth and twentieth centuries.

Recently, however, the idea that education is *the* means by which existing society, with all its divisions, is reproduced has been strongly argued by social scientists, some sociologists and neo-Marxists. This view has been propagated with considerable force by the leading French sociologist, Pierre Bourdieu, who, in his *Reproduction in Education, Society and Culture* (1970) and other writings has advanced a set of tightly argued logically related propositions which lead to the conclusion that the educational structure, together with the pedagogical processes embodied within it, operates to ensure the reproduction of existing social categories, classes or groups. 'The School as Conservative Force', the title of one of Bourdieu's most influential articles, presents his general view very clearly. From this standpoint, education is certainly not seen as a means of bringing about social change.

At just this time (late 1960s, early 1970s) very similar views were expressed elsewhere. In the United States, for instance, Samuel Bowles and Herbert Gintis, in *Schooling in Capitalist America* (1976) argued very ingeniously what has come to be described as the 'correspondence theory'; that the educational structure and ethos 'corresponds' to the structure and ethos of the institutions of monopoly capitalism – and, furthermore, that they necessarily must act in this way. The schools, then, are in no position to challenge existing social structures. A few years earlier, in 1966 and 1972 respectively, social scientists in the United States published two highly influential reports, each based on a mass of contemporary data. These, (the Coleman Report and the Jencks Report, as they were known) both reached similar conclusions, popularly encapsulated in the phrase 'schools make no difference' – that is, schooling was shown to have no significant effect either on the pattern of income distribution or on life chances.[7] This again seemed to indicate that education could hardly promote social change.

This was also the view of the leading French Marxist, Louis Althusser, who in 1970, published his well-known essay entitled 'Ideology and Ideological State Apparatuses'. Althusser argued that the education system had taken the place of the Church as the chief means by which the dominant ideology of a class society was perpetuated, and so that society itself. Teachers were inevitably subsumed as agents of ideological domination, and nothing they could do could have any significant effect. Those who took a radical stance, holding that their actions as teachers could have some effect on the nature of society and even bring about social change were, said Althusser, 'a kind of hero', but one could only pity the futility of their efforts.[8]

Oddly enough these fatalistic views, advanced by radicals and neo-Marxists, chimed in with those of conservative educationists who sought to reverse the promise of the transformation of the 1960s. The result was a sort of unholy alliance between ideologists of the left and right, both of which now operated to disempower, or devalue, the claim that educational change could and did affect social change.

Historical study leads to a different conclusion from that of the social scientists just cited. Educational systems, whether centrally controlled (as in France and until recently the Soviet Union) or where primarily locally controlled (as in the United States and in England and Wales) do appear, at least at certain historical periods, to achieve a degree of autonomy from determination by a centralized state or by powerful structural (economic and social) forces. As England is the country I know best, having studied educational developments since 1780 in some detail, I shall take my examples from the experience of this country, though similar examples could certainly be taken from elsewhere.

There is no doubt whatever that the upthrust which took place in the late nineteenth century, already described, was largely, if not entirely, the outcome of a number of disparate local, or regional initiatives and activity. The primary role was certainly played here by the local School Boards, directly elected, as we have seen, since 1870, having powers to raise local rates to finance local developments. Board (elementary) schools certainly also received a subvention from the state, but the right to raise money from the rates gave considerable powers to local Boards to speed up development and to direct it in the manner these thought fit. Hence the upsurge of new, higher level types of schools and colleges which boded still further advances in the future. The School Boards' electoral system comprised an advanced form of proportional representation, unlike parliamentary representation in Britain; this ensured that all the major political and religious groupings could be represented on the School Boards, so that positive policies at this level achieved a genuine consensus.

It was these conditions which, at that time, certainly allowed a degree of autonomy to the local 'alternative' systems which emerged with some rapidity in the 1880s and especially the 1890s. Indeed so far was this perceived to be the case that, very early in the twentieth century, a conservative government determined to put an end to this threat (as it was perceived). The steps taken by this government have already been outlined. The 1902 Education Act, and related measures, were clearly designed to halt this upthrust from below, and to bring developments in secondary and higher education more directly under central control. These measures involved the actual abolition of the School Boards as we have seen. They also involved clear central control and limitation of secondary education (in the new county grammar schools), as well as a very precise central control over the curriculum in these schools. All this, I would argue, indicates that education had very definitely achieved a certain autonomy and was therefore in a position to effect social change. It was this autonomy which was directly threatened by the series of parliamentary and administrative measures which focused around the 1902 Education Act.

A strikingly similar pattern of events has taken place more recently in England, relating to the upthrust of the 1960s.[9] Here again there can be no question that the main educational developments at this period were the direct outcome of widespread local, popular activity determined to put an end to the fractured, diversive system of the past and to substitute something more generous, more equitable, more suited to the growing aspirations of the mass of the parents. This locally based movement was the force that lay behind the struggle for the single, comprehensive secondary school as well as the movement to abolish early and rigid streaming in primary schools. Very many examples could be given of the widespread activities which ensured that local education authorities all over the country voted democratically to make the transition to comprehensive education in spite of consistent, and long established, opposition to this policy by both Conservative *and* Labour governments in the whole period 1945–1963. It was the strength of local movements of this kind which finally forced governments of both persuasions to modify their policies so that the Labour government elected in 1964 finally decided fully to encourage this transition.

But, precisely as in the late nineteenth century, these advances provoked a backlash. A series of measures brought in, again by Conservative governments in the 1980s, culminating in the 1988 Education Act were designed to circumscribe, or, even destroy, the degree of autonomy which education had once again won back, following the constraining measures at the start of the century. The 1988 Act, as is well known, aims once again to reduce the power of local authorities over their 'systems'. Schools are encouraged to 'opt out' from local authority control; new types of school directly financed by the central state are being established (for instance, city technology colleges); financial control of schools is being devolved from local authorities; a centrally determined curriculum involving mass testing of all pupils covering the ages five to sixteen is being imposed on all maintained schools. So the relative autonomy achieved by local authorities by the 1960s is being destroyed, while that achieved also by the teachers, in terms of influence over the curriculum, is also being swept away. The 1988 Act accorded the Secretary of State for Education and Science some three hundred new powers. To obviate the experience of the 1960s, it seems, direct central state control over all important aspects of education at all levels is being imposed – or such, at least, is the intention. It is evident that the more the educational system is successfully subjected to a strict central control, the *less* scope there is to affect social change.

What conclusion can we reach? It seems clear that the English experience, at least, indicates that there have been periods of more or less rapid educational advance, based on local, popular movements and implying a critique of the existing social order together with its institutional support network – that is, carrying with it the implication of perhaps even radical social change. Such periods have been followed by periods of reaction characterized by measures preventing further developments, reducing the scope for local, popular control and imposing previously unacceptable levels of direct central control – the objective clearly being to obstruct further change, either educational or social. Where measures of this kind achieve primacy the link between educational and social change is broken; education resumes its conservative function of ensuring reproduction of existing social relations in Bourdieu's sense. There is, then, no simple answer to the question as to whether education can effect social change. The relation between education and society varies over time, and in respect to different circumstances. Nor is there anything fixed or determined about this relationship.

There is, then, considerable scope for human action in determining development – and this is the important point to bear in mind.

EDUCATION AS A SITE OF STRUGGLE

Any interpretation of educational change must take account of the fact that different social classes and groupings develop and articulate policies, and indeed a general outlook, reflecting their own needs and aspirations. Advanced industrial societies are, of course, riven by contradictions and divisions between opposing social forces. Such divisions and the conflicts to which they give rise, are necessarily reflected in the world of education – sometimes directly. The result is that education becomes, and is best seen as, a site of struggle between what are often opposing, or at least antagonist social forces. Such conflicts can become acute, as the historical record shows very clearly.

This interpretation was borne in on me when I first tried to make sense of developments in England during the late eighteenth and nineteenth centuries. Finally the model that seemed to 'fit' developments most clearly and logically was the three class model delineated in the writings and analysis of Karl Marx who, of course, derived much of his own material from the data of English industrialization. From the mid-late eighteenth century there took place an energetic development of capitalism which brought into being, and strengthened, the industrial and commercial middle class as a specific sector, one which rapidly became conscious of itself as a class in the early nineteenth century and which now articulated a specific educational policy both for its own members and for the newly developing working class.

With the growth of factory production at this time there also came into being a working class, also now becoming conscious of itself as a class, a process brilliantly analysed by Edward Thompson in his classic study, *The Making of the English Working Class* (1963). The harsh conditions of early capitalism forced this *class* to study and analyse their circumstances in the struggle for a better life. As it gained force and power in the early nineteenth century the nascent working class also articulated an educational policy, sought knowledge for themselves, and established a very wide network of educational activities which reached a climax in the Chartist period (1838–1848), and again later towards the end of the century.

At the start of the nineteenth century these two classes naturally confronted the hegemony of the aristocracy and gentry – the landowners – who traditionally had ruled the country through the eighteenth century and earlier. At the start of the century there developed an alliance between capitalists and workers aiming to force concessions from the ruling forces. Following their relative success in the passage of the Reform Act of 1832, however, this alliance was disrupted and, with the rapid development of industry through the century, and so of the size and strength of the working class, the middle class gradually formed an alliance and even fused with the gentry and aristocracy. The outcome was the establishment, by the end of the century, of a hierarchical education system catering separately for each social level, with the so-called 'public' schools (Eton, Winchester) at the top and the elementary schools for the working class at the bottom. So the scene was set for further struggles.

Using this model as a basis, it was possible to analyse the very complex educational developments in England in the nineteenth century in a way that seemed enlightening and that comprehended contemporary movements both in the institutional field and in that of ideas (relating to educational aims and purposes). Though published now over thirty years ago,[10] no alternative interpretation has been advanced, while the theses put forward have in fact been generally accepted both by educational and social historians. Later volumes in this (historical) series, one covering the period 1870–1920, another the inter-war period 1920–1940 and a fourth, recently published, the war and post-war periods 1940–1990 continue this analysis, although the three class model adopted for the first volume ceases to be appropriate certainly from the early twentieth century.[11] But that education continues to act as a site of struggle between opposing social forces certainly remains the case through the twentieth century and up to today. Indeed, at the moment of writing, it is more evident than ever.

One thing that emerges very clearly is the insistent pressure, from below, to open up the educational system and to ensure fuller access by disadvantaged classes and groups. This pressure meets continuous resistance from those social forces that wish to retain and strengthen existing hierarchical structures in order to ensure that education fulfils its favoured role of facilitating the reproduction of a class divided society. It is the continuous nature of this struggle that ensures that educational development never proceeds in a simple linear form, with everything improving all the time (as education historians of the past often presented the matter). On the contrary, educational development is the outcome of hard, and often very sharp struggles. Advances are recorded, or achieved, when conditions are favourable; retreats at other times.

The nature, procedures and structures of educational systems are clearly of profound significance in terms of human development. It is natural that there should be hard fought battles on these issues. This is why education can best be seen as a site of struggle.

THE IMPORTANCE OF HISTORICAL STUDY

In a seminal little book, published fifty years ago in 1940, Sir Fred Clarke, then Director of the Institute of Education, University of London, argued for a new approach to the history of education.[12] This should interpret thought and practice in the past in the light of conflicting social interests and their political expression. It is from this conflict of interests, as Clarke consistently emphasized, that educational change has emerged – in a form tempered by the political settlement arrived at, as well as compromises of thought and practice.

This is, in fact, the direction that historical studies have taken over the past decades in the United Kingdom, the USA and throughout Europe generally. In an essay on this topic written twenty five years ago, I argued that students, teachers – indeed all those concerned with the educational enterprise – would find the historical approach highly relevant to their work in schools and colleges of all types. By setting educational developments in their historical perspective, such study and knowledge 'opens the teachers' eyes to the real nature of their work'. It is the most difficult thing in the world, the essay continued, 'to view *objectively* a system in which one is immediately involved'. Historical study can be a powerful means to this end. 'It enables the student to understand that educational "principles" contain historical components, some of which may no longer be relevant – or, in the light of advancing knowledge, viable – and which are, therefore, open to reconsideration.' The same applies to institutions which have often changed in the past and will certainly be changed in the future. 'There is, perhaps, no more liberating influence than the knowledge that things have not always been as they are and need not remain so.'[13]

Fred Clarke also laid great stress, and correctly in my view, on the need for 'critical awareness' in teachers, and on the place of historical study in promoting this outlook. In his book he argued that to live unquestioningly in the immediate present is to run the danger of developing a conditioned response to current practice: a set of attitudes unconsciously determined rather than consciously formed. The individual teacher, after completing his or her training, enters a school which is part of an immense, ongoing system, governed by rules and procedures which have built up over time and over which he or she has no apparent control. By their very nature, educational institutions tend to be conservative – resistant to changes made necessary by economic and social developments quite outside the schools. Unless the teachers develop a critical awareness as to their role and function, such systems may become dominated by routinism and so lose touch with the wider society in which they exist and which they serve. Historical understanding can alert teachers to this danger, and, together with the critical awareness that Fred Clarke stressed, can provide the motivation for that innovation and change which is essential if education is to make the contribution to social advance which is, in essence, its *raison d'être*. Such an approach not only lends a new interest and excitement to the job of teaching, it should also ensure that the crucial contribution the teaching profession can make to more human social objectives is widely recognized and appreciated by society as a whole.

For all these reasons, I suggest, the historical study of education is important. Such study should surely form part of the teacher's induction as a student, and should be represented in initial training courses in colleges and universities. But the student, preparing to teach, inevitably focuses his or her mind and energies primarily on acquiring the classroom skills needed to survive in schools and to operate as an effective teacher. It is only when he or she has acquired these basic skills that minds and energies are freed for more intensive study of the social determinants of education. It is at this stage, through in-service courses and similar approaches, that the serious and committed teacher can most fruitfully give time and energy to historical study and reading. At this stage such study is most rewarding; indeed it is essential as the means of completing the formation of a truly professional teacher.

I have attempted, in this essay, to set out some of the main conclusions I have reached as a result of the detailed study involved in the production of four volumes covering the history of education in England from 1780 to the present day (1990). The focus is broadly on the relations between educational and social change since this is the crucial issue that confronts the historian. The complexities of this relationship are, of course, many and varied, and far greater than indicated here. These cannot be dealt with in a short essay. I have, therefore, attempted to focus only on essentials. I hope that students and teachers, in particular, may find this contribution helpful.

NOTES

1. Joan Simon, 'The History of Education in *Past and Present*', *Oxford Review of Education*, 3, 1 (1977).
2. Elie Halevy, *Imperialism and the Rise of Labour*, 1961 ed.
3. For Priestley's views and those of the English Enlightenment, see Brian Simon, *Studies in the History of Education, 1780–1870*, London, 1960, Chapter 1.
4. David McCallum, *The Social Production of Merit: Education, Psychology and Politics in Australia 1900–1950*, London, 1990.
5. Higher Education, Report of the Committee on Higher Education (the Robbins Report), Cmnd 2165, 1963.
6. For Vernon and Floud's evidence to the Robbins Committee, see *Higher Education, Report*, Part II, *Evidence.*
7. James Coleman *et al.*, *Equality of Education Opportunity*, Washington, 1966; Christopher Jencks *et al.*, *Inequality: A Reassessment of the Effect of Family and Schooling in America*, New York, 1972. My analysis of the work of Bowles and Gintis, Bourdieu (in the previous paragraph) and Althusser (in the next) draws on my essay 'Can Education Change Society?', in Brian Simon, *Does Education Matter?* London, 1985.
8. Louis Althusser, Ideology and Ideological State Apparatuses, in *Lenin and Philosophy and Other Essays*, London, 1970, pp121–173.
9. The term England is used here rather than Britain, since Scottish developments in this period differ strikingly from English.
10. As *Studies in the History of Education, 1780–1870*, London, 1960. This volume was later retitled as *The Two Nations and the Educational Structure, 1780–1870*, London, 1974.
11. *Education and the Labour Movement, 1870–1920*, London, 1965; *The Politics of Educational Reform, 1920–1940*, London, 1974; *Education and the Social Order, 1940–1990*, London, 1991.
12. Fred Clarke, *Education and Social Change*, London, 1940.
13. Brian Simon, 'The History of Education', in J W Tibble, ed., *The Study of Education*, London, 1966.

6

CULTURE, MIND AND EDUCATION

Jerome Bruner

INTRODUCTION

Jerome Bruner (born 1915) is one of the best known and influential psychologists of the twentieth century. His books: *The Process of Education* and *Towards a Theory of Instruction* have been widely read and become recognised as classics. Jerome Bruner's reflections on education in *The Culture of Education* (1996), from which this edited chapter is taken, show the impact of the changes in his thinking since the 1960s. Bruner developed the concept of discovery learning which promoted learning as a process of constructing new ideas based on current or past knowledge. This chapter focuses on the subject of cultural psychology and its implications for education. Cultural psychology deals with how individuals make sense of the world; how they engage with established systems of shared meaning, with the beliefs, values, and symbols of the culture at large. It concentrates on how individuals construct 'realities' based on common cultural narratives and symbols. Modern pedagogy, Bruner claims, is moving to the view that the child should be aware of his or her own thought processes and that achieving skills and accumulating knowledge are insufficient by themselves. In this chapter, Bruner discusses the model of the mind and its implications for education.

KEY QUESTIONS

Bruner outlines two broad ways in which human beings organise and manage their knowledge, which he calls: logical-scientific thinking and narrative thinking.

1. Which of these dominates teaching in English schooling?
2. Is there a difference in pedagogical approach between early years, primary, secondary, further and higher?

FURTHER READING

Bruner, in his work, has outlined four dominant models of pedagogy. The first model views the pupil as an imitative learner and focuses on passing on skills and 'know-how' through example and demonstrative action. The second model views pupils as learning from didactic teaching. It is based on the idea that learners should be presented with facts and rules of action which are to be learned, remembered, and then applied. The third model sees pupils as thinkers and revolves around how the pupil makes sense of his or her world. It stresses the value of discussion and collaboration. The fourth model views pupils as knowledgeable and stresses the management of 'objective' knowledge. He explains this in detail in *The Process of Education* (Harvard University Press, Cambridge, MA, 1960), which argues that schooling and curricula should be constructed to foster intuitive 'graspings'. Bruner makes the case for a 'spiral curriculum' in this book. Also worth reading is *Toward a Theory of Instruction* (Belkapp Press, Cambridge, MA, 1966) and *The Relevance of Education* (Norton, New York, 1977). In this last book Bruner applied his theories to infant development.

This Reading links with Chapters 2, 7 and 8 of *The Routledge Education Studies Textbook.*

I

[. . .] Fundamental changes [. . .] have been altering conceptions about the nature of the human mind in the decades since the cognitive revolution. These changes, it now seems clear in retrospect, grew out of two strikingly divergent conceptions about how mind works. The first of these was the hypothesis that mind could be conceived as a computational device. This was not a new idea, but it had been powerfully reconceived in the newly advanced computational sciences. The other was the proposal that mind is both constituted by and realized in the use of human culture. The two views led to very different conceptions of the nature of mind itself, and of how mind should be cultivated. Each led its adherents to follow distinctively different strategies of inquiry about how mind functions and about how it might be improved through 'education'.

The first or *computational* view is concerned with *information processing:* how finite, coded, unambiguous information about the world is inscribed, sorted, stored, collated, retrieved, and generally managed by a computational device. It takes information as its given, as something already settled in relation to some preexisting, rule-bound code that maps onto states of the world. This so-called 'well-formedness' is both its strength and its shortcoming, as we shall see. For the process of knowing is often messier, more fraught with ambiguity than such a view allows.

Computational science makes interesting general claims about the conduct of education, though it is still unclear what specific lessons it has to teach the educator. There is a widespread and not unreasonable belief that we *should* be able to discover something about how to teach human beings more effectively from knowing how to program computers effectively. One can scarcely doubt, for example, that computers provide a learner with powerful aids in mastering bodies of knowledge, particularly if the knowledge in question is well defined. A well-programmed computer is especially useful for taking over tasks that, at last, can be declared 'unfit for human production'. For computers are faster, more orderly, less fitful in remembering, and do not get bored. And of course, it is revealing of our own minds and our human situation to ask what things we do better or worse than our servant computer.

It is considerably more uncertain whether, in any deep sense, the tasks of a teacher can be 'handed over' to a computer, even the most 'responsive' one that can be theoretically envisioned. Which is not to say that a suitably programmed computer cannot lighten a teacher's load by taking over some of the routines that clutter the process of instruction. But that is not the issue. After all, books came to serve such a function after Gutenberg's discovery made them widely available.

The issue, rather, is whether the computational view of mind itself offers an adequate enough view about how mind works to guide our efforts in trying to 'educate' it. It is a subtle question. For in certain respects, 'how the mind works' is itself dependent on the tools at its disposal. 'How the *hand* works', for example, cannot be fully appreciated unless one also takes into account whether it is equipped with a screwdriver, a pair of scissors, or a laser-beam gun. And by the same token, the systematic historian's 'mind' works differently from the mind of the classic 'teller of tales' with his stock of combinable myth-like modules. So, in a sense, the mere existence of computational devices (and a theory of computation about their mode of operating) can (and doubtless will) change our minds about how 'mind' works, just as the book did.

This brings us directly to the second approach to the nature of mind – call it *culturalism.* It takes its inspiration from the evolutionary fact that mind could not exist save for culture. For the evolution of the hominid mind is linked to the development of a way of life where 'reality' is represented by a symbolism shared by members of a cultural community in which a technical-social way of life is both organized and construed in terms of that symbolism. This symbolic mode is not only shared by a community, but conserved, elaborated, and passed on to succeeding generations who, by virtue of this transmission, continue to maintain the culture's identity and way of life.

Culture in this sense is *superorganic.* But it shapes the minds of individuals as well. Its individual expression inheres in *meaning making,* assigning meanings to things in different settings on particular occasions. Meaning making involves situating encounters with the world in their appropriate cultural contexts in order to know 'what they are about'. Although meanings are 'in the mind', they have their origins and their significance in the culture in which they are created. It is this cultural situatedness of meanings that assures their negotiability and, ultimately, their communicability. Whether 'private meanings' exist is not the point; what is important is that meanings provide a basis for cultural exchange. On this view, knowing and communicating are in their nature highly interdependent, indeed virtually inseparable. For however much the individual may seem to operate on his or her own in carrying out the quest for meanings, nobody can do it unaided by the culture's symbolic systems. It is culture that provides the tools for organizing and understanding our worlds in communicable ways. The distinctive feature of human evolution is that mind evolved in a fashion that enables human beings to utilize the tools of culture. Without those tools, whether symbolic or material, man is not a 'naked ape' but an empty abstraction.

Culture, then, though itself man-made, both forms and makes possible the workings of a distinctively human mind. On this view, learning and thinking are always *situated* in a cultural setting and always dependent upon the utilization of cultural resources. Even individual variation in the nature and use of mind can be attributed to the varied opportunities that different cultural settings provide, though these are not the only source of variation in mental functioning.

Like its computational cousin, culturalism seeks to bring together insights from psychology, anthropology, linguistics, and the human sciences generally, in order to reformulate a model of mind. But the two do so for radically different purposes. Computationalism, to its great credit, is interested in any and all ways in which information is organized and used – information in the well-formed and finite sense mentioned earlier, regardless of the guise in which information processing is realized. In this broad sense, it recognizes no disciplinary boundaries, not even the boundary between human and non-human functioning. Culturalism, on the other hand, concentrates exclusively on how human beings in cultural communities create and transform meanings.

I want to set forth in this [. . .] chapter some principal motifs of the cultural approach and explore how these relate to education. But before turning to that formidable task, I need first to dispel the shibboleth of a necessary contradiction between culturalism and computationalism. For I think the apparent contradiction is based on a misunderstanding, one that leads to gross and needless over-dramatization. Obviously the approaches are very different, and their ideological overspill may indeed overwhelm us if we do not take care to distinguish them clearly. For it surely matters ideologically what kind of 'model' of the human mind one embraces. Indeed, the model of mind to which one adheres even shapes the 'folk pedagogy' of schoolroom practice [. . .]. Mind as equated to the power of association and habit formation privileges 'drill' as the true pedagogy, while mind taken as the capacity for reflection and discourse on the nature of necessary truths favors the Socratic dialogue. And each of these is linked to our conception of the ideal society and the ideal citizen.

Yet in fact, neither computationalism nor culturalism is so linked to particular models of mind as to be shackled in particular pedagogies. Their difference is of quite a different kind. Let me try to sketch it.

The objective of computationalism is to devise a formal redescription of *any* and *all* functioning systems that manage the flow of well-formed information. It seeks to do so in a way that produces foreseeable, systematic outcomes. One such system is the human mind. But thoughtful computationalism does *not* propose that mind is like some particular 'computer' that needs to be 'programmed' in a particular way in order to operate systematically or 'efficiently'. What it argues, rather, is that any and all systems that process information must be governed by specifiable 'rules' or procedures that govern what to do with inputs. It matters not whether it is a nervous system or the genetic apparatus that takes instruction from DNA and then reproduces later generations, or whatever. This is the ideal of Artificial Intelligence, so-called. 'Real minds' are describable in terms of the same AI generalization – systems governed by specifiable rules for managing the flow of coded information.

But, as already noted, the rules common to all information systems do not cover the messy, ambiguous, and context-sensitive processes of meaning making, a form of activity in which the construction of highly 'fuzzy' and metaphoric category systems is just as notable as the use of specifiable categories for sorting inputs in a way to yield comprehensible outputs. Some computationalists, convinced a priori that even meaning making can be reduced to AI specifications, are perpetually at work trying to prove that the messiness of meaning making is not beyond their reach. The complex 'universal models' they propose are sometimes half-jokingly referred to by them as 'TOEs', an acronym for 'theories of everything'. But though they have not even come near to succeeding and, as many believe, will probably never in principle succeed, their efforts nonetheless are interesting for the light they shed on the divide between meaning making and information processing.

The difficulty these computationalists encounter inheres in the kinds of 'rules' or operations that are possible in computation. All of them, as we know, must be specifiable in advance, must be free of ambiguity, and so on. They must, in their ensemble, also be computationally consistent, which means that while operations may alter with feedback from prior results, the alterations must also adhere to a consistent, prearranged systematicity. Computational rules may be contingent, but they cannot encompass unforeseeable contingencies. Thus Hamlet cannot (in AI) tease Polonius with ambiguous banter about 'yonder cloud shaped like a camel, nay 'tis backed like a weasel', in the hope that his banter might evoke guilt and some telltale knowledge about the death of Hamlet's father.

It is precisely this clarity, this prefixedness of categories that imposes the most severe limit on computationalism as a medium in which to frame a model of mind. But once this limitation is recognized, the alleged death struggle between culturalism and computationalism evaporates. For the meaning making of the culturalist, unlike the information processing of the computationalist, is in principle interpretive, fraught with ambiguity, sensitive to the occasion, and often after the fact. Its 'ill-formed procedures' are like 'maxims' rather than like fully specifiable rules. But they are hardly unprincipled. Rather, they are the stuff of *hermeneutics*, an intellectual pursuit no less disciplined for its failure to produce the click-clear outputs of a computational exercise. Its model case is text interpretation. In interpreting a text, the meaning of a part depends upon a hypothesis about the meanings of the whole, whose meaning in turn is based upon one's judgment of meanings of the parts that compose it. But [. . .] a wide swath of the human cultural enterprise depends upon it. Nor is it clear that the infamous 'hermeneutic circle' deserves the knocks it gets from those in search of clarity and certainty. After all, it lies at the heart of meaning making.

Hermeneutic meaning making and well-formed information processing are incommensurate. Their incommensurability can be made evident even in a simple example. Any input to a computational system must, of course, be encoded in a specifiable way that leaves no room for ambiguity. What happens, then, if (as in human meaning making) an input needs to be encoded according to the context in which it is encountered? Let me give a homely example involving language, since so much of meaning making involves language. Say the input into the system is the word *cloud*. Shall it be taken in its 'meteorological' sense, its 'mental condition' sense, or in some other way? Now, it is easy (indeed necessary) to provide a computational device with a 'look-up' lexicon that provides alternative senses of *cloud*. Any dictionary can do it. But to determine *which* sense is appropriate for a particular context, the computational device would also need a way of encoding and interpreting all contexts in which the word *cloud* might appear. That would then require the computer to have a look-up list for all possible contexts, a 'contexticon'. But while there are a finite number of words, there are an infinite number of contexts in which particular words might appear. Encoding the context of Hamlet's little riddle about 'yonder cloud' would almost certainly escape the powers of the best 'contexticon' one could imagine!

There is no decision procedure known that could resolve the question whether the incommensurability between culturalism's meaning making and computationalism's information processing could ever be overcome. Yet, for all that, the two have a kinship that is difficult to ignore. For once meanings are established, it is their formalization into a well-formed category system that *can* be managed by computational rules. Obviously one loses the subtlety of context dependency and metaphor in doing so: *clouds* would have to pass tests of truth functionality to get into the play. But then again, 'formalization' in science consists of just such maneuvers: treating an array of formalized and operationalized meanings 'as if' they were fit for computation. Eventually we come to believe that scientific terms actually were born and grew that way: decontextualized, disambiguated, totally 'lookuppable'.

There is equally puzzling commerce in the other direction. For we are often forced to interpret the output of a computation in order to 'make some sense' of it – that is, to figure out what it 'means'. This 'search for the meaning' of final outputs has always been customary in statistical procedures such as factor analysis where the association between different 'variables', discovered by statistical manipulation, needed to be interpreted hermeneutically in order to 'make sense'. The same problem is encountered when investigators use the computational option of parallel processing to discover the association between a set of coded inputs. The final output of such parallel processing similarly needs interpretation to be rendered meaningful. So there is plainly some complementary relationship between what the computationalist is trying to explain and what the culturalist is trying to interpret, a relationship that has long puzzled students of epistemology.

[. . .] Suffice to say that in an undertaking as inherently reflexive and complicated as characterizing 'how our minds work' or how they might be made to work better, there is surely room for two perspectives on the nature of knowing. Nor is there any demonstrable reason to suppose that without a single and legitimately 'true' way of knowing the world, we could only slide helplessly down the slippery slope that leads to relativism. It is surely as 'true' to say that Euclid's theorems are computable as to say, with the poet, that 'Euclid alone has looked on beauty bare'.

II

To begin with, if a theory of mind is to be interesting educationally, it should contain some specifications for (or at least implications bearing on) how its functioning can be improved or altered in some significant way. All-or-none and once-for-all theories of mind are not educationally interesting. More specifically, educationally interesting theories of mind contain specifications of some kind about the 'resources' required for a mind to operate effectively. These include not only instrumental resources (like mental 'tools'), but also settings or conditions required for effective operations – anything from feedback within certain time limits to, say, freedom from stress or from excessive uniformity. Without specification of resources and settings required, a theory of mind is all 'inside-out' and of limited applicability to education. It becomes interesting only when it becomes more 'outside-in', indicating the kind of world needed to make it possible to use mind (or heart!) effectively – what kinds of symbol systems, what kinds of accounts of the past, what arts and sciences, and so on. The approach of computationalism to education tends to be inside-out – though it smuggles the world into the mind by inscribing bits of it in memory, as with our earlier dictionary example, and then relies on 'look-up' routines. Culturalism is much more outside-in, and although it may contain specifications about mental operations *eo ipso,* as it were, they are not as binding as, say, the formal requirement of computability. For the approach of the computationalist to education is indeed bound by the constraint of computability – that is, whatever aids are offered to mind must be operable by a computational device.

When one actually examines how computationalism has approached educational issues, there seem to be three different styles. The first of these consists in 'restating' classical theories of teaching or learning in a computable form. But while some clarity is gained in so doing (for example, in locating ambiguities), not much is gained by way of power. Old wine does not improve much for being poured into differently shaped bottles, even if the glass is clearer. The classic reply, of course, is that a computable reformulation yields 'surplus insight'. Yet 'association theory', for example, has gone through successive translations from Aristotle to Locke to Pavlov to Clark Hull without much surplus yield. So one is justifiably impatient with new claims for veiled versions of the same – as with many so-called PDP 'learning models'.

But in fact, computationalism can and does do better than that. Its second approach begins with a rich description or protocol of what actually transpires when somebody sets out to solve a particular problem or master a particular body of knowledge. It then seeks to redescribe what has been observed in strict computational terms. In what order, for example, does a subject ask for information, what confuses him, what kinds of hypotheses does he entertain? This approach then asks what might be going on computationally in devices that operate that way, for instance, like the subject's 'mind'. From this it seeks to reformulate a plan about how a learner of this kind might be helped – again within limits of computability. John Bruer's interesting book is a nice example of what can be gained from this fresh approach.[1]

But there is an even more interesting third route that computationalists sometimes follow. The work of Annette Karmiloff-Smith[2] provides an example if taken in conjunction with some abstract computational ideas. All complex 'adaptive' computational programs involve redescribing the output of prior operations in order both to reduce their complexity and to improve their 'fit' to an adaptation criterion. That is what 'adaptive' means: reducing prior complexities to achieve greater 'fitness' to a criterion. An example will help. Karmiloff-Smith notes that when we go about solving particular problems, say language acquisition, we characteristically 'turn around' on the results of a procedure that has worked locally and try to redescribe it in more general, simplified terms. We say, for example, 'I've put an s at the end of that noun to pluralize it; how about doing the same for *all* nouns?' When the new rule fails to pluralize *woman,* the learner may generate some additional ones. Eventually, he ends up with a more or less adequate rule for pluralizing, with only a few odd 'exceptions' left over to be handled by rote. Note that in each step of this process that Karmiloff-Smith calls 'redescription', the learner 'goes meta', considering how he is thinking as well as what he is thinking about. This is the hallmark of 'metacognition', a topic of passionate interest among psychologists – but also among computational scientists.

That is to say, the rule of redescription is a feature of *all* complex 'adaptive' computation, but in the present instance, it is also a genuinely interesting *psychological* phenomenon. This is the rare music of an overlap between different fields of inquiry – if the overlap turns out to be fertile. So, REDESCRIBE, a TOE-like rule for adaptive computational systems that also happens to be a good rule in human problem solving, may turn out to be a 'new frontier'. And the new frontier may turn out to be next door to educational practice.

So the computationalist's approach to education seems to take three forms as noted. The first reformulates old theories of learning (or teaching, or whatever) in computable form in the hope that the reformulation will yield surplus power. The second analyzes rich protocols and applies the apparatus of computational theory to them to discern better what might be going on computationally. Then it tries to figure out how the process can be helped. This, in effect, is what Newell, Shaw, and Simon did in their work on the General Problem Solver,[3] and what is currently being done in studies of how 'novices' become 'experts'. Finally there is the happy fortuity where a central computational idea, like 'redescription', seems to map directly onto a central idea in cognitive theory, like 'metacognition'.

The culturalist approaches education in a very different way. Culturalism takes as its first premise that education is not an island, but part of the continent of culture. It asks first what function 'education' serves in the culture and what role it plays in the lives of those who operate within it. Its next question might be why education is situated in the culture as it is, and how this placement reflects the distribution of power, status, and other benefits. Inevitably, and virtually from the start, culturalism also asks about the enabling resources made available to people to cope, and what portion of those resources is made available through 'education', institutionally conceived. And it will constantly be concerned with constraints imposed on the process of education – external ones like the organization of schools and classrooms or the recruitment of teachers, and internal ones like the natural or imposed distribution of native endowment, for native endowment may be as much affected by the accessibility of symbolic systems as by the distribution of genes.

Culturalism's task is a double one. On the 'macro' side, it looks at the culture as a system of values, rights, exchanges, obligations, opportunities, power. On the 'micro' side, it examines how the demands of a cultural system affect those who must operate within it. In that latter spirit, it concentrates on how individual human beings construct 'realities' and meanings that adapt them to the system, at what personal cost, with what expected outcomes. While culturalism implies no particular view concerning inherent psychobiological constraints that affect human functioning, particularly meaning making, it usually takes such constraints for granted and considers how they are managed by the culture and its instituted educational system.

Although culturalism is far from computationalism and its constraints, it has no difficulty incorporating its insights – with one exception. It obviously cannot rule out processes relating to human meaning making, however much they do not meet the test of computability. As a corollary, it cannot and does not rule out subjectivity and its role in culture. Indeed, as we shall see, it is much concerned with *inter*subjectivity – how humans come to know 'each other's minds'. In both these senses, culturalism is to be counted among the 'sciences of the subjective'. And, in consequence, I shall often refer to it as the 'cultural psychological' approach, or simply as 'cultural psychology'. For all that it embraces the subjective in its purview and refers often to the 'construction of reality', cultural psychology surely does not rule out 'reality' in any ontological sense, it argues (on epistemological grounds) that 'external' or 'objective' reality can only be known by the properties of mind and the symbol systems on which mind relies.

A final point relates to the place of emotion and feeling. It is often said that all 'cognitive psychology', even its cultural version, neglects or even ignores the place of these in the life of mind. But it is neither necessary that this be so nor, at least in my view, is it so. Why should an interest in cognition preclude feeling and emotion? Surely emotions and feelings are represented in the processes of meaning making and in our constructions of reality. Whether one adopts the Zajone view that emotion is a direct and unmediated response to the world with subsequent cognitive consequences, or the Lazarus view that emotion requires prior cognitive inference, it is still 'there', still to be reckoned with.[4] And as we shall see, particularly in dealing with the role of schools in 'self construction, it is very much a part of education.

III

Let me now set out some tenets that guide a psycho-cultural approach to education. In doing so I shall commute back and forth between questions about the nature of mind and about the nature of culture, for a theory of education necessarily lies at the intersect between them. We shall, in consequence, constantly be inquiring about the interaction between the powers of individual minds and the means by which the culture aids or thwarts their realization. And this will inevitably involve us in a never-ending assessment of the fit between what any particular culture deems essential for a good, or useful, or worthwhile way of life, and how individuals adapt to these demands as they impinge on their lives. We shall be particularly mindful of the resources that a culture provides in making this fit possible. These are all matters that relate directly to how a culture or society manages its system of education, for education is a major embodiment of a culture's way of life, not just a preparation for it.

Here, then, are the tenets and some of their consequences for education.

1   *The perspectival tenet.* First, about meaning making. The meaning of any fact, proposition, or encounter is relative to the perspective or frame of reference in terms of which it is construed. A treaty that legitimizes the building of the Panama Canal, for example, is an episode in the history of North American imperialism. It is also a monumental step in the history of inter-ocean transportation, as well as a landmark in man's effort to shape nature to his own convenience at whatever cost. To understand well what something 'means' requires some awareness of the alternative meanings that can be attached to the matter under scrutiny, whether one agrees with them or not.

Understanding something in one way does not preclude understanding it in other ways. Understanding in any one particular way is only 'right' or 'wrong' from the particular perspective in terms of which it is pursued. But the 'rightness' of particular interpretations, while dependent on perspective, also reflects rules of evidence, consistency, and coherence. Not everything goes. There are inherent criteria of rightness, and the possibility of alternative interpretations does not license all of them equally. A perspectival view of meaning making does *not* preclude common sense or 'logic'. Something that happens a century after an event cannot be taken as a 'cause' or 'condition' of that event. I shall return to this issue of common-sense, logic, and reason in a later tenet.

Interpretations of meaning reflect not only the idiosyncratic histories of individuals, but also the culture's canonical ways of constructing reality. Nothing is 'culture free', but neither are individuals simply mirrors of their culture. It is the interaction between them that both gives a communal cast to individual thought and imposes a certain unpredictable richness on any culture's way of life, thought, or feeling. There are, as it were 'official' versions of all of these – 'Frenchmen are realistic', for example – and some of them are even inscribed in the law or in widely accepted kinship practices. And of course, they are also portrayed (often ambiguously and even problematically) in a culture's literature and its folk theories.

Life in culture is, then, an interplay between the versions of the world that people form under its institutional sway and the versions of it that are products of their individual histories. It rarely conforms to anything resembling a cookbook of recipes or formulas, for it is a universal of all cultures that they contain factional or institutional interests. Nonetheless, any particular individual's idiosyncratic interpretations of the world are constantly subject to judgment against what are taken to be the canonical beliefs of the culture at large. Such communal judgments, though often governed by 'rational' and evidentiary criteria, are just as often dominated by commitments, tastes, interests, and expressions of adherence to the culture's values relating to the good life, decency, legitimacy, or power. In consequence of all of the foregoing, a culture's judgments about the idiosyncratic construals of its members are rarely univocal. And to cope with this ever-present cultural multivocality, every society requires some 'principle of tolerance', a phrase that David Richards has used to characterize the way in which constitutional systems cope with contending interests and their interpretive claims.[5]

An 'official' educational enterprise presumably cultivates beliefs, skills, and feelings in order to transmit and explicate its sponsoring culture's ways of interpreting the natural and social worlds. And as we shall see later, it also plays a key role in helping the young construct and maintain a concept of Self. In carrying out that function, it inevitably courts risk by 'sponsoring', however implicitly, a certain version of the world. Or it runs the risk of offending some interests by openly examining views that might be taken as like the culture's canonically tabooed ones. That is the price of educating the young in societies whose canonical interpretations of the world are multivocal or ambiguous. But an educational enterprise that fails to take the risks involved becomes stagnant and eventually alienating.

It follows from this, then, that effective education is always in jeopardy either in the culture at large or with constituencies more dedicated to maintaining a status quo than to fostering flexibility. The corollary of this is that when education narrows its scope of interpretive inquiry, it reduces a culture's power to adapt to change. And in the contemporary world, change is the norm.

In a word, the perspectival tenet highlights the interpretive, meaning-making side of human thought while, at the same time, recognizing the inherent risks of discord that may result from cultivating this deeply human side of mental life. It is this double-facing, Janus-like aspect of education that makes it either a somewhat dangerous pursuit or a rather drearily routine one.

2   *The constraints tenet.* The forms of meaning making accessible to human beings in any culture are constrained in two crucial ways. The first inheres in the nature of human mental functioning itself. Our evolution as a species has specialized us into certain characteristic ways of knowing, thinking, feeling, and perceiving. We cannot, even given our most imaginative efforts, construct a concept of Self that does not impute some causal influence of prior mental states on later ones. We cannot seem to accept a version of our own mental lives that denies that what we thought before affects what we think now. We are obliged to experience ourselves as

invariant across circumstances and continuous across time. Moreover, to pick up a theme that will concern us later, we need to conceive of ourselves as 'agents' impelled by self-generated intentions. And we see others in the same way. In answer to those who deny this version of selfhood on philosophical or 'scientific' grounds, we reply simply, 'But that's how it is: can't you *see*?' All this despite the fact that there have always been rhetorically compelling philosophers (or in more recent centuries, psychologists) who have denied this 'folk psychological' view and even called it mischievous.

Indeed, we even institutionalize these so-called folk beliefs. Our legal system takes it as a given and constructs a *corpus juris* based upon notions like 'voluntary consent', 'responsibility', and the rest. It does not matter whether 'selfhood' can be proved scientifically or whether it is merely a 'fiction' of folk psychology. We simply take it as in the 'nature of human nature'. Never mind what critics say. 'Common sense' asserts it to be so. To be sure, we bend slightly for the critics. The law, typically, meets its critics by enunciating 'principled exceptions' – as in the extension and clarification of the *mens rea* doctrine.

Such intrinsic constraints on our capacities to interpret are by no means limited only to subjective concepts like 'selfhood'. They even limit our ways of conceiving of such presumably impersonal, 'objective' matters as time, space, and causality. We see 'time' as having a homogeneous continuity – as flowing evenly whether measured by clocks, phases of the moon, climatic changes, or any other form of recurrence. Discontinuous or quantal conceptions of time offend common sense to such an extent that we come to believe that continuous time is the state of nature that we experience directly. And this despite the fact that Immanuel Kant, one of the most highly honored philosophers in the Western tradition, made so strong a case for time and space as categories of mind rather than facts of nature. Faced with the fact, adduced by anthropologists, that there are local cultural variations in conceptions of time and space, and that these have practical implications in a culture's ways of life and thought, we tend to 'naturalize' them by labeling them exotic. It seems to be a human universal that we nominate certain forms of interpreted experience as hard-edged, objective realities rather than 'things of the mind'. And it is widely believed, both among lay people and scientists, that the 'nominees' for such objective status reflect certain natural or native predispositions to think and interpret the world in a particular way.

These universals are generally considered to constitute the 'psychic unity of mankind'. They can be considered as limits on human capacity for meaning making. And they require our attention because they presumably reduce the range of the perspectival tenet discussed in the preceding section. I think of them as constraints on human meaning making, and it is for that reason that I have labeled this section 'the constraints tenet'. These constraints are generally taken to be an inheritance of our evolution as a species, part of our 'native endowment'.

But while they may reflect the evolution of the human mind, these constraints should not be taken as man's *fixed* native endowment. They may be common to the species, but they also reflect how we represent the world through language and folk theories. And they are not immutable. Euclid, after all, finally altered our way of conceiving of, even looking at space. And in time, doubtless, Einstein will have done the same. Indeed, the very predispositions that we take to be 'innate' most often require shaping by exposure to some communally shared notational system, like language. Despite our presumably native endowment, we seem to have what Vygotsky called a Zone of Proximal Development,[6] a capacity to recognize ways beyond that endowment. The famous slave-boy in Plato's *Meno* was indeed capable of certain 'mathematical' insights (at least in response to the questions posed by the masterful Socrates). Would his insights have been possible without the queries of Socrates?

The educational implications that follow from the foregoing are both massive and subtle. If pedagogy is to empower human beings to go beyond their 'native' predispositions, it must transmit the 'toolkit' the culture has developed for doing so. It is a commonplace that any math major in a halfway decent modern university can do more mathematics than, say, Leibniz, who 'invented' the calculus – that we stand on the shoulders of the giants who preceded us. Obviously, not everybody benefits equally from instruction in the culture's toolkit. But it hardly follows that we should instruct only those with the most conspicuous talent to benefit from such instruction. That is a political or economic decision that should never be allowed to take on the status of an evolutionary principle. Decisions to cultivate 'trained incompetencies' will concern us presently.

I mentioned *two* constraints on human mental activity at the start of this discussion. The second comprises those constraints imposed by the symbolic systems accessible to human minds generally – limits imposed, say, by the very nature of language – but more particularly, constraints imposed by the different languages and notational systems accessible to different cultures. The latter is usually called the Whorf–Sapir hypothesis[7] – that thought is shaped by the language in which it is formulated and/or expressed.

As for the 'limits of language', not much can be said with any certainty – or with much clarity. It has never been clear whether our ability to entertain certain notions inheres in the nature of our minds or in the symbolic systems upon which mind relies in carrying out its mental operations. Is it in mind or in language that it is 'necessary' that something cannot be both A and not-A? Or is it 'in the world' – except for the part of the world covered by quantum theory? Is it in the structure of natural language that the world divides into subjects and predicates, or is this a reflection of how human attention works naturally?

Some have gone to the fanciful length of likening language to an instinct. But that dubious claim relates only to the formal syntax of language and is belied, in the main, by the profusion of expressive forms that mark its *use* – the pragmatics of language. The crafts of the storyteller, the orator, the gossip, or the poet/novelist, while caught in the web of syntax, hardly seem constrained by that fact. And as literary linguists continue to remind us, novelists keep surprising us by inventing new genres, still using the 'old' language.

As for the Whorf–Sapir hypothesis, its power and reach are also still not clearly understood. But as with the 'limits of language' question, it poses an interesting question for the cultural psychology of education. All that is known for sure is that consciousness or 'linguistic awareness' seems to reduce the constraints imposed by any symbolic system. The real victims of the limits of language or of the Whorfian hypothesis are those least aware of the language they speak.

But as the greatest linguist of our century, Roman Jakobson, long ago noted,[8] the *metalinguistic* gift, the capacity to 'turn around' on our language to examine and transcend its limits, is within everybody's reach. There is little reason to believe that anybody, even the speech-disabled, cannot be helped to explore more deeply the nature and uses of his language. Indeed, the spread of literacy may itself have increased linguistic awareness just by virtue of externalizing, decontextualizing, and making more permanent 'what was said', as David Olson has recently argued.[9]

The pedagogical implications of the foregoing are strikingly obvious. Since the limits of our inherent mental predispositions can be transcended by having recourse to more powerful symbolic systems, one function of education is to equip human beings with the needed symbolic systems for doing so. And if the limits imposed by the languages we use are expanded by increasing our 'linguistic awareness', then another function of pedagogy is to cultivate such awareness. We may not succeed in transcending all the limits imposed in either case, but we can surely accept the more modest goal of improving thereby the human capacity for construing meanings and constructing realities. In sum, then, 'thinking about thinking' has to be a principal ingredient of any empowering practice of education.

3   *The constructivism tenet.* This tenet has already been implied in all that has gone
before. But it is worth making explicit. The 'reality' that we impute to the 'worlds'
we inhabit is a constructed one. To paraphrase Nelson Goodman,[10] 'reality is made,
not found'. Reality construction is the product of meaning making shaped by traditions and by a culture's toolkit of ways of thought. In this sense, education must be
conceived as aiding young humans in learning to use the tools of meaning making
and reality construction, to better adapt to the world in which they find themselves
and to help in the process of changing it as required. In this sense, it can even be conceived as akin to helping people become better architects and better builders.

4   *The interactional tenet.* Passing on knowledge and skill, like any human exchange,
involves a subcommunity in interaction. At the minimum, it involves a 'teacher'
and a 'learner' – or if not a teacher in flesh and blood, then a vicarious one like a
book, or film, or display, or a 'responsive' computer.

It is principally through interacting with others that children find out what the culture is
about and how it conceives of the world. Unlike any other species, human beings deliberately teach each other in settings outside the ones in which the knowledge being taught will
be used. Nowhere else in the animal kingdom is such deliberate 'teaching' found – save
scrappily among higher primates. To be sure, many indigenous cultures do not practice as
deliberate or decontextualized a form of teaching as we do. But 'telling' and 'showing' are
as humanly universal as speaking.

It is customary to say that this specialization rests upon the gift of language. But perhaps more to the point, it also rests upon our astonishingly well developed talent for 'inter-
subjectivity' – the human ability to understand the minds of others, whether through
language, gesture, or other means. It is not just words that make this possible, but our
capacity to grasp the role of the settings in which words, acts, and gestures occur. We are
the intersubjective species par excellence. It is this that permits us to 'negotiate' meanings
when words go astray.

Our Western pedagogical tradition hardly does justice to the importance of inter-
subjectivity in transmitting culture. Indeed, it often clings to a preference for a degree of
explicitness that seems to ignore it. So teaching is fitted into a mold in which a single, presumably omniscient teacher explicitly tells or shows presumably unknowing learners
something they presumably know nothing about. Even when we tamper with this model,
as with 'question periods' and the like, we still remain loyal to its unspoken precepts. I
believe that one of the most important gifts that a cultural psychology can give to education is a reformulation of this impoverished conception. For only a very small part of educating takes place on such a one-way street – and it is probably one of the least successful
parts.

So back to the innocent but fundamental question: how best to conceive of a subcommunity that specializes in learning among its members? One obvious answer would be
that it is a place where, among other things, learners help each other learn, each according
to her abilities. And this, of course, need not exclude the presence of somebody serving in
the role of teacher. It simply implies that the teacher does not play that role as a monopoly,
that learners 'scaffold' for each other as well. The antithesis is the 'transmission' model
first described, often further exaggerated by an emphasis on transmitting 'subject matter'.
But in most matters of achieving mastery, we also want learners to gain good judgment, to
become self-reliant, to work well with each other. And such competencies do not flourish
under a one-way 'transmission' regimen. Indeed, the very institutionalization of schooling
may get in the way of creating a subcommunity of learners who bootstrap each other.

Consider the more 'mutual' community for a moment. Typically, it models ways of
doing or knowing, provides opportunity for emulation, offers running commentary,
provides 'scaffolding' for novices, and even provides a good context for teaching

deliberately. It even makes possible that form of job-related division of labor one finds in effective work groups: some serving pro tem as 'memories' for the others, or as record keepers of 'where things have got up to now', or as encouragers or cautioners. The point is for those in the group to help each other get the lay of the land and the hang of the job.

One of the most radical proposals to have emerged from the cultural-psychological approach to education is that the classroom be reconceived as just such a subcommunity of mutual learners, with the teacher orchestrating the proceedings. Note that, contrary to traditional critics, such subcommunities do not reduce the teacher's role nor his or her 'authority'. Rather, the teacher takes on the additional function of encouraging others to share it. Just as the omniscient narrator has disappeared from modern fiction, so will the omniscient teacher disappear from the classroom of the future.

There is obviously no single formula that follows from the cultural-psychological approach to interactive, intersubjective pedagogy. For one thing, the practices adopted will vary with subject: poetry and mathematics doubtless require different approaches. Its sole precept is that where human beings are concerned, learning (whatever else it may be) is an interactive process in which people learn from each other, and not just by showing and telling. It is surely in the nature of human cultures to form such communities of mutual learners. Even if we are the only species that 'teaches deliberately' and 'out of the context of use', this does not mean that we should convert this evolutionary step into a fetish.

5   *The externalization tenet.* A French cultural psychologist, Ignace Meyerson,[11] first enunciated an idea that today, a quarter-century after his death, now seems both obvious and brimming with educational implications. Briefly, his view was that the main function of all collective cultural activity is to produce 'works' – *oeuvres,* as he called them, works that, as it were, achieve an existence of their own. In the grand sense, these include the arts and sciences of a culture, institutional structures such as its laws and its markets, even its 'history' conceived as a canonical version of the past. But there are minor oeuvres as well: those 'works' of smaller groupings that give pride, identity, and a sense of continuity to those who participate, however obliquely, in their making. These may be 'inspirational' – for example, our school soccer team won the county championship six years ago, or our famous Bronx High School of Science has 'produced' three Nobel Laureates. Oeuvres are often touchingly local, modest, yet equally identity-bestowing, such as this remark by a 10-year-old student: 'Look at *this* thing we're working on if you want to see how *we* handle oil spills.'

The benefits of 'externalizing' such joint products into oeuvres have too long been overlooked. First on the list, obviously, is that collective oeuvres produce and sustain group solidarity. They help *make* a community, and communities of mutual learners are no exception. But just as important, they promote a sense of the division of labor that goes into producing a product: Todd is our real computer wonk, Jeff's terrific at making graphics, Alice and David are our 'word geniuses', Maddalena is fantastic at explaining things that puzzle some of the rest of us. One group . . . even devised a way to highlight these 'group works' by instituting a weekly session to hear and discuss a report on the class's performance for the week. The report, presented by a 'class ethnographer' (usually one of the teaching assistants), highlights *overall* rather than individual progress; it produces 'metacognition' on the class's oeuvre and usually leads to lively discussion.

Works and works-in-progress create *shared* and *negotiable* ways of thinking in a group. The French historians of the so-called *Annales* school, who were strongly influenced by Meyerson's ideas, refer to these shared and negotiable forms of thought as *mentalités*, styles of thinking that characterize different groups in different periods living under various circumstances. The class's approach to its 'weekly ethnography' produces just such a *mentalité*.

I can see one other benefit from externalizing mental work into a more palpable oeuvre, one that we psychologists have tended to ignore. Externalization produces a *record* of our mental efforts, one that is 'outside us' rather than vaguely 'in memory'. It is somewhat like producing a draft, a rough sketch, a 'mock-up'. 'It' takes over our attention as something that, in its own right, needs a transitional paragraph, or a less frontal perspective there, or a better 'introduction'. 'It' relieves us in some measure from the always difficult task of 'thinking about our own thoughts' while often accomplishing the same end. 'It' embodies our thoughts and intentions in a form more accessible to reflective efforts. The process of thought and its product become interwoven, like Picasso's countless sketches and drawings in reconceiving Velasquez's *Las Meninas*. There is a Latin motto, 'scientia dependit in mores', knowledge works its way into habits. It might easily be retranslated as 'thinking works its way into its products'.

All viable cultures, Ignace Meyerson noted, make provisions for conserving and passing on their 'works'. Laws get written down, codified, and embodied in the procedure of courts. Law schools train people in the ways of a 'profession' so that the *corpus juris* can be assured for the future. These 'hard copy' externalizations are typically supported as well by mythlike ones: the indomitable Lord Mansfield bringing the skepticism of Montaigne and Montesquieu into English law, the equally indomitable Mr Chief Justice Holmes injecting a new, Darwinian 'realism' into American jurisprudence, and even John Mortimer's fictional Rumpole struggling commonsensically against the legal pedants. What finally emerges is a subtle mix of starchy procedures and their informal human explication.

Obviously, a school's classroom is no match for the law in tradition-making. Yet it can have long-lasting influence. We carry with us habits of thought and taste fostered in some nearly forgotten classroom by a certain teacher. I can remember one who made us relish as a class 'less obvious' interpretations of historical happenings. We lost our embarrassment about offering our 'wilder' ideas. She helped us invent a tradition. 1 still relish it. Can schools and classrooms be designed to foster such tradition-inventing? Denmark is experimenting with keeping the same group of children and teachers together through all the primary grades – an idea that goes back to Steiner. Does that turn 'work' into 'works' with a life of their own? Modern mobility is, of course, the enemy of all such aspirations. Yet the creation and conservation of culture in shared works is a matter worth reflecting upon. Nor are we without good examples in our own time. Sarah Lightfoot has documented how certain public high schools create a sense of their enduring meaning,[12] and Michael Cole's 'computer networking' seems to yield the interesting by-product of widely separated groups of children finding a wider, more enduring, and palpable world through contact with each other by e-mail.[13]

Externalizing, in a word, rescues cognitive activity from implicitness, making it more public, negotiable, and 'solidary'. At the same time, it makes it more accessible to subsequent reflection and metacognition. Probably the greatest milestone in the history of externalization was literacy, putting thought and memory 'out there' on clay tablets or paper. Computers and e-mail may represent another step forward. But there are doubtless myriad ways in which jointly negotiated thought can be communally externalized as oeuvres – and many ways in which they can be put to use in schools.

6   *The instrumentalism tenet.* Education, however conducted in whatever culture, always has consequences in the later lives of those who undergo it. Everybody knows this; nobody doubts it. We also know that these consequences are instrumental in the lives of individuals, and even know that, in a less immediately personal sense, they are instrumental to the culture and its various institutions (the latter are discussed in the following tenet). Education, however gratuitous or decorative it may seem or profess to be, provides skills, ways of thinking, feeling, and

speaking, that later may be traded for 'distinctions' in the institutionalized 'markets' of a society. In this deeper sense, then, education is never neutral, never without social and economic consequences. However much it may be claimed to the contrary, education is always political in this broader sense.

There are two pervasive considerations that need to be taken into account in pursuing the implications of these hard-edged facts. One has to do with *talent;* the other with *opportunity.* And while the two are by no means unrelated, they need to be discussed separately first. For, as in the recent book by Herrnstein and Murray,[14] the two are often confounded – as if opportunity followed talent like its shadow.

About talent, it is by now obvious that it is more multifaceted than any single score, like an IQ test, could possibly reveal. Not only are there many ways of using mind, many ways of knowing and constructing meanings, but they serve many functions in different situations. These ways of using mind are enabled, indeed often brought into being, by learning to master what I earlier described as a culture's 'toolkit' of symbolic systems and speech registers. There is thinking and meaning making for intimate situations different in kind from what one uses in the impersonal setting of a shop or office.

Some people seem to have great aptitude in using certain powers of mind and their supporting registers, others less. Howard Gardner has made a good case for certain of these aptitudes (he calls them 'frames of mind') having an innate and universal basis – like the ability to deal with quantitative relations, or with linguistic subtleties, or with skilled movement of the body in dance, or with sensing the feelings of others.[15] And he is engaged in constructing curricula for fostering these differing aptitudes.

Beyond the issue of differing native aptitudes, however, it is also the case that different cultures place different emphasis upon the skilled use of different modes of thought and different registers. Not everybody is supposed to be numerate, but if you occupy the role of engineer, you're something of a queer duck if you're not. But everybody is supposed to be passingly competent in managing interpersonal relations. Different cultures distribute these skills differently. The French even have an expression that refers to the 'shape' of one's trained capabilities, 'professional deformation' in literal translation. And these very rapidly get 'typed' and consolidated through training and schooling: girls used to be considered more 'sensitive' to poetry, were given more experience in it, and more often than not *became* more sensitive. But this is a harmless example of the kinds of considerations that affect the *opportunity* young people have for developing the skills and ways of thinking that they will later trade for distinctions and rewards in the larger society.

There are many uglier features of opportunity that blight lives far more profoundly. Racism, social-class entitlements, and prejudice, all of them amplified by the forms of poverty they create, have powerful effects on how much and how we educate the young. Indeed, even the so-called innate talents of children from 'socially tainted' backgrounds are altered before they ever get to school – in ghettos, barrios, and those other settings of poverty, despair, and defiance that seem to suppress and divert the mental powers of the young who 'grow up' in them. Indeed, it was principally to counteract these early blighting effects of poverty (and, of course, racism) that Head Start was founded [. . .]. But schools themselves, given that they are locally situated, also tend to continue and perpetuate the subcultures of poverty or defiance that initially nipped or diverted children's 'natural' talents of mind in the first place.

Schools have always been highly selective with respect to the uses of mind they cultivate – which uses are to be considered 'basic', which 'frills', which the school's responsibility and which the responsibility of others, which for girls and which for boys, which for working-class children and which for 'swells'. Some of this selectivity was doubtless based on considered notions about what the society required or what the individual needed to get along. Much of it was a spillover of folk or social class tradition. Even the more recent and seemingly obvious objective of equipping all with 'basic literacy' is premised on moral-political grounds, however pragmatically those grounds may be justified. School curricula and classroom 'climates' always reflect inarticulate cultural values as well as explicit plans; and these values are never far removed from considerations of social class, gender, and the prerogatives of social power. Should girls, to take a case pending before the US Supreme Court, be admitted into state-supported military academies formerly reserved for young men? Is affirmative action a covert form of discrimination against the middle class?

Nothing could be more expressive of a culture than the conflicts and compromises that swirl around quasi-educational questions of this order. What is striking in most democratic states is that the compromises that emerge initially get buried in the rhetoric of official blandness, after which (and partly as a result of which) they become candidates for bitter and rather poorly considered attack. All children should have the same curricula? Of course. And then there is an expose of what 'the same' means in the schools, say, of a South Bronx ghetto and those in suburban Forest Hills. With increased community awareness, formerly innocent issues like curriculum soon become political ones – and quite appropriately so. The trouble, of course, is that purely political debate specializes in oversimplification. And these are not simple issues.

So the 'underground curriculum' continues to loom larger – a school's way of adapting a curriculum to express its attitudes toward its pupils, its racial attitudes, and the rest. And in the community's politicized reaction, political slogans become at least as determinative of educational policy as do theories about the cultivation of the multiple powers of mind.

Surely one of the major educational tenets of a cultural psychology is that the school can never be considered as culturally 'free standing'. *What,* it teaches, what modes of thought and what 'speech registers' it actually cultivates in its pupils, cannot be isolated from how the school is situated in the lives and culture of its students. For a school's curriculum is not only *about* 'subjects'. The chief subject matter of school, viewed culturally, is school itself. That is how most students experience it, and it determines what meaning they make of it.

This, of course, is what I mean by the 'situatedness' of school and school learning. Yet, for all its pervasiveness, there is little question that, with thought and will, it can be changed. Change can occur even by little symbolic innovations – like creating a chess club in a ghetto school, and providing real coaching. Joining the chess club (indeed, *having* a chess club) in a mainly black Harlem middle school creates a quite different communal self-image than joining one (or having one) in Cincinnati's well-to-do Walnut Hills. And winning the National Junior High School Chess Team Championship for Mott High Middle School in Harlem is no ho-hum matter. In some cryptic way it can mean 'beating the oppressor at his own brainy games'. But bits of symbolism scarcely touch the problem at large.

None of this is new. What does the cultural psychologist have to say about such matters? Certainly one general thing: education does not stand alone, and it cannot be designed as if it did. It exists in a culture. And culture, whatever else it is, is also about power, distinctions, and rewards. We have, in the laudable interest of protecting freedom of thought and instruction, officially buffered schools against political pressures. School is 'above' politics. In some important sense, this is surely true – but it is a threadbare truth. Increasingly, we see something quite different. For, as it were, the secret is out. Even the so-called man in the street knows that how one equips minds matters mightily later in our postindustrial, technological era. The public, to be sure, has a rather unformed sense of this – and certainly the press does. But they are aware. The *New York Times* carried as front-page news in the spring of 1995 that achievement levels had gone up in the city's schools; and Dublin's *Irish Times* in the summer of that same year carried on its front page the news that

Irish students had scored 'above the average' in a comparative study of reading ability in European schools.

Why not, then, treat education for what it is? It has always been 'political', though cryptically so in more settled, less aware times. There has now been a revolution in public awareness. But it has not been accompanied by a comparable revolution in our ways of taking this awareness into account in the forging of educational policies and practices. All of which is not to propose that we 'politicize' education, but simply that we recognize that it is already politicized and that its political side needs finally to be taken into account more explicitly, not simply as though it were 'public protest'. I will return to this issue in more detail later in this chapter.

7   *The institutional tenet.* My seventh tenet is that as education in the developed world becomes institutionalized, it behaves as institutions do and often must, and suffers certain problems common to all institutions. What distinguishes it from others is its special role in preparing the young to take a more active part in other institutions of the culture. Let us explore now what this implies.

Cultures are not simply collections of people sharing a common language and historical tradition. They are composed of institutions that specify more concretely what roles people play and what status and respect these are accorded – though the culture at large expresses its way of life through institutions as well. Cultures can also be conceived as elaborate exchange systems, with media of exchange as varied as respect, goods, loyalty, and services. Exchange systems become focalized and legitimized in institutions which provide buildings, stipends, titles, and the rest. They are further legitimized by a complex symbolic apparatus of myths, statutes, precedents, ways of talking and thinking, and even uniforms. Institutions impose their 'will' through coercion, sometimes implicit as in incentives and disincentives, sometimes explicit as in restriction backed by the power of the state, such as the disbarring of a lawyer or the refusal of credit to a defaulting merchant.

Institutions do the culture's serious business. But for all that, they do so through an unpredictable mix of coercion and voluntarism. I say 'unpredictable' because it remains perpetually unclear both to participants in a culture and to those who observe it from 'outside' when and how the power of enforcement will be brought to bear by those delegated or otherwise thought privileged to use it. So if it can be said that a culture's institutions do 'serious business', it can equally be said that it is often ambiguous and uncertain business.

It is also characteristic of human cultures that individuals rarely owe allegiance to any single institution: one 'belongs' to a family of origin and one by marriage, an occupational group, a neighborhood, as well as to more general groups like a nation or a social class. Each institutional grouping struggles to achieve its distinctive pattern of rights and responsibilities. This adds further to the inherent ambiguity of life in culture. As Waller Lippmann and John Dewey long ago pointed out,[16] how any given individual forms his interpretation on issues of public concern will usually involve him in a conflict of interests and identities. For while institutions may complement each other functionally, they also compete for privilege and power. Indeed, the power of a culture inheres in its capacity to integrate its component institutions through a dialectic of conflict resolution.

Institutions, as Pierre Bourdicu has suggested,[17] provide the 'markets' where people 'trade' their acquired skills, knowledge, and ways of constructing meanings for 'distinctions' or privileges. Institutions often compete in getting their 'distinctions' prized above those of others, but the competition must never be 'winner take all', for institutions are mutually dependent upon each other. Lawyers and businessmen need each other as much as patients and doctors do. So, as in Diderot's delightful *Jacques le fataliste et son maître*, bargaining for distinction becomes a subtle game, often a source of sly humor. The struggle for distinction seems to be a feature of all cultures.

While all this may at first seem remote from schools and the process of education, the remoteness is an illusion. Education is up to its elbows in the struggle for distinctions. The very expressions *primary, secondary,* and *tertiary* are metaphors for it. It has even been argued recently that the 'new' bourgeoisie in France after the Revolution used the schools as one of their principal tools for 'turning around' the system of prestige and distinction previously dominated by the aristocracy and gentry of the *ancien régime.* Indeed, the very concept of a meritocracy is precisely an expression of the new power that schools are expected to exercise in fixing the distribution of distinctions in contemporary bureaucratic society.

It was the 'tug' of institutional competition that mainly concerned us in the preceding section, often converted into a more conventionalized political form. I commented there that there had been an 'evolution in awareness' about education. Let me pursue that now. Few democracies today are short of cultural critics who bring educational issues before the public, sometimes vividly: a Paulo Freirc in Latin America, a Pierre Bourdieu in France, a Neil Postman in America, or an A. H. Halsey in Britain. There is lively public discussion of education in virtually every developed country of the world. Despite that, most countries still lack public forums for informed consideration of educational issues. I believe such forums are crucial for responding to and, indeed, informing the kinds of politicized debates discussed earlier. But they are emerging. And though they may not turn out to be as stately or noncontroversial as Her Majesty's Inspectorate of Education in Queen Victoria's class-dominated days, they at least are bringing education out from behind its screen of 'neutrality'. We already have some foretaste of what is to come, as when the President of the United States discusses educational issues on television with a selected forum of experts and participants, or when Shirley Williams, formerly Britain's Minister of Education, instituted widely covered broadcasts of regional discussions. Many regional Italian teachers' unions now hold annual discussion meetings on the state and progress of education, with provincial ministers and leading researchers actively in attendance. In the United States, where sectarian acrimony often increases faster than responsible and informed discussion, many state governors have established quasi-official groups at whose meetings pending state policy decisions on education get discussed. The goals of education seem again to have become a topic worthy of study as well as debate.

But there is more to the matter than public opinion and the need to inform it. For, as I remarked at the outset, educational systems are themselves highly institutionalized, in the grip of their *own* values. Educators have their own usually well informed views about how to cultivate and how to 'grade' the human mind. And like other institutions, education perpetuates itself and its practices: by establishing graduate schools of education, *grandes écoles* like the École Normale Supérieure in France, even elite academies like the chartered National Academy of Education in America and the informal All Souls Group in Britain. And as often happens, it invents durable ways of distributing skills, attitudes, and ways of thinking in the same old unjust demographic patterns. A reliable example of this can be found in procedures for examining students that, somehow, long outlive exposés of their unfairness to less privileged groups in the population. In consequence, the goodness of fit between school practices and society's demands comes increasingly under scrutiny.

Yet, in a sense, the public discussions that occur in consequence of this scrutiny are by no means strictly about 'education'. It is not simply that we are trying to reevaluate the balance between schools as a fixed Educational Establishment, on the one side, and a set of well-established needs of the culture, on the other. The issues are much broader than that. They have to do with the emerging role of women in society, with the vexing problem of the ethnic loyalties of the children of guest workers, with minority rights, with sexual mores, with unmarried mothers, with violence, with poverty. The Educational Establishment, for all its fingertip expertise in dealing with educational routines, has little by way of established doctrine for dealing with such problems. Nor do other institutions within the culture, though they nonetheless seem always tempted to 'blame education' for its particular set of troubles – whether it be the falling competitiveness of the auto industry, the increase in births out of wedlock, or violence on the streets.

It is astonishing how little systematic study is devoted to the institutional 'anthropology' of schooling, given the complexity of its situatedness and its exposure to the changing social and economic climate. Its relation to the family, to the economy, to religious institutions, even to the labor market, is only vaguely understood. But suggestive work is beginning. I find it encouraging that one distinguished contributor to this current debate on the role of education in the economy is no less a figure than the serving Secretary of Labor in the Clinton administration. His discussion of the place of symbolic 'meta-skills' in *The Work of Nations* could serve as a policy document in our times. And one wonders, indeed, whether the institutional challenges of our changing society might call not only for the proverbial New Man, but also for some New Institutions (as Daniel Bell suggests).[18]

Let me offer two such institutions, though entirely in the spirit of illustration. Each is intended to address the range of institutional questions just discussed – both very much in the spirit of the culturalist approach. Each takes for granted that there is a reciprocal relation between education and the other major institutional activities of a culture: communication, economics, politics, family life, and so on. The first is designed to recognize the shortage of useful information on such crucial matters, the second that we lack a deliberative apparatus that can convert useful knowledge into wise policy alternatives.

In connection with the first of these, gathering useful information, what I envision is something that might be called an 'anthropology' of education, a term that for me goes far beyond the collection of 'classroom ethnographies', however helpful such exercises have been. This kind of 'anthropology' should be dedicated to work on the situatedness of education in the society at large – to its institutions, as just noted, but also to 'crisis' problems like poverty and racism. Or, in a word, what role does schooling play in coping with or exacerbating the 'predicament of culture' that James Clifford has described so vividly?[19]

Well, there is no such 'field' as this one, really: only a lot of scattered investigators working in different, academic departments. So, one invents a field and even legitimizes it by granting a broad charter to, say, a National Institute of Education, to be financed (in the interest of maintaining the 'compromise control' mentioned earlier) by federal, state, and private foundation support and sponsorship. And since these are all thoughts that come even before a 'drawing board' gets involved, I will also suggest that such an institute not be exclusively for research, but also for consultation. But let me turn to the other institutional invention, this one concerned principally with forging possible policy alternatives in a setting of competing institutions.

We still have reason to celebrate Clemenceau's remark that war is too important to leave to the generals. Not generals alone – too many other interests and constituencies are affected. In this same sense, as I've tried to make clear in this [. . .] chapter, education is too consequential to too many constituencies to leave to professional educators. And I'm sure most thoughtful professionals would agree. Thus, to bring judgment, balance, and a broader social commitment to the educational scene in America, we would need to engage 'the best and the brightest' as well as the most publicly committed to the task of formulating alternative policies and practices. I know this is not easy, but imagine a task force or a board whose members were recruited from many 'walks of life', as we like to put it. It might take many different forms: its only requirement is that it be made up of those who have achieved a reputation for their acumen, their fair-mindedness, and their public commitment. Imagine such a body as a White House Board, say, in the spirit of the Board of Economic Advisers or the National Security Council, with the function of advising the President of the United States on educational issues in the broad sense, including the impact of federal policy generally on the conduct of education, and vice versa. Or a more vigorous model might be the Federal Reserve Board, though obviously such a model would violate the American constitutional mandate of leaving education to the 'several states'. In any case, I offer these suggestions in the spirit of recognizing that education is not a freestanding institution, not all island, but part of the continent.

Having, offered these rather grandiose examples, I must conclude this discussion of 'institutionalization' on a more homely note. Improving education requires teachers who understand and are committed to the improvements envisioned. So banal a point would scarcely be worth mentioning were it not so easily overlooked by many efforts at educational reform. We need to equip teachers with the necessary background training to take an effective part in reform. The people who run them make institutions. However thoughtful our educational plans may become, they must include a crucial place for teachers. For ultimately, that is where the action is.

8   *The tenet of identity and self-esteem.* I have put this tenet late in the list. For it is so pervasive as to implicate virtually all that has gone before. Perhaps the single most universal thing about human experience is the phenomenon of 'Self', and we know that education is crucial to its formation. Education should be conducted with that fact in mind.

We know 'Self' from our own inner experience, and we recognize others as selves. Indeed, more than one distinguished scholar has argued that self-awareness requires as its necessary condition the recognition of the Other as a self. Though there are universals of selfhood – and we will consider two of them in a moment – different cultures both shape it differently and set its limits in varying ways. Some emphasize autonomy and individuality, some affiliation; some link it closely to a person's position in a divine or secular social order, some link it to individual effort or even to luck. Since schooling is one of life's earliest institutional involvements outside the family, it is not surprising that it plays a critical role in the shaping of Self. But I think this will be clearer if we first examine two aspects of selfhood that are regarded as universal.

The first is *agency*. Selfhood, most students of the subject believe, derives from the sense that one can initiate and carry out activities on one's own. Whether this is 'really' so or simply a folk belief, as radical behaviorists would have us believe, is beyond the scope of this inquiry. I shall simply take it as so. People experience themselves as agents. But then too, any vertebrate distinguishes between a branch *it* has shaken and one that has shaken *it*. So there must be something more to selfhood than the recognition of simple sensorimotor agentivity. What characterizes human selfhood is the construction of a conceptual system that organizes, as it were, a 'record' of agentive encounters with the world, a record that is related to the past (that is, 'autobiographical memory', so-called) but that is also extrapolated into the future – self with history and with possibility. It is a 'possible self' that regulates aspiration, confidence, optimism, and their opposites. While this 'constructed' self-system is inner, private, and suffused with affect, it also extends outward to the things and activities and places with which we become 'ego-involved' – William James's 'extended self'. Schools and school learning are among the earliest of those places and activities.

But just as important as the inner psychodynamics of selfhood are the ways in which a culture institutionalizes it. All natural languages, for example, make obligatory grammatical distinctions between agentive and patientive forms: *I hit him; he hit me.* And even the simplest narratives are built around, indeed depend upon, an agent-Self as a protagonist with his or her own goals operating in a recognizable cultural setting. There is a moral aspect to selfhood as well, expressed simply by such ubiquitous phenomena as 'blaming yourself' or 'blaming another' for acts committed or outcomes that result from our acts. At a more evolved level, all legal systems specify (and legitimize) some notion of *responsibility* by which Self is endowed with obligation in regard to some broader cultural authority – confirming 'officially' that we, our Selves, are presumed to be agents in control of our own actions.

Since agency implies not only the capacity for initiating, but also for completing our acts, it also implies *skill* or *know-how*. Success and failure are principal nutrients in the development of selfhood. Yet we may not be the final arbiters of success and failure, which are often defined from 'outside' according to culturally specified criteria. And school is where the child first encounters such criteria – often as if applied arbitrarily. School judges the child's performance, and the child responds by evaluating himself or herself in turn.

Which brings us to a second ubiquitous feature of selfhood: *evaluation.* Not only do we experience self as agentive, we evaluate our efficacy in bringing off what we hoped for or were asked to do. Self increasingly takes on the flavor of these valuations. I call this mix of agentive efficacy and self-evaluation 'self-esteem'. It combines our sense of what we believe ourselves to be (or even hope to be) capable of and what we fear is beyond us.

How self-esteem is experienced (or how it is expressed) varies, of course, with the ways of one's culture. Low esteem sometimes manifests itself in guilt about intentions, sometimes simply in shame for having been 'found out'; sometimes it is accompanied by depression, even to the point of suicide, sometimes by defiant anger. In some cultures, particularly those that emphasize achievement, high self-esteem increases level of aspiration; in others it leads to status display and standing pat. There may even be an individual temperamental component in how people deal with threatened self-esteem – whether one blames oneself, others, or circumstances.

Only two things can be said for certain and in general: the management of self-esteem is never simple and never settled, and its state is affected powerfully by the availability of supports provided from outside. These supports are hardly mysterious or exotic. They include such homely resorts as a second chance, honor for a good if unsuccessful try, but above all the chance for discourse that permits one to find out why or how things didn't work out as planned. It is no secret that school is often rough on children's self-esteem, and we are beginning to know something about their vulnerability in this area. Ideally, of course, school is supposed to provide a setting where our performance has fewer esteem-threatening consequences than in the 'real world', presumably in the interest of encouraging the learner to 'try things out'. Yet radical critics, like Paulo Freire,[20] have argued that school often metes out failures to those children the society would later 'exploit'. And even moderate critics, like Roland Barthes and Pierre Bourdieu, make the provocative case that school is principally an agent for producing, say, 'little Frenchmen and Frenchwomen' who will conform to the niche where they will end up.[21]

Obviously there are other 'markets' where even school children can 'trade' their skills for distinctions, to use Bourdieu's interesting terms again. And these 'markets' often compensate for sensed failure in school – as when 'street smarts' are traded on the market of petty crime, or when defiance of the majority community earns black teenagers respect among their peers. School, more than we have realized, competes with myriad forms of 'anti-school' as a provider of agency, identity, and self-esteem – no less at a middle-class suburban mall than on the ghetto streets.

Any system of education, any theory of pedagogy, any 'grand national policy' that diminishes the school's role in nurturing its pupils' self-esteem fails at one of its primary functions. The deeper problem – from a cultural-psychological point of view, but in workaday common sense as well – is how to cope with the erosion of this function under modern urban conditions. [. . .] Schools do not simply equip kids with skills and self-esteem or not. They are in competition with other parts of society that can do this, but with deplorable consequences for the society. America manages to alienate enough black ghetto boys to land nearly a third of them in jail before they reach the age of thirty.

More positively, if agency and esteem are central to the construction of a concept of Self, then the ordinary practices of school need to be examined with a view to what contribution they make to these two crucial ingredients of personhood. Surely the 'community of learners' approach mentioned earlier contributes to both. But equally, the granting of more responsibility in setting and achieving goals in all aspects of a school's activities could also contribute – everything from maintenance of a school's physical plant to a share in decisions about academic and extracurricular projects to be undertaken. Such a conception, earlier so dear to the progressive tradition in education, is also in the image of the constitutional principle that (in a democracy) rights and responsibilities are two sides of the same coin. If, as I noted at the outset, school is an entry into the culture and not just a preparation for it, then we must constantly reassess what school does to the young student's conception of his own powers (his sense of agency) and his sensed chances of being able to cope with the world both in school and after (his self-esteem). In many democratic cultures, I think, we have become so preoccupied with the more formal criteria of 'performance' and with the bureaucratic demands of education as an institution that we have neglected this personal side of education.

9   *The narrative tenet.* I want finally to leapfrog over the issue of school 'subjects' and curricula in order to deal with a more general matter: the mode of thinking and feeling that helps children (indeed, people generally) create a version of the world in which, psychologically, they can envisage a place for themselves – a personal world. I believe that story making, narrative, is what is needed for that, and I want to discuss it briefly in this final tenet.

I still hold firmly to the views expressed in my earlier work about subject-matter teaching: the importance of giving the learner a sense of the generative structure of a subject discipline, the value of a 'spiral curriculum', the crucial role of self-generated discovery in learning a subject matter, and so forth. The issue I want to address now has to do more directly with the issue of how growing children create meanings from school experience that they can relate to their lives in a culture. So let me turn to narrative as a mode of thought and as a vehicle of meaning making.

I shall begin with some basics. There appear to be two broad ways in which human beings organize and manage their knowledge of the world, indeed structure even their immediate experience: one seems more specialized for treating of physical 'things', the other for treating of people and their plights. These are conventionally known as *logical-scientific* thinking and *narrative* thinking. Their universality suggests that they have their roots in the human genome or that they are (to revert to an earlier tenet) givens in the nature of language. They have varied modes of expression in different cultures, which also cultivate them differently. No culture is without both of them, though different cultures privilege them differently.

It has been the convention of most schools to treat the arts of narrative – song, drama, fiction, theater, whatever – as more 'decoration' than necessity, something with which to grace leisure, sometimes even as something morally exemplary. Despite that, we frame the accounts of our cultural origins and our most cherished beliefs in story form, and it is not just the 'content' of these stories that grip us, but their narrative artifice. Our immediate experience, what happened yesterday or the day before, is framed in the same storied way. Even more striking, we represent our lives (to ourselves as well as to others) in the form of narrative. It is not surprising that psychoanalysts now recognize that personhood implicates narrative, 'neurosis' being a reflection of either an insufficient, incomplete, or inappropriate story about oneself. Recall that when Peter Pan asks Wendy to return to Never

Never Land with him, he gives as his reason that she could teach the Lost Boys there how to tell stories. If they knew how to tell them, the Lost Boys might be able to grow up.

The importance of narrative for the cohesion of a culture is as great, very likely, as it is in structuring an individual life. Take law as an illustration. Without a sense of the common trouble narratives that the law translates into its common law writs, it becomes arid. And those 'trouble narratives' appear again in mythic literature and contemporary novels, better contained in that form than in reasoned and logically coherent propositions. It seems evident, then, that skill in narrative construction and narrative understanding is crucial to constructing our lives and a 'place' for ourselves in the possible world we will encounter.

It has always been tacitly assumed that narrative skill comes 'naturally', that it does not have to be taught. But a closer look shows this not to be true at all. We know now, for example, that it goes through definite stages, is severely impaired in brain damage of certain kinds, fares poorly under stress, and ends up in literalism in one social community while becoming fanciful in a neighboring one with a different tradition. Observe law students or young lawyers preparing their final arguments for litigation or mock court and it will quickly be plain that some people have the knack more than others – they have simply learned how to make a story believable and worth thinking about.

Feeling at home in the world, knowing how to place oneself into self-descriptive stories, is surely not made easier by the enormous increase in migration in the modern world. It is not easy, however multicultural your intentions, to help a ten-year-old create a story that includes him in the world beyond his family and neighborhood, having been transplanted from Vietnam to the San Fernando Valley, from Algeria to Lyons, from Anatolia to Dresden. If school, his *pied-a-terre* outside the family, can't help him, there are alienated countercultures that can.

None of us know as much as we should about how to create narrative sensibility. Two commonplaces seem to have stood the test of time. The first is that a child should 'know', have a 'feel' for, the myths, histories, folktales, conventional stories of his or her culture (or cultures). They frame and nourish an identity. The second commonplace urges imagination through fiction. Finding a place in the world, for all that it implicates the immediacy of home, mate, job, and friends, is ultimately an act of imagination. So, for the culturally transplanted, there is the imaginative challenge of the fiction and 'quasi-fiction' that takes him or her into the world of possibilities – as in the novels of a Maxine Hong Kingston or the poems of a Maya Angelou. And for any schoolboy pondering how it all came about, there is a Simon Schama narratively restoring the human plights to the 'dead certainties' of the past, to use his telling phrase.[22]

Obviously, if narrative is to be made an instrument of mind on behalf of meaning making, it requires work on our part – reading it, making it, analyzing it, understanding its craft, sensing its uses, discussing it. These are matters much better understood today than a generation ago.

All of which is not intended to undervalue the importance of logical-scientific thinking. Its value is so implicit in our highly technological culture that its inclusion in school curricula is taken for granted. While its teaching may still be in need of improvement, it has become strikingly better since the curriculum reform movements of the 1950s and 1960s. But it is no secret that for many of the young now in school, 'science' has come to seem 'inhuman' and 'uncaring' and 'off-putting' – despite the first-class efforts of science and mathematics teachers and their associations. Indeed, the image of science as a human and cultural undertaking might itself be improved if it were also conceived as a history of human beings overcoming received ideas – whether Lavoisier overcoming the dogma of phlogiston, Darwin rethinking respectable creationism, or Freud daring lo look under the smug surface of our self-satisfaction. We may have erred in divorcing science from the narrative of culture.

[…]

NOTES

1. J. Bruer, *Schools for Thought: A Science of Learning in the Classroom* (Cambridge, Mass., MIT Press, 1993).
2. A. Karmiloff-Smith, *A Functional Approach to Child Language: A Study of Determiners and Reference* (Cambridge, Cambridge University Press, 1979); A. Karmiloff-Smith, *Beyond Modularity: A Developmental Perspective on Cognitive Science* (Cambridge, Mass., MIT Press, 1992).
3. A. Newell and H. A. Simon, *Human Problem Solving* (Englewood Cliffs, N.J., Prentice-Hall).
4. R. B. Zajonc, Feeling and thinking: preferences need no inferences, *American Psychologist*, 35 (1980): 151–75; R. S. Lazarus, A cognitivist's reply to Zajone on emotion and cognition, *American Psychologist*, 36 (1981): 222–3; R. S. Lazarus, Thoughts on the relations between emotion and cognition, *American Psychologist*, 37 (1982): 1019–24; R. B. Zajonc, On the primary of affect, *American Psychologist*, 39 (1984): 117–23; R. S. Lazarus, On the primary of cognition, *American Psychologist*, 39 (1984): 124–9.
5. D. A. J. Richards, *Toleration and the Constitution* (New York, Oxford University Press, 1986); D. A. J. Richards, *Foundation of American Constitutionalism* (New York, Oxford University Press, 1989).
6. Vygotsky, *Thought and Language* (Cambridge, Mass., MIT Press, 1962).
7. B. L. Whorf, *Language, Thought, and Reality: Selected Writings* (Cambridge, Mass., Technology Press of MIT, 1956).
8. R. Jakobson, Poetry of grammar and grammar of poetry, in R. Jakobson, *Selected Writings, III: Poetry of Grammar and Grammar of Poetry* (The Hague, Mourton, 1981).
9. D. A. Olson, *The World on Paper: The Conceptual and Cognitive Implications of Writing and Reading* (Cambridge, Cambridge University Press, 1994).
10. N. Goodman, *Ways of Worldmaking* (Indianapolis, Hackett, 1978).
11. I. Meyerson, *Les Fonctions Psychologiques et les Oeuvres* (Paris, J. Vrin, 1948); I. Meyerson, *Ecrits, 1920–1983: Pour une Psychologie Historique* (Paris, Presses Universitaires de France, 1987).
12. S. L. Lightfoot, *The Good High School: Portraits of Character and Culture* (New York, Basic Books, 1983).
13. M. Cole and A. V. Bclayeva, Computer-mediated joint activity and the problem of mental development, *Soviet Journal of Psychology*, 12 (1991): 133–41.
14. R. J. Herrnslein and C. Murray, *The Bell Curve: Intelligence and Class Structure in American Life* (New York, Free Press, 1994).
15. H. Gardner, *Frames of Mind: The Theory of Multiple Intelligences* (New York, Basic Books, 1983).
16. W. Lippmann, *Public Opinion* (New York: Harcourt, Brace, 1927); J. Dewey, *The Public and its Problems* (Chicago, Swallow Press, 1954).
17. P. Bourdieu, *Language and Symbolic Power* (Cambridge, Mass., Harvard University Press, 1991).
18. R. B. Reich, *The Work of Nations: Preparing Ourselves for Twenty-first-Century Capitalism* (New York, Knopf, 1991); D. Bell, *The Coming of Post-Industrial Society: A Venture in Social Forecasting* (New York, Basic Books, 1976).
19. J. Clifford, *The Predicament of Culture: Twentieth-Century Ethnography, Literature and Art* (Cambridge, Mass., Harvard University Press, 1988).
20. P. Freire, *Pedagogy of the Oppressed* (new rev. 20th anniversary ed) (New York, Continuum, 1994).
21. P. Bourdieu, *Distinction: A Social Critique of the Judgment of Taste* (Cambridge, Mass., Harvard University Press, 1984); R. Barthes, Toys, in R. Barthes, *Mythologies* (New York, Hill & Wang, 1982).
22. S. Schama, *Dead Certainties: Unwarranted Speculations* (New York, Knopf, 1991).

7

EXPLAINING SOCIOECONOMIC INEQUALITIES IN STUDENT ACHIEVEMENT

The role of home and school factors

Gary N. Marks, John Cresswell and John Ainley

INTRODUCTION

Gary Marks, John Cresswell and John Ainley are based in Australia. They have completed work on a wide variety of projects with work that focuses on school effectiveness, wealth, poverty and financial stress and income dynamics. This paper examines 'the extent that material [e.g. money, housing, etc.], social [e.g. access to social networks] and cultural resources [e.g. ease at dealing with the dominant culture] and schools account for the relationship between socio-economic background and student achievement among 15 year olds in 30 countries'. The authors suggest that cultural and material resources are important while social resources are less so. 'Together, the two resources – material and cultural resources – explain about a third of the effect of socioeconomic background on reading achievement' (p. 122) It is possible that forms of educational differentiation (e.g. children attending different schools or different classes depending on the results of tests of ability or aptitude) 'can strengthen socioeconomic inequalities in education' (p. 126).

KEY QUESTIONS

1. Do you think that schools should be open to all in a local community or do you think that schools should, in the context of a full common curriculum, offer specialist expertise to particular individuals or groups?

2. If schools did offer specialist expertise (e.g. one would specialise perhaps in maths while another focused on modern foreign languages), would it be appropriate for schools to decide who should be allowed to join the school?

FURTHER READING

The authors point to the importance of cultural factors in achievement and so the work of Bourdieu is relevant (e.g. Bourdieu, P. (1973) 'Cultural reproduction and social reproduction' in Brown, R. (ed.) *Knowledge, Education, and Cultural Change: Papers in the Sociology of Education*, pp. 71–112. Tavistock, London. There are always many controversies about achievement and equality. A recent example of differences of opinion can be seen in the Education section of *The Guardian* newspaper from 26 August 2008 (see www.guardian. co.uk/education/2008/aug/26/schools.socialexclusion).

This Reading links with Chapters 5 and 9 and Debate 3 of *The Routledge Education Studies Textbook.*

SOCIOECONOMIC INEQUALITIES IN EDUCATION

Socioeconomic inequalities in education are an important issue for both researchers and policy-makers. Regardless of political perspective, all agree that, in a democratic society, socioeconomic inequalities in educational outcomes should be minimal. Such inequality has been demonstrated in countless studies and many of the policy initiatives in education over the past half century have been aimed at reducing these inequalities. However, policies directed at reducing educational inequality have not proved unequivocally successful. Although some evidence suggests that there has been a decline in the influence of socioeconomic background on educational outcomes in most industrialized countries (Rijken, 1999; Sieben, 2001), few would claim that it no longer has significance.

The processes by which socioeconomic background influences educational inequality are not well understood. In this paper, we distinguish four types of explanations based on the extent to which they emphasize the importance of material, cultural, and social factors and school systems.

Material, social, and cultural resources

Material resource explanations focus on the roles of poverty, income, and wealth. Explanations emphasizing material resources contend that differential access to material resources generates differences in student performance. Wealthy families can "buy" educational success for their children by sending them to expensive elite schools, buying houses in desirable school districts, or paying for out-of-school tutors. In contrast, poor families may not be able to afford basic educational resources, such as a student desk and textbooks.

There is empirical evidence that income and wealth are related to student achievement and other educational outcomes (Alexander & Eckland, 1974, 1975; Jencks *et al.*, 1972, 1979; Orr, 2003; Pong & Ju, 2000). Teachman (1987) found that the level of educational resources was related to results in achievement tests, even when parental education and other factors had been taken into account. However, the effect of family income on test scores is generally weaker than that for parent's education (Fejgin, 1995; Ganzach, 2000). However, in developing countries where sizeable proportions of students are deprived of basic resources, material resources are likely to be a more important component of socioeconomic inequality in education.

There are clear policy implications if material resources prove to be largely responsible for socioeconomic inequalities in education. Governments can provide financial support in the form of scholarships, stipends, allowances for textbooks and other educational materials, and tax deductions for educational expenses. Alternatively, they could increase funding to schools in low income areas.

Another group of explanations emphasize the role of social relationships; stronger connections between students, schools, parents, and the local community promote educational success. Social capital theory argues that social networks and social relationships have a substantial impact on a variety of social outcomes. Coleman (1987, 1988) provides the most well-known theory of social capital and educational outcomes. He argues that children do better in schools that have a more closely knit network (community) around them, where parents, teachers, and the local community interact and facilitate educational success. Its relationship with socioeconomic status is more tenuous than for material or cultural resources but high status families are "better connected" in that they are more likely to know people who can more effectively help their children's educational and labor market outcomes. In addition, they are less likely to be in contact with people who may undermine their children's educational or labor market success. However, the empirical evidence for the importance of social capital for student achievement is not strong. Much of the research concerns school dropout and completion rates, rather than student performance. Furthermore, the definitions of social capital can be wide including disciplinary climate, mother's marital status, and family size (see Parcel & Dufur, 2001), which arguably fall outside the concept of social capital. McNeal (1999) concludes that social capital is a salient factor for behavioral but not for cognitive outcomes.

The policy implications are less clear if social networks are a major contributor to socioeconomic inequalities in education. Although it is generally agreed that close and high quality relationships between students, parents, schools, and the local community are desirable, it is difficult for governments to devise and implement policy initiatives that strengthen these relationships.

A further group of explanations include those explanations that focus on cultural differences between high and lower status families and what this implies for student performance. A home environment conducive to intellectual pursuits and the arts may promote student performance. Bourdieu's theory of cultural capital (1973, 1984) is the most well-known theory that provides a cultural explanation to differences in educational outcomes. He argues that children from high status backgrounds are advantaged since they have similar cultural understandings to those which underlie the education system, so are judged very favorably by the system's gatekeepers: teachers, schools, and assessment authorities. Such cultural understandings are likely to be especially important in the humanities and social sciences. Cultural factors, such as ease at dealing with the dominant culture, are likely to be less important in mathematics and the sciences.

There is evidence showing that cultural factors influence educational outcomes. DiMaggio (1982) shows that US children from "cultured" backgrounds receive higher grades, net of their measured cognitive ability. Cultural behavior was also found to influence educational attainment, college attendance, and college graduation (DiMaggio & Mohr, 1985). Sullivan (2001) concluded that linguistic ability and cultural knowledge affects students' scores in the British General Certificate of Education. Focusing on parents rather than students, their participation in cultural activities affects a range of their children's educational outcomes in Australia, Germany, and The Netherlands (Crook, 1997; De Graaf, De Graaf & Kraaykamp, 2000; De Graaf, 1986). De Graaf, Ganzeboom & Kalmijn (1989) found that the cultural dimension of occupational status had a stronger effect on children's education than the material dimension. Several international studies of student achievement have found that the number of books in the home – a crude indicator of the intellectual environment of the home – shows relatively strong correlations with student achievement (Comber & Keeves, 1973, p. 259; Keeves & Saha, 1992, pp. 174–175).

If cultural factors are largely responsible for socioeconomic inequalities in education, then there are few policy options. Policy-makers may endeavor to address implicit cultural biases toward "high" culture in the curriculum but this may mean discarding some of the most celebrated aspects of a nation's history. A less radical response would be to encourage students from lower socioeconomic backgrounds to be interested in 'high' culture rather than assume they have little interest.

Schools

School systems also figure in explanations of socioeconomic inequality in education. School systems that reward ability and effort rather than social origins, may substantially reduce the extent of social reproduction between generations. Conversely, school systems may increase social inequality by assisting less talented and less motivated students from advantaged backgrounds and creating barriers to academically able students from lower socioeconomic backgrounds.

Schools may be involved in the socioeconomic inequalities in education in a number of ways. Wealthy families can buy a superior education for their children by sending them to high-fee elite private schools or purchase homes in the catchment areas of high performing public schools. In countries with tracked school systems, the allocation of students to the more academic school tracks may be biased towards students from higher socioeconomic backgrounds. Within schools, school authorities may be more likely to allocate students from higher socioeconomic backgrounds to more prestigious curriculum tracks or academic locations.

In most countries, there are different types of schools – government and private schools, religious and ethnic schools, and comprehensive, academic, and vocational schools. School type is often associated with particular educational and occupational pathways. In some countries, an elite private school education is a first step in a pathway that leads to high-level professional or administrative positions. In many European countries, attendance at highly academic schools is almost a prerequisite for university entrance. Similarly, vocational schools prepare students for entry to the workplace, usually in the trades. Although comprehensive schools cater for students with a range of academic and social characteristics, the presence of other school types means that such schools will almost certainly be associated with particular educational and occupational pathways.

In many countries, especially in Europe, school systems are tracked; students are assigned to different school types officially on the basis of prior performance. These tracks range from purely academic tracks to vocational tracks and prepare students for different educational and labor market destinations. The age at which students are first assigned to tracks differs between countries. Tracking occurs at 10 years of age in Austria and Germany, at 11 in the Czech Republic and Hungary, at 12 in Belgium, Mexico, and The Netherlands, at 13 in Luxembourg, and at 14 in Italy and Korea. In other countries, tracking occurs later at 15 or 16 years of age. There are differences between school systems in the ability to move between tracks and the extent that the curriculum differs between tracks. In some countries – Australia, Canada, New Zealand, the United Kingdom, and the United States – there are no official school tracks but there are, to varying extents, fee paying schools.

Within school types, individual schools can contribute to their students' performance. The popular image is that there are "good" schools that deliver desirable education outcomes and undesirable "bad" schools. Furthermore, there is a range of school characteristics – resources, academic and disciplinary climates, the quality of teachers, teaching practices, the curriculum, and leadership by the principal – which, to varying degrees, influence students' educational outcomes (Greenwald, Hedges, & Laine, 1996; Lee & Bryk, 1989; Schreiber, 2002).

Within individual schools, students may also be allocated to different academic locations. As with tracking, some streams are academically orientated and designed for students who are likely to attend university. Other locations prepare students for other forms of post-secondary education or direct entry to the workforce. As with tracks, streams differ in the material presented and the expectations placed on students.

The extent to which schools influence educational outcomes has been the subject of a great deal of research. School differences in achievement vary enormously across educational contexts, largest in countries with highly tracked school systems and considerably smaller in comprehensive systems (Organization for Economic Cooperation and Development [OECD], 2001). Meta-analysis of a large number of studies across several countries concluded that the average between-school variation was around 19% of the total variation in student achievement. Although this figure, equivalent to a correlation of nearly 0.45, is large compared to other correlates of student achievement, only in a small minority of schools is student performance substantially higher or lower than expected based on students' individual social and academic characteristics. After adjusting for initial differences, such as prior school performance and social background, the (average) between-school variance is around 8% (Scheerens & Bosker, 1997).

Between- and within-school differences are likely to be stronger for mathematics and the sciences than for reading. Reading is taught in early primary school and is well-established by the end of primary school. In contrast, mathematics and science are "cumulative" and are taught at different levels according to the student's ability to cope with the material. Highly academic schools or locations within schools are likely to be teaching these subjects at a much higher level. Furthermore, the socioeconomic biases favoring students from higher socioeconomic backgrounds may be stronger for mathematics and science because they tend to be more important in selection for post-secondary school study. Therefore, it is expected that school factors will be more important in mediating the relationship between socioeconomic background and student performance in mathematics and science than for reading.

In contrast to educational inequalities produced by social and cultural factors, school-based educational inequalities can be addressed directly by government initiatives. For example, governments can increase the overall funding of schools deemed as disadvantaged, and directly fund specific resources such as classrooms, libraries, laboratories, and teachers. One of the most common policy initiatives of post-war governments has been to reduce or abolish tracking. These policies were established as a way of reducing socioeconomic inequalities in educational outcomes. Generally, tracking and other forms of educational differentiation were viewed as biased in favor of students from higher socioeconomic backgrounds. Therefore, socioeconomic inequalities are perpetuated as students from lower socioeconomic backgrounds were assigned to tracks that did not provide opportunities for higher education (see Muller & Shavit, 1998). In Britain, the 11 plus examinations (which was the basis for the allocation of students to different tracks) were abolished and the proportion of students in comprehensive schools was increased at the expense of academically orientated grammar schools (Kerckhoff, 1993). Similar reforms reducing educational selectivity were carried out in Scotland and Sweden (Gamoran, 1996; Hout and Dohan, 1996). In Australia, technical schools have been abolished in some states. Although it is unclear if such reforms were successful, there remains a general view that educational differentiation, both between and within schools, is associated with a greater socioeconomic inequality in educational outcomes.

Evaluation

The main point emerging from the above discussion is that material, social, and cultural resources and school systems are associated with educational outcomes and are likely to contribute to socioeconomic inequalities in education. It is important to note that these explanations are not mutually exclusive; the ability to buy education success is limited if there are few or no high-fee-paying private schools or little difference in the performance of schools in rich and poor areas. Similarly, cultural explanations can involve school systems. For students familiar with the dominant culture to achieve greater success, there needs to be a match of their cultural understandings with that prevailing in the curriculum and methods of assessment. Although most theories endeavoring to account for socioeconomic inequalities in education include elements from each group of explanations, they can be distinguished by the importance they attribute to families' material, cultural, and social resources and school systems.

Therefore, the purpose of this paper is to examine the relative importance of material, social, and cultural resources and schools, in accounting for socioeconomic inequalities in education. This examination is conducted with data from 30 countries to investigate whether the relative contributions of these groups of factors are similar across countries or if there are substantial cross-national differences.

DATA, MEASURES, AND METHODS

Data

The data are from the OECD Programme for International Student Assessment (PISA), which, in the year 2000, investigated student achievement in three domains, reading, mathematics, and science, among some 172,000 15-year-old students in over 6,000 schools across 32 countries. A two-stage sample was drawn first sampling schools with probabilities proportional to size and then randomly selecting 15-year-old students within schools. Participating countries included all the OECD countries at the time and several non-OECD countries (Brazil, Latvia, Liechtenstein, and the Russian Federation). Since the Japanese data for the parental occupation and education has very high levels of missing data, Japan was not included in these analyses. The sample for Liechtenstein was too small for its data to be included in these analyses. A failure to reach satisfactory sampling requirements meant that data from The Netherlands were excluded from the international comparisons in the initial PISA report (OECD, 2001), but, as international comparisons are not the main focus of this paper, data from The Netherlands have been included here. Details on the data and sampling procedures can be found in the PISA initial and technical reports (OECD, 2001, 2002).

Measures

The outcomes measure investigated here is student achievement in reading, mathematics, and science. Item Response Theory (IRT) modeling was used to create scores standardized at an international mean of 500 and standard deviation of 100. Students' scores are in the form of five plausible values rather than a single score. These measures were constructed by the PISA consortium and are included in the datasets publicly available. Details on the construction of the achievement measures can be found in the PISA technical report (OECD, 2002). In this paper, the focus is on reading achievement since this was the major domain in PISA 2000. All sampled students were tested in reading whereas about half were tested in mathematics and science.

The other measures used in this paper were constructed by the authors. Socioeconomic background (SEB) is a composite measure comprising father's and mother's occupation and education. It was necessary to construct a composite measure of all four variables since all relate to the socioeconomic level of the family. Preliminary analyses showed that each has an influence on reading achievement, net of the effects of the other three indicators. Therefore, to some extent each is tapping into a unique aspect of socio-economic background. The measure of socioeconomic background was constructed as a sheaf variable, converting the effects of all four constituent variables on student achievement across all three domains, within countries, into a single variable (Whitt, 1986). If students were missing on one or more of the constituent variables, information from the nonmissing variables was used. The resulting measure was standardized within countries to a mean of zero and a standard deviation of one.

Information on parents' occupation was obtained from the student questionnaire. Parental occupations were coded according to the International Standard Classification of Occupation 1988 (ISCO-88), as provided by the International Labour Office. ISCO-88 is a four-digit hierarchical coding schema comprising 390 different occupational categories. These codes were converted to occupational status scores using the International Socio-economic Index (ISEI), which ranges from 16 to 90. The index was constructed by iteratively estimating the scores assigned to (4-digit ISCO-88) occupational groups that maximize the effect of occupation status on income. Ganzeboom and Treiman (1996) provide details on its construction and list ISCO-88 occupational titles with their respective ISEI scores.

Information on the educational attainment of each parent was elicited by two questions. The first asked for the level of school education completed. The second asked whether the parent had completed a tertiary qualification. The national project managers were responsible for composing questions meaningful to students in their country. The responses to these questions were classified according to the International Standard Classification of Education (ISCED) schema (OECD, 1999). A measure of educational attainment was constructed for each parent. Parental education was coded to one of seven categories: No Schooling, Primary School, Middle Secondary School, Higher Secondary School (Nonacademic), Higher Secondary School (Academic), Tertiary Education (Nonacademic), and Tertiary Education (Academic). Continuous measures were constructed by optimal or criterion scaling, by iteratively assigning scores to these educational categories to maximize the relationships of father's and mother's education with student achievement. This procedure was performed within countries.

It was necessary to construct criterion-scaled measures of parental education since analyses of categorical measures indicated that a continuous measure with identical ordinal and cardinal properties across countries could not be justified. The major problem is the position, relative to the other groups, of the higher secondary and post-secondary nonacademic groups, with trade or technical qualifications.

The components of material resources in the home are wealth and educational resources. The wealth measure comprised the presence or absence in the student's home of: a dishwasher, a room for the student, and a link to the internet; and the number of mobile phones, televisions, computers, cars, and bathrooms in the home. The educational resources index comprised: possession of a dictionary, a quiet place to study, a desk for study, textbooks, and the number of calculators in the home. Both variables were combined into a single variable by the sheaf variable method.

"Social resources" was constructed from questions on how often do the student's parents discuss how well they were doing at school, eat the main meal around a table, and spend time just talking to the student. These items had positive correlations with achievement scores. This index is more a direct measure of student–parent relations than social capital. However, the questionnaire included a number of items intended to measure social capital which asked the extent to which the student's parents, brothers and sisters, other relations, and friends of their parents *worked* with the student on the student's schoolwork. In almost all instances and countries, the bivariate correlations between frequency of involvement of others with schoolwork and student achievement were negative, suggesting that academically weaker students work more often with adults.[1] Therefore, these items were not incorporated in the measure of "social resources."

"Cultural resources" in the home was measured by two variables: books in the home and cultural possessions (such as works of art and classic literature). "Books in the home" was based on the single question asking how many books there were in the family home. The "cultural possessions" index comprised the presence (or absence) in the family home of classic literature, books of poetry, and works of art. This index measures parental interest and involvement with high culture. An item on the number of musical instruments in the home was not used since it showed weak intercorrelations with the other items. In addition, data on students' own participation in cultural activities was not included in the measure of cultural resources since students' participation relates to personality, talents and interests, as well as cultural background. The composite measure of cultural resources was also constructed as a sheaf variable.

The items comprising wealth, educational materials, and cultural possessions were identified by principal component analyses. Missing data were minimized by using items on which the case had nonmissing data. If data were missing on more than a third of the constituent items in an index, the case was not included in the analyses.

There are two measures relating to school systems: "academic location" and "individual schools." Academic location comprises two components, grade and school program. There are two main reasons why grade is expected to be associated with student achievement. First, the academically more able students are more likely to be found in a higher grade than their same aged peers. Similarly, the academically less able students are more likely to repeat a grade (in countries where grade progression is not automatic) or start school at a later age, and thus be in a grade lower than their age peers. The second reason relates to the curriculum. Students in higher grades are exposed to more complex concepts and more difficult problems. Therefore, students in higher grades perform better than students of the same age in lower grades.

"School program" is an important aspect of academic location. In tracked school systems, all students in a particular school will be taking the same program. Some tracks are preparation for university, while others are preparation for vocational education or direct entry to the labor force. In comprehensive systems, students in the same school may be taking different courses, or different combinations of subjects. Although not as formal as tracked systems, in most countries academic and vocational programs can be distinguished. Students in the academic programs most often show higher scores in achievement tests than students in nonacademic programs.

Information on school program was elicited by a single question asking students what type of program they are in at school. Individual countries were responsible for composing a question appropriate to their national context. However, the response categories had to correspond to an international standard, the ISCED. This classification separates academic, vocational, and work preparation programs at two levels, upper and middle secondary school. For these analyses, the small number of students in the C group "work preparation" were grouped with students in the vocational programs. The categories of programs used in these analyses are: Academic Program (Lower Level), Nonacademic Program (Lower Level), Academic Program (Higher Level), and Nonacademic Program (Higher Level). ISCED is summarized in the ISCED manual (OECD, 1999, pp. 33–46).

In several countries, the ISCED classification did not identify formal school tracks. Germany is well known for its tracked school system but almost all 15-year-olds were correctly assigned to the lower academic track (ISCED 2A). Similarly, almost all students in Italy were assigned to ISCED 3A; in Switzerland, 82% were assigned to ISCED 2A; and in The Netherlands, students were assigned to either lower nonacademic or higher academic programs. In these countries, the distribution of students across program areas is better indicated by differences between schools rather than school program.

Academic location is a composite of grade and school program. It was constructed as a composite (sheaf) variable which maximizes the combined effect of both variables within countries. The resulting sheaf variable is a continuous variable assigning scores to students on the basis of their academic location and its relationship with the composite measure of student achievement. Within countries, the measure was standardized to a mean of zero and a standard deviation of one. For Canada, Finland, and Norway, a composite measure of academic location was based on grade since there were no program differences identified in the PISA study. For Iceland, all students were in the same grade and in the same program so the measure of academic program had no variance.

"Individual schools" is the second measure relating to school systems. There are two reasons for including a categorical measure of individual schools. Individual schools cover tracks or subtracks not formally identified in the ISCED schema. Second, individual schools cover other differences between schools (for example between private and public, rich and poor, academic and technical) that may contribute to the relationship between socioeconomic background and student performance. The schools that students attended were identified during sampling and students attending the same school were assigned the same unique school code.

Analyses

The analysis involved assessing the effects of socioeconomic background (SEB) on reading achievement with and without controls for material, social, and cultural resources and school variables. The extent to which the effects decline indicates the extent to which home resources and schools account for the effects of socioeconomic background on reading achievement. If, for example, the effects of socioeconomic background decline substantially when controlling for cultural resources in the home, then it can be concluded that it is cultural differences that are responsible for much of the effect of socioeconomic background.

The effects of socioeconomic background are presented as regression coefficients that show the average change in achievement score for a one standard deviation increase in socioeconomic background. Each regression coefficient and standard error was calculated by averaging the results obtained from separate analyses of the five plausible values. The standard errors associated with the regression coefficients have been adjusted to take into account the cluster design of the sample and sample stratification (if employed). In the tables, statistical significance is indicated in the usual way (*** $0.001 < P$, ** $0.001 < P < 0.01$, *$0.01 < P < 0.05$).

Estimates for models that controlled for achievement differences between individual schools were obtained through a multilevel modeling procedure that estimates the effects for attending individual schools.[2]

All analyses were weighted to reflect the population of 15-year-old students in each country.

RESULTS

Table 1 presents the effects of socioeconomic background on reading achievement from the analysis of eight models. The first column shows the effects of socioeconomic background without any control variables (Model 1). Columns 2 to 4 show its effects controlling for material, social, and cultural resources, respectively (Models 2–4). Column 5 shows its effects controlling for material and cultural resources and column 6, its effects controlling for all three resources (Models 5 and 6). The last three models add school factors to Model 5. Tables 2 and 3 present the estimates from the same models for achievement in mathematics and science.

Table 1 Effects of socioeconomic background (SEB) on reading achievement with and without controls for cultural, social, and material resources and school variables

Net of	No controls	Material resources	Social resources	Cultural resources	Material and cultural resources	Material, social, and cultural resources	Material and cultural resources + academic location	Material and cultural resources + individual schools	Material and cultural resources + academic location and individual schools
Model	1	2	3	4	5	6	7	8	9
Australia	36***	31***	34***	28***	25***	25***	23***	21***	18***
Austria	35***	31***	34***	25***	23***	23***	11***	10***	9***
Belgium	51***	42***	48***	42***	37***	37***	19***	17***	10***
Brazil	34***	22***	31***	29***	20***	20***	15***	11***	9***
Canada	29***	25***	28***	22***	20***	20***	18***	17***	15***
Czech Republic	43***	35***	35***	32***	28***	26***	20***	11***	12***
Denmark	39***	35***	36***	31***	30***	29***	29***	28***	27***
Finland	24***	22***	24***	17***	16***	16***	16***	16***	16***
France	38***	30***	37***	28***	24***	23***	11***	11***	9***
Germany	49***	40***	43***	35***	31***	30***	22***	11***	8***
Greece	33***	27***	32***	24***	21***	22***	13***	9***	9***
Hungary	46***	40***	45***	28***	26***	27***	16***	5***	5***
Iceland	28***	27***	27***	23***	23***	22***	23***	22***	22***
Ireland	32***	25***	31***	24***	21***	21***	20***	18***	17***
Italy	28***	25***	28***	20***	19***	19***	15***	6***	5***
Korea	19***	16***	16***	12***	12***	11***	6***	4***	4***
Latvia	30***	27***	29***	21***	21***	21***	19***	12***	12***
Luxembourg	43***	33***	40***	29***	26***	25***	12***	17***	11***
Mexico	39***	29***	37***	31***	25***	25***	18***	8***	7***
The Netherlands	35***	31***	31***	29***	25***	23***	21***	13***	11***
New Zealand	38***	29***	36***	29***	24***	24***	23***	21***	20***
Norway	35***	28***	32***	24***	22***	22***	22***	21***	21***

Table 1 *Continued*

Net of	No controls	Material resources	Social resources	Cultural resources	Material and cultural resources	Material, social, and cultural resources	Material and cultural resources + academic location	Material and cultural resources + individual schools	Material and cultural resources + academic location and individual schools
Model	1	2	3	4	5	6	7	8	9
Poland	33***	27***	31***	24***	21***	21***	7**	1	1
Portugal	40***	28***	37***	27***	22***	22***	10***	13***	8***
Russian Federation	31***	26***	29***	23***	22***	21***	19***	14***	13***
Spain	32***	28***	31***	23***	20***	20***	14***	17***	10***
Sweden	30***	28***	30***	21***	21***	21***	20***	19***	19***
Switzerland	46***	41***	44***	37***	34***	34***	25***	20***	19***
United Kingdom	42***	36***	40***	31***	29***	29***	29***	22***	21***
United States	40***	26***	38***	27***	20***	20***	16***	14***	12***
Average	36	30	34	27	24	23	18	14	13

Note: Regression coefficients denoting the change in score for a one standard deviation difference in SEB. ***$0.001 < P$; **$0.001 < P < 0.01$; *$0.01 < P < 0.05$.

Table 2 Effects of socioeconomic background (SEB) on mathematics achievement with and without controls for cultural, social, and material resources and school variables

Net of Model	No controls 1	Material resources 2	Social resources 3	Cultural resources 4	Material and cultural resources 5	Material, social, and cultural resources 6	Material and cultural resources + academic location 7	Material and cultural resources + individual schools 8	Material and cultural resources + academic location and individual schools 9
Australia	35***	31***	34***	30***	25***	27***	25***	25***	22***
Austria	33***	27***	32***	25***	23***	21***	10***	9***	7***
Belgium	50***	41***	49***	43***	37***	37***	20***	19***	13***
Brazil	40***	22***	37***	34***	20***	20***	14***	13***	10***
Canada	25***	21***	24***	21***	20***	18***	17***	16***	15***
Czech Republic	42***	34***	38***	34***	28***	28***	23***	15***	15***
Denmark	32***	27***	30***	26***	30***	23***	22***	22***	21***
Finland	22***	19***	22***	18***	16***	17***	16***	17***	17***
France	35***	27***	34***	29***	24***	23***	11***	13***	10***
Germany	45***	38***	43***	34***	31***	31***	24***	13***	11***
Greece	36***	28***	36***	26***	21***	22***	12***	10***	10***
Hungary	47***	41***	47***	35***	26***	33***	23***	13***	13***
Iceland	22***	22***	22***	17***	23***	16***	17***	17***	17***
Ireland	29***	21***	28***	22***	21***	17***	18***	17***	17***
Italy	24***	20***	23***	16***	19***	14***	10***	5**	4**
Korea	26***	22***	23***	18***	12***	16***	9***	6***	6***
Latvia	23***	19***	22***	17***	21***	15***	14***	10***	9***
Luxembourg	34***	25***	32***	24***	26***	21***	8*	14***	8***
Mexico	35***	25***	34***	26***	25***	20***	13***	8***	7***
The Netherlands	32***	27***	31***	25***	25***	21***	17***	9***	7***
New Zealand	37***	29***	36***	31***	24***	26***	25***	24***	23***
Norway	28***	22***	27***	20***	22***	18***	17***	18***	17***

Table 2 *Continued*

Net of	No controls	Material resources	Social resources	Cultural resources	Material and cultural resources	Material, social, and cultural resources	Material and cultural resources + academic location	Material and cultural resources + individual schools	Material and cultural resources + academic location and individual schools
Model	1	2	3	4	5	6	7	8	9
Poland	35***	27***	33***	26***	21***	22***	12***	6**	5*
Portugal	37***	25***	34***	27***	22***	21***	12***	16***	11***
Russian Federation	27***	21***	25***	20***	22***	16***	15***	12***	10***
Spain	34***	28***	33***	23***	20***	20***	14***	18***	11***
Sweden	32***	29***	33***	24***	21***	24***	23***	23***	22***
Switzerland	41***	35***	39***	33***	34***	29***	21***	18***	16***
United Kingdom	38***	32***	36***	29***	29***	26***	26***	18***	18***
United States	41***	26***	39***	29***	20***	22***	17***	16***	14***
Average	34	27	33	26	24	22	17	15	13

Note: Regression coefficients denoting the change in score for a one standard deviation difference in SEB. ***$0.001 < P$; **$0.001 < P < 0.01$; *$0.01 < P < 0.05$.

■ **Table 3** Effects of socioeconomic background (SEB) on science achievement with and without controls for cultural, social, and material resources and school variables

Net of	No controls	Material resources	Social resources	Cultural resources	Material and cultural resources	Material, social, and cultural resources	Material and cultural resources + academic location	Material and cultural resources + individual schools	Material and cultural resources + academic location and individual schools
Model	1	2	3	4	5	6	7	8	9
Australia	30***	31***	29***	22***	20***	19***	18***	16***	15***
Austria	34***	31***	34***	27***	23***	24***	13***	10***	9***
Belgium	51***	42***	49***	41***	35***	35***	17***	17***	10***
Brazil	34***	22***	34***	31***	22***	22***	19***	18***	16***
Canada	27***	25***	26***	22***	21***	20***	19***	19***	17***
Czech Republic	39***	35***	35***	29***	25***	24***	19***	12***	13***
Denmark	43***	35***	42***	36***	34***	34***	34***	32***	32***
Finland	22***	22***	21***	16***	15***	15***	15***	15***	15***
France	43***	30***	42***	34***	30***	30***	16***	17***	15***
Germany	44***	40***	42***	31***	28***	27***	22***	12***	10***
Greece	31***	27***	30***	23***	21***	22***	13***	10***	10***
Hungary	49***	40***	49***	34***	32***	33***	22***	13***	13***
Iceland	21***	27***	20***	16***	15***	15***	15***	14***	14***
Ireland	30***	25***	29***	24***	21***	21***	20***	19***	18***
Italy	26***	25***	26***	19***	17***	17***	13***	8***	6***
Korea	21***	16***	18***	14***	13***	12***	5*	3	3
Latvia	30***	27***	29***	22***	21***	21***	20***	15***	14***
Luxembourg	36***	33***	34***	24***	21***	21***	9***	14***	9***
Mexico	31***	29***	29***	23***	19***	18***	14***	7***	7***
The Netherlands	37***	31***	33***	30***	28***	26***	23***	17***	14***
New Zealand	40***	29***	39***	33***	27***	28***	26***	25***	24***
Norway	30***	28***	29***	21***	18***	18***	18***	18***	17***
Poland	32***	27***	31***	24***	21***	21***	11***	5	3

Table 3 *Continued*

Net of	No controls	Material resources	Social resources	Cultural resources	Material and cultural resources	Material, social, and cultural resources	Material and cultural resources + academic location	Material and cultural resources + individual schools	Material and cultural resources + academic location and individual schools
Model	1	2	3	4	5	6	7	8	9
Portugal	33***	28***	31***	22***	18***	18***	9***	12***	8***
Russian Federation	27***	26***	25***	19***	19***	19***	17***	13***	12***
Spain	36***	28***	36***	26***	24***	24***	18***	22***	15***
Sweden	26***	28***	27***	19***	18***	19***	17***	17***	17***
Switzerland	47***	41***	46***	38***	37***	37***	29***	24***	23***
United Kingdom	40***	36***	38***	30***	28***	27***	28***	20***	20***
United States	39***	26***	38***	27***	21***	21***	18***	15***	13***
Average	34	30	33	26	23	23	18	15	14

Note: Regression coefficients denoting the change in score for a one standard deviation difference in SEB. ***0.001 < P; **0.001 < P < 0.01; *0.01 < P < 0.05.

Across countries, the average effect of socioeconomic background is 36 score points; in other words, a one standard deviation increase in socioeconomic background is associated with an increase of 36 score points in reading achievement. The strongest effects of socioeconomic background were found in Belgium (51 score points), Germany (49), Hungary (46), Switzerland (46), Luxembourg (43), the United Kingdom (42), Portugal (40), and the United States (40). The weakest effects were found in Korea (19), Finland (24), Italy (28), and Canada (29).

For mathematics and science, the findings were very similar (Tables 2 and 3). The tables show that, in most countries, socioeconomic inequalities in student achievement are, contrary to expectations, slightly stronger in reading than for mathematics and science.

These findings provide some indication of the relationship between tracking and socioeconomic inequalities in education. There is a tendency for countries with tracked school systems in which selection occurs at a young age, such as Belgium, the Czech Republic, Germany, and Hungary, to show stronger relationships and countries which are not tracked or where tracking occurs at a later age, such as Canada and Finland, show the weakest effects. However, there are several notable exceptions; Austria has a similar tracked system to Germany but shows a much weaker effect for socioeconomic background. Similarly, the United States and the United Kingdom are untracked systems but show higher than average effects for socioeconomic background.

Impact of material, social, and cultural resources

Material resources account for part of the influence of socioeconomic background on reading achievement. When controlling for material resources, the average effect of socioeconomic background, across countries, declines by 6 score points – a reduction of around 17% (Model 2). Brazil stands out as a country where material resources are relatively more important; the effect of socioeconomic background decreases by about 35%. Material resources also substantially reduce the impact of socioeconomic background in the United States (where the effect is reduced by 33%), Portugal (30%), and Mexico (26%). Material resources explain little of the influence of socioeconomic background in Iceland, Sweden, Finland, Latvia, Denmark, and Italy. The negligible impact of material resources in the Scandinavian countries may reflect the lower levels of income inequality in these countries. These patterns were generally repeated for mathematics and science achievement (Tables 2 and 3).

In most countries, social resources explain little of the effect of socioeconomic background on reading achievement. Social resources reduce the average effect of socioeconomic background by only 2 score points from 36 to 34 (Model 3). Countries where social resources alone, explain moderate amounts of the effect of socioeconomic background are the Czech Republic (where the effect of socioeconomic background is reduced by 8 score points), Germany (6), and The Netherlands (4). In the other countries, social resources had only a negligible or no impact on the effect of socioeconomic background. The strong impact of social resources on the effects of socioeconomic background on reading achievement in the Czech Republic was not replicated for mathematics and science.

Of the three resources investigated here, "cultural resources" explains a greater proportion of the influence of socioeconomic background. The inclusion of cultural resources reduces the average effect of socioeconomic background from 36 to 27 score points, a reduction of around 25% (Model 4). The decline in the effect of socioeconomic background was largest in Hungary (where the effect of socioeconomic background decreased by 39%), Korea (37%), Luxembourg (33%), the United States (33%), Portugal (33%),

Norway (31%), Latvia (30%), and Sweden (30%). In contrast, cultural resources explained relatively little of the effect of socioeconomic background in Brazil (15%), Iceland (16%), The Netherlands (17%), and Belgium (18%). Similar patterns were found for mathematics and reading.

Together, the two resources – material and cultural resources – explain about a third of the effect of socioeconomic background on reading achievement. Across these countries, the effect of socioeconomic background declined from 36 to 24 score units, a decline of one third (Model 5). These two resources account for sizeable proportions of the influence of socioeconomic background in many countries: the United States (50%), Portugal (45%), Hungary (44%), Brazil (41%), Luxembourg (40%), and France, Germany, and Norway (37%). In contrast, for Iceland these two resources explained only 18% of the effect of socioeconomic background. Other countries where these resources explained a smaller proportion were Denmark (23%) and Switzerland (26%). Therefore, material and cultural resources in the home account for between one fifth and one half of the influence of socioeconomic background on reading achievement. They account for similar proportions of the effects of socioeconomic background on mathematics and science achievement.

"Social resources" adds little additional explanatory power after accounting for the effects of material and cultural resources. This result is demonstrated by little or no difference in the effects of socioeconomic background net of material and cultural resources, and net of all three resources (compare effects for socioeconomic background in Models 5 and 6). In all countries except the Czech Republic, the effects of socioeconomic background are the same or almost the same. Therefore, "social resources" is not included in subsequent analyses on the impact of school factors.

School factors

Three models (7, 8, and 9) include school factors. They build on analyses of the effects of socioeconomic background net of material and cultural resources in the home (Model 5). In addition to material and cultural resources, Models 7 and 8 control for students' academic location and individual schools, respectively. Model 9 shows the effects of socioeconomic background net of cultural and material resources, academic location, and individual schools. Since measures of academic location were not constructed for Canada, Finland, Iceland, and Norway, the effects of socioeconomic background could not be estimated for models that include academic location.

The addition of academic location further reduces the effect of socioeconomic background on reading beyond that achieved by material and cultural resources. The average declines from 24 score points to 18 score points, a decrease of 25%. There are a number of countries where academic location considerably reduces the impact of socioeconomic background: Poland (where the effect of socioeconomic background is reduced by a further 67%), Portugal (55%), France (54%), Luxembourg (54%), Austria (52%), Korea (50%), Belgium (48%), Greece (38%), and Hungary (38%). The reduction in the effect of socioeconomic background with the addition of academic location was minimal in a number of countries: Australia, Denmark, Ireland, Latvia, New Zealand, Sweden, and the United Kingdom. For the United States, a country without established school tracks but within-school curriculum tracking, academic location further reduced the effect of socioeconomic background on reading by 25%.

Controlling for the effects of individual schools with the introduction of a multilevel model also substantially reduces the impact of socioeconomic background, beyond that obtained by material and cultural resources. Controlling for individual schools reduced the effect of socioeconomic background on reading from 24 score points to 14 score points, a decline of 42%. The reduction is greatest in tracked school systems: Poland (where the effect of socioeconomic background is reduced by a staggering 95%), Hungary (81%), Italy (68%), Mexico (68%), Korea (67%), Germany (65%), the Czech Republic (60%), Greece (57%), Austria (56%), France (54%), Belgium (54%), The Netherlands (48%), Brazil (45%), Switzerland (41%), and Portugal (41%). Controlling for achievement differences between individual schools made little difference to the effects of socioeconomic background on reading in Finland, Iceland, Norway, Demark, and Sweden. Moderate reductions were found in Australia (16%), the United Kingdom (24%), and the United States (30%).

Controlling for material and cultural resources, academic location, and the effect of individual schools explains a large proportion of the effect of socioeconomic background on reading. Across countries, the effect decreased from 36 score points to 13. Across these countries, over 60% of the effect of socioeconomic background on reading achievement is accounted for by the material and cultural resources in the home, academic location, and differences between individual schools.

The final model performed best in Poland, where 97% of the effects of socioeconomic background is accounted for by home resources and school factors. Model 9 also accounted for large proportions of the effect of socioeconomic background in many other countries: Hungary (89%), Germany (84%), Italy (82%), Mexico (82%), Belgium (80%), Portugal (80%), Korea (79%), France (76%), Austria (74%), Luxembourg (74%), Brazil (74%), Greece (73%), the Czech Republic (72%), and the United States (70%).

These resources and schools accounted for less than 50% of the effect of socioeconomic background in Iceland (22%), Denmark (31%), Sweden (37%), Norway (40%), Ireland (47%), New Zealand (47%), and Canada (48%). In Australia, these factors account for 50% of the effects of socioeconomic background on reading achievement. Almost identical patterns were found for mathematics and science achievement.

DISCUSSION

The PISA project aims to provide policy-makers in participating countries with an analysis of the achievement of students nearing the end of compulsory schooling. Although the major focus of the PISA project is to compare the performance of education systems in preparing their students for future life, another focus is examination of the equity of educational outcomes within countries. The initial PISA report (OECD, 2001) includes a detailed discussion of the effect of socioeconomic background on student performance and examines the size of this effect in different countries. It has been found that this effect varies markedly between the countries. This paper extends that work by looking at the degree to which social, material, and cultural resources and schools can explain the effect of socioeconomic background on student achievement. An understanding of the effect of these factors can provide policy-makers the opportunity to implement more focused reforms.

Social resources, as measured here, explain little of the effect of socioeconomic background on student achievement. It could be argued that the measure of social resources is inappropriate but it should be kept in mind that this and other international data show almost invariably negative relationships between the involvement of family and other adults with schoolwork and student achievement. This does not mean that social capital is unimportant for educational outcomes but supports McNeal's (1999) contention that the social relationships surrounding the student are important for behavioral outcomes such as dropping out of school but less important for cognitive outcomes, such as achievement.

The most striking finding from these analyses is the importance of cultural factors in socioeconomic inequalities in education. Cultural resources accounted for sizeable proportions of the effect of socioeconomic background in Hungary, Korea, Luxembourg, the United States, and Portugal and had a stronger impact than material resources in most other countries. Therefore, it can be concluded that, in general, cultural resources play a more important role in socioeconomic inequalities in student achievement than material resources in the home.

There is no indication that in less wealthy countries material resources are more important and in wealthy countries cultural resources are more important. Material resources are a particularly important component in socioeconomic inequalities in education in Brazil, Portugal, Mexico, but also the United States. The stronger impact of material resources in the United States may reflect greater inequality in income and wealth there than in most other industrialized countries. Countries that showed the weakest impact of cultural resources on the effect of socioeconomic background were Belgium, Brazil, Iceland, and The Netherlands. Apart from Brazil, these countries cannot be considered poor. Similarly, of the countries in which cultural resources produces the largest declines in the effects of socioeconomic background – Hungary, Korea, Luxembourg, the United States, and Portugal – only Luxembourg and the United States would be considered wealthy countries.

There is no evidence that cultural factors play a greater role in socioeconomic inequalities in reading than in mathematics and science. In most instances the findings were almost identical. Bourdieu's theory of cultural capital focuses on high or "elite" culture. If familiarity with elite culture was important then cultural factors should have played a larger role for reading achievement than for mathematics and science. Furthermore, additional analyses suggest that "books in the home" is a more important component of cultural resources in regard to student achievement than cultural possessions. Therefore, these findings lend support to the hypothesis that cultural factors are important but do not support Bourdieu's theory of cultural capital. A "literary" or "bookish" home environment is likely to be an indicator of the academic environment of the home; the extent to which parents participate in and value learning. Just as highly academic environments in schools enhance educational success so do highly academic home environments. This explains why cultural resources are just as important in accounting for socioeconomic inequalities in mathematics and science as for reading.

Similarly, it was expected that schools and locations within schools would play a greater role in mediating the relationship between socioeconomic background and student performance in mathematics and science than for reading. For mathematics and science there are larger differences in the complexity of the material taught, between schools in different tracks or between upper or lower curriculum tracks within schools, than for reading which unlike mathematics or science is not formally taught in secondary school. However, there was no evidence that school factors had a greater role in socioeconomic inequalities in performance in mathematics and science than in reading. The role of school factors is general.

The generally stronger effects of socioeconomic background in highly differentiated systems do suggest that tracking and other forms of educational differentiation *can* strengthen socioeconomic inequalities in education. If socioeconomic criteria are involved in the allocation of students to different academic locations (so it is not entirely based on student ability) and there is greater achievement growth in the higher academic tracks and locations then the relationship between socioeconomic background and achievement will be strengthened. Therefore, highly differentiated systems can magnify socioeconomic inequalities in education. This explanation suggests that the problem is not tracking or other forms of educational differentiation as such, but the criteria used to allocate students and/or differences in the academic environment between locations in school systems. If this explanation is valid, the policy responses are clear: Ensure that the allocation of students to different academic locations should be based on objective measures of student performance; delay the allocation of students to different locations since the effects of socioeconomic background tend to be stronger among younger students, allow movement between tracks and minimize differences in the learning environment between tracks. Such policies should reduce socioeconomic inequalities in education in highly differentiated school systems.

NOTES

1. Other international achievement studies of middle secondary school students also show negative relationships between measures of parental involvement and achievement. Thorndike (1973, p. 75) notes that the relationship between parental help for homework and reading achievement was across countries consistently negative. A composite measure "home help" incorporates the homework measure and "helping with speaking" and "helping with writing" again showed negative correlations with reading achievement. A nine-item attitude scale "home support", comprising items on whether the students' father and mother enjoy doing mathematics, are able to help with the students' work in mathematics, are very interested in helping, think that mathematics is important, encourage the student to learn as much mathematics as possible, and want the student to do very well in mathematics, was either negatively associated or had no relationship with mathematics achievement (Kifer & Robitalle, 1989, pp. 188–190; Schmidt & Kifer, 1989, p. 224).
2. The SAS program PROC MIXED was used to estimate the effects of socioeconomic background when controlling for school differences in achievement (Littell, Milliken, Stroup & Wolfinger, 1996).

REFERENCES

Alexander, K. L. and Eckland, B. K. (1974) Sex differences in the educational attainment process. *American Sociological Review* **39**, pp. 668–682.

Alexander, K. L. and Eckland, B. K. (1975) Basic attainment processes: A replication and extension. *Sociology of Education* **48**, pp. 457–495.

Bourdieu, P. (1973) Cultural reproduction and social reproduction. In Brown R. (ed.) *Knowledge, education, and cultural change: Papers in the sociology of education*, pp. 71–112. Tavistock, London.

Bourdieu, P. (1984) *Distinction: A social critique of the judgement of taste.* Harvard University Press, Cambridge, MA.

Coleman, J. S. (1987) Families and schools. *Educational Researcher* **16**:6, pp. 32–38.

Coleman, J. S. (1988) Social capital in the creation of human capital. *American Journal of Sociology* **94**:Supplement, pp. S95-S120.

Comber, L. C. and Keeves, J. P. (1973) *Science education in nineteen countries: International studies in evaluation.* Almquist & Wiksell, Stockholm – New York: John Wiley & Sons.

Crook, C. J. (1997) *Cultural practices and socio-economic attainment.* Greenwood Press, Westport, CT.

De Graaf, N. D., De Graaf, P. M. and Kraaykamp, G. (2000) Parental cultural capital and educational attainment in The Netherlands: A refinement of the cultural capital perspective. *Sociology of Education* **73**:2, pp. 92–111.

De Graaf, P. (1986) Parents' financial and cultural resources, grades, and transitions to secondary school in Federal Republic of Germany. *European Sociological Review* **4**:3, pp. 209–221.

De Graaf, P. M., Ganzeboom, H. B. G. and Kalmijn, M. (1989) Cultural and economic dimensions of occupational status. In Jansen, W., Dronkers, J. and Verrips, K. (eds) *Similar or different? Continuities in research on social stratification*, pp. 53–74. SISWO, Amsterdam.

DiMaggio, P. (1982) Cultural capital and school success: The impact of status culture participation on the grades of U.S. high school students. *American Sociological Review* **47**, pp. 189–201.

DiMaggio, P. and Mohr, J. (1985) Cultural capital, educational attainment and martial selection. *American Journal of Sociology* **90**:6, pp. 1231–1261.

Fejgin, N. (1995) Factors contributing to the academic excellence of American Jewish and Asian students. *Sociology of Education* **68**:1, pp. 18–30.

Gamoran, A. (1996) Curriculum standardization and equality of opportunity in Scottish secondary education: 1984–90. *Sociology of Education* **69**, pp. 1–21.

Ganzach, Y. (2000) Parent's education, cognitive ability, educational expectations and educational attainment. *British Journal of Educational Psychology* **70**, pp. 419–441.

Ganzeboom, H. B. and Treiman, D. J. (1996) Internationally comparable measures of occupational status for the 1988 International Standard Classifications of Occupations. *Social Science Research* **25**, pp. 201–239.

Greenwald, R., Hedges, L. and Laine, R. (1996) The effect of school resources on student achievement. *Review of Educational Research* **66**, pp. 361–396.

Hout, M. and Dohan, D. P. (1996) Two paths to educational opportunity: Class and educational selection in Sweden and education selection in Sweden and the United States. In Erikson, R. and Jonsson, J. O. (eds) *Can education be equalized? The Swedish case in comparative perspective*, pp. 207–232. Westview, Boulder, CO.

Jencks, C., Smith, M., Acland, H., Bane, M. J., Ginitis, D., Heyns, B. and Michelson, S. (1972) *Inequality. A reassessment of family and schooling in America*. Basic Books, New York.

Jencks, C., Bartlett, S., Corcan, M., Crouse, J., Eaglesfield, D., Jackson, G., McClelland, K., Mueser, P., Olneck, M., Swartz, J., Ward, S. and Williams, J. (1979) *Who gets ahead? The determinants of economic success in America*. Basic Books, New York.

Keeves, J. P. and Saha, L. J. (1992) Home background factors and educational outcomes. In Keeves, J. (ed) *The IEA study of science III: Changes in science education and achievement 1970 to 1984*, pp. 165–186. Pergamon, Oxford, UK.

Kerckhoff, A. C. (1993) Educational attainment in a changing education system: The case of England and Wales. In Blossfeld, H.-P. and Shavit, Y. (eds) *Persistent inequality: Changing educational attainment in thirteen countries*, pp. 134–154. Westview, Boulder, CO.

Kifer, E. and Robitalle, D. F. (1989) Attitudes, preferences and opinions. In Robitaille, D. F. and Garden, R. A. (eds) *The IEA study of mathematics II: Contexts and outcomes of school mathematics*, pp. 178–208. Pergamon Press, Oxford, UK.

Lee, V. E. and Bryk, A. S. (1989) A multilevel model of the social distribution of high school achievement. *Sociology of Education* **62**:3, pp. 172–192.

Littell, R. C., Milliken, G. A., Stroup, W. W. and Wolfinger, R. D. (1996) *SAS system for mixed models*. SAS Institute, Cary, NC.

McNeal, R. B. J. (1999) Parental involvement as social capital: Differential effectiveness on science achievement, truancy and dropping out. *Social Forces* **78**:1, pp. 117–145.

Muller, W. and Shavit, Y. (1998) The institutional embeddedness of the stratification process: A comparative study of qualifications and occupations in thirteen countries. In *From school to work. A comparative study of educational qualifications and occupational destinations*, pp. 1–48. Clarendon Press, Oxford, UK.

Organization for Economic Cooperation and Development (1999) *Classifying educational programmes. Manual for ISCED-97 implementation in OECD countries*. Author, Paris.

Organization for Economic Cooperation and Development (2001) *Knowledge and skills for life. First results from the OECD programme for international student assessment*. Author, Paris.

Organization for Economic Cooperation and Development (2002) *PISA 2000 technical report*. Author, Paris.

Orr, A. J. (2003) Black-white differences in achievement: The importance of wealth. *Sociology of Education* **76**:4, pp. 281–304.

Parcel, T. L. and Dufur, M. J. (2001) Capital at home and at school: Effects on student achievement. *Social Forces* **79**:3, pp. 881–912.

Pong, S. -L. and Ju, D. -B. (2000) The effects of change in family structure and income on dropping out of middle and high school. *Journal of Family Issues* **21**:2, pp. 147–167.

Rijken, S. (1999) *Educational expansion and status attainment. A cross-national and over-time comparison.* Inter-University Center for Social Science Theory and Methodology, The Netherlands.

Scheerens, J. and Bosker, R. (1997) *The foundations of educational effectiveness.* Pergamon Press, Oxford, UK.

Schmidt, W. H. and Kifer, E. (1989) Exploring relationships across systems population A. In Robitaille, D. F. and Garden, R. A. (eds) *The IEA study of mathematics II: Contexts and outcomes of school mathematics.* Pergamon Press, Oxford, UK.

Schreiber, J. B. (2002) Institutional and student factors and their influence on advanced mathematics achievement. *Journal of Educational Research* **95**:5, pp. 274–286.

Sieben, I. (2001) *Sibling similarities and social stratification: The impact of family background across countries and cohorts.* Inter-University Center for Social Science Theory and Methodology, The Netherlands.

Sullivan, A. (2001) Cultural capital and educational attainment. *Sociology*, **35**:4, pp. 893–912.

Teachman, J. D. (1987) Family background, educational resources, and educational attainment. *American Sociological Review* **52**, pp. 548–557.

Thorndike, R. L. (1973) *Reading comprehension education in fifteen countries. An empirical study: Vol. 3.* John Wiley & Sons, New York.

Whitt, H. P. (1986) The sheaf coefficient: A simplified and expanded approach. *Social Science Research* **15**, pp. 174–189.

THE EFFECT OF CHILDHOOD SEGREGATION ON MINORITY ACADEMIC PERFORMANCE AT SELECTIVE COLLEGES

Douglas S. Massey and Mary J. Fischer

INTRODUCTION

Douglas Massey is Henry G. Bryant Professor of Sociology and Public Affairs at Princeton University, USA. He is a very high-profile prolific academic with a highly significant body of work with positions including being President of the American Academy of Political and Social Science and a very large publication list including, for example, the 2007 book *Categorically Unequal: the American Stratification System* (Russell Sage Foundation, New York). Mary J. Fischer has collaborated with Massey on many projects and publications. She is assistant professor in sociology at the University of Connecticut, USA with interests including stratification and racial/ethnic disparities.

In this article, they use data from the National Longitudinal Survey of Freshman of 4,000 men and women in 1999. Although they focus on students in selective institutions they show that "those coming of age in a [racially/ethnically] segregated environment were less prepared academically and socially for college life and were more exposed to violence and disorder while growing up". They argue that "the evidence overwhelmingly shows that separate is rarely, if ever equal. Rather the segregation of minorities is almost always used as a deliberate tool of subordination to perpetuate inequality between minority and majority groups".

KEY QUESTIONS

1. Do you find the way in which Massey and Fischer focus on traditional evidence of achievement to be acceptable?

2. If we notice differences between ethnic/racial groups should we assert that institutional racism exists?
3. What are the issues that would need to be discussed before such an assertion could be accepted?

FURTHER READING

In the UK, evidence about the nature of differential achievement across racial/ethnic groups has been explored by Steve Strand of the University of Warwick, see www.guardian.co.uk/education/2008/sep/05/raceineducation.raceinschools. Government data and information about strategies to improve achievement can be seen at: www.standards.dfes.gov.uk/ethnicminorities. It is important not to neglect work completed some time ago. Current debates need to be seen in context. The work of Barry Troyna is very valuable. The Report of the Committee of Enquiry into the Education of Children from Ethnic Minority Groups Education for all Cmnd. 9453, Her Majesty's Stationery Office, London, 1985 (popularly known as the Swann report) is still important.

This Reading links with Chapters 6 and 9 and Debate 4 of *The Routledge Education Studies Textbook.*

INTRODUCTION

The United States is still a racially segregated society. Although de jure segregation was prohibited by federal legislation in the 1960s, a variety of de facto mechanisms operate to keep segregation high in both schools (Orfield and Eaton 1996) and neighbourhoods (Massey and Denton 1993). Recent analyses of census and school data reveal that current levels of segregation are not much different from those prevailing in 1970, just after the passage of the 1968 Fair Housing Act (Orfield and Sanni 1999; Iceland, Weinberg, and Steinmetz 2002). Although desegregation efforts have been relatively successful in employment, media, retail, and public accommodation, they have lagged behind in schools and housing.

A large literature documents the harmful consequences of segregation on the life chances of individuals, beginning with the pioneering work of Myrdal (1944) and Clark (1965) and continuing through the recent efforts of Massey and Denton (1993) and Orfield and Eaton (1996). Research has shown that students in minority-dominant schools receive lower-quality education than those attending schools where whites and/or Asians predominate (Orfield and Eaton 1996). People living in minority-dominant neighbourhoods likewise experience elevated concentrations of poverty, which operate to lower the odds of success across a variety of socio-economic dimensions (Brooks-Gunn, Duncan, and Aber 1997; Sampson, Morenoff, and Gannon-Rowley 2002).

Prior research, however, has mostly focused on the *contemporaneous* effects of segregation, seeking to determine how racial isolation and concentrated poverty in schools and neighbourhoods influence concurrent socio-economic outcomes. Few studies have considered the *long-term consequences* of segregation, tracing out the effects of social isolation on socio-economic outcomes that are expressed long after the segregated circumstances were actually experienced.

Although primary and secondary schools remain highly segregated by race and ethnicity, desegregation efforts have been more successful in colleges and universities.

Within institutions of higher learning, race-conscious admission policies have transformed former bastions of white privilege into more representative reflections of American society (Bowen and Bok 1998). From the early 1970s through the middle 1990s race-conscious college admissions were the norm throughout the United Sates. Although recent attacks on affirmative action have rolled back race-conscious policies at public universities in a growing number of states, race continues to be taken into account in admissions at selective private institutions, and it continues in many public schools as well.

The use of race or ethnicity as a criterion in college admissions creates a natural experiment to study the long-term effects of segregation. Employing racial criteria to achieve a racially diverse student body invariably selects some students who grew up in minority-dominant environments and others who did not. The simultaneous entry of minority students from integrated and segregated backgrounds into a common competitive arena allows us to measure and study the long-term consequences of childhood segregation on academic performance. In this article we draw on a new source of data, the National Longitudinal Survey of Freshmen [NLSF], to consider how segregation experienced while growing up influences later academic performance in college or university, as assessed by the grade point average earned in the first few terms of study.

We begin our analysis by showing the relative number of white, Asian, Latino, and black students in our sample who grew up in integrated, mixed, and segregated circumstances. We then consider how school quality, academic preparation, social preparation, psychological preparation, family stress, and exposure to disorder and violence vary by minority composition of neighbourhood. We end by determining the effect of prior segregation on the grade point average earned by respondents during their first three terms of college, and identify which conditions associated with segregation are responsible for its effect on academic performance.

SEGREGATION AND ACADEMIC ACHIEVEMENT

Segregation experienced in childhood can influence later academic performance through a variety of channels, some obvious and some not so readily apparent. Perhaps the clearest pathway is through the quality of education itself. To the extent that mainstream society is reluctant to invest scarce resources in minority schools and neighbourhoods, people growing up in segregated settings will receive lower quality instruction and fewer neighbourhood services. On average, they will be taught by less able teachers, using substandard materials, in more dilapidated circumstances (Kozol 1991) and they will live in neighbourhoods with higher crime, greater poverty, and more physical dilapidation (Massey, Condran, and Denton 1987; Massey and Fong 1990). As a result, students who grow up in minority-dominant schools and neighbourhoods can be expected to arrive on campus less prepared academically for the challenges of a rigorous and competitive academic environment.

Segregation may also leave students unprepared socially for the diversity they will encounter on campus. For those students who grow up entirely within minority-dominant settings, the behaviours, norms, and attitudes they encounter in college may be unfamiliar and intimidating. The feeling of 'not belonging' may cause unease and anxiety that interferes with academic motivations and performance, especially when reinforced by subtle and not-so-subtle exclusion by white peers (see Allen, Epps, and Hannif 1991; Feagin, Vera, and Imani 1996).

Segregation may also affect a student's psychological preparation for college by undermining feelings of self-esteem and self-efficacy. Poor, segregated neighbourhoods, in particular, have been shown to contain residents who feel that they have little influence on their surroundings and who share a strong sense of powerlessness and vulnerability that prevents them from acting (Sampson, Raudenbush, and Earls 1997; Sampson, Morenoff, and Earls 1999). To the extent that a lack of collective efficacy becomes internalized at the individual level, it can be expected to influence other domains of life, such as academics.

The degree of segregation experienced while growing up also influences college achievement in ways that are less obvious. Because racial segregation interacts with the distribution of income to concentrate poverty geographically (Massey and Fischer 2000), it also concentrates any characteristics that are associated with poverty (Massey and Denton 1993). Given that crime, health, and delinquency are associated with socio-economic deprivation, segregation therefore ends up concentrating them as well to create an unusually threatening, hostile, and unhealthy social environment (Massey 2001, 2004). To the extent that students and their families come from segregated schools and neighbourhoods, therefore, two consequences follow.

First, it is more likely that negative life events will occur to people they know and care about, causing stress to flow towards them through their social networks. Even though minority students may leave segregated schools and neighbourhoods far behind, it is likely that many of their friends and relatives will continue to live, work, and play in minority-dominant settings. Because these settings evince higher rates of crime, delinquency, and physical distress, members of their social circle are more likely to become sick, killed, injured, or otherwise victimized by crime, accidents, and illness.

In addition to experiencing stress indirectly through social networks, respondents from segregated backgrounds are also quite likely to experience chronic stress directly in the places where they work and study (Massey 2004). People living in poor, segregated neighbourhoods are personally exposed to high rates of violence and delinquency over long periods of time, bringing about repeated activation of the body's stress response syndrome (LeDoux 1996; Kotulak 1997). Chronic exposure to stress has been found to have relatively strong effects on cognition – reducing memory, increasing frustration, limiting attention, and compromising the physiology of learning (James *et al.* 1987; McEwan 1992, 2002; Diamond and Rose 1993, 1994; Goleman 1995; Bremner 2002). Thus, students growing up in segregated environments may have developed cognitive traits that undermine their academic performance, even holding constant overall aptitude.

DATA AND METHODS

Childhood segregation thus potentially undermines collegiate academic performance in several ways: (1) by depressing the quality of schooling and lowering academic preparation; (2) by isolating students to render them socially and psychologically unprepared for campus life; (3) by producing a surfeit of negative events within the student's social network to produce stress indirectly; and (4) by exposing students directly to stressful environments while growing up to compromise cognitive development along one or more dimensions.

Sorting out these various influences requires unusually detailed data on the racial composition of schools and neighbourhoods at different points in the life cycle, along with information on their socio-economic characteristics and psychological correlates, all linked to indicators of later academic achievement. The NLSF provides such a source of data. It is a probability sample of students entering a set of selective U.S. colleges and universities as freshmen in the autumn of 1999. Some thirty-five schools were asked to participate in the study, including all the institutions studied by Bowen and Bok (1998) plus the University of California at Berkeley. The survey was sponsored by a grant from the Andrew W. Mellon Foundation, whose president (Bowen) contacted each institution's president or chancellor to request his or her support.

In most cases the request was favourably received. Only seven institutions declined or were otherwise unable to participate (Duke, Hamilton, Morehouse, Spelman, Vanderbilt, Wellesley, and Xavier), yielding an institutional participation rate of 80 per cent. In the remaining twenty-eight institutions, 4,573 randomly selected respondents were approached and 3,924 face-to-face interviews were completed, for an overall response rate of 86 per cent. The sample included 998 whites, 959 Asians, 916 Latinos, and 1,051 African Americans. The survey was designed to gather extensive information about respondents prior to entering college and to measure in some detail their initial attitudes, motivations and perceptions.

A detailed description of the sample is available from Massey *et al.* (2003) and the institutions and their basic characteristics are listed in Appendix A. The sample includes students from elite private universities such as Princeton, Penn, and Yale; selective liberal arts colleges such as Swarthmore, Williams, and Kenyon; and selective public institutions such as the University of California at Berkeley, the University of Michigan, and the University of North Carolina. Three women's colleges were included in the sample (Bryn Mawr, Barnard, and Smith) along with one historical black institution (Howard University). The admission rate varied in schools from a low of 11 per cent to a high of 79 per cent and averaged 40 per cent. The median combined SAT score of entering students ranged from 1,105 to 1,450 and averaged 1,243. By any standard, the schools are quite selective.

The baseline questionnaire asked detailed questions about the neighbourhood environments experienced by respondents at three critical junctures in the life course: at age six, when they were beginning primary school; at age 13, when they were entering adolescence and middle school; and during their senior year in high school, when they were 17–18 years old and preparing to leave for college. At each point, respondents were asked to describe the racial composition of the neighbourhood they lived in, along with the extent to which they witnessed various manifestations of disorder (homelessness, prostitution, gang activities, drug paraphernalia, etc.) and violence (gunshots, muggings, shootings, stabbings, etc.).

We defined 'neighbourhood' as a three-block radius around the respondent's house. To assess the validity of these self reports, we matched students' home addresses with geocoded tract data from the 2000 Census and correlated census figures with racial compositions reported on the survey. The correlation between the census black percentage and that reported by respondents during their senior year was 0.83, whereas the corresponding correlations for white and Latino percentages were around 0.79. Thus self-reported neighbourhood composition accounts for around 64 per cent of the variance in tract composition, indicating that our data correspond closely to ecological reality. Given that census tracts are much larger spatial units than those we employed (a three-block radius around the respondent's home), we would not expect the correlation to be perfect. To the extent that self-reports of neighbourhood characteristics are unreliable, of course, it will be more difficult to find significant relationships between them and later academic outcomes, yielding a conservative bias to the analysis.

Respondents were also asked to estimate the racial composition and academic quality of the schools which they attended, the kinds of academic and non-academic resources they contained, and the frequency with which they witnessed various manifestations of social disorder within them (smoking, drinking, drug taking, graffiti, tardiness, skipping classes, cutting school, etc.), along with the extent to which they remembered witnessing certain indicators of violence (fighting, guns, knives, shootings, stabbings, etc.).

Having reported in some detail on the schools and neighbourhoods in which they came of age, respondents were asked to contemplate their current thoughts and feelings, answering detailed questions about their educational aspirations and their confidence in achieving various educational goals. They also responded to a series of standard survey items on self-esteem and self-efficacy developed by Rosenberg and Simmons (1971) and reported on the social, economic, and demographic characteristics of the households in which they grew up.

The baseline interviews were followed by a series of shorter telephone surveys designed to determine how respondents fared on campus after arrival. The follow-up surveys were administered in the spring of 2000 and the spring of 2001, when most students were freshmen and then sophomores. The respective follow-up response rates were 95 per cent and 89 per cent. Whereas the independent variables used in our analysis come from the baseline survey, the dependent variable, academic achievement, is measured from the two follow-up surveys: grades earned during the autumn and spring terms of academic year 1999–2000 and the autumn of academic year 2000–2001. In an earlier pilot survey carried out in 1998 at the University of Pennsylvania, we matched self-reported grades to official records and found that respondents' grade reports were quite accurate (Massey *et al.* 2003).

PATTERNS OF SEGREGATION

We measured segregation using the relative number of blacks and Latinos present in a respondent's school and neighbourhood at ages 6, 13, and 18 (i.e., during the senior year of high school). We computed the average percentage minority (African Americans plus Latinos) in each setting, and then weighted proportionately across person years to determine a subject's overall segregation in childhood. We pooled blacks and Latinos because both groups have relatively high rates of poverty, so that neighbourhoods with high concentrations of blacks and Latinos tend to have higher poverty rates and the social ills that accompany them (see Massey and Denton 1993).

The resulting figures give the average minority composition for the schools and neighbourhoods inhabited by respondents from age 6 to 18. For purposes of tabular presentation, we classify each respondent as having come from a predominantly white, racially mixed, or predominantly minority background prior to entering college. Respondents from a *predominantly white background* grew up in schools and neighbourhoods where blacks and Latinos together averaged less than 30 per cent of the population; those from a *mixed background* came of age in settings that averaged 30 per cent to 69 per cent black or Latino; and those from *predominantly minority backgrounds* spent their time in settings that averaged 70 per cent minority or greater. Table 1 shows the distribution of whites, Asians, Latinos, and blacks by level of neighbourhood and school segregation.

As can be seen, the vast majority of white and Asian students came of age in settings where relatively few minority group members were present: 94 per cent of whites and 91 per cent of Asians grew up in predominantly white neighbourhoods that contained very few minority residents. Likewise, 84 per cent of the whites and 82 per cent of Asians attended

■ **Table 1** Relative integration of neighbourhoods and schools experienced while growing up: respondents to National Longitudinal Survey of Freshmen (weighted)

Level of Segregation	Whites	Asians	Latinos	Blacks
Neighbourhood				
Majority	94.0	90.6	54.4	35.8
Mixed	5.3	8.8	22.1	27.1
Minority	0.7	0.6	23.6	37.1
School				
Majority	84.0	82.4	48.4	37.8
Mixed	15.6	17.0	31.7	40.1
Minority	0.4	0.6	20.0	22.2

schools in which blacks and Latinos together made up less than 30 per cent of the student body (and typically much less). Although a few students in each group grew up in racially mixed schools or neighbourhoods, only a fraction of one per cent of either whites or Asians had experience in a minority-dominant social setting.

In contrast to the relative homogeneity of white and Asian backgrounds, Latinos and especially blacks experienced a diversity of school and neighbourhood compositions while growing up. With respect to neighbourhoods, 54 per cent of Latinos and 36 per cent of blacks grew up in a predominantly white setting while 24 per cent of the former and 37 per cent of the latter came of age in minority-dominant areas. The respective figures living in racially mixed neighbourhoods were 22 per cent and 27 per cent. We observe a similar range of experiences with respect to school composition. Among blacks, 38 per cent attended predominantly white schools, 40 per cent mixed schools, and 22 per cent predominantly minority schools. Among Latinos, the respective figures were 20 per cent in segregated institutions, 32 per cent in mixed schools, and 48 per cent in predominantly white settings.

SEGREGATION AND FAMILY CIRCUMSTANCES

The first panels in Table 2 show family background characteristics for whites and Asians, along with those for blacks and Latinos broken down by level of segregation. Only 11 per cent of whites came from families in which at least one parent is foreign-born, compared to 92 per cent of Asian students. Blacks and Latinos from predominantly white settings are

▦ **Table 2** Indicators of neighbourhood, school, and peer environment experienced while growing up: respondents to National Longitudinal Survey of Freshmen

	Whites	Asians	Latinos and Blacks by Segregation		
			Majority	Mixed	Minority
Demographic Background					
Foreign Born Parent (%)	11.11	91.67	42.12	38.86	38.66
Intact Family (%)	81.96	84.4	70.91	54.26	46.26
Number Siblings 18 and younger	0.9	0.84	0.82	85.98	1.02
Parental Socioeconomic Background					
No College (%)	9.32	15.85	18.46	32.79	54.20
One College Degree (%)	9.92	10.01	17.89	20.00	15.19
Two College Degrees (%)	15.23	15.85	12.97	9.51	10.88
One Advanced Degree (%)	35.77	31.39	28.50	26.72	10.66
Two Advanced Degrees (%)	29.56	26.59	22.08	10.82	8.84
Economic Disadvantage Index	0.737	0.87	1.05	1.38	1.52
Correlates of Segregation Academic Preparation					
Number AP Courses	3.25	3.84	2.72	2.61	2.38
High School GPA	3.78	3.79	3.66	3.57	3.61
Self-Rated Preparation	6.74	6.34	6.58	6.39	5.52
Social Preparation	14.15	14.76	13.86	12.81	12.83
Psychological Preparation	50.91	48.34	51.85	52.11	52.39
Family Stress	26.44	35.63	42.79	53.62	58.84
Environmental Stress	24.10	25.07	27.28	40.86	57.51
Cognitive Skills					
Percentile on SAT or ACT	92.06	92.70	86.23	80.24	72.96

slightly more likely to have a foreign-born parent (42%) than those coming from mixed or predominantly blacks or Latino contexts (39%).

Differences in family structure are more pronounced by degree of segregation. While at least 82–84 per cent of whites and Asians grew up in an intact mother-father household, the percentage of blacks and Latinos coming from intact households declines dramatically as we move from predominantly white contexts (71%) to predominantly minority contexts (46%). The number of siblings under the age of 18 in the household also rises with black and Latino concentration, meaning that fewer resources must be divided among a greater number of dependants.

There are also significant differences in parental socio-economic characteristics among groups. The parents of white and Asian students are, on average, highly educated, with the large majority of both groups coming from households where both parents at least have a college degree. This pattern stands in contrast to that displayed by Latinos and blacks, whose parental socio-economic circumstances appear to vary considerably by level of segregation. Blacks and Latinos who grew up in predominantly white settings have, on average, parents who are nearly as educated as those of whites and Asians. In contrast, 32 per cent of blacks and Latinos who grew up in racially mixed settings came from households in which neither parent had a college degree, as did over half of blacks and Latinos coming from predominantly minority settings.

To assess socio-economic status, we considered three indicators of parental economic disadvantage: whether the respondent's family *did not* own the home the respondent lived in during the senior year, whether the respondent's family was ever on welfare while the respondent was growing up, and whether the respondent's family had applied for financial aid for the respondent to attend college. Although at least 60 per cent of whites and Asians applied for financial aid, fewer than 10 per cent of each group reported that their family had ever been on welfare; a similarly small percentage reported that their family did not own the home they lived in during the respondent's senior year. Blacks and Latinos coming of age in predominantly white settings displayed similarly low levels of family economic disadvantage, with only 16 per cent reporting that their parents did not own their home, 9 per cent reporting their family was ever on welfare, and 80 per cent reporting that they had applied for financial aid.

For those growing up in predominantly minority settings, however, evidence of economic disadvantage was far more prevalent, with 33 per cent reporting that their family did not own the home they lived in, 28 per cent reporting that their family was ever on welfare, and 93 per cent reporting that they had applied for financial aid to attend college. These items were summed together to create a composite index of socio-economic disadvantage which is reported in Table 2 and has a Cronbach's alpha of 0.41. Although this alpha value is rather low, the model's fit was the same whether we used all three variables or the single index. Moreover, none of the constituent variables was statistically significant in predicting academic achievement. We thus used the index of socio-economic disadvantage to conserve degrees of freedom.

THE CORRELATES OF SEGREGATION

In theory, segregation need be neither advantageous nor disadvantageous for children growing up. If a society really could be constructed in such a way that racially distinct domains were 'separate but equal', then perhaps little harm would result from segregation into racially separate schools or neighbourhoods. Unfortunately, the evidence overwhelmingly shows that separate is rarely, if ever, equal. Rather, the segregation of minorities is almost always used as a deliberate tool of subordination to perpetuate inequality between minority and majority groups (Myrdal 1944; Massey and Denton 1993; Orfield and Eaton 1996).

Academic preparation

In addition to estimating the racial and ethnic composition of schools and reporting on frequency of transgressions within them, the NLSF also asked respondents to report on various indicators of preparation for college (we also examined indicators of school quality but they added no explanatory power to the analysis). The bottom panel of Table 2 begins by summarizing the number of advanced placement [AP] courses that respondents took in high school. Asians took the most AP courses, with an average of 3.8, followed by whites at around 3.3. Then in descending order came blacks and Latinos from majority-dominant backgrounds (2.7), those from mixed backgrounds (2.6) and those from predominantly minority settings (2.4). Thus, although Latinos and blacks were less likely than either Asians or whites to complete advanced placement courses, they were *much less likely* to have done so if they grew up in predominantly minority as opposed to predominantly majority settings.

The next line in the panel on academic preparation considers high school grade point average. This measure, of course, does not control for the quality or difficulty of classes taken. Nonetheless, it provides a general indicator of achievement according to local standards. Although differences between groups are not large, they are consistent with earlier patterns. Whereas whites and Asians report average GPAs of around 3.8, and that for blacks and Latinos from integrated backgrounds was 3.7, those coming of age in mixed and predominantly minority circumstances had GPAs of around 3.6.

These 'objective' differentials were echoed by the respondent's own perceptions. When asked themselves to rate how well their high school had prepared them for college on a 1 to 10 scale, whites as well as black and Latino respondents from predominantly white settings reported roughly comparable degrees of preparation, with average values of 6.7 or 6.6. Interestingly, despite objective evidence to the contrary, Asians felt less well prepared, assigning themselves an average rating of only 6.3. Their self-assessed preparation was even lower than that reported by blacks and Latinos from racially mixed backgrounds (6.4); but as before the least prepared were blacks and Latinos who grew up in predominantly minority circumstances (5.5).

In the interests of parsimony, we initially attempted to combine these measures into a single summated rating scale of academic preparation, but the resulting index had low reliability and each indicator proved to have a strong, significant, and independent effect on educational achievement. Hence, we elected to use the three separate measures of academic preparation in our regression analyses.

Social and psychological preparation

As argued above, segregation might also influence the degree to which entering freshmen are socially and psychologically prepared for college. By social preparation we mean the ability of a student to act autonomously in pursuing educational goals irrespective of social context. Social activities on campus can at times be seductive and if pursued to excess may undermine academic performance. It is important that students display a certain autonomy with respect to peer influences: to be able to say 'no' to a night of carousing with friends and go to the library instead.

We measured the degree to which respondents were susceptible to peer influence by asking them how much they agreed or disagreed with seven statements pertaining to their high school years, such as 'I thought and acted like others'; 'I valued the same thing as others', 'I worried about what others thought of me', and 'I did things so that others would like me'. Each of eight such items was coded 0 to 4, so that a higher score indicated less sensitivity to peer influence and more individual autonomy. The resulting index, which had a possible range of 0 to 32 and a Cronbach's alpha of .629, is reported in Table 2. Further details of its construction are provided in Massey *et al.* (2003). Given the fairly high reliability score, we decided to use the index of psychological preparation rather than separate items, thus conserving degrees of freedom.

Psychological preparation was relatively high for whites and Asians but lower in mixed and minority dominant neighbourhoods. The autonomy index for whites stood at 14.2, nearly the same as that for Asians (14.8). The index for blacks and Latinos growing up in majority dominant neighbourhoods was slightly lower at 13.9, but the index dropped another point for minorities coming of age in mixed and minority-dominant environments, with an index value of around 12.8, some 3.5 per cent below that of whites.

We also sought to measure the degree of *psychological* preparation for life in a very competitive academic environment using measures of self-esteem and self-efficacy developed by Rosenberg and Simmons (1971) and replicated in such studies as the National Educational Longitudinal Survey and the High School and Beyond Survey. The scale of self-esteem summarized the extent of agreement or disagreement with ten statements about self-worth, such as 'I am a person of worth equal to others', 'I have a number of good qualities', and 'I am inclined to feel I am a failure'. Each item was coded 0 to 4 such that a higher value indicated a higher self-appraisal. Summing across all items yielded a scale with a potential range of 0–40 and a reliability of .855. On this measure, Asians displayed the lowest degree of self-esteem, with an average index of 30.3, compared with a value of 32.0 for whites. However, blacks and Latinos generally displayed *higher* levels than whites or Asians irrespective of segregation. If anything, the self-esteem of minorities actually *increased slightly* from predominantly white (32.8) to predominantly minority (33.5) settings.

The scale of self-efficacy was created from items that asked respondents their extent of agreement or disagreement with statements such as 'I don't have control over the direction of my life' and 'every time I try to get ahead something stops me'. Six items were coded 0–4 to yield a summated rating scale of self-efficacy that ranged from 0 to 24 and had an alpha of 0.69. There was less inter-group variation on this scale, although once again blacks and Latinos tended to have a *higher* sense of self-efficacy than either whites or Asians. Whereas average self-efficacy was rated at around 19.0 for minorities at all levels of segregation, the self-rating of Asians stood at 18.0 while whites were more similar at 18.9.

The foregoing scales provide little evidence that blacks and Latinos are less psychologically prepared for the rigours of college study than members of other groups. Indeed, they generally report higher levels of self-efficacy and self-esteem than either whites or Asians. Because of the high degree of consistency between these two measures of psychological preparation, we combined them into a single that ranged from 0 to 64 and had an alpha of .875. This index is presented in Table 2. As with the constituent indices, Asians displayed the lowest level of psychological preparation (48.3) and blacks and Latinos in minority-dominant neighbourhoods evinced the highest (52.4), with whites and minorities in integrated and mixed neighbourhoods lying in-between.

Family stress

Ongoing family stress was measured using a severity-weighted index of negative events that occurred to the relatives of respondents. Students were asked to report whether during their freshman or sophomore year one of the following ten events had occurred: an unmarried sister became pregnant; a sibling dropped out of school; an immediate family member went on welfare; an immediate family member went into drug or alcohol rehab; any family member had become a crime victim; any family member had been in trouble with the law; an immediate family member became ill or disabled; an immediate family member became homeless; a parent died; or a close relative died.

In order to weight these events according to severity, we used the Holmes-Rahe Social Adjustment Scale (Holmes and Rahe 1967; Holmes and Masuda 1974). Following Charles *et al.* (2004), we matched the foregoing to the corresponding analogue on the Holmes-Rahe scale and assigning the relevant number of 'life change units'. The Holmes-Rahe scale ranges from 11 (the weight assigned minor violations of the law, such as getting a traffic ticket) to 100 (the death of a spouse). We then computed a weighted scale of family stress as follows: FSI = ?E_i HRS$_i$, where FSI is the family stress index, E_i refers to life event I, and HRS$_i$ refers to the associated Holmes-Rahe scale score.

On the resulting scale, which varied from 0 to 454, whites reported the lowest average score at 26.4, followed by Asians at 35.6. Among blacks and Latinos, however, a familiar pattern emerged. Those who grew up in predominantly white contexts scored an average of 42.8 on the family stress index, slightly higher than that of Asians; but family stress rose substantially as minority concentration increased. Blacks and Latinos who grew up in minority-dominant schools and neighbourhoods reported levels of family stress that were 2.2 times higher (58.8) than those reported by whites, while those growing up in mixed neighbourhoods displayed a value that was twice as high (53.6). Although the Cronbach's alpha for the severity weighted index was relatively low at .336, when we entered the items individually none was found to predict academic achievement at the 5 per cent level, so we went forward with a single index to conserve degrees of freedom and because the composite index served as a better predictor, despite its low reliability.

Environmental stress

As already mentioned, we measured sources of stress in the respondent's childhood environment by asking the frequency with which he or she witnessed different manifestations of disorder and violence at ages 6, 13, and 18. Examples of disorder included homelessness, prostitution, gang activities, drug paraphernalia, drug vending, drug using, public drunkenness, and graffiti. Indicators of violence included fighting, gunshots, stabbings, shootings, and muggings. At age six, respondents reported whether they ever saw these things. We coded every 'yes' as 1 and every 'no' as 0. At ages 13 and 18, respondents estimated the relative frequency with which they observed each transgression: never, rarely, sometimes, often, or very often, which we coded from 0 to 4.

The procedures we used to derive indices violence and disorder are described in detail by Massey *et al.* (2003). Basically we added the frequency ratings at ages 6, 13 and 18 to create a summated rating scale for disorder and violence that had a Cronbach's alpha of 0.90. Although this scale was highly reliable, it was misleading in that it weighed each transgression equally. That is, witnessing a student holding a knife got the same weight in the index as seeing another student being stabbed by a knife. In order to factor in the severity of each manifestation of disorder and violence, we weighted each event by its severity using the index of crime severity developed by Sellin and Wolfgang (1964). Specifically, we took each manifestation of disorder or violence and matched it to the nearest transgression listed on the Sellin-Wolfgang schedule, which was calibrated using the National Survey of Crime Severity (Wolfgang *et al.* 1985). After assigning the associated scale value to each item, we computed a weighted sum of frequencies, yielding an index of violence and disorder with a range of 0 to 187 and a robust alpha of 0.780. For details about the items included in the indices and their Sellin-Wolfgang weights see Appendix B of Massey *et al.* (2003).

The resulting scale of disorder and violence provides an indicator of environmental stress experienced by respondents as they grew up within specific schools and neighbourhoods. As can be seen, the degree of environmental stress for whites, Asians, and Latinos and blacks from majority-dominant backgrounds was modest. The index of environmental stress was 24.1 for whites, 25.1 for Asians, and 27.3 for Latinos and blacks from integrated settings. As minority concentration rose, however, the degree of exposure to violence and disorder rose markedly, reaching 40.9 for those from mixed neighbourhoods (70% higher than whites) and 57.5 for those from minority-dominant settings (2.4 times greater than whites). Exposure to environmental stressors is thus markedly higher among minority students who come from segregated school and neighbourhood backgrounds.

SEGREGATION AND COLLEGE ACHIEVEMENT

So far we have shown that students entering selective colleges and universities in the autumn of 1999 arrived with different levels of academic, social and psychological preparation, and with different degrees of exposure to family and environmental stress, depending on whether they grew up in minority-dominant, mixed, or majority-dominant settings. Nearly all whites (93%) and Asians (89%) grew up in predominantly white surroundings. In contrast, a sizeable portion of Latinos and particularly blacks grew up in minority dominant neighbourhoods, and a significant fraction attended minority-dominant schools. Averaging across schools and neighbourhoods by age we found that around 36 per cent of blacks came from a predominantly white background, 38 per cent came from a racially mixed background, and 26 per cent came from a predominantly minority background. The respective figures for Latinos were 53 per cent, 26 per cent, and 20 per cent.

Thus, prior school and neighbourhood segregation clearly differentiates the experience of African American and Latino students attending selective schools in the United States. The issue we now address is whether this heterogeneity of experience with respect to childhood segregation carries any implications for later college performance. That is, does growing up under predominantly minority circumstances affect the grades earned by blacks and Latinos at college or university, and if so, how much and why? To answer these questions we estimated a series of regression models that predicted the cumulative grade point earned by respondents during their first three terms of college from the average minority composition of the schools and neighbourhoods they experienced while growing up along with the key correlates of segregation we have identified. Owing to the clustered nature of the sample, we estimate regressions using robust standard errors. The results of the analysis are shown in Table 3.

The leftmost equation regresses cumulative GPA on dummy variables for group membership. Across the first three terms of college or university, white students earned an average grade point of 3.317. The GPA for Asians was slightly but not significantly lower at 3.296. In contrast, the cumulative grade point earned by blacks and Latinos was both substantively and statistically lower. After three terms in college, the cumulative GPA for Latinos stood at 3.090 (computed by adding the intercept of 3.317 to the Latino coefficient of – (0.227) whereas that for blacks stood at 2.950 (3.317 – 0.0367). Both differences are highly significant in statistical terms (p<0.001). Group effects account for around 11 per cent of the variance in cumulative GPA across the first three terms of college.

The next equation to the right adds in segregation as a predictor while controlling for family demographic status and parental socio-economic background. Adding in these variables increases the amount of variance explained to around 15 per cent and reduces but does not eliminate the inter-group differences in grade point average. Holding constant these factors, whites are predicted to earn a grade point of 3.189 compared with 3.027 for Latinos and 2.925 for blacks. Thus the black–white gap is reduced by around 40 per cent by controlling segregation, family status, and socio-economic status. Among the newly added independent variables, the strongest predictor of college GPA appears to be parental education. As the number of college and advanced degrees held by a student's parents grows, the GPA he or she is predicted to earn steadily increases. Once parental education is controlled, neither family demographic background nor household economic disadvantage has a significant independent effect. Prior segregation, however, continues

Table 3 Effect of segregation on cumulative grade point average earned during first three semesters at college or university: respondents to National Longitudinal Survey of Freshmen

	B	SE	B	SE	B	SE	B	SE
Racial–Ethnic Background								
Asian	−0.021	0.018	−0.030	0.028	−0.022	0.016	−0.00561	0.01977
Latino	−0.237***	0.020	−0.162***	0.027	−0.121***	0.021	−0.12428***	0.02479
Black	−0.367***	0.024	−0.264***	0.026	−0.179***	0.025	−0.17077***	0.02462
Neighbourhood and School Background								
Average Minority Percentage			−0.0013**	0.0004	−0.001+	0.000	−0.00027	0.00044
Family Background								
Foreign Born Parent (%)			0.030	0.021	0.026	0.015	0.0119	0.01752
Intact Family (%)			0.028	0.019	−0.003	0.020	−0.00749	0.02006
Number Siblings 18 and younger			−0.004	0.008	−0.004	0.007	−0.00679	0.0087
Parental Socioeconomic Background								
One College Degree (%)			0.031	0.023	0.008	0.020	0.02105	0.02428
Two College Degrees (%)			0.105***	0.022	0.069**	0.023	0.04573+	0.02491
One Advanced Degree (%)			0.117***	0.028	0.070**	0.024	0.06214**	0.01951
Two Advanced Degrees (%)			0.225***	0.029	0.147***	0.027	0.11662***	0.02781
Index of Economic Disadvantage			−0.005	0.013	−0.010	0.011	−0.00486	0.01154
Correlates of Segregation								
Academic Preparation								
Number AP Courses					0.013**	0.004	0.00803+	0.00461
High School GPA					0.440***	0.028	0.41038***	0.02651
Self-Rated Preparation					0.030***	0.003	0.02817***	0.00289
Social Preparation								
Susceptibility to Peers					0.011**	0.002	0.01069***	0.00181
Psychological Preparation								
Esteem and Efficacy					0.001	0.001	0.00253+	0.00134

Table 3 *Continued*

	B	SE	B	SE	B	SE	B	SE
Family Stress								
Negative Events in Family					-0.000090	0.000127	-0.00031*	0.00015
Environmental Stress								
Exposure to Violence and Disorder					-0.001**	0.000331	-0.00093*	0.00039
Cognitive Ability								
Percentile on SAT or ACT							0.00417***	0.00153
Intercept	3.317***	0.022	3.189***	0.0447	1.198351***	0.12263	0.92149***	0.16613
R-squared	0.106		0.1501		0.2989		0.3264***	
N =	3699		3447		3375		2732	

*** $p<0.001$, ** $p<0.01$, * $p<0.05$, + $p<0.10$

to have a robust effect on grade point independently of family socio-economic and demographic status. Shifting a student from a completely integrated to a completely segregated background is expected to lower his or her cumulative GPA by 0.13 points ($p<0.01$).

The third equation to the right adds in the various correlates of segregation already discussed. This operation nearly doubles the variance explained (to around 29%), reduces the apparent effect of segregation to marginal significance ($p<0.10$), and further restricts inter-group differentials in GPA, reducing the black–white gap by more than half (though it still remains statistically significant). The reduction of segregation's effect to marginal significance suggests that its negative effect on GPA is substantially accounted for by the five correlates we have identified.

Not surprisingly, indicators of academic preparation are very strongly related to GPA. For each advance placement course taken, GPA rises by 0.015 points, whereas each point of high school GPA raises college GPA by 0.455 points and each point of self-rated preparation raises it by 0.03 points. Thus, one important reason that students who grew up in minority-dominant settings earn lower grades in college is that by virtue of their prior segregation they were less prepared academically to do well.

Whereas neither psychological preparation (a student's perceived self-esteem and self-efficacy) nor family stress (the accumulation of negative events in the student's kinship network) appear to account for segregation's negative effect on college GPA, both social preparation (susceptibility to peer influence) and environmental stress (exposure to disorder and violence in schools and neighbourhoods) play a significant role. As susceptibility to peer influence increases, GPA progressively declines ($p<0.01$); and as childhood exposure to social disorder and violence rise, GPA likewise steadily falls ($p<0.01$). Thus growing up in a minority-dominant environment leaves students more vulnerable to negative peer influences and also because it exposes them to elevated levels of violence and disorder that have long-term effects on academic performance.

These performance effects are not necessarily through the impairment of cognitive ability per se, but appear to operate through other aspects of cognition, such as attention and memory. This conclusion is demonstrated in the rightmost equation, which adds in a measure of cognitive skill – the percentile that each respondent reported earning on the SAT or ACT test, which is required at most colleges and universities. Note that the degrees of freedom are reduced because not all respondents reported test scores, which suggests some caution in interpreting results. Nonetheless, as logically expected, cognitive skills (at least those measured by the SAT or ACT) rather strongly predict cumulative GPA ($p<0.001$). Every percentile point increase in the test score raises the cumulative grade point by around 0.004 points. Shifting a student's score from the 9th to the 99th percentile would thus add around 0.36 to his or her GPA.

Despite the strong effect of cognitive skills on GPA, controlling for this variable only modestly increases the variance explained to around 33 per cent and it does not significantly reduce inter-group differentials in grade performance. Moreover, although the effect of environmental stress is slightly reduced, the change is not significant and its influence remains strong; so whatever effect that exposure to childhood disorder and violence has on college academic performance, it does not operate through the cognitive skills captured by the ACT or SAT tests.

CONCLUSIONS

This analysis drew on a representative sample of the 1999 cohort of freshmen entering twenty-eight selective colleges and universities to explore the long-term consequences of segregation. We showed that whereas upwards of 90 per cent of Asian and white students grew up within social milieu dominated by whites, only a third of black and half of Latino students did so. Indeed, a quarter of African Americans and a fifth of Latinos came of age under conditions of high racial minority isolation, attending schools and living in neigh-bourhoods that were at least 70 per cent black or Latino; and these students, remember, are among the most elite in the nation. The distribution of black and Latino college students in general would undoubtedly be skewed even more towards racially isolated upbringings.

Our data also indicate that separate is by no means equal. Black and Latino students who grew up under conditions of segregation were less prepared academically than those coming from majority-dominant settings. Indeed, those minority students who were fortunate enough to grow up in a predominantly majority context generally experienced a quality of schooling and level of academic preparation comparable to those of whites and Asians.

We also considered how social and psychological preparation for college varied by level of childhood segregation. We found little evidence that minority students were hampered psychologically by the experience of childhood segregation, at least in terms of self-esteem and self-confidence. If anything, black and Latino students who come of age in minority-dominant environments exhibited *higher* levels of self-esteem, self-efficacy, and self-confidence than those growing up in integrated settings, and much higher levels than whites and Asians as well.

We did find, however, evidence that students growing up in a predominantly minor-ity context were more susceptible to negative peer influences, although differences between those from integrated and segregated backgrounds were not great. Far more stark was the degree of variation in exposure to social disorder and violence by level of segre-gation. We showed that blacks and Latinos who came of age in integrated surroundings were generally exposed to levels of disorder and violence that were comparable to the lev-els experienced by whites and Asians. As segregation increased, however, the risk of exposure to disorder and especially violence multiplied greatly.

Given the foregoing disadvantages of a segregated upbringing, we were not surprised to find that the degree of school and neighbourhood segregation experienced between the ages of 6 and 18 was strongly associated with diminished academic performance later, as measured by the GPA earned during the first three terms of college or university. When we entered the correlates of segregation into a regression equation predicting GPA we found that four background factors explained most of segregation's effect on GPA: parental edu-cation, academic preparation, social preparation, and environmental stress.

Although these differences in average GPA between groups may seem small, they could have large implications when considered in light of student aspirations. This is of par-ticular relevance to this population because black students in the sample express a stronger desire than whites to go on to graduate and professional school (Massey *et al.* 2003). Given the competitive nature of graduate and professional school admissions, small differences in GPA can result in big differences in the probability of being accepted into a programme.

Given the continued segregation of blacks and Hispanics from other groups in schools and neighbourhoods, the effects we observe on achievement are not likely to dis-appear any time soon without some type of intervention. Colleges and universities need to be aware of how a student's background may affect their performance in college in unex-pected ways. We found that growing up in a minority-dominant environment leaves stu-dents more vulnerable to negative peer influences and exposes them to elevated levels of violence and disorder that have a negative impact on later college achievement. It is also important to reiterate that because our sample is of minority students at elite colleges and universities, the problems described herein are likely to be more widespread among minority students in less selective institutions.

The mechanism by which long-term exposure to violence translates into depressed academic performance in college or university cannot be established here. We do know, however, that they do not seem to operate through general cognitive ability, as the intro-duction of SAT or ACT scores does not alter the strength of the effect of environmental stress in separate regressions. Our working hypothesis is that long-term exposure to stressful neighbourhoods acts to reduce long- and short-term memory, limit attention, and lower frustration thresholds (see Bremner 2002; McEwan 2002). These cognitive traits, in addition to academic aptitude, are critical for academic achievement.

REFERENCES

Allen, Walter R., Epps, Edgar G. and Haniff, Nesha Z. (1991) *College in Black and White: African American Students in Predominantly White and in Historically Black Public Universities.* State University of New York Press, Albany, NY.

Bowen, William G. and Bok, Derek (1998) *The Shape of the River: Long-Term Consequences of Considering Race in College and University Admissions.* Princeton University Press, Princeton.

Bremner, J. Douglas (2002) *Does Stress Damage the Brain? Understanding Trauma-Related Disorders from a Mind-Body Perspective.* Norton, New York.

Brooks-Gunn, Jeanne, Duncan, Greg J. and Aber, Lawrence (eds) (1997) *Neighbourhood Poverty Volumes I and II.* Russell Sage Foundation, New York.

Clark, Kenneth B. (1965) *Dark Ghetto: Dilemmas of Social Power.* Harper and Row, New York.

Charles, Camille Z., Dinwiddie, Gneisha and Massey, Douglas S. (2004) The continuing consequences of segregation: family stress and college academic performance. *Social Science Quarterly* 85:5, pp. 1353–1373.

Feagin, Joe R., Vera, Hernan and Imani, Nikitah O. (1996) *The Agony of Education: Black Students at White Colleges and Universities.* Routledge, New York.

Diamond, D.M. and Rose, G.M. (1993) Psychological stress interferes with working, but not reference, spatial memory. *Society for Neuroscience Abstracts* 19, pp. 366–374.

Diamond, D.M. and Rose, G.M. (1994) Stress impairs LTP and hippocampal-dependent memory. *Annals of the New York Academy of Sciences* 746, pp. 411–414.

Goleman, Daniel (1995) *Emotional Intelligence.* Bantam, New York.

Holmes, T.H. and Masuda, M. (1974) Life change and illness susceptibility. In Dohrenwend, B.S. and Dohrenwend, B.P. (eds) *Stressful Life Events: Their Nature and Effects*, pp. 45–72. Wiley, New York.

Holmes, T. H. and Rahe, R.H. (1967) The social readjustment rating scale. *Journal of Psychosomatic Research* 11, pp. 213–218.

Iceland, John, Weinberg, Daniel H. and Steinmetz, Erica (2002) *Racial and Ethnic Residential Segregation in the United States 1980–2000.* U.S. Bureau of the Census, Washington, DC.

James, Sherman A., Strogatz, David S., Wing, Steven B. and Ramsey, Diane L. (1987) Socioeconomic status, John Henryism, and hypertension in blacks and whites. *American Journal of Epidemiology* 126, pp. 664–673.

Kotulak, Ronald (1997) *Inside the Brain: Revolutionary Discoveries of How the Mind Works.* Andrews McMeel Publishing, Chicago.

Kozol, Jonathan (1991) *Savage Inequalities: Children in America's Schools.* Crown Publishers, New York.

Ledoux, Joseph (1996) *The Emotional Brain: The Mysterious Underpinnings of Emotional Life.* Simon and Schuster, New York.

Massey, Douglas S. (2001) Segregation and violent crime in urban America. In Anderson, Elijah and Massey, Douglas S. (eds) *Problem of the Century: Racial Stratification in the United States*, pp. 317–346. Russell Sage Foundation, New York.

Massey, Douglas S. (2004) Segregation and stratification: a biosocial perspective. *The DuBois Review: Social Science Research on Race* 1, pp. 1–19.

Massey, Douglas S., Charles, Camille Z., Lundy, Garvey F. and Fischer, Mary J. (2003) *The Source of the River: The Social Origins of Freshmen at America's Selective Colleges and Universities.* Princeton University Press, Princeton.

Massey, Douglas S., Condran, Gretchen A. and Denton, Nancy (1987) The effect of residential segregation on black social and economic well-being. *Social Forces* 66, pp. 29–56.

Massey, Douglas S. and Denton, Nancy (1993) *American Apartheid: Segregation and the Making of the Underclass.* Harvard University Press, Cambridge.

Massey, Douglas S. and Fischer, Mary J. (2000) How segregation concentrates poverty. *Ethnic and Racial Studies* 23, pp. 670–691.

Massey, Douglas S. and Fong, Eric (1990) Segregation and neighborhood quality: blacks, Hispanics, and Asians in the San Francisco metropolitan area. *Social Forces* 69, pp. 15–32.

McEwen, Bruce S. (1992) Paradoxical effects of adrenal steroids on the brain: protection v ersus degeneration. *Biological Psychiatry* 31, pp. 177–199.

McEwen, Bruce S. (2002) *The End of Stress As We Know It.* Joseph Henry Press, Washington, DC.

Myrdal, Gunnar (1944) *An American Dilemma: The Negro Problem and Modern Democracy, Volume I.* Harper and Row, New York.

Orfield, Gary and Eaton, Susan E. (1996) *Dismantling Desegregation: The Quiet Reversal of Brown v. Board of Education.* W.W. Norton & Company, New York.

Orfield, Gary and Sanni, Christine (1999) *Resegregation in American Schools* Harvard Civil Rights Project, Harvard Law School, Cambridge.

Rosenberg, Morris and Simmons, Roberta G. (1971) *Black and White Self-Esteem: The Urban School Child.* American Sociological Association, Washington, DC.

Sampson, Robert J., Morenoff, Jeffrey D. and Earls, Felton (1999) Beyond social capital: social dynamics of collective efficacy for children. *American Sociological Review* 64, pp. 633–642.

Sampson, Robert J., Morenoff, Jeffrey D. and Gannon-Rowley, Thomas (2002) Assessing 'neighbourhood effects': social processes and new directions in research. *Annual Review of Sociology* 28, pp. 443–478.

Sampson, Robert J., Raudenbush, Steven and Earls, Felton (1997) Neighbourhoods and violent crime: a multilevel study of collective efficacy. *Science* 277, pp. 918–924.

Sellin, Thornsten and Wolfgang, Marvin E. (1964) *The Measurement of Delinquency.* Wiley, New York.

Wolfgang, Marvin E., Figlio, Robert M., Tracey, Paul E. and Singer, Simon I. (1985) *The National Survey of Crime Severity.* U.S. Government Printing Office, Washington, DC.

APPENDIX A

Descriptive statistics for variables in analysis: respondents to National Longitudinal Survey of Freshmen.

	Mean	SD	Min	Max
Demographic Background				
Foreign Born Parent (%)	0.51	0.50	0.00	1.00
Intact Family (%)	0.72	0.45	0.00	1.00
Number Siblings 18 and younger	0.87	0.86	0.00	7.00
Parental Socioeconomic Background				
No College (%)				
One College Degree (%)	0.14	0.35	0.00	1.00
Two College Degrees (%)	0.13	0.34	0.00	1.00
One Advanced Degree (%)	0.29	0.45	0.00	1.00
Two Advanced Degrees (%)	0.22	0.41	0.00	1.00
Economic Disadvantage Index	1.03	0.76	0.00	3.00
Correlates of Segregation				
Academic Preparation				
Number AP Courses	3.09	1.98	0.00	10.00
High School GPA	3.71	0.33	1.67	4.00
Self-Rated Preparation	6.39	2.94	0.00	10.00
Social Preparation	10.33	4.58	0.00	30.40
Psychological Preparation	50.84	7.90	20.00	64.00
Family Stress	40.43	54.94	0.00	354.00
Environmental Stress	31.46	24.75	0.00	187.38
Cognitive Skills				
Percentile on SAT or ACT	87.52	14.90	2.00	99.00
CumGPA Sophomore Year	3.162	0.474	0.00	4.000

APPENDIX B

Indicators of institutional quality for colleges and universities included in the NLSF.

Categories and Schools	Median SAT Top 10% of class	% Freshmen in	Acceptance Rate	Alumni Giving Rate
Historically Black Colleges				
Howard University, Washington, D.C.	1105	18	56	9
Schools with 1000+ Black Students				
University of Michigan, Ann Arbor	–	63	64	13
University of North Caroline, Chapel Hill	1250	68	39	31
University of Californian, Berkeley	1315	98	27	18
Schools with 500–1000 Black Students				
Columbia University, New York City	1400	87	14	32
Emory University, Atlanta	1355	90	42	39
Miami University, Ohio	–	32	79	21
Northwestern University, Evanston Illinois	1385	83	32	29
Penn State University, University Park P.A.	1190	42	49	21
Stanford University, Palo Alto California	1455	88	15	37
Tulane University, New Orleans	1292	52	78	21
University of Pennsylvania, Philadelphia	1400	91	26	40
Schools with 100–500 Black Students				
Georgetown University, Washington D.C.	1350	78	23	30
Oberlin College, Ohio	1325	59	50	43
Princeton University, Princeton New Jersey	1450	92	11	66
Rice University, Houston Texas	1415	86	27	39
Tufts University, Somerville Massachusetts	1340	70	32	30
University of Notre Dame, South Bend Indiana	1345	83	35	48
Washington University, St. Louis	1355	79	34	37
Wesleyan University, Middletown Conn	1365	70	29	49
Williams College, Williamstown Massachusetts	1410	84	23	60
Yale University	1465	95	16	49

APPENDIX B *(continued)*

Categories and Schools	Median SAT Top 10% of class	% Freshmen in	Acceptance Rate	Alumni Giving Rate
Schools with <100 Black Students				
Barnard College, New York City	1315	73	37	40
Bryn Mawr College, Bryn Mawr Pennsylvania	1300	61	59	52
Denison University, Ohio	1215	52	69	43
Kenyon College, Gambier Ohio	1295	50	68	47
Smith College, Northampton Massachusetts	1280	52	56	47
Swarthmore College, Swarthmore Pennsylvania	1418	82	22	56
Average	1243	71	40	37

Source: *U.S. News and World Report*, September 1, 2000.

9 RECLASSIFYING UPWARD MOBILITY

Femininity and the neo-liberal subject

Valerie Walkerdine

INTRODUCTION

Valerie Walkerdine (currently Professor in the School of Social Sciences at Cardiff University) is the author of many significant publications with recent books including: Walkerdine, V., Lucey H. and Melody, J. (2002) *Growing Up Girl: Psychosocial Explorations of Gender & Class* (Palgrave, London; New York University Press, New York) and Walkerdine, V. (2007) *Children, Gender, Video Games: Towards a Relational Approach to Multi-Media* (Palgrave Macmillan, London).

She is a member of the Culture, Subject, Economy research group that explores the possibility of creating and working within a new space, which attempts to transcend certain boundaries between disciplines specified by a number of dualisms such as: Individual/Society; Macro/Micro; Culture/Economy; Interiority/Exteriority.

The work shown here recognises that concepts of class have altered significantly in light of a changed labour market but suggests that class is still important. Walkerdine suggests that this article 'aims to explore how we might think about the ways that "class" enters the production of subjectivities in the present. In particular the article explores the way in which narratives of upward mobility are lived as success and failure, hope and despair for some young women entering the labour market in Britain at the turn of the millennium. The multiplicity and fracturing of past and present, belonging, not belonging, the dreams, aspirations and defences are explored in some detail'.

KEY QUESTIONS

1. What is the relationship between women and notions and practices of social class?
2. Is this relationship changed in the light of what could be called 'neo-liberalism'?
3. Should we consider that women in different economic positions will respond differently in relation to social class or is gender a unifying force?
4. To what extent or in what ways are the subjectivities discussed by Walkerdine significant in relation to lived experience: what is the connection (if any) between the perceptions of oneself and others and 'realities'?
5. What is the role of educators in these situations?

FURTHER READING

The examples of Walkerdine's work as mentioned above are useful for locating this article in a wider context. The references given at the end of the article are all worth exploring. Perhaps in particular it will be useful to read Skegg's 1997 book *Formations of Class and Gender*, in which notions of respectability are discussed. Classic works that explore gender and education are, of course, vital foundational material that will allow the familiarity that students need to engage fully with the issues that Walkerdine raises.

This Reading links with Chapters 4 and 9 of *The Routledge Education Studies Textbook.*

INTRODUCTION

In the 1950s and 1960s, the moment of post-war Britain, there was considerable emphasis on the possibility of escape from the working class on the basis of an upward mobility made possible by educational success within state grammar schools. Discussions of upward mobility focused entirely on the working-class boy (Douglas, 1964; Halsey *et al.*, 1980) and the production of a more egalitarian society based on occupational mobility. This fitted neatly with a clear concern about the male manual worker as the bearer of working-class identity. Alongside this was a clear implication that working-class men were the carriers of resistance and radicality, with women often being understood as a conservative force. Indeed, Douglas saw the position of the mother as central to the possibility of successful upward mobility for boys. Thus, within these discourses, women could never be unproblematically the bearers of working-class identity (Reay, 1998). Indeed, many media portrayals have presented women as the driving force for respectability and upward mobility (pace Hyacinth in the television classic *Keeping up Appearances*) and, as Beverley Skeggs (1997) demonstrates clearly, the issue of respectability is an important one for working-class women in the present, who are marked more by the categorisation of their sexuality (rough/respectable/slut) and by the possibility of entry into upward mobility through their production of themselves as worthy of marriage to a middle-class man. Skeggs's (1997) study of working-class women's concerns about being judged in relation to entry into a department store brings this issue into very clear focus. While for many working-class men and women in the post-war period, there was a conflict between working class belonging and educational and occupational aspiration, I would argue that it was women who were always positioned more ambivalently in relation to class in the first place, and whose combination of pain and desire went largely unrecognised. At the turn of the millennium, a very different political and economic landscape configures the place of class differently.

In this article, I want to explore how we might understand re/classification and femininity through the positioning of the female worker as the mainstay of the neo-liberal economy, and the place of upward mobility through education and work as the feminine site of the production of the neo-liberal subject. As the recent study by Walkerdine *et al.* (2001) makes clear, educational attainment for girls in Britain is still deeply and starkly divided on traditional class lines, so that the possibility of entering the new female professional labour market is still incredibly difficult for young women from families who, in 1970s terms, were judged as working class through parental occupation and education. While this article does not address those educational trajectories explicitly, it seeks to explore the intersections of gender and class by thinking about the new labour market demands as demands for upward mobility. While it can be argued that social mobility itself has not increased, the number of working-class women entering service work has. This kind of work, together with the increase in access to university, provides the possibility of a life envisaged as much more tied to the possibilities of being traditionally related to middle-class status. Thus, the new labour market demands can be understood as aiming to produce a subject in the image of the middle class.

My own work on class began with an attempt to explore 'being working class' as an aspect of my own subjectivity, an aspect hidden and occluded by my status as a middle-class academic and also as the object of a surveillant gaze within social science research (Walkerdine, 1991, 1997). This was very caught up with an understanding of the issue of upward mobility and the terrifying invitation to belong in a new place, which was simultaneously an invitation to feel shame about what one had been before and indeed to understand the people with whom I had grown up as part of a growing political problem, a conservative and reactionary force, not the bedrock of a revolution. While economic issues are deeply implicated in this work, the issue of subjectivity does not entirely depend upon them: the place of the past in the present, within a change of class and status, seems to me to be of huge importance now in relation to a changed economic organisation. However, it is also important in relation to the changed political context of neo-liberalism on the one hand and the shifting points of production and consumption and movements of peoples, brought about by late modernity and globalisation, on the other.

CLASS/IFICATION

The use of the term 'class' as a mode of classification is taken to have begun with Booth, the founder of the Salvation Army in the nineteenth century, and was therefore always a moralised category. The mapping of areas of cities in terms of the spread of disease, and of crime, went alongside the emergence of psychology as a tool for the classification of types of personality and intelligence. Sociology and psychology became the twin disciplines through which class was produced as a truth through which the urban population of industrialised cities could be managed. This mode of classification of the population became, following Marx, also the basis of an emancipatory politics and an account of economic exploitation and oppression. It seems to me that there are two issues at stake here: the first is an understanding of the historicity of the use of class in technologies of subjectification and the second is the way in which the economics of capitalism have and have not changed. When I and others wish to hang onto the use of class in relation to subjectivities, it is because the exploitation and oppression which class politics signals, though changed, has not ceased and no other political discourse has emerged to explain or mobilise around these issues, that is, the issue of inequalities associated with social and economic difference. It is how such differences and the oppression and pain that they bring can be spoken, that we need urgently to address inside a political space that seems to deny its existence at the very moment that class is taken to be an anachronistic concept. However, a theorisation of class as a universal concept of sociology, an overarching discourse of the subject, is rendered deeply problematic by post-foundational theorising within the social sciences and humanities. The issue becomes one of how it is possible to think about both the place it has in the making of subjects now and the possibility of talking about exploitation and oppression in terms of social, cultural and economic differences which have not gone away and which therefore need to be understood as a central part of any politics in the present. So, my interest here is the discourses and narratives through which class has been understood and the place of those in producing modes of subjectification and subjectivity, including the meaning and possibility of upward mobility. The history of technologies of class/ification would allow us to understand the changed ways in which class has functioned as a technology of the social and of the subject. While this short article is not the place to rehearse an understanding of the emergence of class as such a technology or to chart the historical changes in the discourses of class/ification, I do want to suggest that a shift in modes of regulation which we might think about coheres around the movement from practices of policing and external regulation to technologies of self-regulation in which subjects come to understand themselves as responsible for their own regulation and the management of themselves is understood as central to a neo-liberal project in which class differences are taken to have melted away. The neo-liberal subject is the autonomous liberal subject made in the image of the middle class.

The emergence of systems of classification in English cities cohered around area and the person. So, for example, a concern with the spread of disease and crime, by mapping parts of cities, was mirrored by a set of scientific discourses concerning the criminal. Thus, the inauguration of the twin poles of sociology and psychology set the stage for the ways in which class was to be understood and utilised as a technology of social regulation in the twentieth century. By the 1950s, there was concern with post-war occupational class mobility, where mothers were understood as central to the good academic performance of working-class boys (Douglas, 1964). By the 1960s, these had developed into studies of maternal deprivation, with debates raging about the relative importance of nature and nurture in producing an intelligence that would allow mobility through education (Bowlby, 1971). Increasingly, the social problem of inequality was understood as produced through the pathologisation of working-class practices, which were understood as simultaneously reproducing poverty and inequality at home, school, work and also as producing affluent workers (Halsey, 1980), with the embourgeoisement and the 'end of the working class' (Gorz, 1982) being incessantly announced.

It is these processes which, we could argue, have reached their zenith in what has been termed neo-liberalism. By now, the subject is understood by many sociologists (e.g. Giddens, 1994) as having been completely freed from traditional ties of location, class and gender and to be completely self-produced. The affluent worker has given way to the embourgeoisement of the population and so the end of the working class is taken to have arrived. Freed from the ties of class, the new worker is totally responsible for their own destiny and so techniques and technologies of regulation focus on the self-management of citizens to produce themselves as having the skills and qualities necessary to succeed in the new economy. So, for example, in an Australian pilot study of the new workers (Walkerdine *et al.*, in preparation), a secretary in her thirties describes her continual overwork in a succession of jobs. In each she thinks herself not good enough and in each she gradually works longer and longer hours in order to perform her job to the standards she sets. In each job too the managers she works for gradually begin to pile work on her and ignore the huge number of hours she is working because she is so good. When asked in an interview to explain why she works likes this, she uses a psychological narrative which relates to her relation to her father and his idea that she was never good enough. One of the many interesting aspects of this is that not once does the secretary refer to a discourse of exploitation: it becomes the Othered and suppressed discourse. Any problems are caused by her failure, her pathology or her standards, not by the impossibility of the amount of work she is expected to do or the exploitative way in which the managers benefit hugely from her overwork. So, what I am saying is that the sets of political and economic changes which have led to neo-liberalism (the loss of power of trade unions, the end of jobs for life, the increase in short-term contracts etc.) have emerged alongside a set of discourses and practices already well in place, but in which certain discourses and practices of class which stress class as oppositional have been replaced by those which stress that the possibility of upward mobility has, in a sense, now become a necessity.

Nikolas Rose (1999) argues in respect of the relation of scientific psychology to liberalism that 'the new forms of regulation do not crush subjectivity. They actually fabricate subjects – human men, women and children capable of bearing the burdens of liberty'

(p. viii). He later talks of 'the obligation to be free', through the celebration of the values of autonomy and self-realisation, in which 'each individual must render his or her life meaningful as if it were the outcome of individual choices made in furtherance of a biographical project of self-realization' (p. ix). Although Rose is talking about the project of liberalism in general, I argue that these forms of regulation are becoming more intense in the present period because of the huge changes taking place in the global labour market. In this context, the nature of work is being transformed in terms of the kind of work available, its gendered nature and its contractual basis, and the forms, imperatives and distributed outcomes of education are also in a period of major transformation.

Jobs for life are being replaced by a constantly changing array of jobs, small businesses and employment contracts. In such an economy, it is the flexible and autonomous subject who is demanded to be able to cope with constant change in work, income and lifestyle and with constant insecurity. It is the flexible and autonomous subject who negotiates, chooses, succeeds in the array of education and retraining forms that form the new 'lifelong learning' and the 'multiple career trajectories' that have replaced the linear hierarchies of the education system of the past and the jobs for life of the old economy (cf. Giddens's [1991] 'reflexive project' of the self as a key marker of this new period of history; Gee's [1999] 'shape-shifting portfolio person'; du Gay's [1996] 'entrepreneur of oneself'). It is argued that these times demand a subject who is capable of constant self-invention. Such a subject is presumed by, as well as being the intended product of, contemporary forms of education and training, and is a subject who is propped up and supported by a whole array of psychological support, most particularly forms of counselling and therapy. Thus, psychological practices have a central role in that they have to constantly prop up the self-invented subject. While self-realisation is what is expected of the life project and one in which success is judged by the psychological capacities to succeed, the ability to handle uncertainty, the never knowing where work will come from etc., in fact produces an almost inevitable failure that will be lived as a personal failing, hence the necessity for forms of counselling and therapy intended to prop up the fragile subject, to keep the illusion of a unitary subject intact. Containing this kind of subject and the containment of fracturing and fragmentation is a key task for neo-liberal and globalised economies which are no longer willing to provide long-term forms of support. The issue is that, in the Foucauldian sense, the practices of subjectification produce a constantly failing subject who has to understand their position in essentially personal and psychological terms. It is, of course, a deep irony that the subject of neo-liberalism is actually produced as multiple, having to cope with existing in a number of different discourses and positions: the subject who is supposed to be able to choose who they are from a myriad offerings, who can make themselves. But, this subject is actually also supposed to be sustained by a stable centre, an ego capable of resilience.

We no longer have a large manufacturing base which provides the pivot for an understanding of social stratification based on class divisions. What used to be the working class is now dispersed into service industries based on individual contracts, piecework, home work and work in call centres, with jobs for life having disappeared. Women's employment is divided between those who have education and skills to enter the professional and managerial sector and those who leave school with little or no qualifications and enter a labour market defined mostly by poorly paid, often part-time work, little job security and periods of unemployment. We are witnessing the complete collapse of civil society, thus, the attempt to further develop the psychological and social characteristics of the Robinson Crusoe economic man of liberalism (even if that man is now female) has to be created at this conjuncture as a subject who can cope without strong community roots or ties, hence the desire to make subjects responsible for their own lives through networks of 'social capital'. This leaves us with a situation where governments are grappling with the need to find ways to keep the social and political order among people for whom all the previous practices of social and community cohesion, including class and trade union membership, have been largely destroyed and where the massive sell-off of public utilities to bolster finance capital has meant the decline of welfare provision. I want to put these changes together with the place of psychology needed to prop up the autonomous and self-invented subject that Rose talks about. One way in which governments can keep order is to make citizens responsible for their own self-regulation by producing discourses in which success as a constantly changing successful entrepreneur of oneself is possible. Psychology has a central role in providing both the discourses through which the psychologised self is understood and the clinical discourses and practices which put that subject together again after the inevitable failure. Equally important are the discourses through which that success and failure is understood and therefore the techniques of self-regulation and management which both inscribe the subject and allow him or her to attempt to refashion themselves as a successful subject: the subject of neo-liberal choice. While the failure of this project is inevitable because the autonomous and multiple self is an impossible fiction, it is a fiction constantly held up as possible. Discourses of this impossibility function as counter-narratives, which I think we are beginning to see in an anti-globalisation politics which takes as its first refusal the refusal to consume and therefore to become that subject. However, most likely are the many narratives of failure lived as psychopathology and inadequacy and the practices and discourses which defend against failure by the bolstering of a subject position which denies the possibility of failure or contradiction.

So, in this context, upward mobility becomes a central trope of class/ification in which women and the qualities ascribed to femininity have a central place. The centrality of psychological discourse for explaining as pathology distress experienced by working-class women in their bid for upward mobility, or even simple respectability, is made clear by Walkerdine (1991, 1997; film, 1991), Skeggs (1997) and Lawler (1999). I would argue further that it is the qualities ascribed to femininity which are understood as the central carriers of the new middle-class individuality, building upon the long-established incitement to women to become producers of themselves as objects of the gaze. They are to look the part, sound the part and, moreover, they can make themselves and their homes over to conform to this middle-class aesthetic.

The concept of the 'makeover' has been a staple of women's magazines for many years (I remember wanting to turn my and my sister's shared bedroom into a 'bedsitting room' with the aid of furniture rearrangement and 'scatter cushions' in the early 1960s, and of course, even at that time I studied the hair, dress and make-up makeovers offered to readers and longed to rearrange my own appearance to be prettier and more fashionable, and took pride in making my own clothes in fashionable styles). So, today, television viewers are incited to rearrange their homes to make them fashionable, even if they have little money, by utilising leftover pots of paint and scraps from the garden shed or storeroom. We could hardly argue that these incitements are new but I think they are now more intense (there are at least four weekly programmes on home makeovers on commercial terrestrial television in Australia), and in some sense, unlike earlier moments, the upwardly mobile subject has nowhere else to go. In a 1997 BBC television series called *The Missing Postman*, the gendered nature of the problem of the change in the labour market and subsequent problems of finding work becomes clear. A redundant postman becomes a hero because he refuses to give up, becoming a fugitive by delivering his last sack of letters by bicycle all over the country. His wife, by contrast, while he is away, transforms herself into a fashionable interior decorator by doing a complete makeover on her home. While he is unable to let go of the position of masculine working-class subject and, in fact, has no other job to go to, her makeover is a sign of her new and more exciting place within the new economy and the relative positions of (working-class) women and men within it. So, if the working class, as understood typically in terms of a male manual worker, allied to trade union struggles and a particular form of politics, barely any longer exists in the West, what was once understood as upward mobility takes on a different and more central place, a place in which both women and men are incited to become self-reflexive subjects, to be looked at and in that sense feminised and in charge of their own biography in Rose's sense, but in which the feminine takes on a particular significance. So, we have the erosion of a discourse of the working class, which is also pushing onto women the old place of the displacement of radicality onto a middle-class conservatism, while at the same time bringing in values of emotionality, caring and introspection – the values of a psychology and interiority usually ascribed to women. Women can thus become understood as the carriers of all that is both good and bad about the new economy in the sense that the erosion of a discourse of classed identity can also be seen as a feminisation. In this sense, we are certainly not witnessing any lessening of inequality or exploitation – far from it – but I would claim that this inequality is differently lived because low-paid manual and service workers are constantly enjoined to improve and remake themselves as the freed consumer, the 'entrepreneur of themselves'. I want therefore to understand the discourses and narratives through which 'upward mobility' is lived for women in the present.

Both Skeggs (1997) and I (Walkerdine 1991, 1997; film, 1991) make a similar point about the unremitting nature of what Skeggs calls the 'doubts and insecurities of living class that working-class women endure on a daily basis' (p. 167). Indeed, I argued in 1991 and showed in my documentary film, *Didn't She Do Well*, that the understanding of what Pheterson (1993) calls 'daily routine humiliation' elicits considerable pain and a whole defensive organisation, sets of desires, avoidances, practices designed to make the pain bearable, to make it go away, to pursue other possibilities of being, to develop practices of being, coping, hoping, longing, shame, guilt and so forth, and that these are understood as personal failures when all there is available to understand these is an individual psychological discourse. In *Didn't She Do Well* I explored narratives of upward mobility presented by a group of professional women who had grown up working class in Britain at different historical moments and who had all made a transition to the middle class by virtue of education and professional work. A common theme for these women was the issue of what we might call a 'survival guilt' in which they felt that it was not acceptable for them to have survived and prospered when their families, and particularly their fathers, had suffered greatly and families had to live in poverty, illness, doing without. One of the women also talked about the way in which she found life with her parents boring because they had nothing to say and she longed for another life. She saw her chance in the 1960s by reading about becoming an au pair in a women's magazine. Subsequently, she left home and eventually became a university lecturer. However, as she put it, she could never fully accept the 'life that she had been given a ticket for' and in fact worked only part-time so that she never actually had much money and made sure that she stayed close to other academics from the working class. What is clear about her narrative is that she does not want to go back to that place of pain, poverty and silence yet she feels that she has no right to belong in the new place without taking those less fortunate with her. We could understand her strategy of part-time work as being one which meant that she still carried with her something from her parents, that is, their suffering (Ricoeur, 1996). By this act, she still remained their daughter. Upward mobility was something which for her was met with deep ambivalence. She could not go back, but she could also not go fully forward. Her own poverty was the only psychic and material link she had with her parents and could not therefore be severed. This theme is echoed by Lawler's (1999) work on narratives of upward mobility for women in which 'the fantasy of "getting out and getting away" may be achieved only at the price of entering another set of social relations, in which the assumed pathology of their (working-class women's) history and their desires is brought home to them more intensely' (p. 19).

So, I want to argue that we need to understand upward mobility as having a deeply defensive aspect. The discourses through which to read upward mobility present it as a freeing, a success. This discourse, transported into the popular narratives of a women's magazine, was what provided a vehicle for the fantasy of moving away from pain and silence and provided a material means for doing so – earning money as an au pair. Thus, defences and desires (which, of course, can also be defensive) work through popular narratives, formal discourses[1].

CHANGING PLACES

I will refer to one example from Walkerdine *et al.*'s (2001) study of transition to womanhood in 1990s Britain. I want to focus on one young woman whose family bought their council house during the period of the Conservative government under Margaret Thatcher, which introduced a 'Right to Buy' scheme, under which working-class people could become homeowners.

Lisa's family lived in a Victorian house in a socially mixed area of London, the house having been bought by the council to add to their housing stock at some point. The family bought the house under the Right to Buy scheme and meticulously did it up in the current fashionable style of restoration, with the aid of books on Victorian decor from the public library. During the housing boom of the 1980s they sold the house and moved to the North of England, to the small town where Lisa's maternal grandmother had grown up, where the houses were much cheaper. With the proceeds of the sale of the council house, they were able to buy a cottage in a village setting, which they set about extending and renovating, also setting up a franchise of the watch and clock repair business that Lisa's father had worked for in the extension. The cottage had some considerable land on which Lisa kept a horse.

What I want to explore here is Lisa's narratives of her subjectivity, taken from interviews and a video diary made by her at the age of 18. In particular, I want to concentrate on the way in which she understands herself as a subject as a young child in a council house in London and the transformations she makes to become a young, middle-class country businesswoman in the North.

I want to make some reference to the study of pariahs and parvenus by the sociologist, Zygmunt Bauman (2001), who makes a particular case that modernity is the moment of the parvenu. 'Modernity', says Bauman:

> proclaimed no order untouchable, as all untouchable orders were to be replaced with a new, artificial order where roads are built that lead from the bottom to the top and so no-one belongs anywhere forever. Modernity is thus the hops of the pariah. But the pariah could stop being pariah only by becoming – struggling to become – parvenu. And the parvenu, having never washed out the stain of his origin, laboured under a constant threat of deportation back to the land he tried to escape. Deportation in case he failed; deportation in case he succeeded too spectacularly for the comfort of those around. (p. 225)

What struck me about this powerful passage is that the process Bauman describes as one of a difficult and shaky self-invention is certainly one of modernism, but it is, I think, speeded up and broadened under neo-liberalism – we are all parvenus (indeed, why else should there have been a recent television series called *Faking It* in which the aim was to see if people could pass for what they are not and get away with it?). What Bauman makes clear, though, is that the self-invention involves a journey, a material and imagined transformation of status. This is certainly what Lisa and her family undergo, but it is also what the apparent classless self-invention involves. The apparently limitless possibilities are all possibilities of being SOMEBODY. What I think Bauman describes powerfully is that the changes in status sanctioned by modernity carry with them some very difficult emotions which the parvenu must always carry with them and which are absolutely central to their beingness. In striving to remake him or herself, the parvenu, according to Bauman, must simultaneously want to belong in some other place, a place that must be achieved entirely through the remaking processes of the subject themselves and which simultaneously contains the threat of being not good enough and the threat of being too good. How, then, does the subject as parvenu manage to hold all this together without breaking down? If there is no way to go except forward, back being impossible, and yet going forward demands an impossible, shaky act of ventriloquism, then its demands on the subject in terms of a commodification of the self, the constant reinvention, are immense.

Lisa's family sought to remake themselves as middle-class country people by the purchase and subsequent sale of their council house and the move north. What I want to think about is the way in which Lisa understands her old childhood subjectivity as a working-class girl in a council house and how she understands and fantasises her new subjectivity. I want to argue that she imagines remaking herself and this demands a complete negation of her Other self. She then engages in powerful and pleasurable fantasies about the kind of woman she wants to become. Held inside these fantasies, though, is a painful Other, that which she fears that she is and wants not to be.

Lisa presents to the camera in her video diary a model of an English countrywoman: her hair, the pearl necklace, the twinset. It is as though, for the world, the remake has been a success. Yet, in the interview she tells a narrative of depression, eating disorders and unhappiness set against the relentless story of becoming a horse riding middle-class country lady and a career woman. Everything in the old life is presented as Other. At one point she talks about her father growing up in a council house and that she now looks down on people who live in council houses. Yet it wasn't just her father, of course, who grew up in a council house, but her until the age of eight. Why does she 'forget' this part of her own history? I suggest that she forgets her history for the same reason that she claims not to have had a childhood ('Once I broke down and cried because I said I've had no childhood'; 'I think I was an adult from birth'), that it is too difficult to bear the fact that she now 'looks down' on that part of herself who lived in a council house. Far easier to forget it, claim it didn't exist in order to better remake herself as the country lady and career woman she should always have been.

She describes the village in which she lives as being close to the area where the BBC television series *Heartbeat* was filmed. This is a nostalgic fictional series about a country police force and community set in the 1960s, which presents a cosy, friendly and white rural England. She presents the village where she lives as full of friendly locals, who hail her as she passes on her horse. She reads the magazine *Horse and Hound*, a conservative and upper-class country magazine favoured by the hunting, shooting and fishing set. She presents herself as totally immersed in the community and describes how she, like the locals in the nearby small town, crosses over the road so as not to walk directly in front of the local Indian restaurant to show the Asian owners that they are not welcome. Yet this is a young woman who grew up until the age of eight in a multicultural inner-city setting and who, by her own admission at interview, knew all about Indian festivals like Divali and Indian deities. It is as though Lisa wants to be more local than the locals (an idea that Bauman works with) and to do so, she must take another subject position that risks negating her past. The past therefore has to be reworked. I suggest that Lisa's statement that she didn't have a childhood is an attempt to operate as though there were no Other to have to dismiss. Its only remnants, then, are the depression and eating disorders – testimony to the problems of living this identity as though it were all there. As with the women in *Didn't She Do Well* and those interviewed by Lawler (1999), the present is lived in relation to the shame of the past and the fear of exposure and ridicule.

But, in addition to this, she is attempting to create herself as a career woman with certain tastes and style, what I think we can term a whole aesthetics of herself, to remake herself in the image of the country middle-class career woman:

> I want the business to grow and I want to say – I think the main point is that making a name for myself, because you know as – you know, you're getting more money round here – you've got big cars and you've got bigger houses and people are starting to take a note of you, yeah – and I think that sort of the most important thing to me is my status.
>
> I've got lots of suits – a lot of business suits. When I'm out with my friends I like to be the person that turns the heads rather than my friends.

She works with her father, training to be a horologist (the term she uses rather than a watch and clock repairer). She likes to wear business suits, fantasises a 90-year-old billionaire with a heart defect as her 'ideal man', never having children, living in a stylish and uncomfortable house and driving a Mercedes:

> I love looking the part, and I can't wait to drive the Mercedes … I'll look the part when I step outside the Merc.

I argue that she performs this aesthetic, this commodification of herself through the complex manifestations of signs, discourses, practices, narratives, that constitute her immersion in this life, yet everything that is not present in this performance contains that other narrative, the narrative of being Other, now pushed into the place opposite to the position she now holds. Her world, her self is marked as:

Country
Middle class
Conservative
Successful
White
Adult and away from
The city
Working class
Childish
Black
Unhappy

Little by little in the interview, a story emerges in which she is rejected for being overweight (' "you're fat, you know", "oh go away!" '), rejected for being a Londoner ('they would say "she's a Londoner, keep her out" '), depressed ('I literally nearly had a nervous breakdown'), not eating ('I lost so much weight and I thought this is great you know, I can do this again like yeah – and that's when I just started going around with just like a packet of crisps for the whole day and I was feeling dizzy and sick and I thought, no, this isn't right') and feeling that she had no childhood, is tired of trying to succeed and longs to be accepted into this new place. So the narrative of the parvenu, the mimetic narrative which aims to produce as reality that identity which she fantasises being ('I'll probably have a very sort of flashy, sort of snobby lifestyle'), is a narrative which displaces and avoids the rejection which accompanies the narrative of Otherness, the narrative condemned to psychopathology because illness (depression and eating disorders) is the only way in which it can be spoken. Only the relentless pursuit of this new narrative identity and the 'success' implied within it can quieten the other insistent narrative in order to attempt the impossible task, as Bauman says, the complete displacement of the what one was.

Lisa wants to be a businesswoman, which is not the same identity as a villager – she wants to have a particular position – one of high status and a lifestyle that demands money and high levels of consumption, which are to be financed by the marriage to the billionaire.

It is not just fitting into the village, but this other fantasy of the businesswoman that is important. They intersect to inscribe her and she reads the village through *Heartbeat* and *Horse and Hound*. Work is central now and so the creation of a desirable work identity is crucial for her, as for all the young women in the study. It is through becoming the businesswoman that she is able to finance the consumption that she fantasises. It seems as though it is the business suits, flash cars and stylish home that create in fantasy the possibility of an Other space, an Other life, a life in which depression and eating disorders do not exist because this is the life of wealth and success. Thus, what I am saying is that it is the fantasy of being that Other, the desire to be that Other, which is absolutely central for us to understand. It is how that desire positions her in the practice of working, of upward mobility, produces the practices of self-management through which she can be inscribed in those identities to which she aspires. And always this desire must be set against its Other, that which it defends against, the other positions – not only, I think, that which she has left behind in London but what it would mean not to have money and wealth. These other positions are to some extent medicalised and psychologised and presented in the form of illness: depression and eating disorders, the available ways for articulating and living the impossibility of success, of arrival, of being a unitary subject.

As Gonnick (2001) says, to 'become somebody', the task of neo-liberalism, is an impossible task, revealing 'the delusionary character of self-determining, individualistic and autonomous ideas of subjectivity' (p. 204). What the examples reveal is the problem of contradiction between positions, possible identities, identifications and the shaky move between them. Bauman (2001) calls this 'ambivalence', that is, the discursive place where there is a slip or sliding, ambiguity between classifications. It is this, not this. He argues that discursively this is a problem for narrative organisation in that it is difficult to hold something as existing within opposing narratives and discourses. He argues further that the single and simple discursive classification is what makes possible the fiction of the rational unitary and autonomous subject – I am this. Therefore the failure to classify, that he calls ambivalence, is experienced as great pain and anxiety for the subject because it is lived as a failure to become the desired singular subjectivity, the subjectivity that one can consume oneself into being. By contrast, he argues that unemployed people experience complete boredom and breakdown because they cannot become a consuming subject, the subject for which happiness is apparently possible – I will become this person and then I will be happy ever after. So, the goal of happiness is invested in the endless becoming of the unitary subject through turning oneself into a commodity and thereby owning the means to consume. It is a pleasure endlessly displaced and postponed, glimpsed in snatches of holidays, acquisitions as though it were life. It contains failure inside it as an inevitability. It is that failure which psychology is constantly asked to remedy. I suggest that this gives us a glimpse of how class is both lived and elided within the present and allows us to understand the discourses and narratives of the upwardly mobile neo-liberal subject and the problems and the necessity to work with the complex intersection of narratives and discourses, Other and occluded narratives, through which gendered and classed subjectivity within the present might be understood.

NOTE

1. Although psychoanalysis classically understands the defences as constituted through a process of a universalised developmental sequence and therefore prior to the secondary influence of discourses and narratives, it could be argued, following Lacan, that the mobius strip of inside and outside, in which the inside is the outside and vice versa, provides a way of moving beyond such a position. However, Lacanian work still retains a central discourse of a universal human subject which is in opposition to discursive and narrative approaches' refusal of interiority (see Walkerdine, 2002). In using the term 'defences' here, I am wanting to suggest that there are non-

conscious, non-rational connections between discourses and narratives and that these are held in a complex relationship and that some kind of understanding of these connections is necessary beyond an account of narratives and discourses. I recognise that the issue of the relationship of a concept of defences to a more general psychic organisation is important, but it is beyond the scope of this article to explore it.

REFERENCES

Bauman, Z. (2001) Pariahs and parvenus, in: P. Beilharz (Ed.) *The Bauman Reader* (Oxford, Blackwell).

Bowlby, J. (1971) *Attachment and Loss*, vol. 1 (Harmondsworth, Penguin).

Douglas, J.W.B. (1964) *The Home and the School* (Glasgow, McGibbon & Kee).

Du Gay, P. (1996) *Consumption and Identity at Work* (London, Sage).

Gee, J. (1999) New people in new worlds: networks, the new capitalism and schools, in: B. Cope & M. Kalantzis (Eds) *Multiliteracies: literacy learning and the design of social futures*, pp. 43–68 (London, Routledge).

Giddens, A. (1991) *Modernity and Self-identity: self and society in the late modern age* (Oxford, Polity Press).

Giddens, A. (1994) *Beyond Left and Right* (Oxford, Polity Press).

Gonnick, M. (2001) Unpublished PhD thesis, Ontario Institute for Studies in Education.

Gorz, A. (1982) *Farewell to the Working Class* (London, Pluto).

Halsey, A.H., Heath, A.F. & Ridge, J.M. (1980) *Origins and Destinations: family, class and education in modern Britain* (Oxford, Clarendon Press).

Lawler, S. (1999) 'Getting out and getting away': women's narratives of class mobility, *Feminist Review*, 63, pp. 3–23.

Pheterson, G. (1993) Historical and material determinants of psychodynamic development, in: J. Adleman & G. Enguidanos (Eds) *Racism in the Lives of Women* (New York, Haworth Press).

Reay, D. (1998) Rethinking social class: qualitative perspectives on class and gender, *Sociology*, 32, pp. 259–275.

Ricoeur, P. (1996) A new ethos for Europe, in: R. Kearney (Ed.) *The Hermeneutics of Action* (London, Sage).

Rose, N. (1999) *Governing the Soul*, 2nd edn (London, Free Association Books).

Skeggs, B. (1997) *Formations of Class and Gender* (London, Sage).

Walkerdine, V. (1991) Film: *Didn't She Do Well* (Working Pictures).

Walkerdine, V. (1991) *Schoolgirl Fictions* (London, Verso).

Walkerdine, V. (1997) *Daddy's Girl: young girls and popular culture* (London, Macmillan).

Walkerdine, V. (2002) Psychology, post modernity and neo-liberalism, keynote address to the 'Politics of Psychological Knowledge Conference', Free University of Berlin.

Walkerdine, V., Bansel, P. & Mueller, F. (in preparation) *Psychological discourse and narratives of work in the new labour market*.

Walkerdine, V., Lucey, H. & Melody, J. (2001) *Growing up Girl: psychosocial explorations of gender and class* (London, Palgrave).

SECTION 2

CONTEXTS
Making education work

CERTIFYING THE WORKFORCE
Economic imperative or failed social policy?

Alison Wolf, Andrew Jenkins and Anna Vignoles

INTRODUCTION

All three authors are based at the University of London (all three have strong connections to the Institute of Education, although Wolf is now based at King's College). They have published very widely on matters to do with education, focussing on inequality, widening participation and labour market policy.

In this paper, the authors examine the outcomes of education policies that are directed towards economic ends. Governments have relied on targets and emphasised certification. Data from a large national longitudinal survey are used to examine factors that affect the acquisition of formal additional qualifications and whether those qualifications lead to increased earnings for their holders. The authors argue that 'the results strongly suggest that current policies are failing even on their own terms'. Explanations for this failure are given by suggesting that many qualifications are acquired for non-wage and non-productivity-related reasons; that gaining a new qualification does not necessarily mean that new skills have been acquired and that there may be a lack of demand among employers for the skills that have been developed.

KEY QUESTIONS

1. Is education an example of investment or consumption?
2. Are schools institutions that an economically successful society can afford to provide as young people and others are kept out of the labour market or are schools the means by which jobs and wealth are created?
3. If you see that this cannot be answered in simple mutually exclusive terms, then what sort of issues need to be considered before we can work towards greater clarity?

FURTHER READING

The authors' concern with the nature and pursuit of certification relates to longstanding debates in education. One of the classic discussions on this issue is given in Dore, R. (1977) *The Diploma Disease: Education, Qualification and Development* (University of California Press, Berkeley). The relationship between the economy and education is explored with very different conclusions by Barnett, C. (1996) *The Audit of War: The Illusion and Reality of Britain as a Great Nation* (Pan, London), and by Rubinstein, W. (1993) *Capitalism, Culture and Decline in Britain* (Routledge, London). More recent and less academic work can be seen on government websites that focus on enterprise (e.g. http://curriculum.qca.org.uk/ key-stages-3-and-4/cross-curriculum dimensions/enterprise/index.aspx?return=/search/ index.aspx%3FfldSiteSearch%3Denterprise).

This Reading links with Chapter 10 and Debate 3 of *The Routledge Education Studies Textbook.*

INTRODUCTION

During the last quarter of the twentieth century the education policies of European and North American governments became increasingly directed towards immediate economic goals, especially in the post-compulsory, further and adult sectors. This development reflected concerns over increased global competition and each country's own economic performance and has been informed by a rather simplistic version of human capital theory. The development of the population's (and so the workforce's) skills came to be regarded as both a critical, and a sure-fire, way of improving productivity. Within the education sector governments have correspondingly directed support towards the development of vocational skills and towards courses and activities of apparently direct relevance to the workplace (Green *et al.*, 2000; Grubb & Lazerson, 2004; Organisation for Economic Cooperation and Development [OECD], 2004a, b).

In Britain the policy rationale is similar to that expressed in other developed nations, but there are, nonetheless, distinctive features to the UK case. It is not simply that the country has embraced the idea of reshaping education for economic ends with particular enthusiasm (see Coffield, 2002a; Wolf, 2002). Policy has been bound up, to an unusually high degree, with debate over the whole structure of the UK economy: first, in relation to a level of performance which, until the 1990s, was markedly poorer than that of major neighbours and competitors and, more recently, over whether, in spite of apparent economic revival, the economy remains caught in a 'low skill equilibrium' which bodes ill for the future (see Keep, 1999; Coffield, 2004). In addition, the UK has been distinctive in the policy tools it has favoured, notably, as discussed below, its use of quantitative targets tied to a centrally controlled 'national qualification framework'.

The domination of education policy by economic objectives has been much remarked on in the policy literature, and the ideological perspectives underlying New Labour's policies, in particular, have been subject to detailed analysis (see especially, in this journal, articles by Coffield, 2002a, 2004; Lloyd & Payne, 2003a, b; see also Taylor, 2005). However, evaluation of the impact of policy on individuals has been constrained by a lack of detailed, micro-level data.

This paper helps to fill this gap. Following an overview of the relevant policy environment and using a combination of new and previously published findings, it discusses the experiences since 1990 of a large sample of UK adults who have undertaken formal education and training. Their experiences allow us to evaluate the impact of government policies designed to increase skill levels and formal accreditation, especially among the less skilled. The paper first looks at participation patterns and secondly examines the economic outcomes of formal, accredited training. Many of these outcomes are markedly at odds with governments' expectations and intentions. The latter part of the paper discusses possible explanations for these findings, drawing on both the national and the international context, and implications for the current policy debate.

THE POLICY CONTEXT

The idea that 'lifelong learning' is increasingly important for emerging 'learning societies' has passed into conventional wisdom. Within the European Union (EU) it was first identified formally as a strategic priority in the 1993 White Paper on *Growth, competitiveness and employment*, and the following year a White Paper on *Teaching and learning: towards the learning society* identified lifelong learning as a necessary response to the arrival of the 'information society', to internationalization (globalization) and to technical change. The European Parliament and Council declared 1996 the European Year of Lifelong Learning, identifying lifelong learning as 'a key factor . . . for a European model of competitiveness and growth'. The 2000 Lisbon Strategy, intended to make the EU 'the most competitive and dynamic knowledge-based economy in the world by 2010', includes 'giving higher priority to lifelong learning as a basic component of the European social model'. In 2002 the Council agreed a resolution on lifelong learning (2002/C 163/01) reaffirming its importance and in 2004 the EU agreed on five shared education benchmarks, one of which is a target for at least 80% of 25–59-year-olds to participate in lifelong learning.

The OECD, encompassing the world's richest countries outside as well as within Europe, is an enthusiastic promoter of human capital formation as a means to growth (see, for example, OECD, 2004a) and specifically of lifelong learning, which is 'vital to sustained economic progress and social cohesion in the "new economy"' (OECD, 2000). In 1996 (the European Year of Lifelong Learning) the OECD Education Ministers adopted a mandate to 'make lifelong learning for all a reality'. An OECD Policy Brief on lifelong learning emphasized that the 'lifelong learning approach' is fuelled by the 'increased pace of globalisation and technological change' (OECD, 2004b, p. 2) and by 'serious deficiencies in skills and competencies in the OECD labour force' (p. 3).

Although learning as a means to personal fulfilment or cultural development may be mentioned in passing, the focus of such documents is overwhelmingly on productivity and economic success. It is therefore not surprising to find that governments have increasingly favoured vocational training over general education for adults. Green *et al.* (2000) reviewed education and training policy throughout the EU for the period 1985–1999 and found a uniform preoccupation with links between education and the economy and direction of funding towards overtly vocational adult programmes.

The UK, as noted above, has been particularly active in its promotion of 'education for growth'. The dominant concerns of a succession of governments and ministers are encapsulated in the following quotes, each from major White Papers:

> The Government's plans to improve and develop the education and training system [are] . . . a response to the rising demand from employers for more and higher level skills to meet the growing challenge from overseas competitors in world markets (Department of Education and Science [DES], 1991, p. 1).

> Learning is the key to prosperity. Investment in human capital will be the foundation of success in the knowledge-based global economy of the twenty-first century. (Department for Education and Employment [DfEE], 1998, p. 1).
>
> Nationally, the UK faces a major challenge in ensuring our workforce is equipped ... to compete in a global market place ... we have too few people trained. (Department for Education and Skills [DfES], 2005, p. 5).

During much of the late twentieth century Britain's economic problems sparked a search for culprits and remedies. Education and training failures became favourite contenders (Barnett, 1986; Prais, 1995; Sanderson, 1999). Comparisons of the qualification levels of British workers (low) and of German and French workers (high) became and indeed remain staples of policy discourse, with government determined to increase the numbers of workers with vocational qualifications as a means of raising productivity. For example, in evidence to the House of Commons Education and Skills Committee in 2005 the DfES argued that 'If we look at the relationship between ourselves and our European competitors, I think the figure is that about 20% of the [productivity] difference between ourselves and them is down to the skills of the workforce' (House of Commons Education and Skills Committee, 2005, p. 10; see also National Skills Task Force, 2000; DfES, 2003, 2005). (The 20% figure has become standard in government statements but is an 'informed judgement' rather than established by empirical analysis.)

In their analysis British policy-makers tread a well-worn path. For example, at much the same time as the DfES was testifying to the Commons Committee, Germany's Chancellor Schroeder was using exactly the same arguments to promote university reform in Germany. What has been highly distinctive, however, is the major policy tool adopted by successive UK governments, the use of qualification targets as a driver of and proxy for skills acquisition.

An overarching framework is provided by the National Education and Training Targets. Originally promoted by the Confederation of British Industry (CBI) and then adopted by successive governments (Wolf, 2002), they set down targets for proportions of young people and adults attaining formal qualifications at different levels. The targets were originally expressed in terms of National Vocational Qualifications (NVQs) at different levels. NVQs were developed by the government during the late 1980s and early 1990s as the launch pad for an intended qualification-based up-skilling of the entire employed workforce (Jessup, 1991; Wolf, 2001). More recent formulations of the targets involve qualifications of all types, and all qualifications offered in publicly supported programmes and institutions other than universities must now be approved and classified within a National Qualifications Framework (see Appendix). This is operated by the Qualifications and Curriculum Agency (QCA), which assigns each qualification a formal level from 1 to 5 (although the QCA is now reclassifying them into eight levels).

Targets drive education policy directly because they are incorporated into Public Services Agreements, which originate with the Treasury and provide accountability measures for public services investment and provision. The DfES thus becomes answerable to the Treasury (and Downing Street) for the 'delivery' of aggregate quantitative targets and in turn disaggregates them and passes specific ones to the agencies it funds. Progress towards them consequently dominates civil service thinking.

The targets of which the general public is most aware are probably those for attainment at Key Stage 2 (age 11) and at GCSE (age 16). However, the education and training of adults, the subject of this paper, has been especially strongly affected. Further education funding has been tied increasingly to the provision of formally accredited courses (which because they are qualification bearing can count towards the targets). In addition, some of the funding in mainstream further education, and a great deal of the funding received by independent 'training providers', who cater particularly for the unemployed and workplace-based training, is 'output related', meaning that payment is directly tied to whether or not learners actually achieve a formal award. This has obvious implications for the type and level of qualification for which learners are entered by providers who need to 'make' their targets, and also exerts pressure on assessors (Eraut *et al.*, 1996; Mager *et al.*, 2000).

The two adult targets currently receiving most emphasis involve basic skills and 'level 2' awards. (The third major target for the post-compulsory age group, involving 50% participation in higher education, has been downplayed in the last few years, following heavy public criticism. It was very important in the first and early in the second post-1997 Labour administrations.) The basic skills target is for 1,500,000 adults to improve their basic skill levels between 2001 and 2007, with an interim target of 750,000 by 2004. The level 2 target is to reduce the number of adults in the workforce who lack a level 2 qualification by at least 40% by 2010, with 1,000,000 to achieve a level 2 between 2003 and 2006.

The importance attached to these targets reflects the preoccupation with economic objectives discussed above, although, as we will show, it is not necessarily based on any empirical evidence that these targets can contribute to the economic objectives set. Moreover, associated policies increasingly direct subsidies straight to the workplace, to employees and/or employers. Companies now have a statutory obligation to support Union Learning Representatives in the workplace and public funding for the Union Learning Fund supports Union Learning Representative training and promotion of workplace-based learning programmes. Employer Training Pilots were introduced in selected areas by the Treasury in 2003, as a precursor to a national policy, announced in a 2005 White Paper (DfES, 2005). The National Employer Training Programme will direct an increasing proportion of further and adult education funding towards adults in employment and will supposedly be demand led, 'built up from the employers' business needs, and delivered in the workplace' (DfES, 2005, p. 11).

Companies have always spent significant amounts of money on in-house training. However, there is a substantial theoretical literature arguing that 'market failure' is likely, i.e. that the amount of training paid for by employers is likely to be less than is optimal for the economy overall (see, for example, Booth & Snower, 1996; Acemoglu & Pischke, 1999). This is a major justification for the activist role which, as noted earlier, has been adopted by many governments in promoting 'lifelong learning', although there have been and remain major disagreements, in the UK and elsewhere, over the desirability of forcing companies to spend prescribed amounts on training, directly or via levies.

Ensuring progress towards key targets is the major concern of the Learning and Skills Council (LSC), the unitary funding body for further education and training established in 2001. The LSC replaced a structure in which further education and training were dealt with separately (largely through the Further Education Funding Council and the local Training and Enterprise Councils or TECs). Analysts of the new structure agree that it is highly focused on national strategic objectives, at the expense of local flexibility (Ramsden *et al.*, 2004; Coffield *et al.*, 2005). In the immediate future this means a continuing interest in basic skills provision and a major emphasis on 'level 2' qualifications.

The distinctive education policy tools adopted by UK governments partly reflect a general enthusiasm for targets in public sector management. Qualifications are easy to count and so they are an obvious way of setting and measuring progress towards targets in education and training and once the National Targets had been introduced, the approach became self-perpetuating. But it has also been argued strongly by government policymakers that qualifications (as compared to uncertificated training) have greater potential to increase economic efficiency because they provide clear signals to employers about holders' skills and potential productivity and so improve the allocation and use of labour (Jessup, 1991; Jenkins & Wolf, 2005). Hence, while the rhetoric around the new National Employer Training Programme emphasizes that it will be 'demand-led' and respond to employers' needs and preferences, in practice the entitlement will reflect government ideas on how to promote productivity: the entitlement is to 'free training to a first full Level 2 *qualification*' (DfES, 2005, p. 18, emphasis added).

ADULT LEARNERS IN BRITAIN: HOW MANY AND WHO?

That successive UK governments have shared the goal of increasing economically relevant learning by adults is clear enough. But what evidence is there that the policy has actually achieved its goals?

Information on the numbers and characteristics of British adult learners is highly sensitive to the way questions are posed (Jenkins & Wolf, 2004). However, there are two surveys which have provided repeated measures over a period of years, using consistent question formats. The Labour Force Survey is conducted by all EU member states and collects data on, among other things, qualification levels and participation in training or learning activities in the four week period prior to the survey. In recent years UK data show about one in five adults aged 25–64 reporting participating in training or learning: a figure which is almost identical to the levels reported by Scandinavian countries and much higher than for southern Europe (OECD, 2003).

Participation is more common among the more educated: an international and universal pattern (Bélanger & Valdivielso, 1997). Again, patterns for the UK are very close to those for northern Europe, while in Southern Europe the gap between the more and less educated is substantially greater (OECD, 2003). High participation rates are also reported for employer-provided workplace training. Around one-third of individuals in the UK who have some sort of qualification receive workplace training. This has risen from 30% in 1999. However, among unqualified individuals only one in ten currently receives workplace training in the relevant time period, a figure that is largely unchanged since 1999 (Office for National Statistics, 2005). The other major source of repeated measures is the NIACE surveys of adult participation in learning (with, in this case, the target population comprising anyone aged 17 or over).[1] Over the last 10 years, the results show a little over one in five adults reporting participation in learning at the time of questioning and about 40% having participated at some time in the last three years. The NIACE surveys also show stable participation patterns (allowing for the usual year on year fluctuations in a moderately sized survey). The one exception is evidence of a significant decline in participation among those aged 65 or over[2] (see Sargant, 2000; Aldridge & Tuckett, 2004).

A similar pattern of stability is apparent in the Labour Force Survey data on qualifications. Gorard and associates have used these to examine progress towards all the national lifelong learning targets (for the proportion of the workforce holding level 2, 3 or 4 qualifications) and conclude that recorded increases mostly reflect the feed-through of school-leavers who are more formally qualified than their predecessors and that 'there is little suggestion that the qualifications of adults while they are adults has improved much since 1991' (Gorard *et al.*, 1999, p. 86; see also Gorard *et al.*, 2002). The Skills for Life interim target of 750,000 adults improving their basic skills between 2001 and 2004 has been met and might suggest major expansion in this area. However, since adults are, for target purposes, defined as anyone over 16, success was entirely predictable on the basis of pre-existing enrolment and qualification trends. Sixty-eight per cent of those participating in Skills for Life (basic skills) courses are aged 16–18 years, while 75% are under 25 (Meadows & Metcalf, 2005).

Overall we know of no data suggesting that there have been significant increases in adult enrolment, if we define 'adult' as the 25–64 age group of conventional survey usage. The limitation of the sources cited, however, is that they are based on cross-sectional data. Although the Labour Force Survey and the NIACE surveys collect repeated measures, the sample of individuals is not the same. This makes it hard to track detailed participation trends.

However, data do exist with which to address these issues in a UK context, notably longitudinal data from the National Child Development Study (NCDS). The NCDS is a continuing longitudinal survey of people living in Great Britain who were born there between 3 and 9 March 1958. They have been interviewed six times: in childhood and adolescence, and also in 1991 (age 33) and 2000 (age 42). The NCDS database for each cohort member includes attainment on a variety of tests taken at the ages of seven and 11 (including reading and mathematics), school and family background variables (e.g. parents' education, father's social class, indicators of financial difficulties and type of school), initial and later education and training, employment status and wages. Among the information collected at the most recent interview (at age 42) were formal qualifications[3] taken since the age of 33 (when previously interviewed) and current enrolment on qualification-bearing courses.[4]

These data offer us a much clearer picture of how far recent government policies have succeeded in shifting participation patterns and also whether the qualifications adults obtain have any discernible effects on their working lives. We have, specifically, useable data for 9829 cohort members, although missing data on some variables means that the actual sample size varies between analyses.

Seventy per cent of the NCDS cohort reported undertaking some form of training or course during the period 1991–2000 (and many reported more than one form). One-third acquired a qualification of some description (33% of the sample, 30% of males and 36% of females). In addition, 31% reported undertaking non-certificated training at work at some point during 1991–2000 and 24% undertook some form of non-certificated 'leisure' learning. Respondents were also asked about current learning activity. Ten per cent reported that they were currently involved in a course leading to a qualification, with women again more heavily represented.

Between 1981 and 1991 34% reported taking a qualification-bearing or access course, so there appears to be no overall drop-off in cohort members' involvement with certificated learning. (In contrast, the NIACE surveys regularly report significant declines in the incidence of learning between those in their 20s and their 30s. This may reflect differences in sample size and composition:[5] the NIACE results on age-related participation do not differentiate between certificated and uncertificated learning.)

Table 1 shows what type of qualifications respondents reported they had obtained. ('Vocationally related' qualifications are qualifications such as BTEC Diplomas or general NVQs. What are conventionally thought of as vocational awards are classified as occupational in the National Framework.) Readers should note that this shows total number of qualifications obtained by the sample and that many respondents obtained more than one. As noted earlier, 33% of the total sample obtained one or more formal qualifications between 1991 and 2000 (18.5% obtained just one, 7.5% obtained two and 7% obtained more than two).[6]

As Table 1 makes evident, qualification-oriented lifelong learning led predominantly to occupational qualifications, rather than academic or vocationally related qualifications. Government policy has focused on occupational qualifications, and adult certification thus follows the desired pattern. Notably, 16% of the sample obtained occupational qualifications at level 1 of the framework. These include NVQ level 1, lower level RSA qualifications and other low level qualifications, such as Pitmans level 1 and HGV licences. Some 7% of the sample obtained occupational qualifications at level 2 (the

■ **Table 1** NCDS cohort members obtaining qualifications between ages 33 and 42 by National Qualifications Framework levels and type

	n	%
Academic Level 1	23	0.23
Academic Level 2	214	2.18
Academic Level 3	108	1.10
Academic Level 4	360	3.66
Academic Level 5	130	1.32
Vocationally related Level 1	16	0.16
Vocationally related Level 2	156	1.59
Vocationally related Level 3	104	1.06
Vocationally related Level 4	98	1.00
Occupational Level 1	1541	15.68
Occupational Level 2	702	7.14
Occupational Level 3	276	2.81
Occupational Level 4	402	4.09
Occupational Level 5	273	2.78
Total sample[a]	9829	100

[a] Note that individuals may acquire more than one qualification during this period.

subject of one of the current high priority targets), which include City and Guilds part 1 and NVQ level 2 qualifications. Relatively small numbers took academic qualifications between the ages of 33 and 42, the exception being the 360 (approximately 4%) who obtained level 4, namely degrees or higher education diplomas.

But are these learners the individuals whom the government wishes to target? And is policy succeeding in increasing uptake by the less skilled? As noted above, adult learning in the UK, in common with the rest of the developed world, is much more common for those from higher social classes and with higher levels of formal education. For example, data from the NIACE survey indicate that in 2004, 54% of people in classes A and B, but only 25% in classes D and E reported some learning (Aldridge & Tuckett, 2004; see also Beinart & Smith, 1998, for a multivariate analysis using data from the National Adult Learning Survey). The NCDS sample is no different. For example, only 20% of those who left school without any formal qualifications report that they obtained one in the previous decade, while 35% of those who acquired A-levels also acquired further qualifications.

Since the 1990s were a period of constant government activity in this area, we used multivariate analysis to investigate the predictors of participation at either end of the decade. This allows us to look at the effects of different variables while controlling for the fact that they tend to be highly intercorrelated. (This is notably the case for education, occupation, income and class of origin.) We specified a standard probit model (see Jenkins *et al.*, 2002) incorporating variables which previous research indicated were important in explaining participation levels. Table 2 (for men) and Table 3 (for women) show which variables had a significant impact, first, on the likelihood of undertaking qualification-bearing courses between 1991 and 2000 and, second, on the likelihood of being on one in 2000. (Separate analyses are needed because the labour market participation patterns of males and females are radically different.) These indicate whether, using the same individuals and with constant measures and definitions, there were changes by the end of the 1990s, as government policy intended.

Table 2 summarizes the variables which are significantly associated with the probability of males having completed, or being engaged in, qualification-bearing learning.

■ **Table 2** Determinants of the decision to undertake qualification-bearing courses: males ($n = 3878$)

	Undertaking or completing a course 1991–2000	Enrolment on a qualification-bearing course 2000
Obtained a qualification 1991–2000	N/A	Significant at 1% level
Ability at age 11[a]	Significant at 5% level	Not significant
Unemployed in 1991	Significant at 1% level	Not significant
Union membership	Significant at 1% level	Significant at 5% level
Work for public sector	Significant at 5% level	Significant at 1% level
School qualifications (base case none)		
CSEs	Significant at 5% level	Not significant
<5 O-levels	Significant at 5% level	Not significant
>5 O-levels	Significant at 5% level	Not significant
A-level	Significant at 10% level	Not significant
Post-school qualifications		
Mid-level vocational	Significant at 1% level	Not significant

For a full specification of this model, including non-significant variables included, see Jenkins *et al.* (2002).
[a] The ability measure is an index derived from reading, mathematics and general ability tests taken at age 11.

For the period up to 2000 we find, as in other studies, that school performance is quite strongly related to the likelihood of obtaining a qualification: for example, as compared with those who left school with no qualifications, both men who left with CSEs and those with five or more O-levels are 9% more likely to obtain qualifications. (Post-school qualifications generally show no effects.) Being unemployed in 1990 is associated, for male respondents, with a 17% greater chance of taking a qualification-bearing course in the next nine years (compared with the employed). Union members are 6% more likely than

■ **Table 3** Determinants of the decision to undertake qualification-bearing courses: females ($n = 4213$)

	Undertaking or completing a course 1991–2000	Enrolment on a qualification-bearing course 2000
Obtained a qualification 1991–2000	N/A	Significant at 1% level
Out of labour force 1991	Negatively related: 5% level	Negatively related: 10% level
Ability at age 11[a]	Significant at 1% level	Not significant
Union membership	Significant at 1% level	Significant at 10% level
Worked in public sector	Not significant	Not significant
School qualifications (base case none)		
CSEs	Significant at 5% level	Significant at 1% level
<5 O-levels	Significant at 1% level	Significant at 1% level
>5 O-levels	Significant at 1% level	Significant at 1% level
A-levels	Significant at 1% level	Significant at 1% level
Post-school qualifications		
Mid-level vocational	Significant at 1% level	Not significant

For a full specification of this model, including non-significant variables included, see Jenkins *et al.* (2002).
[a] The ability measure is an index derived from reading, mathematics and general ability tests taken at age 11.

non-members to have achieved a qualification and private sector employees 4% less so. In contrast, family background and firm size did not have a significant independent effect on the likelihood of obtaining a qualification.[7]

When we look at the factors associated with participation in 2000 (reported by 8% of men in the sample) we find that, in contrast, prior qualifications do not impact on the likelihood of participating in a course. This does not mean education has become irrelevant. Its effect is captured by what is now, for men, the single most important predictor of participation, namely having obtained a qualification during 1991–2000. While some unqualified men were obtaining qualifications in their 30s, it is also the case that the most educated men were far more likely to participate in adult learning during those years and that those who acquired more qualifications then were in turn 11% more likely to be enrolled at the age of 42. Nonetheless, the fact that education level appears to have no additional impact on enrolment in 2000 provides some weak support for the idea that participation shifted somewhat in the desired direction, away from the most educated men, though not to the point where less favourable backgrounds are positively associated with learning.

For women, as Table 3 indicates, the pattern is more complex. For acquisition of qualifications between 1991 and 2000, the impact of both the ability variable and the initial education variables is much greater for women. In most instances the marginal effects are double. Thus, whilst having five or more O-levels increases the probability of acquiring more qualifications by around 9% for men, the impact for women is nearer 19%. Post-school qualifications and family background factors are also significant to a greater degree than for men. Overall, it would seem that succeeding first time around (having better skills, getting more qualifications) is powerfully associated with acquiring qualifications in later life in the case of women.

Women were more likely to be enrolled on qualification-bearing courses in 2000 than were men: 12% rather than 8% reported involvement. As for men, the most powerful predictor of enrolment in 2000 was having previously acquired qualifications, something which is itself again strongly related to prior education level. Those who had acquired one or more between 1991 and 2000 were 11% more likely to be doing so again at the time of interview in 2000. Moreover, in contrast to men, higher levels of school attainment remained independently significant in predicting who was more likely to participate at this point (although the marginal effects were considerably reduced). Overall, participation patterns for women give little indication of any significant move in the direction intended by government policy.

MOTIVATIONS FOR UNDERTAKING LIFELONG LEARNING

As we have seen, the most common form of lifelong learning leading to a qualification is a relatively low level occupational award (see Table 1), which is presumably intended to improve specific occupational skills rather than provide a general 'second chance' educational ladder. This is certainly consistent with recent UK governments' desire to steer learning in directions which will (supposedly) increase workplace productivity. In the next section we discuss whether there is any evidence of such productivity increases actually occurring, but first we examine whether adult learners themselves see their activities in economic terms. The motivation data discussed here relate specifically to award-bearing courses. As one might expect, when asked about motivation with respect to any sort of formal learning or course that had been undertaken, respondents place relatively less emphasis on work-related outcomes (Aldridge & Tuckett, 2002).

When the NCDS respondents were interviewed in 2000, rather little information was, unfortunately, collected about their motives for taking courses. Only if they were actually on a course at the time of interview was their reason for enrolling collected: in this

■ **Table 4** Perceived probable results of current courses leading to qualification: percentage selecting each (NCDS respondents, 2000; n = 1029)

	n	%
Get a new job	225	21.9
Change to a different type of work	190	18.5
Learn new skills for current job	397	38.6
Able to do job better	377	36.6
Get a pay rise in current job	118	11.5
Get promotion in current organization	133	12.9
Get more job satisfaction	301	29.3
Other job-related outcomes	193	18.8
None of these things	176	17.1
Total sample	1029	

case they were shown a card with possible prespecified outcomes from their course and asked which they thought might actually happen (up to a maximum of eight). Table 4 gives responses for the 1029 respondents (the pattern for which is similar for men and women). They are, as can be seen, overwhelmingly job related, although this no doubt reflects, in good part, the nature of the options offered.

Only 20% of respondents claimed that they were on a course for reasons which had nothing to do with work. Almost twice as many saw this type of learning as an opportunity to do a job better or to learn new skills. Significant numbers wanted to facilitate a change in their employment, either to a new job or to a different type of work. However, only around one in ten workers expected their current course to lead to a pay rise in their current job, compared with more than a quarter who expected to get more job satisfaction as a result.

In 1991 (NCDS sweep 5) all respondents had been asked in some detail not only about courses taken in the previous decade (i.e. 1981–1991, between the ages of 23 and 33) but also about their motivation for taking these. Motives for undertaking courses leading to qualifications (as opposed to leisure courses) and access courses were recorded for the two most recent courses taken, with qualification courses taking priority over access courses if the respondent had done both. For each up to three reasons could be specified.

The question was phrased as follows: 'Did you start this course mainly because you needed it for the job you were doing or taking up at the time; because you thought it would lead to a better job later; or mainly for another reason?'. The other reasons were recorded verbatim and coded later. Given this phrasing, a predominance of job-related reasons would probably be expected. However, it is noteworthy that many of the verbatim responses also turned out to be work related.[8] In all, 3830 (33.6%) of the sample reported taking qualification-based or access courses during 1981–1991; 3157 or 82% of these learners gave a work-related reason.

These responses suggest substantial agreement between learners and policy-makers regarding the purpose of certificated adult learning. The form of response may also, however, make adult learners' motivation seem less complex and sophisticated than is really the case. The sensitivity of findings to wording and analysis is highlighted by some more recent data collected in 2004–2005 as part of an ongoing study of employed adults undertaking government supported, qualification-bearing workplace learning (for a full description of this study see Evans & Wolf, 2005a). The sample of 295 is much smaller than the 1000-odd NCDS respondents enrolled on courses in 2000, but unlike them is made up entirely of individuals from the government's priority target group, namely

■ **Table 5** Reasons for undertaking training: adults in government-supported workplace programmes 2004–2005 ($n = 295$)

Reason for undertaking course	One reason for undertaking course (%)	Most important reason for undertaking course (%)
Increase skills for current job	32.5	14.2
Prepare for future job	21.4	8.5
Develop skills in general	53.6	32.9
Increase skills of use at home (e.g. to help children)	15.6	4.7
Other (open-ended)	24.7	

employed adults with few formal qualifications. All were following workplace-based courses in which there was at least some formal 'basic skills' content and all were volunteers. They were asked why they were taking the course and offered four pre-specified possible reasons and the opportunity to volunteer other reasons. As Table 5 shows, work-related reasons, while important, are by no means dominant.

Funding for workplace basic skills instruction is promoted by the government as a way to reduce presumed substantial losses to employers resulting from basic skill deficiencies among workers. A figure often cited is that poor basic skills cost firms around £10,000,000,000 in 1999. [See, for example, the Moser report, which led to the major 'Skills for Life' initiative to improve adult basic skills (DfEE, 1999). See also Ananiadou *et al.* (2003) for a critique of the research base for this figure.]

However, employers involved in the study of workplace programmes which we have just cited appear to be far from convinced either that their workers are suffering from some major skill deficit which reduces their productivity or that the training they receive will have immediate pay-offs for the enterprise. Like their employees, they appear to have a far more nuanced view of the links between training, pay and productivity than do Whitehall policy-makers.

The managers responsible for organizing the programmes were offered a list of 10 predefined possible benefits to the company from the course and asked, first, which were of any relevance to the company and, second, which was seen as the single most important.[9] Of the 20 interviewed to date only two identified acquisition of job-related skills as critical. Overall, managers identified an average of seven options as relevant, but only half included acquisition of job-specific skills in their list. The two managers who identified job-related skills as very important both ran care homes (and were the only ones to do so). Here, new regulations have created demands for higher literacy levels among workers as well as requiring employees to acquire formal qualifications (NVQs) as a condition of the home remaining open.[10]

THE ECONOMIC IMPACT OF LIFELONG LEARNING

To policy-makers the direct link between 'lifelong learning', skills enhancement and prosperity appears self-evident. Given this general assumption, what is surprising is not that many adult learners agree, but that, as we have seen, many have no great expectations of wage or career gains. However, as Coffield pointed out in his summary of findings from the ESRC's large Learning Society Programme (Coffield, 2000, p. 8) there is actually no hard evidence at all to support these firmly held beliefs about the impact of education for adults.

In the case of initial (including initial post-compulsory) education for the young, there is clear evidence that more education benefits the learner. Those with more initial education (e.g. upper secondary certificates, university degrees) have higher earnings and lower unemployment rates. While it may be difficult to tell how much this is a reward for the higher skills acquired through education and how much a result of educated people's actual or presumed higher ability and attractiveness to employers, the financial 'returns' to such education are very clear (OECD, 2004a; Dearden *et al.*, 2005; Machin & Vignoles, 2005).

There is also a moderate amount of good quantitative data on the impact of employer-provided and uncertificated workplace training (largely French, American and Dutch). This is summarized in Ananiadou *et al.* (2004, p. 299), who concluded that, 'In general – though not universally – the literature finds strong evidence of wage effects of training for individuals'. Overall:

> A great deal of the training currently provided by employers has a major direct impact on recipients' wages. . . . It seems reasonable to conclude that these wage gains reflect, at least in part, substantive changes in the productivity and value of the employee to the employer. (Ananiadou *et al.*, 2004, p. 303; see also Barrett & Hovels, 1998)

No such wealth of evidence is available for publicly supported 'lifelong learning', whether in the form of adult education or supported workplace training. With the exception of degrees (to which we return below), little is known nationally or internationally about the economic impact of qualifications gained in adulthood.

The NCDS data set is therefore unusual and valuable in allowing us to examine some of the concrete effects of 'lifelong learning' and, specifically, of acquiring qualifications. If the government is correct, then newly qualified learners will become more productive (by acquiring new skills and also because the qualification 'signal' helps employers put the right people in the right jobs). As a result, they should also be paid more.

As we have seen, the assumption that education and training make people more productive, and so help increase overall wealth, lies at the centre of modern governments' education policy. However, there are likely to be wide variations in the extent to which any productivity increases translate directly into higher wages for the newly skilled or newly qualified (Wolf, 2004). In some cases, notably where employees find it very hard to move to a new job, the benefits may all be captured by the employer. Often, they may be shared, with the employee receiving some increase in remuneration and the employer also receiving benefits, and higher profits.

The less free the labour market, the less one can expect a one-to-one relationship between greater productivity and higher pay. This affects public sector services generally, since pay scales are normally established centrally. More generally, countries differ in the degree to which they insist on a licence to practise various occupations and tie this to officially recognized qualifications or diplomas. Such licensing arrangements are almost universal in the case of doctors, nurses and lawyers, but there are enormous differences between, say, the UK and Germany in the number of regulated occupations which can only be practised by the formally qualified. There are also large differences (e.g. between France and the UK) in whether or not central wage bargaining agreements guarantee wage rises on receipt of additional diplomas.

The more occupations that are licensed, the more likely it is that some diplomas will lead directly to pay benefits (since a formally closed occupation is now open to the diploma-holder). How far such licensing protects the public and ensures high standards and how far it reflects the successful creation of monopolies and costly barriers to entry is an empirical question, with the balance varying from occupation to occupation.

Clearly, however, it further affects one's ability to interpret pay changes as reflections of individual productivity. Nonetheless, pay is, in practice, the only useable measure of productivity available to us. In the current UK labour market we consider that it is likely to bear some, albeit an imperfect, relationship to underlying skills and skill changes. Our governments certainly believe that it is a valid measure and consistently interpret higher graduate wages as clear evidence of the economic benefits of higher education (Wolf, 2002).

We therefore examined the impact on earnings in 2000 of formal qualifications obtained by the NCDS sample between 1991 and 2000. The effect was estimated controlling for: early attainment on academic tests;[11] school qualifications; highest post-school qualifications obtained before 1991; type of school attended; parental education; family circumstances, including parental interest; job characteristics (union membership, firm size, sector). (See Jenkins *et al.*, 2004, for the full specification of this model, including all marginal effects.) Each of these variables has been found to be an important determinant of earnings in one or more previous studies (see, for example, Choudhury, 1994; Rees & Shah, 1995; Green *et al.*, 1996; Hildreth, 1999). For example, since public sector wages are on average lower, we need to allow for sector in our model. Only then can we be sure that we are identifying the wage effects of lifelong learning, as opposed to the (negative) wage effects of being in the public sector.

Table 6 summarizes the main results. They are clear and indeed stark. By and large, there are no widespread wage effects from qualification-bearing learning. Certain sub-groups may benefit. In particular, females who acquired degree level qualifications (general level 4) earned on average 8% more and females and males who gained higher degree (level 5) awards earned 22% and 15% more, respectively, than those who acquired no formal qualifications between ages 33 and 42. For males these high level academic awards are the only ones with significant positive earnings effects. However, women also benefit from level 3 and 4 occupational awards (with average 8% and 9% wage premiums).

■ **Table 6** Impact on wages in 2000 of formal qualifications gained since 1991

Qualification acquired	Males[a] (*n* = 2819)	Females[a] (*n* = 2960)
Academic level 1	Negative effect (5% level)	No significant effects
Academic level 2	No significant effects	No significant effects
Academic level 3	No significant effects	No significant effects
Academic level 4	No significant effects	Positive effect (1% level)
Academic level 5	Positive effect (5% level)	Positive effect (1% level)
Occupational level 1	No significant effects	No significant effects
Occupational level 2	Negative effect (1% level)	Negative effect (5% level)
Occupational level 3	No significant effects	Positive effect (5% level)
Occupational level 4	No significant effects	Positive effect (1% level)
Occupational level 5	No significant effects	No significant effects
Vocationally related level 1	No significant effects	No significant effects
Vocationally related level 2	No significant effects	No significant effects
Vocationally related level 3	No significant effects	No significant effects
Vocationally related level 4	No significant effects	No significant effects
Vocationally related level 5	No significant effects	No significant effects

[a] Base case no qualifications gained.
Estimates control for ability and prior educational attainments, for family background and for job characteristics. Results are for OLS regression of log hourly wages in 2000 on explanatory variables (see Jenkins *et al.*, 2004, for full details of the specification).

There is no evidence at all for earnings gains from the relatively low level qualifications (levels 1 and 2) favoured by current policy. Instead, the data show a significant negative impact on wages associated with acquiring an occupational level 2 certificate (e.g. an NVQ2). For men it is associated with wages that are 10% lower and for women with wages 7% lower than the base case (of no new qualifications post-1991). The lowest level of academic qualification is also associated with lower earnings for men, but so few people took these in their 30s (12 people in the whole sample) that this result must be treated with caution. In contrast, 353 people took level 2 occupational qualifications (and 807 took them at level 1).

One possibility which might explain the apparent lack of impact of qualifications on earnings is that many of the people who acquired low level qualifications already had higher ones. For example, some might be managerial or supervisory workers who acquired low level NVQs as a way of demonstrating up-to-date acquaintance with specific vocational skills or for regulatory reasons. We therefore analysed the impact of qualifications looking only at those respondents who had actually increased their highest level of qualification between 1991 and 2000.

Five per cent of the sample had raised their academic qualification level, 15% their occupational qualification level and 11% had acquired a qualification whose level was higher than their highest one (of any sort) had been in 1991. This compares with 34% who acquired some form of new qualification. Of those with no qualifications in 1991, 17% had acquired one by 2000, mostly at level 1 or 2, while 15% of those whose highest level was level 1 in 1991 had improved on this, and so had 12% of those who were at level 2 in 1991. In comparison, 11% with a level 3 in 1991 had acquired a level 4 or 5 qualification and 8% of those with level 4 acquired a level 5.

We examined whether increasing one's highest level of qualification between 1991 and 2000 earned a wage premium. Because numbers were fairly small we had to merge qualification levels and simply look at whether any increase in level affected wages, using the same full set of control variables as before. We were not able, for example, to compare the effects of raising the highest level from level 1 to level 2 with those of moving from level 3 to level 4.

As so often (Dearden *et al.*, 2005), the effects appear substantially different for men and women. For men, it made no difference whether the qualification obtained from 1991 onwards was at a higher level than the qualifications obtained earlier in life or not: either way there was no significant effect on wages. However, for women, increasing the highest qualification held in the course of the 1990s did have a significantly positive effect on wages, raising them on average five percentage points, while obtaining a qualification without increasing the highest level did not influence wages.[12]

The NCDS data also indicate that acquiring a qualification may be associated with movement from outside the labour force (or being unemployed) into employment.[13] Those out of work at the beginning of the period were more likely to be in work at the end of the period if they had undertaken qualification-bearing courses meanwhile. The causal chain here is not clear or simple: among the group that both obtained a qualification and moved into the labour market between 1991 and 2000, roughly one-third undertook their learning before (re)entry, one-third at the time of entry and one-third after (re)entering employment. However, further analysis using duration models showed that qualifications did have a positive impact on the probability of women making the transition into employment (Jenkins, 2004).

We have already noted the absence of hard evidence on whether 'lifelong learning', and specifically lower level vocational awards, is of general benefit to learners. There have, however, been some studies of degree acquisition which are broadly consistent with our findings and show earning gains, although not always very large ones. Steel and Sausman (1997) compared mature graduates and those who graduated at the 'usual' age of 21.

They concluded that rates of return for more mature graduates were lower than, but quite close to, those obtained by early graduates.[14] Blundell *et al.* (1997) concluded that for the NCDS cohort, men who began their course at over 21 but completed it by age 33 earned a return about seven percentage points lower, while starting after age 21 did not appear to have any detrimental effect on women's earnings at 33. Egerton (2000) used data from the General Household Surveys (GHS) for the years 1983–1992 and defined a mature graduate as one who had obtained a first degree after the age of 25 or who completed a higher degree after the age of 28. She found that mature male graduates earned substantially less than early graduates.[15] Egerton and Parry (2001) also utilised the GHS for the years 1983–1992 to obtain estimates of rates of return for both male and female mature graduates. Mature male graduates had a rate of return of just 1.5% over those with A-levels, while for mature women the figure was 5.6%. In contrast, male early graduates earned rates of return of between 6% and 10% and female early graduates earned returns of between 22% and 27%.

Our results are thus consistent with other research insofar as it exists. They also call into question the basic assumption of current government policy, for they indicate that few types of qualification appear to have any significant impact on earnings. This conclusion is strengthened if one takes into account that individuals who undertake this form of learning may not be randomly selected from the population as a whole. Instead, such lifelong learners may be more able and motivated, factors that are likely to have an independent positive impact on their earnings. The results also need to be set alongside a large body of research that found relatively short spells of unaccredited employer training were often associated with substantial wage gains: a finding which also holds true for the same NCDS cohort which failed to benefit financially from accredited learning (Vignoles *et al.*, 2004).

DISCUSSION AND CONCLUSIONS

Commentators on the education policy of both the Labour government since 1997 and its Conservative predecessors agree that it has been overwhelmingly preoccupied with human capital formation. This restricted set of objectives is also often criticized for ignoring and indeed undermining other key functions of a national education system (see, for example, Coffield, 2002a, b; Wolf, 2002; Lloyd & Payne, 2003a). The findings discussed here suggest strongly that, even on their own terms, current policies are not successful.

Large numbers of adults are obtaining formal qualifications, most of them work oriented in nature. Moreover, while the individuals who undertake this type of lifelong learning are likely to be more educated and skilled, there is also some 'upskilling' of the type prioritized by government policy. A good number of low skilled individuals are achieving new qualifications at higher levels than before. Yet, when we examine the effect of such qualifications on earnings, very little positive impact can be found.

Before discussing these findings with reference to other commentaries and critiques of current policy, it is important to ask whether our findings reflect peculiarly British circumstances or a more general phenomenon. Unfortunately, very little empirical evidence is available for other countries. We know that, as in the UK, adult learners in other developed countries tend to give work-related reasons for undertaking courses (van der Kamp, 1997). We also know that throughout the world short-term training courses for the unemployed have poor outcomes in terms of employment and earnings (see, for example, Heckman, 1999; Grubb & Lazerson, 2004). However, our interest here is in the impact of formal qualifications on the earnings of the adult population as a whole, and particularly those of the low skilled (but predominantly employed) labour force. It would have been particularly interesting to compare UK findings with those of a more regulated labour market, with more formal provision for rewarding additional qualifications.[16] Unfortunately, however, very few countries have longitudinal data from which to evaluate the effects of mainstream adult ('lifelong') learning.

The two countries for which there are relevant comparative data are the USA and Sweden. In the USA a longitudinal survey of adult women found very clear positive wage effects for on-the-job training, in line with many other studies, but no clear positive pay-offs to formal education after the age of 30 (Hill, 2001). The bulk of relevant US evidence, however, relates to the General Educational Development (GED) certificate, which can be gained by high school dropouts and adult immigrants and is formally equivalent to a high school diploma. At present almost 500,000 adults a year obtain the GED.

Labour market data clearly show that the GED certificate does have value and that certificate holders earn more than those without a high school diploma, but also that its worth is significantly less than a 'normal' high school diploma. This difference is best explained not in terms of the cognitive skills or academic attainment associated with the two diplomas, but by employers using the diplomas as signals not merely of skills but also of attitudes and likely work ethic (see especially Cameron & Heckman, 1993; Murnane *et al.*, 1999). The GED evidence confirms that adults who obtain certificates may indeed be viewed as more valuable (and productive) than those who do not. However, it is also important to emphasize that the diploma is generally acquired by young adults (under 30), that it is not a vocational certificate and that it is a single qualification with a long history and very high recognition levels across the country.

Swedish data are more immediately relevant to the UK case because of similarities in government policies between the two countries. The component of Swedish adult education which is most remarked upon and admired abroad is 'popular', unaccredited learning, run in myriad study circles affiliated to study associations and in the 'folk high schools'. But, as Rubenson (1997, p. 72) pointed out, from 1967 onwards increased public funding for the sector was, as a matter of official policy, aimed mainly at developing 'forms of adult education that would effectively contribute to the advancement of the Swedish economy'.[17] Four out of five participants in adult education in the mid-1990s were receiving some form of employer support or sponsorship, which is in turn underpinned by legislation, collective agreements and training allowances from the National Labour-market Board. Rubenson concluded that 'the increase in the total participation rate since the early 1980s is almost exclusively due to more and more people reporting employer-sponsored activities. . . . [This] has radically altered the Swedish landscape of adult education' (Rubenson, 1997, p. 78).

Longitudinal analysis of the impact of participation in Swedish adult sub-degree education indicates rather few economic benefits for participants (Ekstrm, 2003). The adult programmes studied are equivalent (although not identical) to regular upper secondary education and designed as a 'second chance' for adults, and attract around 150,000 participants a year in a population of 9,000,000. For Swedish-born adults participating between 1988 and 1995[18] Ekström found that earnings in 2000 were significantly lower for participating men, on average by 3.5% (at the 1% significance level), compared with non-participants matched with respect to age, prior educational level, marital status, residence, entry date and pre-programme earnings. For Swedish-born women and male immigrants there were no significant programme effects either way. Only for female immigrants was there a positive effect (at the 10% significance level), giving an earnings increase of 9%.

Overall, therefore, the international evidence for 'mainstream' educational qualifications obtained in adult life indicates economic gains for some groups, at a considerably lower level than for young learners, and none at all for others. There is also nothing to suggest that the UK data reflect unique characteristics of the country's labour market, although there are likely to be major differences between it and countries where large numbers of occupations require formal licences to practice.

British, and especially English, governments' enthusiasm for qualification targets meanwhile shows no sign of abating, with 'leisure' and other non-award-bearing courses increasingly squeezed to make room for certificated learning. Can we explain the apparent failure of adult learners to reap any financial rewards for their new certificates and what does it imply for the impact of the next wave of initiatives?

There are several possible and not mutually exclusive explanations for our findings, all of which receive some support from other research evidence and recent commentary. The first is that a substantial proportion of these qualifications are acquired for non-wage- and non-productivity-related reasons. The second is that gaining a qualification may not mean that the holder has actually acquired new skills. The third is that many of the skills being taught and/or certified do not command any wage premium because of a lack of demand for them among employers.

As we have seen, most qualification-bearing learning does appear to be work oriented and taken for job-related reasons. However, one in five NCDS respondents and more than two in five adults on workplace basic skills courses cite non-job factors as the reason for acquiring a qualification in adulthood. If lifelong learning results in skills or knowledge unrelated to individuals' jobs, one would not necessarily expect this to lead to higher productivity or wages for these workers.

The survey evidence may also, as discussed above, overstate the importance of work-related reasons. Furthermore, even when job related, the learning may still not be undertaken with a view to increasing a person's productivity or wages. Our work has suggested that workers in the public sector who are union members and who work in large firms are more likely to obtain occupational qualifications. Their workplaces are also, on average, more subject to regulation relating to concerns over health and safety, quality assurance and public accountability (while wages are set more by collective agreement than by managers' responses to individual productivity).

We may therefore hypothesise that, in at least some cases, individuals and establishments invest in qualifications because of institutional demands to do so, rather than to increase earnings or productivity. Some interesting research by Cooke *et al.* (2000) sheds some light on this. It was carried out as part of the ESRC's Learning Society Programme (1994–2000), which is the major single source of in-depth research on adult learning in the contemporary UK.[19] A number of projects, including Cooke's, examined workplace-based and employer-sponsored learning in sectors where there had either been a major increase in the amount of training or where training had been significantly affected by government policy and initiatives.

Cooke and colleagues focused on three sectors (care, construction and engineering) in which there has been heavy promotion and/or uptake of NVQs in recent years. The care sector has probably been the sector of the labour market in which NVQs have had their greatest effect, both proportionately and in terms of overall numbers affected. This is a sector where there has been very rapid growth in employment and where there was little or no tradition of qualifications for lower skilled workers. Now NVQs are used by government as a way of monitoring quality. Employers must ensure their staff obtain them in order to secure certification and that they continue in operation.

Cooke and co-workers reported in their discussion of care workers, 'In this sector ...NVQs... were not held in high esteem' (Cooke *et al.*, 2000, p. 215). To the extent that such qualifications are used as a way of demonstrating compliance for audit purposes and attest to existing skills rather than developing new ones, they are unlikely to produce significant income effects.[20] This is consistent with our argument that some qualifications, especially occupational ones, may be acquired for reasons other than to improve skills and productivity.

The second, and complementary, explanation as to why there is little wage gain from this type of certified lifelong learning is that the qualifications which adults acquire do not necessarily increase their substantive skills at all.

The National Health Service is a major example of a sector in which training expanded greatly in the 1990s, and research, also for the Learning Society Programme, by Hewison *et al.* (2000) (see also Dowswell *et al.*, 1998) indicated how many of those involved felt they were effectively forced into training rather than opting in, and how rarely they described or experienced the training as involving substantive increases in their skills. Stanton (1996) also documented the harmful effects on quality of the output-related funding regime adopted in the 1990s for government funded training programmes offering lower level vocational qualifications. As noted earlier, a large part of training providers' funding was made available only when and if a trainee acquired formal certification, the said certification also being, for the most part, under the control of the training establishment. Eraut *et al.* (1996) studied NVQs specifically and found major problems with the quality and reliability of the assessment and that the system often failed to encourage systematic skill acquisition by those working for the awards.

In other cases qualifications may indeed signal skills acquisition, but not at levels any higher than, and possibly lower than, equivalent uncertified workers. (So one would not expect the certified to obtain higher wages, other things being equal.) Again, this is illustrated by the research by Cooke *et al.* (2000). They reported a general belief that the construction standards associated with NVQs represent a decline as compared with the past (Cooke *et al.*, 2000, pp. 213–214), while in engineering, those employers (somewhat over half) who had adopted NVQs 'admitted that the qualifications parallel the training they would have been doing anyway' (Cooke *et al.*, 2000, p. 213). If the major difference between certificated and non-certificated workers is not their skill levels or the amount of training they have received, but simply whether their employers have decided, or been persuaded, to introduce a system of formal awards then, at least in the short term, significant wage gains associated with certification are unlikely.

The third possible explanation for the finding of minimal returns to certified lifelong learning is that the skills being acquired are not in demand. In other words, adults are acquiring new skills, signalled by formal certification, but are unable to obtain higher wages because the labour market does not make use of these. There is consequently no increase in economic productivity which can be passed through (in part) to the worker.

This third scenario lies at the heart of current policy debate over UK skills policy, notably as conducted in this journal (see especially Keep, 1997; Coffield, 2002b, 2004; Lloyd & Payne, 2003a, b). Successive governments' emphasis on human capital formation as the core of education policy, in the UK and elsewhere, has been based on the assumption that skill levels are a critical determinant of productivity and growth levels. It has also until recently been assumed, at least implicitly, that intervention on the supply side, to increase skill levels, will feed through into the economy more or less automatically.

Both these assumptions are questionable. Skills are only one consideration among many in firms' (or public sector organizations') strategy making, and a third or fourth order one at that (Keep, 1999). In the UK in those sectors which have shown the greatest growth and improvement in recent years, shortfalls in training and skill development seem to have been insignificant factors in explaining either decline or revival (Owen, 1999). In many parts of the economy there appears to be no obvious 'skill shortage', even at the craft and technician levels most often identified as problematic (Wolf, 2004). The large-scale study of *Work skills in Britain* (Felstead *et al.*, 2002), commissioned by the DfES, indicated that if skills shortages were evaluated in terms of broad categories of skill levels required (levels 1–4, in line with the National Qualifications Framework), the only category for which there were more job openings than people qualified at the relevant level was that of 'no formal qualifications required'.

Of course, this finding is quite consistent with the existence of serious and persistent shortages of specific skills (in, for example, construction or mathematics teaching). It is also entirely compatible with the existence of a 'low-skill equilibrium' (Finegold & Soskice, 1988) in which many firms are able to remain profitable using low skill, low value-added strategies and have no motivation to make the difficult move to a high value-added strategy which would, among many other things, require them to utilize higher skilled workers (see, for example, Skills Task Force, 2000).

This point has been made repeatedly by researchers, arguing that governments' emphasis on the supply of qualifications and skills must lead to disappointment in the absence of a demand for skills from employers. At one level it might seem that this argument has been won. The Performance and Innovation Unit in the Cabinet Office carried out a major review of workforce development issues in 2001, with an academic panel which included some of the foremost academic commentators in this area and duly published a report entitled *In demand: adult skills in the 21st century* (Performance and Innovation Unit, 2001).

The report's emphasis on the importance of fostering demand for skills among employers is echoed in the recent White Paper on skills (DfES, 2005), whose proposals, notably the new National Employer Training Programme, will supposedly increase the extent to which skill formation responds to employer demands and current needs in a direct, firm-specific way. The shift in policy emphasis to the demand side is also reflected in the remit given to the Sector Skills Councils (which have replaced National Training Organizations) and to the overarching Sector Skills Development Agency. However, at this stage it is still unclear how these initiatives might motivate or help companies move to higher skill, higher value-added strategies.

Coffield (2004) has pointed out that it is the supply side (colleges and other providers) that is actually being subjected to increasing regulation and control, while employer activity remains entirely voluntary. But it is also true that employers are not in fact able to request public support for the skills or training that they see as relevant to up-skilling or strategic change. They must operate within the confines of funding tied to particular approved national qualifications. Under current schemes (Employer Training Pilots, ESF, Skills for Life, etc.) the dominant experience of all but the largest employers is not of initiating government funded training. It is of being approached by 'cold-call' providers who offer to deliver and assess training, free, with minimal involvement by the employer or of working with unions to provide a personal development initiative rather than a commercial one (Evans & Wolf, 2005b). There seems to be no reason why the new programmes should be any different. On the contrary, a continuing mismatch between skill provision and employer demand seems likely, with a consequent lack of economic returns to certification.

In summary, it seems likely that all three identified factors play a role in explaining the failure of formal qualifications to deliver earning gains. Such a failure in all probability reflects a corresponding failure to increase productivity to any significant degree. Overall, the evidence discussed here further strengthens criticisms of current government policies in the area of adult education and skills for being seriously misconceived in design and execution.

Our focus here has been on the qualification-bearing awards that continue to receive priority. But in closing, it is worth emphasizing that current policies are not the only option, whether one is concerned with personal development or with human capital formation itself. We have noted, at a number of points, that uncertificated, employer-designed and employer-organized training generally does lead to wage gains for recipients. As for 'leisure courses', as they have come to be known dismissively, their value to society goes well beyond the individual development and self-improvement that previous generations accepted as self-evidently worthwhile. Participation in such learning also shows significant, measurable effects in terms of health, citizenship and life satisfaction (Feinstein & Hammond, 2004). There are clear messages here for policy-makers interested in the welfare of the citizenry and willing to resist the largely pointless pursuit of qualification targets in favour of a more genuinely 'evidence-based' approach.

ACKNOWLEDGEMENTS

Support for the research described here was received from the DfES funded Centre for the Economics of Education and from the ESRC Teaching and Learning Research Programme (grant RES-139-25-0120) and is gratefully acknowledged. Opinions are, of course, entirely the authors' own.

APPENDIX

National qualifications framework

General (Academic)
- Level 5 Higher Degree
- Level 4 Degree
- HE Diploma
- Level 3 A-level
- AS-level
- Scottish Highers
- Scottish Certificate of 6th Year Studies
- Level 2 GCSE grade A*–C
- O levels grade A–C
- O levels grade D–E
- CSE grade 1
- Scottish standard grades 1–3
- Scottish lower or ordinary grades
- Level 1 GCSE grade D–G
- CSEs grades 2–5
- Scottish standard grades 4–5
- Other Scottish school qualification

Vocationally related (Applied)
- Level 4 BTEC Higher Certificate/Diploma
- HNC/HND
- Level 3 Advanced GNVQ
- BTEC National Diploma
- ONC/OND
- Level 2 Intermediate GNVQ
- BTEC First Certificate
- BTEC First Diploma
- Level 1 Foundation GNVQ
- Other GNVQ

Occupational (Vocational)

■ Level 5 NVQ level 5
■ PGCE
■ Professional degree level qualifications
■ Level 4 NVQ level 4, Nursing/paramedic
■ Other teacher training qualification
■ City & Guilds Part 4
■ RSA Higher Diploma
■ Level 3 NVQ level 3
■ City & Guilds Part 3/Final/Advanced Craft
■ RSA Advanced Diploma
■ Pitmans level 3
■ Level 2 NVQ level 2
■ Apprenticeships
■ City & Guilds Part 2/Craft/Intermediate
■ City & Guilds Part 1/Other
■ RSA First Diploma
■ Pitmans level 2
■ Level 1 NVQ level 1
■ Other NVQ
■ Units towards NVQ
■ RSA Certificate/Other
■ Pitmans level 1
■ Other vocational qualifications
■ HGV

NOTES

1. Information on the characteristics of British adult learners is also available from a number of one-off survey sources (see La Valle & Finch, 1999; Hillage *et al.*, 2000), which produce figures ranging from 40% to 70% for participation, over specified time periods, in formal or informal learning.
2. The stability in participation reported by NIACE surveys is slightly surprising, since further education numbers have risen considerably during this period. However, there are a number of possible explanations, including increased participation levels among 16–19-year-olds and more efficient collation and reporting of all enrolments by colleges.
3. Qualifications were coded using the official National Qualifications Framework (referred to earlier). This distinguishes three types of qualifications, each with five levels. The categories used are shown in the Appendix. This framework produces a large number of different categories, but has the advantage of more precisely identifying the type of qualification acquired.
4. Information was also collected, in the 2000 sweep, about courses and training taken that did not lead to qualifications. For an analysis of these data see Vignoles *et al.* (2004).
5. The NIACE sample is typically about half the size of the NCDS one used here, and spread across all relevant age groups.
6. Two per cent of the sample reported acquiring more than four qualifications during the period.
7. Respondents were also less likely to have obtained a qualification if they had attended a school other than a comprehensive, grammar, secondary modern or public. This residual 'other' category (which includes special schools) involved only a small number of respondents.
8. These other reasons were coded as:

1. needed it for the job you were doing at the time;
2. because you thought it would lead to a better job later;
3. to gain promotion;
4. because moving to another job;
5. to improve chances of getting any job;
6. interest/for knowledge/keep mind active;
7. to acquire/improve a specific area of knowledge, ability or skill;
8. as a qualification for other courses;
9. compulsory, as part of current job/arranged by employer;
10. place on course available.

9. Improve job-specific skills; improve 'soft' skills (e.g. team working); offer general development, increase morale; reduce errors; reduce absenteeism; reduce turnover; improve health and safety; increase confidence; help staff be receptive to change.
10. The care home learners in the sample were not enrolled on NVQs at the time of study, but were taking specific literacy qualifications. The sample as a whole included learners working for NVQs of various types.
11. Attainment tests at 11 rather than at 7 were used here since they explained a greater amount of variance.
12. The precise changes associated with a change in highest level of qualification held were as shown in Table N1.

■ **Table N1** Changes associated with a change in highest level of qualification held

	Robust				
	Coefficient	SE	t	p > |t|	
Male wages 2000					
Dependent variable, wage in 2000					
No change in level	−0.033	0.021	−1.590	0.112	
Level increased	−0.004	0.025	−0.160	0.872	
n					3283
r^2					0.222
Female wages 2000					
Dependent variable, wage in 2000					
No change in level	−0.027	0.018	−1.490	0.138	
Level increased	0.048	0.022	2.160	0.031[a]	
n					3454
r^2					0.284

[a] Significant at 5% level.
Control variables were highest school qualification, highest post-school qualification, mathematics and reading age 7 test scores, type of school, mother and father's years of education, father's SES, finances in 1974, union membership, employed in large firm in 2000, employed in public sector in 2000.

13. Eighteen per cent of 1991 respondents were out of the labour market at the time of interview. Seventy-one per cent of this group ($n = 1260$) made the transition into the labour market at some point during the next 10 years. Of this group, 372 also undertook qualification-bearing courses and we looked at the pattern of learning in relation to employment entry. Thirty-three per cent completed the learning and then entered employment, 42% entered employment and then obtained a qualification and 25% did both simultaneously. The pattern for

those who changed jobs and undertook qualification-bearing courses between 1991 and 2000 is very similar.

14. Social returns for male graduates averaged over all age groups were estimated at 6–8%, compared with 7–9% for males who had entered higher education at age 18. The gap in private returns was slightly wider, at 9–11% for all entrants, compared with 11–13% for 18-year-old males.

15. £31 per week less in 1999 prices. Lower mature graduate pay was explained by a number of factors. Social origin was important, with fewer mature graduates having a middle class background. The institution of education also mattered, since mature graduates had a higher probability of having attended a polytechnic (note that the study covers the period up to 1992).

16. The non-UK labour market which is most studied by British training experts is undoubtedly the German. However, the highly structured element of German training, and the one which gives access to regulated employment, is the apprenticeship system, which is for the young and is not normally open to adults. Training for adults is far less regulated and is generally not tied to formal qualifications.

17. Between 1997 and 2002, in response to the Swedish recession, targeted education programmes for the unemployed/disadvantaged groups with relatively low academic skills were also emphasized. The 'Adult Education Initiative' for the unemployed moved large sums of money into adult education programmes rather than vocational training.

18. Participants in the special time-limited Adult Education Initiative directed at the unemployed were excluded from the sample.

19. The full title of the programme was The Learning Society: knowledge and skills for employment. It was funded by the Economic and Social Research Council to a total of £2.5 million and supported 14 projects based in universities and institutions across the UK (see especially Coffield, 2000).

20. If only certificated employees were allowed to practise, and certification opportunities were in short supply, then certificate holders could extract a rent (in the form of higher wages), but this does not appear to be the case in the care sector at present. On the contrary, government programmes underwrite the cost of accreditation and encourage training providers to sign up employers and workers.

REFERENCES

Acemoglu, D. and Pischke, J.-S. (1999) Beyond Becker: training in imperfect labor markets. *Economic Journal* 109, pp. 112–142.

Aldridge, F. and Tuckett, A. (2002) *Two steps forward, one step back.* NIACE, Leicester, UK.

Aldridge, F. and Tuckett, A. (2004) Business as usual? *Adults Learning*, pp. 22–24.

Ananiadou, K., Jenkins, A. and Wolf, A. (2003) *The benefits to employers of raising workplace basic skills levels: a review of the literature.* NRDC, London.

Ananiadou, K., Jenkins, A. and Wolf, A. (2004) Basic skills and workplace learning: what do we actually know about their benefits? *Studies in Continuing Education* 26:(2), pp. 289–308.

Barnett, C. (1986) *The audit of war: the illusion and reality of Britain as a great nation.* Macmillan, London.

Barrett, A. and Hovels, B. (1998) Towards a rate of return on training: assessing the research on the benefit of employer-provided training. *European Journal of Vocational Training* 14, pp. 28–35.

Beinart, S. and Smith, P. (1998) *National adult learning survey 1997.* Department for Education and Employment, Sheffield, UK.

Bélanger, P. and Valdivielso, S. (eds) (1997) *The emergence of learning societies: who participates in adult learning?* Pergamon, Oxford.

Blundell, R., Dearden, L., Goodman, A. and Reed, H. (1997) *Higher education, employment and earnings in Britain.* Institute for Fiscal Studies, London.

Booth, A. L. and Snower, D. G. (eds) (1996) *Acquiring skills.* Cambridge University Press, Cambridge, UK.

Cameron, S. V. and Heckman, J. J. (1993) *Determinants of young male schooling and training choices*, NBER Working Paper 4327. National Bureau of Economic Research, Cambridge, MA.

Choudhury, S. (1994) New evidence on public sector wage differentials. *Journal of Applied Economics* 26:(3), pp. 259–266.

Coffield, F. (ed) (2000) *Differing visions of a learning society* 1. The Policy Press, Bristol, UK.

Coffield, F. (2002a) *A new strategy for learning and skills: beyond 101 initiatives.* Institute of Education, London.

Coffield, F. (2002b) Britain's continuing failure to train: the birth pangs of a new policy. *Journal of Education Policy* 17:(4), pp. 483–498.

Coffield, F. (2004) Alternative routes out of the low skills equilibrium: a rejoinder to Lloyd and Payne. *Journal of Education Policy* 19:(6), pp. 733–740.

Coffield, F., Steer, R., Hodgson, A., Spours, K., Edward, S. and Finlay, I. (2005) A new learning and skills landscape? The central role of the Learning and Skills Council. *Journal of Education Policy* 20:(5), pp. 631–655.

Cooke, P., Cockrill, A., Scott, P., Fitz, J. and Davies, B. (2000) Working and learning in Britain and Germany: findings of a regional study. In Coffield, F. (ed) *Differing visions of a learning society* 1, The Policy Press, Bristol, UK.

Dearden, L., Blundell, R. and Sianesi, B. (2005) Measuring the returns to education. In Machin, S. and Vignoles, A. (eds) *What's the good of education? The economics of education in the UK.* Princeton University Press, Princeton, NJ.

Department of Education and Science (DES) (1991) *Education and training for the 21st century.* HMSO, London.

Department for Education and Employment (DfEE) (1998) *The learning age: a renaissance for a new Britain.* DfEE, London.

Department for Education and Employment (DfEE) (1999) *Improving literacy and numeracy: a fresh start.* DfEE, London.

Department for Education and Skills (DfES) (2003) *21st century skills. Realising our potential.* DfES, London.

Department for Education and Skills (DfES) (2005) *Skills: getting on in business, getting on at work, Overview.* DfES, London.

Dowswell, T., Hewison, J. and Millar, B. (1998) Enrolled nurse conversion: trapped into training. *Journal of Advanced Nursing* 28, pp. 540–547.

Egerton, M. (2000) Pay differentials between early and mature graduate men: the role of state employment. *Journal of Education and Work* 13:(3), pp. 289–306.

Egerton, M. and Parry, G. (2001) Lifelong debt: rates of return to mature study. *Higher Education Quarterly* 55:(1), pp. 4–27.

Ekstrm, E. (2003) *Earning effects of adult secondary education in Sweden*, Working paper 2003:16. Institute for Labour Market Policy Evaluation, Stockholm, Sweden.

Eraut, M., Steadman, S., Trill, J. and Porkes, J. (1996) *The assessment of NVQs*, Research Report 4. University of Sussex Institute of Education, Brighton.

European Commission (1993) *Growth, competitiveness, employment: the challenges and ways forward into the 21st century – White Paper.* European Commission, Brussels – COM (93)700.

European Commission (1995) *White Paper on education and training, teaching and learning – towards the learning society.* European Commission, Brussels – COM (95)590.

Evans, K. and Wolf, A. (2005a) *Enhancing 'Skills for Life': adult basic skills and workplace learning.* Institute of Education, London – Annual Progress Report to ESRC.

Evans, K. and Wolf, A. (2005b) Institute of Education, London.

Feinstein, L. and Hammond, C. (2004) The contribution of adult learning to health and social capital. *Oxford Review of Education* 30:(2), pp. 199–221.

Felstead, A., Gallie, D. and Green, F. (2002) *Work skills in Britain 1986–2001*. DfES and SKOPE, London.

Finegold, D. and Soskice, D. (1988) The failure of training in Britain: analysis and prescription. *Oxford Review of Economic Policy* 4:(3), pp. 21–53.

Gorard, S., Fevre, R. and Rees, G. (1999) The apparent decline of informal learning. *Oxford Review of Education* 25:(4), pp. 437–454.

Gorard, S., Rees, G. and Selwyn, N. (2002) The 'conveyor belt effect': a re-assessment of the impact of National Targets for lifelong learning. *Oxford Review of Education* 28:(1), pp. 75–89.

Green, A., Wolf, A. and Leney, T. (2000) *Convergence and divergence in European education and training systems.* Institute of Education, London.

Green, F., Machin, S. and Manning, A. (1996) The employer size–wage effect: is monopsony the explanation? *Oxford Economic Papers* 48, pp. 433–455.

Grubb, W. N. and Lazerson, M. (2004) *The education gospel: the economic power of schooling.* Harvard University Press, Cambridge, MA.

Heckman, J. (1999) *Policies to foster human capital*, Working Paper 7288. National Bureau of Economic Research, Cambridge, MA.

Hewison, J., Dowswell, T. and Miller, B. (2000) Changing patterns of training provision in the National Health Service: an overview. In Coffield, F. (ed) *Differing visions of a learning society* 1. The Policy Press, Bristol, UK.

Hildreth, A. (1999) What has happened to the union wage differential in Britain in the 1990s? *Oxford Bulletin of Economics and Statistics* 61:(1), pp. 5–32.

Hill, E. T. (2001) Post-school age training among women: training methods and labour market outcomes at older ages. *Economics of Education Review* 20, pp. 181–191.

Hillage, J., Uden, T., Aldridge, F. and Eccles, J. (2000) *Adult learning in England: a review.* Institute for Employment Studies, Brighton, UK – Report 369.

House of Commons Education and Skills Committee (2005) *National skills strategy: sixth report of session 2004–5. Volume II, oral and written evidence*, p. 10. House of Commons, London.

Jenkins, A. (2004) *Women, lifelong learning and employment*, Discussion Paper 39. Centre for the Economics of Education, London.

Jenkins, A. and Wolf, A. (2004) *Regional variations in adult learning and vocational training: evidence from NCDS and WERS 98*, Discussion Paper 37. Centre for the Economics of Education, London.

Jenkins, A. and Wolf, A. (2005) Employers' selection decisions: the role of qualifications and tests. In Machin, S. and Vignoles, A. (eds) *What's the good of education? The economics of education in the UK.* Princeton University Press, Princeton, NJ.

Jenkins, A., Vignoles, A., Wolf, A. and Galindo-Rueda, F. (2002) *The determinants and effects of lifelong learning*, Discussion Paper 19. Centre for the Economics of Education, London.

Jenkins, A., Vignoles, A., Wolf, A. and Galindo-Rueda, F. (2004) The determinants and labour market effects of lifelong learning. *Applied Economics* 35, pp. 1711–1721.

Jessup, G. (1991) *Outcomes: NVQs and the emerging model of education and training.* Falmer, London.

Keep, E. (1997) 'There's no such thing as society . . .': some problems with an individual approach to creating a Learning Society. *Journal of Education Policy* 12:(6), pp. 457–471.

Keep, E. (1999) UK's VET policy and the 'Third Way': following a high skills trajectory or running up a dead end street? *Journal of Education and Work* 12:(3), pp. 323–346.

La Valle, I. and Finch, S. (1999) *Pathways in adult learning research*, Report RR 137. Department for Education and Employment, London.

Lloyd, C. and Payne, J. (2003a) The political economy of skill and the limits of educational policy. *Journal of Education Policy* 18:(1), pp. 85–107.

Lloyd, C. and Payne, J. (2003b) Forget birth pains, we haven't got past the conception stage yet. A reply to Frank Coffield's 'Britain's continuing failure to train: the birth pangs of a new policy'. *Journal of Education Policy* 18:(5), pp. 563–568.

Machin, S. and Vignoles, A. (eds) (2005) *What's the good of education? The economics of education in the UK.* Princeton University Press, Princeton, NJ.

Mager, C., Robinson, P., Fletcher, M., Stanton, G., Perry, A. and Westwood, A. (2000) *The new learning market.* IPPR and FEDA, London.

Meadows, P. and Metcalf, H. (2005) *Evaluation of the impact of 'Skills for Life' learning. Report on sweep 1.* DfES, London.

Murnane, R. J., Willett, J. B. and Tyler, J. H. (1999) *Who benefits from obtaining a GED? Evidence from high school and beyond*, Working Paper Series 7172. National Bureau of Economic Research, Cambridge, MA.

National Skills Task Force (2000) *Skills for all: proposals for a national skills agenda.* DfEE, London.

Office for National Statistics (2005) *Labour force survey.* Office for National Statistics, London.

Organisation for Economic Cooperation and Development (OECD) (2000) *Where are the resources for lifelong learning?* OECD, Paris.

Organisation for Economic Cooperation and Development (OECD) (2003) *Beyond rhetoric: adult learning policies and practices.* OECD, Paris.

Organisation for Economic Cooperation and Development (OECD) (2004a) *Education at a glance: OECD indicators.* OECD, Paris.

Organisation for Economic Cooperation and Development (OECD) (2004b) *Policy brief: lifelong learning.* OECD, Paris.

Owen, G. (1999) *From Empire to Europe: the decline and revival of British industry since the Second World War.* HarperCollins, London.

Performance and Innovation Unit (PIU) (2001) *In demand: adult skills in the 21st century.* PIU, London.

Prais, S. J. (1995) *Productivity, education and training. An international perspective.* Cambridge University Press, Cambridge, UK.

Ramsden, M., Bennet, R. and Fuller, C. (2004) The Learning and Skills Council and the institutional infrastructure for post-16 education and training: an initial assessment. *Journal of Education and Work* 17:(4), pp. 397–420.

Rees, H. and Shah, A. (1995) Public–private sector wage differentials in the UK. *Manchester School* 63:(1), pp. 52–68.

Rubenson, K. (1997) Sweden: the impact of the politics of participation. In Belanger, P. and Valdivielso, S. (eds) *The emergence of learning societies: who participates in adult learning?* Pergamon, Oxford.

Sanderson, M. (1999) *Education and economic decline in Britain 1870 to the 1990s.* Cambridge University Press, Cambridge, UK.

Sargant, N. (2000) *The learning divide revisited: a report on the findings of a UK-wide survey on adult participation in education and learning.* National Institute of Adult Continuing Education, Leicester, UK.

Skills Task Force (2000) *Skills for all: research report from the National Skills Task Force.* DfEE, London.

Stanton, G. (1996) *Output related funding and the quality of education and training.* International Centre for Research on Assessment, Institute of Education, London.

Steel, J. and Sausman, C. (1997) *The contribution of graduates to the economy – rates of return.* HMSO, London – (Dearing Committee) Report no 7.

Taylor, R. (2005) Lifelong learning and the Labour governments 1997–2004. *Oxford Review of Education* 31:(1), pp. 101–118.

van der Kamp, M. (1997) The Netherlands: impacts of a new policy environment. In Belanger, P. and Valdivielso, S. (eds) *The emergence of learning societies: who participates in adult learning?* Pergamon, Oxford.

Vignoles, A., Galindo-Rueda, F. and Feinstein, L. (2004) The labour market impact of adult education and training: a cohort analysis. *Scottish Journal of Political Economy* 51, pp. 266–280.

Wolf, A. (2001) Qualifications and assessment. In Aldrich, R. (ed) *A century of education*, pp. 206–227. RoutledgeFalmer, London.

Wolf, A. (2002) *Does education matter? Myths about education and economic growth*. Penguin, London.

Wolf, A. (2004) Education and economic performance: simplistic theories and the policy consequences. *Oxford Review of Economic Policy* 20:(2), pp. 315–333.

11

EDUCATION AS A SOCIAL FUNCTION

John Dewey

INTRODUCTION

John Dewey (1859–1952) was a philosopher, one of whose principal considerations was pragmatism in which knowledge arose as the individual interacts with his or her environment. He was interested in the connections between education and civil society and proposed not just engagement by formal means such as voting but by developing a well-informed population who would be able to understand and act in society. In this extract from his key work *Democracy and Education*, Dewey discusses the nature of environment, the links that exist between education and the environment and the ways in which educators can act to ensure max- imum benefit for learners. Dewey became known as a 'progressive' (this is not the same as saying that Dewey would have accepted all that was said and done in his name) advocating child-centred experiential education. His ideas about the connection between education and civil society and the importance of environment rather than didactic teaching of knowledge had a powerful influence on many educators. He was active on a number of fronts: he influenced the development of what became the National Association for the Advancement of Colored People, supported women's rights, and led the Dewey Commission which condemned Stalin's actions against Trotsky.

KEY QUESTIONS

1. What is 'child-centred education'?
2. How does it differ from supposedly 'traditional' education?
3. What are the potential advantages and limitations to 'child-centred education'?
4. Do you think that schools should be concerned with preparing learners to understand and be active within civil society or would this be a negative form of social engineering?

FURTHER READING

There are several good overviews of Dewey's work, which include Pring, R. (2008) *John Dewey*. Continuum Library of Educational Thought (4) (Continuum, London) and Ryan, A. (1997) *John Dewey And the High Tide of American Liberalism* (W. W. Norton & Company, New York). An argument against the supposedly Dewey-influenced excesses of liberal education can be seen in Bloom, A. (1987) *The Closing of the American Mind* (Simon and Schuster, New York).

This Reading links with Chapter 11 and Debate 1 of *The Routledge Education Studies Text- book*.

THE NATURE AND MEANING OF ENVIRONMENT

We have seen that a community or social group sustains itself through continuous self-renewal, and that this renewal takes place by means of the educational growth of the immature members of the group. By various agencies, unintentional and designed, a society transforms uninitiated and seemingly alien beings into robust trustees of its own resources and ideals. Education is thus a fostering, a nurturing, a cultivating, process. All of these words mean that it implies attention to the conditions of growth. We also speak of rearing, raising, bringing up – words which express the difference of level which education aims to cover. Etymologically, the word education, means just a process of leading or bringing up. When we have the outcome of the process in mind, we speak of education as shaping, forming, molding activity – that is, a shaping into the standard form of social activity. In this chapter we are concerned with the general features of the *way* in which a social group brings up its immature members into its own social form.

Since what is required is a transformation of the quality of experience till it partakes in the interests, purposes, and ideas current in the social group, the problem is evidently not one of mere physical forming. Things can be physically transported in space; they may be bodily conveyed. Beliefs and aspirations cannot be physically extracted and inserted. How then are they communicated? Given the impossibility of direct contagion or literal inculcation, our problem is to discover the method by which the young assimilate the point of view of the old, or the older bring the young into like-mindedness with themselves.

The answer, in general formulation, is: By means of the action of the environment in calling out certain responses. The required beliefs cannot be hammered in; the needed attitudes cannot be plastered on. But the particular medium in which an individual exists leads him to see and feel one thing rather than another; it leads him to have certain plans in order that he may act successfully with others; it strengthens some beliefs and weakens others as a condition of winning the approval of others. Thus it gradually produces in him a certain system of behavior, a certain disposition of action. The words "environment," "medium" denote something more than surroundings which encompass an individual. They denote the specific *continuity* of the surroundings with his own active tendencies. An inanimate being is, of course, continuous with its surroundings; but the environing circumstances do not, save metaphorically, constitute an environment. For the inorganic being is not *concerned* in the influences which affect it. On the other hand, some things which are remote in space and time from a living creature, especially a human creature, may form his environment even more truly than some of the things close to him. The things with which a man *varies* are his genuine environment. Thus the activities of the astronomer vary with the stars at which he gazes or about which he calculates. Of his immediate surroundings, his telescope is most intimately his environment. The environment of an antiquarian, as an antiquarian, consists of the remote epoch of human life with which he is concerned, and the relics, inscriptions, etc., by which he establishes connections with that period.

In brief, the environment consists of those conditions that promote or hinder, stimulate or inhibit, the *characteristic* activities of a living being. Water is the environment of a fish because it is necessary to the fish's activities – to its life. The north pole is a significant element in the environment of an arctic explorer, whether he succeeds in reaching it or not, because it defines his activities, makes them what they distinctively are. Just because life signifies not bare passive existence (supposing there is such a thing), but a way of acting, environment or medium signifies what enters into this activity as a sustaining or frustrating condition.

THE SOCIAL ENVIRONMENT

A being whose activities are associated with others has a social environment. What he does and what he can do depend upon the expectations, demands, approvals, and condemnations of others. A being connected with other beings cannot perform his own activities without taking the activities of others into account. For they are the indispensable conditions of the realization of his tendencies. When he moves he stirs them and reciprocally. We might as well try to imagine a business man doing business, buying and selling, all by himself, as to conceive it possible to define the activities of an individual in terms of his isolated actions. The manufacturer moreover is as truly socially guided in his activities when he is laying plans in the privacy of his own countinghouse as when he is buying his raw material or selling his finished goods. Thinking and feeling that have to do with action in association with others is as much a social mode of behavior as is the most overt cooperative or hostile act.

What we have more especially to indicate is how the social medium nurtures its immature members. There is no great difficulty in seeing how it shapes the external habits of action. Even dogs and horses have their actions modified by association with human beings; they form different habits because human beings are concerned with what they do. Human beings control animals by controlling the natural stimuli which influence them; by creating a certain environment in other words. Food, bits and bridles, noises, vehicles, are used to direct the ways in which the natural or instinctive responses of horses occur. By operating steadily to call out certain acts, habits are formed which function with the same uniformity as the original stimuli. If a rat is put in a maze and finds food only by making a given number of turns in a given sequence, his activity is gradually modified till he habitually takes that course rather than another when he is hungry.

Human actions are modified in a like fashion. A burnt child dreads the fire; if a parent arranged conditions so that every time a child touched a certain toy he got burned, the child would learn to avoid that toy as automatically as he avoids touching fire. So far, however, we are dealing with what may be called *training* in distinction from educative teaching. The changes considered are in outer action rather than in mental and emotional dispositions of behavior. The distinction is not, however, a sharp one. The child might conceivably generate in time a violent antipathy, not only to that particular toy, but to the class of toys resembling it. The aversion might even persist after he had forgotten about the original burns; later on he might even invent some reason to account for his seemingly irrational antipathy. In some cases, altering the external habit of action by changing the environment to affect the stimuli to action will also alter the mental disposition concerned in the action. Yet this does not always happen; a person trained to dodge a threatening blow, dodges automatically with no corresponding thought or emotion. We have to find, then, some differentia of training from education.

A clue may be found in the fact that the horse does not really share in the social use to which his action is put. Someone else uses the horse to secure a result which is advantageous by making it advantageous to the horse to perform the act – he gets food, etc. But the horse, presumably, does not get any new interest. He remains interested in food, not in the service he is rendering. He is not a partner in a shared activity. Were he to become a copartner, he would, in engaging in the conjoint activity, have the same interest in its accomplishment which others have. He would share their ideas and emotions.

Now in many cases – too many cases – the activity of the immature human being is simply played upon to secure habits which are useful. He is trained like an animal rather than educated like a human being. His instincts remain attached to their original objects of pain or pleasure. But to get happiness or to avoid the pain of failure he has to act in a way agreeable to others. In other cases, he really shares or participates in the common activity. In this case, his original impulse is modified. He not merely acts in a way agreeing with the actions of others, but, in so acting, the same ideas and emotions are aroused in him that animate the others. A tribe, let us say, is warlike. The successes for which it strives, the achievements upon which it sets store, are connected with fighting and victory. The presence of this medium incites bellicose exhibitions in a boy, first in games, then in fact when he is strong enough. As he fights he wins approval and advancement; as he refrains, he is disliked, ridiculed, shut out from favorable recognition. It is not surprising that his original belligerent tendencies and emotions are strengthened at the expense of others, and that his ideas turn to things connected with war. Only in this way can he become a fully recognized member of his group. Thus his mental habitudes are gradually assimilated to those of his group.

If we formulate the principle involved in this illustration, we shall perceive that the social medium neither implants certain desires and ideas directly, nor yet merely establishes certain purely muscular habits of action, like "instinctively" winking or dodging a blow. Setting up conditions which stimulate certain visible and tangible ways of acting is the first step. Making the individual a sharer or partner in the associated activity so that he feels its success as his success, its failure as his failure, is the completing step. As soon as he is possessed by the emotional attitude of the group, he will be alert to recognize the special ends at which it aims and the means employed to secure success. His beliefs and ideas, in other words, will take a form similar to those of others in the group. He will also achieve pretty much the same stock of knowledge since that knowledge is an ingredient of his habitual pursuits.

The importance of language in gaining knowledge is doubtless the chief cause of the common notion that knowledge may be passed directly from one to another. It almost seems as if all we have to do to convey an idea into the mind of another is to convey a sound into his ear. Thus imparting knowledge gets assimilated to a purely physical process. But learning from language will be found, when analyzed, to confirm the principle just laid down. It would probably be admitted with little hesitation that a child gets the idea of, say, a hat by using it as other persons do; by covering the head with it, giving it to others to wear, having it put on by others when going out, etc. But it may be asked how this principle of shared activity applies to getting through speech or reading the idea of, say, a Greek helmet, where no direct use of any kind enters in. What shared activity is there in learning from books about the discovery of America?

Since language tends to become the chief instrument of learning about many things, let us see how it works. The baby begins of course with mere sounds, noises, and tones having no meaning, expressing, that is, no idea. Sounds are just one kind of stimulus to direct response, some having a soothing effect, others tending to make one jump, and so on. The sound h-a-t would remain as meaningless as a sound in Choctaw, a seemingly inarticulate grunt, if it were not uttered in connection with an action which is participated in by a number of people. When the mother is taking the infant out of doors, she says "hat" as she puts something on the baby's head. Being taken out becomes an interest to the child; mother and child not only go out with each other physically, but both are *concerned* in the going out; they enjoy it in common. By conjunction with the other factors in activity the sound "hat" soon gets the same meaning for the child that it has for the parent; it becomes a sign of the activity into which it enters. The bare fact that language consists of sounds which are *mutually intelligible* is enough of itself to show that its meaning depends upon connection with a shared experience.

In short, the sound h-a-t gains meaning in precisely the same way that the thing "hat" gains it, by being used in a given way. And they acquire the same meaning with the child which they have with the adult because they are used in a common experience by both. The guarantee for the same manner of use is found in the fact that the thing and the sound are first employed in a *joint* activity, as a means of setting up an active connection between the child and a grown up. Similar ideas or meanings spring up because both persons are engaged as partners in an action where what each does depends upon and influences what the other does. If two savages were engaged in a joint hunt for game, and a certain signal meant "move to the right" to the one who uttered it, and "move to the left" to the one who heard it, they obviously could not successfully carry on their hunt together. Understanding one another means that objects, including sounds, have the same value for both with respect to carrying on a common pursuit.

After sounds have got meaning through connection with other things employed in a joint undertaking, they can be used in connection with other like sounds to develop new meanings, precisely as the things for which they stand are combined. Thus the words in which a child learns about, say, the Greek helmet originally got a meaning (or were understood) by use in an action having a common interest and end. They now arouse a new meaning by inciting the one who hears or reads to rehearse imaginatively the activities in which the helmet has its use. For the time being, the one who understands the words "Greek helmet" becomes mentally a partner with those who used the helmet. He engages, through his imagination, in a shared activity. It is not easy to get the *full* meaning of words. Most persons probably stop with the idea that "helmet" denotes a queer kind of headgear a people called the Greeks once wore. We conclude, accordingly, that the use of language to convey and acquire ideas is an extension and refinement of the principle that things gain meaning by being used in a shared experience or joint action; in no sense does it contravene that principle. When words do not enter as factors into a shared situation, either overtly or imaginatively, they operate as pure physical stimuli, not as having a meaning or intellectual value. They set activity running in a given groove, but there is no accompanying conscious purpose or meaning. Thus, for example, the plus sign may be a stimulus to perform the act of writing one number under another and adding the numbers, but the person performing the act will operate much as an automaton would unless he realizes the meaning of what he does.

THE SOCIAL MEDIUM AS EDUCATIVE

Our net result thus far is that social environment forms the mental and emotional disposition of behavior in individuals by engaging them in activities that arouse and strengthen certain impulses, that have certain purposes and entail certain consequences. A child growing up in a family of musicians will inevitably have whatever capacities he has in music stimulated, and, relatively, stimulated more than other impulses which might have been awakened in another environment. Save as he takes an interest in music and gains a certain competency in it, he is "out of it"; he is unable to share in the life of the group to which he belongs. Some kinds of participation in the life of those with whom the individual is connected are inevitable; with respect to them, the social environment exercises an educative or formative influence unconsciously and apart from any set purpose.

In savage and barbarian communities, such direct participation (constituting the indirect or incidental education of which we have spoken) furnishes almost the sole influence for rearing the young into the practices and beliefs of the group. Even in present-day societies, it furnishes the basic nurture of even the most insistently schooled youth. In accord with the interests and occupations of the group, certain things become objects of high esteem; others of aversion. Association does not create impulses or affection and dislike, but it furnishes the objects to which they attach themselves. The way our group or class does things tends to determine the proper objects of attention, and thus to prescribe the directions and limits of observation and memory. What is strange or foreign (that is to say outside the activities of the groups) tends to be morally forbidden and intellectually suspect. It seems almost incredible to us, for example, that things which we know very well could have escaped recognition in past ages. We incline to account for it by attributing congenital stupidity to our forerunners and by assuming superior native intelligence on our own part. But the explanation is that their modes of life did not call for attention to such facts, but held their minds riveted to other things. Just as the senses require sensible objects to stimulate them, so our powers of observation, recollection, and imagination do not work spontaneously, but are set in motion by the demands set up by current social occupations. The main texture of disposition is formed, independently of schooling, by such influences. What conscious, deliberate teaching can do is at most to free the capacities thus formed for fuller exercise, to purge them of some of their grossness, and to furnish objects which make their activity more productive of meaning.

While this "unconscious influence of the environment" is so subtle and pervasive that it affects every fiber of character and mind, it may be worthwhile to specify a few directions in which its effect is most marked. First, the habits of language. Fundamental modes of speech, the bulk of the vocabulary, are formed in the ordinary intercourse of life, carried on not as a set means of instruction but as a social necessity. The babe acquires, as we well say, the *mother* tongue. While speech habits thus contracted may be corrected or even displaced by conscious teaching, yet, in times of excitement, intentionally acquired modes of speech often fall away, and individuals relapse into their really native tongue. Secondly, manners. Example is notoriously more potent than precept. Good manners come, as we say, from good breeding or rather are good breeding; and breeding is acquired by habitual action, in response to habitual stimuli, not by conveying information. Despite the never ending play of conscious correction and instruction, the surrounding atmosphere and spirit is in the end the chief agent in forming manners. And manners are but minor morals. Moreover, in major morals, conscious instruction is likely to be efficacious only in the degree in which it falls in with the general "walk and conversation" of those who constitute the child's social environment. Thirdly, good taste and aesthetic appreciation. If the eye is constantly greeted by harmonious objects, having elegance of form and color, a standard of taste naturally grows up. The effect of a tawdry, unarranged, and overdecorated environment works for the deterioration of taste, just as meager and barren surroundings starve out the desire for beauty. Against such odds, conscious teaching can hardly do more than convey second-hand information as to what others think. Such taste never becomes spontaneous and personally engrained, but remains a labored reminder of what those think to whom one has been taught to look up. To say that the deeper standards of judgments of value are framed by the situations into which a person habitually enters is not so much to mention a fourth point, as it is to point out a fusion of those already mentioned. We rarely recognize the extent in which our conscious estimates of what is worth while and what is not, are due to standards of which we are not conscious at all. But in general it may be said that the things which we take for granted without inquiry or reflection are just the things which determine our conscious thinking and decide our conclusions. And these habitudes which lie below the level of reflection are just those which have been formed in the constant give and take of relationship with others.

THE SCHOOL AS A SPECIAL ENVIRONMENT

The chief importance of this foregoing statement of the educative process which goes on willynilly is to lead us to note that the only way in which adults consciously control the land of education which the immature get is by controlling the environment in which they act, and hence think and feel. We never educate directly, but indirectly by means of the environment. Whether we permit chance environments to do the work, or whether we design environments for the purpose makes a great difference. And any environment is a chance environment so far as its educative influence is concerned unless it has been deliberately regulated with reference to its educative effect. An intelligent home differs from an unintelligent one chiefly in that the habits of life and intercourse which prevail are chosen, or at least colored, by the thought of their bearing upon the development of children. But schools remain, of course, the typical instance of environments framed with express reference to influencing the mental and moral disposition of their members.

Roughly speaking, they come into existence when social traditions are so complex that a considerable part of the social store is committed to writing and transmitted through written symbols. Written symbols are even more artificial or conventional than spoken; they cannot be picked up in accidental intercourse with others. In addition, the written form tends to select and record matters which are comparatively foreign to everyday life. The achievements accumulated from generation to generation are deposited in it even though some of them have fallen temporarily out of use. Consequently as soon as a community depends to any considerable extent upon what lies beyond its own territory and its own immediate generation, it must rely upon the set agency of schools to insure adequate transmission of all its resources. To take an obvious illustration: The life of the ancient Greeks and Romans has profoundly influenced our own, and yet the ways in which they affect us do not present themselves on the surface of our ordinary experiences. In similar fashion, peoples still existing, but remote in space, British, Germans, Italians, directly concern our own social affairs, but the nature of the interaction cannot be understood without explicit statement and attention. In precisely similar fashion, our daily associations cannot be trusted to make clear to the young the part played in our activities by remote physical energies, and by invisible structures. Hence a special mode of social intercourse is instituted, the school, to care for such matters.

This mode of association has three functions sufficiently specific, as compared with ordinary associations of life, to be noted. First, a complex civilization is too complex to be assimilated *in toto*. It has to be broken up into portions, as it were, and assimilated piecemeal, in a gradual and graded way. The relationships of our present social life are so numerous and so interwoven that a child placed in the most favorable position could not readily share in many of the most important of them. Not sharing in them, their meaning would not be communicated to him, would not become a part of his own mental disposition. There would be no seeing the trees because of the forest. Business, politics, art, science, religion, would make all at once a clamor for attention; confusion would be the outcome. The first office of the social organ we call the school is to provide a simplified environment. It selects the features which are fairly fundamental and capable of being responded to by the young. Then it establishes a progressive order, using the factors first acquired as means of gaining insight into what is more complicated.

In the second place, it is the business of the school environment to eliminate, so far as possible, the unworthy features of the existing environment from influence upon mental habitudes. It establishes a purified medium of action. Selection aims not only at simplifying but at weeding out what is undesirable. Every society gets encumbered with what is trivial, with dead wood from the past, and with what is positively perverse. The school has the duty of omitting such things from the environment which it supplies, and thereby doing what it can to counteract their influence in the ordinary social environment. By selecting the best for its exclusive use, it strives to reënforce the power of this best. As a society becomes more enlightened, it realizes that it is responsible *not* to transmit and conserve the whole of its existing achievements, but only such as make for a better future society. The school is its chief agency for the accomplishment of this end.

In the third place, it is the office of the school environment to balance the various elements in the social environment, and to see to it that each individual gets an opportunity to escape from the limitations of the social group in which he was born, and to come into living contact with a broader environment. Such words as "society" and "community" are likely to be misleading, for they have a tendency to make us think there is a single thing corresponding to the single word. As a matter of fact, a modern society is many societies more or less loosely connected. Each household with its immediate extension of friends makes a society; the village or street group of playmates is a community; each business group, each club, is another. Passing beyond these more intimate groups, there is in a country like our own a variety of races, religious affiliations, economic divisions. Inside the modern city, in spite of its nominal political unity, there are probably more communities, more differing customs, traditions, aspirations, and forms of government or control, than existed in an entire continent at an earlier epoch.

Each such group exercises a formative influence on the active dispositions of its members. A clique, a club, a gang, a Fagin's household of thieves, the prisoners in a jail, provide educative environments for those who enter into their collective or conjoint activities, as truly as a church, a labor union, a business partnership, or a political party. Each of them is a mode of associated or community life, quite as much as is a family, a town, or a state. There are also communities whose members have little or no direct contact with one another, like the guild of artists, the republic of letters, the members of the professional learned class scattered over the face of the earth. For they have aims in common, and the activity of each member is directly modified by knowledge of what others are doing.

In the olden times, the diversity of groups was largely a geographical matter. There were many societies, but each, within its own territory, was comparatively homogeneous. But with the development of commerce, transportation, intercommunication, and emigration, countries like the United States are composed of a combination of different groups with different traditional customs. It is this situation which has, perhaps more than any other one cause, forced the demand for an educational institution which shall provide something like a homogeneous and balanced environment for the young. Only in this way can the centrifugal forces set up by juxtaposition of different groups within one and the same political unit be counteracted. The intermingling in the school of youth of different races, differing religions, and unlike customs creates for all a new and broader environment. Common subject matter accustoms all to a unity of outlook upon a broader horizon than is visible to the members of any group while it is isolated. The assimilative force of the American public school is eloquent testimony to the efficacy of the common and balanced appeal.

The school has the function also of coordinating within the disposition of each individual the diverse influences of the various social environments into which he enters. One code prevails in the family; another, on the street; a third, in the workshop or store; a fourth, in the religious association. As a person passes from one of the environments to another, he is subjected to antagonistic pulls, and is in danger of being split into a being having different standards of judgment and emotion for different occasions. This danger imposes upon the school a steadying and integrating office.

SUMMARY

The development within the young of the attitudes and dispositions necessary to the continuous and progressive life of a society cannot take place by direct conveyance of beliefs, emotions, and knowledge. It takes place through the intermediary of the environment. The environment consists of the sum total of conditions which are concerned in the execution of the activity characteristic of a living being. The social environment consists of all the activities of fellow beings that are bound up in the carrying on of the activities of any one of its members. It is truly educative in its effect in the degree in which an individual shares or participates in some conjoint activity. By doing his share in the associated activity, the individual appropriates the purpose which actuates it, becomes familiar with its methods and subject matters, acquires needed skill, and is saturated with its emotional spirit.

The deeper and more intimate educative formation of disposition comes, without conscious intent, as the young gradually partake of the activities of the various groups to which they may belong. As a society becomes more complex, however, it is found necessary to provide a special social environment which shall especially look after nurturing the capacities of the immature. Three of the more important functions of this special environment are: simplifying and ordering the factors of the disposition it is wished to develop; purifying and idealizing the existing social customs; creating a wider and better balanced environment than that by which the young would be likely, if left to themselves, to be influenced.

CURRICULUM REFORM AND CURRICULUM THEORY

A case of historical amnesia

Ivor F. Goodson

INTRODUCTION

Ivor Goodson is Professor of Learning Theory at the Education Research Centre, University of Brighton. He has produced a series of books which aim to explore the curriculum as a site of social contestation and social distribution. The series 'Studies in Curriculum History' was commissioned by Falmer Press in 1984 and led to the publication of over 20 books which established the history and sociology of curriculum construction. His own contributions to the series elaborate the relationship between curriculum and society. In this chapter, Goodson introduces us to the historical study of the school curriculum and draws out some of the implications of such study for the teaching profession and the construction of the subjects that are taught and learnt in our schools. Goodson reviews the research on the historical patterns, followed by specific subjects in the English secondary school curriculum and compares this review with work done in the history of French psychiatric knowledge in the nineteenth century.

KEY QUESTIONS

1. How do subjects gain academic respectability in the school curriculum?
2. Explain how Goodson offers new possibilities for curriculum development and reform in a post-modernist age.

FURTHER READING

The series 'Studies in Curriculum History' published by Falmer Press is a good start for anyone interested in the history of curriculum development in English education. Goodson has written a number of books in the series including: *Social Histories of the School Curriculum*; *Defining the Curriculum*; *The Making of Curriculum*; *Studying School Subjects* and *Subject Knowledge*.

This Reading links with Chapters 10, 11, 15 and 16 of *The Routledge Education Studies Textbook*.

INTRODUCTION

The school curriculum is a social artifact, conceived of and made for deliberate human purposes. It is therefore a supreme paradox that in many accounts of schooling the written curriculum, this most manifest of social constructions, has been treated as a 'given'. Moreover, the problem has been compounded by the fact that it has often been treated as a neutral given embedded in an otherwise meaningful and complex situation. Yet in our own schooling we know very well that while we loved some subjects, topics or lessons, we hated others. Some we learnt easily and willingly, others we rejected wholeheartedly. Sometimes the variable was the teacher, or the time, or the room, or us, but often it was the form or content of the curriculum itself. Of course, beyond such individualistic responses there were, and are, significant collective responses to curriculum and when patterns can be discerned they suggest this is far from a 'neutral' factor.

Why then, has so little attention been given to the making of curriculum? We have a social construction which sits at the heart of the process by which we educate our children. Yet in spite of the patchy exhortations of sociologists, sociologists of knowledge in particular, one looks in vain for serious study of the process of social construction that emanates as curriculum. The reasons for this lacuna in our social and educational studies can be focused on two specific aspects: first, the nature of curriculum as a source for study; second, associated with this, questions relating to the methods we employ in approaching the study of curriculum.

Here, I shall deal with some of the problems involved in employing curriculum as a source. Part of the problem has already been mentioned: namely that many accounts of schooling accept the curriculum as a given, an inevitable and essentially unimportant variable. (Of course, some important work in the fields of curriculum studies and sociology of knowledge have provided a continuing challenge to this kind of curriculum myopia.) But once it is accepted that the curriculum itself is an important source for study a number of further problems surface, for 'the curriculum' is a perennially elusive and multifaceted concept. The curriculum is such a slippery concept because it is defined, redefined and negotiated at a number of levels and in a number of arenas. It would be impossible to arbitrate over which points in the ongoing negotiations were critical. In addition, the terrain differs substantially according to local or national structures and patterns. In such a shifting and unfocused terrain it is plainly problematic to try to define common ground for our study. After all, if there is a lacuna in our study it is likely to be for good reasons.

The substantial difficulties do not, however, mean, as has often been the case to date, that we should ignore the area of curriculum as social construction completely or focus on 'minute particulars' that are amenable to focused study. Part of the problem is, I believe, resolvable. This resolution turns on identifying common ground or, conceptualized another way, some areas of stability within the apparent fluidity and flux of curriculum.

We should remember that a great deal of the most important scholarship on curriculum, certainly on curriculum as a social construction, took place in the 1960s and early

1970s. This was, however, a period of considerable change and flux everywhere in the Western world; and nowhere more so than in the world of schooling in general and curriculum in particular. For such a burgeoning of critical curriculum scholarship to happen during such times was both encouraging and, in a sense, symptomatic. The emergence of a field of study of curriculum as social construction was an important new direction. But, while itself symptomatic of a period of social questioning and criticism this burgeoning of critical scholarship was not without its down-side.

I believe that down-side has two aspects which are important as we begin to reconstitute our study of schooling and curriculum. First, influential scholars in the field often took a value position which assumed that schooling should be reformed, root and branch – 'revolutionized', the 'maps of learning redrawn'. Second, this scholarship took place at a time when a wide range of curriculum reform movements (which themselves carried a cadre of scholarly advisers) were actively seeking to do precisely this, 'to revolutionize school curricula'. Therefore it was unlikely that scholars or curriculum reformers would wish to focus upon, let alone concede, the areas of stability, of unchallengeable 'high ground' that may have existed within the school curriculum.

One might characterize curriculum reform in the 1960s as a sort of 'tidal wave'. Everywhere the waves created turbulence and activity but actually they only engulfed a few small islands; more substantial land masses were hardly affected at all, and on dry land the mountains, the high ground, remained completely untouched. As the tide now rapidly recedes the high ground can be seen in stark silhouette. If nothing else, our scrutiny of the curriculum reform should allow recognition that there is not only high ground but common ground in the world of curriculum.

Standing out more clearly than ever on the new horizon is the school subject, the 'basic' or 'traditional' subject. Throughout the Western world there is exhortation of but also evidence about a 'return to basics', a reconstitution of 'traditional subjects'. In England and Wales, for instance, the 'new' National Curriculum defines a range of subjects to be taught as a 'core' curriculum in all schools. The subjects thereby reinstated bear an uncanny resemblance to the list which generally defined secondary school subjects in the 1904 Regulations. *The Times Educational Supplement* commented about this reassertion of traditional subject dominance: 'The first thing to say about this whole exercise is that it unwinds 80 years of English (and Welsh) educational history. It is a case of go back to Go.' In the early years of the twentieth century the first state secondary schools were organized. Their curriculum was presented by the national Board of Education under the detailed guidance of Sir Robert Morant:

> The course should provide for instruction in the English Language and Literature, at least one Language other than English, Geography, History, Mathematics, Science and Drawing, with due provision for Manual Work and Physical Exercises, and in a girls' school for Housewifery. Not less than 4½ hours per week must be allotted to English, Geography and History; not less than 3½ hours to the Language where one is taken or less than 6 hours where two are taken; and not less than 7½ hours to Science and Mathematics, of which at least 3 must be for Science.

But in looking at the new National Curriculum, we find that: 'The 8–10 Subject timetable which the discussion paper draws up has as academic a look to it as anything Sir Robert Morant could have dreamed up.'[1] Likewise, in scrutinizing an earlier curriculum history in the US high school, Kliebard has pointed to the saliency of the 'traditional' school subjects in the face of waves of curriculum reform initiatives from previous decades. He characterizes the school subject within the US high school curriculum at this time as 'the Impregnable Fortress'.[2]

Let us return to the conceptualization of curriculum as our source of study, for it remains elusive and slippery, even in these times of centrality and tradition where we return to basics. In the 1960s and 1970s critical studies of curriculum as social construction pointed to the school classroom as the site wherein the curriculum was negotiated and realized. The classroom was the 'centre of action', 'the arena of resistance'. By this view what went on in the classroom *was* the curriculum. The definition of curriculum – the view from the high ground and the mountains – was, it was thought, not just subject to redefinition at classroom level but quite simply irrelevant. Interestingly, some recent British work on the National Curriculum continues this myopia, focusing on resistance and redefinition at school level while signally failing to analyse the ideological and political battles over curriculum at the state level.

Such a view, and such a standpoint from which to begin to study curriculum, is, I think, unsustainable (and I would argue further, from my own social location, morally and politically unconscionable). Certainly the high ground of the written curriculum is subject to renegotiation at lower levels, notably the classroom. But the view, common in the 1960s, that it is therefore irrelevant is much less common nowadays. Initiatives such as the National Curriculum should have demolished such commonly held complacencies. In the high ground what is to be 'basic' and 'traditional' is reconstituted and reinvented. The 'given' status of school subject knowledge is therein reinvented and reasserted. But this is more than political manoeuvring or rhetoric: such re-assertion affects the discourse about schooling and relates to the 'parameters of practice'. In the 1990s it would, I think, be folly to ignore the central importance of the redefinition of the written curriculum. The written curriculum is the visible and public testimony of selected rationales and legitimating rhetoric for schooling. I have argued elsewhere that in England and Wales the written curriculum

> both promulgates and underpins certain basic intentions of schooling as they are operationalized in structures and institutions. To take a common convention in pre-active curriculum, the school subject: while the written curriculum defines the rationales and rhetoric of the subject, this is the only tangible aspect of a patterning of resources, finances and examinations and associated material and career interests. In this symbiosis, it is as though the written curriculum provides a guide to the legitimating rhetorics of schooling as they are promoted through patterns of resource allocation, status attribution and career distribution. In short, the written curriculum provides us with a testimony, a documentary source, a changing map of the terrain: it is also one of the best official guide books to the institutionalized structure of schooling.[3]

What is most important to stress is that the written curriculum, notably the convention of the school subject, has, in this instance, not only symbolic but also practical significance: symbolic in that certain intentions for schooling are thereby publicly signified and legitimated; practical in that these written conventions are rewarded with finance and resource allocation and with the associated work and career benefits.

Our study of the written curriculum should afford a range of insights into schooling. But it is important to stress that such study must be allied to other kinds of educational study – in particular studies of school process, of school texts, of school assessment and of the history of pedagogy. This must be grounded within an understanding of the general social and economic history of the times, as the current salience of 'markets', privatization and globalization indicates; for schooling is comprised of the interlinked matrix of these elements and, indeed, other vital ingredients. With regard to schooling and to curriculum in particular, the final question is 'Who gets what and what do they do with it?'

The definition of written curriculum is part of this story. And that is not the same as asserting a direct or easily discernible relationship between the preactive definition of written curriculum and its interactive realization in classrooms. It is, however, to assert that the written curriculum most often sets important parameters for classroom practice (not always, not at all times, not in all classrooms, but 'most often'). The study of written curriculum will, first, increase our understanding of the influences and interests active at the preactive level. Second, this understanding will further our knowledge of the values and purposes represented in schooling and the manner in which preactive definition, notwithstanding individual and local variations, may set parameters for interactive realization and negotiation in the classroom and school, as well as for discourse construction and textual production.

Studies of the preactive in relationship to the interactive are, then, where we should end. But for the moment so neglected is the study of the preactive definition of written curriculum that no such marriage of methodologies could be consummated. The first step is plainly to undertake a range of studies of the definitions of written curriculum and, in particular, to focus on the 'impregnable fortress' of the school subject.

RECONSTITUTING SCHOOL SUBJECTS: THE EXAMPLE OF ENGLAND AND WALES IN THE 1980s AND EARLY 1990s

Traditionally in England and Wales those stressing 'the basics' have referred to the 3 Rs – reading, writing and arithmetic. In the 1980s and early 1990s it would be fair to say that those with curriculum power were following a new version of the 3 Rs – rehabilitation, reinvention and reconstitution. Often the rehabilitation strategy for school subjects in the 1980s took the form of arguing that good teaching is in fact good subject teaching. This is to seek to draw a veil over the whole experience of the 1960s, to seek to forget that many curriculum reforms were developed to try to provide antidotes to the perceived failures and inadequacies of conventional subject teaching. The rehabilitation strategy is itself in this sense quintessentially ahistorical but paradoxically it is also a reminder of the power of 'vestiges of the past' to survive, revive and reproduce.

In England the 'reinvention' of 'traditional' subjects began in 1969 with the issue of the first collection of Black Papers.[4] The writers in this collection argued that teachers had been too greatly influenced by progressive theories of education, such as the integration of subjects, mixed ability teaching, enquiry and discovery teaching. This resulted in neglect of subject and basic skill teaching and led to reduced standards of pupil achievement and school discipline; the traditional subject was thereby equated with social and moral discipline. The rehabilitation of the traditional subject promised the re-establishment of discipline in both these ways. The Black Papers were taken up by politicians and in 1976 the Labour Prime Minister James Callaghan embraced many of their themes in his Ruskin Speech. Specific recommendations soon followed. In 1979, for instance, following a survey of secondary schools in England and Wales, Her Majesty's Inspectorate drew attention to what they judged to be evidence of insufficient match in many schools between the qualification and experience of teachers and the work they were undertaking;[5] later in a survey of middle schools they found that higher standards of work overall were associated with a greater degree of use of subject teachers.[6]

These assertions and perceptions provided a background to the Department of Education pamphlet *Teaching Quality*. The Secretary of State for Education listed the criteria for initial teacher training courses. The first criteria imposed a requirement that the higher education and initial training of all qualified teachers should include at least two full years' course time devoted to subject studies at a level appropriate to higher education. This requirement therefore 'would recognize teachers' needs for subject expertise if they are to have the confidence and ability to enthuse pupils and respond to their curiosity in their chosen subject fields.'[7]

This final sentence is curiously circular. Obviously if the pupils choose subjects then it is probable that teachers will require subject expertise. But this is to foreclose a whole debate about whether they should choose traditional subjects as an educational vehicle. Instead, we have a political *fait accompli* presented as a dispassionate educational choice. In fact the students have no choice except to embrace 'their chosen subject fields'. The political rehabilitation of subjects by political diktat is presented as pupil choice.

In *Teaching Quality,* the issue of the match between the teachers' qualifications and their work with pupils, first raised in the 1979 HMI document, is again employed. We learn that 'the Government attach high priority to improving the fit between teachers' qualifications and their tasks as one means of improving the quality of education.'[8] The criterion for such a fit is based on a clear belief in the sequential and hierarchical pattern of subject learning: 'All specialist subject teaching during the secondary phase requires teachers whose study of the subject concerned was at a level appropriate to higher educa- tion, represented a substantial part of the total higher education and training period and built on a suitable A level base.'[9]

The beginning of subject specialization is best evidenced where the issue of non- subject based work in schools is scrutinized. Many aspects of school work take place out- side (or beside) subject work – studies of school process have indeed shown how integrated, pastoral and remedial work originates because pupils, for one reason or another, do *not* achieve in traditional subjects. Far from accepting the subject as an educa- tional vehicle with severe limits if the intention is to educate all pupils, the document seeks to rehabilitate subjects even in those domains which often originate from subject 'fall-out'.

> Secondary teaching is not all subject based, and initial training and qualifications cannot provide an adequate preparation for the whole range of secondary school work. For example, teachers engaged in careers or remedial work or in providing group courses of vocational preparation, and those given the responsibility for meeting 'special needs' in ordinary schools, need to undertake these tasks not only on the basis of initial qualifications but after experience of teaching a specialist sub- ject and preferably after appropriate post-experience training. Work of this kind and the teaching of interdisciplinary studies are normally best shared among teachers with varied and appropriate specialist qualifications and expertise.[10]

The rehabilitation of school subjects has become the mainstay of government thinking about the school curriculum. In many ways the governmental and structural support offered to school subjects as the organizing device for secondary schooling is reaching unprecedented levels. Hargreaves has judged that 'more than at any time previously, it seems, the subject is to take an overriding importance in the background preparation and curricular responsibility of secondary school teachers.' But the preferred policy sits along- side a major change in the style of governance of education, for Hargreaves argues that

> nor does that intention on the part of HMI and DES amount to just a dishing out of vague advice. Rather, in a style of centralized policy intervention and review with which we in Britain are becoming increasingly familiar in the 1980s, it is supported by strong and clear declarations of intent to build the achievement of subject match into the criteria for approval (or not) of teacher training courses, and to under- take five yearly reviews of selected secondary schools to ensure that subject match is being improved within them and is being reflected in the pattern of teacher appointments.[11]

The associated issue of increasingly centralized control is also raised in a DES publication on education from 8 to 12 in combined and middle schools.[12] Again, the rehabilitation of school subjects is rehearsed in a section on the need to 'extend teachers' subject knowledge'. Rowland has seen the document as 'part of an attempt to bring a degree of centralized control over education'. He states that 'Education 8 to 12 may well be interpreted by teachers and others as recommending yet another means in the trend towards a more schematicized approach to learning in which the focus is placed even more firmly on the subject matter rather than the child.' He adds cryptically that the evidence it provides actually 'points to the need to move in quite the opposite direction'.[13] His reservations about the effects of rehabilitating school subjects are shared by other critics. Hargreaves has noted that one effect of the strategy 'will be to reinforce the existing culture of secondary teaching and thereby inhibit curricular and pedagogic innovation on a school-wide front'.[14]

The various government initiatives and reports since 1976 have shown a consistent tendency to return to 'basics', to re-embrace 'traditional' subjects. This government project, which spans both Labour and Conservative administrations, has culminated in the 'new' National Curriculum. The curriculum was defined in a consultative document, *The National Curriculum 5–16*. This was rapidly followed in the wake of the Conservatives' third election victory by the passing of the Education Reform Act in the House of Commons in 1988. The Act defines the National Curriculum, certain common curricular elements which are to be offered to pupils of compulsory school age. While it is presented as a striking new political initiative, comparison with the 1904 Regulations shows the remarkable degree of historical resonance. The National Curriculum comprises: the 'core' subjects of mathematics, English and science; and the 'foundation' subjects of history, geography, technology, music, art, physical education and (for secondary pupils) a modern foreign language.[15]

DEVELOPING HISTORICAL PERSPECTIVES

Following the frustrating results of curriculum reform efforts in the 1960s and their substantial dismantling and reversal in the 1980s and early 1990s, the arguments for historical study are now considerable indeed. The contemporary power of those 'vestiges of the past', traditional school subjects, has been evidenced with instances drawn from Great Britain. To argue for curricular change strategies that ignored history would surely be an improbable, if not impossible, route in the current situation. Yet as we shall see this has been the dominant posture of curricular activists and theorists in the twentieth century. It is time to place historical study at the centre of the curriculum enterprise, to exhume the early work on curricular history, and the spasmodic subsequent work, and systematically to rehabilitate the study of the social construction of school subjects and the school curriculum.

The written curriculum is identified as a major but neglected historical source with which to develop our investigations of schooling. It becomes clear that just as the search for new sources moves us into neglected territory so too the search for an associated modality of study will require methods seldom used or at least seldom integrated in the study of schooling. Methods are required which allow us to study curriculum as it impinges on individual experiences of schooling as well as the experiences and social activities of social groups. Exploring curriculum as social construction allows us to study, indeed exhorts us to study, the intersection of individual biography and social structure. The emergence of curriculum as a concept came from a concern to direct and control individual teachers' and pupils' classroom activities. The definition of curriculum developed over time as part of an institutionalized and structured pattern of state schooling. Our methods therefore have to cover the analysis of individual lives and biographies as well as of social groups, structures and forces.

For this reason we should employ a range of methods from life histories of individual teachers through to histories of school subjects where the interplay of groups and structures is scrutinized. Relationships between individual and collective, between action and structures, are perennially elusive. However, our studies may either accept or exacerbate fragmentation or seek integration. Life history study pursued alongside the study of more collective groupings and milieux might promote better integration. The difficulty of integration is partly a problem of dealing with modes and levels of consciousness. The life history helps penetrate the individual subject's consciousness and also attempts to map the changes in that consciousness over the life cycle. But at the individual level as at other levels we must note that change is structured, but that structures change. The relationship between the individual and wider structures is central to our investigations but again it is through historical studies that such investigations might be most profitably pursued: 'Our chance to understand how smaller milieux and larger structures interact, and our chance to understand the larger causes at work in these limited milieux, thus require us to deal with historical materials.'[16]

The problems of elucidating the symbiosis of the individual and the social structure can be seen in the assessment of the broad goals of curriculum or schooling. The discerning of 'regularities', 'recurrences' or patterns is particularly elusive at the level of the individual life (and consciousness). Walter Feinberg has noted that 'once we understand that a goal is identified in terms of something that is reasonably distinctive and that establishes relevance by postulating a continuity to otherwise discrete acts then we can see that goals may belong to individuals, but they may also belong to individuals as they are related to each other in acts or institutions.' He provides an example of people in America moving westwards, 'colonizing the west', which they did for many reasons:

> Some went to escape debt, others to make a fortune; some went to farm, others to pan gold, or to sell merchandise; some went as soldiers, others as trappers and hunters. Whereas it is perfectly proper to speak about the continuity of any series of acts performed by an individual in terms of a goal it is equally appropriate to speak of a whole series of acts performed by different individuals along with the acts of the government that supported them, such as the Homestead Act and the building of railroads, in terms of the *general* goal of settling the west. It is this way of speaking that allows us to make sense of all these acts and to see them as forming some kind of continuous meaningful event.[17]

The dangers of 'abstraction' to the general level are evidential and can be seen when Feinberg adds: 'Moreover, it is equally appropriate to speak of the goal as beginning with the movement of the first settlers west, even though these people may not have had a whisper of an idea about the overall historical significance of their act.'

Understood in this manner, structural change provides a facilitating arena for a range of individual actions which then feed into and act upon this initial change. Consciousness of the significance of the action differs according to the time period in question and the level of scrutiny – hence a series of individual 'dreams' and actions build up into a movement to 'colonize' a vast territory. Likewise, with schooling and curriculum discerning regularities, recurrences and patterns allows analysis and assessment of goals and intentions. 'To begin to characterise these goals by looking back to the origins of the school system itself is not necessarily to claim that the goals were fully understood at the time. It is simply to say that in the light of these goals we can understand some of the major lines of continuity between the activity of the past and the activity of the present.'[18]

Development of our studies of curriculum at individual and collective level demands that our historical analyses work across the levels of individual lives and group action and assess relations between individuals, between groups and between individuals and groups. Such work is reminiscent of Esland's early exhortations to develop frameworks 'for the analysis of the knowledge which constitutes the life world of teachers and pupils in particular educational institutions, and the epistemological traditions in which they collectively participate'. The intentions are very similar: 'trying to focus the individual biography in its sociohistorical context is in a very real sense attempting to penetrate the symbolic drift of school knowledge, and the consequences for the individuals who are caught up in it and attempting to construct their reality through it.'[19] Histories of the symbolic drift of school knowledge raise questions about the patterns of change through which subjects pass. There is a growing body of work on the history of school subjects. These studies reflect a growing interest in the history of curriculum and besides elucidating the symbolic drift of school knowledge raise central questions about past and current 'explanations' of school subjects, whether they be sociological or philosophical.

Above all, this work illustrates the historical background, emergence and construction of the political economy of curriculum. The structure of resources and finance and the attribution of status and careers are linked to a system that has developed since the foundation of state schooling. This structure impinges on both individual intentions and collective aspirations. By focusing our studies on the historical emergence and reconstruction of structures and the ongoing activities of individuals and groups we might progressively alleviate the current amnesia. The written curriculum would begin to emerge as a major battleground where the futures and lives of generations of school students are influenced in crucial, yet so far substantially mystified, ways.

NOTES

1. *Times Educational Supplement* (1987) 1904 and all that, *TES*, 31 July: 2.
2. Kliebard, H. (1986) *The Struggle for the American Curriculum 1893–1958*, London: Routledge and Kegan Paul, p. 269.
3. Goodson, I. F. (1988) *The Making of Curriculum – Collected Essays*, London, New York and Philadelphia: Falmer Press, p. 16.
4. Cox, C. B. and Dyson, A. E. (eds) (1969) *Fight for Education: a Black Paper*, London: The Critical Quarterly Society. Followed by Cox, C. B. and Boyson, R. (eds) (1975) *The Black Paper 1975*, London: Dent.
5. Her Majesty's Inspectorate (1979) *Aspects of Secondary Education*, London: HMSO.
6. Her Majesty's Inspectorate (1983) *9–13 Middle Schools – an Illustrative Survey*, London: HMSO.
7. Department of Education and Science (1983) *Teaching Quality*, London: HMSO, p. 19, para. 64 (i).
8. Ibid., p. 9, para. 29.
9. Ibid., p. II, para. 37.
10. Ibid., para. 40.
11. Hargreaves, A. (1984) Curricular policy and the culture of teaching: some prospects for the future. Mimeo. See, for a later version, Chapter 4 of Hargreaves, A. (1989) *Curriculum and Assessment Reform*, Milton Keynes: Open University Press.
12. Department of Education and Science (1985) *Education 8 to 12 in Combined and Middle Schools: an HMI Survey*, London: HMSO.
13. Rowland, S. (1987) Where is primary education going? *Journal of Curriculum Studies*, 19(1): 90.
14. Hargreaves (1984), op. cit.
15. DES (1987) *The National Curriculum 5–16*, London: HMSO.
16. Wright Mills, C. (1970) *The Sociological Imagination*, Harmondsworth: Penguin, p. 165.

17. Feinberg, W. (1983) *Understanding Education: Towards a Reconstruction of Educational Enquiry*, Cambridge: Cambridge University Press, p. 86.
18. Ibid. See Goodson (1988), op. cit., pp. 62–3.
19. Esland, G. M. (1971) Teaching and learning as the organisation of knowledge. In M. F. D. Young (ed.) *Knowledge and Control: New Directions for the Sociology of Education*, London: Collier Macmillan, p. 111.

13

THE COMMON STRANDS OF PEDAGOGY AND THEIR IMPLICATIONS

Judith Ireson, Peter Mortimore and Susan Hallam

INTRODUCTION

This edited chapter has been written by three authors from the Institute of Education, University of London. Judith Ireson is Professor of Psychology and Peter Mortimore is the former Director of the Institute. As a professor of education, he has written widely and commented on many contemporary issues in education, particularly school effectiveness and improvement. Susan Hallam is also a professor with expertise in the psychology of education. This chapter has taken from *Understanding Pedagogy and its Impact on Learning* edited by Peter Mortimore and is the final chapter in the book which summarises the diversity of approaches to pedagogy in different phases of education discussed in the book as a whole. The chapter effectively outlines what we know about pedagogy and presents some of the implications for teaching in the future. The authors call for a wide-ranging debate on pedagogy and specifically in the area of the aims of teaching. This chapter is a good introduction to a discussion of pedagogy and the conditions under which it is more effective in education.

KEY QUESTIONS

1. What pedagogies develop the knowledge, understanding, abilities, habits of mind, and ways of knowing and problem solving that define a biologist, an accountant, or a sociologist?
2. What assumptions about teaching and learning underlie how teachers teach in a discipline?

FURTHER READING

Jenny Leach and Robert Moon have written an excellent book on *Learners and Pedagogies* (Sage, London) which has become a set book for universities in the UK and internationally. *Culture and Pedagogy* (Blackwell, Oxford) by Robin Alexander compares primary and secondary schooling in England, France, India, Russia, and the United States and reveals how teaching, learning, and pedagogic discourse are shaped not just by the decisions of the teacher but also by school values and organisation, national policy, the balance of political control, the tensions and ambiguities of the democratic ideal, and by culture and history.

This Reading links with Chapter 12 and Debate 5 of *The Routledge Education Studies Textbook*.

We will endeavour to answer the question 'What do we now know about effective pedagogy?'. We will also comment on what we still do not know about this important topic. We will explore whether the age or stage of the learner makes a difference to the pedagogy used. Finally, we will set out what we see as the major lessons and implications for pedagogy in the future.

Before addressing these questions, however, it may be helpful to comment on some of the economic and labour force trends which are affecting the context of learning currently. These are important because pedagogy cannot be considered in isolation. It has to be considered in relation to the aims of education. What should these be? Teaching people the basic skills of literacy and numeracy is crucially important but there are many additional cultural tools that they will need to master if they are to have productive and satisfying lives in the twenty-first century.

Four major developments have had an impact on the English education system and hence on its pedagogy. First, the world trade markets have become acutely competitive and are increasingly dominated by large and mobile multinational companies, able to relocate their business to areas with skilled but cheap labour. Second, higher education, once a small scale enterprise catering for about ten per cent of the age group, has expanded such that a third of all school leavers – and a significant number of older people – now expect to participate in it. Third, during the second half of the twentieth century there has been an explosion of knowledge. To take just two examples of radical scientific developments: the biomolecular and quantum revolutions have given mankind the ability to alter and synthesize new forms of life and, perhaps ultimately, to control matter; and the information and computing technologies providing instant access to information, are transforming much of our working and our social lives. Fourth, the emergence of international studies of educational performance has made governments acutely aware of comparisons of the outputs of different systems.

Changes in the world economy will place different demands on students in secondary, further and higher education. New demands will also be made on teachers in these sectors. The expansion of higher education requires that pedagogy meets the needs of a greater diversity of learners. Moreover, it is no longer sufficient for learners to demonstrate that they have acquired a specific knowledge base from courses. They now enter the workplace with the expectation that their learning will continue and the realization that they will need the skills constantly to adapt to changing patterns of work. These requirements for continued learning and adaptation call for specific personal qualities and attitudes. Individuals must be willing and able to continue learning and they must be willing and able to adapt to new demands and challenges.

WHAT DO WE KNOW ABOUT EFFECTIVE PEDAGOGY?

If we take as our yardstick the most general definition of pedagogy – 'Any conscious activity designed by one person to bring about learning in another' – we can address the question of effectiveness through the idea of fitness for purpose. By this we mean that teaching methods are aligned with the needs of the learner and with the desired learning outcomes. A particular pedagogy will be effective if it is:

■ clear about its goals
■ imbued with high expectations and capable of providing motivation
■ technically competent and appropriate to its purpose
■ theoretically sophisticated.

A pedagogy which has clear goals

A major problem at the heart of our consideration of pedagogy is that there has been little explicit discussion of goals within the education system. The question 'What are we teaching for?' is surprisingly seldom posed or answered. There was little discussion of general principles when the National Curriculum was being designed during the late 1980s. Instead, separate Subject Task Groups were given responsibility for drawing up a framework of attainment targets and these focused on the curriculum structure and assessment. There was little debate about the aims of education, which in the very broad terms of the Education Reform Act were 'to promote the spiritual, moral, cultural, mental and physical development of pupils' (DES, 1988). In time, each of the Task Groups concerned with the curriculum subjects formulated aims for their subject but, even taken together, these do not add up to a set of overarching national aims for education.

There has been a similar lack of clarity about the aims of pre-school education, where there is debate as to whether academic achievement or personal and social development should be the priority. Likewise in further, continuing and higher education, there is a tension between needs for personal development, the needs of industry and commerce and the requirements of academic work. In the absence of clear aims, the competitive climate that currently exists at national and international level has a powerful influence. An increasingly common pragmatic – but none the less limited – view is that the sole aim of teaching is to improve learners' performance in those national assessments and examinations whose results are in the public domain and are therefore open to scrutiny at home and abroad.

We would be among the first to support the view that a principal aim of teaching should be to enable as many people as possible to achieve as much as they can during their life time. For too long, in our judgement, young people from less advantaged backgrounds have underachieved (Mortimore and Whitty, 1997). To make closing the gap between the achievements of the advantaged and the disadvantaged a major aim of teaching will require a restructuring of our current educational system. In higher education, Government initiatives such as the establishment of the Open University, the turning of polytechnics into universities and many of the developments in further and higher education, including the proposed University of Industry, have began to move in this direction.

We also believe that our democratic political system requires an education in citizenship. The responsibilities of the individual in a democratic system are both personal and social. The personal aspects include taking responsibility for maintaining oneself and one's dependants and abiding by the laws of the land. The social aspects include paying one's taxes, contributing to the care of those unable to work and fulfilling one's electoral duties. In addition, good citizens need to develop critical and reflective awareness, to make informed choices and to take responsibility for their own decisions. This requires the systematic acquisition of knowledge, understanding, attitudes and competencies. Within the educational system, therefore, individuals need to learn to deal with choice within a carefully structured framework of progression.

It is well recognized that choice and self-determination can also exert powerful, positive influences on motivation. Despite this, much of our current school system offers little choice for pupils. Where, at fourteen, pupils have been offered a modular curriculum with guided choice, the adoption of such a system is reported to have improved pupil motivation (Ireson and McCallum, in press). Beyond the secondary school years, learner choice tends to increase, although training is often task or job specific. However, some companies have recognized the importance of personal motivation and have developed successful schemes in which training has been broadened to accommodate individual interests (Hougham *et al.*, 1991).

This brings us back to the question of the aims of education. Should education encourage individuals to pursue their own interests or should the needs of society take priority over individual wishes? Are the two, in fact, mutually exclusive? One starting point for discussion of the aims of education might be to ask parents, teachers and students what they think are the important goals of education. Surveys carried out in America (e.g. Goodlad, 1983) demonstrate that pupils, parents and teachers rated four general goals as important for schools. These were academic (including critical thinking as well as basic skills), vocational (relating to employment), social and civic (relating to preparation for entry into civic society) and personal (relating to the development of individual responsibility, self-confidence, creativity and thinking for oneself).

In a similar exercise undertaken in Britain, Raven (1994) found that pupils rated most highly personal qualities such as being confident, able to take the initiative in introducing changes, and being independent. They gave priority to qualities which were self-determined, self-motivated and forward-looking. They valued high grades, but mainly because these provided access to occupational opportunities and privilege, rather than because they valued the subject matter itself. Teachers' values were broadly similar to those of the pupils but were generally more prescriptive and rated the content of the curriculum more highly. Parents and pupils tended to value school mainly as a preparation for the world of work. Similarly, a high proportion of students in higher education see their education as a means of improving their employment prospects (*The Independent,* 10th December, 1998).

It is clear that careful thinking and informed debate are needed on the nature of the aims of education in all institutions committed to furthering learning. The debate will also necessarily involve a consideration of the values underlying the issue of inclusion. There are few occupations which require the simple, repetitive actions of industrial production lines. Increasingly, robots are performing these tasks. Most occupations require self-motivation, ability to take the initiative and to solve problems; many also require leadership and management skills.

The Movimento da Escola Moderna (MEM) set out its goals for early childhood with great clarity. These goals included: an initiation into democratic life; the re-institution of values and social meanings; and the co-operative reconstruction of culture. Pupils, parents and staff could be in no doubts as to what MEM was trying to achieve. At the other extreme, the Connective Model of vocational education sets out its goals as helping learners to experience different combinations of theoretical and practical learning and enabling them to relate their formal programmes of study to trends in labour and work organization. In other words, the students were being offered the opportunity to learn about business organization and provided with an opportunity to develop personal and social skills in this setting.

Evaluation of the effectiveness of pedagogy can only be made in relation to its aims. Establishing clear aims within each educational phase would enable the development of an appropriate pedagogy for each phase. Further, establishing clear overarching aims which provide a lifespan framework within which all formal teaching and learning could be understood would facilitate the development of a structured learning progression for each individual.

A pedagogy which is imbued with high expectations and capable of promoting motivation

A number of authors stressed the importance of high expectations in all forms of pedagogy. The problem is that high expectations cannot be assigned; they have to spring naturally from the belief and aspirations of the teacher and learner. They have to be genuine or they become counterproductive. We know from empirical research that expectations are passed between teacher and learner in subtle, often undetected, ways (Mortimore *et al.*, 1988). Underpinning teachers' attitudes to the capabilities of their students is their belief about intelligence. If teachers believe that intelligence is largely innate and unchangeable and if their students find learning difficult, they are unlikely to be able to adopt high expectations for their students. If, on the other hand, teachers believe that intelligence can be modified by experience, they will be more likely to pitch their expectations positively. This applies throughout all phases of education.

The emphasis on high expectations marks out the approach of the High/Scope Project. A strong Vygotskian influence takes a stage further the emphasis on continuous planning and review that is found in Reggio Emilia and provides a structured approach in all its routines. The same positive approach can be found in the work of Bruner, in many of the accounts of studies of school effectiveness (Mortimore, 1998) and in the references to mastery learning. High expectations also play a part in work experience, in 'on the job' training and in participation in university courses.

Learners' orientations to learning

An important theme is the need to develop pedagogies that will encourage and support learners to take control of their own learning. With appropriate support, active control over learning fosters a mastery orientation towards achievement.

A mastery orientation to learning is linked with numerous beneficial motivational characteristics, including a preference for challenging work, high persistence in the face of difficulty and a focus on learning as a goal in itself (Ames and Ames, 1992; Dweck and Leggett, 1988; Nicholls, 1989). Learners with a mastery orientation are more likely to use effective learning strategies; to monitor their own learning, checking that they understand the meaning of their work, and to relate learning in formal education to their own experience (Meece, 1991; Rogers, 1990). The concept of a mastery orientation, which has largely been developed and applied in relation to school-age learners, resonates with the concept of deep learning, studied in student populations in secondary school (Selmes, 1987), further education (Strang, 1997) and higher education (Entwistle, 1992; Marton and Booth, 1997). The student who adopts a deep approach to learning makes the effort to understand and connect ideas. In contrast to the mastery orientation, a helpless or 'work-avoidant' orientation is linked with numerous negative motivational characteristics, including an avoidance of challenge, low persistence in the face of difficulties and the use of superficial learning strategies. This pattern is one that leads learners into a downward spiral of achievement.

A mastery or deep approach to learning, however, does not always work to the learner's advantage. In an education system which is governed by fixed syllabuses and courses of study, students who become too absorbed in a topic or piece of work may leave insufficient time to cover the syllabus. Generally, learners adapt to the learning situations in which they find themselves and maximize their potential for success. For instance, the evidence suggests that to cope with the demands of higher education, students tend to move from the adoption of a deep approach prior to starting their course towards a more surface approach as they proceed through it. Learners have to regulate their interest and organize their time so that they complete the work set and obtain the best grades they can. This may mean adopting a surface approach to satisfy course requirements.

Grades can be a powerful source of motivation and undoubtedly spur learners on to make greater effort, who otherwise might give up. They can also provide useful information about one's performance relative to others in a class or subject which may subsequently feed in to decisions about choice of courses and careers. However, too great an emphasis on grades can undermine learning – particularly if grades form a major part of judgements about self-worth (Covington, 1992) or where the emphasis is on rote learning for regurgitation in examinations at the expense of understanding.

Metacognition and self-regulation

A first step towards self-regulation is to become aware of one's own learning. This awareness can be developed from a very early age, as Siraj-Blatchford has pointed out. Programmes such as the Reggio Emilia provide a means for children to reflect on their learning and to see their efforts and ideas validated and considered important by their teachers. In a similar vein, Pramling has demonstrated that children in the first years of school can start to take control over their learning if the meta-cognitive aspects of learning are introduced to them in appropriate ways (Pramling, 1996).

Gipps and MacGilchrist comment on the current focus in primary education on the academic content of the curriculum and call for an increased emphasis on meta-cognition. In other countries, particularly the United States, programs have been developed to increase children's use of learning strategies and their awareness of their learning. Examples include Informed Strategies for Learning (Paris *et al.,* 1984), Reciprocal Teaching (Palinscar and Brown, 1989) and Cognitive Apprenticeship (Brown *et al.,* 1989). Although these programmes differ from one another in their theoretical roots, they are all embedded within a curriculum area. They also include pedagogic elements to enhance teachers' and learners' awareness and understanding of the process of learning and, in particular, of the need for positive expectations.

The evidence from secondary and higher education shows mixed effects of programmes designed to promote meta-cognitive skills. While some have been successful (Biggs, 1987; Weinstein *et al.,* 1988) others have not (Howe, 1991). This is in part because learners tend not to transfer their knowledge of strategies between learning situations. The degree of success of meta-cognitive programmes, therefore, depends crucially on the extent to which they are embedded within the curriculum and the current learning environment. Where they are not integrated, they can increase the adoption of a surface approach to learning. Learning about learning cannot be successful if it is taught as an 'add on'. It must be integrated with the knowledge which is being acquired.

Learners' and teachers' beliefs in their ability to succeed

In academic situations, beliefs about their ability to succeed influence both students' and teachers' motivation and coping. For students, their perceived self-efficacy means their belief in their ability to regulate their own learning and to master different academic subjects. For teachers, it means their belief in their personal efficacy to motivate and promote their students' learning. Bandura argues that, in the current information age with the rapidly accelerating growth of knowledge, a major goal of education should be to equip young people with the intellectual tools, efficacy beliefs and intrinsic interests they need in order to educate themselves throughout their lifetime (Bandura, 1995).

Teachers' beliefs in their own personal efficacy also influence their classroom practice. Those who have a high sense of efficacy tend to support the development of students' intrinsic motivation and academic self-determination. They also have a positive impact on student attainment (Ashton and Webb, 1986; Tschannen-Moran *et al.,* 1998). In addition, teachers' belief in their own efficacy offers them some protection from stressful experiences in schools. Those who have a strong sense of self-efficacy are more likely to deal with academic problems by directing their efforts at resolving the problems, whereas those who have a weak sense of efficacy are more likely to attempt to avoid the problems. A teacher's sense of efficacy is built up primarily through experience of successfully moti-vating and promoting students' learning. A student's sense of efficacy is built up primarily through experiences of successful self-regulation and learning. For this to occur, teaching must be appropriately matched to enable the student to experience reasonable challenge. While success in the early stages of learning is important – failure creates expectations of failure which may be difficult to dispel – setting very easy work which may guarantee suc-cess may also lead to boredom and therefore is not a long term solution.

For those who experience failure during their education, the emotional responses to learning linger on and may have to be confronted in later life. Common emotions are a lack of confidence in the ability to learn, anxiety or a general lack of efficacy, which may inhibit the learner from engaging in formal learning. In schools, pupils disengage in a variety of ways, such as playing truant or daydreaming; beyond school, adults simply avoid further formal learning. As Hodgson and Kambouri point out, the lecturer's awareness of adults' previous learning experience is an important factor in their work, since adults frequently carry with them a sense of failure from their school days. The situation is similar in further education where part of the educator's work is to help motivate those who have become disaffected from learning. Those who leave school with few or no qualifications are less likely to participate in continuing education than their better qualified peers. In England and Wales, it is estimated that only about half the adult population has engaged in any kind of education or training since leaving school. Those who do participate tend to be young, male, mobile and from higher socio-economic groups (McGivney, 1993).

A pedagogy which is technically competent and appropriate for its purpose

Teaching is a complex task. A number of the chapters in this book have attempted to iden-tify the assorted components that contribute to its totality. Even though it is possible to list the characteristics of an effective teacher, the anecdotal evidence of newspaper columns such as 'My best teacher' (in the *Times Educational Supplement)* illustrates just how often it is the unusual or the quirky approaches which feature in people's recollections. Never-theless, the preparation of teaching programmes, presentation of ideas and information, setting of suitable assignments and provision of appropriate feedback all require a high level of technical competence.

Fitness for purpose

Earlier in this chapter, we introduced the notion of 'fitness for purpose'. The term implies an alignment between the needs of the learner, the desired learning outcomes and the tasks and activities designed by the teacher to achieve those outcomes. It includes assessment appro-priate for particular forms of learning. There are two aspects of alignment that we would like to highlight. The first is the alignment of the learning activity with the learner's capabilities. By this we mean that a reasonable match is achieved between the learner's current under-standing and skill and the new learning presented. Within special education, as Corbett and Norwich argue, considerable effort has been invested in the development of techniques of task and needs analysis to enable teachers more accurately to target their teaching to meet learners' needs. Behavioural analytic models exemplify this approach, with detailed analy-ses of the needs of the individual learner in relation to particular goals and objectives. Opti-mal teaching methods are then developed in order to help achieve those objectives.

These ideas have been adopted in recent years in relation to target setting for schools and in the National Literacy Strategy. Although behavioural methods may not be appro-priate for all kinds of learning and learners, there can be value in the approach. Similar methods are used to teach complex workplace activities such as team working.

Formative assessment, combined with tutoring programmes, can also help establish learners' needs but, to be effective, it must be rigorous and theoretically well grounded. Corbett and Norwich usefully point to the distinction between three types of educational needs: those that are common to all; those that are specific or distinct; and those that are individual. All learners will have some individual needs which would require a specific adaptation of any general pedagogical approach in order to achieve a perfect alignment of learning tasks with their capabilities.

In addition to their role in establishing learners' needs, techniques of formative assessment provide a very powerful means of providing support for learning. Used well, this type of assessment can help students to develop the capacity to undertake assessment of their own learning. Assessment techniques, such as profiling, also encourage older students to set up their own action plans, assess their own work, discuss curriculum goals and review progress with their teachers. Black and Wiliam (1998), in a comprehensive review, demonstrate that formative assessment can raise attainment to a remarkable level. It can also have powerful effects on student motivation and learning (Broadfoot, 1996). However, its importance is not universally recognized: for instance, the majority of lecturers in higher education tend to view the role of assessment as summative rather than formative and do not appreciate how much assessment can help students to learn (Ramsden, 1992).

Aligning teaching methods and learning outcomes

The second form of alignment we wish to consider is between teaching methods, tasks and learning outcomes. Certain teaching methods appear to be better suited to achieve particular learning outcomes. Methods that emphasize efficient one way communication, such as lectures and class presentations, may assist students in obtaining and understanding information – the lower order objectives of teaching according to Bloom's taxonomy, although the evidence from higher education suggests that this may not always be the case. Methods which utilize communication between learners, or that involve discussion between teacher and students, tend to be more useful in helping students to achieve the higher order objectives of analysis, synthesis and evaluation.

There is also evidence that teachers' task assignment tends to emphasize quantity rather than quality and concentrates on the lower, rather than the higher, forms of learning (Kerry, 1984; Stodolsky, 1988). This appears to be true across all phases of education. On the one hand, the preponderance of knowledge acquisition and comprehension is not surprising, given that a major role of formal education is to impart new information and skills. On the other hand, the challenge facing education as a whole is to develop a pedagogy which will equip students to deal with the uncertainty and unpredictability inherent in the world today.

In similar vein, Noss and Pachler argue that access to the information available through new technology renders untenable the role of the teacher as the source of all knowledge. Other skills, such as organizing and making sense of large amounts of information, need to be given a higher priority. If we are to take up these challenges then teaching methods will need to be aligned to achieve more complex learning outcomes.

Challenge and interest in learning

Fitness for purpose also involves the teacher in presenting sufficient challenge for the learner. If the task merely repeats what is already known, the learner will find it boring yet if it presents too much that is unfamiliar, the learner will be overwhelmed. Finding the optimal level of challenge for the learner is a key pedagogical skill in all phases of education, although to date it has been given most attention in school level education. It is important to distinguish here between the types of learning defined by curriculum analysts and the level of challenge for an individual learner. From the students' perspective, the acquisition and comprehension of knowledge can present considerable challenges, even though such tasks may not be considered by educators to be the most challenging types of learning.

Whereas challenge and interest fuel learning, boredom detracts from it. Students in post-compulsory education have choices and can opt out or drop out of courses they find uninteresting or ill-suited to their needs. Pupils in schools, however, do not have this freedom. In a recent survey, more than half of Year 9 pupils said they were bored in some lessons. Lessons in secondary schools may be uninteresting because of the curriculum content, the teacher's approach or because pupils simply do not engage with the topic (Mortimore, 1998). But cognitive challenge, relevance, variety of activities including well designed discussions and thought-provoking activities can make even the most difficult subjects interesting.

A pedagogy which is theoretically sophisticated

If there are to be radical changes in pedagogy to equip young people for the future, then teachers and lecturers must have an understanding of learning processes and the factors which affect them. They must also be learners too, a point made in several chapters of this book. For example, if teachers are to enable learners to develop a better awareness of their own learning, they too will need to develop awareness of their own learning, along with pedagogic strategies to encourage it. As Siraj-Blatchford reported, children who attended pre-school centres where staff had a dynamic understanding of children's learning and a positive view of their own influence on their pupils made better progress in literacy and numeracy. But teachers and lecturers also need a positive environment in which to learn – one which is rich in knowledge and supportive.

Teachers and lecturers as learners

Developing pedagogies to assist students in developing skills for the twenty-first century, for instance, dealing with large amounts of information or using advanced technological tools, involves experimentation and provides some risk for both teachers and learners. Both parties have to leave the security of their structured lesson or lecture. Teachers may be asked to demonstrate their own processes of problem solving, including all the uncertainties and false starts involved in, for example, creative writing or solving mathematical problems. Learners may be asked to reveal and discuss their methods for essay writing, solving problems or writing a composition. They may be afraid of looking foolish if they fail or if their strategy is judged unfavourably. The creation of a safe, accepting, and non-judgmental environment is essential for this type of learning.

Connecting theory and practice

The theoretical basis of new pedagogic initiatives needs to be established, researched and debated if teachers are take on the role of the architects rather than the bricklayers of learning. Theory is an important element in any formal learning. It serves to order thinking and to provide explanations. Yet, in recent times, there has been an enforced separation between theoretical and practical knowledge and a public belittling of theory within education. The establishment of a General Teaching Council and the newly formed Institute of Learning and Teaching may lead to a recognition of the need for all kinds of teachers to ground their teaching skills in theories of learning. It remains to be seen whether the theoretical knowledge underpinning pedagogy and the research evidence for particular teaching approaches are given sufficient priority in courses for teachers and lecturers. Teachers and lecturers in all phases of education require an understanding of the principles on which teaching is based, in addition to practical skills, if they are to be able to use their knowledge flexibly and intelligently. In the past, teaching methods based on reflection have underplayed the importance of a theoretical knowledge base. It is important that the new National Literacy Strategy does not fall into the same trap.

Connecting learning in different contexts

A number of authors in this book have stressed how academic learning is enhanced when it is perceived as relating to real life. However, learners sometimes experience difficulties in making the connections between formal learning and real life contexts. Formal learning situations generate expectations and understandings of acceptable ways of doing things which govern learners' approaches to the tasks that they may be faced with. For example, students use different strategies to solve the same problems in different lessons in school (Saljo and Wyndham, 1993) and adults use different strategies for arithmetical calculation depending on whether they are in informal or formal settings (Lave and Wenger, 1991). Griffiths and Guile point to activity theory, as developed by Engstrom and others, as a fruitful avenue for the development of pedagogies linking school and work contexts. Promoting ways in which learning can be generalized to other contexts is a problem that has long taxed educators. It continues to do so.

Currently, in England, there is a tendency to see learning in rather polarized terms, linked to different ideas about human potential and to different views of epistemology. In crude terms, on one side are those who consider learning to be mainly a process of acquiring knowledge. On the other are those who see learning as the development of understanding and of conceptual change. The former tend to view extrinsic motivation as the fuel for learning whilst the latter see curiosity and the desire for competence as primary sources of motivation. In reality, both are required for the development of expertise in any field (Glaser, 1984). Ways of thinking are, to a great extent, embedded within knowledge structures. While an individual may acquire a range of strategies for problem solving, learning, or achieving understanding these cannot be transferred successfully to other domains unless the individual possesses the relevant knowledge base. An expert problem solver in one field, e.g. psychology, will not be an expert problem solver in nuclear physics without developing an extensive knowledge base in nuclear physics. Many educationalists intuitively have recognized this and try to find a balance between these two extreme positions. Similarly, learners are motivated by a variety of factors, including the promise of rewards, fascination with a subject, the desire to please a 'significant other' or, for some, the desire to get ahead of peers. Different motivators come into play in different situations for different individuals and it seems to us that pedagogy needs to be sufficiently flexible to accommodate this variety.

WHAT DO WE STILL NOT KNOW ABOUT PEDAGOGY?

Despite the surveys undertaken by some of the authors of this book, there remain a number of key pedagogical issues about which we know very little. The following five examples illustrate the point.

■ *Whether it is equally beneficial to teach those who find learning easy with those who find it difficult*

This argument lies at the heart of controversies about inclusion, selection, streaming and setting. The evidence for and against integration or segregation of different sorts of learners is often contradictory. At present, segregation of learners increases through the primary and secondary phases of education. In the post-compulsory phases, selection segregates learners but learners, themselves, also select courses and exercise some control over their learning. As with so many policy issues, the question cannot be considered without taking account of the aims of education. What does society wish to achieve through its system of education? With a clear set of aims established, educators and those involved in research may then address how they might best be achieved. Controversy arises where discussions about educational and institutional structures are undertaken without relation to the purposes for which they are intended. For instance, evidence from accumulated research on streaming has indicated that it tends to increase the gap in achievement between those in the bottom and top sets and has a detrimental effect on the self-esteem of those in the lower sets. If society requires a small proportion of well educated individuals and a greater mass of unskilled labour then it may be the best way of achieving this end. If, on the other hand, a society is required where everyone has high levels of skill then it is unlikely that streaming will be the appropriate means to attain this aim.

■ *How much the adoption of particular assessment techniques influences the pedagogy chosen by teachers and the strategies adopted by learners*

In 1979, Elton and Laurillard argued persuasively on the basis of their research that assessment is the driving force in determining teaching and learning strategies. The American literature similarly asserts that 'teaching to test' and 'learning for test' are common reactions to formal assessment. Where test data are taken as a measure of teachers' accountability, the more 'high stakes' the process becomes and the more likely it is that a 'backwash' effect will be discerned (Biggs and Moore, 1993). If learning is driven by assessment then to achieve the desired learning outcomes requires that the assessment procedures reflect precisely the aims of the pedagogy. In the UK, national testing throughout the school years is still in its infancy and opportunities to target it specifically on higher order attainments are often defeated by the need to produce reliable – and hence defensible – measures. This also influences students' behaviour. Not surprisingly, some adopt strategies solely to get through tests and examinations regardless of whether such strategies involve any real changes in understanding.

■ *How much the features of a disadvantaged life (poorer housing, health care, diet and emotional stress caused by relative poverty) impact on the pedagogy of schools and colleges*

There is mounting evidence that, in a competitive education system, socioeconomic disadvantage has a negative impact on the learning of pupils. However, as Mortimore and Whitty (1997) point out, data do not yet exist which could document the amount of improvement that particularly effective schools are able to endow on disadvantaged pupils. Whether learners who experience material or economic disadvantage would benefit from a different – perhaps more structured – pedagogy is yet to be researched. Entry to higher education is also influenced by social class with the lower classes being under-represented. In further and higher education, increasingly students are taking paid employment to support themselves, particularly where financial help is not available from their families. Where long hours are worked this can have detrimental effects on studying (Hodgson and Spours, 1998). Economic disadvantage has effects which continue beyond the school years. The question for society is whether educational aims should encompass the promotion of equity of opportunity and if so how this aim might be achieved.

■ *How much ICT should change traditional approaches to pedagogy*

ICT offers an opportunity to transform the pedagogy traditionally adopted in formal learning situations. In higher education, the Teaching and Learning Technology Programme has generated a number of multi-media and interactive packages and simulations designed to extend the quality of teaching. There are interactive educational programmes available for schools and for individual learners to use on PCs at home. Many relate to the National Curriculum, Key Stage tests or national examinations at 16 or 18. Schools are also making increasing use of the Internet and available software in a range of subject domains. Despite the increased availability of ICT, the question remains as to the extent to which ICT can and should replace more traditional forms of teaching. Is a scenario likely in the foreseeable future where most learning takes place individually through interactive learning packages and institutions of learning as we know them, for instance, schools, colleges, universities disappear?

■ *Whether it is equally beneficial to both parties to teach girls and boys together and if so in what phases of education*

Although this has not been raised directly in most of the chapters in the book, there are advocates of the idea that it is best to educate girls and boys separately in secondary schools. Because girls develop physically, emotionally and intellectually at a different pace to boys, arguments are made that progress for both would be better if their education was undertaken separately. The evidence to support these arguments is inconclusive at the moment and there are many possible confounding factors. There is also the question of why segregation should be in adolescence and not in other phases of education. Are there particular concerns about the education of adolescents that are distinct from learners of other ages? A fruitful approach might be to consider the common and distinct needs of boys and girls and how these might be met within a broadly co-educational environment. In addition, the personal and social development needs of young people must be considered alongside their academic attainment.

DOES THE AGE OR STAGE OF THE LEARNER MAKE A DIFFERENCE?

Teachers of different aged learners are often seen as very different. The stereotype personified in Joyce Grenfell's early childhood teacher is very different to that of David Lodge's university 'History Man'. Such teachers work in contrasting institutions, exist in different cultures and hold very different images of their status. Yet they share many of the same aims and adopt similar pedagogical techniques. Both are trying to promote learning. Both are seeking to elicit motivation. Both have access to specialized knowledge. Both use feedback to guide and develop the learner's own skills.

As we have seen, there are probably more similarities than differences between children's and adults' learning. The basic mechanisms by which we learn do not change over our lifetime although they may become less efficient in old age. This is compensated for by greater knowledge and expertise. The main differences are that children know less than adults and are less self conscious as learners. Adult learners have become expert in many everyday activities which they can perform effortlessly and without conscious thought. They have more knowledge of particular topics and much more general knowledge. Also, they may have gained more control over themselves and their emotions, although this is not always the case.

All learners, however, whether children or adults, appear to benefit from a sense of control over their learning and the chance to understand and to apply their knowledge. They also benefit from challenge and an ethos in which learning is valued. In the current education system in England there is little continuity in pedagogy from one phase of education to the next and little opportunity for learners to achieve continuity and progression in their control and self-regulation of learning.

At present, young people in primary and secondary schools have very little control over their own learning. Ironically, the secondary phase is probably the most restrictive of all, at a time when young people are striving to become independent and look forward to the time when they will support themselves. Yet they are seldom permitted to take any control or responsibility for their own learning, although in higher education this is an accepted and essential responsibility. An important aim for education in the future might be the establishment of a planned and progressive increase in the learner's responsibility in relation to their own learning as they progress through each phase of education.

THE LESSONS AND IMPLICATIONS FOR THE FUTURE

Patterns of employment in this country have changed dramatically during the past fifty years. We have moved from an industrial to a service-based economy. Fewer factories employ unskilled manual labour. Employment is less secure, with more part-time and temporary work and a concomitant requirement for flexibility and resourcefulness. This applies across all occupations, from the least to the most skilled. The shift to a service-based economy places different types of demands on those who perform less skilled work. Social and inter-personal skills are in greater demand. Team working and flexible, transferable skills are required in many occupations. Given these changes, we should now consider if it is possible to identify forms of pedagogy that will best equip our young people for the future.

One way of tackling this task is to consider the characteristics that will be required of young people in the future and then to establish overarching aims for the entire education system which will cumulatively enable them to develop the necessary skills and knowledge. We do not claim to have a ready list of such characteristics (indeed we would contend there is a need for them to be debated in the country as a whole) but there are probably several that most people would agree are essential. These would include a good general education, including literacy and numeracy, and a knowledge of science, humanities and the arts. Young people also need to have a range of learning and self-regulatory strategies and the confidence to use them effectively. To these we would also add creativity, flexibility and the ability to obtain and evaluate knowledge in new topics and subjects. These characteristics require skills in locating, interpreting and evaluating information from a range of sources, including the electronic media. Faced with an enormous variety of possible occupations and careers, people also need to acquire self-knowledge, so that they can find a niche where they will be satisfied and competent. Perhaps we should encourage personal development and 'spend less time ranking children and more time helping them to identify their natural competencies and gifts and cultivate those' as Gardner recently suggested (Gardner, 1996).

One of Vygotsky's ideas, subsequently developed by Wertsch (1985), was that cultures assist development by enabling members of society to appropriate and use a range of tools. For Vygotsky, tools were both physical objects (such as hammers) and conceptual systems or ways of thinking. Could this be extended to include pedagogic tools? Marton and Booth (1997) have argued that one of the most important ways in which we, as humans, differ from other animals is in how we explicitly and deliberately teach our children and each other. Alongside this is our ability to learn deliberately and to take conscious control of our own learning. Our knowledge and thinking about the complex and challenging process of teaching may provide us with powerful cultural tools to enhance learning in the next generations. These tools may be the key to our culture's survival.

So how can we respond to the Vygotskian idea of cultural tools, place them within a pedagogical framework, and make generalizations from the debates which have emerged from this book?

Six key ideas stand out:

1. *The term pedagogy is seldom dearly defined*

   Pedagogy has been seen by many within and outside the teaching profession as a somewhat vague concept. Even amongst continental educationalists – where the term is much more commonly used – it is seldom clearly defined and, as a result, is used fairly generally. Yet it could offer those involved with teaching a useful conceptual framework with which to examine their own professional practice and those outside of this group a way to understand the often complex approaches that are needed. Further, the time for a consideration of pedagogy is ripe. The technological revolution currently underway on the one hand demands and yet also offers an opportunity for a reappraisal and evaluation of current pedagogical practice with a view to examining its appropriateness for the needs of the future – with or without assistance from information and communications technology.

2. *There is no pedagogical panacea*

   Different learners at different ages and stages require different methods of teaching in order to achieve optimum learning of different kinds. There is no simple recipe for effective teaching in any phase of education. Teachers need to develop a full repertoire of skills and techniques designed to achieve different types of learning outcome. This process takes time and involves training, practice and reflection. It is ongoing throughout the careers of teachers whichever phase of education they work in and is optimized where teachers are in a supportive environment and can adopt a mastery approach to their own learning. Allowance needs to be made for this in the demands made on teachers' working lives.

3. *Teachers are important*

   Whatever the age or stage of learners, it is clear that teachers are crucially important. They need to devote themselves to the needs of their students but must be aware they cannot do the learning for them. As so many of the authors have stressed, teaching is a highly sophisticated activity in which thousands of judgements are made in course of a single day. Teachers – in their attempts to promote learning – have to provide information, challenge their learners to find information themselves, assess understanding, measure skills and provide formative feedback. Most of all, they have to inspire in their learners the desire to learn and reinforce their self-confidence. They will achieve this more readily if they have high self-esteem themselves and are regarded as members of a respected profession rather than one that faces constant criticism.

4. *Context matters*

   The arenas for learning, whether kindergarten, schoolroom, lecture hall, workplace or other 'life' setting, bring with them sets of expectations about learning and behaviour. Transferability of learning from one setting to another does not happen automatically. Learners have to develop the skills of boundary crossing. Such skills are enormously important to the ability to succeed in modern life. But for some young learners, feelings of powerlessness and of being a captive audience can get in the way and can inhibit learning.

   For teachers, this often means that issues of power and control become mixed up with pedagogical concerns. Control can become the first priority, learning the second. Pedagogy may be selected to facilitate control and not necessarily be the best teaching strategy for the desired learning outcome. If pupils have to be wooed to learn – and punished if they refuse to conform to the norms of the school – what hope is there of enlisting them as active learners at school or in their future lives? And what hope is there of them benefiting from the natural learning that appears to occur in other aspects of life? Commentators sometimes juxtapose the ease of 'real life' learning with the difficulties of school learning. But this misses the point that for young pupils, it is *school* rather than the worlds of pop music, premier league football or super models that is the 'real world'. These other worlds may exist but for most pupils will be unattainable. Yet young people seem to learn about these worlds very easily. Is this because the concepts are relatively simple or because motivation is so strong? The evidence would suggest the latter (Morris *et al.,* 1985). The compliance expected of school pupils (for very good institutional reasons) can act as a barrier to effective learning. This, as we have seen, is very different to the position of the adult learner who has much greater personal power and is generally in a learning environment because they wish to be there. The increasing trend for work place learning may mean, however, that some adults lose the voluntarism that has been an important part of the adult learning tradition.

5. *There are some general pedagogic principles*
   Some pedagogical principles for teachers can be formulated, though only at a very general level. From the literature searches undertaken by various authors it appears to be beneficial if teachers:

   – are clear about their aims and share them with learners
   – plan, organize and manage their teaching effectively
   – try to formulate the highest expectations about the potential capabilities of learners and their level of progress
   – endeavour to provide positive formative feedback to all their students
   – recognize the distinctiveness of individual learners within a general context of inclusivity
   – provide learning tasks which will challenge and interest and which are aligned to appropriate assessment procedures
   – seek to relate academic learning to other forms of learning and promote 'boundary crossing' skills
   – make explicit the rules and, at times, the hidden conventions of all learning institutions so that all learners become aware of ways in which they will be judged
   – include an understanding of metacognition in their objectives so that all learners can benefit from this knowledge and – as they advance through their learning careers – take increasing responsibility for their own learning
   – motivate and enthuse learners.

6. *Teachers are learners too*
   Finally, as so many of the authors have argued, it is important that the teacher remains a learner. Not only is our knowledge about the world growing at an increasingly rapid pace, but our knowledge of how learning takes place is also developing. It is imperative that teachers – with their many skills and experiences – continue to increase their own capabilities. Governments cannot do this for teachers – no matter how much they may want to do so. The teaching profession, itself, must set about becoming a learning profession. In England, the creation of a General Teaching Council and the Institute for Learning and Teaching in Higher Education will provide opportunities for this to take place.

To conclude, a wide-ranging debate is needed which focuses on the aims of education as well as pedagogy. This debate should take a broad view of learning through the lifespan, to develop a coherent framework for the lifelong development of learning skills. At present, the changes experienced by learners, as they move from one institution or setting to another, are governed to a large extent by the structures and forms of the institutions, rather than by a coherent strand of development in learning. The debate about aims that we propose should seek the views of all those who have a stake in education, including learners of all ages and stages as well as employers and – through the government – the wider society. But it must be led by teachers so that the profession will own the debate and will thus be most likely to take the conclusions into its own practice.

REFERENCES

Ames, C. and Ames, A. (1992) Classrooms: goals, structures and student motivation, *Journal of Educational Psychology*, 84(3): 261–271.

Ashton, P. T. and Webb, R. B. (1986) *Making a Difference: Teachers' Sense of Efficacy and Student Achievement*, New York: Longman.

Bandura, A. (1995) Exercise of personal and collective self-efficacy, in A. Bandura (ed.) *Self-Efficacy in Changing Societies*, Cambridge: Cambridge University Press.

Biggs, J. B. (1987) *Student Approaches to Learning and Studying*, Hawthorn, Victoria: Australian Council for Educational Research.

Biggs, J. B. and Moore, P. J. (1993) *The Process of Learning*, New York: Prentice Hall.

Black, P. and Wiliam, D. (1998) Assessment and classroom learning, *Assessment in Education*, 5(1): 7–73.

Broadfoot, P. (1996) Educational assessment: the myth of measurement, in P. Woods (ed.) *Contemporary Issues in Teaching and Learning*, London: Routledge.

Brown, J. S., Collins, A. and Duguid, P. (1989) Situated cognition and the culture of learning, *Educational Researcher*, 18(1): 32–42.

Covington, M. (1992) *Making the Grade: A Self-Worth Perspective on Motivation and School Achievement*, New York: Cambridge University Press.

Department of Education and Science (1988) *The Education Reform Act*, London: HMSO.

Dweck, C. S. and Leggett, E. L. (1988) Self-theories and goals: A social-cognitive approach to motivation and personality, *Psychological Review*, 95(2): 256–273.

Elton, L. R. and Laurillard, D. (1979) Trends in research on student learning, *Studies in Higher Education*, 4: 87–102.

Entwistle, N. (1992) *The Impact of Teaching on Learning Outcomes in Higher Education: A Literature Review*, Sheffield: CVCP.

Gardner, M. (1996) *New York Times Educational Supplement*, Nov. 3.

Glaser, R. (1984) Education and thinking: the role of knowledge, *American Psychologist*, 3: 93–104.

Goodlad, J. (1983) *A Place Called School*, New York: McGraw Hill.

Hodgson, A. and Spours, K. (1998) Pushed too far, *Times Educational Supplement*, December 11.

Hougham, J., Thomas, J. and Sisson, K. (1991) Ford's EDAP scheme: a round table discussion, *Human Resource Management Journal*, 1(3): 77–91.

Howe, M. (1991) Learning to learn: A fine idea but does it work?, *Education Section Review of the British Psychological Society*, 15(2): 43–57.

Ireson, J. and MacCallum, B. (in press) *Innovative Grouping Practices in Secondary Schools*, A Report for the Department of Education and Employment.

Kerry, T. (1984) Analysing the cognitive demand made by classroom tasks in mixed ability classes, in E. Wragg (ed.) *Classroom Teaching Skills*, London: Croom Helm.

Lave, J. and Wenger, E. (1991) *Situated Cognition: Legitimate Peripheral Participation*, Cambridge: Cambridge University Press.

Marton, F. and Booth, S. (1997) *Learning and Awareness*, Mahwah, NJ: Lawrence Erlbaum.

McGiveney, V. (1993) Participation and non-participation: a review of the literature, in R. Edwards, S. Sieminski and D. Zeldin (eds.), *Adult Learners, Education and Training*, Milton Keynes: Open University Press.

Meece, J. (1991) The classroom context and students' motivational goals, in M. Maehr and P. Pintrich (eds.) *Advances in Motivation and Achievement*, Vol. 7, Greenwich, Conn.: JAI Press.

Morris, P. E., Tweedy, M. and Gruneberg, M. M. (1985) Interest, knowledge and the memorising of soccer scores, *British Journal of Psychology*, 76: 415–425.

Mortimore, P. (1998) *The Road to Improvement: Reflections on School Effectiveness*, Lisse: Swcts & Zeitlinger.

Mortimore, P., Sammons, P., Stoll, L., Lewis, D. and Ecob, R. (1988) *School Matters*, Wells: Open Books (reprinted 1995, London: Paul Chapman).

Mortimore, P. and Whitty, J. (1997) *Can School Improvement Overcome the Effects of Disadvantage?* London: Institute of Education.

Nicholls, J. G- (1989) *The Competitive Ethos and Democratic Education*, Cambridge, MA: Harvard University Press.

Palinscar, A. M. and Brown, A. M. (1989) Classroom dialogues to promote self-regulated comprehension, in J. S. Brophy (ed.) *Advances in Research on Teaching*, Vol. 1, London: JAI Press.

Paris, S. G., Cross, D. R. and Lipson, M. Y. (1984) Informed strategies for learning: a program to improve children's reading awareness and comprehension, *Journal of Educational Psychology*, 76: 1239–1252.

Pramling, I. (1996) Understanding and empowering the child as a learner, in D. Olson and N. Torrance (eds.) *The Handbook of Education and Human Development*, Oxford: Blackwell.

Ramsden, P. (1992) *Learning to Teach in Higher Education*, London: Routledge.

Raven, J. (1994) *Managing Education for Effective Schooling: The Most Important Problem is to Come to Terms with Values*, Oxford: Oxford Psychologists Press.

Rogers, C. R. (1990) Motivation in the primary years, in C. Rogers and P. Kutnick (eds.) *The Social Psychology of the Primary School*, London: Routledge.

Saljo, R. and Wyndham, J. (1993) Solving problems in the formal setting: an empirical study of the school as a context for thought, in S. Chaiklin and J. Lave (eds.) *Understanding Practice*, Cambridge: Cambridge University Press.

Selmes, I. P. (1987) *Improving Study Skills*, London: Hodder and Stoughton.

Stodolsky, S. S. (1988) *The Subject Matters: Classroom Activity in Math and Social Studies*, Chicago: University of Chicago Press.

Strang, A. (1997) Motivation for effective independent learning, *Education Section Review of the British Psychological Society*, 21(2): 26–35.

Tschannen-Moran, M., Hoy, A. W. and Hoy, W. K. (1998) Teacher efficacy: its meaning and measure, *Review of Educational Research*, 68(2): 202–248.

Vygotsky, L. 5. (1978) *Mind in Society*, Cambridge: Cambridge University Press.

Weinstein, C. S., Goetz, E. T. and Alexander, P. A. (eds.) (1988) *Learning and Study Strategies: Issues in Assessment, Instruction and Evaluation*, New York: Academic Press.

Wertsch, J. V. (1985) *Vygotsky and the Social Formation of Mind*, Cambridge: Cambridge University Press.

14

BEYOND TESTING
Towards a theory of educational assessment

Caroline Gipps

INTRODUCTION

Professor Gipps has, since 2005, been Vice Chancellor of Wolverhampton University. For the previous six years she was Deputy Vice Chancellor at Kingston University, in Surrey, and prior to that Professor of Education and Dean of Research at the Institute for Education in London. She trained as a psychologist, primary school teacher and test developer. She has written about some of her work focusing on the changes taking place 'from psychometrics to educational assessment, from a testing and examination culture to an assessment culture'. This shift involves the use of a broader range of methods to achieve a wide range of purposes (not just grading and certification but the making of diagnostic judgements in order to enhance learning) and an increased professional sophistication that explored criterion (assessment of a particular target), norm (assessment in the context of what others achieve) and ipsative (assessment in light of what an individual has previously achieved) referencing.

KEY QUESTIONS

1. It might be possible to avoid testing but is it possible to avoid assessment? In other words, can we ever stop ourselves as teachers or learners making judgements about the extent to which we are making progress?
2. Do you feel that it is easier and/or more acceptable to assess in particular areas of school life? (For example, can you assess certain types of mathematical understanding with relative ease but would not want to try to assess spirituality?)

FURTHER READING

The Qualifications and Curriculum Authority has enthusiastically embraced assessment for learning, the key principles of which are outlined at: www.qca.org.uk/qca_4336.aspx and discussed by Black and Wiliam (see Black, P. and Wiliam, D. (1998) *Inside the Black Box*, King's College, London School of Education). See also Assessment Reform Group (1999)

> *Assessment for Learning: Beyond the Black Box* (University of Cambridge, Cambridge). There is an interesting discussion of relevant issues in Gardner, J. (ed.) (2006) *Assessment and Learning* (Sage, London).

This Reading links with Chapters 8, 9 and 13 of *The Routledge Education Studies Textbook*.

ASSESSMENT PARADIGMS

Introduction

Assessment is undergoing a paradigm shift, from psychometrics to a broader model of educational assessment, from a testing and examination culture to an assessment culture. There is a wider range of assessment in use now than there was twenty-five years ago: teacher assessment, standard tasks, coursework, records of achievement as well as practical and oral assessment, written examinations and standardized tests. There is criterion-referenced assessment, formative assessment and performance-based assessment, as well as norm-referenced testing. In addition, assessment has taken on a high profile and is required to achieve a wide range of purposes: it has to support teaching and learning, provide information about pupils, teachers and schools, act as a selection and certificating device, as an accountability procedure, and drive curriculum and teaching. These new forms and range of purposes for assessment mean that the major traditional model underpinning assessment theory, the psychometric model, is no longer adequate, hence the paradigm shift.

A paradigm is a set of interrelated concepts which provide the framework within which we see and understand a particular problem or activity. The paradigm within which we work determines what we look for, the way in which we construe what we observe, and how we solve emerging problems. A paradigm shift or 'scientific revolution' occurs when the old paradigm is unable to deal with an outstanding problem (Kuhn, 1970). This is written as part of the attempt to reconceptualize assessment in education in the 1990s. There has been over the last decade an explosion of developments in assessment and a number of key actors have been reconceptualizing the issues. The aim of this text is to bring together much of this work to discuss and synthesize it in an attempt to further our understandings and practice in educational assessment: to develop the theory of educational assessment.

We need to develop a new way of thinking about assessment to deal with the issues that are emerging as assessment takes on this broader definition and purpose. For example, one outstanding problem which we have in assessment is how to reconceptualize traditional reliability (the 'accuracy' of a score) in terms of assuring quality, or warranting assessment-based conclusions, when the type of assessment being used is not designed according to psychometric principles and for which highly standardized procedures are not appropriate.

I use the term theory to refer to a vehicle for explanation and prediction, a framework that will allow us to understand, explain and predict. Theories, as devices for organizing and giving meaning to facts, are built up through the process of analytical work: abstract, conceptual analysis is the vehicle for isolating crucial dimensions and constituents. My aim is that through this analysis we will come to have a better understanding of the design, functioning, impact, as well as inappropriate uses, of assessment within the new paradigm.

It is important too, given the much wider and more significant role given to assessment, that these issues are made clear to a wider audience. This is therefore aimed at all those who work in and around education and are interested in assessment: teachers and administrators, advisors, lecturers, policy-makers and other educational researchers.[1]

We set the scene by looking at purpose and fitness for purpose in assessment, the traditional psychometric paradigm and what we see as the new educational assessment paradigm.

Fitness for purpose

I have already referred to reliability of assessment (by this we mean the extent to which an assessment would produce the same, or similar, score if it was given by two different assessors, or given a second time to the same pupil using the same assessor) which goes alongside validity (by this is meant the extent to which an assessment measures what it purports to measure) but there is more to testing and assessment than technical issues of reliability and validity. Assessments (which I use here to include tests, examinations, practicals, coursework, teacher observations and assessment) come not only in a range of forms but with different purposes and underlying philosophies; these determine the range of appropriate use for an assessment. The first question to be asked then when considering the form of assessment to be used is 'what is the assessment for?' For example assessment to support learning, offering detailed feedback to the teacher and pupil, is necessarily different from assessment for monitoring or accountability purposes (for a start it is much more detailed). We must first ask the question *'assessment for what?'* and then design the assessment programme to fit.

I take the view that the prime purpose of assessment is professional: that is assessment to support the teaching/learning process. But, government, taxpayers and parents also want to know how the education system and individual schools are performing and they must have access to such information. A major, though not the only, element of this information is pupil performance as measured by tests and examinations. Assessment carried out for these purposes is likely to be more superficial since it needs to be relatively quick and manageable and needs to be more reliable than that to support learning. One can picture it as a form of survey (using postal questionnaires) as opposed to an in-depth study (using detailed interviews). Somewhere in between these two extremes of testing to support learning or for accountability purposes lies assessment for certification purposes, as with our public exams at 16 and 18: this assessment has to be both detailed (to provide comprehensive coverage) and reasonably reliable (so that we may have confidence that the results are comparable from one school to another and from one part of the country to another) though in other countries, for example Germany, this is not seen as an issue.

The problem that we have to confront is that tests designed for purposes other than to support learning – the huge quantities of multiple choice standardized tests in the USA, and the formal written exam in the UK – have had, we now realize, unwanted and negative effects on teaching and the curriculum. The stultifying effect of public exams on the secondary system in England has been pointed out by the HMI (1979 and 1988), and was a prime mover in the shift towards GCSE with its emphasis on a broader range of skills assessed, a lessening of emphasis on the timed exam and an opening up of the exam to a broader section of the age cohort. (All of this was brought in and supported by the same government which is now retrenching to a formal, exclusive, written exam, but that is another story.) The limiting and damaging effect of standardized multiple-choice tests in the USA has also been well documented and analyzed in recent years (for example, Resnick and Resnick, 1992). But assessment for monitoring and accountability purposes will not go away; on the contrary, a number of countries in the developing world are using assessment even more to gear up their education systems: in the USA, in New Zealand, in

Australia as in Great Britain governments have linked economic growth with educational performance and are using assessment to help determine curriculum, to impose high 'standards' of performance and, in New Zealand and Britain, countries which have taken on board the New Right marketplace model, as a market signal to aid parental choice and competition between schools (Murphy, 1990; Willis, 1992a).

Mindful of the distorting effects of assessment for these purposes, the task assessment specialists must address is how best to design accountability assessment which will provide good quality information about pupils' performance without distorting good teaching (and therefore learning) practice. We must also explore other forms of assessment which can be used alongside accountability assessment to support learning, and criteria by which we can evaluate them. This is not to say that traditional standardized tests and examinations have no role to play in assessment policy, but that we need to design assessment programmes that will do what is required of them and have a positive impact on teaching and learning.

This brings us to the second question which should be asked, but almost never is: *what kind of learning do we wish to achieve?*' for we know now that different forms of assessment encourage, via their effect on teaching, different styles of learning. If we wish to foster higher order skills including application of knowledge, investigation, analyzing, reasoning and interpretation for *all our pupils,* not just the élite, then we need our assessment system to reflect that.

But a failure to articulate the relationship between learning and assessment has resulted 'in a mismatch between the high quality learning described in policy documents as desirable and the poor quality learning that seems likely to result from associated assessment procedures' (Willis, 1992b, p. 1).

We need to put on to the assessment agenda issues of learning style and depth. We must articulate the model of learning on which we are to base new developments in assessment over the next decade if we are to develop a sound model and one which will achieve the results we wish for it. After all, the original psychometrics was based on a theory of intelligence, while multiple choice standardized tests were based on a behaviourist model of learning: educational assessment for the next century must be based on our best current understanding of theories of learning.

In considering assessment paradigms I shall look first at the traditional psychometric model, which is where testing in education began, and then look at what has come to be called educational assessment and how it differs from the psychometric model.

Psychometrics

The science of psychometrics developed from work on intelligence and intelligence testing. The underlying notion was that intelligence was innate and fixed in the way that other inherited characteristics such as skin colour are. Intelligence could therefore be measured (since it was observable like other characteristics) and on the basis of the outcome individuals could be assigned to streams, groups or schools which were appropriate to their intelligence (or 'ability' as it came to be seen). Thus the traditional psychometric testing model was essentially one of limitation: measuring attributes which are a property of the individual and which were thought to be fixed. This notion of limitation is seen now to be a major disadvantage of the psychometric approach. Assessment to support learning, by contrast, aims to help the individual to develop and further his/her learning: it is enabling rather than limiting. Another feature of psychometrics is the interpretation of scores in relation to norms: norm-referencing grades an individual's performance in relation to that of his/her peers, that is in terms of relative performance rather than their absolute performance. Norm-referenced tests are designed to produce familiar proportions of high, medium and low scorers. Since students cannot control the performance of other students they cannot control their own grades; this is now widely considered to be an unfair approach for looking at pupils' educational performance.

With the psychometric model comes an assumption of the primacy of technical issues, notably standardization, reliability and limited dimensionality. If individuals are to be compared with one another then we need to be certain that the test or assessment was carried out in the same way for all individuals, scored in the same way and the scores interpreted in the same way. Standardization is thus vital as is the technical reliability of the test within this model. These requirements can have a negative effect on the construct validity and curricular impact of the test since only some material and certain tasks are amenable to this type of testing.

Along with psychometric theory and its formulae and quantification comes an aura of objectivity; such testing is scientific and therefore the figures it produces must be accurate and meaningful. The measurements which individuals amass via such testing: IQ scores, reading ages, rankings, etc. thus come to have a powerful labelling potential.

But the psychometric paradigm has two other problematic assumptions which have been articulated more recently (Berlak *et al.*, 1992; Goldstein, 1992 and 1993).

The first is the *assumption of universality,* which means that a test score has essentially the same meaning for all individuals; this implies that a score on a standardized reading test represents the individual's ability to read (the performance is extrapolated from the test to reading in the general sense) and that what this means is universally accepted and understood.

A key factor in this argument is the 'construct'; a construct is a term used in psychology to label underlying skills or attributes. A construct is an explanatory device, so-called because it is a theoretical construction about the nature of human behaviour. In test development the construct being assessed is defined before the test is developed: this is to make sure that the test assesses the attribute that it is supposed to, that it is 'valid'. In the case of reading a detailed definition of the construct 'reading' would include accuracy and fluency in reading both aloud and silently, comprehension of material, interest in reading, etc. Thus a test which had high construct validity (i.e. which actually assesses reading adequately) should address each of these aspects of the skill. In fact, standardized tests of reading tend to assess only one aspect of the reading skill, for example, comprehension of simple sentences. This means that such a standardized reading test score does not represent the individual's ability to read in the widest sense, and therefore that the meaning of the score cannot be universally understood (since the user of the score would need to know which aspect of reading had been tested).

The second assumption is that of *unidimensionality* which relates to the conceptualization of constructs and impacts on the techniques used for analyzing test items. The assumption (within psychometric theory) is that the items in a test should be measuring a single underlying attribute. Thus when items are designed for a test they are first screened for obvious biases in terms of stereotypes either in the language or the pictures. The 'pilot' test is then given to a sample of students (which should be similar in characteristics to the intended sample). Item analysis is then carried out to get rid of items which are 'discrepant', i.e. items which do not correlate highly with the total score, because the test is meant to assess only one attribute. Items which have a high correlation with the total score are said to have high 'discrimination' while those which have low correlations are poor discriminators and are usually either dropped or modified. This approach comes from factor analysis techniques and the aim with a 'good' test would be to produce one which had only one underlying factor. This practice has two effects: first it implies an artificial simplicity of measured constructs since many attributes are in fact multi-dimensional as in the example of reading given above. Second, if the original group of items chosen actually measures more than one attribute and only a few items relate to one of these attributes these few items will inevitably have low correlation with the final score and therefore be eliminated from the final test. Thus they will be excluded from the test because they are different from the rest, the majority, of the items. The result will be a test measuring a single attribute, but the interpretations made from the score to a broader conceptualization of the construct will be invalid (and the measured construct will be determined by the original choice of items which might have been balanced in the direction of the second attribute which would then become the main attribute).

Since many of the attributes or skills which we measure in tests are multi- rather than unidimensional we can see that forcing tests into a unidimensional structure is illogical based as it is on the unproved assumption of unidimensionality. Item response models of item analysis, including the Rasch model, are predicated on the factor analysis model assuming a single underlying factor and this is the basis of critiques of these models (see Goldstein, 1992; Goldstein and Wood, 1989).

Around the 1950s the benefits of the application of psychological measurement in educational settings producing tests such as intelligence tests (including group tests used in the 11+) aptitude tests and the like began to be questioned. This criticism of the psychometric approach had two main foci. First the notion of limitation and the belief that tests are measuring a property of the individual; its focus was, critics argued, on the degree of ineducability of the child which arises from defects in the child or his/her home and parents rather than considering problems in teaching, curriculum, etc. (Meredith, 1974, quoted in Wood, 1986; Walkerdine, 1984).

The second was that the key feature of reliability requires the standardization of administration and tasks as well as scoring. Tests based on psychometric theory have as a prime requirement measurement properties amenable to statistical analysis: reliability and norm-referencing are the prime concerns. This has profound implications for the style of task assessed, the limited ways in which tasks can be explained to pupils and the required non-interaction of the tester. As a result of having to meet these requirements, issues of validity and usefulness to teachers have sometimes been overridden or ignored.

Around the time of the publication of Bloom's *Taxonomy of Educational Objectives* in the late 1950s, educators began to articulate a need for assessment which was specifically for educational purposes and could be used in the cycle of planning, instruction, learning and evaluation. This was termed educational measurement.

Educational measurement

Wood (1986) cites Glaser's 1963 paper on criterion-referenced testing was cited as a watershed in the development of educational measurement, i.e. the separation of educational assessment from classical psychometrics. Glaser's paper made the point that the emphasis on norm-referenced testing stemmed from the preoccupation of test theory with aptitude, selection and prediction. Wood maintains that every development in educational assessment since Glaser's criterion-referenced testing paper is based on the criterion-referenced model. There are enormous problems in the development of this kind of assessment, that results from criterion-referenced assessment can also be used for norm-referenced type purposes, and indeed norms are often used to set and interpret criteria of performance. But nevertheless, the point is well made, that in order to move away from a *norm*-referenced approach the only other reference we have come up with is that of criteria or standards, whether the result is described as criterion-referenced assessment, graded assessment, or standards-referenced assessment. There are different philosophies and techniques underlying these approaches but what they all have in common is that they do not interpret performance in relation to norms.

Educational measurement, by contrast with psychometrics, aims to devise tests which look at the individual as an individual rather than in relation to other individuals and to use measurement constructively to identify strengths and weaknesses individuals might have so as to aid their educational progress.

To find out 'How well' rather then 'How many' requires a quite different approach to test construction. Wood's definition of educational measurement therefore is that it:

1. deals with the individual's achievement relative to himself rather than to others;
2. seeks to test for competence rather than for intelligence;
3. takes place in relatively uncontrolled conditions and so does not produce 'well-behaved' data;
4. looks for 'best' rather than 'typical' performances;
5. is most effective when rules and regulations characteristic of standardized testing are relaxed;
6. embodies a constructive outlook on assessment where the aim is to help rather than sentence the individual.

and is happy to accept that this is 'thinking not of how things often are but rather of how they might or even ought to be . . .' (Wood, 1986, p. 194).

Where Wood uses the term competence (rather than intelligence) he is referring to the product of education, training or other experience rather than being an inborn or natural characteristic, as intelligence. We could more comfortably now use 'attainment' or 'achievement'. He argues that a powerful reason why educational measurement should not be based on psychometric theory is that the performances or traits being assessed have different properties: 'achievement data arise as a direct result of instruction and are therefore crucially affected by teaching and teachers' (p. 190). Aptitude and intelligence, by contrast, are traits which are unaffected by such factors, he claims. Achievement data are therefore 'dirty' compared with aptitude data and should not/cannot be analyzed using models which do not allow for some sort of teaching effect.

Looking for best rather than typical performance (the fourth principle on Wood's list) relates to Vygotsky's *zone of proximal development*. In educational assessment tester and pupil would collaborate to produce the best performance of which the pupil is capable, given help from an adult, rather than withholding such help to produce typical performance.

This also relates to the competence/performance distinction: competence refers to what a person can do under ideal circumstances, while performance refers to what is actually done under existing circumstances, competence thus includes the ability to access and utilize knowledge structures, as well as motivational, affective and cognitive factors that influence the response. 'Thus, a student's competence might not be revealed in either classroom performance or test performance because of personal or circumstantial factors that affect behaviour' (Messick, 1984). Elaborative procedures are therefore required to elicit competence; examination procedures tend to produce non-elaborated performance, i.e. they test at the lower rather than upper thresholds of performance (a profoundly non-Vygotskyian notion). This competence/performance distinction is a useful one to make in the consideration of educational assessment, but so that we do not get drawn into the question of whether we can infer competence from performance (i.e. the deep ability from the surface performance) we should think instead in terms of *best* performance. Wood concludes his paper with a plea for teachers to see test and examination results as saying something about their teaching rather than just about the pupil; he cites their reluctance to do this as the reason why teachers make so little use of test results (Gipps and Goldstein, 1983). 'How do you persuade teachers to trust tests?' is Wood's parting question.

What is interesting to see is how the agenda has changed in only ten years since Wood's seminal paper: a major development in educational assessment in England is now teachers' own classroom based assessment, while in the USA it is 'performance' or 'authentic' assessment in which (the latter at least) the teacher is centrally involved. In other words, the teacher has moved centre stage as an actor in assessment rather than being a simple administrator of 'better' tests devised elsewhere, the scenario when Wood was writing. Because of these developments educational measurement has now become called more generally educational assessment; this is largely because 'measurement' implies a precise quantification, which is not what the educational assessment paradigm is concerned with. I shall now look at some of the key authors who have elaborated and defined educational assessment.

Educational assessment

Glaser (1990) makes the case that assessment must be used in support of learning rather than just to indicate current or past achievement. Glaser's own work in the area of novice/expert performance indicates that there are characteristics of learners which differentiate experts from novices across a range of domains. 'As competence in a domain grows, evidence of a knowledge base that is increasingly *coherent, principled, useful* and *goal-oriented* is displayed. Assessment can be designed to capture such evidence' (ibid, p. 477). 'Assessment should display to the learner models of performance that can be emulated and also indicate the assistance, experiences and forms of practise required by learners as they move towards more competent performance' (ibid, p. 480).

The sort of assessment that Glaser has in mind here are: portfolios of accomplishments; situations which elicit problem-solving behaviour which can be observed and analyzed; dynamic tests that assess responsiveness of students to various kinds of instruction; and 'scoring procedures for the procedures and products of reasoning'. In other words we need a much wider range of assessment strategies to assess a broader body of cognitive aspects than mere subject-matter acquisition and retention.

Glaser's point is that assessment must offer 'executable advice' to both students and teachers; knowledge must be assessed in terms of its constructive use for further action. 'Once mastered, the skills and knowledge of a domain should be viewed as enabling competencies for the future' (ibid); in other words the assessments must themselves be useful and must focus on the student's ability to use the knowledge and skills learnt.

Raven on the other hand (Berlak *et al.*, 1992) argues that we must develop assessments which assess performance in relation to valued goals, rather than separating cognitive, affective and conative factors (and indeed failing to assess the latter two). He also argues that we need approaches which assess them in a unified way, since people do not become competent in activities which they do not value. Raven's general argument, that we should move outside the cognitive, is to be welcomed and resonates with some of the ideas from cognitive science and learning theory in relation to the importance of metacognitive processes in performance.

Goldstein (1992) argues that we need to stop seeing testing as a static activity which has no effect on the pupil. On the contrary, the pupil is participating in a learning procedure, he argues, and his/her state will be altered at the end of it. For example, successfully completing early items in a test might boost confidence and result in a higher overall performance than failing, or being unable to complete, early items. Thus we should have a more interactive model of assessment which does not assume that an individual's ability to respond to items remains constant during the test. The more 'authentic' the assessment becomes, Goldstein argues, the more important it is to question the assumption that nothing happens to the student during the process of assessment.

'Authentic assessment' is a term used largely in the USA where the intention is to design assessment which moves away from the standardized, multiple-choice type test towards approaches where the assessment task closely matches the desired performance and takes place in an authentic, or classroom, context. Performance-based assessment, more commonly called performance assessment, aims to model the real learning activities that we wish pupils to engage with, for example, written communication skills and problem-solving activities, so that assessment does not distort instruction. Briefly, the intention in performance assessment is to capture in the test task the same demands for critical thinking and knowledge integration as required by the desired criterion performance. The Standard Assessment Tasks outlined in the blueprint for the National Curriculum assessment programme in England and Wales (DES, 1988) are good examples of performance assessment. Performance assessments demand that the assessment tasks themselves are real examples of the skill or learning goals, rather than proxies. They support good teaching by not requiring teachers to move away from concepts, higher order skills, in depth projects, etc. to prepare for the tests. The focus is more likely to be on thinking to produce an answer than on eliminating wrong answers as in multiple choice tests. '. . . insights about how to develop and evaluate such tasks come not from the psychometric literature . . . but from research on learning in subject matter fields' (Shepard, 1991). However, when such tasks are required to support psychometric principles such as reliability and standardization, in order to be used in accountability settings, they fall short since that is not the purpose for which they have been designed.

The issue for performance assessment, as some see it, is how can tasks developed from, for example, diagnostic interviews be adapted for large scale administration and offer some level of confidence in comparability of results (which is necessary for accountability purposes). An alternative view is that we cannot force performance assessment into a psychometric model and that what we need is a range of approaches: more formal testing on a psychometric model for monitoring and accountability purposes and teacher-based approaches on an educational assessment model for assessment to support learning. This still leaves us with the question of whether assessment for certification and selection purposes can be more broadly conceived (as for example, the GCSE) to offer both beneficial impact on teaching *and* sufficient reliability for public credibility.

The dilemma that we face is that there are increased demands for testing at national level which must offer comparability, at the same time as our understanding of cognition and learning is telling us that we need assessment to map more directly on to the processes we wish to develop, including higher order skills, which makes achieving such comparability more difficult. Attempting to resolve this dilemma is part of the purpose of this text. There is no doubt we are faced with a paradigm clash, and the question is whether educational assessment can offer high quality assessments for a range of purposes.

In relation to our first question 'assessment for what?' Stiggins (1992) is one of those who take the view that assessment for accountability purposes and classroom-based assessment are so fundamentally different that we should not seek to merge or blend the two, for example, by making standardized tests more 'performance based' or by making classroom based assessment more standardized. While the test developer is looking to isolate traits that are common to all, to extract single elements from complex reality and to assess parts, the teacher seeks to understand and describe the 'complex reality of the individual child, attending to what is unique and changeful' (ibid, p. 1). Stiggins refers to these as 'trickle down' and 'trickle up' testing systems: in the first, data are gathered for use at the local or national level and eventually filters down to the teacher, while in the latter, data are gathered in the classroom and are aggregated upward to other levels of decision-making.

Trickle down testing is characterized by standardization first and foremost and may be paper and pencil or performance assessment; a good test is one that has high reliability, validity and efficiency and whose assessor remains a neutral observer; the results are largely used for accountability purposes (and in the UK we would add certification); the need for efficient scoring means that the 'fidelity' of results may be sacrificed; testing occurs at most once a year; the content represents a shallow sample from a broad domain; tests are timed; results are reported summatively, often with norm-referencing and involve considerable delay. (Validity essentially relates to the extent to which a test measures what it was designed to measure. If it does not measure what it purports to measure then its use is misleading.)

Trickle up testing, on the other hand, is essentially non-standardized and involves a wide range of activity but its purpose is to gather information for use in decision-making in the classroom; a sound assessment is one that allows understanding of the teaching/learning process for the student and the teacher is assessor, user and interpreter of results, i.e. s/he has an interactive role. The results are used by teachers to identify students' needs, assign them to teaching groups and to evaluate their teaching and courses; by students for feedback on their learning which in turn helps to determine their academic self-esteem and attitude to school; by parents to monitor progress and shape their view of the child's academic potential. This assessment takes place almost continuously; the content represents a deep sample from narrowly defined domains with a broad array of achievement targets being assessed; whilst they may be standardized *within* the class and may be timed, the criterion of comparability is likely to give way to the criterion of maximizing students' demonstrated level of competence in order to maximize motivation. Results will be used formatively and summatively and may not always be represented as scores or grades; feedback will be speedy.

Stiggins' paper takes us beyond the commonly used formative/summative[2] distinction, but he is making the same point that others do (Harlen *et al.*, 1992): assessment for formative purposes has quite different properties and qualities from that used summatively for accountability purposes. Any attempt to use formative assessment for summative purposes will impair its formative role. Not everyone takes this position of course and throughout this text I shall be exploring issues which are central to this problem: the relationship between formative and summative assessment, 'trickle up' and 'trickle down' testing, assessment for accountability purposes and that to support learning.

The legacy of psychometrics

The impact of psychometrics goes beyond the specifics of item design and test construction to a broader range of implications: the emphasis on relative ranking, rather than actual accomplishment; the privileging of easily quantifiable displays of skills and knowledge; the assumption that individual performances, rather than collaborative forms of cognition, are the most powerful indicators of educational progress; the notion that evaluating educational progress is a matter of scientific measurement (Wolf *et al.*, 1991). Thus we have tests that rank student performances rather than describe their level of learning in a meaningful way; the most useful form of information is taken to be comparison between individuals or groups, hence items are chosen to distinguish between students rather than because they represent the construct being assessed; and the presentation of performance in a normal curve has led to the belief that because the group of students at the bottom are well below average they cannot learn as much as others. These are all legacies of the psychometric model of testing which developed from the theory of intelligence.

Although American writers refer to the need to change the culture of teachers if we are to move them away from a reliance on norms, and to change their belief that formal exams and tests are necessary in order to make students work hard, the situation in the UK is different. We have not had the same reliance on standardized tests as in the USA: our public exams sit firmly within the performance assessment model while authentic assessment in the guise of RoA and pupil portfolios have been widely accepted as good assessment techniques. In addition, the early experience of having to do SATs at age 7 and 14 together with the teacher assessment element of National Curriculum assessment in England and Wales suggests that our teachers are no newcomers to the wide variety of assessment methods, so that a different culture of assessment clearly exists in the UK. But the problem that we have in the UK is that these developments, and this culture, are being eroded as a strongly right wing government puts assessment for market place and account-ability purposes on a traditional, examination model at the top of the agenda and down-grades other approaches.

The particular problem for the USA is that currently new forms of assessment are being held up as *the way* of changing the system and reforming education. Not that this is new: 'Nearly every large educational reform effort of the last few years has either mandated a new form of testing or expanded uses of existing testing' (Pipho, 1985). But, as Haney and Madaus (1989) point out technologies of educational assessment will not of themselves cure the ills in the education system that have been associated with standardized testing (see also Miller and Seraphine, 1992; Shepard, 1991). The same promise was also held for Measure-ment Driven Instruction (Mehrens, 1992). Various authors (for example, Mehrens, 1992; Wiggins, 1989; Miller and Seraphine, 1992) point out that the problem for performance assessment in changing the system is that (as already pointed out) it is not particularly amenable to use for large-scale accountability purposes; there are also serious concerns about equity issues in relation to performance assessment in the USA (Baker and O'Neil, 1994). Furthermore, the same teaching-to-the-test problems may occur with teachers focus-ing on the particular part of the skill that is being assessed, rather than the wider domain. Also, that assessment alone will not develop higher-order skills in the absence of clearly delineated teaching strategies that foster the development of higher order thinking in pupils.

An agenda for educational assessment

What we need is a more measured, analytical, approach to assessment in education. We need to resist the tendency to think in simplistic terms about one particular form of assessment being better than another: consideration of form without consideration of purpose is wasted effort. We must develop and propagate a wider understanding of the effect of assessment on teaching and learning for assessment does not stand outside teaching and learning but stands in dynamic interaction with it. We need also to foster a system which supports multiple meth-ods of assessment while at the same time making sure that each one is used appropriately.

In the shift from the limiting, psychometric model with its emphasis on ranking and statistically derived distributions to a new model we need to focus on pupil achievement. This involves a shift away from a norm-referenced approach towards one in which what pupils can and cannot do is stated. This requires the production of descriptions of per-formance as in the English National Curriculum. However, this in itself is problematic, since such descriptions will tend to be hierarchical or developmental and, as the research on learning and cognition makes clear, individual learning is idiosyncratic rather than ordered and the 'building-block' model of learning is inappropriate.

There are also implications for how we report performance: the use of a single over-all figure as a test result does not fit with current notions of describing pupils' performance in terms of what they can do, or indeed with the complexity of the domains being assessed. It is the legacy of psychometrics that compels us to want data from assessment that we can use to add up, make averages and standard deviations. The integrity of educational assess-ment requires that we look at profiles of pupils' performance across and within domains. This requires a rethinking of the ways in which information is presented at group level for evaluation or accountability purposes: we must devise alternative ways of presenting results that do not do violence to the domain and the rich judgments made. Details of what pupils have achieved across the broad range of the domain can be provided by 'qualitative' descriptors, or by denoting the level or grade attained within different strands or themes of the subjects and skills assessed. At the back of this argument is a belief that assessment on which so many resources are used should be, not only to measure, but also to inform the educational process. To collapse or aggregate these levels or grades to provide a single figure for reporting is to lose detailed information. When scores must be aggregated for reporting then we need to use models which result in the least loss of information and to make the rules explicit.

But the most difficult part of the agenda is in relation to technical issues. Previous notions about the importance of high-agreement reliability have to be reconsidered, both because of the changing nature of the assessments and because we are assessing more complex tasks in a range of contexts. Traditional internal consistency approaches cannot be used with many of the newer developments in assessment so we need to generate other ways of ensuring consistency and comparability where these are important. Considerable effort has gone in to a reconceptualizing of validity over the last five years but we need to evaluate this development and to see whether the reconceptualization is entirely helpful. Finally, we need to consider ethical issues in the framework which will guide our development and use of assessment, bearing in mind the enormous influence that assessment has on pupils' lives.

A FRAMEWORK FOR EDUCATIONAL ASSESSMENT

To recap, a paradigm is a set of interrelated concepts that frames research in a scientific field. The paradigm within which we work determines the way in which we understand and construe what we observe, as well as how we generate the universe of discourse; it constitutes the framework in which observations are made and interpreted, and directs which aspects we attend to.

> A paradigm shift redefines what scientists see as problems, and reconstitutes their tool kit for solving them. Previous models and methods remain useful to the extent that certain problems the old paradigm addresses are still meaningful, and the solutions it offers are still satisfactory, but now as viewed from the perspective of the new paradigm.
>
> (Mislevy, 1993, p. 4)

What we are observing in assessment is a shift in practice from psychometrics to educational assessment, from a testing culture to an assessment culture. However, it is not just that we wish to move beyond testing and its technology, but that the shift involves a much deeper set of transformations, hence the paradigm shift: our underlying conceptions of learning, of evaluation and of what counts as achievement are now radically different from those which underpin psychometrics.

The message of this reading is that assessment is an important part of education, and that whenever possible it must be of a type suitable to and used for the enhancement of good quality learning. This is not to say that traditional standardized tests and examinations have no role to play in assessment policy, but that we need to design assessment programmes that will have a positive impact on teaching and learning.

What it proposes is a form of educational assessment which will take up more by way of teacher and pupil time, but if it is true to the principles of educational assessment, it will support the teaching and learning of *important* skills and concepts at both basic and higher levels and the time will be deemed well-spent.

Educational assessment: a broader definition

Having already discussed educational assessment, it is now time to develop the definition:

■ Educational assessment recognizes that domains and constructs are multi-dimensional and complex; that assessing achievement is not an exact science; and that the interaction of pupil, task and context is sufficiently complex to make generalization to other tasks and contexts dubious. These issues are well understood in the literature but ignored within much test and examination development because they are inconvenient (Satterley, 1994).

■ In educational assessment clear standards are set for performance against which pupils will be assessed; these and assessment processes are shared with pupils (progressively so as they get older); pupils are encouraged to monitor and reflect on their own work/performance (with the positive and constructive help of teachers) so that they become self-monitoring learners in the metacognitive mode. Feedback to pupils, which is a key factor in the assessment process, emphasizes mastery and progress, not comparison with other pupils.

■ Educational assessment encourages pupils to think rather than tick alternatives or regurgitate facts. (But it is teachers who have to encourage pupils to organize and integrate ideas, to interact with material, to critique and evaluate the logic of an argument.) Good quality assessment needs to have good quality tasks so that pupils are not wasting their time: the tasks need to be anchored in important and relevant subject matter and the nature and mode of the task needs to be based on what we know about equitable and engaging assessment tasks.

■ Assessment which elicits an individual's best performance involves tasks that are concrete and within the experience of the pupil (an equal access issue); presented clearly (the pupil must understand what is required of her if she is to perform well); relevant to the current concerns of the pupil (to engender motivation and engagement); and in conditions that are not threatening (to reduce stress and enhance performance) (after Nuttall, 1987).

■ Assessment criteria are more holistic than in criterion-referenced assessment as originally conceived, to allow for the assessment of complex skills; this can be supported by having exemplars which allow teachers and others to interpret the criteria/standards.

■ Educational assessment involves grading or scoring by teachers or trained raters; in order to enhance consistency of scoring teachers need to understand the scoring categories and the levels of performance associated with them. This can be achieved through a process of moderation and provision of exemplars. These exemplars and moderation procedures need to be made available to all the teachers involved in any particular assessment scheme. The exemplars and standards can also serve the purpose of explicating to teachers the nature of the skill or concepts being taught and assessed.

■ In the culture of testing (Wolf *et al.*, 1991) it is the number of items correct, not the overall quality of response, that determines the score. In educational assessment we move away from the notion of a score, a single statistic, and look at other forms of describing achievement including 'thick' description of achievement and profiles of performance, what Wolf and colleagues call 'differentiated portraits of student performance' (p. 62). Aggregation of complex data to produce a simple (simplistic) figure is in many instances misleading and unless strict mastery rules are followed (for example 90 per cent correct) actually may provide 'untrue scores' which do not allow valid inferences about the component skills.

■ Teachers' own assessments of pupils are a key component within educational assessment. Such assessment can be interactive in order to engage fully with pupils and to gauge their understanding and misconceptions; it can support or scaffold the learning process and can evaluate performance in a range of contexts. The importance of informal teacher assessment is beginning to be recognized at policy level: it is now time that this recognition is translated into proper preparation and training of teachers in assessment principles and practice, including observation and questioning. Evidence is widespread that teachers are not well trained in assessment; but to get the full benefit out of educational assessment teachers need to be assessment literate.

▪ Teachers cannot assess well subject matter they do not understand just as they cannot teach it well. Teachers have to understand the constructs which they are assessing (and therefore what sort of tasks to set); they have to know how to get at the pupil's knowledge and understanding (and therefore what sort of questions to ask); and how to elicit the pupil's best performance (which depends on the physical, social and intellectual context in which the assessment takes place).

▪ Educational assessment is not high stakes: the publication of test data at class and school level distorts the educational process and encourages 'cheating' of various kinds; teachers and pupils cannot avoid this: they are caught in a trap. Using performance based assessment where high stakes external tests are unavoidable, together with teacher assessment, will mitigate the worst effects on teaching but even this, if stakes are too high, will promote assessed activities and therefore teaching to the performance assessment task, rather than to the domain or the higher level skill. When high stakes tests and exams allow a high proportion of pupils to fail there are self-esteem and motivation problems for low-scoring pupils with the concomitant risk of drop-out. Assessment against clear standards, in a low-stakes programme, with constructive feed-back and a focus on the individual's own performance in relation to the standard and to his/her own previous performance, rather than comparison with others, is more likely to maintain the engagement of pupils and retain them in the system.

This account of educational assessment is not academic ivory-towered hyperbole: every statement in this section is supported by the research evidence. Neither is it wishful thinking; we can develop assessment in this way and we must. We have to develop our assessment policy and practice in line with the educational assessment paradigm otherwise our attempts to raise educational standards and get the best out of our education system will be disappointed. The world has moved on: assessment is more pervasive and important than it was twenty years ago and the type of education needed to see us into the next century both as individuals and as a society has changed: basic skills are not enough – the majority of the population, not just the elite, needs to become flexible thinkers, reasoners and intelligent novices, and to believe that they can do so. A pervasive and narrow formal testing and examining system in a high-stakes setting will not allow this to happen.

I will expand on some of the main issues, but first I consider the design of assessment programmes.

Design of assessment programmes

The tension between assessment for accountability purposes and to support learning is not restricted to the UK. In a review of assessment for the OECD the two key themes were:

1. Testing national standards, a new political imperative: the use of assessment for monitoring and accountability in national systems, especially in terms of nationwide testing of pupils' achievement in basic skills or core subjects of the curriculum;

2. New approaches to assessment, a paradigm shift towards integrating assessment with learning: continuous assessment using pupils' regular work rather than formal examinations or standardized tests, records of achievement, portfolios, practical tasks, school-based assessment by teachers and self-assessment by pupils, using

results as feedback to help define objectives and encourage learners to take responsibility for their own learning.

Theme 1 may be seen as in conflict with Theme 2, the second being favoured by the professionals in education, against pressure for the first from politicians, parents, and administrators. As a result, there is an ideological divide between those who hope to raise standards by more extensive testing and those who hope to improve the quality of learning by changing assessment methods (Nisbet, 1993, p. 28).

In France, Germany, the Netherlands, Spain, Sweden, the UK and the USA the dilemma was apparent and the same.

Stiggins (1992) gets to the heart of the matter when he points out that centralized assessment for accountability purposes, what he characterizes as trickle-down testing, cannot meet the needs of teachers for assessment information.

Only high-quality classroom assessments developed and conducted under the control of the teacher can serve that teacher's needs well. We will begin to use our assessment resources wisely to the maximum benefit of students when we acknowledge these differences and begin to distribute assessment resources so as to ensure quality in both contexts (ibid, p. 2).

In other words, it is not an either-or issue, but a fitness for purpose issue. The same assessment cannot be used for a range of purposes. Designing assessments with fitness for purpose in mind will mean that a range of assessments is used; the acceptance of a range of types of assessments from traditional formal written examination to teachers' own assessments (via standardized tests, performance assessments, portfolios and RoA) will have valuable spin-offs in terms of fairness (a range of approaches allows pupils who are disadvantaged by one assessment to compensate on another provided that they carry comparable weight) and cost (performance assessment and portfolios are expensive in terms of pupil and teacher time, standardized tests are less so).

We need to move the debate away from false dichotomies: criterion-referenced assessment versus norm-referenced assessment, standardized tests versus performance assessment; they are as unhelpful as the quantitative *versus* qualitative research method argument. What we need is to understand the value of each approach and to follow the fitness for purpose principle; some approaches then, of course, may be seen to have little value. Messick (1992) argues for a realistic mixture of decontextualized structured exercises and contextualized performance-based tasks on the grounds that both basic and higher order skills need assessing. This combination is in any case necessary to ensure full construct representation and to balance the advantages of time-intensive depth of assessment within a domain with broader domain-coverage.

One model for designing assessment programmes is to use teacher assessment and portfolio assessment at the individual child level for formative purposes; APU/NAEP type surveys at the school district and national level for accountability purposes using light sampling and matrix sampling; and a mixture of moderated teacher assessment with optional use of good quality tasks from item banks, carrying national statistics, for school-level accountability purposes and parental/community feedback (Harlen *et al.*, 1992).

Using only a light sample in order to reduce the stakes is possible for national and local district level accountability purposes. It may also be acceptable to light-sample large schools in order to get school level performance and accountability data; but this approach will not work for smaller schools where light sampling does not provide enough pupils for an acceptable sample size. Furthermore, those who advocate light sampling in order to reduce the stakes and costs associated with authentic assessment (for example, Popham, 1993) ignore the certificating and selecting role of assessment: this cannot be carried out on a sample – it must include all pupils and it will be high stakes. The broader and more performance-based is the assessment for this purpose the 'better' will be the impact on teaching. We are thus back in the conundrum of how performance-based we can afford to make assessment for certification and selection purposes.

Alongside using a variety of approaches it is important to reduce the stakes associated with any single one. It is publication in the (local) press that seems most to influence the stakes as far as teachers are concerned (and the *perception* of the significance of results is what counts). So we need to look for other ways of communicating how well schools are doing than using league tables, for example embedding results within detailed prospectuses.

The original blueprint for the National Curriculum assessment programme in England and Wales (DES, 1988) matched in many ways Frederiksen and Collins' (1989) blueprint for the design of a systemically valid testing system. These include first, a set of tasks that cover the spectrum of knowledge, skills and strategies needed for the activity or domain being tested. Second, a list of 'primary traits' for each task must be made available to teachers and students; the traits should cover knowledge and skills necessary to do well in that activity, for example for expository writing the primary traits might be clarity, persuasiveness, memorability and enticingness. Third, a library of exemplars of all levels of performance of the primary traits with explanation of how they were judged; this would ensure reliability of scoring and help pupils to understand what is required of them. Fourth, there needs to be a training system for scoring the tests reliably; this should be extended to teachers, pupils *and* administrators of the testing system, indeed teachers should encourage pupils to carry out self-assessment. Frederiksen and Collins also discuss fostering improvement on the test through: employing forms of assessment that enhance learning; practice in self-assessment; detailed feedback on performance in relation to the primary traits; and multiple levels of success so that through repeated testing students can strive for higher levels of performance. This blueprint incorporates many of our requirements for an educational assessment programme.

If teacher assessments and performance assessments are used for high-stakes purposes then they must offer comparability of results. It is possible to do this as the GCSE in the UK demonstrates, *but* it is very time and labour intensive and relies on the involvement of teachers. Supporting such a system requires: clear statements of looked-for performance, comprehensive scoring schemes, training of raters, group moderation to ensure comparability across tasks and raters, some form of statistical moderation if appropriate, and an auditing process to check the processes and results. It can be done at one or two points in a school system if there is the political will to support this type of assessment model.

Arguments about the impact of assessment do not by and large apply to the devices used for diagnostic assessment, or to teachers' informal formative assessment in the classroom but to the high-status, high-stakes forms of testing which are used for certification, selection and accountability purposes. This is because tests for these purposes are the ones that have most power within the system and as a result of this power the tests shape the curriculum and teaching. We need to accept that any significant assessment program will have an impact on teachers and pupils so we must put this into the design consideration of a test program.

Ethics and equity

Raising the stakes enhances the ethical dimension in assessment. The higher the stakes the greater the likelihood of cheating and unethical practices and the more important it is that assessment practice be equitable. There is, however, a confusion over equity within the educational assessment model, in performance assessment in particular. Performance assessment, which is often conflated with educational assessment, is sometimes promoted because it is 'more fair' (but for an alternative view from minority groups, see Baker and O'Neil, 1994); this is a serious misconception of the theoretical rationale underpinning educational assessment. The underlying assumption of most traditional psychometrics is one of fixed abilities and therefore limitation; in educational assessment performance is seen to be dependent on context and motivation and is essentially interactive and elastic. Thus the concept is a positive one with the corollary that in assessment all pupils must be given the opportunity to show what they can do, that it is possible to maximize learning, and that assessment should try to get the best performance out of pupils. But it is still true that some groups may have been better prepared for assessment including performance assessment than others. As an example, Linn *et al.* (1991) give the use of calculator-based problems: pupil access to calculators may be quite inequitable and if problems using calculators are part of an accountability or certificating assessment then there is an equal access issue. So, the conception is enabling, but individual assessments may still be inequitable.

The ethics of assessment demand that the constructs and assessment criteria are made available to pupils and teachers, and that a range of tasks and assessments be included in an assessment programme. These requirements are consonant with enhancing construct validity in any case.

We need to be clear about what counts as proper preparation of pupils in any assessment programme. If there are preparation practices which are considered to be unethical then they should be spelled out. The other side of the coin is that teachers and schools have a commitment to teach pupils the material on which they are going to be assessed. To this requirement we should add proper preparation of teachers so that they understand the basic issues in assessment and are equipped to carry out good formative assessment.

The more that teachers are involved in generating or carrying out assessment, through discussing the standards, how to generate best performance, what counts as meeting the criteria, etc., the more teachers will be empowered in the educative process rather than technicians carrying out an imposed curriculum and testing programme.

Given the detailed, and as yet poorly understood, effect of context (Murphy, 1993) on performance, the evidence that girls attend to context in an assessment task more than do boys, and the ability of changes in the context of the task to alter the construct being assessed this is an area of validity which demands detailed study. We certainly need to define the context of an assessment task and the underlying constructs and make sure they reflect what is taught.

Context has a crucial role in both learning and assessment: the learning and performance of a skill interacts with the context in which it takes place. Assessing in a decontextualized way (as in the baldest of multiple-choice questions) is possible but limiting; it is important, however, to strip away irrelevant context from an assessment task since that will cause construct-irrelevance variance. Messick (1992) describes an approach called 'cross-contextual measurement' in which performance on the same skill across contexts is assessed in order to 'develop an aggregate measure of the construct across a variety of item contexts in an effort to balance the effects of different student backgrounds and interests' (ibid, p. 25). The findings would also allow one to generalize performance to a broader construct domain. This is essentially what happens in teacher assessment, but is likely to be too time-consuming for external assessment for accountability purposes (which is when one is most likely to generalize).

Paradigm shift

The most challenging task in developing a theory of educational assessment is that of reconceptualizing reliability. Underlying this challenge is a shift in our world view. The psychometric model carried with it a notion of objectivity – that ability or attainment is a property of the individual which can be reliably (accurately) measured and that the resulting 'score' is unaffected by context or the testing situation. We now know however that performance is very much context bound, affected by motivation and the assessment mode itself. It is also construed according to the perspectives and values of the assessor –

whether it is the one who designs the assessment and marking scheme or the one who grades the open-ended performances. We do not therefore see assessment as a scientific, objective, activity, this we now understand to be spurious.

Assessment is not an exact science, and we must stop presenting it as such. This is of course part of the post-modern condition – a suspension of belief in the absolute status of 'scientific' knowledge (Gipps, 1993; Torrance, 1993). The modernist stance suggests that it is possible to be a disinterested observer, while the post-modernist stance indicates that such detachment is not possible: we are social beings who construe the world according to our values and perceptions. The constructivist paradigm does not accept that reality is fixed and independent of the observer; rather reality is constructed by the observer, thus there are multiple constructions of reality. This paradigm would then deny the existence of such a thing as a 'true score'.

The shift from a psychometric model of assessment to an educational model has a parallel in the experimental versus naturalistic evaluation paradigms. Eisner (1993) elaborated the comparisons between curriculum evaluation and pupil assessment (also called evaluation in the USA) and a similar move towards qualitative approaches in both disciplines which he ascribes to the general dissatisfaction with education and its outcomes and a realization that standards will not be raised by having tough assessment policies. It is improving the quality of teaching and what goes on in schools that will raise standards:

> . . . we find ourselves exploring new routes to excellence, partly because we have recognized that mandates do not work, partly because we have come to realize that the measurement of outcomes on instruments that have little predictive or concurrent validity is not an effective way to improve schools, and partly because we have become aware that unless we can create assessment procedures that have more educational validity than those we have been using, change is unlikely.

(ibid, p. 224)

Evaluation within the constructivist and naturalistic paradigms rejects the traditional criteria of reliability, validity and generalizability and looks instead for qualities such as trustworthiness and authenticity (Guba and Lincoln, 1989). We need similarly to reconceptualize the concepts of reliability and generalizability in relation to assessment, and the educational evaluation literature is a potential source.

Trustworthiness according to Guba and Lincoln is based on *credibility, transferability* and *dependability. Credibility* comes from prolonged engagement and persistent observation, i.e. regular on-going assessment in the classroom, and including parents in the dialogue about pupil performance. *Transferability* could replace the notion of generalizability: since performance is context bound the assessor must specify the context in which a particular achievement was demonstrated. Others then judge whether this will be transferable to other contexts; these are referred to as the sending and receiving contexts respectively: the more the sending and receiving contexts are alike the more likely is transfer. It is this description which, through providing extensive information about the sending context, allows judgments about transferability to be made. Dependability replaces traditional reliability, it is related to the process of assessment and the judgments made which must be open to scrutiny. Guba and Lincoln suggest that this be achieved through an audit process – possibly like the quality control process in moderation. *Authenticity* is to do with the extent to which the relevant constructs (and this means all the stakeholders' constructs) are fairly and adequately covered in the assessment. The fairness aspect of authenticity suggests that *all* groups' constructs are included rather than just the test developer's.

Assessment is developing a wider meaning better to represent pupils' broad range of achievement. For example, the descriptions of pupil achievement in RoA are akin to a qualitative form of assessment. Such 'thick description' (Guba and Lincoln, 1989) is a key feature of naturalistic forms of evaluation and one can say is also necessary for a full understanding of what it is pupils know, understand and can do and in what contexts. So we can use profiles of performance in reporting individual attainment for use by parents and teachers. What the qualitative approach to assessment makes difficult, however, is comparison because the detailed description does not easily condense to a single figure, or even a set of figures. But to wish to do this is to confuse the two paradigms and to misunderstand the purpose of newer approaches to assessment.

But first, what can be salvaged, if anything, from the traditional concepts of validity and reliability?

Validity issues

More has been written about validity in recent years than about any other aspect of assessment practice. Messick's expanded view of validity incorporates evidence of construct validity (which supports test-score interpretation) and social consequences of test use. While Messick's conception has not been seriously challenged, neither is it being adopted in practice probably because it is too complex and all-embracing. While a number of authors (Linn, Baker and Dunbar, 1991; Harnisch and Mabry, 1993) suggest expanding the validity framework what I believe is needed, as Shepard (1993) also points out, is a simplified framework with some priorities identified. To keep expanding the validity framework, whilst accepting the dictum that construct validation is a never-ending process, is to make the validation task so demanding that test and assessment developers cannot (and do not) engage with it.

Shepard (1993) argues that Messick's validity studies when operationalized start 'with a traditional investigation of test score meaning and then adds test relevance, values, and social consequences. Orchestrated this way, typical validity investigations never get to consequences'. Shepard suggests instead that we need to identify which validity questions must be answered to defend a test use and which are less immediate questions. The direct question then is 'What does a testing practice claim to *do*?' (p. 408). An indication of the labyrinthine nature of validity studies is that a test has to be validated for each use: evidence collected to support the interpretations and uses of test scores for individuals does not necessarily support the interpretations and policy uses of the results when aggregated to give data about schools or districts. If a test has not been validated for a particular purpose, then using it for that purpose is highly questionable, particularly if the purpose is high stakes for individuals.

The criticism of Messick's approach is not that his conceptualization is *wrong*, but that it is inappropriate because it is inoperable. The concern is that test developers will simply opt out of the consequential aspect of validity studies because the process is never ending. The danger then is that the responsibility for making judgments about valid test use – assuming the test developer claims evidence of construct validity – will fall to test users. This is not appropriate since, with the widespread publication of test results, virtually every member of the public with an interest in education and schools including parents of school-aged children, and the pupils themselves, is a user of test results.

Most test users cannot carry out validity studies, and so it is the test developer's role to articulate the uses to which a particular test may be put. For this we can pose the question: For what use, and of which construct, is this a valid indicator? Test developers must address this question as a priority in the design of tests and their evaluation of construct validity. This implies an opening up of the test's constructs to users and for test developers to commit themselves to appropriate test use. In assessment programmes designed for accountability purposes, which will in practice be used at a range of levels, independent evaluation of consequences must be carried out; funding of this should be the responsibility of the policy making authority – national or local – which is responsible for commissioning the assessment. The onus must then be on the publisher of results to present them 'fairly', whether it be central government, LEA, local newspaper or school, that is: to state clearly what the results can appropriately be used for and what they cannot, and to contextualize the results when they are used to compare institutions, etc. To summarize:

■ the test developer must articulate the constructs assessed and appropriate test use;
■ for accountability testing the policy-making authority must commission evaluation of the consequences of test use;
■ the 'publisher' of results must present them fairly and with contextual information: of the institution in relation to league tables, of the actual assessment in relation to individuals.

This implies rethinking the partnership between, and responsibilities of, developers, policy-makers and test users. Finally, researchers and evaluators in assessment need to continue to simplify the validity concept so that it becomes manageable.

Studies of consequential validity are particularly important for newer forms of assessment given the promises that are held out for them. In particular in the USA if performance assessment is to do what is hoped for it in terms of broadening teaching, then one thing that needs to be evaluated is whether, in a high-stakes setting, teaching takes place to the task or to the broader domain. Although we have high stakes performance assessment in the UK we have not researched this particular issue.

The pupils' views about the tasks will also be important in order to gauge the impact on pupil motivation and other behavioural effects. This research agenda will, however, require a new focusing of effort: effort is most marked in developing new assessments and setting up new assessment policy. Little or no effort is characteristically put into evaluating the effects of the assessment programme or any adverse impact once it is introduced.

Reliability

Whilst rethinking validity is a question of prioritizing and specifying the responsibility of test developer, policy-maker and user, reliability needs a much more radical approach. Educational assessment does not operate on the assumption of unidimensionality, results are not forced into a normal distribution, fewer items are used, assessment conditions are not fully standardized. Thus many of the statistical approaches used to evaluate reliability in standardized tests are simply not appropriate. In any case we no longer conceive of 'accurate' measurement and 'true scores'. Where traditional reliability measures are not appropriate we need to drop the term reliability and instead use, I suggest, *comparability,* which is based on consistency. The level of comparability demanded for any assessment will be related to its use: for example, if performance assessment is used for accountability purposes then great care will need to be taken to ensure comparability; for teacher assessment for formative purposes comparability is of lesser concern. Consistency leading to comparability is achieved by assessment tasks being presented in the same way to all pupils assessed; assessment criteria being interpreted in the same way by all teachers; and pupil performance being evaluated according to the same rubric and standards by all markers.

This is not as radical a suggestion as it might at first appear. The evidence for high technical reliability in examinations is weak to say the least (Satterley, 1994). Furthermore, the interaction of student with task is such a great source of variation that the relatively small number of tasks assessed even in traditional examinations does not offer results which are robust enough to warrant generalization. Teacher assessment over time and task, if done well, is better equipped to reach a dependable conclusion about students' work. Furthermore, in assessment carried out by teachers and used within the classroom, the importance of comparability may give way to the importance of maximizing the pupil's performance.

Some assessment theorists, for example, Frederiksen and Collins (1989) believe that in educational assessment we must move away from a sampling model of measurement towards a performance model 'where the quality of performance and the fairness of scoring are crucial but where the replicability and generalisability of the performance are not'(Moss, 1992, p. 250). For some forms of assessment we may need to give up on generalizability altogether:

> Rather than attempting to estimate and to predict future performance on a construct such as mathematics understanding, some new assessments simply credit a specific, complex accomplishment in and of itself, without the burden of prediction or the constraints of domain generality.
>
> (Baker, O'Neil and Linn, 1991, p. 14)

Reliability and validity are important dimensions of traditional test development, acting essentially as quality assurance devices and still have a role to play in developing some forms of assessment. But for educational assessment, however, we need other indicators of quality and I will now discuss some of these, before proposing a check-list of alternative criteria for evaluating the quality of assessment.

Alternative criteria of quality in educational assessment

Curriculum fidelity is a useful alternative criterion for evaluating assessment when that assessment is linked to a specified or National Curriculum: we need to have a broad coverage of the curriculum because of the well-rehearsed problems of assessing only examinable tasks. The concept of curriculum fidelity is particularly useful for teacher assessment (and authentic assessment), because it has the advantage of being easier to specify than construct validity, since curriculum is more apparent than are underlying constructs. The notion of curriculum fidelity is in fact consonant with construct validity: construct underrepresentation is analogous with poor curriculum fidelity.

Dependability is a term which is coming back into use; it attempts to recognize the tension between reliability and validity. Dependability is the 'intersection of reliability and validity' (Wiliam, 1993), in other words an assessment is dependable to the extent that it is both content valid and reliable. Harlen (1994) defines quality in assessment similarly as 'the provision of information of the highest validity and optimum reliability suited to a particular purpose and context' (p. 2). This is useful in that it relates to fitness-for-purpose, but for assessment for which traditional measures of reliability are not suitable we may prefer to define dependability as the highest validity and optimum consistency and comparability for a particular purpose.

In relation to performance assessment and teacher assessment what we must do to assure comparability, and in the name of equity and fairness, is to tie the assessment to criteria, to provide training in observation and questioning, and support group moderation to get consistency across, and indeed within, schools *and* to limit the damaging effects of teacher stereotyping (Gipps and Murphy, 1994).

Public credibility is a criterion (McGaw, 1993) which would be particularly important for high-stakes or accountability testing and is rather different from Cuba and Lincoln's concept of credibility. This criterion is important since test users and the general public need to be reassured that results are *consistent* (from one administration to another) and *comparable* (from one school or assessor to another).

Generalization is dubious with performance assessment: not only is performance heavily task and context dependent but the time each task takes means that we are unlikely to be able to get enough tasks to generalize within the domain, never mind outside it. Pupil performance is quite unpredictable; we know that from work in cognitive psychology and learning theory. So to pretend that we can generalize widely is to delude ourselves and others. Instead of generalizability we can focus on *transferability* and this involves much more description of the context in which the assessment took place: since performance is context-bound we must specify the context in which a particular achievement was demonstrated. Performance cannot be generalized beyond the context of assessment although test users often do this. Context description will at least allow for a more informed judgment about possible transferability. With complex constructs and skills it may be more appropriate to credit a specific complex accomplishment in and of itself without the burden of generalizing to, or beyond, the domain as we do at university level with, for example, dissertations.

What we wish good quality assessment to do, therefore, is to elicit quality performance, within a well-defined context; it must then be scored fairly (in a way that the pupil understands) and consistently (across teachers and pupils).

To the definition of educational assessment we can now therefore add a checklist of alternative indicators to assure quality in educational assessment:

■ *Curriculum fidelity:* this implies that the construct, domain or curriculum is well specified and there is a broad coverage of the curriculum (if not of each domain) in the assessment.
■ *Comparability:* this is achieved through *consistency of approach* to the assessment by teachers; a *common understanding of assessment criteria;* and that performance is evaluated fairly, that is, according to the same rubric by all markers. These can be achieved by a combination of training, moderation and provision of exemplars.
■ *Dependability:* this emerges from evidence of curriculum fidelity, consistency and comparability, as will.
■ *Public credibility.*
■ *Context description:* this requires that detailed information about context be available so that we may make informed judgments about transferability.
■ *Equity:* this requires that a range of indicators be used in an assessment programme to offer pupils multiple opportunities to achieve.

These alternative criteria of quality in educational assessment, and the rethinking of reliability and generalizability, are still relatively untried. The debate has been rumbling in the literature for a number of years, but research in educational assessment is uncoordinated and the technical base is somewhat weak and underconceptualized. The hope is that this framework will act as an impetus en route to developing good quality educational assessment.

There are those who criticize educational assessment for having no underlying theoretical rationale (for example, Hansen, 1993): it is seen simply as a new bandwagon which criticizes psychometrics without putting anything substantive in its place. What I hope I have shown is that educational assessment, which has the learner at its core, has a theoretical base in theories of learning, motivation and evaluation. That the main area in which development is needed is the 'technical' one, but what is needed is not a technology as such, but a radically different way of conceptualizing purpose, and quality, in assessment.

We must acknowledge the difference between highly standardized testing procedures, performance-based tasks used by teachers or as part of an external testing programme, and teacher assessment. If we move teacher assessment and performance assessment too closely towards standardization in order to satisfy traditional reliability, we are in danger of throwing out the baby with the bath water. The search for objectivity in assessment is not only futile but can be destructive; the alternative criteria proposed will allow us to ensure quality in educational assessment without resorting to highly standardized and narrow testing procedures with all that this implies for teaching and learning.

That some of these criteria are qualitative rather than quantitative is all to the good, since we need to stop supporting the notion of assessment as an objective activity or exact science (see also Broadfoot, 1994). If we wish to continue to include performance assessment and teacher assessment in assessment programmes we must develop these criteria and their use. Otherwise many new developments will be pushed out of formal assessment practice because they fail to meet the traditional criteria of quality. These newer forms of assessment are important because of what they offer by way of impact on teaching and learning practice and broad curriculum coverage.

The message for policy-makers is that assessment programmes, even for accountability purposes, need to include a range of types of assessment to provide manageability in terms of cost and time, construct representation, depth of assessment and broad domain coverage, and in terms of fairness to different groups of pupils.

We need to persuade politicians and policy makers of the importance of lowering the stakes associated with assessment whenever possible, particularly at the level of the teacher and school. With assessment for certification and selection purposes high stakes are unlikely to be reduced and therefore the style and content of assessment tasks is particularly crucial. We also need to persuade policy-makers of their responsibility for evaluation of the educational and social consequences of test use at every level.

The message for assessment developers is that, particularly for assessment for selection and certification, high quality tasks requiring extended responses and a range of modes are important to encourage good impact on teaching and curriculum: we need to design accountability assessment which will provide good quality information about pupils' performance without distorting good teaching practice. These are not impossible demands. Furthermore, the constructs assessed and appropriate test use must always be articulated. The development of other forms of assessment which can be used alongside accountability assessment to support learning must also continue as a priority.

Finally, any assessment model, policy or programme will only be as good as the teachers who use it: devalue the role of teachers and deprofessionalize their training and no assessment technology will replace their skill. It is teachers who teach the concepts and skills, prepare pupils for the assessments, feedback to pupils and parents and move learners on in the appropriate direction. To limit the role of teachers in assessment would be the ultimate misconstrual of the process of teaching and learning. To embrace educational assessment, with the professional involvement of well-trained teachers, will be to harness a powerful tool for learning.

NOTES

1. However, we do assume a basic knowledge of testing and assessment; readers who are new to the area are advised to read *Assessment: A Teacher's Guide to the Issues* (1993), by Gipps and Stobart, first.
2. Formative assessment takes place during the course of teaching and is used essentially to feed back into the teaching/learning process. Summative assessment takes place at the end of a term or a course and is used to provide information about how much students have learned and how well a course has worked.

REFERENCE

Baker, E. and O'Neil, H. (1994) 'Performance assessment and equity: A view from the USA', *Assessment in Education*, 1, 1.

Baker, E., O'Neil, H. and Linn, R. (1991) *'Policy and validity prospects for performance-based assessment'*, paper presented at APA annual meeting, August.

Berlak, H., Newmann, F., Adams, E., Archbald, D., Burgess, T., Raven, J. and Romberg, T. (1992) *Towards a New Science of Educational Testing and Assessment*, New York, State University of New York Press.

Broadfoot, P. (1994) *Educational Assessment: The Myth of Measurement*, Inaugural Lecture, University of Bristol.

DES (1988) *National Curriculum Task Group on Assessment and Testing: A Report*, London, DES/WO. (the TGAT Report)

Eisner, E. (1993) 'Reshaping assessment in education: Some criteria in search of practice', *Journal Curriculum Studies*, 25, 3, pp. 219–33.

Frederiksen, J. and Collins, A. (1989) 'A systems approach to educational testing', *Educational Researcher*, 18, 9, pp. 27–32.

Gipps, C. (1993) 'The profession of educational research', BERA Presidential Address, *British Educational Research Journal*, 19, 1, pp. 3–16.

Gipps, C. and Goldstein, H. (1983) *Monitoring Children: An Evaluation of the Assessment of Performance Unit*, London, Heinemann Educational Books.

Gipps, C. and Murphy, P. (1994) *A Fair Test? Assessment, Achievement and Equity*, Milton Keynes, Open University Press.

Glaser, R. (1990) 'Toward new models for assessment', *International Journal of Educational Research*, 14, 5, pp. 475–83.

Goldstein, H. (1992) *Recontextualising Mental Measurement*, London, ICRA Research Working Paper, ULIE. [Published in *Educational Mreasurement: Issues and Practice* 1994, Vol. 13, 1.]

Goldstein, H. (1993) 'Assessing group differences', *Oxford Review of Education*, 19, 2, pp. 141–50.

Goldstein, H. and Wood, R. (1989) 'Five decades of item response modelling', *British Journal of Mathematical and Statistical Psychology*, 42, pp. 139–67.

Guba, E. and Lincoln, Y. (1989) *Fourth Generation Evaluation*, London Sage.

Haney, W. and Madaus, G. (1989) 'Searching for alternatives to standardised tests: The whats, whys and whithers', *Phi Delta Kappa*, 70, 9, pp. 683–7.

Hansen, J. (1993) *'Assessment in the year 2001: The darkness and the light'*, paper presented at the NCME Conference, April, Atlanta.

Harlen, W. (Ed) (1994) *Enhancing Quality in Assessment*, BERA Policy Task Group on Assessment, Paul Chapman Publishers.

Harlen, W., Gipps, C., Broadfoot, P. and Nuttall, D. (1992) 'Assessment and the improvement of education', *The Curriculum Journal*, 3, 3.

Harnisch, D. and Mabry, L. (1993) 'Issues in the development and evaluation of alternative assessments', *Journal of Curriculum Studies*, 25, 2, pp. 179–87.

Kuhn, T.S. (1970) *The Structure of Scientific Revolutions*, Chicago, IL, University of Chicago Press.

Linn, R.L., Baker, E. and Dunbar, S. (1991) 'Complex, performance-based assessment: Expectations and validation criteria', *Educational Researcher*, 20, 8, pp. 15–21.

McGaw, B. (1993) *Presidential Address*, IAEA Conference, May, Mauritius.

Mehrens, W. (1992) 'Using performance assessment for accountability purposes', *Educational Measurement: Issues and Practice*, spring, pp. 3–20.

Messick, S. (1984) 'The psychology of educational measurement', *Journal of Educational Measurement*, 21, pp. 215–38.

Messick, S. (1992) *The Interplay of Evidence and Consequences in the Validation of Performance Assessments*, Research Report ETS, July.

Miller, D. and Seraphine, A. (1992) *'Teaching to the test with alternative assessment'*, paper presented at the NCME conference, April, San Francisco.

Mislevy, R.J. (1993) *'Test theory reconceived'*, paper presented at the NCME conference, April, Atlanta.

Moss, P.A. (1992) 'Shifting conceptions of validity in educational measurement: Implications for performance assessment', *Review of Educational Research*, 62, 3, pp. 229–58.

Murphy, P. (1993) *'Some teacher dilemmas in practising authentic assessment'*, paper presented to the AERA Conference, April, Atlanta.

Murphy, R. (1990) 'National assessment proposals: Analysing the debate' in Flude, M. and Hammer, M. (Eds) *The Education Reform Act 1988*, London, Falmer Press.

Nisbet, J. (1993) 'Introduction' in *Curriculum Reform: Assessment in Question*, Paris, OECD.

Nuttall, D. (1987) 'The validity of assessments', *European Journal of Psychology of Education*, 11, 2, pp. 109–18.

Pipho, C. (1985) 'Tracking the reforms, Part 5: Testing – can it measure the success of the reform movement?', *Education Week*, 22 May, p. 19, quoted in Haney, W. and Madaus, G. (1989).

Popham, J. (1993) 'Circumventing the high costs of authentic assessment', *Phi Delta Kappan*, February.

Resnick, L.B. and Resnick, D.P. (1992) 'Assessing the thinking curriculum: New tools for educational reform', in Gifford, B. and O'Connor, M. (Eds) *Changing Assessments: Alternative Views of Aptitude, Achievement and Instruction*, London, Kluwer Academic Publishers.

Satterly, D. (1994) 'The quality of external assessment', in Harlen, W. (Ed) *Enhancing Quality in Assessment*, Paul Chapman Publishers.

Shepard, L. (1991) 'Psychometricians' beliefs about learning', *Educational Researcher*, 20, 7.

Shepard, L. (1993) 'Evaluating test validity', *Review of Research in Education*, 19, pp. 405–50.

Stiggins, R.J. (1992) 'Two disciplines of educational assessment', paper presented at ECS Assessment Conference June 1992, Boulder, Colorado. In Press: *Measurement and Evaluation in Counseling and Development*.

Torrance, H. (1993) *'Assessment, curriculum and theories of learning: Some thoughts on assessment and postmodernism'*, paper presented to ESRC/BERA Seminar, June, Liverpool.

Walkerdine, V. (1984) 'Developmental psychology and the child centred pedagogy' in Henriques, J. *et al.* (Eds) *Changing the Subject: Psychology, Social Regulation and Subjectivity*, London, Methuen.

Wiggins, G. (1989) 'A true test: Toward more authentic and equitable assessment' *Phi Delta Kappa*, 70, pp. 703–13.

Wiliam, D. (1993) *'Reconceptualising validity, dependability and reliability for National Curriculum assessment'*, paper given to BERA Conference, Liverpool.

Willis, D. (1992a) 'Educational assessment and accountability: A New Zealand case study', *Journal of Education Policy*, 7, 2.

Willis, D. (1992b) *'Learning and assessment: Exposing the inconsistencies of theory and practice'*, paper presented at ULIE, March.

Wolf, D., Bixby, J., Glenn, J. and Gardner, H. (1991) 'To use their minds well: Investigating new forms of student assessment', *Review of Research in Education*, 17, pp. 31–74.

Wood, R. (1986) 'The agenda for educational measurement', in Nuttall, D. (Ed) *Assessing Educational Achievement*, London, Falmer Press.

15

FROM TECHNICAL RATIONALITY TO REFLECTION-IN-ACTION

Donald A. Schön

INTRODUCTION

Donald Schön (1931–1997) was Ford Professor of Urban Studies and Education at Massachusetts Institute of Technology (MIT). At the time of his death, Schön was Ford professor emeritus and senior lecturer in the School of Architecture and Planning. Schön, a philosopher, tried to help educators teach professionals how to be competent in practice. He is credited with creating the concept of the reflective practitioner. The concept of a reflective practitioner is developed in Schön's published works, which include *The Reflective Practitioner* (Temple Smith, London) and *Educating the Reflective Practitioner* (Jossey Bass, San Francisco). This edited chapter, taken from *The Reflective Practitioner*, focuses on bringing 'reflection' into the centre of an understanding of what professionals do. He argues against 'technical-rationality' as the grounding of professional knowledge. The notions of reflection-in-action, and reflection-on-action were central to Schön's efforts in this area. The former is sometimes described as 'thinking on our feet'. It involves looking to our experiences, connecting with our feelings, and attending to our theories in use. It entails building new understandings to inform our actions in the situation that is unfolding. This edited chapter examines the move from technical rationality to reflection-in-action and explores the process involved in various instances of professional judgement. The impact of Schön's work on reflective practice has been significant, with many training and education programmes for teachers adopting his core ideas of the reflective practitioner.

KEY QUESTIONS

1. What is the kind of knowing in which competent practitioners engage?
2. Can it be applied successfully to teacher education and training?
3. In what ways is professional knowledge similar to the kinds of knowledge presented in academic textbooks?
4. In what sense, if any, is there intellectual content in professional practice?

FURTHER READING

For two critical accounts of Schön's ideas, the reader should look at Smith, M. K. (2001) 'Donald Schön: learning, reflection and change', in the *Encyclopedia of Informal Education* and Usher, R. *et al.* (1997) *Adult Education and the Postmodern Challenge* (Routledge, London). Schön's own work which followed *The Reflective Practitioner* in 1987, entitled *Educating the Reflective Practitioner*, developed his thinking by explaining how the reflective practicum works and detailing the implications for improving professional education.

This Reading links with Chapter 14 of *The Routledge Education Studies Textbook.*

THE DOMINANT EPISTEMOLOGY OF PRACTICE

According to the model of Technical Rationality – the view of professional knowledge which has most powerfully shaped both our thinking about the professions and the institutional relations of research, education, and practice – professional activity consists in instrumental problem solving made rigorous by the application of scientific theory and technique. Although all occupations are concerned, on this view, with the instrumental adjustment of means to ends, only the professions practice rigorously technical problem solving based on specialized scientific knowledge.

The model of Technical Rationality has exerted as great an influence on scholarly writing about the professions as on critical exposés of the role of the professions in the larger society. In the 1930s, for example, one of the earliest students of the professions asserted that

> it is not difficult to account in general for the emergence of the new professions. Large-scale organization has favored specialization. Specialized occupations have arisen around the new scientific knowledge.[1]

In a major book on the professions, published in 1970, Wilbert Moore embraced Alfred North Whitehead's distinction between a profession and an avocation. An avocation is "the antithesis to a profession" because it is "based upon customary activities and modified by the trial and error of individual practice."[2] In contrast, Moore said, a profession

> involves the application of general principles to specific problems, and it is a feature of modern societies that such general principles are abundant and growing.[3]

The same author argues further that professions are highly specialized occupations, and that

> the two primary bases for specialization within a profession are (1) the substantive field of knowledge that the specialist professes to command and (2) the technique of production or application of knowledge over which the specialist claims mastery.[4]

Finally, a recent critic of professional expertise sees the professional's claim to uniqueness as a ". . . preoccupation with a specialized skill premised on an underlying theory."[5]

The prototypes of professional expertise in this sense are the "learned professions" of medicine and law and, close behind these, business and engineering. These are, in Nathan Glazer's terms, the "major" or "near-major" professions.[6] They are distinct from such "minor" professions as social work, librarianship, education, divinity, and town planning. In the essay from which these terms are drawn, Glazer argues that the schools of the minor professions are hopelessly nonrigorous, dependent on representatives of academic disciplines, such as economics or political science, who are superior in status to the professions themselves. But what is of greatest interest from our point of view, Glazer's distinction between major and minor professions rests on a particularly well-articulated version of the model of Technical Rationality. The major professions are "disciplined by an unambiguous end – health, success in litigation, profit – which settles men's minds,"[7] and they operate in stable institutional contexts. Hence they are grounded in systematic, fundamental knowledge, of which scientific knowledge is the prototype,[8] or else they have "a high component of strictly technological knowledge based on science in the education which they provide."[9] In contrast, the minor professions suffer from shifting, ambiguous ends and from unstable institutional contexts of practice, and are *therefore* unable to develop a base of systematic, scientific professional knowledge. For Glazer, the development of a scientific knowledge base depends on fixed, unambiguous ends because professional practice is an instrumental activity. If applied science consists in cumulative, empirical knowledge about the means best suited to chosen ends, how can a profession ground itself in science when its ends are confused or unstable?

The systematic knowledge base of a profession is thought to have four essential properties. It is specialized, firmly bounded, scientific, and standardized. This last point is particularly important, because it bears on the paradigmatic relationship which holds, according to Technical Rationality, between a profession's knowledge base and its practice. In Wilbert Moore's words,

> If every professional problem were in all respects unique, solutions would be at best accidental, and therefore have nothing to do with expert knowledge. What we are suggesting, on the contrary, is that there are sufficient uniformities in problems and in devices for solving them to qualify the solvers as professionals . . . professionals apply very general principles, *standardized* knowledge, to concrete problems . . .[10]

This concept of "application" leads to a view of professional knowledge as a hierarchy in which "general principles" occupy the highest level and "concrete problem solving" the lowest. As Edgar Schein has put it,[11] there are three components to professional knowledge:

1. An *underlying discipline* or *basic science* component upon which the practice rests or from which it is developed.
2. An *applied science* or *"engineering"* component from which many of the day-to-day diagnostic procedures and problem-solutions are derived.
3. A *skills and attitudinal* component that concerns the actual performance of services to the client, using the underlying basic and applied knowledge.[12]

The application of basic science yields applied science. Applied science yields diagnostic and problem-solving techniques which are applied in turn to the actual delivery of services. The order of application is also an order of derivation and dependence. Applied science is said to "rest on" the foundation of basic science. And the more basic and general the knowledge, the higher the status of its producer.

When the representatives of aspiring professions consider the problem of rising to full professional status, they often ask whether their knowledge base has the requisite properties and whether it is regularly applied to the everyday problems of practice. Thus, in an article entitled "The Librarian: From Occupation to Profession,"[13] the author states that the central gap is of course the failure to develop a general body of scientific knowl-edge bearing precisely on this problem, in the way that the medical profession with its auxiliary scientific fields has developed an immense body of knowledge with which to cure human diseases.

The sciences in which he proposes to ground his profession are "communications theory, the sociology or psychology of mass communications, or the psychology of learning as it applies to reading."[14] Unfortunately, however, he finds that

> most day-to-day professional work utilizes rather concrete rule-of-thumb local reg-ulations and rules and major catalog systems . . . The problems of selection and organization are dealt with on a highly empiricist basis, concretely, with little refer-ence to general scientific principles.[15]

And a social worker, considering the same sort of question, concludes that "social work is already a profession" because it has a basis in

> theory construction via systematic research. To generate valid theory that will pro-vide a solid base for professional techniques requires the application of the scien-tific method to the service-related problems of the profession. Continued employment of the scientific method is nurtured by and in turn reinforces the ele-ment of *rationality* . . .[16]

It is by progressing along this route that social work seeks to "rise within the professional hierarchy so that it, too, might enjoy maximum prestige, authority, and monopoly which presently belong to a few top professions."[17]

If the model of Technical Rationality appeared only in such statements of intent, or in programmatic descriptions of professional knowledge, we might have some doubts about its dominance. But the model is also embedded in the institutional context of pro-fessional life. It is implicit in the institutionalized relations of research and practice, and in the normative curricula of professional education. Even when practitioners, educators, and researchers question the model of technical rationality, they are party to institutions that perpetuate it.

As one would expect from the hierarchical model of professional knowledge, research is institutionally separate from practice, connected to it by carefully defined rela-tionships of exchange. Researchers are supposed to provide the basic and applied science from which to derive techniques for diagnosing and solving the problems of practice. Prac-titioners are supposed to furnish researchers with problems for study and with tests of the utility of research results. The researcher's role is distinct from, and usually considered superior to, the role of the practitioner.

> In the evolution of every profession there emerges the researcher-theoretician whose role is that of scientific investigation and theoretical systematization. In technological professions, a division of labor thereby evolves between the theory-oriented and the practice-oriented person. Witness the physician who prefers to attach himself to a medical research center rather than to enter private practice . . .[18]

In a similar vein, Nathan Glazer speaks of the sociologist, political scientist, or economist who, when he is invited to bring his discipline to the school of a minor profession, mani-fests a level of status disturbingly superior to that of the resident practitioners. And in schools of engineering, which have been transformed into schools of engineering science, the engineering scientist tends to place his superior status in the service of values different from those of the engineering profession.[19]

The hierarchical separation of research and practice is also reflected in the normative curriculum of the professional school. Here the order of the curriculum parallels the order in which the components of professional knowledge are "applied." The rule is: first, the relevant basic and applied science; then, the skills of application to real-world problems of practice. Edgar Schein's study of professional education led him to describe the dominant curricular pattern as follows:

> Most professional school curricula can be analyzed in terms of the form and timing of these three elements [of professional knowledge]. Usually the professional curriculum starts with a common science core followed by the applied science elements. The attitudinal and skill components are usually labelled "practicum" or "clinical work" and may be provided simultaneously with the applied science components or they may occur even later in the professional education, depending upon the availability of clients or the ease of simulating the realities that the professional will have to face.[20]

Schein's use of the term "skill" is of more than passing interest. From the point of view of the model of Technical Rationality institutionalized in the professional curriculum, real knowledge lies in the theories and techniques of basic and applied science. Hence, these disciplines should come first. "Skills" in the use of theory and technique to solve concrete problems should come later on, when the student has learned the relevant science – first, because he cannot learn skills of application until he has learned applicable knowledge; and secondly, because skills are an ambiguous, secondary kind of knowledge. There is something disturbing about calling them "knowledge" at all.

Again, medicine is the prototypical example. Ever since the Flexner Report, which revolutionized medical education in the early decades of this century, medical schools have devoted the first two years of study to the basic sciences – chemistry, physiology, pathology – as "the appropriate foundation for later clinical training."[21] Even the physical arrangement of the curriculum reflects the basic division among the elements of professional knowledge:

> The separation of the medical school curriculum into two disjunctive stages, the preclinical and the clinical, reflects the division between theory and practice. The division also appears in the location of training and in medical school facilities. The sciences of biochemistry, physiology, pathology and pharmacology are learned from classrooms and laboratories, that is, in formal academic settings. More practical training, in clinical arts such as internal medicine, obstetrics and pediatrics, takes place in hospital clinics, within actual institutions of delivery.[22]

And teaching roles tend to reflect the same division:

> Medical school faculties tend to be divided between the PhD's and MD's, between teachers of basic science and those in clinical programs.[23]

Even though the law might be thought to have a dubious basis in science, the introduction of the still-dominant pattern of legal education – by Christopher Columbus Langdell at Harvard University in the 1880s and 1890s – followed the normative curricular model. In his address before the Harvard Law School in 1886, Langdell argued that "first, law is a science, and secondly . . . all available materials of that science are contained in printed books."[24] Langdell claimed that legal education is better conducted in a law school than in a lawyer's office because legal study is based upon broad, scientifically determined principles which cut across state lines.

> For Langdell claimed law was a science . . . this meant that its principles could be developed from analysis of prior court decisions and could be used to predict subsequent ones. Just as Charles William Eliot was introducing the experimental laboratory into the study of natural sciences at Harvard, so it was Langdell's claim, with the study of previously decided cases.[25]

Even the famous "case method" was originally grounded in the belief that the teaching of scientific principles should precede the development of skills in their application.

In his recent review of the Harvard School of Business Administration, the school which first adapted Langdell's method to management education, Derek Bok, the current president of Harvard University, argues against case method. His argument reveals both his implicit belief in the normative curriculum of professional education and his adherence to the model of technical rationality.

Bok begins by noting that case teaching has certainly helped to keep professors "closely involved with the activities of real corporations" and has "forced them to work continuously at their teaching."[26] But he worries that

> although the case is an excellent device for teaching students to *apply* theory and technique, it does not provide an ideal way of communicating concepts and analytic methods in the first instance.[27]

Exclusive concentration on cases leaves students little time to "master analytic technique and conceptual material" – a limitation that has become more critical as "the corporate world grows more complex" – and it prevents faculty from engaging in "intensive work to develop better generalizations, theories and methods that can eventually be used to attack corporate problems in more effective ways."[28] What is especially interesting in this argument is its misreading of what many business case teachers would consider the heart of their teaching: carefully guided analysis of innumerable cases drawn from real-world business contexts in order to help students develop the generic problem-solving skills essential to effective management. Although some of the strongest advocates of case teaching admit that they cannot define these skills or relate them to general theory, they believe that the case method stands on its own unique merits.[29] President Bok has made a contrary assumption. He assumes that the business school faculty accepts both the mission to develop "better generalizations, theories and methods" and the normative idea of a curriculum which places general principles and methods before the skills of application. To faculty members who think they are engaged in a very different sort of educational enterprise, he argues from an unquestioned belief in a normative curriculum which derives from the model of Technical Rationality.

THE ORIGINS OF TECHNICAL RATIONALITY

It is striking that the dominant model of professional knowledge seems to its proponents to require very little justification. How comes it that in the second half of the twentieth century we find in our universities, embedded not only in men's minds but in the institutions themselves, a dominant view of professional knowledge as the application of scientific theory and technique to the instrumental problems of practice?

The answer to this question lies in the last three hundred years of the history of Western ideas and institutions. Technical Rationality is the heritage of Positivism, the powerful philosophical doctrine that grew up in the nineteenth century as an account of the rise of science and technology and as a social movement aimed at applying the achievements of science and technology to the well-being of mankind. Technical Rationality is the Positivist epistemology of practice. It became institutionalized in the modern university, founded in the late nineteenth century when Positivism was at its height, and in the professional schools which secured their place in the university in the early decades of the twentieth century.

EMERGING AWARENESS OF THE LIMITS OF TECHNICAL RATIONALITY

Although it was in the early decades of the twentieth century that occupations professionalized and professional schools sought their places in the universities, it was World War II that gave a major new impetus both to the Technological Program and to the Positivist epistemology of practice.

In World War II, technologists drew upon scientific research as never before. Vannevar Bush created the first large-scale national research and development institute, the National Research and Development Corporation. The new discipline of operations research grew out of the American and British efforts to use applied mathematics for bomb tracking and submarine search. And the Manhattan project became the very symbol of the successful use of science-based technology for national ends. Its lesson seemed to be this: If a great social objective could be clearly defined, if a national commitment to it could be mustered, if unlimited resources could be poured into the necessary research and development, then any such objective could be achieved. The greatest beneficiary of this lesson was the institution of research and development itself. But as a side effect, there was also a reinforcement of the idea of scientific research as a basis for professional practice.

Following World War II, the United States government began an unparalleled increase in the rate of spending for research. As government spending for research increased, research institutions proliferated. Some were associated with the universities, others stood outside them. All were organized around the production of new scientific knowledge and were largely promoted on the basis of the proposition that the production of new scientific knowledge could be used to create wealth, achieve national goals, improve human life, and solve social problems. Nowhere was the rate of increase in research spending more dramatic, and nowhere were the results of that spending more visible, than in the field of medicine. The great centers of medical research and teaching were expanded, and new ones were created. The medical research center, with its medical school and its teaching hospital, became the institutional model to which other professions aspired. Here was a solid base of fundamental science, an equally solid body of applied clinical science, and a profession which had geared itself to implement the ever-changing products of research. Other professions, hoping to achieve some of medicine's effectiveness and prestige, sought to emulate its linkage of research and teaching institutions, its hierarchy of research and clinical roles, and its system for connecting basic and applied research to practice.

The prestige and apparent success of the medical and engineering models exerted a great attraction for the social sciences. In such fields as education, social work, planning, and policy making, social scientists attempted to do research, to apply it, and to educate practitioners, all according to their perceptions of the models of medicine and engineering. Indeed, the very language of social scientists, rich in references to measurement, controlled experiment, applied science, laboratories, and clinics, was striking in its reverence for these models.

In the mid-1950s, the Soviet launching of Sputnik gave a further impetus to national investment in science and technology. Sputnik shocked America into increased support for science, especially basic science, and created a new sense of urgency about the building of a society based on science. Suddenly we became acutely aware of a national shortage of professionals – scientists and engineers, but also physicians and teachers – who were seen as necessary to the development and application of scientific knowledge. It was the cumulative impact of these national responses to World War II and Sputnik which set the stage for the triumph of professionalism, the triumph celebrated in the *Daedalus* issue of 1963.

Between 1963 and 1982, however, both the general public and the professionals have become increasingly aware of the flaws and limitations of the professions.

From the perspective of Technical Rationality, professional practice is a process of problem *solving*. Problems of choice or decision are solved through the selection, from available means, of the one best suited to established ends. But with this emphasis on problem solving, we ignore problem *setting*, the process by which we define the decision to be made, the ends to be achieved, the means which may be chosen. In real-world practice, problems do not present themselves to the practitioner as givens. They must be constructed from the materials of problematic situations which are puzzling, troubling, and uncertain. In order to convert a problematic situation to a problem, a practitioner must do a certain kind of work. He must make sense of an uncertain situation that initially makes no sense. When professionals consider what road to build, for example, they deal usually with a complex and ill-defined situation in which geographic, topological, financial, economic, and political issues are all mixed up together. Once they have somehow decided what road to build and go on to consider how best to build it, they may have a problem they can solve by the application of available techniques; but when the road they have built leads unexpectedly to the destruction of a neighborhood, they may find themselves again in a situation of uncertainty.

It is this sort of situation that professionals are coming increasingly to see as central to their practice. They are coming to recognize that although problem setting is a necessary condition for technical problem solving, it is not itself a technical problem. When we set the problem, we select what we will treat as the "things" of the situation, we set the boundaries of our attention to it, and we impose upon it a coherence which allows us to say what is wrong and in what directions the situation needs to be changed. Problem setting is a process in which, interactively, we *name* the things to which we will attend and *frame* the context in which we will attend to them.

Even when a problem has been constructed, it may escape the categories of applied science because it presents itself as unique or unstable. In order to solve a problem by the application of existing theory or technique, a practitioner must be able to map those categories onto features of the practice situation. When a nutritionist finds a diet deficient in lysine, for example, dietary supplements known to contain lysine can be recommended. A physician who recognizes a case of measles can map it onto a system of techniques for diagnosis, treatment, and prognosis. But a unique case falls outside the categories of applied theory; an unstable situation slips out from under them. A physician cannot apply standard techniques to a case that is not in the books. And a nutritionist attempting a planned nutritional intervention in a rural Central American community may discover that the intervention fails because the situation has become something other than the one planned for.

Technical Rationality depends on agreement about ends. When ends are fixed and clear, then the decision to act can present itself as an instrumental problem. But when ends are confused and conflicting, there is as yet no "problem" to solve. A conflict of ends cannot be resolved by the use of techniques derived from applied research. It is rather through the nontechnical process of framing the problematic situation that we may organize and clarify both the ends to be achieved and the possible means of achieving them.

Similarly, when there are conflicting paradigms of professional practice, such as we find in the pluralism of psychiatry, social work, or town planning, there is no clearly established context for the use of technique. There is contention over multiple ways of framing the practice role, each of which entrains a distinctive approach to problem setting and solving. And when practitioners do resolve conflicting role frames, it is through a kind of inquiry which falls outside the model of Technical Rationality. Again, it is the work of naming and framing that creates the conditions necessary to the exercise of technical expertise.

We can readily understand, therefore, not only why uncertainty, uniqueness, instability, and value conflict are so troublesome to the Positivist epistemology of practice, but also why practitioners bound by this epistemology find themselves caught in a dilemma. Their definition of rigorous professional knowledge excludes phenomena they have learned to see as central to their practice. And artistic ways of coping with these phenomena do not qualify, for them, as rigorous professional knowledge.

This dilemma of "rigor or relevance" arises more acutely in some areas of practice than in others. In the varied topography of professional practice, there is a high, hard ground where practitioners can make effective use of research-based theory and technique, and there is a swampy lowland where situations are confusing "messes" incapable of technical solution. The difficulty is that the problems of the high ground, however great their technical interest, are often relatively unimportant to clients or to the larger society, while in the swamp are the problems of greatest human concern. Shall the practitioner stay on the high, hard ground where he can practice rigorously, as he understands rigor, but where he is constrained to deal with problems, of relatively little social importance? Or shall he descend to the swamp where he can engage the most important and challenging problems if he is willing to forsake technical rigor?

REFLECTION-IN-ACTION

When we go about the spontaneous, intuitive performance of the actions of everyday life, we show ourselves to be knowledgeable in a special way. Often we cannot say what it is that we know. When we try to describe it we find ourselves at a loss, or we produce descriptions that are obviously inappropriate. *Our knowing is ordinarily tacit, implicit in our patterns of action and in our feel for the stuff with which we are dealing. It seems right to say that our knowing is in our action.*

Similarly, the workaday life of the professional depends on tacit knowing-in-action. Every competent practitioner can recognize phenomena – families of symptoms associated with a particular disease, peculiarities of a certain kind of building site, irregularities of materials or structures – for which he cannot give a reasonably accurate or complete description. In his day-to-day practice he makes innumerable judgments of quality, for which he cannot state adequate criteria, and he displays skills for which he cannot state the rules and procedures. Even when he makes conscious use of research-based theories and techniques, he is dependent on tacit recognitions, judgments, and skillful performances.

On the other hand, both ordinary people and professional practitioners often think about what they are doing, sometimes even while doing it. Stimulated by surprise, they turn thought back on action and on the knowing which is implicit in action. They may ask themselves, for example, "What features do I notice when I recognize this thing? What are the criteria by which I make this judgment? What procedures am I enacting when I perform this skill? How am I framing the problem that I am trying to solve?" Usually reflection on knowing-in-action goes together with reflection on the stuff at hand. There is some puzzling, or troubling, or interesting phenomenon with which the individual is trying to deal. As he tries to make sense of it, he also reflects on the understandings which have been implicit in his action, understandings which he surfaces, criticizes, restructures, and embodies in further action.

It is this entire process of reflection-in-action which is central to the "art" by which practitioners sometimes deal well with situations of uncertainty, instability, uniqueness, and value conflict.

Knowing-in-action. Once we put aside the model of Technical Rationality, which leads us to think of intelligent practice as an *application* of knowledge to instrumental decisions, there is nothing strange about the idea that a kind of knowing is inherent in intelligent action. Common sense admits the category of know-how, and it does not stretch common sense very much to say that the know-how is *in* the action – that a tightrope walker's know-how, for example, lies in, and is revealed by, the way he takes his trip across the wire, or that a big-league pitcher's know-how is in his way of pitching to a batter's weakness, changing his pace, or distributing his energies over the course of a game. There is nothing in common sense to make us say that know-how consists in rules or plans which we entertain in the mind prior to action. Although we sometimes think before acting, it is also true that in much of the spontaneous behavior of skillful practice we reveal a kind of knowing which does not stem from a prior intellectual operation. As Gilbert Ryle has put it,

> What distinguishes sensible from silly operations is not their parentage but their procedure, and this holds no less for intellectual than for practical performances. "Intelligent" cannot be defined in terms of "intellectual" or "knowing *how*" in terms of "knowing *that*"; "thinking what I am doing" does not connote "both thinking what to do and doing it." When I do something intelligently . . . I am doing one thing and not two. My performance has a special procedure or manner, not special antecedents.[30]

And Andrew Harrison has recently put the same thought in this pithy phrase: when someone acts intelligently, he "acts his mind."[31]

Over the years, several writers on the epistemology of practice have been struck by the fact that skillful action often reveals a "knowing more than we can say." They have invented various names for this sort of knowing, and have drawn their examples from different domains of practice.

As early as 1938, in an essay called "Mind in Everyday Affairs," Chester Barnard distinguished "thinking processes" from "non-logical processes" which are not capable of being expressed in words or as reasoning, and which are only made known by a judgment, decision, or action.[32] Barnard's examples include judgments of distance in golf or ball-throwing, a high-school boy solving quadratic equations, and a practiced accountant who can take "a balance sheet of considerable complexity and within minutes or even seconds get a significant set of facts from it."[33] Such processes may be unconscious or they may occur so rapidly that "they could not be analyzed by the persons in whose brain they take place."[34] Of the high-school mathematician, Barnard says, memorably, "He could not write the text books which are registered in his mind."[35] Barnard believes that our bias toward thinking blinds us to the non-logical processes which are omnipresent in effective practice.

Michael Polanyi, who invented the phrase "tacit knowing," draws examples from the recognition of faces and the use of tools. If we know a person's face, we can recognize it among a thousand, indeed, among a million, though we usually cannot tell how we recognize a face we know. Similarly, we can recognize the moods of the human face without being able to tell, "except quite vaguely,"[36] by what signs we know them. When we learn to use a tool, or a probe or stick for feeling our way, our initial awareness of its impact on our hand is transformed "into a sense of its point touching the objects we are exploring."[37] In Polanyi's phrase, we attend "from" its impact on our hand "to" its effect on the things to which we are applying it. In this process, which is essential to the acquisition of a skill, the feelings of which we are initially aware become internalized in our tacit knowing.

Chris Alexander, in his *Notes Toward a Synthesis of Form,*[38] considers the knowing involved in design. He believes that we can often recognize and correct the "bad fit" of a form to its context, but that we usually cannot describe the rules by which we find a fit bad or recognize the corrected form to be good. Traditional artifacts evolve culturally through successive detections and corrections of bad fit until the resulting forms are good. Thus for generations the Slovakian peasants made beautiful shawls woven of yarns which had been dipped in homemade dyes. When aniline dyes were made available to them, "the glory of the shawls was spoiled."[39] The shawlmakers had no innate ability to make good shawls but "were simply able, as many of us are, to recognize bad shawls and their own mistakes. Over the generations . . . whenever a bad one was made, it was recognized as such, and therefore not repeated."[40] The introduction of aniline dyes disrupted the cultural process of design, for the shawl-makers could not produce wholly new designs of high quality; they could only recognize "bad fit" within a familiar pattern.

Ruminating on Alexander's example, Geoffrey Vickers points out that it is not only artistic judgments which are based on a sense of form which cannot be fully articulated:

> artists, so far from being alone in this, exhibit most clearly an oddity which is present in all such judgments. We can recognize and describe deviations from a norm very much more clearly than we can describe the norm itself.[41]

For Vickers, it is through such tacit norms that all of us make the judgments, the qualitative appreciations of situations, on which our practical competence depends.

Psycholinguists have noted that we speak in conformity with rules of phonology and syntax which most of us cannot describe.[42] Alfred Schultz and his intellectual descendants have analyzed the tacit, everyday know-how that we bring to social interactions such as the rituals of greeting, ending a meeting, or standing in a crowded elevator.[43] Birdwhistell has made comparable contributions to a description of the tacit knowledge embodied in our use and recognition of movement and gesture.[44] In these domains, too, we behave according to rules and procedures that we cannot usually describe and of which we are often unaware.

In examples like these, knowing has the following properties:

- There are actions, recognitions, and judgments which we know how to carry out spontaneously; we do not have to think about them prior to or during their performance.
- We are often unaware of having learned to do these things; we simply find ourselves doing them.
- In some cases, we were once aware of the understandings which were subsequently internalized in our feeling for the stuff of action. In other cases, we may never have been aware of them. In both cases, however, we are usually unable to describe the knowing which our action reveals.

It is in this sense that I speak of knowing-in-action, the characteristic mode of ordinary practical knowledge.

Reflecting-in-action. If common sense recognizes knowing-in-action, it also recognizes that we sometimes think about what we are doing. Phrases like "thinking on your feet," "keeping your wits about you," and "learning by doing" suggest not only that we can think about doing but that we can think about doing something while doing it. Some of the most interesting examples of this process occur in the midst of a performance.

Big-league baseball pitchers speak, for example, of the experience of "finding the groove":

> Only a few pitchers can control the whole game with pure physical ability. The rest have to learn to adjust once they're out there. If they can't, they're dead ducks.

> [You get] a special feel for the ball, a kind of command that lets you repeat the exact same thing you did before that proved successful.
>
> Finding your groove has to do with studying those winning habits and trying to repeat them every time you perform.[45]

I do not wholly understand what it means to "find the groove." It is clear, however, that the pitchers are talking about a particular kind of reflection. What is "learning to adjust once you're out there"? Presumably it involves noticing how you have been pitching to the batters and how well it has been working, and on the basis of these thoughts and observations, changing the way you have been doing it. When you get a "feel for the ball" that lets you "repeat the exact same thing you did before that proved successful," you are noticing, at the very least, that you have been doing something right, and your "feeling" allows you to do that something again. When you "study those winning habits," you are thinking about the know-how that has enabled you to win. The pitchers seem to be talking about a kind of reflection on their patterns of action, on the situations in which they are performing, and on the know-how implicit in their performance. They are reflecting *on* action and, in some cases, reflecting *in* action.

When good jazz musicians improvise together, they also manifest a "feel for" their material and they make on-the-spot adjustments to the sounds they hear. Listening to one another and to themselves, they feel where the music is going and adjust their playing accordingly. They can do this, first of all, because their collective effort at musical invention makes use of a schema – a metric, melodic, and harmonic schema familiar to all the participants – which gives a predictable order to the piece. In addition, each of the musicians has at the ready a repertoire of musical figures which he can deliver at appropriate moments. Improvisation consists in varying, combining, and recombining a set of figures within the schema which bounds and gives coherence to the performance. As the musicians feel the direction of the music that is developing out of their interwoven contributions, they make new sense of it and adjust their performance to the new sense they have made. They are reflecting-in-action on the music they are collectively making and on their individual contributions to it, thinking what they are doing and, in the process, evolving their way of doing it. Of course, we need not suppose that they reflect-in-action in the medium of words. More likely, they reflect through a "feel for the music" which is not unlike the pitcher's "feel for the ball."

Much reflection-in-action hinges on the experience of surprise. When intuitive, spontaneous performance yields nothing more than the results expected for it, then we tend not to think about it. But when intuitive performance leads to surprises, pleasing and promising or unwanted, we may respond by reflecting-in-action. Like the baseball pitcher, we may reflect on our "winning habits"; or like the jazz musician, on our sense of the music we have been making; or like the designer, on the misfit we have unintentionally created. In such processes, reflection tends to focus interactively on the outcomes of action, the action itself, and the intuitive knowing implicit in the action.

Let us consider an example which reveals these processes in some detail.

In an article entitled "If you want to get ahead, get a theory," Inhelder and Karmiloff-Smith[46] describe a rather unusual experiment concerning "children's processes of discovery in action."[47] They asked their subjects to balance wooden blocks on a metal bar. Some of the blocks were plain wooden blocks, but others were conspicuously or inconspicuously weighted at one end. The authors attended to the spontaneous processes by which the children tried to learn about the properties of the blocks, balance them on the bar, and regulate their actions after success or failure.

They found that virtually all children aged six to seven began the task in the same way:

all blocks were systematically first tried at their geometric center.[48]

And they found that slightly older children would not only place all blocks at their geometric center but that

> when asked to add small blocks of varying shapes and sizes to blocks already in balance, they added up to ten blocks precariously one on top of the other at the geometric center rather than distributing them at the extremities.[49]

They explain this persistent and virtually universal behavior by attributing to the children what they call a "theory-in-action": a "geometric center theory" of balancing, or, as one child put it, a theory that "things always balance in the middle."

Of course, when the children tried to balance the counter-weighted blocks at their geometric centers, they failed. How did they respond to failure? Some children made what the authors called an "action-response."

> They now placed the very same blocks more and more systematically at the geometric center, with only very slight corrections around this point. They showed considerable surprise at not being able to balance the blocks a second time ("Heh, what's gone wrong with this one, it worked before") . . . Action sequences then became reduced to: Place carefully at geometric center, correct very slightly around this center, abandon all attempts, declaring the object "impossible" to balance.[50]

Other children, generally between the ages of seven and eight, responded in a very different way. When the counterweighted blocks failed to balance at their geometric centers, these children began to de-center them. They did this first with conspicuously counter-weighted blocks. Then

> gradually, and often almost reluctantly, the 7 to 8 year olds began to make corrections also on the inconspicuous weight blocks . . . At this point, we observed many pauses during action sequences on the inconspicuous weight items.[51]

Later still,

> As the children were now really beginning to question the generality of their geometric center theory, a negative response at the geometric center sufficed to have the child rapidly make corrections toward the point of balance.[52]

And finally,

> children paused *before* each item, roughly assessed the weight distribution of the block by lifting it ("you have to be careful, sometimes it's just as heavy on each side, sometimes it's heavier on one side"), inferred the probable point of balance and then placed the object immediately very close to it, without making any attempts at first balancing at the geometric center.[53]

The children now behaved as though they had come to hold a theory-in-action that blocks balance, not at their geometric centers, but at their centers of gravity.

This second pattern of response to error, the authors call "theory-response." Children work their way toward it through a series of stages. When they are first confronted with a number of events which refute their geometric center theories-in-action, they stop and think. Then, starting with the conspicuous-weight blocks, they begin to make corrections away from the geometric center. Finally, when they have really abandoned their earlier theories-in-action, they weigh all the blocks in their hands so as to infer the probable point of balance. As they shift their theories of balancing from geometric center to center of gravity, they also shift from a "success orientation" to a "theory orientation." Positive and negative results come to be taken not as signs of success or failure in action but as information relevant to a theory of balancing.

It is interesting to note that as the authors observe and describe this process, they are compelled to invent a language. They describe theories-in-action which the children themselves cannot describe.

> Indeed, although the (younger) child's action sequences bear eloquent witness to a theory-in-action implicit in his behavior, this should not be taken as a capacity to conceptualize explicitly on what he is doing and why.[54]

Knowing-in-action which the child may represent to himself in terms of a "feel for the blocks," the observers redescribe in terms of "theories." I shall say that they convert the child's know*ing*-in-action to know*ledge*-in-action.

A conversion of this kind seems to be inevitable in any attempt to talk about reflection-in-action. One must use words to describe a kind of knowing, and a change of knowing, which are probably not originally represented in words at all. Thus, from their observations of the children's behavior, the authors make verbal descriptions of the children's intuitive understandings. These are the authors' theories about the children's knowing-in-action. Like all such theories, they are deliberate, idiosyncratic constructions, and they can be put to experimental test:

> just as the child was constructing a theory-in-action in his endeavor to balance the blocks, so we, too, were making on-the-spot hypotheses about the child's theories and providing opportunities for negative and positive responses in order to verify our own theories![55]

Reflecting-in-practice. The block-balancing experiment is a beautiful example of reflection-in-action, but it is very far removed from our usual images of professional practice. If we are to relate the idea of reflection-in-action to professional practice, we must consider what a practice is and how it is like and unlike the kinds of action we have been discussing.

The word "practice" is ambiguous. When we speak of a lawyer's practice, we mean the kinds of things he does, the kinds of clients he has, the range of cases he is called upon to handle. When we speak of someone practicing the piano, however, we mean the repetitive or experimental activity by which he tries to increase his proficiency on the instrument. In the first sense, "practice" refers to performance in a range of professional situations. In the second, it refers to preparation for performance. But professional practice also includes an element of repetition. A professional practitioner is a specialist who encounters certain types of situations again and again. This is suggested by the way in which professionals use the word "case" – or project, account, commission, or deal, depending on the profession. All such terms denote the units which make up a practice, and they denote types of family-resembling examples. Thus a physician may encounter many different "cases of measles"; a lawyer, many different "cases of libel." As a practitioner experiences many variations of a small number of types of cases, he is able to "practice" his practice. He develops a repertoire of expectations, images, and techniques. He learns what to look for and how to respond to what he finds. As long as his practice is stable, in the sense that it brings him the same types of cases, he becomes less and less subject to surprise. His knowing-in-practice tends to become increasingly tacit, spontaneous, and automatic, thereby conferring upon him and his clients the benefits of specialization.

On the other hand, professional specialization can have negative effects. In the individual, a high degree of specialization can lead to a parochial narrowness of vision. When a profession divides into subspecialties, it can break apart an earlier wholeness of experience and understanding. Thus people sometimes yearn for the general practitioner of earlier days, who is thought to have concerned himself with the "whole patient," and they sometimes accuse contemporary specialists of treating particular illnesses in isolation from the rest of the patient's life experience. Further, as a practice becomes more repetitive and routine, and as knowing-in-practice becomes increasingly tacit and spontaneous, the practitioner may miss important opportunities to think about what he is doing. He may find that, like the younger children in the block-balancing experiment, he is drawn into patterns of error which he cannot correct. And if he learns, as often happens, to be selectively inattentive to phenomena that do not fit the categories of his knowing-in-action, then he may suffer from boredom or "burn-out" and afflict his clients with the consequences of his narrowness and rigidity. When this happens, the practitioner has "over-learned" what he knows.

A practitioner's reflection can serve as a corrective to over-learning. Through reflection, he can surface and criticize the tacit understandings that have grown up around the repetitive experiences of a specialized practice, and can make new sense of the situations of uncertainty or uniqueness which he may allow himself to experience.

Practitioners do reflect *on* their knowing-in-practice. Sometimes, in the relative tranquility of a postmortem, they think back on a project they have undertaken, a situation they have lived through, and they explore the understandings they have brought to their handling of the case. They may do this in a mood of idle speculation, or in a deliberate effort to prepare themselves for future cases.

But they may also reflect on practice while they are in the midst of it. Here they reflect-in-action, but the meaning of this term needs now to be considered in terms of the complexity of knowing-in-practice.

A practitioner's reflection-in-action may not be very rapid. It is bounded by the "action-present," the zone of time in which action can still make a difference to the situation. The action-present may stretch over minutes, hours, days, or even weeks or months, depending on the pace of activity and the situational boundaries that are characteristic of the practice. Within the give-and-take of courtroom behavior, for example, a lawyer's reflection-in-action may take place in seconds; but when the context is that of an antitrust case that drags on over years, reflection-in-action may proceed in leisurely fashion over the course of several months. An orchestra conductor may think of a single performance as a unit of practice, but in another sense a whole season is his unit. The pace and duration of episodes of reflection-in-action vary with the pace and duration of the situations of practice.

When a practitioner reflects in and on his practice, the possible objects of his reflection are as varied as the kinds of phenomena before him and the systems of knowing-in-practice which he brings to them. He may reflect on the tacit norms and appreciations which underlie a judgment, or on the strategies and theories implicit in a pattern of behavior. He may reflect on the feeling for a situation which has led him to adopt a particular course of action, on the way in which he has framed the problem he is trying to solve, or on the role he has constructed for himself within a larger institutional context.

Reflection-in-action, in these several modes, is central to the art through which practitioners sometimes cope with the troublesome "divergent" situations of practice.

When the phenomenon at hand eludes the ordinary categories of knowledge-in-practice, presenting itself as unique or unstable, the practitioner may surface and criticize his initial understanding of the phenomenon, construct a new description of it, and test the new description by an on-the-spot experiment. Sometimes he arrives at a new theory of the phenomenon by articulating a feeling he has about it.

When he finds himself stuck in a problematic situation which he cannot readily convert to a manageable problem, he may construct a new way of setting the problem – a new frame which, in what I shall call a "frame experiment," he tries to impose on the situation.

When he is confronted with demands that seem incompatible or inconsistent, he may respond by reflecting on the appreciations which he and others have brought to the situation. Conscious of a dilemma, he may attribute it to the way in which he has set his problem, or even to the way in which he has framed his role. He may then find a way of integrating, or choosing among, the values at stake in the situation.

The following are brief examples of the kinds of reflection-in-action which I shall illustrate and discuss at greater length later on.

An investment banker, speaking of the process by which he makes his judgments of investment risk, observes that he really cannot describe everything that goes into his judgments. The ordinary rules of thumb allow him to calculate "only 20 to 30 percent of the risk in investment." In terms of the rules of thumb, a company's operating numbers may be excellent. Still, if the management's explanation of the situation does not fit the numbers, or if there is something odd in the behavior of the people, that is a subject for worry which must be considered afresh in each new situation. He recalls a situation in which he spent a day with one of the largest banks in Latin America. Several new business proposals were made to him, and the bank's operating numbers seemed satisfactory. Still, he had a gnawing feeling that something was wrong. When he thought about it, it seemed that he was responding to the fact that he had been treated with a degree of deference out of all proportion to his actual position in the international world of banking. What could have led these bankers to treat him so inappropriately? When he left the bank at the end of the day, he said to his colleague, "No new business with that outfit! Let the existing obligations come in, but nothing new!" Some months later, the bank went through the biggest bankruptcy ever in Latin America – and all the time there had been nothing wrong with the numbers.

An ophthalmologist says that a great many of his patients bring problems that are not in the book. In 80 or 85 percent of the cases, the patient's complaints and symptoms do not fall into familiar categories of diagnosis and treatment. A good physician searches for new ways of making sense of such cases, and invents experiments by which to test his new hypotheses. In a particularly important family of situations, the patient suffers simultaneously from two or more diseases. While each of these, individually, lends itself to familiar patterns of thought and action, their combination may constitute a unique case that resists ordinary approaches to treatment.

The ophthalmologist recalls one patient who had inflammation of the eye (uveitis) combined with glaucoma. The treatment for glaucoma aggravated the inflammation, and the treatment for uveitis aggravated the glaucoma. When the patient came in, he was already under treatment at a level insufficient for cure but sufficient to irritate the complementary disease.

The ophthalmologist decided to remove all treatment and wait to see what would emerge. The result was that the patient's uveitis, a parasitic infection, remained in much reduced form. On the other hand, the glaucoma disappeared altogether, thus proving to have been an artifact of the treatment. The opthalmologist then began to "titrate" the patient. Working with very small quantities of drugs, he aimed not at total cure but at a reduction of symptoms which would allow the patient to go back to work. (Seven lives depended on his 5000 ocular cells!) The prognosis was not good, for uveitis moves in cycles and leaves scars behind which impede vision. But for the time being, the patient was able to work.

In his mid-thirties, sometime between the composition of his early work *The Cossacks* and his later *War and Peace,* Lev Nikolayevitch Tolstoy became interested in education. He started a school for peasant children on his estate at Yasnaya Polanya, he visited Europe to learn the latest educational methods, and he published an educational journal, also called *Yasnaya Polanya.* Before he was done (his new novel eventually replaced his interest in education), he had built some seventy schools, had created an informal teacher-training program, and had written an exemplary piece of educational evaluation.

For the most part, the methods of the European schools filled him with disgust, yet he was entranced by Rousseau's writings on education. His own school anticipated John Dewey's later approach to learning by doing, and bore the stamp of his conviction that good teaching required "not a method but an art." In an essay, "On Teaching the Rudiments," he describes his notion of art in the teaching of reading:

> Every individual must, in order to acquire the art of reading in the shortest possible time, be taught quite apart from any other, and therefore there must be a separate method for each. That which forms an insuperable difficulty to one does not in the least keep back another, and vice versa. One pupil has a good memory, and it is easier for him to memorize the syllables than to comprehend the vowellessness of the consonants; another reflects calmly and will comprehend a most rational sound method; another has a fine instinct, and he grasps the law of word combinations by reading whole words at a time.
>
> The best teacher will be he who has at his tongue's end the explanation of what it is that is bothering the pupil. These explanations give the teacher the knowledge of the greatest possible number of methods, the ability of inventing new methods and, above all, not a blind adherence to one method but the conviction that all methods are one-sided, and that the best method would be the one which would answer best to all the possible difficulties incurred by a pupil, that is, not a method but an art and talent.
>
> . . . Every teacher must . . . by regarding every imperfection in the pupil's comprehension, not as a defect of the pupil, but as a defect of his own instruction, endeavor to develop in himself the ability of discovering new methods . . .[56]

An artful teacher sees a child's difficulty in learning to read not as a defect in the child but as a defect "of his own instruction." So he must find a way of explaining what is bothering the pupil. He must do a piece of experimental research, then and there, in the classroom. And because the child's difficulties may be unique, the teacher cannot assume that his repertoire of explanations will suffice, even though they are "at the tongue's end." He must be ready to invent new methods and must "endeavor to develop in himself the ability of discovering them."

Over the last two years, researchers at the Massachusetts Institute of Technology have undertaken a program of in-service education for teachers, a program organized around the idea of on-the-spot reflection and experiment, very much as in Tolstoy's art of teaching. In this Teacher Project,[57] the researchers have encouraged a small group of teachers to explore their own intuitive thinking about apparently simple tasks in such domains as mathematics, physics, music, and the perceived behavior of the moon. The teachers have made some important discoveries. They have allowed themselves to become confused about subjects they are supposed to "know"; and as they have tried to work their way out of their confusions, they have also begun to think differently about learning and teaching.

Early in the project, a critical event occurred. The teachers were asked to observe and react to a videotape of two boys engaged in playing a simple game. The boys sat at a table, separated from one another by an opaque screen. In front of one boy, blocks of various colors, shapes, and sizes were arranged in a pattern. In front of the other, similar blocks were lying on the table in no particular order. The first boy was to tell the second one how to reproduce the pattern. After the first few instructions, however, it became clear that the second boy had gone astray. In fact, the two boys had lost touch with one another, though neither of them knew it.

In their initial reactions to the videotape, the teachers spoke of a "communications problem." They said that the instruction giver had "well-developed verbal skills" and that the receiver was "unable to follow directions." Then one of the researchers pointed out that, although the blocks contained no green squares – all squares were orange and only triangles were green – she had heard the first boy tell the second to "take a green square." When the teachers watched the videotape again, they were astonished. That small mistake had set off a chain of false moves. The second boy had put a green thing, a triangle, where the first boy's pattern had an orange square, and from then on all the instructions became problematic. Under the circumstances, the second boy seemed to have displayed considerable ingenuity in his attempts to reconcile the instructions with the pattern before him.

At this point, the teachers reversed their picture of the situation. They could see why the second boy behaved as he did. He no longer seemed stupid; he had, indeed, "followed instructions." As one teacher put it, they were now "giving him reason." They saw reasons for his behavior; and his errors, which they had previously seen as an inability to follow directions, they now found reasonable.

Later on in the project, as the teachers increasingly challenged themselves to discover the meanings of a child's puzzling behavior, they often spoke of "giving him reason."

In examples such as these, something falls outside the range of ordinary expectations. The banker has a feeling that something is wrong, though he cannot at first say what it is. The physician sees an odd combination of diseases never before described in a medical text. Tolstoy thinks of each of his pupils as an individual with ways of learning and imperfections peculiar to himself. The teachers are astonished by the sense behind a student's mistake. In each instance, the practitioner allows himself to experience surprise, puzzlement, or confusion in a situation which he finds uncertain or unique. He reflects on the phenomena before him, and on the prior understandings which have been implicit in his behavior. He carries out an experiment which serves to generate both a new understanding of the phenomena and a change in the situation.

When someone reflects in action, he becomes a researcher in the practice context. He is not dependent on the categories of established theory and technique, but constructs a new theory of the unique case. His inquiry is not limited to a deliberation about means which depends on a prior agreement about ends. He does not keep means and ends separate, but defines them interactively as he frames a problematic situation. He does not separate thinking from doing, ratiocinating his way to a decision which he must later convert to action. Because his experimenting is a kind of action, implementation is built into his inquiry. Thus reflection-in-action can proceed, even in situations of uncertainty or uniqueness, because it is not bound by the dichotomies of Technical Rationality.

Although reflection-in-action is an extraordinary process, it is not a rare event. Indeed, for some reflective practitioners it is the core of practice. Nevertheless, because professionalism, is still mainly identified with technical expertise, reflection-in-action is not generally accepted – even by those who do it – as a legitimate form of professional knowing.

Many practitioners, locked into a view of themselves as technical experts, find nothing in the world of practice to occasion reflection. They have become too skillful at techniques of selective inattention, junk categories, and situational control, techniques which they use to preserve the constancy of their knowledge-in-practice. For them, uncertainty is a threat; its admission is a sign of weakness. Others, more inclined toward and adept at reflection-in-action, nevertheless feel profoundly uneasy because they cannot say what they know how to do, cannot justify its quality or rigor.

For these reasons, the study of reflection-in-action is critically important. The dilemma of rigor or relevance may be dissolved if we can develop an epistemology of practice which places technical problem solving within a broader context of reflective inquiry, shows how reflection-in-action may be rigorous in its own right, and links the art of practice in uncertainty and uniqueness to the scientist's art of research. We may thereby increase the legitimacy of reflection-in-action and encourage its broader, deeper, and more rigorous use.

NOTES

1. A.M. Carr-Saunders, *Professions: Their Organization and Place in Society* (Oxford: The Clarendon Press, 1928). Quoted in Vollmer and Mills, eds., *Professionalization* (Englewood Cliffs, N.J.: Prentice-Hall, 1966), p. 3.
2. Wilbert Moore, *The Professions* (New York: Russell Sage Foundation, 1970), p. 56.
3. Ibid.
4. Ibid., p. 141.
5. Jethro Lieberman, *Tyranny of Expertise* (New York: Walker and Company), p. 55.
6. Nathan Glazer, "Schools of the Minor Professions," *Minerva*, (1974): 346.
7. Ibid., p. 363.
8. Ibid., p. 348.
9. Ibid., p. 349.
10. Moore, *The Professions*, p. 56.
11. Edgar Schein, *Professional Education* (New York: McGraw-Hill, 1973), p. 43.
12. Ibid., p. 39.
13. William Goode, "The Librarian: From Occupation to Profession," reprinted in Vollmer and Mills, *Professionalization*, p. 39.
14. Ibid.
15. Ibid.
16. Ernest Greenwood, "Attributes of a Profession," reprinted in Vollmer and Mills, *Professionalization*, p. 11.
17. Ibid., p. 19.
18. Ibid., p. 12.
19. Harvey, Brooks, "Dilemmas of Engineering Education," *IEEE Spectrum* (February 1967): 89.
20. Schein, *Professional Education*, p. 44.
21 Barry Thorne, "Professional Education in Medicine," in *Education for the Professions of Medicine, Law, Theology and Social Welfare* (New York: McGraw-Hill, 1973), p. 30.
22. Ibid., p. 31.
23. Ibid.
24. Alan Gartner, *Preparation of Human Service Professionals* (New York: Human Sciences Press, 1976), p. 80.
25. Ibid., p. 93.
26. Derek Bok, "The President's Report," reprinted in *The Harvard Magazine*, (May-June 1979): 83.
27. Ibid., p. 84.
28. Ibid.
29. From private conversations with three Harvard Business School faculty members.
30. Gilbert Ryle, "On Knowing How and Knowing That," in *The Concept of Mind* (London: Hutcheson, 1949), p. 32.
31. Andrew Harrison, *Making and Thinking* (Indianapolis: Hackett, 1978).
32. Chester Barnard, in *The Functions of the Executive* (Cambridge, Mass.: Harvard University Press, 1968, first published 1938), p. 302.
33. Ibid., p. 305.
34. Ibid., p. 302.
35. Ibid., p. 306.
36. Michael Polanyi, *The Tacit Dimension*, (New York: Doubleday and Co., 1967), p. 4.
37. Ibid., p. 12.
38. Chris Alexander, *Notes Toward a Synthesis of Form*, (Cambridge, Mass.: Harvard University Press, 1968).
39. Ibid., p. 53.

40. Ibid., p. 55.
41. Geoffrey Vickers, unpublished memorandum, MIT, 1978.
42. The whole of contemporary linguistics and psycholinguistics is relevant here – for example, the work of Chomsky, Halle, and Sinclair.
43. Alfred Schutz, *Collected Papers* (The Hague: Nijhoff, 1962).
44. Ray L. Birdwhistell, *Kinesics and Context* (Philadelphia: University of Pennsylvania Press, 1970).
45. Jonathan Evan Maslow, "Grooving on a Baseball Afternoon," in *Mainliner* (May 1981): 34.
46. Barbel Inhelder and Annette Karmiloff-Smith, "If you want to get ahead, get a theory," *Cognition* 3, 3: 195–212.
47. Ibid., p. 195.
48. Ibid., p. 202.
49. Ibid., p. 203.
50. Ibid.
51. Ibid., p. 205.
52. Ibid.
53. Ibid.
54. Ibid., p. 203.
55. Ibid., p. 199.
56. Leo Tolstoy, "On Teaching the Rudiments," in *Tolstoy on Education*, Leo Wiener, ed. (Chicago and London: University of Chicago Press, 1967).
57. The staff of the Teachers' Project consisted of Jeanne Bamberger, Eleanor Duckworth, and Margaret Lampert. My description of the incident of "giving the child reason" is adapted from a project memorandum by Lampert.

Ivan D. Illich

INTRODUCTION

Ivan Illich (1926–2002) was a highly influential thinker and radical educator who was deeply sceptical of an institutionalised society that depended upon professional experts in fields such as medicine and education. Rather than formal schooling he preferred the notion of learning through informal 'webs'. Existing schools he argued did no more than 'confuse teaching with learning, grade advancement with education, a diploma with competence and fluency with the ability to say something new'. There are many significant controversies surrounding Illich. Some of those controversies relate to his work as a Catholic priest and educator who came into conflict with the Vatican. Some see Illich as a radical liberal who foresaw the potential of technology in education and the personalised learning agenda (and who would have railed against their institutionalisation). Others see him as a political innocent who although calling for freedom and a heightened emphasis on the needs of the poor was actually pursuing a libertarian agenda that would most support the already powerful.

KEY QUESTIONS

1. Does technology provide the means to develop new forms of learning?
2. Do you feel that Illich was a radical whose ideas supported the less powerful?

FURTHER READING

Other works by Illich are of interest, especially *Tools for Conviviality* (1973). Many books about professionalism relate directly to Illich's work (whether or not Illich is mentioned explicitly); some examples include Derber, C., Schwartz, W. A. and Magrass, Y. (1990) *Power in the Highest Degree: Professionals and the Rise of a New Mandarin Order* (Oxford, Oxford University Press) and Cunningham, B. (2008) *Exploring Professionalism* (Bedford Way Papers, London). The power of technology as a means by which young people can learn democratically is explored in publications such as Bennett, W. L. (2008) *Civic Life Online: Learning How Digital Media Can Engage Youth* (The MIT Press, Cambridge, MA).

This Reading links with Chapter 15 and Debate 2 of *The Routledge Education Studies Textbook.*

Many students, especially those who are poor, intuitively know what the schools do for them. They school them to confuse process and substance. Once these become blurred, a new logic is assumed: the more treatment there is, the better are the results; or, escalation leads to success. The pupil is thereby 'schooled' to confuse teaching with learning, grade advancement with education, a diploma with competence, and fluency with the ability to say something new. His imagination is 'schooled' to accept service in place of value. Medical treatment is mistaken for healthcare, social work for the improvement of community life, police protection for safety, military poise for national security, the rat race for productive work. Health, learning, dignity, independence and creative endeavour are defined as little more than the performance of the institutions which claim to serve these ends, and their improvement is made to depend on allocating more resources to the management of hospitals, schools and other agencies in question.

In this essay, I will show that the institutionalization of values leads inevitably to physical pollution, social polarization and psychological impotence: three dimensions in a process of global degradation and modernized misery. I will explain how this process of degradation is accelerated when non-material needs are transformed into demands for commodities; when health, education, personal mobility, welfare or psychological healing are defined as the result of services or 'treatments'. I do this because I believe that most of the research now going on about the future tends to advocate further increases in the institutionalization of values and that we must define conditions which would permit precisely the contrary to happen. We need research on the possible use of technology to create institutions which serve personal, creative and autonomous interaction and the emergence of values which cannot be substantially controlled by technocrats. We need counterfoil research to current futurology.

I want to raise the general question of the mutual definition of man's nature and the nature of modern institutions which characterizes our world view and language. To do so, I have chosen the school as my paradigm, and I therefore deal only indirectly with other bureaucratic agencies of the corporate state: the consumer-family, the party, the army, the Church, the media. My analysis of the hidden curriculum of school should make it evident that public education would profit from the deschooling of society, just as family life, politics, security, faith and communication would profit from an analogous process.

I begin my analysis, in this first essay, by trying to convey what the deschooling of a schooled society might mean.

Not only education but social reality itself has become schooled. It costs roughly the same to school both rich and poor in the same dependency. The yearly expenditure per pupil in the slums and in the rich suburbs of any one of twenty US cities lies in the same range – and sometimes is favourable to the poor.* Rich and poor alike depend on schools and hospitals which guide their lives, form their world view, and define for them what is legitimate and what is not. Both view doctoring oneself as irresponsible, learning on one's own as unreliable, and community organization, when not paid for by those in authority, as a form of aggression or subversion. For both groups the reliance on institutional treatment renders independent accomplishment suspect. The progressive underdevelopment of self- and community-reliance is even more typical in Westchester than it is in the northeast of Brazil. Everywhere not only education but society as a whole needs 'deschooling'.

Welfare bureaucracies claim a professional, political and financial monopoly over the social imagination, setting standards of what is valuable and what is feasible. This monopoly is at the root of the modernization of poverty. Every simple need to which an

---

* Penrose B. Jackson, *Trends in Elementary and Secondary Education Expenditures; Central City and Suburban Comparisons 1965 to 1968*, U S Office of Education, Office of Program and Planning Evaluation, June 1969.

institutional answer is found permits the invention of a new class of poor and a new defi-nition of poverty. Ten years ago in Mexico it was the normal thing to be born and to die in one's own home and to be buried by one's friends. Only the soul's needs were taken care of by the institutional church. Now to begin and end life at home become signs either of poverty or of special privilege. Dying and death have come under the institutional man-agement of doctors and undertakers.

Once basic needs have been translated by a society into demands for scientifically produced commodities, poverty is defined by standards which the technocrats can change at will. Poverty then refers to those who have fallen behind an advertised ideal of con-sumption in some important respect. In Mexico the poor are those who lack three years of schooling, and in New York they are those who lack twelve.

The poor have always been socially powerless. The increasing reliance on institu-tional care adds a new dimension to their helplessness: psychological impotence, the inability to fend for themselves. Peasants on the high plateau of the Andes are exploited by the landlord and the merchant – once they settle in Lima they are, in addition, dependent on political bosses, and disabled by their lack of schooling. Modernized poverty combines the lack of power over circumstances with a loss of personal potency. This modernization of poverty is a world-wide phenomenon, and lies at the root of contemporary underdevel-opment. Of course it appears under different guises in rich and in poor countries.

It is probably most intensely felt in US cities. Nowhere else is poverty treated at greater cost. Nowhere else does the treatment of poverty produce so much dependence, anger, frustration and further demands. And nowhere else should it be so evident that poverty – once it has become modernized – has become resistant to treatment with dollars alone and requires an institutional revolution.

Today in the United States the black and even the migrant can aspire to a level of professional treatment which would have been unthinkable two generations ago, and which seems grotesque to most people in the Third World. For instance, the US poor can count on a truant officer to return their children to school until they reach seventeen, or on a doctor to assign them to a hospital bed which costs sixty dollars per day – the equivalent of three months' income for a majority of the people in the world. But such care only makes them dependent on more treatment, and renders them increasingly incapable of organizing their own lives around their own experiences and resources within their own communities.

The poor in the United States are in a unique position to speak about the predicament which threatens all the poor in a modernizing world. They are making the discovery that no amount of dollars can remove the inherent destructiveness of welfare institutions, once the professional hierarchies of these institutions have convinced society that their minis-trations are morally necessary. The poor in the US inner city can demonstrate from their own experience the fallacy on which social legislation in a 'schooled' society is built.

Supreme Court Justice William O. Douglas observed that 'the only way to establish an institution is to finance it'. The corollary is also true. Only by channelling dollars away from the institutions which now treat health, education and welfare can the further impov-erishment resulting from their disabling side-effects be stopped.

This must be kept in mind when we evaluate federal aid programmes. As a case in point, between 1965 and 1968 over three thousand million dollars were spent in US schools to offset the disadvantages of about six million children. The programme is known as Title One. It is the most expensive compensatory programme ever attempted anywhere in education, yet no significant improvement can be detected in the learning of these 'dis-advantaged' children. Compared with their classmates from middle-income homes, they have fallen further behind. Moreover, in the course of this programme, professionals dis-covered an additional ten million children labouring under economic and educational handicaps. More reasons for claiming more federal funds are now at hand.

This total failure to improve the education of the poor despite more costly treatment can be explained in three ways:

1. Three thousand million dollars are insufficient to improve the performance of six million children by a measurable amount; *or*
2. The money was incompetently spent: different curricula, better administration, further concentration of the funds on the poor child, and more research are needed and would do the trick; *or*
3. Educational disadvantage cannot be cured by relying on education within the school.

The first is certainly true so long as the money has been spent through the school budget. The money indeed went to the schools which contained most of the disadvantaged children, but it was not spent on the poor children themselves. These children for whom the money was intended comprised only about half of those who were attending the schools that added the federal subsidies to their budgets. Thus the money was spent for custodial care, indoctrination and the selection of social roles, as well as education, all of which functions are inextricably mingled in the physical plants, curricula, teachers, administrators and other key components of these schools, and, therefore, in their budgets.

The added funds enabled schools to cater disproportionately to the satisfaction of the relatively richer children who were 'disadvantaged' by having to attend school in the company of the poor. At best a small fraction of each dollar intended to remedy a poor child's disadvantages in learning could reach the child through the school budget.

It might be equally true that the money was incompetently spent. But even unusual incompetence cannot beat that of the school system. Schools by their very structure resist the concentration of privilege on those otherwise disadvantaged. Special curricula, separate classes or longer hours only constitute more discrimination at a higher cost.

Taxpayers are not yet accustomed to permitting three thousand million dollars to vanish from the Department of Health, Education and Welfare as if it were the Pentagon. The present Administration may believe that it can afford the wrath of educators. Middle-class Americans have nothing to lose if the programme is cut. Poor parents think they do, but, even more, they are demanding a control of the funds meant for their children. A logical way of cutting the budget and, one hopes, of increasing benefits is a system of tuition grants such as that proposed by Milton Friedman and others. Funds would be channelled to the beneficiary, enabling him to buy his share of the schooling of his choice. If such credit were limited to purchases which fit into a school curriculum, it would tend to provide greater equality of treatment, but would not thereby increase the equality of social claims.

It should be obvious that even with schools of equal quality a poor child can seldom catch up with a rich one. Even if they attend equal schools and begin at the same age, poor children lack most of the educational opportunities which are casually available to the middle-class child. These advantages range from conversation and books in the home to vacation travel and a different sense of oneself, and apply, for the child who enjoys them, both in and out of school. So the poorer student will generally fall behind so long as he depends on school for advancement or learning. The poor need funds to enable them to learn, not to get certified for the treatment of their alleged disproportionate deficiencies.

All this is true in poor nations as well as in rich ones, but there it appears under a different guise. Modernized poverty in poor nations affects more people more visibly but also – for the moment – more superficially. Two-thirds of all children in Latin America leave school before finishing the fifth grade, but these *'desertores'* are not therefore as badly off as they would be in the United States.

Few countries today remain victims of classical poverty, which was stable and less disabling. Most countries in Latin America have reached the 'take-off' point towards economic development and competitive consumption, and thereby towards modernized poverty: their citizens have learned to think rich and live poor. Their laws make six to ten years of school obligatory. Not only in Argentina but also in Mexico or Brazil the average citizen defines an adequate education by North American standards, even though the chance of getting such prolonged schooling is limited to a tiny minority. In these countries the majority is already hooked on school, that is, they are schooled in a sense of inferiority towards the better schooled. Their fanaticism in favour of school makes it possible to exploit them doubly: it permits increasing allocation of public funds for the education of a few and increasing acceptance of social control by the many.

Paradoxically, the belief that universal schooling is absolutely necessary is most firmly held in those countries where the fewest people have been – and will be – served by schools. Yet in Latin America different paths towards education could still be taken by the majority of parents and children. Proportionately, national savings invested in schools and teachers might be higher than in rich countries, but these investments are totally insufficient to serve the majority by making even four years of school attendance possible. Fidel Castro talks as if he wanted to go in the direction of deschooling when he promises that by 1980 Cuba will be able to dissolve its university since all of life in Cuba will be an educational experience. At the grammar-school and high-school level, however, Cuba, like all other Latin American countries, acts as though passage through a period defined as the 'school age' were an unquestionable goal for all, delayed merely by a temporary shortage of resources.

The twin deceptions of increased treatment, as actually provided in the United States – and as merely promised in Latin America – complement each other. The Northern poor are being disabled by the same twelve-year treatment whose lack brands the Southern poor as hopelessly backward. Neither in North America nor in Latin America do the poor get equality from obligatory schools. But in both places the mere existence of school discourages and disables the poor from taking control of their own learning. All over the world the school has an anti-educational effect on society: school is recognized as the institution which specializes in education. The failures of school are taken by most people as a proof that education is a very costly, very complex, always arcane and frequently almost impossible task.

School appropriates the money, men and goodwill available for education and in addition discourages other institutions from assuming educational tasks. Work, leisure, politics, city living and even family life depend on schools for the habits and knowledge they presuppose, instead of becoming themselves the means of education. Simultaneously both schools and the other institutions which depend on them are priced out of the market.

In the United States the per capita costs of schooling have risen almost as fast as the cost of medical treatment. But increased treatment by both doctors and teachers has shown steadily declining results. Medical expenses concentrated on those above forty-five have doubled several times over a period of forty years with a resulting 3 per cent increase in life expectancy in men. The increase in educational expenditures has produced even stranger results; otherwise President Nixon could not have been moved in the spring of 1970 to promise that every child shall soon have the 'Right to Read' before leaving school.

In the United States it would take eighty thousand million dollars per year to provide what educators regard as equal treatment for all in grammar and high school. This is well over twice the thirty-six thousand million now being spent. Independent cost projections prepared at the Department of Health, Education and Welfare and the University of Florida indicate that by 1974 the comparable figures will be 107 thousand million dollars as against the forty-five thousand million now projected, and these figures wholly omit the enormous costs of what is called 'higher education', for which demand is growing even faster. The United States, which spent nearly eighty thousand million dollars in 1969 for 'defence' including its deployment in Vietnam, is obviously too poor to provide equal schooling. The President's committee for the study of school finance should ask not how to support or how to trim such increasing costs, but how they can be avoided.

Equal obligatory schooling must be recognized as at least economically unfeasible. In Latin America the amount of public money spent on each graduate student is between 350 and 1500 times the amount spent on the median citizen (that is, the citizen who holds the middle ground between the poorest and the richest). In the United States the discrepancy is smaller, but the discrimination is keener. The richest parents, some 10 per cent, can afford private education for their children and help them to benefit from foundation grants. But in addition they obtain ten times the per capita amount of public funds if this is compared with the per capita expenditure made on the children of the 10 per cent who are poorest. The principal reasons for this are that rich children stay longer in school, that a year in a university is disproportionately more expensive than a year in high school, and that most private universities depend – at least indirectly – on tax-derived finances.

Obligatory schooling inevitably polarizes a society; it also grades the nations of the world according to an international caste system. Countries are rated like castes whose educational dignity is determined by the average years of schooling of its citizens, a rating which is closely related to per capita gross national product, and much more painful.

The paradox of the schools is evident: increased expenditure escalates their destructiveness at home and abroad. This paradox must be made a public issue. It is now generally accepted that the physical environment will soon be destroyed by biochemical pollution unless we reverse current trends in the production of physical goods. It should also be recognized that social and personal life is threatened equally by HEW pollution, the inevitable by-product of obligatory and competitive consumption of welfare.

The escalation of the schools is as destructive as the escalation of weapons but less visibly so. Everywhere in the world school costs have risen faster than enrolments and faster than the GNP; everywhere expenditures on school fall even further behind the expectations of parent, teacher and pupils. Everywhere this situation discourages both the motivation and the financing for large-scale planning for non-schooled learning. The United States is proving to the world that no country can be rich enough to afford a school system that meets the demands this same system creates simply by existing, because a successful school system schools parents and pupils to the supreme value of a larger school system, the cost of which increases disproportionately as higher grades are in demand and become scarce.

Rather than calling equal schooling temporarily unfeasible, we must recognize that it is, in principle, economically absurd, and that to attempt it is intellectually emasculating, socially polarizing and destructive of the credibility of the political system which promotes it. The ideology of obligatory schooling admits of no logical limits. The White House recently provided a good example. Dr Hutschnecker, the 'psychiatrist' who treated Mr Nixon before he was qualified as a candidate, recommended to the President that all children between six and eight be professionally examined to ferret out those who have destructive tendencies, and that obligatory treatment be provided for them. If necessary, their re-education in special institutions should be required. This memorandum from his doctor the President sent for evaluation to HEW. Indeed, preventive concentration camps for pre-delinquents would be a logical improvement over the school system.

Equal educational opportunity is, indeed, both a desirable and a feasible goal, but to equate this with obligatory schooling is to confuse salvation with the Church. School has become the world religion of a modernized proletariat, and makes futile promises of salvation to the poor of the technological age. The nation-state has adopted it, drafting all citizens into a graded curriculum leading to sequential diplomas not unlike the initiation rituals and hieratic promotions of former times. The modern state has assumed the duty of enforcing the judgement of its educators through well-meant truant officers and job requirements, much as did the Spanish kings who enforced the judgements of their theologians through the conquistadors and the Inquisition.

Two centuries ago the United States led the world in a movement to disestablish the monopoly of a single church. Now we need the constitutional disestablishment of the monopoly of the school, and thereby of a system which legally combines prejudice with discrimination. The first article of a bill of rights for a modern, humanist society would correspond to the First Amendment to the US Constitution: 'The State shall make no law with respect to the establishment of education.' There shall be no ritual obligatory for all.

To make this disestablishment effective, we need a law forbidding discrimination in hiring, voting or admission to centres of learning based on previous attendance at some curriculum. This guarantee would not exclude performance tests of competence for a function or role, but would remove the present absurd discrimination in favour of the person who learns a given skill with the largest expenditure of public funds or – what is equally likely – has been able to obtain a diploma which has no relation to any useful skill or job. Only by protecting the citizen from being disqualified by anything in his career in school can a constitutional disestablishment of school become psychologically effective.

Neither learning nor justice is promoted by schooling because educators insist on packaging instruction with certification. Learning and the assignment of social roles are melted into schooling. Yet to learn means to acquire a new skill or insight, while promotion depends on an opinion which others have formed. Learning frequently is the result of instruction, but selection for a role or category in the job market increasingly depends on mere length of attendance.

Instruction is the choice of circumstances which facilitate learning. Roles are assigned by setting a curriculum of conditions which the candidate must meet if he is to make the grade. School links instruction but not learning – to these roles. This is neither reasonable nor liberating. It is not reasonable because it does not link relevant qualities or competences to roles, but rather the process by which such qualities are supposed to be acquired. It is not liberating or educational because school reserves instruction to those whose every step in learning fits previously approved measures of social control.

Curriculum has always been used to assign social rank. At times it could be prenatal: karma ascribes you to a caste and lineage to the aristocracy. Curriculum could take the form of a ritual, of sequential sacred ordinations, or it could consist of a succession of feats in war or hunting, or further advancement could be made to depend on a series of previous princely favours. Universal schooling was meant to detach role assignment from personal life history: it was meant to give everybody an equal chance to any office. Even now many people wrongly believe that school ensures the dependence of public trust on relevant learning achievements. However, instead of equalizing chances, the school system has monopolized their distribution.

To detach competence from curriculum, inquiries into a man's learning history must be made taboo, like inquiries into his political affiliation, church attendance, lineage, sex habits or racial background. Laws forbidding discrimination on the basis of prior schooling must be enacted. Laws, of course, cannot stop prejudice against the unschooled – nor are they meant to force anyone to intermarry with an autodidact – but they can discourage unjustified discrimination.

A second major illusion on which the school system rests is that most learning is the result of teaching. Teaching, it is true, may contribute to certain kinds of learning under certain circumstances. But most people acquire most of their knowledge outside school, and in school only in so far as school, in a few rich countries, has become their place of confinement during an increasing part of their lives.

Most earning happens casually, and even most intentional learning is not the result of programmed instruction. Normal children learn their first language casually, although faster if their parents pay attention to them. Most people who learn a second language well do so as a result of odd circumstances and not of sequential teaching. They go to live with their grandparents, they travel, or they fall in love with a foreigner. Fluency in reading is also more often than not a result of such extracurricular activities. Most people who read widely, and with pleasure, merely believe that they learned to do so in school; when challenged, they easily discard this illusion.

But the fact that a great deal of learning even now seems to happen casually and as a by-product of some other activity defined as work or leisure does not mean that planned learning does not benefit from planned instruction and that both do not stand in need of improvement. The strongly motivated student who is faced with the task of acquiring a new and complex skill may benefit greatly from the discipline now associated with the old-fashioned schoolmaster who taught reading, Hebrew, catechism or multiplication by rote. School has now made this kind of drill teaching rare and disreputable, yet there are many skills which a motivated student with normal aptitude can master in a matter of a few months if taught in this traditional way. This is as true of codes as of their encipherment; of second and third languages as of reading and writing; and equally of special languages such as algebra, computer programming, chemical analysis, or of manual skills like typing, watchmaking, plumbing, wiring, TV repair; or for that matter dancing, driving and diving.

In certain cases acceptance into a learning programme aimed at a specific skill might presuppose competence in some other skill, but it should certainly not be made to depend upon the process by which such prerequisite skills were acquired. TV repair presupposes literacy and some maths; diving, good swimming; and driving, very little of either.

Progress in learning skills is measurable. The optimum resources in time and materials needed by an average motivated adult can be easily estimated. The cost of teaching a second Western European language to a high level of fluency ranges between four and six hundred dollars in the United States, and for an Oriental tongue the time needed for instruction might be doubled. This would still be very little compared with the cost of twelve years of schooling in New York City (a condition for acceptance of a worker into the Sanitation Department) – almost fifteen thousand dollars. No doubt not only the teacher but also the printer and the pharmacist protect their trades through the public illusion that training for them is very expensive.

At present schools pre-empt most educational funds. Drill instruction which costs less than comparable schooling is now a privilege of those rich enough to bypass the schools, and those whom either the army or big business sends through in-service training. In a programme of progressive deschooling of US education, at first the resources available for drill training would be limited. But ultimately there should be no obstacle for anyone at any time of his life to be able to choose instruction among hundreds of definable skills at public expense.

Right now educational credit good at any skill centre could be provided in limited amounts for people of all ages, and not just to the poor. I envisage such credit in the form of an educational passport or an 'edu-credit card' provided to each citizen at birth. In order to favour the poor, who probably would not use their yearly grants early in life, a provision could be made that interest accrued to later users of cumulated 'entitlements'. Such credits would permit most people to acquire the skills most in demand, at their convenience, better, faster, cheaper and with fewer undesirable side-effects than in school.

Potential skill teachers are never scarce for long because, on the one hand, demand for a skill grows only with its performance within a community and, on the other, a man exercising a skill could also teach it. But, at present; those using skills which are in demand and do require a human teacher are discouraged from sharing these skills with others. This is done either by teachers who monopolize the licences or by unions which protect their trade interests. Skill centres which would be judged by customers on their results, and not on the personnel they employ or the process they use, would open unsuspected working opportunities, frequently even for those who are now considered unemployable. Indeed, there is no reason why such skill centres should not be at the work place itself, with the employer and his work force supplying instruction as well as jobs to those who choose to use their educational credits in this way.

In 1956 there arose a need to teach Spanish quickly to several hundred teachers, social workers and ministers from the New York Archdiocese so that they could communicate with Puerto Ricans. My friend Gerry Morris announced over a Spanish radio station that he needed native speakers from Harlem. Next day some two hundred teenagers lined up in front of his office, and he selected four dozen of them – many of them school dropouts. He trained them in the use of the US Foreign Service Institute (FSI) Spanish manual, designed for use by linguists with graduate training, and within a week his teachers were on their own – each in charge of four New Yorkers who wanted to speak the language. Within six months the mission was accomplished. Cardinal Spellman could claim that he had 127 parishes in which at least three staff members could communicate in Spanish. No school programme could have matched these results.

Skill teachers are made scarce by the belief in the value of licences. Certification constitutes a form of market manipulation and is plausible only to a schooled mind. Most teachers of arts and trades are less skilful, less inventive and less communicative than the best craftsmen and tradesmen. Most high-school teachers of Spanish or French do not speak the language as correctly as their pupils might after half a year of competent drills. Experiments conducted by Angel Quintero in Puerto Rico suggest that many young teenagers, if given the proper incentives, programmes and access to tools, are better than most schoolteachers at introducing their peers to the scientific exploration of plants, stars and matter, and to the discovery of how and why a motor or a radio functions.

Opportunities for skill-learning can be vastly multiplied if we open the 'market'. This depends on matching the right teacher with the right student when he is highly motivated in an intelligent programme, without the constraint of curriculum.

Free and competing drill instruction is a subversive blasphemy to the orthodox educator. It dissociates the acquisition of skills from 'humane' education, which schools package together, and thus it promotes unlicenced learning no less than unlicenced teaching for unpredictable purposes.

There is currently a proposal on record which seems at first to make a great deal of sense. It has been prepared by Christopher Jencks of the Center for the Study of Public Policy and is sponsored by the Office of Economic Opportunity. It proposes to put educational 'entitlements' or tuition grants into the hands of parents and students for expenditure in the schools of their choice. Such individual entitlements could indeed be an important step in the right direction. We need a guarantee of the right of each citizen to an equal share of tax-derived educational resources, the right to verify this share and the right to sue for it if denied. It is one form of a guarantee against regressive taxation.

The Jencks proposal, however, begins with the ominous statement that 'conservatives, liberals and radicals have all complained at one time or another that the American educational system gives professional educators too little incentive to provide high-quality education to most children'. The proposal condemns itself by proposing tuition grants which would have to be spent on schooling.

This is like giving a lame man a pair of crutches and stipulating that he uses them only if the ends are tied together. As the proposal for tuition grants now stands, it plays into the hands not only of the professional educators but of racists, promoters of religious schools and others whose interests are socially divisive. Above all, educational entitlements restricted to use within schools play into the hands of all those who want to continue to live in a society in which social advancement is tied not to proven knowledge but to the learning pedigree by which, it is supposedly acquired. This discrimination in favour of schools which dominates Jencks's discussion on refinancing education could discredit one of the most critically needed principles for educational reform: the return of the initiative and accountability for learning to the learner or his most immediate tutor.

The deschooling of society implies a recognition of the two-faced nature of learning. An insistence on skill drill alone could be a disaster; equal emphasis must be placed on other kinds of learning. But if schools are the wrong places for learning a skill, they are even worse places for getting an education. School does both tasks badly, partly because it does not distinguish between them. School is inefficient in skill instruction especially because it is curricular. In most schools a programme which is meant to improve one skill is chained always to another irrelevant task. History is tied to advancement in maths, and class attendance to the right to use the playground.

Schools are even less efficient in the arrangement of the circumstances which encourage the open-ended, exploratory use of acquired skills, for which I will reserve the term 'liberal education'. The main reason for this is that school is obligatory and becomes schooling for schooling's sake: an enforced stay in the company of teachers, which pays off in the doubtful privilege of more such company. Just as skill instruction must be freed from curriculur restraints, so must liberal education be dissociated from obligatory attendance. Both skill-learning and education for inventive and creative behaviour can be aided by institutional arrangement, but they are of a different, frequently opposed nature.

Most skills can be acquired and improved by drills, because skill implies the mastery of definable and predictable behaviour. Skill instruction can rely, therefore, on the simulation of circumstances in which the skill will be used. Education in the exploratory and creative use of skills, however, cannot rely on drills. Education can be the outcome of instruction, though instruction of a kind fundamentally opposed to drill. It relies on the relationship between partners who already have some of the keys which give access to memories stored in and by the community. It relies on the critical intent of all those who use memories creatively. It relies on the surprise of the unexpected question which opens new doors for the inquirer and his partner.

The skill instructor relies on the arrangement of set circumstances which permit the learner to develop standard responses. The educational guide or master is concerned with helping matching partners to meet so that learning can take place. He matches individuals starting from their own, unresolved questions. At the most he helps the pupil to formulate his puzzlement since only a clear statement will give him the power to find his match, moved like him, at the moment, to explore the same issue in the same context.

Matching partners for educational purposes initially seems more difficult to imagine than finding skill instructors and partners for a game. One reason is the deep fear which school has implanted in us, a fear which makes us censorious. The unlicenced exchange of skills – even undesirable skills – is more predictable and therefore seems less dangerous than the unlimited opportunity for meeting among people who share an issue which for them, at the moment, is socially, intellectually and emotionally important.

The Brazilian teacher Paulo Freire knows this from experience. He discovered that any adult can begin to read in a matter of forty hours if the first words he deciphers are charged with political meaning. Freire trains his teachers to move into a village and to discover the words which designate current important issues, such as the access to a well or the compound interest on the debts owed to the *patron*. In the evening the villagers meet for the discussion of these key words. They begin to realize that each word stays on the blackboard even after its sound has faded. The letters continue to unlock reality and to make it manageable as a problem. I have frequently witnessed how discussants grow in social awareness and how they are impelled to take political action as fast as they learn to read. They seem to take reality into their hands as they write it down.

I remember the man who complained about the weight of pencils: they were difficult to handle because they did not weigh as much as a shovel; and I remember another who on his way to work stopped with his companions and wrote the word they were discussing with his hoe on the ground: '*agua*'. Since 1962 my friend Freire has moved from exile to exile, mainly because he refuses to conduct his sessions around words which are preselected by approved educators, rather than those which his discussants bring to the class.

The educational matchmaking among people who have been successfully schooled is a different task. Those who do not need such assistance are a minority, even among the readers of serious journals. The majority cannot and should not be rallied for discussion around a slogan, a word or a picture. But the idea remains the same: they should be able to meet around a problem chosen and defined by their own initiative. Creative, exploratory learning requires peers currently puzzled about the same terms or problems. Large universities make the futile attempt to match them by multiplying their courses, and they generally fail since they are bound to curriculum, course structure and bureaucratic administration. In schools, including universities, most resources are spent to purchase the time and motivation of a limited number of people to take up predetermined problems in a ritually defined setting. The most radical alternative to school would be a network or service which gave each man the same opportunity to share his current concern with others motivated by the same concern.

Let me give, as an example of what I mean, a description of how an intellectual match might work in New York City. Each man, at any given moment and at a minimum price, could identify himself to a computer with his address and telephone number, indicating the book, article, film or recording on which he seeks a partner for discussion. Within days he could receive by mail the list of others who recently had taken the same initiative. This list would enable him by telephone to arrange for a meeting with persons who initially would be known exclusively by the fact that they requested a dialogue about the same subject.

Matching people according to their interest in a particular title is radically simple. It permits identification only on the basis of a mutual desire to discuss a statement recorded by a third person, and it leaves the initiative of arranging the meeting to the individual. Three objections are usually raised against this skeletal purity. I take them up not only to clarify the theory that I want to illustrate by my proposal – for they highlight the deepseated resistance to deschooling education, to separating learning from social control – but also because they may help to suggest existing resources which are not now used for learning purposes.

The first objection is: Why cannot self-identification be based also on an *idea* or an issue? Certainly such subjective terms could also be used in a computer system. Political parties, churches, unions, clubs, neighbourhood centres and professional societies already organize their educational activities in this way and in effect they act as schools. They all match people in order to explore certain ' themes'; and these are dealt with in courses, seminars and curricula in which presumed 'common interests' are prepackaged. Such thememartching is by definition teacher-centred: it requires an authoritarian presence to define for the participants the starting point for their discussion.

By contrast, matching by the title of a book, film, etc., in its pure form leaves it to the author to define the special language, the terms, and the framework within which a given problem or fact is stated; and it enables those who accept this starting point to identify themselves to one another. For instance; matching people around the idea of 'cultural revolution' usually leads either to confusion or to demagoguery. On the other hand, matching those interested in helping each other understand a specific article by Mao, Marcuse, Freud or Goodman stands in the great tradition of liberal learning from Plato's Dialogues, which are built around presumed statements by Socrates, to Aquinas's commentaries on

Peter the Lombard. The idea of matching by title is thus radically different from the theory on which the 'Great Books' clubs, for example, were built: instead of relying on the selection by some Chicago professors, any two partners can choose any book for further analysis.

The second objection asks; Why not let the identification of match seekers include information on age, background, world view, competence, experience or other defining characteristics? Again, there is no reason why such discriminatory restrictions could not and should not be built into some of the many universities – with or without walls – which could use title-matching as their basic organizational device. I could conceive of a system designed to encourage meetings of interested persons at which the author of the book chosen would be present or represented; or a system which guaranteed the presence of a competent adviser; or one to which only students registered in a department or school had access; or one which permitted meetings only between people who defined their special approach to the title under discussion. Advantages for achieving specific goals of learning could be found for each of these restrictions. But I fear that, more often than not, the real reason for proposing such restrictions is contempt arising from the presumption that people are ignorant: educators want to avoid the ignorant meeting the ignorant around a text which they may not understand and which they read *only* because they are interested in it.

The third objection: Why not provide match seekers with incidental assistance that will facilitate their meetings – with space, schedules, screening and protection? This is now done by schools with all the inefficiency characterizing large bureaucracies. If we left the initiative for meetings to the match seekers themselves, organizations which nobody now classifies as educational would probably do the job much better. I think of restaurant owners, publishers, telephone-answering services, department-store managers, and even commuter-train executives who could promote their services by rendering them attractive for educational meetings.

At a first meeting in a coffee shop, say, the partners might establish their identities by placing the book under discussion next to their cups. People who took the initiative to arrange for such meetings would soon learn what items to quote to meet the people they sought. The risk that the self-chosen discussion with one or several strangers might lead to a loss of time, disappointment or even unpleasantness is certainly smaller than the same risk taken by a college applicant. A computer-arranged meeting to discuss an article in a national magazine, held in a coffee shop off Fourth Avenue, would obligate none of the participants to stay in the company of his new acquaintances for longer than it took to drink a cup of coffee, nor would he have to meet any of them ever again. The chance that it would help to pierce the opaqueness of life in a modern city and further new friendship, self-chosen work and critical reading is high. (The fact that a record of personal readings and meetings could be obtained thus by the FBI is undeniable; that this should still worry anybody in 1970 is only amusing to a free man, who willy-nilly contributes his share in order to drown snoopers in the irrelevancies they gather.)

Both the exchange of skills and matching of partners are based on the assumption that education for all means education by all. Not the draft into a specialized institution but only the mobilization of the whole population can lead to popular culture. The equal right of each man to exercise his competence to learn and to instruct is now pre-empted by certified teachers. The teachers' competence, in turn, is restricted to what may be done in school. And, further, work and leisure are alienated from each other as a result: the spectator and the worker alike are supposed to arrive at the work place all ready to fit into a routine prepared for them. Adaptation in the form of a product's design, instruction and publicity shapes them for their role as much as formal education by schooling. A radical alternative to a schooled society requires not only new formal mechanisms for the formal acquisition of skills and their educational use. A deschooled society implies a new approach to incidental or informal education.

Incidental education cannot any longer return to the forms which learning took in the village or the medieval town. Traditional society was more like a set of concentric circles of meaningful structures, while modern man must learn how to find meaning in many structures to which he is only marginally related. In the village, language and architecture and work and religion and family customs were consistent with one another, mutually explanatory and reinforcing. To grow into one implied a growth into the others. Even specialized apprenticeship was a by-product of specialized activities, such as shoemaking or the singing of psalms. If an apprentice never became a master or a scholar, he still contributed to making shoes or to making church services solemn. Education did not compete for time with either work or leisure. Almost all education was complex, lifelong and unplanned.

Contemporary society is the result of conscious designs, and educational opportunities must be designed into them. Our reliance on specialized, full-time instruction through school will now decrease, and we must find more ways to learn and teach: the educational quality of all institutions must increase again. But this is a very ambiguous forecast. It could mean that men in the modern city will be increasingly the victims of an effective process of total instruction and manipulation once they are deprived of even the tenuous pretence of critical independence which liberal schools now provide for at least some of their pupils.

It could also mean that men will shield themselves less behind certificates acquired in school and thus gain in courage to 'talk back' and thereby control and instruct the institutions in which they participate. To ensure the latter we must learn to estimate the social value of work and leisure by the educational give-and-take for which they offer opportunity. Effective participation in the politics of a street, a work place, the library, a news programme or a hospital is therefore the best measuring stick to evaluate their level as educational institutions.

I recently spoke to a group of junior-high-school students in the process of organizing a resistance movement to their obligatory draft into the next class. Their slogan was 'participation – not simulation'. They were disappointed that this was understood as a demand for less rather than for more education, and reminded me of the resistance which Karl Marx put up against a passage in the Gotha programme, which – one hundred years ago – wanted to outlaw child labour. He opposed the proposal in the interest of the education of the young, which could happen only at work. If the greatest fruit of man's labour should be the education he receives from it and the opportunity which work gives him to initiate the education of others, then the alienation of modern society in a pedagogical sense is even worse than its economic alienation.

The major obstacle on the way to a society that truly educates was well defined by a black friend of mine in Chicago, who told me that our imagination was 'all schooled up'. We permit the state to ascertain the universal educational deficiencies of its citizens and establish one specialized agency to treat them. We thus share in the delusion that we can distinguish between what is necessary education for others and what is not, just as former generations established laws which defined what was sacred and what was profane.

Durkheim recognized that this ability to divide social reality into two realms was the very essence of formal religion. There are, he reasoned, religions without the supernatural and religions without gods, but none which does not subdivide the world into things and times and persons that are sacred and others that as a consequence are profane. Durkheim's insight can be applied to the sociology of education, for school is radically divisive in a similar way.

The very existence of obligatory schools divides any society into two realms: some time spans and processes and treatments and professions are 'academic' or 'pedagogic', and others are not. The power of school thus to divide social reality has no boundaries: education becomes unwordly and the world becomes non-educational.

Since Bonhoeffer contemporary theologians have pointed to the confusions now reigning between the Biblical message and institutionalized religion. They point to the experience that Christian freedom and faith usually gain from secularization. Inevitably their statements sound blasphemous to many churchmen. Unquestionably, the educational process will gain from the deschooling of society even though this demand sounds to many schoolmen like treason to the enlightenment. But it is enlightenment itself that is now being snuffed out in the schools.

The secularization of the Christian faith depends on the dedication to it on the part of Christians rooted in the Church. In much the same way, the deschooling of education depends on the leadership of those brought up in the schools. Their curriculum cannot serve them as an alibi for the task: each of us remains responsible for what has been made of him, even though he may be able to do no more than accept this responsibility and serve as a warning to others.

17

SOCIAL NETWORKING AS AN EDUCATIONAL TOOL

Robin Mason and Frank Rennie

INTRODUCTION

Robin Mason was Professor of Educational Technology at the Open University where she was a specialist in the design and practice of online teaching and learning. Frank Rennie is Professor of Sustainable Rural Development at the UHI Millennium Institute in the Highlands and Islands of Scotland. In this work, Mason and Rennie consider student engagement with digital learning resources and online social networking. They explore the different types of resources that are available and the nature of learning that may be promoted. Currently, there is a good deal of debate about the nature and impact of technology in education. For some, technology is the means by which traditional things can be done more easily, more quickly and more engagingly. For others, there is the sense that a new type of learning is within our grasp as new things are learned and new forms of dialogue develop between teachers and learners.

KEY QUESTIONS

1. What claims have been made for the transformational potential of digital media in education?
2. What changes do you think have actually occurred?
3. What do you feel is likely to happen to schooling and education more generally as a result of digital media?

FURTHER READING

A great deal of research is taking place at the Oxford Internet Institute. Summaries of many interesting papers on many aspects of technology and society are available at: www.oii.ox.ac.uk/research. An interesting and rather sceptical view about the value of some educational technology can be seen from Smith, F., Hardman, F. and Higgins, S. (2006) 'The impact of interactive whiteboards on teacher–pupil interaction' in the *National Literacy and Numeracy Strategies British Educational Research Journal* (Vol. 32 No. 3) pp. 437–451. It may be useful to explore particular aspects of society and technology by reading Loader, B. L. (ed.)

(2007) *Young Citizens in the Digital Age* (Routledge, London). An interesting overview of key issues is provided in Andrews, R. and Haythornthwaite, C. (eds) (2007) *The SAGE Handbook of E-learning Research* (Sage, London).

This Reading links with Chapter 16 of *The Routledge Education Studies Textbook.*

YET ANOTHER TREND . . .

The popularity of a wide range of social software, particularly with young people, has led many educators to think that this practice and enthusiasm could be turned to educational use. We aim to show that the roots of social networking are not a paradigm shift from what went before but a growth or development from previous practice and theory. Of course there have been other media which educators were convinced could transform teaching and learning:

- Television and then videoconferencing were going to render most ordinary lecturers redundant because every student would have easy access to outstanding lecturers, with resulting cost savings.
- Computer-based training was going to allow learners to work at their own pace, practicing as often as necessary and receiving programmed feedback from the ever-patient computer.
- Artificial intelligence was going to provide a truly responsive 'tutor' who would 'understand' the student's misunderstandings and respond appropriately.
- Asynchronous computer conferencing was going to support global education in which students from different time zones around the world could take courses from prestigious universities without having to leave home or work.

The list could go on. Educational hype has a long and resilient history of jumping on the latest technology as the means of making education better, cheaper, more available or more responsive. Is social networking going to be any different? Our answer is, probably not, but this may be the wrong question. Ignoring social and technological trends is not the way forward for educators any more than is chasing after every new movement because it is new. If a university were to issue each student with a slate and chalk it would be ludicrous, but equally, to expect all students on all courses to benefit from keeping a blog or creating multimedia items in their e-portfolio, is not a sensible way forward either. What we are advocating is an open mind to the possibility that using some form of social software could be beneficial in most courses, given imaginative course design. The emphasis is squarely on how to use social software creatively, not on any assumption that these tools are predisposed to improving education, reducing costs, widening participation or any future priorities of higher education. These are merely tools; however, as we know, man is a tool-using animal!

WHAT ARE THE TOOLS?

The various tools to be considered in this book are all part of what has been called web 2.0 (O'Reilly, 2005). The underlying practice of web 2.0 tools is that of harnessing collective intelligence, and we have explored the relevance of this for education in a previous book (Rennie & Mason, 2005). As users add new content and new sites, they are connected through hyperlinking so that other users discover the content and link to it, thus the web grows organically as a reflection of the collective activity of the users. O'Reilly cites Amazon as an archetypal example:

> Amazon sells the same products as competitors such as Barnesandnoble.com, and they receive the same product descriptions, cover images, and editorial content from their vendors. But Amazon has made a science of user engagement. They have an order of magnitude, more user reviews, invitations to participate in varied ways on virtually every page – and even more importantly, they use user activity to produce better search results. While a Barnesandnoble.com search is likely to lead with the company's own products, or sponsored results, Amazon always leads with "most popular", a real-time computation based not only on sales but other factors that Amazon insiders call the "flow" around products. With an order of magnitude more user participation, it's no surprise that Amazon's sales also outpace competitors.
>
> (O'Reilly, 2005)

Other examples of social software with relevance to education are:

- Wikipedia is an online encyclopedia in which the content is created and edited entirely by users.
- Folksonomy sites such as delicious and Flickr in which users tag with keywords their photos or other content entries, thus developing a form of collaborative categorization of sites using the kind of associations that the brain uses, rather than rigid, preordained categories.
- Blogging, a form of online diary, adds a whole new dynamism to what was in web 1.0, the personal home page.
- Really Simple Syndication or Rich Site Summary (RSS) is a family of web feed formats used to publish frequently updated digital content, such as blogs, news feeds or podcasts.
- Podcasting is a media file that is distributed over the Internet using syndication feeds, for playback on mobile devices and personal computers.
- E-portfolios encourage students to take ownership of their learning through creating a dynamic, reflective, multimedia record of their achievements.
- Real-time audio and shared screen tools are used for multi-way discussions.

The web has always supported some forms of social interaction, such as computer conferencing, e-mail, and listservs. The level of social interaction they afford has become an established component of distance and even campus-based education. What has changed with web 2.0 is the popularity of social networking sites which, Boyd claims, have three defining characteristics:

1. **Profile.** A profile includes an identifiable handle (either the person's name or nickname) or information about that person (e.g. age, sex, location, interests, etc.). Most profiles also include a photograph and information about last login. Profiles have unique URLs that can be visited directly and updated.
2. **Traversable, publicly articulated social network.** Participants have the ability to list other profiles as "friends" or "contacts" or some equivalent. This generates a social network graph which may be directed ("attention network" type of social network where friendship does not have to be confirmed) or undirected (where the other person must accept friendship). This articulated social network is displayed on an individual's profile for all other users to view. Each node contains a link to the profile of the other person so that individuals can traverse the network through friends of friends of friends.

3. **Semi-persistent public comments.** Participants can leave comments (or testimonials, guestbook messages, etc.) on others' profiles for everyone to see. These comments are semi-persistent in that they are not ephemeral but they may disappear over some period of time or upon removal. These comments are typically reverse-chronological in display. Because of these comments, profiles are a combination of an individual's self-expression and what others say about that individual.

(Boyd, 2006)

These three attributes do not immediately suggest an educational use. However, we will try to demonstrate ways in which they can be integrated in courses and programmes. More recently the term *People Power* on the web has been noted in relation to the success of Hogging, user reviews, and photo sharing (Anderson, 2006); and observers speak of a 'gift culture' on the web whereby users contribute as much as they take. Examples include YouTube, MySpace and Flickr. The primary focus in social networking is participation rather than publishing, which was the primary feature of Web 1.0 activity. Bloch (n.d.) links web 2.0, mashups and social networking as "all intertwined in the brave new Internet, the so-called second phase of the evolution of the online world." The essence of social networking is that the users generate the content. This has potentially profound implications for education.

USER-GENERATED CONTENT

The theoretical benefits of user generated content in education are fairly obvious:

1. Users have the tools to actively engage in the construction of their experience, rather than passively absorbing existing content.
2. Content will be continually refreshed by the users rather than require expensive expert input.
3. Many of the new tools support collaborative work, thereby allowing users to develop the skills of working in teams.
4. Shared community spaces and inter-group communications are a massive part of what excites young people and therefore should contribute to users' persistence and motivation to learn.

However, this assumes a transition between entertainment and education which has never in the past been an obvious or straightforward one. The early champions of educational television had a difficult time persuading learners that this entertaining (but passive) medium could be a tool for active and demanding education. Similarly, how will current users of computer games, blogging, podcasting, and folksonomies be convinced that they can use their favourite tools for getting a degree? O'Reilly suggests that we look at what commercial organisations are doing:

One of the key lessons of the Web 2.0 era is this: *Users add value.* But only a small percentage of users will go to the trouble of adding value to your application via explicit means. Therefore, Web 2.0 companies *set inclusive defaults for aggregating user data and building value as a side-effect of ordinary use of the application.* As noted above, they build systems that get better the more people use them. . . . This architectural insight may also be more central to the success of open source software than the more frequently cited appeal to volunteerism. The architecture of the internet, and the World Wide Web, as well as of open source software projects like Linux, Apache, and Perl, is such that users pursuing their own "selfish" interests build collective value as an automatic by product. Each of these projects has a small core, well-defined extension mechanism, and an approach that lets any well-behaved component be added by anyone, growing the outer layers of what Larry Wall, the creator of Perl, refers to as "the onion." In other words, these technologies demonstrate network effects, simply through the way that they have been designed.

(O'Reilly, 2005)

What is the comparable onion in relation to education? We claim that it is course design. Through appropriate course design, we can help learners to pursue their 'selfish interests' of passing the course, while at the same time adding value to the learning of other students.

Another way of looking at user-generated content, and one that is possibly less contentious, is to see it as a network. In a report from FutureLab, Rudd, Sutch and Facer (2006) note that:

> Castells, for example, argues that the network is now the fundamental underpinning structure of social organisation – that it is in and through networks – both real and virtual – that life is lived in the 21st century. This perspective is also advocated by social commentators such as Demos, who argue that networks are the 'most important organisational form of our time', and that, by harnessing what they describe as 'network logic', the ways we view the world and the tools we use for navigating and understanding it, will change significantly. The ability to understand how to join and build these networks, the tools for doing so and the purpose, intention, rules and protocols that regulate use and communications, therefore, become increasingly important skills. This concept of the 'network society' calls into question what it means to be 'educated' today – what new skills, what new ways of working and learning, what new knowledge and skills will be required to operate in and through these networks? It requires us to ask whether our current education system, premised not upon networks but upon individualised acquisition of content and skills, is likely to support the development of the competencies needed to flourish in such environments.

(Rudd, Sutch, & Facer, 2006, p. 4)

The wise use of web 2.0 technologies in education addresses this call for students to develop 21st century skills. Blogging, wikis, e-portfolios and social networks are all excellent tools for allowing learners to clarify concepts, establish meaningful links and relationships, and test their mental models. Furthermore, they provide a public forum in which the cumulative process of concept formation, refinement, application and revision is fully visible to student peers and teachers. By providing a comprehensive record of how concepts take form through multiple clusters of knowledge, such media can promote more complex and lasting retention of course ideas among students.

(Boettcher, 2007)

WHAT ARE THE LIMITATIONS?

Critics of user-created content refer to a breakdown in the traditional place of expertise, authority and scholarly input. They express concerns about trust, reliability and believability in relation to the move away from the printed word to the more ephemeral digital word (Poster, 1990). The web contains a plethora of unauthenticated, unfiltered information and most students lack the critical skills to penetrate this mass of undifferentiated material. In short, traditional notions of quality in higher education seem to be abandoned in the move to web 2.0 learning.

Another line of criticism is that course designers who use these technologies are merely pandering to the net generation, which is not in their best interests. Carlson notes that "not everyone agrees that Millennials are so different from their predecessors, or that, even if they are different, educational techniques should change accordingly" (Carlson, 2005). These critics feel that new technologies encourage a short attention span and lead students to demand immediate answers, rather than thinking for themselves.

Furthermore, if content is created by users on different systems (e.g. podcasts, blogs, wikis, chat systems, and other social networking software) then it can be difficult to keep track of where everything is, and to access it with ease, both for the users and the casual visitor. This in turn calls for new tools to help users search and integrate across content that may be quite fragmented.

Other commentators question whether social networking has real learning value and point to the superficiality of this informal mode of learning. Learning from websites and online discussion groups is very different from the orientation of formal courses, where stress is laid on learning step by step, just in case one needs it later or for the exam. By contrast informal learning is just-in-time and just the amount necessary to put to immediate use. However, Kapp (2006) argues that:

> We can contemplate whether "real" learning happens with Web 2.0 technologies, we can be philosophical about the value of informal learning versus formal learning, we can tout the virtues of "collective wisdom" but in the end . . . none of that matters.
>
> What matters is that kids are already using Web 2.0 technologies comfortably and effectively. If we old folks (over 30) don't figure out how to effectively use these tools to help the younger generation learn what they need to be successful in our baby boomer-run companies, government agencies and other large organizations then we learning and development folks will be irrelevant. Conducting traditional classroom lectures for these gamers is not going to cut it and neither is our multiple-choice question, e-learning module format. We better stop bad mouthing Web 2.0 or eLearning 2.0 and start using these technologies or be passed up by the "digital natives" as Prensky calls them.
>
> (Kapp, 2006)

Others of the same persuasion apply the dictum, 'If you can't beat them, help them.' They focus on developing critical thinking skills, analysis of the content of websites, and peer commenting on student assignments. In a similar way, Cross (2007) takes a positive stance towards integrating informal learning and web 2.0, and describes an approach which has implications for the role of the teacher:

> Because the design of informal learning ecosystems is analogous to landscape design, I will call the environment of informal learning a learnscape. A landscape designer's goal is to conceptualize a harmonious, unified, pleasing garden that makes the most of the site at hand. A learnscaper strives to create a learning environment that increases the organization's longevity and health, and the individual learner's happiness and well-being. Gardeners don't control plants; managers don't control people. Gardeners and managers have influence but not absolute authority. They can't make a plant fit into the landscape or a person fit into a team. A learnscape is a learning ecology. It's learning without borders.
>
> (Cross, 2007)

STUDIES OF STUDENT BEHAVIOUR

The predictions that students who have grown up with digital media will learn differently and demand a more engaging form of education, have led to a number of studies and surveys of student attitudes, behaviours and uses of technology. A study by Oblinger and

Oblinger (2005) talks about Millennials, those born since 1982, whose learning characteristics are defined as follows:

- Ability to multitask rather than single task
- Preference to learn from pictures, sound and video rather than text
- Preference for interactive and networked activities rather than independent and individual study.

However these characteristics have the following disadvantages:

- Shorter attention spans or choosing not to pay attention
- Lack of reflection
- Relatively poor text literacy
- A cavalier attitude to quality of sources.

Millennials could be described as having hypertext minds, craving interactivity, easily reading visual images, possessing good visual-spatial skills, and having the ability to parallel process. They will prefer learning in teams, will seek to engage with problems and enjoy experiential forms of learning. Another study of millennials by Raines (2002) lists similar characteristics:

- Skilled at teamwork
- Techno-savvy
- Preference for structure
- Desire for entertainment and excitement
- Biased toward experiential activities.

Two European reports, one from Germany (Veen, 2004) and the other from Hungary (Karpati, 2002) both largely confirm the description of millennials outlined in the Oblingers' study. The German report refers to millennials as *Homo Zappiens* because of their habit of using remote controls, and outlines four characteristics:

- Scanning skills
- Multi-tasking
- Processing interrupted information flows
- Non-linear learning.

Not all of these skills, whether positive or negative, can be attributed to social networking, although a number of online gaming sites have web 2.0 characteristics.

An extensive study in the UK of largely pre-university students' use of online technologies (Livingstone & Bober, 2005) has some sobering conclusions:

- Young people lack key skills in evaluating online content and few have been taught how to judge the reliability of online information
- Most online communication is with local friends
- Nearly one quarter of the sample admitted to copying something from the Internet and passing it off as his or her own.

The researchers note, however, that the opportunities and risks of these technologies go hand in hand, and the more users experience the one, the more they experience the other. We turn now to what researchers are investigating in the web 2.0 world.

RESEARCH ISSUES

Web 2.0 research literature

The technologies which have come to dominate the activities of young people have also been taken up by researchers, academics and lecturers as methods of disseminating their thinking and their practice. Much of the literature on the educational use of web 2.0 technologies is online – in blogs, podcasts, wikis and social networking sites. For those trying to keep abreast of developments, it is more important to have the right RSS feeds than the right journal subscriptions.

Of course in many scientific disciplines, printed journals and books have long been an outmoded form of dissemination for research – too late, too inaccessible, and too expensive. Web 1.0 was an improvement over print as a means of transmitting and consuming research. What is different with web 2.0 technologies is that real interaction, peer commenting and collaborative research are actually happening in a distributed, global environment. Knowledge is created, shared, remixed, repurposed, and passed along. In short, web 2.0 is a research network as well as a learning network.

However, do web 2.0 networks constitute research? The 2007 Horizon Report notes that "academic review and faculty rewards are increasingly out of sync with new forms of scholarship". Will academics list blog entries in their CV? The Horizon Report goes on to say "The trends toward digital expressions of scholarship and more interdisciplinary and collaborative work continue to move away from the standards of traditional peer-reviewed paper publication" (New Media Consortium, 2007). The essence of research has always involved notions such as ownership and copyright, objectivity and replicability. Blogging is very different: it is much less formal; it is usually written from a personal point of view, in a personal voice. Wikis do not privilege personal ownership and are ephemeral or at least are constantly changing. Some researchers counter these criticisms by underlining the fact that our relation to knowledge is changing. The shelf life of information is now so short that knowing where to find information is more valuable than knowing any particular piece of information. The capacity to form connections between sources of information, and thereby create useful information patterns, is what is needed in a knowledge economy. Knowledge used to be organised in strictly classified disciplines and subjects, but is increasingly becoming more fluid and responsive, allowing it to be organised in different ways for different purposes. Furthermore, as Stephenson notes:

> Experience has long been considered the best teacher of knowledge. Since we cannot experience everything, other people's experiences, and hence other people, become the surrogate for knowledge. 'I store my knowledge in my friends' is an axiom for collecting knowledge through collecting people.
>
> (Stephenson, n.d.)

Experienced academic bloggers find that this forum for airing ideas and receiving comments from their colleagues helps them to hone their thinking and explore avenues they might otherwise have overlooked. The Horizon Report lists new scholarship and emerging forms of publication as one of its six key trends in 2007 as most likely to have a significant impact in education in the next five years.

> While significant challenges remain before the emerging forms of scholarship we are seeing are accepted, nonetheless, there are many examples of work that is expanding the boundaries of what we have traditionally thought of as scholarship. In the coming years, as more scholars and researchers make original and worthwhile contributions to their fields using these new forms, methods for evaluating and

recognizing those contributions will be developed, and we expect to see them become an accepted form of academic work.

(New Media Consortium, 2007, p. 21)

Knowledge is no longer acquired in a linear manner. We can no longer personally experience and acquire all the learning that we need in order to act. We must derive our competence from forming connections with other people. Blogs and wikis are ideal tools for this and what we see in these tools are examples of networks of growing knowledge and understanding. In terms of the use of web 2.0 tools in education, research on the whole is not to be found in print-based literature. Knowledge and understanding of practice are developing within a network of interactions through web 2.0 tools online.

The changing learner

One of the questions which have arisen due to the phenomenal uptake of new technologies by young people is whether and to what extent learners are changing. That is, what is the effect of computer games, mobile phones, the Internet, and social networking on learners who have grown up with these as an integral part of their environment? The most widely quoted respondent to this question is, of course, Prensky whose papers on 'digital natives' (the net generation for whom everything digital is natural) and 'digital immigrants' (those who have had to learn the language of these technologies as mature adults) have sparked controversy, further studies, and commentators on both sides of the fence (e.g. Allen & Seaman, 2006; Conole, de Laat, Dillon, & Darby, 2006; Kvavik & Caruso, 2005). Prensky (2001a, 2001b) holds that digital natives are different in kind from digital immigrants.

> It is now clear that as a result of this ubiquitous environment and the sheer volume of their interaction with it, today's students think and process information fundamentally differently from their predecessors. These differences go far further and deeper than most educators suspect or realize.
>
> (Prensky, 2001a)

Prensky's conclusions are based (loosely) on research into the neuroplasticity of the brain and he suggests that there may be an actual change in the brains of young people who have spent hours of their growing period as screenagers gaming, interacting online, and creating online content. Owen (2004) counters such sloganising with a reference to Brown and Duguid (2000):

> In this study Brown and Duguid's central theme is that access to information does not equate to knowledge. Brown and Duguid note, much of what we recognise as learning comes from informal social interactions between learners and mentors. These social interactions are difficult to achieve in mediated instruction. They recognise that technology can enhance instruction in remarkable ways; however, it cannot replace the insights that students receive by struggling to make sense of information with both peers and mentors. They contend that the gung-ho tunnel vision of commentators like Prensky – seeing only one way ahead (if all you have is a hammer, everything looks like a nail!), has led to erroneously simplified and unrealistic expectations of what our future in the information age will be like.
>
> (Owen, 2004)

Nevertheless, Owen agrees with Prensky that the tools we use inevitably change how we think, how we learn, what we may think and what we may learn, but he sees this as evolutionary rather than revolutionary. Johnson and Johnson reiterate this point of view:

> Because the nature of technology used by a society influences what the society is and becomes, individuals who do not become technologically literate will be left behind. Influences of a technology include the nature of the medium, the way the medium extends human senses, and the type of cognitive processing required by the medium.
> (Johnson & Johnson, 2004, p. 785)

Johnson and Johnson are confirming the idea already suggested above that educators need to use the tools that are common in the social context of the day, because they are determining the way people learn.

A major piece of research on student reactions to the use of information technology (IT) in education was carried out by Kvavik and Caruso in 2005. Reassuringly, students in this survey still saw faculty knowledge and expertise as the most important element in learning, but the majority wanted instructors to make moderate use of IT, whilst equal numbers wanted extensive use or limited use.

Another aspect of the changing learner is the increasing multiculturalism of most university classes. This is especially true of online, distributed courses, as students from outside the originating institution may be part of each cohort, making a more culturally diverse online environment than was the case for traditional classrooms in the past. Course design manuals used to begin with the process of identifying learners' needs and background knowledge. This may be possible with a relatively homogeneous student body, but becomes impossible in a multicultural context. Cultural backgrounds are inextricably related to how we learn, and hence learning needs of students may well vary by culture. Attitudes to particular content (political correctness, contextuality in meaning-making and views about absolute reality), variations in writing styles (formality, vocabulary, directness), and above all, concepts about the role of the learner and of the teacher (criticism, authority, politeness); these are all culturally specific, and hence highly variable in multicultural learning environments. The practices of peer evaluation, student-generated content, and teacher-as-equal-partner may make students from some non-Western cultures feel uncomfortable and leave them floundering rather than participating. Experienced practitioners of online multicultural environments usually recommend flexibility and openness on the part of course designers. For example, Palloff and Pratt (2003) suggest "recognizing the different ways in which students might respond to instructional techniques online and being sensitive to potential cultural barriers and obstacles is yet another means by which the online classroom can become more culturally sensitive".

Similarly, Henderson (1996) promotes an eclectic paradigm which does not assume that any one instructional pedagogy is immutable but provides an epistemological and pedagogic pluralism that allows students to interact with materials that reflect multiple cultural values and perspectives. Another approach to cultural pluralism is to recognise that every student is individual in his or her learning requirements regardless of cultural background. Providing diversity in types of resources, assessments, communication tools, and learning activities not only creates greater flexibility for all learners to customise their learning, but also provides a self-reinforcing learning environment for creativity and innovation (Price & Rennie, 2005). The issues raised by multicultural classrooms are not new and not restricted to online learning, though they will undoubtedly be exacerbated by web 2.0 technologies.

Collaborative learning

Johnson and Johnson (2004) analyse the history of cooperative and collaborative learning and the way in which these practices have been revitalised by the advent of online learning. They cite a range of studies which demonstrate that cooperative learning online results in higher achievement than individualistic learning. They conclude that "few educational innovations hold the promise that technology-supported cooperative learning does . . ." (p. 806). Jenkins (2006) points out that one of the implications of online collaborative work is that educators need to rethink the individualistic foundations of assessment in higher education. Social networking encourages collective contribution, not individual ownership. Creativity is different in an open source culture. He uses the term *distributed cognition* and outlines the new skills educators need to develop in their learners:

> Applications of the distributed cognition perspective to education suggest that students must learn the affordances of different tools and information technologies, and know which functions tools and technologies excel at and in what contexts they can be trusted. Students need to acquire patterns of thought that regularly cycle through available sources of information as they make sense of developments in the world around them. Distributed intelligence is not simply a technical skill, although it depends on knowing how to use tools effectively; it is also a cognitive skill, which involves thinking across "brain, body, and world." The term "distributed intelligence" emphasizes the role that technologies play in this process, but it is closely related to the social production of knowledge that we are calling collective intelligence.
>
> (Jenkins, 2006, p. 38)

Course design is a particularly important component of successful online collaborative learning. Wenger (1998, p. 229) clarifies the relation between course design and learning: 'Learning [itself] cannot be designed: it can only be designed for – that is, facilitated or frustrated'. The essence of online collaborative course design is the use of activities appropriate to the subject and level of the students. Generic models include: an online debate, joint creation of a website, group presentations, and peer comments on student work. Web 2.0 course design involves collaborative uses of blogs, wikis, e-portfolios and podcasts. These are in their infancy, although educational uses of blogging have a marginally longer history.

Student-centred course design

The issue of student versus teacher centred course design is another long-standing one which continues to evolve with the impact of social networking. Designing a course around the learner's needs is a cornerstone of open and distance learning where it usually involves passing at least some control to the learner over pacing, interaction with the course content, and timing of the assessments in order that part-time students can fit studying around work and family commitments. Garrison and Baynton (1989) argued that control is a dynamic relationship between independence, power and support, and Hall, Watkins and Eller (2003) talk about the need to find a balance between providing the student with enough structure to keep their studying on track, and enough freedom to work creatively and flexibly on the course.

The advent of user or student generated content adds a new dimension to the debate. There are a number of ways in which students can participate in creating the content of a course. Discussions and debates have been standard practice on campuses and have been used regularly in online courses where asynchronous conferences are the established mode of communication. Similarly, the practice of resource-based and problem-based learning pre-dates social networking by some decades. Both of these design models imply that students find appropriate material in order to study the course. Student-generated content takes this a step further by students not just finding content (in the form of resources), but actually creating it (through blogs, wikis, e-portfolios, and other multimedia presentations).

The obvious implication of student-created content is a changing role for the teacher and for the educational institution. There is a need for teachers not only to master the new technologies, but also to understand and capitalise on the pedagogical implications. There is a need for institutions to monitor student access to the technologies and consider what to provide for students and what to leave to social trends to determine. Many of the web services are free and may already be familiar to students from social and informal learning activities outside of their studies.

The Vice Chancellor of the UK Open University, in considering the implications of student-created content for the university, posed the following issues:

> how best we deliver customer service and student support in this new world and how we harness this gift culture to enhance student support with peer-to-peer mentoring and collaborative learning models; how we deal with the shifting boundaries between formal and informal learning. What we see on the Web are people from all over the world creating communities of interest (some of them very sophisticated indeed) on a whole range of subject matter – and what we need to do is ask ourselves how we harness this energy and recognise the learning – if that is indeed useful to people as they negotiate their careers and lives.
>
> (Gourley, 2006)

Mason and Lefrere (2003) define the essence of this move to a sharing environment as involving processes for developing trustworthiness. Jameson, Ferrell, Kelly, and Ryan (2006) also conducted research on the importance of trust in collaborative online learning networks. Course designers need to set up learning systems that recognise the need for building trust and exploit the learners' social networks.

The changing role of the student obviously has implications for the role of the teacher. Beldarrain (2006) notes the transition from teacher as deliverer of knowledge, to facilitator of online interaction. With the advent of student-generated content, she predicts that "the future instructor may have to be more of a partner in learning than a facilitator. The instructor must view the students as contributors of knowledge, and thus allow them to participate in the creation of content" (p. 149). The instructor, therefore, needs to provide feedback and build rapport. Nearly ten years ago, Papert noted that there was a clash between the dominant ideology of curriculum design and the empowerment learners get from games and other technologies which enable the user to take charge of his or her learning (Papert, 1998). Rudd *et al.* (2006) have reiterated this point:

> Currently most discussions about increasing learner 'choice' and 'voice' are focused around giving learners a greater variety of routes through predetermined and predefined subjects and curriculum content. However, a truly personalised system requires that learners will not only have greater choice and influence over the pace, style and content of learning but that they are also supported to become active partners in developing their own educational pathways and experiences.
>
> (p. 7)

Student-centred learning and the technologies which enable them to generate content will continue to have profound effects on the interrelationships of students, teachers, and course content.

BEYOND CONSTRUCTIVIST THEORY

Many researchers consider that course design based on constructivist theories of learning is highly compatible with the use of web 2.0 tools. Constructivist curricula favour an open-ended, negotiable approach which structures activities so that students have opportunities to collaboratively negotiate knowledge and to contextualise learning within an emergent situation. This reflects the two tenets of constructivism: that (1) learning is an active process of constructing knowledge rather than acquiring it, and (2) instruction is a process that involves supporting that construction rather than of communicating knowledge (Duffy & Cunningham, 1996, p. 171).

Through the provision of activities for students to direct their own learning, the designer acknowledges the students' need for autonomy in the learning process in order to construct their own understanding. The provision of realistic or authentic contexts for learning is the basis for many constructivist learning environments, as the purpose is to stimulate learners to relate their thinking to actual practice.

Communication through the learning environment is a key feature of constructivist design, especially where the students are geographically isolated. It is through dialogue in chat rooms, commenting on blogs, collaborating through wikis and self-expression through e-port-folios that students are able to develop as members of their learning community, to create shared understandings, to challenge and to question the key issues of their area of study.

Learners are considered to be distributed, multidimensional participants in a socio-cultural process. This concept moves away from the idea that learning is effective inter-nalising of knowledge, toward one that involves a connection with communities and a pattern of participation in community. It should not be a lonely act of a single person but a matter of being "initiated into the practices of a community, of moving from legitimate peripheral participation to centripetal participation in the actions of a learning community" (Duffy & Cunningham, 1996, p. 181).

Learners in a constructivist environment need to be active and interactive, and web 2.0 software is inherently participative.

> Web 2.0 is where anyone can not only *take* information *down from* it but also create content and upload *to* it. In this respect the Web is not simply a one-way means of *obtaining* knowledge, but also a place where you *interact* with the materials and *annotate* and *contribute* to the content. Such sites frequently display other Web 2.0 characteristics such as automated access through RSS feeds and ability to find related materials through tagging and other social networking devices.
>
> (Stevens, 2006)

Nevertheless, other educators are beginning to look beyond constructivism and to associate it with web 1.0 thinking. For example, Siemens (2004) claims that web 2.0 technologies have changed the learning landscape such that the three pillars of learning theory (behaviourism, cognivitism and constructivism) are no longer adequate for describing the world in which we now are learning:

> Constructivism suggests that learners create knowledge as they attempt to understand their experiences (Driscoll, 2000, p. 376). Behaviorism and cognitivism view knowledge as external to the learner and the learning process as the act of internalizing knowledge. Constructivism assumes that learners are not empty vessels to be filled with knowledge. Instead, learners are actively attempting to create meaning. Learners often select and pursue their own learning. Constructivist principles acknowledge that real-life learning is messy and complex. Classrooms which emulate the "fuzziness" of this learning will be more effective in preparing learners for life-long learning.
>
> Learning theories are concerned with the actual process of learning, not with the value of what is being learned. In a networked world, the very manner of information that we acquire is worth exploring. The need to evaluate the worthiness of learning something is a meta-skill that is applied before learning itself begins. When knowledge is subject to paucity, the process of assessing worthiness is assumed to

be intrinsic to learning. When knowledge is abundant, the rapid evaluation of knowledge is important. Additional concerns arise from the rapid increase in information. In today's environment, action is often needed without personal learning – that is, we need to act by drawing information outside of our primary knowledge. The ability to synthesize and recognize connections and patterns is a valuable skill.

(Siemens, 2004)

He posits instead, a theory he calls connectivism, whose principles he defines as:

■ Learning and knowledge rest in diversity of opinions.
■ Learning is a process of connecting specialized nodes or information sources.
■ Learning may reside in non-human appliances.
■ Capacity to know more is more critical than what is currently known.
■ Nurturing and maintaining connections is needed to facilitate continual learning.
■ Ability to see connections between fields, ideas, and concepts is a core skill.
■ Currency (accurate, up-to-date knowledge) is the intent of all connectivist learning activities.
■ Decision making is itself a learning process. Choosing what to learn and the meaning of incoming information is seen through the lens of a shifting reality. While there is a right answer now, it may be wrong tomorrow due to alterations in the information climate affecting the decision.

(Siemens, 2004)

Connectivism as a theory presents a model of learning that reflects a society in which learning is no longer a personal, individualistic activity. It acknowledges the fact that the ways people learn and function are altered when new tools are used. Siemens is critical of educators for being slow to recognize both the impact of new learning tools and the environmental changes in what it means to learn. Connectivism is his theoretical foundation for the learning skills and tasks needed for learners to flourish in a digital era.

Learning design

A new area of research has emerged recently called Learning Design. It reflects a shift of focus in course design from an emphasis on providing content to an emphasis on designing activities that help students learn through interaction with sources, people and ideas. Learning designs provide a way of representing learning activities so that course designers can easily identify the essence of a design or learning sequence and apply it to their own curriculum area. Through a process of breaking down activities into constituent parts, it guides individuals through the process of creating activities and incidentally, highlights policy and technology implications. It also provides a common vocabulary for course designers to understand how students learn through activities. In short, learning design offers a method for reusing good practice across many disciplines. An example of research in this area comes from Australia:

In a climate where individual institutions are experiencing increased costs at the same time as they face increased demand for more flexible approaches to learning, the Australian Universities Teaching Committee (AUTC) considers there is benefit to be gained in developing shared resources and disseminating successful, generalisable templates between institutions. One product of this assessment is a project, now completed, which is captured here as 'Learning Designs'.

The project was commissioned in 2000 by the AUTC to explore the use of Information and Communication Technologies (ICTs) to facilitate flexible learning opportunities for students by identifying learning designs that have been demonstrated to contribute to high quality learning experiences and determining which learning designs may be redeveloped in a more generic form.

(http://www.learningdesigns.uo\v.edu.au/project/index.htm)

There are a number of learning design tools which have been developed to support the process of course design from creation, through technical implementation, to actual presentation to students. One of these has been developed by researchers at Oxford University and the tool is called Phoebe (http://phoebe-project.conted.ox.ac.uk). Another is the Joint Information Systems Committee (JISC) Pedagogic Planner (http://www.wle.org.uk/d4l/) and a third is called Compendium and was developed at The Open University (http://kmi.open.ac.uk/projects/compendium/). The value of these tools is currently untested on any significant scale. They are essentially decision support tools and some (e.g. the JISC Pedagogic Planner) are highly structured, while others (e.g. Phoebe) are open-ended. Early indications are that some users welcome them and others with different working and thinking practices find it preferable to design on paper or from instinct about what works with students.

OUTCOME-BASED DESIGN

What should drive the process of course design: pedagogical principles, specific problems to be addressed, or tools to be used? It is generally acknowledged that there is no best approach to begin the process of course design. However, there are fashions or trends and currently outcome-based design is in vogue (and definitely out of fashion are technology-driven rationales and teacher-centred approaches).

Learning outcomes are statements of what students will know or be able to do, if they have learned everything in the course. Outcomes are subtly but distinctly different from learning objectives, which are statements of what is going to be taught, although they may be expressed as if the students were going to learn it. Objectives are normally written using behavioural verbs: list, define, calculate, state. Unfortunately behavioural objectives are not so easily adaptable to the higher forms of learning such as understanding and being creative or to critical reflection or transformative learning. With learning outcomes, there is a slight shift from content to process as the outcome is more explicit about how evidence is to be provided, rather than the evidence itself.

Apart from this shift to a focus on process, learning outcomes have also become the driver for the assessment strategy of a course. Coats and Stevenson (2006) claim that it is important to "ensure that assessment strategies and assessment methods support the development of the stated outcomes and enable them to be appropriately assessed." Furthermore, the learning outcomes and their assessment should make a positive contribution to the learning process.

> Good assessment now is that which most closely reflects desired learning outcomes and in which the process of assessment has a directly beneficial influence on the learning process.
>
> (Boud, 1995)

Knowing the expected outcomes and being clear about the criteria that will be used to assess whether or not they have been achieved gives more control to the learner and thus enables him or her to use that assessment as a learning experience. Assessment can be, indeed always is, a learning experience, with or without an outcomes-based approach and clear assessment criteria. The point is that appropriate outcomes and shared criteria can enhance that learning.

How can an educational assessment methodology (or paradigm) that places emphasis on the learners and supposedly encourages them to take more responsibility for their own learning – stressing autonomy and empowerment at the same time – subject that learner to a prescribed curriculum and defined outcomes to learning? One approach to this seeming contradiction is to see assessment as an integrated part of teaching and learning, in which both teacher and student play an interactive role, and in which teaching and learning are seen as complex and socially mediated (Coats & Stevenson, 2006).

Another approach to this contradiction is proposed by Irlbeck, Kays, Jones and Sims (2006) who suggest using emergent models of instructional design, rather than the top-down models in which the 'experts' decide the objectives, assessment criteria, learning outcomes, and activities. Emergent theory suggests a radical alternative – that design should proceed from the ground up using a process of natural selection that will weed out less useful information. Boettcher (2007) sees the unpredictability of a course which is allowed to evolve with the students, as highly engaging:

> Other valuable features of games and simulations are their unpredictability, their interactive qualities, and their infinite variety. Canned, predictable, and static learning resources such as books, preprogrammed tutorials, and linear video experiences are less interesting and less engaging. The more dynamic and interactive the learning experience, the more likely it is that students will invest greater amounts of time in the learning process.
>
> (Boettcher, 2007)

COURSE DESIGN

There is a substantial literature on course design in higher education and particularly so for distributed and distance education (e.g. Gagnon & Collay, 2006; Jochems, van Merrienboer, & Koper, 2003; Rabinowitz, Blumberg, & Everson, 2004). Evidence from the literature on the use of new technologies in education shows that many educators appropriate the new technology – be it computer-based learning, videoconferencing, or computer conferencing – but use them to mirror existing practice rather than to exploit their real affordances. Conole, Oliver, Falconer, Littlejohn, and Harvey (2007) argue that this gap between the potential of technologies and the reality of actual use is due to a number of interconnected issues:

■ Lack of understanding of how they could be used
■ Lack of appropriate guidance at the course design stage
■ Immaturity of the tools
■ Organizational barriers.

Waller (2007) predicts a similar misuse of web 2.0 tools:

> You find nowadays that PowerPoint is inevitable and used with the slightest of excuses. In the main it no longer supports the speaker as it should but instead acts as a crutch . . . . Now we all just stare at the PowerPoint, looking but not seeing, thereby relieving our brain of the tiresome task of seeing what the speaker is saying. Very soon we will have death by podcast as people with uninspiring voices dump what they have to say onto enormous mp3 files. We will have death by short learning programme, rapidly produced by someone who is convinced that this will always produce the required results. We will have death by blogs and wikis and we will be inundated with demands to share what we know in online communities . . . . If these

interventions are not designed by people who know about these things, these events will fail in their purpose . . . .

(Waller, 2007)

The role of the course designer is arguably *more* relevant with web 2.0 tools than with traditional forms of teaching and learning. It is our intention to address this need by providing a framework and above all, examples of how web 2.0 tools can be used appropriately in distributed and distance education settings.

CONCLUSIONS

This synopsis of some of the issues affecting web 2.0 course design has emphasised a number of critical issues. We summarise these in several aphorisms:

1. The medium is only as good as the design of the instructional strategy the educators have used.
2. Cooperation is the watchword, not control. Web 2.0 applications work on the basis of participation not coercion.
3. Course design is no longer about transmission and consumption; it is about co-creating, sharing, repurposing, and above all, interacting.

But as with many areas of web 2.0, the new tools and approaches are only a development or fuller realization of the true potential of the web platform. This gives us a key insight into how to design educational uses for these applications and services.

This overview of the issues related to using web 2.0 tools in education has tried to convey an important concept: that web 2.0 is actually more than a set of tools and services. It is the powerful ideas behind the tools and services that have so much potential for education: the reality of user-generated content, the network effects of mass participation, and the openness and low threshold for easy access. These factors are inherent in the original concept of the web, just as their application to education builds on long established principles of best practice: student engagement and interaction in learning, and student ownership and management of learning.

REFERENCES

Allen, I., & Seaman, J. (2006). Making the grade: Online education in the United States. Retrieved December 12, 2007, from the Sloan Consortium website http://www.sloan-c.org/publications/survey/pdf/making_the_grade.pdf

Anderson, C. (2006, July 14). People power. *Wired Magazine*.

Beldarrain, Y. (2006). Distance education trends: Integrating new technologies to foster student interaction and collaboration. *Distance Education, 27*(2), 139–153.

Bloch, M. (n.d.). Web 2.0, mashups and social networking – What is it all about? Retrieved December 12, 2007, from http://www.tamingthebeast.net/articles6/web2-mashups-social-network.htm

Boettcher, J. (2007). Ten core principles for designing effective learning environments: Insights from brain research and pedagogical theory. *Innovate Journal of Online Education, 3*(3). Retrieved December 12, 2007, from http://innovateonline.info/index.php?view=issue&id=18

Boud, D. (1995). Assessment as learning: Contradictory or complementary? In P. Knight (Ed.), *Assessment for learning*. Pp. 35–48. London: Kogan Page.

Boyd, D. (2006). Social network sites: My definition. Retrieved December 12, 2007, from http://www.zephoria.org/thoughts/archives/2006/11/10/social_network_1.html

Brown, J. S., & Duguid, P. (2000). *Social life of information*. Boston: Harvard Business School Press.

Carlson, S. (2005, October). The net generation goes to college. *The Chronicle of Higher Education*, *52*. Retrieved December 12, 2007, from http://chronicle.com/free/v52/i07/07a03401.htm

Coats, M., & Stevenson, A. (2006, July). *Towards outcomes-based assessment: An unfinished story of triangulation and transformation*. Paper presented at the Association for the Study of Evaluation and Assessment in Education in Southern Africa Conference. Retrieved December 12, 2007, from http://www.open.ac.uk/cobe/docs/ASEASA2006. pdf

Conole, G., de Laat, M., Dillon, T., & Darby, J. (2006). Student experiences of technologies. Joint Information Systems Committee (JISC) Final Report. Retrieved December 12, 2007, from http://www.jisc.ac.uk/media/documents/programmes/elearning_pedagogy/lxp%20project%20final%20report%20dec%2006.pdf

Conole, G., Oliver, M., Falconer, I., Littlejohn, A., & Harvey, J. (2007). Designing for learning. In G. Conole & M. Oliver (Eds.), *Contemporary perspectives in e-learning research: Themes, methods and impact on practice* (pp. 101–120). Abingdon, UK: Routledge Falmer.

Cross, J. (2007). Designing a web-based learning ecology. Retrieved December 12, 2007, from http://infoml.com/?p=697#more-697

Driscoll, M. (2000). *Psychology of learning for instruction*. Needham Heights, MA: Allyn & Bacon.

Duffy, T. M., & Cunningham, D. J. (1996). Constructivism: Implications for the design and delivery of instruction. In D. H. Jonassen (Ed.), *Handbook of research for educational communications and technology* (pp. 170–198). New York: Macmillan.

Gagnon, G., & Collay, M. (2006). *Constructivist learning design: Key questions for teaching to standards*. New York: Sage.

Garrison, D., & Baynton, M. (1989). Beyond independence in distance education: The concept of control. In M. Moore & G. Clark (Eds.), *Readings in principles of distance education* (pp. 3–15). University Park, PA: American Center for the Study of Distance Education.

Gourley, B. (2006). Vice Chancellor's speech to Council, September 26 2006. *Open House*, October.

Hall, R., Watkins, S., & Eller, V. (2003). A model of web-based design for learning. In M. Moore & W. Anderson (Eds.), *Handbook of distance education*. Mahwah, NJ: Erlbaum.

Henderson, L. (1996) Instructional design of interactive multimedia: A cultural critique. *Educational Technology Research and Development*, *44*(4), 86–104.

Jameson, J., Ferrell, G., Kelly, J., Walker, S., & Ryan, M. (2006). Building trust and shared knowledge in communities of e-learning practice: Collaborative leadership in the JISC, eLISA and CAMEL lifelong learning projects. *British Journal of Educational Technology*, *37*(6), 949–967.

Irlbeck, S., Kays, E., Jones, D., & Sims, R. (2006). The phoenix rising: Emergent models of instructional design. *Distance Education*, *37*(2), 171–185.

Jenkins, H. (2006). Confronting the challenges of participatory culture: Media education for the 21st century. Retrieved from New Media Literacy website http://www.projectnml.org/files/working/NMLWhitePaper. pdf

Jochems, W., van Merrienboer, J., & Koper, R. (Eds.). (2003). *Integrated e-learning: implications for pedagogy, technology and organization*. Abingdon, UK: Routledge Falmer.

Johnson, D., & Johnson, R. (2004). Cooperation and the use of technology. In D. Jonassen (Ed.), *Handbook of research on educational communications and technology* (2nd ed.; pp. 1017–1044). Mahwah, NJ: Erlbaum.

Kapp, K. (2006). Gadgets, games and gizmos: Informal learning at Nick.com. Retrieved December 12, 2007, from http://karlkapp.blogspot.com/2006/12/gadgets-games-and-gizmos-informal.html

Karpati, A. (2002). Net generation. Retrieved from http://www.emile.eu.org/Papers1.htm

Kvavik, R., & Caruso, J. (2005). *Study of students and information technology: Convenience, connection, control, and learning* (Vol. 6). Boulder, CO.: Educause Center for Applied Research, Research Study. Retrieved December 12, 2007, from http://www.educause. edu/ir/library/pdf/ers0506/rs/ers0506w.pdf

Livingstone, S., & Bober, M. (2005). UK children go online. Retrieved December 12, 2007, from http://www.york.ac.uk/res/e-society/projects/1.htm

Mason, J., & Lefrere, P. (2003). Trust, collaboration, e-learning and organisational transformation. *International Journal of Training and Development, 7*(4), 259–270.

New Media Consortium. (2007). *The horizon report 2007 edition.* Retrieved December 12, 2007, from The New Media Consortium and Educause website http://www.nmc.org/horizon/2007/report

Oblinger, D., & Oblinger, J. (Eds.). (2005). *Educating the net generation.* Boulder, CO: Educause. Retrieved December 12, 2007, from http://www.educause.edu/ir/library/pdf/pub7101.pdf

O'Reilly, T. (2005). What is Web 2.0? Retrieved December 12, 2007, from http://www.oreillynet.com/pub/a/oreilly/tim/news/2005/09/30/what-isweb-20.html?page=1

Owen, M. (2004). The myth of the digital native. Retrieved December 12, 2007, from http://www.futurelab.org.uk/resources/publications_reports_articles/web_articles/Web_Article561

Pallof, R., & Pratt, K. (2003). *Virtual student: A profile and guide to working with online learners.* San Francisco: Jossey-Bass.

Papert, S. (1998). Does easy do it? Children, games, and learning. *Game Developer.* Retrieved December 12, 2007, from http://www.papert.org/articles/Doeseasydoit.html

Poster, M. (1990). *The mode of information. Poststructuralism and social contexts.* Cambridge, UK: Polity Press.

Prensky, M. (2001a, September/October). Digital natives, digital immigrants. *On the Horizon, 9*(5), 1–6.

Prensky, M. (2001b, November/December). Digital natives, digital immigrants, Part II: Do they really think differently? *On the Horizon, 9*(6), 1–6.

Price, M., & Rennie, F. (2005, June). MSc degrees in managing sustainable mountain/rural development at the UHI Millennium Institute. *Planet, 14,* 2–4. Retrieved December 12, 2007, from http://www.gees.ac.uk/pubs/planet/p14/mpfr.pdf

Raines, C. (2002). Generations at work, managing millennials. Retrieved December 12, 2007, from http://www.generationsatwork.com/articles/millenials.htm

Rabinowitz, M., Blumberg, F., & Everson, H. (Eds.). (2004). *The design of instruction and evaluation: Affordances of using media and technology.* Mahwah, NJ: Erlbaum.

Rennie, F., & Mason, R. (2004). *The connecticon: Learning for the connected generation.* Greenwich, CT: Information Age.

Rudd, T., Sutch, D., & Facer, K. (2006). Opening education: Towards new learning networks. Retrieved December 12, 2007, from http://www.futurelab.org.uk/research/opening_education.htm

Siemens, G. (2004). Connectivism: A learning theory for the digital age. *elearnspace.* Retrieved December 12, 2007, from http://www.elearnspace.org/Articles/connectivism.htm

Stephenson, K. (n.d.). *What knowledge tears apart, networks make whole.* Retrieved December 12, 2007, from http://www.netform.com/html/icf. pdf.

Stevens, V. (2006). Revisiting multiliteracies in collaborative learning environments: Impact on teacher professional development. *Teaching English as a Second Language, 10*(2). Retrieved December 12, 2007, from http://www-writing.berkeley.edu/TESL-EJ/ej38/int.html

Veen, W. (2004). A new force for change: Homo zappiens. *Learning Citizen Cluster Newsletter.* Retrieved December 12, 2007, from http://www.learningcitizen.net/articles/AnewforceforchangeHo.shtml

Waller, V. (2007, January). Are we all learning designers now? *Inside Learning Technologies.* Retrieved December 12, 2007, from http://www.learningtechnologies.co.uk

Wenger, E. (1998). *Communities-of-practice: Learning, meaning and identity.* Cambridge, UK: Cambridge University Press.

18

RETHINKING EDUCATION

James Tooley

INTRODUCTION

James Tooley is Professor of Education Policy at Newcastle University. He has completed a three-year international research programme that explored the nature and extent of private education serving low-income families in Asia and Africa. His research is ongoing into private education in India, China, Nigeria, Kenya and Ghana. His main scholarly work is on the role of the State in education, and on private education, privatisation and public-private partnerships in developing countries. Tooley's edited introductory chapter to his book *Reclaiming Education* was considered controversial by the education community when first published; one reviewer commented that 'Tooley is an extremist: his ideas are outrageous'. His chapter outlines an alternative agenda for education based upon private education and meeting the demands of parents. This chapter presents Tooley's idea that education should be reclaimed from the State and that schooling should be privatised. He goes further, by suggesting that schooling run by the State brings with it undesirable consequences and he proposes a number of controversial solutions.

KEY QUESTIONS

1. What role should there be for the State in educational policy?
2. Has Tooley made a credible case for his conclusion that there is no justification for State intervention in education, in terms of provision, funding and regulation?

FURTHER READING

A number of books and articles have been written on this theme and Joseph Zajda's edited collection *Decentralisation and Privatisation in Education: The Role of the State* (Springer, Berlin, 2006) critically examines the overall interplay between privatisation, decentralisation and the role of the State in education. Another book that pre-dates Tooley's research is *Privatizing Education and Educational Choice: Concepts, Plans, and Experiences* (Praeger, Westport, CT, 1994) by Gary W. Bowman, Simon Hakim, and Paul Seidenstat. Eighteen experts examine the issues surrounding educational choice in public school systems and the voucher system for private schools. They discuss when choice should be considered, methods of implementation, and the extent to which government should be involved.

This Reading links with Chapters 1 and 5 and Debate 1 of *The Routledge Education Studies Textbook.*

A GLOBAL AND HISTORICAL WAKE-UP CALL

There are solutions to the fundamental challenges facing education. The solutions do not require much more from government other than that it leaves education well alone. New global and historical evidence has provided us with radical new ways of thinking about the way education is provided for in society. This evidence can change the way we think about the state, education and 'privatization' – giving education back to the private sector, to markets and civil society.

I lay out an agenda for reclaiming education from *the state*. I show how all the supposed justifications for state intervention in education melt away in the face of this new evidence and new arguments. With these justifications revoked, a moral case for privatization of education *can be made*, grounded firmly in practice, focused on the future. But I explain why we should reclaim education from *the tyranny of schooling*. I go back to first principles about the nature of education, and find the current fashion of putting all our educational expectations into schooling unsatisfactory and bringing undesirable consequences.

THREE FUNDAMENTAL CHALLENGES

My work is not premised on there being a crisis as measured by government statistics, but it is premised on there being challenges to education and choices to be made.

The first challenge is how we are to meet unsatisfied demand for educational opportunities of all kinds. Globally it is estimated that there are 150 million children aged between 6 and 11 who are not in school, 60 per cent of these girls. And fully one quarter of those children who do start primary school drop out. Adult literacy globally remains below 40 per cent. Further and higher education participation rates in most countries in the world are considerably less than 20 per cent of the relevant populations. All these figures are usually taken to mean there is huge unsatisfied demand for education in developing countries. Similar unmet demand is also evident in educational aspirations in any developed country – a recent high-level discussion in the New Zealand education department estimated that if all the demand for further and higher education was to be met by government, it would annually exceed all of current government earnings through taxation! Similar situations are apparent in any other developed country.

Now, the solution to this challenge is presumed to be the same the world over. Whether our education system is top notch, or whether we are a struggling developing country, nonetheless, the solution is always: 'What can government do about it?' Whether in the UK or USA, or in the United Nations or, until very recently, the World Bank, or in a developing country, the proposal is always the same. Educational challenges need a solution from government. But why? Why do we assume we need government here, and not the private sector? Our first challenge leads us to seek evidence about the ways in which 'the private alternative' can satisfy educational demand – and how it has done so historically.

The second challenge raised about education brings us up graphically against what we mean by education. For we find in the various writings concerns which are, to say the least, extremely wide-ranging if not all-encompassing. So we have Professor Barber nervous about 'the problems of the global environment' (1996, p. 17) and the 'descent into hell' felt by the parents of the murdered Liverpool child James Bulger and its ramifications for moral decline in society (p. 19) – sentiments similarly echoed by Melanie Phillips (1996, p. x). Tom Bentley is anxious about the crises in young people's relationships – with marriage break-down featuring highly – depression and suicide amongst young people, and apathy towards governments and voting (1999, ch. 2). But, curiously, the solution to this sweeping range of problems always seems to be couched in terms of what *schools* can do to solve them. I think a Martian, not immersed in our everyday ways of seeing these matters, would find this somewhat puzzling. Perhaps schools are such powerful places that they can solve every problem besetting us – from global warming to adulterous relationships – but it wouldn't be clear at the outset how the place where children spend only 15 per cent of their waking hours would necessarily have such power. However, read these authors and you'll rarely find any discussion about what they think education is and why schools must have such wide-ranging responsibilities. I will not neglect this fundamental area. And this challenge brings us to one of the senses, as noted above, in which we seek to reclaim education – by reclaiming the concept of education from the tyranny of schooling.

The third challenge looks at what society requires from education – in all the ways we understand it. We are worried about inequality – about some children, as noted earlier, having really poor quality of schooling, for example, or about terrible inequalities within countries and also between countries. Some are worried about issues concerning democracy, how to improve it and to reinvigorate what it means to be a citizen. Equality and democracy are the key concerns which lead people to want the state to intervene in education. Others are worried about social cohesion, or crime, or economic growth. What is notable about each of these societal concerns about education is that they have been put forward as justifications in their own right for governments to get involved in education. Without government being involved in these areas, we are told, we will never achieve equality of opportunity or equity. Or we will never achieve real democracy. Or society will disintegrate. The main thrust of this work is to challenge these assumptions. It considers whether these ideals, sincerely held by many, can be satisfied by government, or whether they are aspirations better met outside of the state. This is the fundamental sense in which we are seeking to reclaim education – to reclaim education from the state.

THREE LEVELS OF STATE INTERVENTION

As well as focusing on the three challenges facing education, there is a second strand of discussion woven into the argument. This focuses on the three levels in which states can intervene in education, through provision, funding and regulation (Barr 1993, p. 80) and examines justifications for intervention at each level. Let's be clear on what we mean by each level: states can, for example, *provide* by supplying buildings and employing teachers, *fund* by supplying school places free of charge or heavily subsidized, and *regulate* through having compulsory attendance laws and national curricula and assessment systems. And while we are used to all three aspects being together in state education now, it is important to note that each is independent of the other. In other areas of our lives, for instance, we are accustomed to the state regulating to ensure that all drivers on the road have passed their driving test, but there is no state funding of this, nor state provision of driving schools, both aspects which are left to private initiative. Or we can have state funding of food for the poor, through welfare payments, but no state provision of food shops.

With these distinctions in mind, I examine the justifications given for state intervention, exploring at what level they *might* apply, and then exploring whether they *do* apply. Equity or equality of opportunity is a justification for state intervention which seems to encompass all three levels. Choice is desirable in education – even, paradoxically, for those who don't actually value the act of having to choose.

The 'information problem' is another justification for (at least) state regulation, that parents will not have enough appropriate and relevant information about education on which to base sensible decisions. The state is needed to step in to solve this problem. But, it does not lead to the need for state intervention after all.

Another major justification for state intervention concerns the need for education for democracy, and also democratic control of education.

Building on the three challenges, and exploring the major justifications for the three levels of state intervention, the message is simple: we need to start thinking differently about education. Jolted by recent global and historical evidence, we need to revisit ideas on what education is. From there, we need to imaginatively ponder ways in which we can ensure its presence and delivery in society. And all this will lead us to realize that the *status quo* of state education systems is simply untenable. We will realize that if we want education to be of the highest quality, inclusive of all children and all their varied needs, and to respond to the needs of society and encourage life-long learning, then our current system simply cannot deliver it. There is no point in looking any further to the state. State intervention in education has been a cul-de-sac, a historical experiment with the lives of children. It has not been successful. We must now return from it, to consider something new.

The argument is that there are no moral or ethical justifications for state intervention. The conclusions reached here are that we should do all we can to encourage what I will call from now on 'the private alternative' – in all its diverse and delightful forms, for-profit companies, not-for-profit foundations, the family, philanthropy and other agencies in civil society – to play an ever-increasing role in the delivery of educational opportunities.

THREE FUNDAMENTAL CONFUSIONS

Before we can set off on this journey we need to do some 'intellectual housekeeping' to get rid of three fundamental confusions.

But markets in education don't work . . .

A book has just landed on my desk which has – even I have to reluctantly concede – the very clever title *Trading in Futures: Why markets in education don't work* (Lauder *et al.* 1999). Its title is very much in keeping with the spirit of literally hundreds of books and articles published over the last decade, by educational researchers in universities, educational journalists and concerned others, all proclaiming precisely the same message: that markets in education don't work. Academic books and papers clamour for attention, all heavily critical of recent reforms that have taken place which have purportedly introduced markets into education, in the UK, the USA, Australia, New Zealand, Canada, Chile, Colombia – all over the world in fact. (Professor Lauder and his colleagues are writing about reforms in New Zealand, for example.) Marking essays by students on modular undergraduate education courses, or by students on teacher training courses, one soon becomes aware that there is only one acceptable view on this issue, and that view is hostile towards markets in education. And the students have only got this from their tutors, whose reading lists positively bristle with sources angry at market reforms. It would seem I have my work cut out to engage with every one of these authors to show why, against all this mounting evidence, I still want to put forward the case *for* markets in education. Am I very brave, or just very stupid?

I think I am neither, at least not in this context. For all these books have nothing to do with markets in education as we shall come to understand them in this book. This is the first fundamental misunderstanding which we will have to clear up. All these hundreds of books and articles may be right to be objecting to certain reforms, but these reforms have very little, if anything, to do with markets.

For the education systems which are being objected to in this literature all feature 'choice' reforms, which have as their chief characteristic that parental choice is permitted within a heavily regulated, state provided and funded schooling system. In these choice systems, it is hardly possible for new suppliers to enter the market, such is the near-monopoly offered by the state. And there is definitely no price mechanism operating. But defenders of markets in areas *other* than education do not normally have in mind that the state should be so heavily involved. Markets in food and clothing, for example, have some relatively minimal state regulation, and zero state provision and funding, although in some circumstances there may be some very tiny amount of targeted (indirect) funding for the poor, such as food stamps in the USA or social security cash benefits in the UK. They also feature an open and competitive supply-side, with many competing suppliers from large supermarket chains to corner shops and market stalls. Finally, customer demand and producer supply is co-ordinated through a price mechanism. Crucially, each of these features are necessary, and in combination sufficient, to define a market, and are worth highlighting:

1. No state provision.
2. No state funding (except perhaps for targeted indirect funding for the poor).
3. Relatively minimal regulation.
4. Relatively easy entry for new suppliers.
5. A price mechanism.

Only when all of these features are present together can we say there is a market in education. This is more than a semantic point – we need some term to be able to define what education without the state will look like, and we object to the use of the term 'market' to describe something which is so patently not this.

Interestingly, many of the principal writers in this debate do seem to recognize there is something odd about calling choice reforms 'markets', but then they all promptly drop their misgivings and go on using the unhelpful terminology. So Professor Lauder and his colleagues note that what has been introduced in the choice reforms is 'in reality, quasi or proxy market mechanisms into education', given the lack of a price mechanism and lack of competing suppliers (1999, p. 19). And they do even go as far as considering whether there could ever be 'genuine' market mechanisms in education:

> Suppose, for example, that the condition of allowing schools complete freedom over their budgets . . . was met. Would that make a difference? Would, for example, Sheppard High, which performs so well on raw examination results, expand to include more students?
>
> (p. 135)

But they argue no, basing this on the fact that the successful school wouldn't want to expand – the head told them so! – and 'from her perspective, rightly so. If the apparently successful schools expanded while others closed down, all that would happen is that the problems associated with the schools closing down would be exported to the "successful" schools' (p. 135). It is crucially important to consider what would happen under more genuine market mechanisms, and that their simple dismissal of other possibilities excludes quite radical and dramatic options. So, while possibly being a useful critique of inequality within the New Zealand state system, noting how certain reforms *may* have made things worse in that respect, Professor Lauder and his colleagues do not touch on markets in education, whatever their title claims to the contrary.

Similarly, Professor Michael Barber (1996) also objects to markets. In his *The Learning Game* he harangues the 'market forces' introduced by the Conservative Government – which were precisely the same type of reforms as those introduced in New Zealand, with parental choice introduced into a heavily regulated, state funded and provided system. But again, interestingly, he also notes that what was introduced

> . . . is in fact a very crude model of market forces . . . it is as if a state monopoly in the provision of supermarkets were to be broken down by telling consumers that, from

> now on, they could choose which supermarket they shopped at; but once they had made their choice – assuming the supermarket was not over-subscribed and too full to be able to accept their custom – they would have to do all their shopping there.
>
> (p. 256)

I couldn't have put it better myself – except he also neglects the price mechanism, and the fact that the supermarket would also be state provided and funded. But nonetheless, I think it is a graphic illustration of the problem. But given his awareness that these are not markets in education which he is criticizing, unfortunately he persists in using the language of markets throughout his book. And so again, readers might think that he is criticizing the subject of this book, when in fact he is patently not.

Finally, some of the most important empirical research in England and Wales on 'markets' in education is that conducted by Professor Stephen J. Ball and his colleagues at King's College, London. Again, this work shows the problems which have occurred because of the choice reforms in terms of equity. Again, they call these reforms 'markets';

> Schools in England are now set within the whole paraphernalia of a market system, albeit a market which is strongly politically regulated.
>
> (Gewirtz *et al.* 1995, p. 1)

But not only is it regulated, but it is also, of course, funded and provided by the state, does not have a price mechanism operating, and entrance for new suppliers is severely limited. Again, Professor Ball recognizes that there is something uncomfortable about calling it a market:

> . . . the UK education system is organised as a very strange market indeed . . . The market is thus heavily constrained and singularly constructed by government. Furthermore, the performance indicators of schooling are fixed by the Government . . . Is this 'real' choice? Is this a market? It certainly has the effect of a market in creating competition between schools but the possibilities of invention and entrepreneurship and expressions of minority interests or commitments among parents are severely limited by political control of the market.
>
> (Ball 1993, pp. 8–9)

Agreed. So why call this a market at all?

Perhaps some readers will be rather impatient with this, because they might argue: so even if these aren't real markets, wouldn't real markets just be like these choice systems *but worse*? Wouldn't all these criticisms apply, but even more strongly? London University professors Geoff Whitty and David Halpin and Dr Sally Power argue along these lines. They do concede that 'of course, empirical research on current systems does not, indeed in principle could not, show that total, deregulation would not have beneficial effects', and they continue:

> The *best available evidence* does seem to suggest that going further in the direction of marketization would be unlikely to yield overall improvements in the quality of education and might well have damaging equity effects.
>
> (Whitty *et al.* 1998, p. 128, emphasis added)

I totally disagree with this. I'm not sure that the 'best available evidence' does show this for a start, but even if they are right, it assumes that the state reforms of devolution and choice *are* actually moves towards markets. But to have one's ideas on deregulated education damned because current reforms (which, sorry to keep on repeating it, involve heavy government regulation, provision and funding – where's the free market?) haven't succeeded in promoting quality and equity, seems rather akin to having one's egalitarian impulses damned because of the failure of the Soviet Union.

The point is that there is very little which is recognizable about real markets in these choice systems. Barber's analogy with the supermarkets is helpful here: if food provision was provided, funded, and regulated by the state in the ways that schools are under choice reforms, does anyone believe they would in any way resemble food provision as we know it today? Perhaps I shouldn't leave this as a rhetorical question, but should spell out exactly what I mean for readers. So consider this parable.

Suppose that in the late nineteenth century it had been decided that children needed an adequate diet to grow up into good citizens and employees, and it was observed that not all children were getting this. Hence the state, invoking the 'protection of minors' principle, intervenes to ensure an adequate diet for all children. Through a bold series of ever-more encompassing reforms, starting with the setting up of a National Bread Board through to the creation of the Department for Nutrition, the system, is in place by, say, 1970, whereby the vast majority of children attend Local Nutrition Authority (LNA) kitchens for all their eating requirements. Children are directed to their local kitchen by their LNA, neither they nor their parents have any choice in this matter. Food is provided free at the kitchen, and officials strongly warn against provision of food outside of the kitchen. (In any case, as parents would have to pay for such additional food, there is very little motivation for them to do so.) Attendance at the kitchens is compulsory for all children, and they have to eat three meals a day, at set times. All children have the same amount of food and the same amount of time in which to eat it. If they haven't finished one course when the time is up, they have to move on to the next. They eat their meals in their own part of the kitchen around tables with 30 other children of the same age, supervised by one member of the Feeding Profession. If they do not eat their meals at the set times, they are punished, often by serving them the meal that children least like when everyone else has gone home.

The Nutrition System as outlined comes under mounting pressures. In many kitchens, it is alleged, food is of poor quality, leading to illness and listlessness. Some of the Feeding Profession cannot control their charges, with consequent riotous meal-times. Moreover, it is pointed out that because diet is not centrally prescribed, some kitchens are experimenting with different kinds of food, with disastrous consequences for children thus exposed. Samosas served at one school instead of steak and kidney pie creates a huge national scandal. Questions are asked in the House of Commons. All this seems grossly unfair, particularly as at other institutions, meal-times are orderly and the food good, at least in part. Finally, the children of the rich, it is noted, can afford to opt out of the state system, and have food in restaurants or even, in rare cases, cooked at home by their own parents. This adds to the inequity of the system, because it is agreed that the quality of private restaurants is better than the state kitchens, and because home cooking clearly deprives children of their national nutritional entitlement. It is apparent that urgent reforms are needed.

The party that wins the next election favours 'markets' as a panacea for the country's ills. It introduces market reforms into the public services, including Nutrition. To avoid alienating the Department for Nutrition and the Feeding Profession, the government sets up a National Dietary Division (NDD) and brings out a National Diet (ND), prescribing the quantity, quality, speed of eating, table levels and so on, to take place in all kitchens in the country. To ensure national accountability – so important in a democracy – a testing regime is enhanced, with frequent eating examinations and publication of kitchen (league) tables. But these are not the key market reforms. These, enthuse the politicians, liberate nutritional demand and supply. On the demand side parents are now permitted to choose their preferred kitchen from the two or three in their area. Moreover, whereas previously kitchens had received funding regardless of how many children they had to feed, now they are to be allocated a specific amount for each child. That should keep these kitchens on their toes! On the supply side, kitchens are now given control of much of their budgets and a rather small number of brand-new expensive kitchens opened, with superb modern cooking equipment. With these demand and supply-side revolutions in place, the government presents its Nutrition Market.

However, it is not long before critics begin condemning the market. Says one professor: look how markets exacerbate inequality! For it is clear that, under the reforms, some kitchens are far more popular than others. Lo and behold, just as one could have predicted, the popular kitchens are able to choose between parents. Under the guise of consumer choice, it is the producers who are empowered, not the customers, and particularly not the disadvantaged, who end up in the worst kitchens from which the middle classes have escaped. The debate rages, and when a new government comes into power, under agitation from the Nutrition pressure groups, the market reforms are curtailed.

Let's leave this parable and return to Michael Barber's point, and consider the 'more authentic' market as we know it in Nutrition, or, as we call it, food. Parents can choose in what ways they wish their children to be fed. They purchase food using their own money, and the myriad of these individual choices have an influence on the final price of the food, giving information to suppliers to act according to demand. They can choose uncooked, cooked, or partly cooked food. They choose from an incredible diversity of suppliers, from traditional markets, supermarkets, hypermarkets, late stores, corner shops and wholesalers. Some grow food for themselves. Some eat out for certain meals at restaurants or fast-food stores, or order take-away food. Some eat with friends or extended family. The government is not involved in the funding or provision at all. There is some state intervention in this market for sure. The food suppliers need to conform to safety and informational requirements. Moreover, there are two 'safety nets' to ensure that children don't suffer. If parents are neglectful, there are mechanisms to ensure children are cared for properly. For poor parents, there are money handouts to ensure their children eat properly. These mechanisms, if working properly, enhance but don't undermine the market.

I hope I have written enough to bring out the stark contrast between an authentic market and the 'so-called' one. The tiny aspects of markets which were introduced in the parable are largely insignificant, and indeed, as the critics pointed out may even exacerbate the unfairness of the previous system. Moral of this parable is, I hope, that tinkering with heavy state intervention does not bring about a market, even if the tinkering is introducing some vaguely market-like mechanisms. All we have in education is this tentative tinkering; the so-called market is as different from a more authentic market as the reformed Nutrition System is from the market in food.

Education markets versus education for the market

A second widespread misapprehension about markets in education confuses what we are talking about, markets in education – as we've just defined them – and education geared for the marketplace. Two vehement critics of markets in education, Professor Ruth Jonathan of Edinburgh University (Jonathan 1989, 1997) and Canadian professor James McMurtry (McMurtry 1991), seem to be assuming that markets in education mean that the education delivered will be of a particular vocationally oriented type, i.e. education to equip young people for the marketplace. They don't want education to be narrowly defined in that way, and certainly don't want to forsake the possibility of education understood as being of intrinsic value, or of being involved with disciplines and practices which have no obvious value in business or industry. So this is one reason why they don't like markets in education. However, this is to misunderstand what we are talking about. Here are the two possibilities spelled out in more detail:

■   *Education for the market.* Educational opportunities designed to equip young people for work; or educational opportunities designed by governments to foster greater international economic competitiveness.

■   *Markets in education.* Educational opportunities delivered by markets, i.e. not provided, largely funded or largely regulated by governments, with supply-side liberated and price mechanisms in place.

The first point is: *there is no necessary connection between the two.* Many governments, throughout history and globally, have tried or are trying to provide the first through *increasing* their control over education. As we shall see, this was arguably one of the reasons why the British government intervened in education in the first place in the nineteenth century. Britain needed to remain competitive with Germany and France, whose governments had already intervened in order to achieve greater economic power. Similarly, the governments in Korea and Taiwan and Indonesia have sought to increase international competitiveness by increasing their hold on education, not by letting markets be given free reign. From the opposite direction, it is quite possible that markets in education will not bring about greater international competitiveness and not bring about more focus on vocational preparation. This all depends on what consumers choose to spend their funds on. There are markets in books, now, for example, but this doesn't mean we all spend our funds on books which will improve our business competitiveness, but many of us spend money on books which will improve our minds.The same can be true in a genuine educational market.

The second point is that in this book we are not concerned with the first – education for the market – except of course when it arises as a consequence of the second, markets in education. So no one must read what follows and think we are talking about education narrowly geared to vocational preparation.

Business involvement in education versus education business

Reviewing the quality of educational research for Her Majesty's Chief Inspector of Schools, Chris Woodhead, was in general a pretty grim business, as readers of my report *Educational Research: A critique* may have suspected (Tooley with Darby 1998). However, in all the hundreds of articles surveyed, I did come across one joke, which I liked so much I have since used it, suitably personalized, at several conferences. An article by Professor Rosemary Deem, entitled 'Border territories: a journey through sociology, education and women's studies' (1996), at first seemed a rather unpromising account of yet another woman academic telling her life story, sorry 'auto/biography'. But it was actually quite a lively account, and in it she described how, as an undergraduate, she attended

> a core theory course in which we were all dazzled by Tony Giddens [now the Director of the London School of Economics] . . . unencumbered by lecture notes and wearing a donkey jacket emblazoned across the back with the legend 'Laing'. Whereas then this apparel might have been decoded as showing his empathy with the working class, today anyone wearing a similar jacket might be thought to be sponsored by industry!
>
> (Deem 1996, p. 8)

It is this aspect of education being sponsored by industry which many people assume I am talking about when I speak of markets in education. It is also the subject of severe criticism from Professor Alex Molnar (1996). Similar qualms are raised by Robertson in her book *No More Teachers, No More Books* (1998), from the Canadian perspective, and by Sheila Harty in *Hucksters in the Classroom* (1979) (based on the situation in the USA) and *The Corporate Pied Piper* (1985) (based on findings in Malaysia).

So for example, Professor Molnar objects to Pizza Hut's 'BOOK IT!' literacy programme – which brings as a reward for children's reading 'a salty, high-fat meal', whereas we all know that 'a healthful diet is low in salt, fat, and sugar'. He condemns the involvement of this business in schooling: 'It's understandable that Pizza Hut wants to be associated with reading. It's less clear why schools are willing to undermine their curricula for the promise of a personal pan pizza' (p. 45).

Similarly, Sheila Harty objects to the

> best sales pitch ever advanced in USA schools . . . the Cheesborough Ponds' advertising campaign which promoted Q-Tips cotton swabs through an art contest aimed at primary grades. Student entries for paintings and construction models had to use Q-Tips as the paintbrush, the glue applicator, or the construction material. Prizes amounted to $40,000 worth of USA savings bonds for four winners per grade.
>
> Teachers' chances at a sweepstake drawing were increased with each student who entered the contest. The winning teacher was awarded a paid 'art experience' for two in either Athens, Cairo or Florence. Now that's guaranteed to sell Q-Tips.
>
> (Harty 1994, pp. 91–2)

And Heather-Jane Robertson objects to the way Scholastic, who are publishers and distributors of educational materials, distributed a pamphlet entitled 'Introducing Indonesia' to 77,000 teachers in 1997. The problem was that it was backed by 'the Lippo Bank, the Indonesian government, Mobil, Texaco, and other Suharto-friendly corporations'; because of this it explained that 'sneakers are manufactured in Indonesia not because labour is cheap, but because rubber is a natural resource' (Robertson 1998, p. 211).

In each of these cases we have big business being involved in schools, to promote their brand names, to increase sales, or even to subvert truth in the cause of offering free curriculum materials.

I find that when I'm giving lectures defending the involvement of education businesses or companies in schooling, many in the audience simply assume I am defending this sort of practice. However, this is a crucial misunderstanding, and we need to make a very important distinction to avoid it.

The distinction is between businesses getting involved in schools – for all the kinds of reasons outlined above – and education businesses *whose only business is education* getting involved in schools, or other educational opportunities. It is only the latter which I am seeking to defend, not the former. In fact, I too share an abhorrence of many of the practices revealed by the above three writers. I really don't think other businesses have much role to play in schooling, as will become apparent in what follows. They are liable to distort the educational process, and subvert it to their own ends. But this does *not* mean I am also against education businesses being involved. Professor Molnar puts it succinctly: 'Corporations don't exist either to serve the best interests of schoolchildren or to promote "family" values. Corporations are created to return profits to their owners' (Molnar 1996, p. 47). But this brings out the crucial distinction I wish to make. For real education businesses – the sort I will defend here – *do* exist 'to serve the best interests of schoolchildren' and their families, as well as their shareholders. If they are not serving the interests of children then they will go out of business. The only way they can make profits for their owners is if they provide high-quality educational services. This isn't the case with the other businesses involved with schooling, I agree with Professor Molnar. They want to make profits to shareholders who are not particularly concerned about the educational impact of what they are doing.

So this distinction must be made clear. Incidentally, I do think that the kinds of criticisms raised by Molnar, Robertson and Harty could actually be used *against* their positions in favour of state education. For the strongest part of their arguments against business involvement is that public schools are really gullible to use these materials and promotions from (non-education) businesses:

> Even a cursory look at most of this stuff would be enough to cause most people to wonder why in the world teachers and principals continue to let it into their schools. It takes up valuable learning time and distracts, misinforms, and manipulates the students.
>
> (Molnar 1996, p. 43)

Similarly, Molnar notes the experience of 'one Milwaukee mother', who wanted to reward her child with a book rather than pizza, involved with a Pizza Hut promotion in schools: 'In the clash of values, Pizza Hut prevailed' (p. 45).

What an indictment of state schools in America these examples show, that they can bring in programmes so alien to parents' values – and what a compelling argument for liberating school choice!

ONE FUNDAMENTAL (POTENTIAL) PROBLEM

All this leads to one fundamental problem for me; indeed, some might think it is an insurmountable problem. If I am to present an argument in favour of something that doesn't yet exist in any country, then where is my evidence going to come from to show that it is preferable?

Actually, I think I am in a perfectly symmetrical position to many of those advocates of other reforms which can improve the lot of people. Anyone who argues in favour of more egalitarian education or more democratic education or whatever else is the flavour of the month in left-wing circles also has to concede that there is no evidence to show that these proposals actually do work, for nowhere have their proposals been fully tried. All similar proposals point to an alternative which has not yet been tested and on which, therefore, there is bound to be scant evidence on which to base any debate.

But this brings in the need not for further dwelling on past empirical evidence which may not be relevant, but an examination of the underlying theoretical arguments which support the case. What is needed is philosophical reflection and some greater historical perspective.

REFERENCES

Ball, Stephen J. (1993) 'Education markets, choice and social class: the market as a class strategy in the UK and the USA', *British Journal of Sociology of Education*, 14.1, pp. 3–19.

Barber, Michael (1996) *The Learning Game: Arguments for an Education Revolution*, London: Victor Gollancz.

Barr, Nicholas ([1987] 1993) *The Economics of the Welfare State*, London: Weidenfeld and Nicolson.

Bentley, Tom (1999) *Learning Beyond the Classroom*, London: Routledge.

Deem, Rosemary (1996) 'Border territories: a journey through sociology, education and women's studies', *British Journal of Sociology of Education*, 17.1.

Gewirtz Sharon, Ball, Stephen J. and Bowe, Richard (1995) *Markets, Choice and Equity in Education*, Buckingham and Philadelphia: Open University Press.

Harty, Sheila (1979) *Hucksters in the Classroom: A Review of Industry Propaganda in Schools*, Washington DC: Center for Study of Responsive Law.

Harty, Sheila (1985) *The Corporate Pied Piper: Ideas for International Consumer Action on Business Propaganda in Schools*, Penang, Malaysia: International Organization of Consumer Unions.

Harty, Sheila (1994) 'Pied piper revisited', in Bridges, David and McLaughlin, Terry (eds) *Education and the Market Place*, London: Falmer.

Jonathan, Ruth (1989) 'Choice and control in education: parental rights, individual liberties and social justice', *British Journal of Educational Studies*, 37, pp. 321–38.

Jonathan, Ruth (1997) *Illusory Freedoms: Liberalism Education and the Market*, Oxford: Blackwell (with *Journal of Philosophy of Education*).

Lauder, Hugh, Hughes, David, Watson, Sue, Waslander, Sietske, Thrupp, Martin, Strathdee, Rob, Simiyu, Ibrahim, Dupuis, Ann, McGlinn, Jim and Hamlin, Jennie (1999) *Trading in Futures: Why Markets in Education Don't Work*, Buckingham, Philadelphia: Open University Press.

McMurtry, John (1991) 'Education and the market model', *Journal of Philosophy of Education*, 25(2).

Molnar, Alex (1996) *Giving Kids the Business: The Commercialization of America's Schools*, Boulder, Colorado: Westview Press.

Phillips, Melanie (1996, 3rd edn) *All Must Have Prizes*, London: Warner Books.

Robertson, Heather-Jane (1998) *No More Teachers, No More Books: The Commercialization of Canada's Schools*, Toronto: McClelland & Stewart Inc.

Tooley, James with Darby, Doug (1998) *Educational Research: A Critique*, London: Ofsted.

Whitty, Geoff, Power, Sally and Halpin, David (1998) *Devolution & Choice in Education: The School, the State and the Market*, Buckingham and Philadelphia: Open University Press.

19

MEASURING CATHOLIC SCHOOL PERFORMANCE

James Arthur

INTRODUCTION

James Arthur is Professor of Education and Civic Engagement at the University of Birmingham and the co-editor of this *Reader*. He has written widely on faith schools and education and presented this paper as a conference paper at the Institute of Education, University of London Conference on 'Faith Schools: Consensus or Conflict' in 2004. The paper looks at the major challenges of attempting to evaluate faith schools' performance through a consideration of whether it is possible to measure Catholic school performance from an international perspective. Arthur provides a critical examination of the 'religio-philosophical' effect of faith schools as well as commenting on the measured outcomes and examination results of faith schools. The paper introduces the reader to the international dimension of faith schools, which is often missing from studies in this area.

KEY QUESTIONS

1. Why are faith schools often presented as contested and complex?
2. Is there a justification for them within a State system of education provision?
3. Can secular or State schools learn from the experience and outcomes of faith schools?
4. What can we learn from a consideration of the international perspectives in studying faith schools?

FURTHER READING

Faith Schools: Consensus or Conflict (2005), edited by Roy Gardner, Jo Cairns and Denis Lawton and published by Routledge (Oxon), is an excellent start containing a wide range of views on faith-based schooling and education. *Education in the United Kingdom: Structures and Organisation*, edited by Liam Gearon and published by David Fulton (London) gives a very good introduction to faith schools in the UK and Mark Halstead writes an interesting chapter on the diversity of religious school provision in this volume. The references in both these volumes provide ample further reading opportunities in this expanding field of study.

This Reading links with Chapters 2 and 9 and Debate 4 of *The Routledge Education Studies Textbook*.

INTRODUCTION

On a world basis, Catholic schools continue to expand and they represent the world's largest non-governmental school system. There are over 50 million children attending Roman Catholic schools around the world. This number would be trebled if the Church had the resources to fund new schools. Nevertheless, new Catholic schools continue to open in Vietnam, India, Africa and in Eastern Europe. Thousands of religious schools have been founded since the collapse of communism in Poland, Hungary, Slovakia, Croatia and many other Eastern European countries. Catholic schools, whilst few in number, were also extremely popular under communist governments. In some countries the state relies almost entirely upon the voluntary efforts of the main religious groups in providing schools – this is particularly the case in some African countries. The perceived effectiveness of these schools among parents is one significant factor in explaining this continued expansion.

In Britain, the academic success of Catholic schools has been highlighted, in recent years, by the Office for Standards in Education (OFSTED) Reports and by examination league tables. Andrew Morris (1994, 1997, 1998a and 1998b) has demonstrated that levels of academic achievement in Catholic schools are higher than those in local education authority (LEA) schools. Academic results in Catholic schools are well above LEA and national averages. Earlier studies during the 1960s also indicated that Catholic school academic performance was greater than in comparable schools. The Catholic Education Council (1967) enquiry in 1963–4 found that a higher proportion of school leavers from Catholic schools compared to LEA schools entered full-time higher and further education. Michael Hornsby-Smith (1978:87) also found evidence during the 1970s that Catholics had been more upwardly mobile than the general population. Even the research evidence compiled by John Marks *et al.* (2001), whilst revealing the wide variations of standards among church schools in England, still concluded that faith-based schools, on average, do better in academic terms. Early studies in the United States of America (USA) by Greely and Rossi (1966) also found positive associations between Catholic schooling and academic achievement and future economic prosperity. In continental Europe there has not been a great deal of research in this area, but where such research studies have been conducted, such as in Holland, they indicate that Catholic schools have higher levels of achievement as measured by public tests, especially in primary mathematics and language (Hofman and Hofman 2001).

Differences in pupil admission policies are often perceived as the principal cause of achievement variations between different kinds of school (see Teddie and Reynolds 2000). Consequently, some have suggested that Catholic schools do better because they attract better-educated pupils from more economically stable families, that they are guilty of 'skimming the cream', that they exercise a degree of academic and social selectivity bias in admissions. The evidence in support of these arguments is often anecdotal and potentially unreliable; even the chapter by Schagen and Schagen in this collection goes beyond the evidence available to make unfounded generalisations. Indeed, since the social composition of the British Catholic community has largely been Irish urban working class with origins in poor immigrant families, the evidence would appear to point in the opposite direction. This would also seem to be the case in Australia, New Zealand and the USA, where there is little evidence to suggest that the income and occupation of parents sending their children to Catholic schools in inner-city areas are significantly different from parents who send their children to government or state schools. There is certainly evidence of greater parental involvement in Catholic schools (see Arthur 1994).

Comparisons between schools must be conducted carefully to be valid and would generally include a comparison of the following factors: socio-economic background, parental involvement and the innate ability of pupils. All three factors have the potential to interfere with measured academic outcomes. In addition, because of the diversity of Catholic schools, many of the indicators produced are complex and need to be interpreted with care. Only by understanding and comparing these complex factors can we arrive at a genuine sense of the value-added element of the school. We need to sound another cautionary note here, for there have been a very limited number of studies and data collections in Australia, New Zealand and South Africa, whilst the main studies have been conducted in the USA. Not all countries provide reliable information on the nature and performance of Catholic schools and not all facets of Catholic schooling are covered by the indicators. Together with the USA research evidence, the available statistics and information from the other countries discussed in this paper cover some of these areas of comparison and help us to measure some aspects of Catholic school performance. It provides us with perhaps what might be called evidence for the 'Catholic school effect'. The socio-economic perspective in school effectiveness studies has become dominant in recent years because it relies on quantifiable data that are accessible. It is easier to gain information about cognitive outcomes and socio-economic status than it is to assess the religious ethos of a school. In measuring the effectiveness of Catholic schools we need to measure the extent to which they accomplish what they set out to do. This must include questions about the integration of human learning with religious faith, but few studies have been sophisticated enough to achieve this aim (see Fahy 1992). There has also been no international study of Catholic school effectiveness in terms of academic performance or religious mission.

THE CATHOLIC SCHOOL EFFECT

USA

In the USA the research evidence shows that many Catholic schools in the inner cities take a large share of disadvantaged students. Also in the USA where Roman Catholic schools were once filled with students from poor ethnic families, mostly of European descent, those poor have been replaced by a new urban poor, primarily African-Americans, Hispanics and Asians. Indeed, Hispanics and Asians now have a larger percentage of students in Roman Catholic schools than in public schools (see Neal 1997a).

Given the social and ethnic variety of their intake, it is clear that Catholic schools are among the most successful. In the USA the dedication and commitment of staff is quite simply remarkable. If you work within a Roman Catholic school, your salary will most likely be two-thirds that of the teacher in the local public school. On average, if you are employed as a teacher in a Catholic school in America then you will earn the equivalent of £17,000 per annum, whilst if you were employed in a public school, your salary would be in the region of £27,000. You would also have larger classes to teach.

These Catholic schools do not have the same resources in buildings and teaching materials that public school teachers enjoy. James Coleman (1981; Coleman *et al.* 1982; Coleman and Hoffer 1987), the eminent American sociologist, conducted research into Catholic schools in the 1980s and found the following three things. First, on average, Catholic schools were more educationally effective than public schools. Second, Catholic schools were especially beneficial to students from less advantaged backgrounds. Third, there were strong indications that higher levels of discipline and academic demands accounted in large part for the success of these schools.

Compared to students in public schools, Catholic school students scored about two grade levels higher in mathematics, reading and vocabulary. Coleman found that Catholic schools produced better cognitive outcomes even after family background factors that predict achievement were controlled. The study found that factors that accounted for this were more effective school discipline, fewer student absences, higher enrolments in academic course work and about 50 per cent more homework.

Coleman's research was undertaken in 1980 and 1987. In 1997 Derek Neal (1997a, 1997b), an economics professor at Chicago University, repeated Coleman's surveys. Whilst confirming Coleman's earlier results, Neal found that attendance at Catholic schools increased the chances of graduation by 26 per cent. No less than 97 per cent of students graduated from Catholic schools and 94 per cent went on to College. He also found that African and Hispanic Americans who attended city Catholic schools had a higher graduation rate than whites in city public schools. Attendance at Catholic schools also improved future economic prospects. His research demonstrated that immigrant, minority and disadvantaged children all did better in Catholic schools. The main reason he gives for these findings is the poor quality of alternative public schools in urban areas. In fact, Neal (1997a) concludes that urban minorities are the greatest beneficiaries of Catholic schooling. He says: 'In sum, these results do not indicate that Catholic schools are superior to public schools in general. Rather, they suggest that Catholic schools are similar in quality to suburban public schools, slightly better that the urban public schools that white students usually attend, and much better than the urban public schools that many minorities attend.' On this evidence, Catholic schools might be seen as more inclusive.

Similar studies to Neal's had been conducted previously in various states in the USA. Paul Hill *et al.* (1990) conducted a study of Catholic and public schools in New York with between 85 and 95 per cent intakes of black pupils for the Rand Corporation that revealed the following:

■   Catholic schools graduated 95 per cent of their students each year whilst public schools graduated 50 per cent;
■   65 per cent of Catholic school graduates received the New York Regents diploma whilst only 5 per cent of public school students received this distinction;
■   Catholic school students achieved an average combined standard assessment test (SAT) 1 score of 803 whilst the average combined SAT 1 score for public school students was 642;
■   60 per cent of African-American Catholic school students scored above the national average for African-American students on the SAT 1 whilst less than 30 per cent of public school African American students scored above the average.

It would seem that in SAT scores, high school completions and college entry Catholic schools are more successful, often strikingly so. This is achieved against a backdrop of difficulties with tight finances, shifting demographics and teacher retention. Catholic schools not only pay teachers considerably less, they also spend much less on pupils. Byrk *et al.* (1993) offer a useful interpretation of Catholic school success by focusing on community influences and the social and cognitive climates in USA Catholic schools.

Australia

There is much more limited evidence for the academic performance of Catholic schools in Australia. Nevertheless, there is the research of Marcellin Flynn (1985) who studied 2,041 pupils in 23 schools in 1982 who sat the Higher School Certificate of that year. He discovered that Catholic school pupils were more highly represented in the top 1 per cent of overall Higher School Certificate pupils. His research concluded that Catholic schools have unique positive effects upon the academic results of pupils. His explanation for this was that academic achievement in Catholic schools bears a distinct relation to the pervading values of the school. In other words, the informal climate or ethos of achievement is the result of important characteristics; some of these he identified as:

- ■ the pervasive values of the school;
- ■ the morale and spirit of the pupils;
- ■ the importance of the development of each pupil;
- ■ the pastoral care of the school.

When pupils experience these characteristics in schools they do better in final public examinations.

There is one other source of data that can be employed to compare state and Catholic schools in the Sydney system of schools. The Basic Skills Tests are administered each year to over 10,000 students in Years 3 and 5 to assess pupils' literacy and numeracy skills in the context of learning in the Key Learning Areas of the Australian primary school curriculum. In March 2001 these tests demonstrated that pupils in Catholic primary schools had, on average, higher levels of writing, reading and language skills than did state school pupils (Catholic Education Office, Sydney, 2001). The performance of Sydney Archdiocesan schools has consistently shown higher levels of literacy and numeracy and unofficial tables produced by the press indicate that Catholic schools are extremely well represented on 'Distinguished Achievers Lists' (see *Daily Telegraph* (Australia), 23 December 2001).

In 2000 there were 1,701 Australian Catholic schools educating 355,623 pupils in primary schools and 279,989 pupils in secondary schools, representing 19.7 per cent of all pupils in Australian schools. Catholic schools in Australia have also become extremely popular with non-Catholics with the proportion of non-Catholics admitted to them rising in recent years from 8 per cent to over 21 per cent. In a survey conducted by Kelvin Canavan (1994) it was found that parents ranked the attractiveness of Catholic schools in the following order: first, school discipline, second, quality of teachers, third, the school's value system and fourth, the academic reputation of the school. Consequently, the main reasons for selecting a Catholic school were value related, i.e. disciplinary standards, religious education, better student behaviour, instilling of values and character. This was only then followed by academic reasons, i.e. a higher academic standard of education and academic achievement. The tentative evidence that exists in Australia would indicate that the higher the value-related aims of the school, the higher the academic performance. Research has also indicated that satisfaction and morale levels among teachers in Australian Catholic schools are high (see Ellyn 2001). In a recent longitudinal study of pupils in Catholic schools for the years 1972, 1982, 1990 and 1998 by Flynn and Mok (2002:11) it was also found that pupils attending Catholic schools were generally happy.

New Zealand

In New Zealand there is a system that rates each school by the parents' jobs/incomes. A school in a wealthy area might get a decile rating of 9 whilst in a poor area this could fall to as low as 1 or 2. This system provides a good method of comparing the academic success of schools and on this basis Catholic schools, which are integrated into the State system, are on average between 10 per cent and 20 per cent more successful in public examinations. Several of these schools are also leaders in academic results (Source: New Zealand Catholic Education Office 2001).

However, the New Zealand government has a careful policy of not releasing any statistics which could be interpreted as supporting the idea of league tables, or, for that matter, setting Catholic and other state schools up in comparison with each other. Whilst the government is fully supportive of Catholic schools, there is great sensitivity about providing interpretations of school achievement statistics both by government and Church authorities.

South Africa

Government support for Catholic schools in South Africa is regularly stated in public. However, this has not prevented government subsidy to Catholic schools being substantially reduced in recent years. Nevertheless, parental demand for Catholic schools has been unaffected, despite increased fees levied on poor parents. This can be accounted for by the reputation for high-quality provision that Catholic schools enjoy in South Africa.

For example, St Martin De Porres Roman Catholic Primary School is one of at least nine diocesan Catholic schools situated in Soweto. The annual fee charged by the school in 1999 was R596 whilst the school's annual cost per pupil was R2,676. The government provides a maximum subsidy of 60 per cent of the annual cost per pupil. In comparison, the amount the government pays for each pupil in public primary schools is R3,173 per annum. St Martin's therefore must survive on a combination of government subsidy, church subsidy and pupil fees. Crucially, the school also has the active support and involvement of parents that ranges from painting school buildings to clearing ground for a football pitch. It was Coleman and Hoffer (1987) who drew attention to the social resources available in the functional communities that surround schools: such a community is characterised by a social network with structural consistency, a network of active parents that shapes the social norms and structure within the school community. Through a homogeneous system of norms, a functional community provides a consistent environment for socialisation to take place, and it protects against influences of conflicting values. This kind of community, according to Coleman and Hoffer, influences the outcomes of schooling, especially academic achievement. It could be said that the community represented by the pupils, parents and staff of St Martin's is exactly this kind of community. Teachers are committed and work longer hours for less salary, parents not only pay fees from their extremely modest incomes, but offer their services to the school, and pupils respond by achieving higher scores in public tests than pupils in state schools.

Many schools in South Africa face similar problems to schools in Third World contexts where a great deal of education time is lost due to weather, large classes, crop harvesting, teenage pregnancy, hunger and disease. There is often little homework and low morale among teachers. Evidence (Christie and Potterton 1997) indicates that Catholic schools, particularly in rural settings, seem to ride these problems and spend substantial time on task. There is an ethic of care in Catholic schools where teachers know their pupils, even in large classes. There is also an ideal that motivates staff and pupils that is often absent in state schools.

COMMENTARY

The research studies and data reviewed in this paper offer different explanations for their results. A number of commentators on Catholic schools provide a range of possible reasons for this persistent and positive association between Catholic schools and academic achievement. Many focus on the shared values or ethos of Catholic schooling. Andrew Morris (1997) has suggested that Catholic schools that have a more holistic ethos – a greater proportion of Catholic school pupils and staff who focus on the primary aim of Catholic education (see Arthur 1995) – are even more academically successful. In other words, Catholic schools that have higher levels of agreement about the mission of the school and the degree to which all concerned ensure that the values, attitudes and pedagogical practices, together with parental expectations and support, are consistent with its generally accepted purpose, the more effective the school is likely to be. Flynn's (1985) research would also appear to confirm this. Shokraii (1997) found that in the USA, Catholic schools have fewer vocational courses on offer and more academic-orientated programmes. Catholic schools are also often characterised by a strong sense of community. John Marks *et al.* (2001) has suggested that we should look at teaching methods in Church schools, as opposed to their religious ethos, for an account of their academic success.

But the question remains, how does the Catholic philosophical world and life view influence educational practices in Catholic schools? Catholic Church teaching provides a set of 'givens' in terms of what Catholic education should be about and these givens could be summarised as primarily about developing the theological virtues of faith, hope and love. Academic performance is not neglected, but it is a secondary consideration. Catholic schools will also commonly develop particular core values, often referred to as 'gospel values', which they actively promote. Community and the promotion of the common good are also central, but what kind of community do they perceive themselves to be? Are Catholic schools theological communities of believers or are they more sociological communities of care? Gerald Grace's (2002:125ff) major study of Catholic head teachers in England indicates that Catholic schools still see their mission in terms of promoting faith, community and the social dimension. However, Grace acknowledged that Catholic schools in England had given greater attention to academic performance in school prospectuses and that this development had been largely driven by government legislation. Grace (2002:125) concluded that this emphasis on academic performance was viewed by the head teachers in the sample as an education for service.

Whatever kind of ideological inspiration Catholic schools offer, few would say that academic success is the primary aim of a Catholic school. Examination success is not the measure of a child in a Catholic school. The danger is that to focus on examination success is to view only one element of schooling that may lead many to take this one measurement as evidence of the overall standard of performance in the wider, more diffuse process of Catholic schooling. Whilst a measurable performance indicator is a useful tool, it is not in itself evidence of achieving the aims of Catholic schooling – which is to provide a Catholic educational experience and formation. Grace (2002:142) found some evidence in his study of a stated resistance among head teachers to 'the domination of technical performativity' in English Catholic schools. There appear to me to be two main levels of explanation for the effectiveness of Catholic schools in public examinations that could be briefly raised or characterised under the more diffuse headings of the *religio-philosophical* and the *pedagogical*.

The religio-philosophical

The goals, purposes, values and ideals of the Catholic school are largely predetermined by the Catholic philosophy of life. There is a sense in which all Catholic schools are committed to shared values and beliefs within an authoritative teaching church. This tradition of theological, moral, spiritual, social and intellectual ideas forms the backdrop to Catholic schooling. From this tradition certain premises are derived about human nature and James Hunter (2000) maintains that Catholicism, whilst not hermetically closed to developments in psychology and the social sciences, nevertheless offers resistance to whole-scale absorption of 'child-centred' and 'development' theories into educational practice. Catholicism promotes the dignity of human life and the active duty and service we owe to others, and encourages pupils to give their best with an emphasis on civil duty and obligation to the common good. Consequently, are Catholic schools more able to motivate pupils to a greater extent and strengthen their will so that they give of their best both in and out-side of the classroom? What are the effects of Catholic belief systems on academic study? Much of this religio-philosophical level has simply not been researched, but if Andrew Morris (1997) is right then pupils professing and sharing the Catholic faith or world view in a holistic faith environment will do better in public examinations.

The pedagogical

In all the countries discussed in this paper it appears that teaching methods in Catholic schools emphasise more structured learning and regular homework. There appears to be emphasis on academic performance and high standards of pupil behaviour. Absenteeism appears lower and there is strong parental involvement. Teaching methods are often more traditional and there is a hierarchy of authority that is clear, unambiguous and understood by all in the school community. There is perhaps less 'child-centred' learning and greater emphasis on the authority of the teacher. In some countries the Catholic school day is longer than in state schools and it appears that there are more extra-curricular activities on offer to pupils. Again, the research evidence for this pedagogical effect is fragmented and incomplete, but if Marks *et al.* (2001) are right then it is this area which accounts most for the success of some Catholic schools.

Nevertheless, there appear to be some critical features that help explain Catholic school academic success, particularly among the increasing numbers of ethnic-minority and low-income children admitted to Catholic schools. It is also important to add that the number of non-Catholic children, in all the countries mentioned in this paper, admitted to Catholic schools has increased rapidly in recent years. Nevertheless, priority is still given to Catholics in admissions policies with the justification that Catholic schools offer 'an education in the faith for those of the faith'. Catholic schools constitute a small to large, relatively homogeneous sector of schooling in each of these countries. Whilst more research is needed, the following tentative list of features might help explain the greater academic performance of Catholic schools:

- ▣ An ideological stance that is shared, celebrated and motivates the school commu-nity to respect and honour the innate abilities of self and others;
- ▣ A greater sense of vocational commitment on the part of teachers to sustain a Catholic ethos at some cost to themselves;
- ▣ Greater parental involvement and commitment to the school, including provision of financial support;
- ▣ An emphasis on the pastoral activities of the school with a marked focus on building community with high expectations of behaviour and attendance;
- ▣ An emphasis on a wide range of pedagogical methods, less emphasis on wholesale 'child-centred' approaches and a stronger atmosphere of order;
- ▣ Greater emphasis on academic as opposed to vocational courses, particularly a strong focus on religious education and the humanities;
- ▣ An atmosphere of success and belonging with strong parental support – on average, providing a more homogeneous school system of norms and values.

However, perhaps the most overlooked factor is the quality of available public schools, especially in urban areas as compared to Catholic school provision.

The review of evidence presented here suggests that pupils, on average, in Catholic schools, irrespective of their 'faith orientation', learn more, as measured by public achievement tests, than pupils in State schools – that is, in comparison to pupils of similar social backgrounds and ability levels. There appears to be a persistent and positive association between Catholic schooling and academic achievement that seems to be demonstrated on an international level. However, the evidence is fragmentary and there is therefore a need for an international study of Catholic schools to determine what combination of 'Catholic' and 'school' factors influences academic effectiveness and accounts for the comparative educational achievement of these schools. Most studies at local and national levels have focused on what can be measured in terms of outcomes. Few have addressed the religio-philosophical level which is a much more diffuse area, but such a study is necessary to understand and show how the Catholic Church's teaching on education is both realised within Catholic schools and how it influences, if at all, academic outcomes. A focus on academic success by itself is both narrow and reductionist and is not what Catholic schooling principally sets out to achieve.

REFERENCES

Arthur, J. (1994) 'Parental involvement in Catholic schools: an increasing case of conflict', *British Journal of Educational Studies*, 42(2):174–90.

Arthur, J. (1995) *The Ebbing Tide: Policy and Principles of Catholic Education*, Leominster: Gracewing.

Byrk, A.S., Lee, V.E. and Holland, P.B. (1993) *Catholic Schools and the Common Good*, Cambridge, MA: Harvard University Press.

Canavan, K. (ed.) (1994) *Why do Parents Choose a Catholic School?*, Sydney: Catholic Education Office.

Catholic Education Council (1967) *News Bulletin*, 14:23–9.

Catholic Education Office, Sydney (2001) *Basic Skills Testing Program Report 2001*.

Christie, P. and Potterton, M. (1997) *School Development in South Africa: A Research Project to Investigate Strategic Interventions for Quality Improvement in South African Schools*, Johannesburg: University of the Witwatersrand.

Coleman, J. (1981) 'Public schools, private schools, and the public interest', *The Public Interest*, 64, Summer.

Coleman, J. and Hoffer, T. (1987) *Public, Catholic and Private Schools: The Importance of Community*, New York: Basic Books.

Coleman, J., Hoffer, T. and Kilgore, S. (1982) *High School Achievement: Public, Catholic and Private Schools Compared*, New York: Basic Books.

Ellyn, G. (2001) 'Commitment and satisfaction among parochial teachers', *Catholic Education Journal* (Australia), Spring.

Fahy, P.S. (1992) *Faith in Catholic Schools*, Homebush: St Paul Publications.

Flynn, M. (1985) *The Effectiveness of Catholic Schools*, Homebush: St Paul Publications.

Flynn, M. and Mok, M. (2002) *Catholic Schools 2000: A Longitudinal Study of Year 12 Students in Catholic Schools*, Sydney: Sydney Catholic Education Commission.

Grace, G. (2002) *Catholic Schools: Mission, Markets and Morality*, London: Routledge.

Greely, A.M. and Rossi, P.H. (1966) *The Education of American Catholics*, Chicago, IL: Aldine.

Hill, P.T., Foster, G.E. and Gendler, T. (1990) *High Schools with Character*, Santa Monica, CA: Rand Corporation.

Hofman, R.H. and Hofman, A. (2001) 'School choice, religious traditions and school effectiveness in public and private schools', *International Journal of Education and Religion*, 2(2):144–64.

Hornsby-Smith, M. (1978) *Catholic Education: The Unobtrusive Partner*, London: Sheed and Ward.

Hunter, J.D. (2000) *The Death of Character*, New York: Basic Books.

Marks, J., Burn, J. and Pilkington, P. (2001) *Faith in Education: The Role of the Churches in Education*, London: Civitas.

Morris, A. (1994) 'The academic performance of Catholic schools', *School Organisation*, 14(1): 81–9.

Morris, A. (1997) 'Same mission, same methods, same results? Academic and religious outcomes from different models of Catholic schools', *British Journal of Educational Studies*, 45(4):378–91.

Morris, A. (1998a) 'So far, so good: levels of academic achievement in Catholic schools', *Educational Studies*, 24(1):83–94.

Morris, A. (1998b) 'Catholic and other secondary schools: an analysis of OFSTED inspection reports 1993–1995', *Educational Research*, 40(2):181–90.

Neal, D. (1997a) 'The effects of Catholic secondary schooling on educational attainment', *Journal of Labour Economics*, 15(1):98–123.

Neal, D. (1997b) 'Measuring Catholic school performance', *Public Interest*, (Spring) 127:81–7.

New Zealand Catholic Education Office (2001) *Catholic Schools in New Zealand*, Wellington: The Catholic Bishops Conference of New Zealand.

Shokraii, N.H. (1997) 'Why Catholic schools spell success for America's inner-city children', *Heritage Foundation*, 1128, June.

Teddie, C. and Reynolds, R. (2000) *The International Handbook of School Effectiveness Research*, London: Falmer Press.

20 HOW CHILDREN FAIL

John Holt

INTRODUCTION

John Holt (1923–1985) was known as an opponent of formal schooling and a liberal or progressive thinker and activist. In his books of which *How Children Fail* is the most well known, he suggests that schools are dominated by authoritarianism and this leads to the teaching and the testing of knowledge that is largely useless. This encourages children only to be frightened. He served in the Navy in World War II and later became a teacher and author. Initially he was a critic of schools but did not suggest alternative ways forward. He did for a time embrace home-schooling but was critical of those who did no more than replicate in the home those negative processes that had taken place in the school. In this extract from *How Children Fail*, Holt argues for a reformed view of intelligence (not indicated by test scores) and for honesty about ourselves and what we know and do not know. He argues passionately for 'schools to be places where children learn what they most want to know, instead of what we think they ought to know . . . The idea of the curriculum would not be valid even if we could agree what ought to be in it'.

KEY QUESTIONS

1. If learners were left to follow their own interests would those who were most capable of taking advantage of that freedom benefit more than those who are already marginalised in society?
2. Can we as a society identify and agree upon what should be learned and if so what is it?

FURTHER READING

Meighan, R. (2007) *John Holt: Continuum Library of Educational Thought* (Continuum, London). A number of books appeared around the same time as Holt was writing which, very broadly, were seen as promoting a similar progressive outlook. These books include Postman, N. and Weingartner, C. (1969) *Teaching as a Subversive Activity* (Penguin, Harmondsworth); and Reimer, E. (1971) *School is Dead: an Essay on Alternatives in Education* (Penguin, Harmondsworth).

This Reading links with Chapters 9, 12, 13 and 15 and Debate 5 of *The Routledge Education Studies Textbook.*

SUMMARY

When we talk about intelligence, we do not mean the ability to get a good score on a certain kind of test, or even the ability to do well in school; these are at best only indicators of something larger, deeper, and far more important. By intelligence we mean a style of life, a way of behaving in various situations, and particularly in new, strange, and perplexing situations. The true test of intelligence is not how much we know how to do, but how we behave when we don't know what to do.

The intelligent person, young or old, meeting a new situation or problem, opens himself up to it; he tries to take in with mind and senses everything he can about it; he thinks about *it,* instead of about himself or what it might cause to happen to him; he grapples with it boldly, imaginatively, resourcefully, and if not confidently at least hopefully; if he fails to master it, he looks without shame or fear at his mistakes and learns what he can from them. This is intelligence. Clearly its roots lie in a certain feeling about life, and one's self with respect to life. Just as clearly, unintelligence is not what most psychologists seem to suppose, the same thing as intelligence only less of it. It is an entirely different style of behaviour, arising out of an entirely different set of attitudes.

Years of watching and comparing bright children and the not-bright, or less bright, have shown that they are very different kinds of people. The bright child is curious about life and reality, eager to get in touch with it, embrace it, unite himself with it. There is no wall, no barrier between him and life. The dull child is far less curious, far less interested in what goes on and what is real, more inclined to live in worlds of fantasy. The bright child likes to experiment, to try things out. He lives by the maxim that there is more than one way to skin a cat. If he can't do something one way, he'll try another. The dull child is usually afraid to try at all. It takes a good deal of urging to get him to try even once; if that try fails, he is through.

The bright child is patient. He can tolerate certainty and failure, and will keep trying until he gets an answer. When all his experiments fail, he can even admit to himself and others that for the time being he is not going to get an answer. This may annoy him, but he can wait. Very often, he does not want to be told how to do the problem or solve the puzzle he has struggled with, because he does not want to be cheated out of the chance to figure it out for himself in the future. Not so the dull child. He cannot stand uncertainty or failure. To him, an unanswered question is not a challenge or an opportunity, but a threat. If he can't find the answer quickly, it must be given to him, and quickly; and he must have answers for everything. Such are the children of whom a second-grade teacher once said, 'But my children *like* to have questions for which there is only one answer.' They did; and by a mysterious coincidence, so did she.

The bright child is willing to go ahead on the basis of incomplete understanding and information. He will take risks, sail uncharted seas, explore when the landscape is dim, the landmarks few, the light poor. To give only one example, he will often read books he does not understand in the hope that after a while enough understanding will emerge to make it worth while to go on. In this spirit some of my fifth-graders tried to read *Moby Dick.* But the dull child will go ahead only when he thinks he knows exactly where he stands and exactly what is ahead of him. If he does not feel he knows exactly what an experience will be like, and if it will not be exactly like other experiences he already knows, he wants no part of it. For while the bright child feels that the universe is, on the whole, a sensible, reasonable, and trustworthy place, the dull child feels that it is senseless, unpredictable, and treacherous. He feels that he can never tell what may happen, particularly in a new situation, except that it will probably be bad.

Nobody starts off stupid. You have only to watch babies and infants, and think seriously about what all of them learn and do, to see that, except for the most grossly retarded, they show a style of life, and a desire and ability to learn that in an older person we might well call genius. Hardly an adult in a thousand, or ten thousand, could in any three years of his life learn as much, grow as much in his understanding of the world around him, as every infant learns and grows in his first three years. But what happens, as we get older, to this extraordinary capacity for learning and intellectual growth?

What happens is that it is destroyed, and more than by any other one thing, by the process that we misname education – a process that goes on in most homes and schools. We adults destroy most of the intellectual and creative capacity of children by the things we do to them or make them do. We destroy this capacity above all by making them afraid, afraid of not doing what other people want, of not pleasing, of making mistakes, of failing, of being *wrong*. Thus we make them afraid to gamble, afraid to experiment, afraid to try the difficult and the unknown. Even when we do not create children's fears, when they come to us with fears ready-made and built-in, we use these fears as handles to manipulate them and get them to do what we want. Instead of trying to whittle down their fears, we build them up, often to monstrous size. For we like children who are a little afraid of us, docile, deferential children, though not, of course, if they are so obviously afraid that they threaten our image of ourselves as kind, lovable people whom there is no reason to fear. We find ideal the kind of 'good' children who are just enough afraid of us to do everything we want, without making us feel that fear of us is what is making them do it.

We destroy the disinterested (I do *not* mean uninterested) love of learning in children, which is so strong when they are small, by encouraging and compelling them to work for petty and contemptible rewards – gold stars, or papers marked 100 and tacked to the wall, or *As* on report cards, or honour rolls, or dean's lists, or Phi Beta Kappa keys – in short, for the ignoble satisfaction of feeling that they are better than someone else. We encourage them to feel that the end and aim of all they do in school is nothing more than to get a good mark on a test, or to impress someone with what they seem to know. We kill not only their curiosity but their feeling that it is a good and admirable thing to be curious, so that by the age of ten most of them will not ask questions, and will show a good deal of scorn for the few who do.

In many ways we break down children's convictions that things make sense, or their hope that things may prove to make sense. We do it, first of all, by breaking up life into arbitrary and disconnected hunks of subject matter, which we then try to 'integrate' by such artificial and irrelevant devices as having children sing Swiss folk songs while they are studying the geography of Switzerland, or do arithmetic problems about rail-splitting while they are studying the boyhood of Lincoln. Furthermore, we continually confront them with what is senseless, ambiguous, and contradictory; worse, we do it without knowing that we are doing it, so that, hearing nonsense shoved at them as if it were sense, they come to feel that the source of their confusion lies not in the material but in their own stupidity. Still further, we cut children off from their own common sense and the world of reality by requiring them to play with and shove around words and symbols that have little or no meaning to them. Thus we turn the vast majority of our students into the kind of people for whom all symbols are meaningless; who cannot use symbols as a way of learning about and dealing with reality; who cannot understand written instructions; who, even if they read books, come out knowing no more than when they went in; who may have a few new words rattling around in their heads, but whose mental models of the world remain unchanged and, indeed, impervious to change. The minority, the able and successful students, we are very likely to turn into something different but just as dangerous: the kind of people who can manipulate words and symbols fluently while keeping themselves largely divorced from the reality for which they stand; the kind of people who like to speak in large generalities but grow silent or indignant if someone asks for an example of what they are talking about; the kind of people who, in their discussions of world affairs, coin and use such words as megadeaths and megacorpses, with scarcely a thought to the blood and suffering these words imply. We encourage children to act stupidly, not only by scaring and confusing them, but by boring them, by filling up their days with dull, repetitive tasks that make little or no claim on their attention or demands on their intelligence. Our hearts leap for joy at the sight of a roomful of children all slogging away at some imposed task, and we are all the more pleased and satisfied if someone tells us that the children don't really like what they are doing. We tell ourselves that this drudgery, this endless busywork, is good preparation for life, and we fear that without it children would be hard to 'control'. But why must this busywork be so dull? Why not give tasks that are interesting and demanding? Because, in schools where every task must be completed and every answer must be right, if we give children more demanding tasks they will be fearful and will instantly insist that we show them how to do the job. When you have acres of paper to fill up with pencil marks, you have no time to waste on the luxury of thinking. By such means children are firmly established in the habit of using only a small part of their thinking capacity. They feel that school is a place where they must spend most of their time doing dull tasks in a dull way. Before long they are deeply settled in a rut of unintelligent behaviour from which most of them could not escape even if they wanted to.

*

School tends to be a dishonest as well as a nervous place. We adults are not often honest with children, least of all in school. We tell them, not what we think, but what we feel they ought to think; or what other people feel or tell us they ought to think. Pressure groups find it easy to weed out of our classrooms, texts, and libraries whatever facts, truths, and ideas they happen to find unpleasant or inconvenient. And we are not even as truthful with children as we could safely be, as the parents, politicians, and pressure groups would let us be. Even in the most non-controversial areas of our teaching, the books, and the textbooks we give children present a dishonest and distorted picture of the world.

The fact is that we do not feel an obligation to be truthful to children. We are like the managers and manipulators of news in Washington, Moscow, London, Peking, and Paris, and all the other capitals of the world. We think it our right and our duty, not to tell the truth, but to say whatever will best serve our cause – in this case, the cause of making children grow up into the kind of people we want them to be, thinking whatever we want them to think. We have only to convince ourselves (and we are very easily convinced) that a lie will be 'better' for the children than the truth, and we will lie. We don't always need even that excuse; we often lie only for our own convenience.

Worse yet, we are not honest about ourselves, our own fears, limitations, weaknesses, prejudices, motives. We present ourselves to children as if we were gods, all-knowing, all-powerful, always rational, always just, always right. This is worse than any lie we could tell about ourselves. I have more than once shocked teachers by telling them that when kids ask me a question to which I don't know the answer, I say, 'I haven't the faintest idea'; or that when I make a mistake, as I often do, I say, 'I goofed again'; or that when I am trying to do something I am no good at, like paint in water colours or play a clarinet or bugle, I do it in front of them so they can see me struggling with it, and can realize that not all adults are good at everything. If a child asks me to do something that I don't want to do, I tell him that I won't do it because I don't want to do it, instead of giving him a list of 'good' reasons sounding as if they had come down from the Supreme Court. Interestingly enough, this rather open way of dealing with children works quite well. If you tell a child that you won't do something because you don't want to, he is very likely to accept that as a fact which he cannot change; if you ask him to stop doing something because it drives you crazy, there is a very good chance that, without further talk, he will stop, because he knows what that is like.

We are, above all, dishonest about our feelings, and it is this sense of dishonesty of feeling that makes the atmosphere of so many schools so unpleasant. The people who write books that teachers have to read say over and over again that a teacher must love all the children in a class, all of them equally. If by this they mean that a teacher must do the best he can for every child in a class, that he has an equal responsibility for every child's welfare, an equal concern for his problems, they are right. But when they talk of love they don't mean this; they mean feelings, affection, the kind of pleasure and joy that one person can get from the existence and company of another. And this is not something that can be measured out in little spoonfuls, everyone getting the same amount.

In a discussion of this in a class of teachers, I once said that I liked some of the kids in my class much more than others and that, without saying which ones I liked best, I had told them so. After all, this is something that children know, whatever we tell them; it is futile to lie about it. Naturally, these teachers were horrified. 'What a terrible thing to say!' one said. 'I love all the children in my class exactly the same.' Nonsense; a teacher who says this is lying to herself or to others, and probably doesn't like any of the children very much. Not that there is anything wrong with that; plenty of adults don't like children, and there is no reason why they should. But the trouble is they feel they should, which makes them feel guilty, which makes them feel resentful, which in turn makes them try to work off their guilt with indulgence and their resentment with subtle cruelties – cruelties of a kind that can be seen in many classrooms. Above all, it makes them put on the phoney, syrupy, sickening voice and manner, and the fake smiles and forced, bright laughter that children see so much of in school, and rightly resent and hate.

As we are not honest with them, so we won't let children be honest with us. To begin with, we require them to take part in the fiction that school is a wonderful place and that they love every minute of it. They learn early that not to like school or the teacher is *verboten,* not to be said, not even to be thought. I have known a child, otherwise healthy, happy, and wholly delightful, who at the age of five was being made sick with worry by the fact that she did not like her kindergarten teacher. Robert Heinemann worked for a number of years with remedial students whom ordinary schools were hopelessly unable to deal with. He found that what choked up and froze the minds of these children was above all else the fact that they could not express, they could hardly even acknowledge the fear, shame, rage, and hatred that school and their teachers had aroused in them. In a situation in which they were and felt free to express these feelings to themselves and others, they were able once again to begin learning. Why can't we say to children what I used to say to fifth-graders who got sore at me: 'The law says you have to go to school; it doesn't say you have to like it, and it doesn't say you have to like me either.' This might make school more bearable for many children.

Children hear all the time: 'Nice people don't say such things.' They learn early in life that for unknown reasons they must not talk about a large part of what they think and feel, are most interested in, and worried about. It is a rare child who, anywhere in his growing up, meets even one older person with whom he can talk openly about what most interests him, concerns him, worries him. This is what rich people are buying for their troubled kids when for $25 per hour they send them to psychiatrists. Here is someone to whom you can speak honestly about whatever is on your mind, without having to worry about his getting mad at you. But do we have to wait until a child is snowed under by his fears and troubles to give him this chance? And do we have to take the time of a highly trained professional to hear what, earlier in his life, that child might have told anybody who was willing to listen sympathetically and honestly? The workers in a project called Street-corner Research, in Cambridge, Mass., have found that nothing more than the opportunity to talk openly and freely about themselves and their lives, to people who would listen without judging, and who were interested in them as human beings rather than as problems to be solved or disposed of, has totally remade the lives and personalities of a number of confirmed and seemingly hopeless juvenile delinquents. Can't we learn something from this? Can't we clear a space for honesty and openness and self-awareness in the lives of growing children? Do we have to make them wait until they are in a jam before giving them a chance to say what they think?

*

Behind much of what we do in school lie some ideas, that could be expressed roughly as follows: (1) Of the vast body of human knowledge, there are certain bits and pieces that can be called essential, that everyone should know; (2) the extent to which a person can be considered educated, qualified to live intelligently in today's world and be a useful member of society, depends on the amount of this essential knowledge that he carries about with him; (3) it is the duty of schools, therefore, to get as much of this essential knowledge as possible into the minds of children. Thus we find ourselves trying to poke certain facts, recipes, and ideas down the gullets of every child in school, whether the morsel interests him or not, even if it frightens him or sickens him, and even if there are other things that he is much more interested in learning.

These ideas are absurd and harmful nonsense. We will not begin to have true education or real learning in our schools until we sweep this nonsense out of the way. Schools should be a place where children learn what they most want to know, instead of what we think they ought to know. The child who wants to know something remembers it and uses it once he has it; the child who learns something to please or appease someone else forgets it when the need for pleasing or the danger of not appeasing is past. This is why children quickly forget all but a small part of what they learn in school. It is of no use or interest to them; they do not want, or expect, or even intend to remember it. The only difference between bad and good students in this respect is that the bad students forget right away, while the good students are careful to wait until after the exam. If for no other reason, we could well afford to throw out most of what we teach in school because the children throw out almost all of it anyway.

The notion of a curriculum, an essential body of knowledge, would be absurd even if children remembered everything we 'taught' them. We don't and can't agree on what knowledge is essential. The man who has trained himself in some special field of knowledge or competence thinks, naturally, that his speciality should be in the curriculum. The classical scholars want Greek and Latin taught; the historians shout for more history; the mathematicians urge more maths and the scientists more science; the modern language experts want all children taught French, or Spanish, or Russian; and so on. Everyone wants to get his speciality into the act, knowing that as the demand for his special knowledge rises, so will the price that he can charge for it. Who wins this struggle and who loses depends not on the real needs of children or even of society, but on who is most skilful in public relations, who has the best educational lobbyists, who best can capitalize on events that have nothing to do with education, like the appearance of Sputnik in the night skies.

The idea of the curriculum would not be valid even if we could agree what ought to be in it. For knowledge itself changes. Much of what a child learns in school will be found, or thought, before many years, to be untrue. I studied physics at school from a fairly up-to-date text that proclaimed that the fundamental law of physics was the law of conservation of matter – matter is not created or destroyed. 1 had to scratch that out before I left school. In economics at college I was taught many things that were not true of our economy then, and many more that are not true now. Not for many years after I left college did I learn that the Greeks, far from being a detached and judicious people surrounded by chaste white temples, were hot-tempered, noisy, quarrelsome, and liked to cover their temples with gold leaf and bright paint; or that most of the citizens of Imperial Rome, far from living in houses in which the rooms surrounded an atrium, or central court, lived in multi-storey tenements, one of which was perhaps the largest building in the ancient world. The child who really remembered everything he heard in school would live his life believing many things that were not so.

Moreover, we cannot possibly judge what knowledge will be most needed forty, or twenty, or even ten years from now. At school, I studied Latin and French. Few of the teachers who claimed then that Latin was essential would make as strong a case for it now; and the French might better have been Spanish, or better yet, Russian. Today the schools are busy teaching Russian; but perhaps they should be teaching Chinese, or Hindi, or who-knows-what? Besides physics, I studied chemistry, then perhaps the most popular of all science courses; but I would probably have done better to study biology, or ecology, if such a course had been offered (it wasn't). We always find out, too late, that we don't have the experts we need, that in the past we studied the wrong things; but this is bound to remain so. Since we can't know what knowledge will be most needed in the future, it is senseless to try to teach it in advance, Instead, we should try to turn out people who love learning so much and learn so well that they will be able to learn whatever needs to be learned.

How can we say, in any case, that one piece of knowledge is more important than another, or indeed, what we really say, that some knowledge is essential and the rest, as far as school is concerned, worthless? A child who wants to learn something that the school can't and doesn't want to teach him will be told not to waste his time. But how can we say that what he wants to know is less important than what we want him to know? We must ask how much of the sum of human knowledge anyone can know at the end of his schooling. Perhaps a millionth. Are we then to believe that one of these millionths is so much more important than another? Or that our social and national problems will be solved if we can just figure out a way to turn children out of schools knowing two millionths of the total, instead of one? Our problems don't arise from the fact that we lack experts enough to tell us what needs to be done, but out of the fact that we do not and will not do what we know needs to be done now.

Learning is not everything, and certainly one piece of learning is as good as another. One of my brightest and boldest fifth-graders was deeply interested in snakes. He knew more about snakes than anyone I've ever known. The school did not offer herpetology; snakes were not in the curriculum; but as far as I was concerned, any time he spent learn-ing about snakes was better spent than in ways I could think of to spend it; not least of all because, in the process of learning about snakes, he learned a great deal more about many other things than I was ever able to 'teach' those unfortunates in my class who were not interested in anything at all. In another fifth-grade class, studying Romans in Britain, I saw a boy trying to read a science book behind the cover of his desk. He was spotted, and made to put the book away, and listen to the teacher; with a heavy sigh he did so. What was gained here? She traded a chance for an hour's real learning about science for, at best, an hour's temporary learning about history – much more probably no learning at all, just an hour's worth of daydreaming and resentful thoughts about school.

It is not subject matter that makes some learning more valuable than others, but the spirit in which the work is done. If a child is doing the kind of learning that most children do in school, when they learn at all – swallowing words, to spit back at the teacher on demand – he is wasting his time, or rather, we are wasting it for him. This learning will not be permanent, or relevant, or useful. But a child who is learning naturally, following his curiosity where it leads him, adding to his mental model of reality whatever he needs and can find a place for, and rejecting without fear or guilt what he does not need, is growing – in knowledge, in the love of learning, and in the ability to learn. He is on his way to becom-ing the kind of person we need in our society, and that our 'best' schools and colleges are *not* turning out, the kind of person who, in Whitney Griswold's words, seeks and finds meaning, truth, and enjoyment in everything he does. All his life he will go on learning. Every experience will make his mental model of reality more complete and more true to life, and thus make him more able to deal realistically, imaginatively, and constructively with whatever new experience life throws his way.

We cannot have real learning in school if we think it is our duty and our right to tell children what they must learn. We cannot know, at any moment, what particular bit of knowledge or understanding a child needs most, will most strengthen and best fit his model of reality. Only he can do this. He may not do it very well, but he can do it a hundred times better than we can. The most we can do is try to help, by letting him know roughly what is available and where he can look for it. Choosing what he wants to learn and what he does not is something he must do for himself.

There is one more reason, and the most important one, why we must reject the idea of school and classroom as places where, most of the time, children are doing what some adult tells them to do. The reason is that there is no way to coerce children without making them afraid, or more afraid. We must not try to fool ourselves into thinking that this is not so. The would-be progressives, who until recently had great influence over most American public school education, did not recognize this and still do not. They thought, or at least talked and wrote as if they thought, that there were good ways and bad ways to coerce children (the bad ones mean, harsh, cruel, the good ones gentle, persuasive, subtle, kindly), and that if they avoided the bad and stuck to the good they would do no harm. This was one of their greatest mistakes, and the main reason why the revolution they hoped to accomplish never took hold.

The idea of painless, non-threatening coercion is an illusion. Fear is the inseparable companion of coercion, and its inescapable consequence. If you think it your duty to make children do what you want, whether they will or not, then it follows inexorably that you must make them afraid of what will happen to them if they don't do what you want. You can do this in the old-fashioned way, openly and avowedly, with the threat of harsh words, infringment of liberty, or physical punishment. Or you can do it in the modern way, subtly, smoothly, quietly, by withholding the acceptance and approval which you and others have trained the children to depend on; or by making them feel that some retribution awaits them in the future, too vague to imagine but too implacable to escape. You can, as many skilled teachers do, learn to tap with a word, a gesture, a look, even a smile, the great reservoir of fear, shame, and guilt that today's children carry around inside them. Or you can simply let your own fears, about what will happen to you if the children don't do what you want, reach out and infect them. Thus the children will feel more and more that life is full of dangers from which only the goodwill of adults like you can protect them, and that this goodwill is perishable and must be earned anew each day.

The alternative – I can see no other – is to have schools and classrooms in which each child in his own way can satisfy his curiosity, develop his abilities and talents, pursue his interests, and from the adults and older children around him get a glimpse of the great variety and richness of life. In short, the school should be a great smorgasbord of intellectual, artistic, creative, and athletic activities, from which each child could take whatever he wanted, and as much as he wanted, or as little. When Anna was in the sixth grade, the year after she was in my class, I mentioned this idea to her. After describing very sketchily how a school might be run, and what the children might do, I said, 'Tell me, what do you think of it? Do you think it would work? Do you think the kids would learn anything?' She said, with utmost conviction, 'Oh, yes, it would be wonderful!' She was silent for a minute or two, perhaps remembering her own generally unhappy schooling. Then she said thoughtfully, 'You know, kids really like to learn; we just don't like being pushed around.'

No, they don't; and we should be grateful for that. So let's stop pushing them around, and give them a chance.

SECTION 3

DOING EDUCATION STUDIES

21

WHAT IS EVIDENCE-BASED EDUCATION?

Philip Davies

INTRODUCTION

Philip Davies is currently Deputy Director of the Government Social Research Unit, which is part of the UK Cabinet Office. He previously was Director of Social Sciences in the Department for Continuing Education at Oxford University and a Fellow of Kellogg College, Oxford. The movement for evidence-based practice for enhanced use of research evidence in the work of the professions, started in medicine in the early 1990s. It has grown in influence there, and spread across a number of other fields, including education. This method of research is not without its critics who advise caution in approaching it. In this paper, Davies argues that education should become more evidence-based and by evidence-based, he means searching the research literature in a systematic way to test whether new educational practices are better or worse than those that they replace. It also means conducting new research and evaluation studies. Davies makes a plea for the 'power of evidence' in research to be made available in an accessible way so that teachers and others can improve education practice. He explains that Education Based Research is a set of principles for enhancing educational policy and practice.

KEY QUESTIONS

1. Does evidence-based research produce compelling evidence of effectiveness?
2. Is there any evidence that it builds quality learning environments for students?
3. What are the limitations of evidence-based research in the field of educational studies?
4. How are contradictions between research evidence and professional experience to be resolved?

FURTHER READING

Readers should begin with the references in this paper. In addition, see: Davies, P. (2000) 'The relevance of systematic reviews to educational policy and practice' in *Oxford Review of Education* (Vol. 26 No. 3/4) pp. 365–378; and Davies, H. T. O., Nutley, S. M., and Smith, P. C. (eds) (2000) *What Works? Evidence-Based Policy and Practice in the Public Services* (Policy Press, Bristol) for a general exploration of the method. An interesting and worthwhile paper is presented by Hargreaves, D. (1996) *Teaching As a Research-Based Profession: Possibilities and Prospects* (Teacher Training Agency, London). Finally, a good collection of articles on the theme can be found in Trinder, L. (ed.) (2000) *Evidence-Based Practice: A Critical Appraisal* (Blackwell Science, Oxford).

This Reading links with Chapters 17 and 18 and Debate 6 of *The Routledge Education Studies Textbook.*

INTRODUCTION

In most societies education is constantly being asked to do more and more things, to higher and higher standards, with greater accountability and finite (if not diminishing) resources. Its agenda is often driven by political ideology, conventional wisdom, folklore, and wishful thinking as it strives to meet the needs and interests of the economy, business, employers, law and order, civil society, parental choice, and, at least rhetorically, the children, young people, and adults who make up the learning community (Apple, 1982; Apple and Weis, 1983; Ball, 1990, 1993; Bowles and Gintis, 1976; Giroux, 1983, 1992; Willis, 1977). Much of this impetus represents the triumph of hope over reason, sentiment over demonstrated effectiveness, intuition over evidence. Increasingly, the direction of change in educational thinking and practice is top-down from central governments, think tanks, opinion formers, educational regulators (such as OFSTED), the media, and academic departments whose research is often selective, unsystematic, and prone to political or scientific bias (or both). Some recent examples from the United Kingdom include: the form and content of the National Curriculum; the introduction of standardised tests and league tables as a means of 'raising standards' and supposedly increasing parental choice; the substitution of 'trendy' teaching methods based on activity-based, student-centred, self-directed learning and problem solving, with whole-class teaching based on 'rows and columns' classroom organisation, didactic instruction, and a more passive approach to learning, often by rote.

It is often unclear whether these developments in educational thinking and practice are better, or worse, than the regimes they replace. This is in part because educational activity is often inadequately evaluated by means of carefully designed and executed controlled trials, quasi-experiments, surveys, before-and-after studies, high-quality observational studies, ethnographic studies which look at outcomes as well as processes, or conversation and discourse analytic studies that link micro structures and actions to macro level issues. Moreover, the research and evaluation studies that do exist are seldom searched for systematically, retrieved and read, critically appraised for quality, validity and relevance, and organised and graded for power of evidence. This is the task of evidence-based education.

USING *VS* ESTABLISHING EVIDENCE

Evidence-based education operates at two levels. The first is to utilise existing evidence from worldwide research and literature on education and associated subjects. Educationalists at all levels need to be able to:

- pose an answerable question about education;
- know where and how to find evidence systematically and comprehensively using the electronic (computer-based) and non-electronic (print) media;
- retrieve and read such evidence competently and undertake critical appraisal and analysis of that evidence according to agreed professional and scientific standards;
- organise and grade the power of this evidence; and
- determine its relevance to *their* educational needs and environments.

The second level is to *establish* sound evidence where existing evidence is lacking or of a questionable, uncertain, or weak nature. Practitioners of evidence-based education working at this level need to be able to plan, carry out, and publish studies that meet the highest standards of scientific research and evaluation, incorporating the methods of the social sciences, the natural sciences, and the humanistic and interpretive disciplines. The objective of evidence-based education at this level is to ensure that future research on education meets the criteria of scientific validity, high-quality, and practical relevance that is some-times lacking in existing evidence on educational activities, processes, and outcomes (Hargreaves, 1996, 1997; Hillage *et al.*, 1998; Tooley and Darby, 1998).

This view of evidence-based education is derived quite explicitly from the University of Oxford Master's programme in Evidence-Based Health Care. This programme offers health professionals of all types the opportunity to develop their professional skills whilst maintaining full-time professional practice. A central feature of the Oxford programme in Evidence-Based Health Care is that students learn by attempting to solve clinical and population-based problems that *they* bring to the course. This approach to learning, and teaching, is explicitly based on the problem-solving, self-directed model of adult education developed by Knowles (1990) and derived from the learning theory of Piaget, Bruner, Vygotsky, and the 'constructivist' school of learning (Davies, 1999).

The need for both levels of evidence-based practice in education seems clear. There have been a number of recent criticisms about the gap between the teaching and the research communities, the relevance, applicability and quality of educational research, the non-cumulative nature of good educational research, and its effective dissemination (Hargreaves, 1996, 1997; Hillage *et al.*, 1998. Tooley and Darby, 1998). Hargreaves (1996:7), for instance, has called for an end to:

> second-rate educational research which does not make a serious contribution to fundamental theory or knowledge; which is irrelevant to practice; which is uncoordinated with any preceding or follow-up research; and which clutters up academic journals that virtually nobody reads.

Such broad-brush characterisations of educational research have, not surprisingly, received a strong and critical response from the educational research community (Norris, 1996; Gray, 1996; Edwards, 1996; Hammersley, 1997), and a debate that has often shed more heat than light. There is a risk that observations such as those of Hargreaves may promote a narrowly utilitarian and philistine approach to research and intellectual life. What constitutes the relevance of research, for instance, depends to a large extent on what questions are being asked, in what context, and for what practical ends. The demands of practice in one context may make a seemingly narrow and esoteric piece of research highly relevant and very enlightening for those who use it. Similarly, research that is apparently more generalisable, cumulative, and based on highly representative samples for some purposes may be of little value to those with different practice needs and in quite different contexts from those in which the research took place. There is no such thing as context-free evidence.

Some of the criticisms of educational research, however, do have some validity. Hammersley, who has responded most critically to Hargreaves' 1996 lecture, acknowledges, with apparent sincerity, that educational research does lack a cumulative character and that it needs 'to move to a situation where new research builds more effectively on earlier work, and where greater attention is given to testing competing interpretations of data, whether descriptive or explanatory' (Hammersley, 1997: 144). Also, the claim that there is a gap between educational research and teachers (Hargreaves, 1996; Hillage *et al.*, 1998) is undoubtedly true, though perhaps in different ways to those suggested by these critics. The problem is not so much that teachers do not undertake research, or that they are often excluded from determining the research agenda (both of which may be true), but that there is often not a culture of teachers using research to inform their everyday school practice. Contrary to Hargreaves' claim about medicine, the same situation prevails in many areas of clinical practice. One of the ways in which evidence-based health care has had some influence in recent years is in getting clinicians to be clearer about the clinical problems for which they require solutions, and utilising existing evidence effectively and critically to help them solve these problems. There is no question of evidence replacing clinical judgement or experience, but of uniting these two dimensions of knowledge to provide a sound basis for action. Evidence-based practice can provide a similar basis for professional knowledge and action in education. It can also ensure that those who undertake educational research are properly trained in research methods, and understand its underlying theoretical and methodological principles, thereby enhancing its quality.

SOME OBJECTIONS

Some objections from the educational community to such a model of evidence-based education can be anticipated, and have been expressed by respondents to Hargreaves' (1996) call for teaching to be a research-based profession (Norris, 1996; Gray, 1996; Edwards, 1996; Hammersley, 1997). It is claimed that education is unlike health care, and medicine especially, because its activities, processes, and outcomes are complex and culturally, or contextually, specific. Consequently, it is argued, there are problems of measurement and causation in educational research that are not found in medicine and health care. Medicine and health care, however, face very similar, if not identical, problems of complexity, context-specificity, measurement, and causation that Hammersley (1997) has identified in education. The activities, processes, and outcomes of health care are also highly complex, often indeterminate, and context/culture specific, making their measurement both difficult and controversial (Le Grand and Illsley, 1986; Wilkinson, 1986; Samphier, Robertson and Bloor, 1988; MacBeth, 1996). The generalisability of evidence-based health care is one of its major concerns, as it is of all epidemiology and clinical practice. The uncertain relationship between how people behave in hospitals and in their own and other environments (i.e. ecological validity) is a well documented problem in the medical and health care literature (Christmas *et al.*, 1974; Andrews and Stewart, 1979; Newcombe and Ratcliff, 1979; Davies and Mehan, 1988; Davies, 1996), with clear parallels with students' educational performances in schools and colleges on the one hand and in the 'real world' on the other. Greenhalgh and Worrall (1997) have recently argued that the concept of context-sensitive medicine is appropriate to describe the skill of applying the findings of research to the demands of everyday clinical practice.

So far as the measurement of outcomes is concerned, the only discrete and (usually) uncontroversial outcome of health care is death (or survival). Almost every other outcome of health care depends on whether one is concerned *with* objective or subjective dimensions of health and illness, the contexts within which health and illness occur, or the improvement, maintenance, or deterioration of people's health status. Central to these problems is the interaction of signs and symptoms on the one hand and variations in health and illness behaviour according to social class, gender, ethnicity, and cultural practices on the other. For Hammersley to claim that 'unlike in most areas of medicine, in education the "treatments", consist of symbolic interaction, with all the scope for multiple interpretations and responses which that implies', is to ignore his own detailed knowledge of both medical practice and the extensive sociological work on health and illness that has been inspired by symbolic interactionists such as Goffman (1959, 1963, 1964), Glaser and Strauss (1965, 1967), Davis (1963), Fagerhaugh and Strauss (1977), and Strong (1979).

The claim that medicine and health care are based on the natural sciences and their methodologies, whereas education is much more firmly embedded in social science and its approaches to research and evaluation, is also unsustainable. The rejection of natural science as the only basis of modern health care has come from such diverse sources as Balint (1957), Capra (1982), Laing (1965) and Sacks (1990), and the professional training and accreditation bodies of nursing and almost all allied professions, including medicine.

Similarly, educational research draws upon the methodological principles and practices of the natural and the social sciences. Whilst it is undoubtedly the case that experimental and quasi-experimental research is harder to achieve in many aspects of education than it is in some aspects of health care, it is not unknown in educational research and other areas of social scientific inquiry (Oakley, 1998). Randomised controlled trials are difficult to undertake in evaluations of teaching or learning effectiveness, though their potential has been recognised by some researchers (Boruch *et al.*, 1978; Oakley and Harris, 1996; Oakley, 1998). Consequently, researchers who evaluate educational methods or initiatives tend to rely more heavily on controlled comparisons of matched schools, classrooms, or communities, and to develop models of the effects of extraneous variables (Anderson, 1998).

An associated problem, often mentioned by people in the educational community, is that education is, and must be, concerned with *qualitative* research whereas health care is much more concerned with *quantitative* research and evaluation. This is also a false polemic, and one that is unsustainable when one examines research studies in education and health care. A recent review article on research methods in American educational research concluded that:

> results are consistent with those of other studies in that the most commonly used methods were ANOVA and ANCOVA, multiple regression, bivariate correlation, descriptive statistics, multivariate analysis, non-parametric statistics and t-tests. The major difference in current methodology is the increase in the use of qualitative methods. (Elmore and Woehlke, 1996)

The journals reviewed by Elmore and Woehlke represent the more positivistic tradition of American educational research. Other journals, such as the *Harvard Educational Review, Anthropology and Education Quarterly, Qualitative Studies in Education, Social Psychology of Education,* and *Linguistics and Education* have a tradition of publishing more qualitative research, and the proliferation of articles using qualitative methods and discourse analysis confirms the increase in these types of research in the educational field. This trend is also evident in the British educational research literature.

Another common feature of educational and health care research is the use of systematic reviews and meta-analyses. Indeed, meta-analysis and systematic reviews have their origins in educational research following the pioneering work of Glass (Glass, McGaw and Lee Smith, 1980). Glass's work on meta-analysis, like that of Kulik and Kulik (1989), has been described as 'a form of literature review (that) is not meant to test a hypothesis but to summarise features and outcomes of a body of research' (Bangert-Drowns, 1985). Others in the educational research field (Hunter and Schmidt, 1995; Hedges, 1992; Rosenthal, 1995) have used meta-analysis in a way that is more akin to that found in health care research, as a way of data-pooling and 'the use of statistical methods to combine the results of independent empirical research studies' (Hedges, 1992). Meta-analysis in educational research has the same problems as in health care research, such as ensuring the comparability of different samples, research designs, outcome and process measures, identifying confounding factors and bias, and determining the attributable effects of the intervention(s) being assessed. As Preiss (1988) points out 'the researcher will have several options when cumulating empirical studies and readers will have questions regarding judgment calls made during meta-analysis'.

WHAT IS EVIDENCE?

A key issue in developing evidence-based education, and evidence-based health care, is the uncertainty as to what counts as evidence. For those who ask questions such as 'does educational method (or health care intervention) *x* have a better outcome than educational method (or health care intervention) *y* in terms of achieving outcome *z*, evidence consists of the results of randomised controlled trials or other experimental and quasi-experimental studies. Other types of question, for which valid and reliable evidence is sought in both educational and health care research, require evidence about the strength and pattern of relationships between different variables that effect the processes and outcomes of education (and health care). These are best provided by survey and correlational research using methods such as simple and multiple correlation, regression analysis, and analysis of variance.

Yet other questions are more concerned about the *processes* by which educational and health care activities are undertaken and the *meanings* that education or health care have for different people (e.g. learners/patients, teachers/health care professionals, school governors, health care executives, purchasers, etc.). The ways in which teachers and doctors typify students and patients, and use categories and practices that open up, and close down, opportunities for advancement in education (Cicourel and Kitsuse, 1963; Cicourel and Mehan, 1985; Mehan *et al.*, 1996) or health care (Strong, 1979; Davies, 1979), are important topics about which high quality evidence is needed. Evidence is also required about the *consequences* of educational and health care activities on students' and parents' sense of self and their sense of social worth and identity. These types of question require more qualitative and 'naturalistic' research methods such as ethnography, detailed observations, and face-to-face interviews.

Other evidence may be sought about the patterns and structures of interaction, conversation, and discourse by means of which both educational and health care activities are accomplished. Such questions focus on naturally occurring activities between teachers and students, health professionals and patients, and between professionals. Studies such as those by Button and Lee (1987); Fisher and Todd (1983); Silverman (1987), in health care and by Cazden (1988); Mehan (1977, 1996), and Spindler, D (1982) in education represent types of research and evidence from within the conversation analysis and discourse analysis tradition.

Evidence is also required about ethical issues of educational or health care practice, such as whether or not it is right or warrantable to undertake a particular educational activity or health care intervention. Each of the methodological approaches mentioned above may inform these issues, but none will resolve them without additional considerations about the moral and ethical issues of universal versus selective action, informed choices, social inequalities and social justice, resource allocation and prioritisation, and the values underlying education and health care. There is a considerable literature on the ethics of research and professional practice in health care (Brazier, 1987; Fulford, 1990; Gillon, 1985; Veatch, 1989; Weiss, 1982) and education (Adair, Dushenko and Lindsay, 1985; Frankel, 1987; Kimmel, 1988) which the competent practitioner needs to include in his or her considerations of appropriate evidence for best practice.

BIBLIOGRAPHIC AND DATA-BASE PROBLEMS

A third objection to evidence-based education is that the data-bases which serve educational research are less developed, and contain lower-quality filters, than those found in medical and health care research. It does seem that the ERIC Clearing House for educational research is less universal, comprehensive and systematically indexed than MEDLINE and other data-bases in health care (e.g. CINAHL), social science (SOCIOFILE, PSYCLIT, ECONLIT) and biological sciences (BIOLOGICAL ABSTRACTS), and that many studies in education fail to appear on it. This is an issue of improving the reporting and indexing of educational research and changing its reporting practices.

Educational research has also lacked a centralised data-base for the preparation, maintenance and dissemination of systemic reviews of education such as the Cochrane Collaboration, Best Evidence, and the Centre for NHS Reviews and Dissemination. The Cochrane Collaboration has already begun to assemble a data-base of reviews and meta-analysis of social and educational research. The Social, Psychological and Educational Controlled Trials Register (SPECTR) is an extension of The Cochrane Controlled Trials Register in health care (Milwain, 1998; Petrosino *et al.*, 1999). To date, handsearching, electronic database searching and the searching of reference lists have identified over 5000 references to studies in education, criminology and psychosocial-learning research. These studies do not include research which uses methodologies other than experimental or quasi-experimental designs. Such studies also need systematic identification, review, and critical appraisal if the full range of educational research is to be used in the ways suggested in this paper.

This indicates an urgent need for the development of such infrastructural arrangements in education (see Hillage *et al.*, 1998: 53), and the financial support of central governments and the major research councils to develop and maintain them. The existence of many high-quality educational research centres throughout the world which can undertake systematic reviews and meta-analyses on different aspects of education suggests that a similar network of collaboration in educational research is feasible.

In short, the inadequacy of data-bases and bibliographic sources in education is a real problem, but one that is surmountable with appropriate effort and resources. The need for the continuing professional development of teachers, educational researchers, policy makers, and school governors, so that the principles and practices of evidence-based education can be nurtured and introduced into everyday educational life, is also clearly indicated.

EVIDENCE AND PROFESSIONAL JUDGEMENT

Establishing best practice, in both education and health care, is more than a matter of simply accessing, critically appraising, and implementing research findings. It also involves integrating such knowledge with professional judgement and experience. Much professional practice in education and health care is undertaken on the basis that things have always been done a certain way, or they carry the authority and legitimacy of some charismatic, highly valued practitioner. The role of 'common-sense' and 'back to basics' is also favoured by politicians and those charged with developing national educational policy.

Whilst tradition, charismatic authority, and experience can work against change and the development of best practice, they do have some merit. A teacher's experience and judgement can be much more sensitive to the important nuances of contextual and cultural factors than the findings of research alone, however thorough and valid that research may be. The question of the *relevance* of high-quality research to more local issues of teaching and learning (or treatment and change of health status) has already been noted, and is one which demands the highest levels of professional skill, judgement, and experience. Just as evidence-based health care means 'integrating individual clinical expertise with the best available external evidence from systematic research' (Sackett *et al.*, 1996), so evidence-based education means integrating individual teaching and learning expertise with the best available external evidence from systematic research. Indeed, a central feature of evidence-based education must be the two-way process of broadening the basis of individuals' experience and judgement by locating it within the available evidence, and generating research studies and evidence which explore and test the professional experience of teachers, students and other constituents of learning communities.

CONCLUSION

Education seems to be in a position remarkably similar to that of medicine and health care five or ten years ago. There are many research journals which contain a broad range of reports on research using different methodologies and addressing a diverse range of educational issues. Some of this research is of a high quality, some less so. The demands being made upon teachers and others who provide education call out for educational practice to be based on the best available evidence as well as the professional skills, experience, and competence of teachers. To do this, the educational research literature needs to be better registered, indexed, classified, appraised, and made accessible to researchers and teachers alike.

Educators need access to this research and to be able to search and critically appraise it in order to determine its relevance (or lack of relevance) to *their* schools, students, and educational needs. Whether this is called evidence-based education, research-based education (Hargreaves, 1996), literature-based education (Hammersley, 1997), or context-sensitive practice (Greenhalgh and Worrall, 1997) is immaterial.

Evidence-based education, like evidence-based health care, is not a panacea, a quick fix, cookbook practice or the provider of ready-made solutions to the demands of modern education. It is a set of principles and practices which can alter the way people think about education, the way they go about educational policy and practice, and the basis upon which they make professional judgements and deploy their expertise.

REFERENCES

Adair, J. G., Dushenko, T.W., and Lindsay, R.C.L. (1985) Ethical regulations and their impact on research practices, *American Psychologist*, 40, 59–72.

Anderson, G. (1998) *Fundamentals of Educational Research*. London, The Falmer Press.

Andrews, K. and Stewart, J. (1979) Stroke recovery: he can but does he?, *Rheumatology and Rehabilitation*, 18, 43–48.

Apple, M.W. (1982) *Education and Power*. Boston, Routledge and Kegan Paul.

Apple, M.W. and Weis, L. (1983) *Ideology and Practice in Education: A Political and Conceptual Introduction*. Philadelphia, Temple University Press.

Balint, M. (1957) *The Doctor, His Patient, and the Illness*. London, Tavistock.

Ball, S.J. (1990) *Politics and Policy Making in Education*. London, Routledge.

Ball, S.J. (1993) Market Forces in Education, *Education Review*, 7(1), 8–11.

Bangert-Drowns, R.L. (1985) The meta-analysis debate, *Paper presented at the Annual Meeting of the American Educational Research Association*, Chicago, April 4, 1985.

Boruch, R.F., McSweeney, A.J., and Sonderstrom, E.J. (1978) Randomised field experiments for program planning, development and evaluation, *Evaluation Quarterly*, 2, 655–695.

Bowles, S. and Gintis, H.I. (1976) *Schooling in Capitalist America*. New York, Basic Books.

Brazier, M. (1987) *Medicine, Patients and the Law*. Harmondsworth, Penguin Books.

Button, G. and Lee, J.R.E. (1987) *Talk and Social Organisation*. Clevedon and Philadelphia, Multilingual Matters.

Capra, F. (1982) *The Turning Point: Science, Society and the Rising Culture*. London, Wildwood House.

Cazden, C.B. (1988) *Classroom Discourse*. New York, Heinemann.

Christmas, E.M., Humphrey, M.E., Richardson, A.E., and Smith, E.M. (1974) The response of brain damage patients to a rehabilitation regime, *Rheumatology and Rehabilitation*, 13, 92–97.

Cicourel, A.V. and Kitsuse, J.I. (1963) *Educational Decision Makers*. Indianapolis, Bobbs-Merrill.

Cicourel, A.V. and Mehan, H. (1985) Universal development, stratifying practices, and status attainment, *Research in Social Stratification and Mobility*, 4, 3–27.

Davis, F. (1963) *Passage Through Crisis: Polio Victims and Their Families.* Indianapolis, Bobbs-Merrill.

Davies, P.T. and Mehan, H. (1988) Professional and family understanding of impaired communication, *British Journal of Disorders of Communication*, 23, 141–155.

Davies, P.T. (1979) Motivation, sickness and responsibility in the psychiatric treatment of alcohol problems, *British Journal of Psychiatry*, 134(1), 449–459.

Davies, P.T. (1996) Sociological approaches to health outcomes. In H. Macbeth (ed), *Health Outcomes Reviewed: Biological and Sociological Aspects.* Oxford: Oxford University Press.

Davies, P.T. (1999) Teaching evidence-based health care, in M.G. Dawes, P.T. Davies, A Gray, J. Mant, K. Seers, and R. Snowball (1999) *Evidence-based Practice: A Primer for Health Professionals.* Edinburgh, Churchill Livingstone.

Edwards, T. (1996) The research base of effective teacher education, *British Educational Research Association Newsletter*, Research Intelligence, Number 57, July, 7–12.

Elmore, P.B. and Woehlke, P.L. (1996) Research methods employed in *American Educational Research Journal, Educational Researcher* and *Review of Educational Research, 1978–1995. Paper presented at the Annual Meeting of the American Educational Research Association*, New York, April 8, 1996.

Fagerhaugh, S.Y. and Strauss, A.L., (1977) *Politics of Pain Management: Staff-Patient Interaction.* Menlo Park, Addison-Wesley Publishing Company.

Fisher, S. and Todd, A. (eds) (1983) *The Social Organisation of Doctor-Patient Communication.* Washington D.C., Centre for Applied Linguistics.

Frankel, M.S. (ed) (1987) *Values and Ethics in Organisation and Human Systems Development: An Annotated Bibliography* Washington, D.C., American Association for the Advancement of Science.

Fulford, K.W.M. (1990) *Moral Theory and Medical Practice.* Cambridge, Cambridge University Press.

Gillon, R. (1985) *Philosophical Medical Ethics.* New York, John Wiley.

Giroux, H. (1983) *Theory and Resistance in Education.* London, Heinemann Education Books.

Giroux, H. (1992) *Border Crossing: Cultural Workers and the Politics of Education.* London, Routledge and Kegan Paul.

Glaser, B. and Strauss, A. (1965) *Awareness of Dying.* Chicago, Aldine Publishing Co.

Glaser, B. and Strauss, A. (1967) *The Discovery of Grounded Theory: Strategies for Qualitative Research.* Chicago, Aldine Publishing Co.

Glass, G., McGaw, B., and Lee Smith, M. (1980) *Meta-Analysis in Social Research.* Beverly Hills, Saga Publications.

Goffman, E. (1959) *The Presentation of Self in Everyday Life.* Harmondsworth, Penguin.

Goffman, E. (1963) *Stigma: Notes on the Management of Spoiled Identity.* Harmondsworth, Penguin.

Goffman, E. (1964) *Asylums: Essays on the Social Situation of Mental Patients and Other Inmates.* Harmondsworth, Penguin.

Gray, J. (1996) Track record of peer review: a reply to some remarks by David Hargreaves, *British Educational Research – Association Newsletter*, Research Intelligence, Number 57, July, 5–6.

Greenhalgh, T. and Worrall, J.G. (1997) From EBM to CSM: the evolution of context-sensitive medicine, *Journal of Evaluation in Clinical Practice*, 3(2), 105–8.

Hammersley, M. (1997) Educational research and a response to David Hargreaves, *British Educational Research Journal*, 23(2), 141–161.

Hargreaves, D.H. (1996) *Teaching as a Research-Based Profession: Possibilities and Prospects.* Cambridge, Teacher Training Agency Annual Lecture.

Hargreaves, D.H. (1997) In defence of research for evidence-based teaching: a rejoinder to Martyn Hammersley, *British Educational Research Journal*, 23(4), 405–419.

Hedges, L.V. (1992) Meta-analysis, *Journal of Educational Statistics*, 17(4), 279–296.

Hillage, J., Pearson, R., Anderson, A. and Tamkin, P. (1998) *Excellence in Research on*

Schools, Research Report RR74, Department for Education and Employment Sudbury, DfEE Publications.

Hunter, J.E. and Schmidt, F.L. (1995) The impact of data-analysis methods on cumulative research knowledge: statistical significance testing, confidence intervals and meta-analysis, *Evaluation and the Health Professions*, 18(4), 408–427.

Kimmel, A.J. (1988) *Ethics and Values in Applied Social Research*. Beverly Hills, Saga Publications.

Knowles, M. (1990) *The Adult Learner: A Neglected Species*. Houston, Gulf Publishing Company.

Kulik, J. and Kulik, C.C. (1989) Meta-analysis in education, *International Journal of Educational Research*, 13(3), 220.

Laing, R.D. (1965) *The Divided*. Harmondsworth, Penguin.

Legrand, J. and Illsley, R. (1986) The measurement of inequality in health, *Paper presented to a meeting of the British Association for the Advancement of Science*. Bristol, 1–5 September 1986.

Macbeth, H. (ed) (1996) *Health Outcomes Reviewed: Biological and Sociological Aspects*. Oxford, Oxford University Press.

Mehan, H. (1977) *Learning Lessons*. Cambridge Mass., Harvard University Press.

Mehan, H., Villanueva, I., Hubbard, L. and Lintz, A. (1996) *Constructing School Success*. Cambridge, Cambridge University Press.

Milwain, C. (1998) *Assembling, Maintaining and Disseminating a Social and Educational Controlled Trials Register (SECTR): A Collaborative Endeavour*. Oxford, UK Cochrane Centre.

Newcombe, F. and Ratcliff, G. (1979) Long term psychological consequences of cerebral lesions, in M. Gazzangia (ed), *Handbook of Behavioural Neurobiology*, Vol 2. Chapter 16 New York, Plenum Press.

Norris, N. (1996) Professor Hargreaves, the TTA and evidence-based practice, *British Educational Research Association Newsletter*, Research Intelligence, Number 57, July 2–4.

Oakley, A. and Roberts, H. (eds) (1996) *Evaluating Social Interventions*. Ilford, Essex, Bamados.

Oakley, A. (1998) Experimentation in social science: the case of health promotion, *Social Sciences in Health*, 4(2), 73–88.

Petrosino, A.J., Rounding, C., McDonald, S., and Chalmers, I. (1999) *Improving Systematic Reviews of Evaluations: Preliminary Efforts to Assemble a Social, Psychological and Educational Controlled Trials Register (SPECTR)*, Paper prepared for the meeting on Research Synthesis and Public Policy, University College London, 15/16 July 1999.

Preiss, R.W. (1988) *Meta-Analysis: A Bibliography of Conceptual Issues and Statistical Methods*. Annandale, Virginia, Speech Communication Association.

Rosenthal, R. (1995) Interpreting and evaluating meta-analysis, *Evaluation and the Health Professions*, 18(4), 393–407.

Sackett, D.L., Rosenberg, W., Gray, J.A.M., Haynes, R.B. and Richardson, W. (1996) Evidence-based medicine: what it is and what it isn't, *British Medical Journal* 312, 71–72.

Sacks, O. (1990) Neurology and the soul, *New York Reviews of Books*, 37(18), 44–50.

Samphier, M.L., Robertson, C. and Bloor, M.J. (1988) A possible artefactual component in specific cause mortality gradients. Social class variations in the clinical accuracy of death certificates, *Journal of Epidemiology and Community Health*, 42(2), 138–43.

Silverman, D. (1987) *Communication and Medical Practice: Social Relations in the Clinic*. London and Newbury Park, Sage Publications.

Spindler, D. (ed) (1982) *Doing the Ethnography of Schooling*. New York, Rinehart and Winston.

Strong, P.M. (1979) *The Ceremonial Order of the Clinic: Parents, Doctors and Medical Bureaucracies*. London, Routledge and Kegan Paul.

Tooley J. and Darby, D. (1998) *Education Research: An Ofsted Critique.* London, Ofsted.

Veatch, R.M. (1989) *Medical Ethics.* London, Jones and Bartlett.

Weiss, B.D. (1982) Confidentiality expectations of patients, physicians and medical students, *Journal of the American Medical Association*, 247(19), 2695–2697.

Wilkinson, R.G. (1986) Socio-economic differences in morality: interpreting the data on their size and trends. In R.G. Wilkinson (ed) *Class and Health: Research and Longitudinal Data.* London, Tavistock.

Willis, P. (1977) *Learning to Labour: How Working Class Kids Get Working Class Jobs.* Westmead, Saxon House.

22

TOWARDS A JUDGEMENT-BASED STATISTICAL ANALYSIS

Stephen Gorard

INTRODUCTION

Stephen Gorard is Professor of Education Research at the University of Birmingham. His web pages make clear that he is interested in 'the improvement of education in terms of effectiveness and equity, but my research is "society-wide" and lifelong in scope'. He has used a wide variety of methods. He has completed a very large number of research projects and is a prolific author with publications including Gorard, S. (2008) 'Which students are missing from HE?', *Cambridge Journal of Education* (Vol. 38 No. 3); and Gorard, S. (2008) 'Research impact is not always a good thing: a re-consideration of rates of "social mobility" in Britain', *British Journal of Sociology of Education* (Vol. 29 No. 3) pp. 317–324. These publications are useful for understanding something of Gorard's interests and his ideas as presented in this paper. His wide-ranging use of research methods is connected with the view that statistical analysis is not 'a technical essentially objective process of decision making' but rather that it is 'no different from the analysis of other forms of data, especially those forms often referred to as "qualitative"'. By suggesting that there are three kinds of explanations for observed results (bias, chance and plausible substantive explanations) and asking why the last of these three are often rejected, he argues that we need to be alert to the real nature of statistical analysis.

KEY QUESTIONS

1. To what extent is it worthwhile to think about educational research as either qualitative or quantitative?
2. Should mixed methods always be used?
3. Do you feel that education research may be able (through the use of mixed or single methods) to identify 'what works'?

FURTHER READING

This paper raises questions about the nature of educational research. Recent work explores the emphasis that might be placed on 'what works' through using evidence and undertaking experiments. Some interesting work representing something of the diversity of these debates can be seen in Gage, N. L. (1989) 'The paradigm wars and their aftermath: a "historical" sketch of research on teaching since 1989' in *Educational Researcher* (Vol. 18 No. 7) pp. 4–10; and Creswell, J. W. and Plano Clark, V. L. (2007) *Designing and Conducting Mixed Methods Research* (Thousand Oaks, CA: Sage).

This Reading links with Chapters 17 and 18 and Debate 6 of *The Routledge Education Studies Textbook.*

INTRODUCTION

Statistics are no substitute for judgement. (Henry Clay, 1777–1852)

The paper highlights the role of judgement in statistical decision-making via an imaginary example. It starts from the premise that all statistical analyses involve the format data = model + error, where the error is not merely random variation from sampling but stems from more systematic sources such as non-response, estimation, transcription and propagation. This total error component is an unknown and there is, therefore, no technical way of deciding whether the error dwarfs the other components. Existing techniques are largely concerned with the sampling variation alone. However complex our analysis, at heart it involves a judgement about the probable size of the error in comparison with the size of the alleged findings (whether pattern, trend, difference or effect).

The paper reminds readers of the three common kinds of explanations for observed results: bias, chance and plausible substantive explanations. The paper then re-considers standard practice when dealing with each of these types in turn. It concludes that standard practice needs adjusting in two crucial ways. We need to formally consider, and explain why we reject, a greater range of plausible substantive explanations for the same results. More pressingly, we need to take more notice of the estimated size of any bias relative to the size of the 'effects' that we uncover. This means that the logic of statistical analysis is little different, except in terminology, from the analysis of other forms of data – especially those traditionally referred to as 'qualitative'.

AN EXAMPLE OF JUDGEMENT

Imagine trying to test the claim that someone is able mentally to influence the toss of a perfectly fair coin, so that it will land showing heads more than tails (or vice versa) by a very small amount. We might set up the test using our own set of standard coins, selected from a larger set at random by observers, and ask the claimant to specify in advance whether it is heads (or tails) that will be most frequent. We would then need to conduct a very large number of coin tosses, because a small number would be subject to considerable 'random' variation. If, for example, there were 51 heads after 100 tosses the claimant might try to claim success even though the *a priori* probability of such a result is quite high anyway. If, on the other hand, there were 51 tails after 100 tosses the claimant might claim that this is due to the standard variation, and that their influence towards heads could only be seen over a larger number of trials. We could not say that 100 tosses would provide a definitive test of the claim. Imagine instead, then, one million trials yielding 51% heads. We have at least three competing explanations for this imbalance in heads and tails. First, this could still be an example of normal 'random' variation, although considerably less probable than in the first example. Second, this might be evidence of a slight bias in the experimental set-up such as a bias in one or more coins, the tossing procedure, the readout or the recording of results. The key problem with such bias is that we have no reason to believe that its impact is random in nature. Third, this might be evidence that the claimant is correct; they *can* influence the result.

In outline, this situation is one faced by all researchers using whatever methods, once their data collection and analysis is complete. The finding could have no substantive significance at all (being due to chance). It could be due to 'faults' in the research (such as a selection effect in picking the coins). It could be a major discovery affecting our theoretical understanding of the world (that a person can influence events at a distance). Or it could be a combination of any of these. I consider each solution in turn.

The explanation of pure chance becomes less likely as the number of trials increases.[1] In some research situations, such as coin tossing, we can calculate this decrease in likelihood precisely. In most research situations, however, the likelihood can only be an estimate. In all situations we can be certain of two things – that the chance explanation can never be discounted entirely (Gorard, 2002a), and that its likelihood is mostly a function of the scale of the research. Where research is large in scale, repeatable, conducted in different locations, and so on, then it can be said to have minimised the chance element. In the example of one million coin tosses this chance element is small (less than the 1/20 threshold used in traditional statistical analysis), but it could still account for some of the observed difference (either by attenuating or disguising any 'true' effect).

If we have constructed our experiment well, then the issue of bias is also minimised. There is a considerable literature on strategies to overcome bias and confounds as far as possible (for example, Adair, 1973; Cook & Campbell, 1979). In our coin tossing example we could automate the tossing process, mint our own coins, not tell the researchers which of heads or tails was predicted to be higher, and so on. However, like the chance element, errors in conducting research can never be completely eliminated. There will be coins lost, coins bent, machines that malfunction, and so on. There can even be bias in recording (misreading heads for tails, or reading correctly but ticking the wrong column) and in calculating the results. Again, as with the chance element, it is usually not possible to calculate the impact of these errors precisely (even on the rare occasion that the identity of any error is known). We can only estimate the scale of these errors, and their potential direction of influence on the research. We are always left with the error component as a plausible explanation for any result or part of the result.

Therefore, to be convinced that the finding is a 'true' effect, and that a person can mentally influence a coin toss, we would need to decide that the difference that we have found is big enough for us to reasonably conclude that the chance and error components represent an insufficient explanation. Note that the chance and error components not only have to be insufficient in themselves, they also have to be insufficient in combination. In the coin tossing experiment, is 51% heads in one million trials enough? The answer will be a matter of judgement. It should be an informed judgement, based on the best estimates of both chance and error, but it remains a judgement. The chance element has traditionally been considered in terms of null-hypothesis significance testing and its derivatives, but this approach is seen as increasingly problematic, and anyway involves judgement (see later). But perhaps because it *appears* to have a technical solution, researchers have tended to concentrate on the chance element in practice and to ignore the far more important components of error, and the judgement these entail.

If the difference is judged a 'true' effect, so that a person can mentally influence a coin toss, we should also consider the importance of this finding. This importance has at least two elements. The *practical* outcome is probably negligible. Apart from in 'artificial' gambling games, this level of influence on coin tossing would not make much difference. For example, it is unlikely to affect the choice of who bats first in a five-match cricket test series. If someone could guarantee odds of 3:1 in favour of heads on each toss, then that would be different, and the difference over one million trials would be so great that there could be little doubt it was a true effect. Even if the immediate practical importance is minor, on the other hand, a true effect would involve many changes in our understanding of important areas of physics and biology. This would be important knowledge for its own sake, and might also lead to more usable examples of mental influence at a distance. In fact, this revolution in thinking would be so great that many observers would conclude that 51% was not sufficient, even over one million trials. The finding makes so little immediate practical difference, but requires so much of an overhaul of existing 'knowledge' that it makes perfect sense to conclude that 51% is consistent with merely chance and error. However, this kind of judgement is ignored in many social science research situations, where our over-willing acceptance of what Park (2000) calls 'pathological science' leads to the creation of weak theories based on practically useless findings (Cole, 1994; Davis, 1994; Platt, 1996; Hacking, 1999). There *is* an alternative, described in the rest of this paper.

THE ROLE OF CHANCE

To what extent can traditional statistical analysis help us in making the kind of decision illustrated earlier? The classical form of statistical testing in common use today was derived from agricultural studies (Porter, 1986). The tests were developed for one-off use, in situations where the measurement error was negligible, in order to allow researchers to estimate the probability that two random samples drawn from the same population would have divergent measurements. In a roundabout way, this probability is then used to help decide whether the two samples actually come from two different populations. Vegetative reproduction can be used to create two colonies of what is effectively the same plant. One colony could be given an agricultural treatment, and the results (in terms of survival rates perhaps) compared between the two colonies. Statistical analysis helps us to estimate the probability that a sample of the results from each colony would diverge by the amount we actually observe, under the artificial assumption that the agricultural treatment had been ineffective and, therefore, that all variation comes from the sampling. If this probability is very small, we might conclude that the treatment appeared to have an effect. That is what significance tests are, and what they can do for us.

In light of current practice, it is also important to emphasise what significance tests are not, and cannot do for us. Most simply, they cannot make a decision for us. The probabilities they generate are only estimates, and they are, after all, only probabilities. Standard limits for retaining or rejecting our null hypothesis of no difference between the two colonies, such as 5%, have no mathematical or empirical relevance. They are arbitrary thresholds for decision-making. A host of factors might affect our confidence in the probability estimate, or the dangers of deciding wrongly in one way or another, including whether the study is likely to be replicated (Wainer & Robinson, 2003). Therefore there can be, and should be, no universal standard. Each case must be judged on its merits. However, it is also often the case that we do not need a significance test to help us decide this. In the agricultural example, if all of the treated plants died and all of the others survived (or vice versa), then we do not need a significance test to tell us that there is a very low probability that the treatment had no effect. If there were 1000 plants in the sample for each colony, and one survived in the treated group, and one died in the other group, then again a significance test would be superfluous (and so on). All that the test is doing is formalising the estimates of relative probability that we make perfectly adequately anyway in everyday situations. Formal tests are really only needed when the decision is not clear-cut (e.g. where 600/1000 survived in the treated group but only 550/1000 survived in the control), and since they do not make the decision *for* us, they are of limited practical use even then. Above all, significance tests only estimate a specific kind of sampling error, but give no idea about the real practical importance of the difference we observe. A large enough sample can be used to reject almost any null hypothesis on the basis of a very small difference, or even a totally spurious one (Matthews, 1998).

It is also important to re-emphasise that the probabilities generated by significance tests are based on probability samples (Skinner *et al.*, 1989). They tell us the probability of a difference as large as we found, assuming that the *only* source of the difference between the two groups was the random nature of the sample. Fisher (who pioneered many of today's tests) was adamant that a random sample was required for such tests (Wainer & Robinson, 2003). 'In non-probability sampling, since elements are chosen arbitrarily, there is no way to estimate the probability of any one element being included in the sample … making it impossible either to estimate sampling variability or to identify possible bias' (Statistics Canada, 2003, p. 1). If the researcher does not use a random sample then traditional statistics are of no use since the probabilities then become meaningless. Even the calculation of a reliability figure is predicated on a random sample. Researchers using significance tests with convenience, quota or snowball samples, for example, are making a key category mistake. Similarly, researchers using significance tests on populations (from official statistics perhaps) are generating meaningless probabilities. All of these researchers are relying on the false rhetoric of apparently precise probabilities, while abdicating their responsibility for making judgements about the value of their results. As Gene Glass put it:

> In spite of the fact that I have written stats texts and made money off of this stuff for some 25 years, I can't see any salvation for 90% of what we do in inferential stats. If there is no ACTUAL probabilistic sampling (or randomization) of units from a defined population, then I can't see that standard errors (or t-test or F-tests or any of the rest) make any sense. (cited in Camilli, 1996)

Rather than modelling and inferential techniques, Glass recommends analysis via exploration and discovery (Robinson, 2004).

Added to this is the problem that social scientists are not generally dealing with variables, such as plant survival rates, with minimal measurement error. In fact, many studies are based on latent variables of whose existence we cannot even be certain, let alone how to measure them (e.g. underlying attitudes). In agronomy there is often little difference between the substantive theory of interest and the statistical hypothesis (Meehl, 1998), but in wider science, including social science, a statistical result is many steps away from a substantive result. Added to this are the problems of non-response and participant dropout in social investigations, which also do not occur in the same way in agricultural applications. All of this means that the variation in observed measurements due to the chance factor of sampling (which is *all* that significance tests estimate) is generally far less than the potential variation due to other factors, such as measurement error (Sterne & Smith, 2001, p. 230).

The probability from a test contains the unwritten proviso – assuming that the sample is random with full response, no dropout and no measurement error. The number of social science studies meeting this proviso is very small indeed. To this must be added the caution that probabilities interact, and that most analyses in the information and communication technology age are no longer one-off. Analysts have been observed to conduct hundreds of tests, or try hundreds of models, with the same data-set. Most analysts also start each probability calculation as though nothing prior is known, whereas it may be more realistic and cumulative (and more efficient use of research funding) to build the results of previous work into new calculations. Statistics is not, and should not be, reduced to a set of mechanical dichotomous decisions around a 'sacred' value such as 5%.

As shown at the start of this section, the computational basis of significance testing is that we are interested in estimating the probability of observing what we actually observed, assuming that the artificial null hypothesis is correct. However, when explaining our findings there is a very strong temptation to imply that the resultant probability is actually an estimate of the likelihood of the null hypothesis being true given the data we observed (Wright, 1999). Of course, the two values are very different, although it is possible to convert the former into the latter using Bayes' Theorem (Wainer & Robinson, 2003). Unfortunately this conversion, of the 'probability of the data given the null hypothesis' into the more useful 'probability of the null hypothesis given the data', requires us to use an estimate of the probability of the null hypothesis being true irrespective of (or prior to) the data. In other words, Bayes' Theorem provides a way of adjusting our prior belief in the null hypothesis on the basis of new evidence (Gorard, 2003). But doing so entails a recognition that our posterior belief in the null hypothesis, however well informed, now contains a substantial subjective component.

In summary, therefore, significance tests are based on unrealistic assumptions, giving them limited applicability in practice. They relate only to the assessment of the role of chance, tell us nothing about the impact of errors and do not help decide whether any plausible substantive explanation is true. Even so, they require considerable judgement to use, and involve decisions that need to be explained and justified to any audience.

EFFECT OR ERROR?

Here is a real example of the role of judgement, selected because I was reading it recently and not because it is extreme or particularly problematic (in fact, it comes from a very well-respected and influential source). From their analysis of the 1958 National Childhood Study and 1970 British Cohort Study, Machin and Gregg (2003) found that 'the extent of intergenerational mobility in economic status has reduced substantially over time' (p. 194), and claimed that 'these findings are sizeable and important' (p. 196). This is their conclusion. Their actual finding is that the regression coefficient for individual earnings related to the income of family of origin was 0.17 for both men and women in the 1958 study, but was 0.26 for men and 0.23 in women in the 1970 study. Given that we will assume both a chance element and an error component in both studies, do the figures justify the conclusion? In line with current practice, the authors do not argue the point or set out clearly the logic of their move from the figures to the conclusion (their 'warrant', see later), so it is up to the reader to make the judgement alone. This judgement over social mobility matters because the paper was presented via an influential think-tank to help form the policy-setting agenda for the current government.

Both of these cohort studies originally involved over 16,000 cases selected to be representative of the population of Britain. But this new analysis used only around 2000 cases per cohort from the two studies. Originally, not all individuals were included in the sampling frame anyway (perhaps the families of very severely disabled or terminally ill infants were not approached to participate) so there was some selection bias. Not all of those included in the sampling frame agreed to take part, so there was some volunteer bias among the 16,000. Not all who agreed initially have taken part in successive sweeps, so there is some bias from dropout (only around 70% of the original participants could be traced and were still available to the researchers in 1999; see Bynner *et al.*, 2000). There will also be typical levels of error in reporting, recording, coding, transcription and calculation. Finally, there are systematic differences in the sampling procedures, question formats and question contents between the 1958 and 1970 surveys. We can have no real idea of the overall level and impact of these combined biases, but that is not any reason to ignore them, or their propagation through the complex computations of multiple regression.

Machin and Gregg (2003) report conducting null-hypothesis significance tests, and report that the differences are 'mostly significant' using the standard 5% threshold. But, as we have seen, this approach only addresses the chance element, and only caters for a chance element introduced as a result of random sampling. It does not decide in any way whether the differences between the two surveys are worthy of further attention. In light of the errors in each survey and the other differences between them, it is perfectly reasonable to conclude that statistical significance of the kind reported by the authors is totally consistent with a position that claims there is no real difference. A difference between 0.17 and 0.23, in these circumstances, may not be substantial enough for us to base social policy on.

Even where the difference is judged substantial enough, the argument so far has only considered what may be termed the 'methodological' alternatives such as error and chance. There will also be a large number of substantive alternatives to the conclusions given, and the warrant should also show how the most plausible of these other explanations were considered, and the reasons why they were rejected in favour of the published conclusion. For example, is it possible that individual earnings would become easier to predict from family income if earnings become less variable over time, so the different coefficients may represent not so much less social mobility as less overall social variation in 1970? If this is not possible – because the second survey shows at least as much income variation as the first, for example – then the authors could explain this, thereby eliminating a rival conclusion derived from the same finding.

To recapitulate: all research faces the problem outlined in the introduction, of having at least three types of explanation for the same observed data. The first is the explanation of chance. The second is an explanation based on error such as bias, confounds and 'contamination'. The third type is a substantive explanation, from a range of plausible explanations. Null hypothesis significance tests cater for only the first of these, and only under very unrealistic conditions. What are the alternatives?

WHAT ARE THE ALTERNATIVES?

Suggestions for alternatives include the use of effect sizes, confidence intervals, standard errors, meta-analyses, parameter estimation and a greater use of graphical approaches for examining data. These could be complements to significance testing, but there has also been the suggestion that reporting significance tests should be banned from journals to encourage the growth of useful alternatives (Thompson, 2002).

All of these ideas are welcome, but none is a panacea for the problems outlined so far – chiefly the problem of estimating the relative size of the error component. Most actually address the somewhat simpler but less realistic issue of estimating the variation due to random sampling. Confidence intervals and standard errors are based on the same artificial foundation as significance tests in assuming a probability-based sample with full response and no measurement error, and an ideal distribution of the data (de Vaus, 2002). They are still inappropriate for use both with populations and non-random samples. Even for random samples, minor deviations from the ideal distribution of the data affect the confidence intervals derived from them in ways that have nothing to do with random error (Wright, 2003). In addition, the cut-off points for confidence intervals are just as arbitrary as a 5% threshold used in significance tests (Wainer & Robinson, 2003). In no way do they overcome the need for judgement or replication.

Whereas a significance test is used to reject a null hypothesis, an 'effect size' is an estimate of the scale of divergence from the null hypothesis. The larger the effect size, the more important the result (Fitz-Gibbon, 1985). For example, a standard effect size from a simple experiment might be calculated as the difference between the mean scores of the treatment and control groups, proportional to the standard deviation for that score among the population. This sounds fine in principle, but in practice we will not know the population standard deviation. If we had the population figures then we would probably not be doing this kind of calculation anyway. We *could* estimate the population standard deviation by using the standard deviation for one or both of the two groups, but this introduces a new source of potential error.

■ Table 1 'Effect' of aspirin on heart attacks in two groups

Condition	No heart attack	Heart attack	Total
Aspirin	10,933	104	11,037
Placebo	10,845	189	11,034
Total	21,778	293	22,071

Above all, the use of effect sizes requires considerable caution. Several commentators have suggested that in standardising them they become comparable across different studies, and so we see papers setting out scales describing the range of effect sizes that are substantial and those that are not. They therefore return us to the same position of dealing with arbitrary cut-off points as do confidence intervals and significance tests. Wainer and Robinson (2003) present an example of the folly of such scales. Table 1 summarises the results of a large trial of the impact of regular doses of aspirin on the incidence of heart attacks. A significance test such as chi-squared would suggest a significant difference between these two groups. But the effect size (in this case R-squared) is of the order of magnitude 0.001, which is far too small to be of a practical value, according to scales describing the meaning of effect sizes. On the other hand, there were 85 fewer deaths in the treatment group, which is impressive because of what they represent. The traditional odds ratio of the diagonals is over 1.8, reinforcing the idea that the effect size is misleading in this case.

In fact, of course, 'there is no wisdom whatsoever in attempting to associate regions of the effect-size metric with descriptive adjectives such as "small", "moderate", "large", and the like' (Glass *et al.*, 1981, p. 104). Whether an effect is large enough to be worth bothering with depends on a variety of interlocking factors, such as context, cost-benefit, scale and variability. It also depends on the relative size of the error component because, like all of the attempted technical solutions already stated, effect sizes do nothing to overcome errors. An effect size of 0.1 might be very large if the variability, the costs and the errors in producing it are low, while the benefits are high. Again, we are left only with our judgement and our ability to convey the reasons for our judgements as best we can.

Therefore, while these moves to extend the statistical repertoire are welcome, the lack of agreement about the alternatives, the absence of textbooks dealing with them (Curtis & Araki, 2002) and their need for even greater skill and judgement means that they may not represent very solid progress (Howard *et al.*, 2000). In fact, the alternatives to null hypothesis significance tests are doing little to assist scientific progress (Harlow *et al.*, 1997). The major error component in our findings is not usually due to pure chance. Unfortunately, the vagaries of pure chance are the *only* things that classical statistical analyses allow us to estimate.

DISCUSSION

If the aforementioned points are accepted it can be seen that merely producing a result, such as 51% heads, is not sufficient to convince a sceptical reader that the results are of any importance. In addition to explaining the methods of sampling, data collection and analysis, authors need also to lay out a clear, logical warrant (Gorard, 2002b). A key issue here is clarity of expression in the overt argument that leads from the results to the conclusions (Phillips, 1999). At present, too much social science research seems to make a virtue of being obscure but impressive-sounding – whether it is the undemocratic way in which complex statistical models are presented in journals, or the use of neologisms that are more complex than the concepts they have been, ostensibly, created to describe. Jargon-laden reports go into considerable mathematical detail without providing basic scientific information (Wright & Williams, 2003). Clarity, on the other hand, exposes our judgements to criticism, and our warrant stems from that exposure of the judgement. Transparency does not, in itself, make a conclusion true or even believable, but it forces the analyst to admit the subjectivity of their analysis and allows others to follow their logic as far as it leads them.

Phillips (1999) reminds us that, despite their superficial similarity, falsification is very different to the null hypothesis testing of traditional statisticians. The first approach involves putting our cherished ideas 'on-the-line', deliberately exposing them to the likelihood of failure. It involves considerable creativity in the production of predictions and ways of testing them. The second involves a formulaic set of rules (mis)used to try and eliminate the null hypothesis, and so embrace the cherished alternative hypothesis. As such, it is only a very weak test of the alternative hypothesis. Perhaps, the apparent and soothing 'rigour' of traditional statistics has satisfied both researchers and research users, and so inhibited the search for more truly rigorous ways of testing our ideas. One obvious example of this is the preference among UK social science funders for increasingly complex methods of statistical analysis (the *post hoc* dredging of sullen datasets), over a greater use of quasi-experimental designs. The use of complex techniques should never be allowed to mislead readers into thinking that *any* technique eliminates, or even addresses, the error component. For, 'despite the trapping of modeling, the analysts are not modeling or estimating anything, they are merely making glorified significance tests' (Davis, 1994, p. 190).

Complex statistical methods cannot be used *post hoc* to overcome design problems or deficiencies in datasets. If all of the treated plants in the agricultural example at the start were placed on the lighter side of the greenhouse, with the control group on the other side, then the most sophisticated statistical analysis in the world could not do anything to overcome that bias. It is worth stating this precisely because of the 'capture' of funders by those pushing for more complex methods of probability-based traditional analysis, whereas of course, 'in general, the best designs require the *simplest* statistics' (Wright, 2003, p. 130). Or as Ernest Rutherford bluntly pointed out, 'If your experiment needs statistics, you ought to have done a better experiment' (cited in Bailey, 1967, p. 16). Therefore, a more fruitful avenue for long-term progress would be the generation of better data, open to inspection through simpler and more transparent methods of accounting. Without adequate empirical information, 'to attempt to calculate chances is to convert mere ignorance into dangerous error by clothing it in the garb of knowledge' (Mills, 1843, cited in Porter 1986, pp. 82–83).

Perhaps one reason why research is not typically taught as an exercise in judgement is that judgement seems 'subjective' whereas computation is ostensibly 'objective'. This distinction is often used by commentators to try and reinforce the distinction between a 'qualitative' and a 'quantitative' mode of reasoning and researching. But, in fact, we all combine subjective estimates and objective calculations routinely and unproblematically. Imagine preparing for a catered party, such as a wedding reception. We may know how many invitations we send, and this is an objective number. We may know how much the catering will cost per plate, and this is another objective number. To calculate the cost of the party, we have to use the number invited to help us estimate the number who will attend, and this is a subjective judgement even when it is based on past experience of similar situations. We then multiply our estimate by the cost per plate to form an overall cost. The fact that one of the numbers is based on a judgement with which other analysts might disagree does not make the arithmetic any different, and the fact that we arrive at a precise answer does not make the final estimate any firmer. This last point is well known, yet when they conduct research many people behave as though it were not true. 'Quantitative' researchers commonly eschew the kind of judgement at the heart of their decisions, seeking instead pseudo-technical ways of having the decisions taken out of their hands.

At present, much of science is bedevilled by 'vanishing breakthroughs', in which apparently significant results cannot be engineered into a usable policy, practice or arte-fact. Epidemiology, in particular, and perhaps dietary advice, cancer treatment, genetics and drug development have become infamous for these vanishing breakthroughs. The tra-ditional guidelines for significance tests, and the apparently standardised scales for effect sizes, are producing too many results that literally disappear when scaled up. Social scien-tists' use of statistics is, therefore, retarding progress (Robinson, 2004). When Fisher sug-gested the 5% threshold he realised that this was quite high, but did so because he felt it was more important not to miss possible results than to save time and effort in fruitless work on spurious results. He also assumed that this was relatively safe because he envisaged a far higher level of direct replication in agricultural studies than we see in social science. How-ever, rather than simply lowering the 5% threshold, this paper argues for a recognition that any such threshold is only concerned with the chance explanation. Of much more concern is the relative size of the propagated error component. According to Cox (2001), the key issue is whether the direction of the effect is firmly established and of such magnitude as to make it of 'clinical' importance.

We could always set out to estimate a band of error, and judge its potential impact. This would give us a far more realistic idea of the 'confidence' we can place in our results than any confidence interval. For example, imagine a survey that sets out to include 2000 people. It receives 1000 responses, for a 50% response rate, of which 50% are from men and 50% from women. On one key question, 55% of men respond in a particular way but only 45% of women do. This is clearly a statistically 'significant' result, and it leads to medium-sized 'effect size'. Therefore, traditional approaches lead us to the conclusion that men and women differ in their response to this question. But neither of these measures, nor any of the other alternatives discussed, takes into account the response rate. Since 275 of the men and 225 of the women respond in this particular way, we would need only 50 more of the 500 women non-respondents than the men non-respondents to have responded in a particular way (if they could have been made to respond) for there to be no difference. Put another way, if most non-responders had responded in the same proportions as the actual responders, then we need only assume that 5% of all non-responders would have responded differently for the difference between men and women to disappear. In this case, the difference we observe seems very small in comparison with the non-response. As we add in the potential errors caused at each stage of our survey (measurement and tran-scription error, for example), we may conclude that the difference is not worth investing further effort in because studies of the implementation of research findings show that the signal to noise ratio becomes even weaker as the results are rolled out into policy and practice.

As a rule-of-thumb we could say that we need to be sure that the effect sizes we con-tinue to work with are substantial enough to be worth it. Clearly, this judgement depends on the variability of the phenomenon, its scale and its relative costs and benefits (Schmidt, 1999). It also depends on the acknowledged ratio of effect to potential error. Therefore, an effect size that is worth working with will usually be clear and obvious from a fairly sim-ple inspection of the data. If we have to dredge deeply for any effect, then it is probably 'pathological' to believe that anything useful will come out of it. We cannot specify a min-imum size needed for an effect, but we can say with some conviction that, in our present state of knowledge in social science, the harder it is to find the effect, the harder it will be to find a use for the knowledge so generated. It is probably unethical to continue to use public money pursuing some of the more 'pathological' findings of social science.

Probably the best 'alternative' to many of the problems outlined so far in contem-porary statistical work is a renewed emphasis on judgements of the worth of results (Altman *et al.*, 2000). The use of open, plain but ultimately subjective judgement is prob-ably also the best solution to many of the problems in other forms of current research, such as how to judge the quality of in-depth data analysis or how to link theory and empirical work more closely (Spencer *et al.*, 2003). If this course were adopted it would also have the effect of making it easier for new researchers to adopt mixed methods approaches as routine, without having to worry about which forms of data require a judgement-based analysis rather than a technical one. They *all* do (Gorard, 2004).

NOTE

1. This, of course, is the key advantage of large-scale work, and is usually expressed in terms of reliability. For a fixed budget, therefore, large-scale work is sacrificing depth for reliability.

REFERENCES

Adair, J. (1973) *The human subject.* Little, Brown and Co., Boston, MA.

Altman, D., Machin, D., Bryant, T. and Gardiner, M. (2000) *Statistics with confidence.* BMJ Books, London.

Bailey, N. (1967) *The mathematical approach to biology and medicine.* Wiley, New York.

Bynner, J., Butler, N., Ferri, E., Shepherd, P. and Smith, K. (2000) *The design and conduct of the 1999–2000 surveys of the National Child Development Study and the 1970 British Cohort Study.* Centre for Longitudinal Studies, London – (working paper 1).

Camilli, G. (1996) Standard errors in educational assessment: a policy analysis perspective. *Education Policy Analysis Archives* 4:(4).

Cole, S. (1994) Why doesn't sociology make progress like the natural sciences? *Sociological Forum* 9:(2), pp. 133–154.

Cook, T. and Campbell, D. (1979) *Quasi-experimentation: design and analysis issues for field settings.* Rand McNally, Chicago, IL.

Cox, D. (2001) Another comment on the role of statistical methods. *British Medical Journal* 322, p. 231.

Curtis, D. and Araki, C. (2002) Effect size statistics: an analysis of statistics textbooks, paper presented at American Educational Research Association, New Orleans.

Davis, J. (1994) What's wrong with sociology? *Sociological Forum* 9:(2), pp. 179–197.

de Vaus, D. (2002) *Analyzing social science data: 50 key problems in data analysis.* Sage, London.

Fitz-Gibbon, C. (1985) The implications of meta-analysis for educational research. *British Educational Research Journal* 11:(1), pp. 45–49.

Glass, G., McGaw, B. and Smith, M. (1981) *Meta-analysis in social research.* Sage, Beverley Hills, CA.

Gorard, S. (2002a) The role of causal models in education as a social science. *Evaluation and Research in Education* 16:(1), pp. 51–65.

Gorard, S. (2002b) Fostering scepticism: the importance of warranting claims. *Evaluation and Research in Education* 16:(3), pp. 136–149.

Gorard, S. (2003) Understanding probabilities and re-considering traditional research methods training. *Sociological Research Online* 8:(1).

Gorard, S. (2004) *Combining methods in educational and social research.* Open University Press, London.

Hacking, I. (1999) *The social construction of what?* Harvard University Press, London.

Harlow, L., Mulaik, S. and Steiger, J. (1997) *What if there were no significance tests?* Lawrence Erlbaum, Marwah, NJ.

Howard, G., Maxwell, S. and Fleming, K. (2000) The proof of the pudding: an illustration of the relative strengths of null hypothesis, meta-analysis, and Bayesian analysis. *Psychological Methods* 5:(3), pp. 315–332.

Machin, S. and Gregg, P. (2003) A lesson for education. *New Economy* 10:(4), pp. 194–198.

Matthews, R. (1998) *Statistical snake-oil: the use and abuse of significance tests in science.* European Science and Environment Forum, Cambridge – (working paper 2/98).

Meehl, P. (1998) The power of quantitative thinking, speech delivered upon receipt of the James McKeen Cattell Fellow award at the American Psychological Society Meeting. Washington, DC.

Park, R. (2000) *Voodoo science: the road from foolishness to fraud.* Oxford University Press, Oxford.

Phillips, D. (1999) How to play the game: a Popperian approach to the conduct of research. In Zecha, G. (ed.) *Critical rationalism and educational discourse.* Rodopi, Amsterdam.

Platt, J. (1996) *A history of US Sociological Research Methods 1920–1960.* Cambridge University Press, Cambridge.

Porter, T. (1986) *The rise of statistical thinking.* Princeton University Press, Princeton, NJ.

Robinson, D. (2004) An interview with Gene Glass. *Educational Researcher* 33:(3), pp. 26–30.

Schmidt, C. (1999) *Knowing what works: the case for rigorous program evaluation.* Institute for the Study of Labor, Bonn – (IZA DP 77).

Skinner, C., Holt, D. and Smith, T. (1989) *Analysis of complex surveys.* John Wiley and Sons, Chichester.

Spencer, L., Ritchie, J., Lewis, J. and Dillon, L. (2003) *Quality in qualitative evaluation: a framework for assessing research evidence.* Cabinet Office Strategy Unit, London.

Statistics Canada (2003) *Non-probability sampling* – Available online at: www.statcan.ca/english/power/ch13/ (accessed 5 January 2004).

Sterne, J. and Smith, G. (2001) Sifting the evidence – what's wrong with significance tests. *British Medical Journal* 322, pp. 226–231.

Thompson, B. (2002) What future quantitative social science could look like: confidence intervals for effect sizes. *Educational Researcher* 31:(3), pp. 25–32.

Wainer, H. and Robinson, D. (2003) Shaping up the practice of null hypothesis significance testing. *Educational Researcher* 32:(7), pp. 22–30.

Wright, D. (1999) Science, statistics and the three 'psychologies'. In Dorling, D. and Simpson, L. (eds) *Statistics in society.* Arnold, London.

Wright, D. (2003) Making friends with your data: improving how statistics are conducted and reported. *British Journal of Educational Psychology* 73, pp. 123–136.

Wright, D. and Williams, S. (2003) How to produce a bad results section. *The Psychologist* 16:(12), pp. 646–648.

23

THE OBVIOUSNESS OF SOCIAL AND EDUCATIONAL RESEARCH RESULTS

N. L. Gage

INTRODUCTION

Nathaniel Gage (1917–2008) was an educational psychologist who led the Stanford University (USA) Center for Research and Development of Teaching, and his numerous roles included that of president of the American Educational Research Association and founding editor of the journal *Teaching and Teacher Education*. His output includes a book (*A Conception of Education*) published posthumously in 2008. He is most widely known for what he referred to as a scientific approach to teaching and this article discusses in a lively and provocative manner reactions to research results. When people say to researchers "well, we knew that already", Gage suggests that there may simply be a willingness to accept a coherent argument. There are significant implications in what Gage writes in this article for how we should interpret research and how we should try to make the most of the valuable human approach to teaching that is reliant on "hunch" and the extent to which we should be influenced by scientifically derived data.

KEY QUESTIONS

1. Identify three examples of educational practice that you regard as obviously 'good'.
2. Make connections between that 'good' practice and research evidence. Does the evidence exist?
3. If there is currently no research evidence available, what sort of research would you need to do in order to make a more confident judgement about what seems to be obviously worthwhile?

FURTHER READING

Gage's ideas link to debates about what works. Contrasting views about the nature of evidence in education can be seen in: *European Educational Research Journal* (Vol. 7 No. 1, 2008) in papers by: Slavin, R. E. 'Evidence-based reform in education: what will it take?', pp. 124–128 and Bridges, D. 'Evidence-based reform in education: a response to Robert Slavin', pp. 129–133; and in Hammersley, Martyn (ed.) (2007) *Educational Research and Evidence-Based Practice* (Sage, London).

This Reading links with Chapters 17 and 18 and Debate 6 of *The Routledge Education Studies Textbook.*

Is what we find out in social and educational research old hat, stale, platitudinous? Are the results of such research mere truisms that any intelligent person might know without going to the trouble of doing social or educational research?

THE IMPORTANCE OF THE OBVIOUSNESS QUESTION

The obviousness question has important ramifications. It can influence the motivation of any person who is thinking about doing social or educational research. Why do research if you are not going to find anything new, anything not already known? Obviousness also relates to the justification of social science departments and schools of education in expecting or requiring their faculties and graduate students to do social and educational research. It also concerns government funding policies, such as those of the National Science Foundation and the National Institute of Mental Health that support social research, and those of the U.S. Department of Education, particularly the Office of Educational Research and Improvement, that support educational research. Foundations, school boards, state legislatures, and Congressional committees need to be convinced, before they put up the money, that social and educational research will produce something that any intelligent adult might not already know.

So, the issue of obviousness, apart from piquing our intellectual curiosity, has tremendous practical importance. Unless social and educational researchers face that issue, they may lack motivation to do research and lose societal support expressed in dollars.

THE CHARGE OF OBVIOUSNESS

Does anyone really hold that social and educational research yields only the obvious? I begin with an old joke attributed to James T. Farrell, the novelist who became famous in the 1930s for *Studs Lonigan.* Farrell was quoted in those days as having defined a sociologist as someone who will spend $10,000 to discover the location of the nearest house of ill fame. He actually used a less polite term, and nowadays he would have said a quarter of a million dollars. I also remember a fellow graduate student who could always get a laugh by referring to the content of some of his textbooks as "unctuous elaborations of the obvious."

Schlesinger's critique

The first serious piece of writing that I know of that made the same charge appeared in 1949 in *The Partisan Review.* It was in a review by Arthur Schlesinger, Jr., of the two volumes of *The American Soldier,* which had just been published. *The American Soldier* was written by a group led by Samuel A. Stouffer, who later became a professor of sociology at Harvard. It reported on the work done by sociologists and other social scientists in surveying, with questionnaires and interviews, the attitudes of American soldiers during World War II. The first volume, subtitled "Adjustment During Army Life," dealt with soldiers' attitudes during training, and the second, subtitled "Combat and Its Aftermath," dealt with soldiers' attitudes while they were engaged with the enemy and risking their lives. As a young assistant professor, I found the two books impressive for their methodological thoroughness, sophisticated interpretation, and theoretical formulations of such concepts as "relative deprivation."

So I was taken aback after some months when I discovered a review of those two volumes by Arthur Schlesinger, Jr., the distinguished historian. Then a young professor at Harvard University, Schlesinger had just won a Pulitzer Prize for his *Age of Jackson*. Witty and vituperative, Schlesinger's review also denounced what he considered the pretensions of social scientists. Schlesinger wrote:

> Does this kind of research yield anything new? . . . [T]he answer . . . is easy. Most of the *American Soldier* is a ponderous demonstration in Newspeak of such facts as these: New recruits do not like noncoms; front-line troops resent rear-echelon troops; combat men manifest a high level of anxiety as compared to other soldiers; married privates are more likely than single privates to worry about their families back home. Indeed, one can find little in the 1,200 pages of text and the innumerable surveys which is not described more vividly and compactly and with far greater psychological insight, in a small book entitled *Up Front* by Bill Mauldin. What Mauldin may have missed will turn up in the pages of Ernie Pyle. (p. 854)

Lazarsfeld's examples

At about the same time as Schlesinger, Paul Lazarsfeld, a professor of sociology at Columbia University, also reviewed *The American Soldier*. Lazarsfeld (1949) was clearly aware of the same problem of obviousness. He wrote:

> [I]t is hard to find a form of human behavior that has not already been observed somewhere. Consequently, if a study reports a prevailing regularity, many readers respond to it by thinking "of course, that is the way things are." Thus, from time to time, the argument is advanced that surveys only put into complicated form observations which are already obvious to everyone.
>
> Understanding the origin of this point of view is of importance far beyond the limits of the present discussion. The reader may be helped in recognizing this attitude if he looks over a few statements which are typical of many survey findings and carefully observes his own reaction. A short list of these, with brief interpretive comments, will be given here in order to bring into sharper focus probable reactions of many readers.
>
> 1. Better educated men showed more psychoneurotic symptoms than those with less education. (The mental instability of the intellectual as compared to the more impassive psychology of the man-in-the-street has often been commented on.)
> 2. Men from rural backgrounds were usually in better spirits during their Army life than soldiers from city backgrounds. (After all, they are more accustomed to hardships.)

3.   Southern soldiers were better able to stand the climate in the hot South Sea Islands than Northern soldiers. (Of course. Southerners are more accustomed to hot weather.)
4.   White privates were more eager to become non-coms than Negroes. ([Because of their having been deprived of opportunity for so many years], the lack of ambition among Negroes was [quite understandable].)
5.   Southern Negroes preferred Southern to Northern white officers [because Southerners were much more experienced in having interpersonal interactions with Negroes than Northern officers were].
6.   As long as the fighting continued, men were more eager to be returned to the States than they were after the Germans surrendered [because during the fighting, soldiers were in danger of getting killed, but after the surrender there was no such danger]. (pp. 379–380)

Keppel's position

For a later sample of the worry about obviousness, we can turn to an essay by Frank Keppel, titled "The Education of Teachers," which appeared in 1962 in a volume of talks on American education by American scholars that had been broadcast by radio to foreign audiences. Keppel had left the deanship of the Harvard Graduate School of Education to serve as U.S. Commissioner of Education under President Kennedy. As Commissioner he led the movement that resulted in the Elementary and Secondary Education Act of 1965, the first major effort in the U.S. to improve the education of children from low-income families. In his article, Keppel (1962) indicated that some people question the principles that have emerged from psychological studies of teaching and learning. Without committing himself as to whether he agreed, he summed up the critics' arguments this way:

> The efforts to use scientific methods to study human behavior seem to them [the critics] ridiculous if not impious. The result is a ponderous, pseudo-scientific language which takes ten pages to explain the obvious or to dilute the wisdom long ago learned in humanistic studies. . . . To build an art of teaching on the basis of the "behavioral sciences," they suggest, is to build on sand. (p. 91)

Conant's position

The very next year, obviousness was mentioned again, by another prestigious educator, namely, James Bryant Conant, who had been president of Harvard University for 20 years, and then the U.S. High Commissioner (and eventually the U.S. ambassador) in West Germany. During World War II, he had been a member of the highest scientific advisory committees, including the one that led to the production of the atom bomb. When he returned from Germany, he devoted himself almost exclusively to educational problems. In 1963, he published a book titled *The Education of American Teachers,* in which he reported on his studies of teacher education programs and schools – studies made through much interviewing, reading, and visiting. His book gained extremely wide and respectful attention. Yet, when I looked into it, as an educational psychologist, I couldn't help being dismayed by Conant's assertion that educational psychology largely gives us merely common-sense generalizations about human nature – generalizations that are "for the most part highly limited and unsystematized generalizations, which are the stock in trade of every day life for all sane people" (p. 133).

Phillips's critique

These references to obviousness take us only into the 1960s. Did the attacks disappear after that? Or are there more recent statements on the obviousness of educational and social research results? In 1985, a volume of papers appeared on the subject of instructional time, which had been central in a variety of formulations, such as John B. Carroll's model of school learning, Benjamin Bloom's mastery approach to teaching, and the concept of academic engaged time developed by Charles Fisher and David Berliner. All of these writers seemed to agree that the more time students spent in studying, practicing, and being engaged with the content or skills to be learned, the greater the related learning they achieved. The correlations between academic engaged time and achievement were not perfect, of course, because outside of the laboratory, correlations are never perfect, even in the natural sciences and certainly not in the social and behavioral sciences.

The subject of instructional time thus received a lot of attention in many articles and several books, including the edited volume, *Perspectives on Instructional Time,* to which the philosopher of the social sciences, Denis Phillips (1985), contributed a chapter entitled "The Uses and Abuses of Truisms." Here Phillips first cited Hamlyn, also a philosopher, who had criticized the work of Piaget. Hamlyn had asked his readers to try to imagine a world in which Piaget's main ideas were untrue:

> a world where children mastered abstract and complex tasks before concrete and simple ones, for example. Such a world would differ crazily from our own, and one gets the sense that many of Piaget's views are unsurprising and necessarily (if not trivially) true. (p. 311)

Phillips then raised the same kind of question about the research on instructional time: "What sort of world would it be if children learned more the *less* time they spent on a subject? If achievement were not related to the time spent engaged on a topic?" (p. 311). So, just as with Piaget's major findings, "one gets the sense that these findings [about instructional time] are almost necessarily (and perhaps even trivially) true" (p. 311). "Indeed, it suddenly seems strange to dress up these truisms as 'findings'" (p. 312).

Phillips then went on to make a distinction between truisms and statements that are trivially true. "[T]he latter are, in effect, a subgroup of the former. A truism is a statement the truth of which is self-evident or obvious . . . whereas a trivially true statement is one that is true by virtue of the meaning of the terms involved (e.g., 'All colored objects are colored,' or 'All bachelors are unmarried')" (p. 312). He went on to say that 'It is easier to keep a small group of children working on a task than it is a large group' is a truism, for it is obviously true, but it is not true by virtue of the meanings of the terms involved (p. 312). Phillips also pointed out that:

> truisms and statements that are trivially true are not thereby *trivial*. The terms *truism* and *trivially true* refer to the patentness of the truth of statements, whereas *trivial* refers to their degree of value or usefulness. The two do not automatically go together; many a statement the truth of which is far from obvious is of no practical use . . . and many truisms are vitally important and even theoretically significant ("The sky is dark at night" [this truism bears on the theory of the expanding universe]). (p. 313)

Furthermore,

> truisms uncovered by researchers, then, are not necessarily trivial. But on the other hand *truisms do not require research in order to be uncovered.* Agencies would be

wasting money if they awarded grants to researchers who wanted to determine if all bachelors in the United States were unmarried, or if the sky is dark at night, or if small groups are easier to control than large groups. (p. 313, emphasis added)

In short

Let me summarize the argument so far. I have presented a series of opinions quite damaging to the notion that social and educational research yields results that would not already be known to any intelligent and thoughtful citizen. These opinions are hard to ignore. Extremely estimable people – Farrell, Schlesinger, Keppel, Conant, Lazarsfeld, and Phillips – all have made statements that might well give pause to any sensible person considering the pursuit of social and educational research or any organization being asked to part with money to support such research. I have presented these statements in chronological order extending from novelist James T. Farrell in the mid-1930s to philosopher Denis Phillips in the mid-1980s.

EMPIRICAL EXAMINATION OF OBVIOUSNESS

One noteworthy characteristic of all of these criticisms is that they were what might be called nonempirical or, at least, not systematically and formally empirical. Informal and personal, the appraisals were not made with any great specificity, detail, explicitness, or exactitude. Presumably, Schlesinger had not actually compared the statements of results reported in *The American Soldier* with statements made by Bill Mauldin or Ernie Pyle. He did not perform a content analysis of the two kinds of reports about soldiers to show in any literal way that the sociologists' statements of results had been anticipated by the insights of the cartoonist and the journalist. The same point can be made about what was said by Keppel and Conant: They did not go into any detail, or become at all specific, to support their allegations. However, the sociologist Lazarsfeld did go into detail and referred to specific results, namely, soldiers' attitudes of various kinds. Phillips referred to specific findings about instructional time, or time on task, and also findings about size of group or class size.

Rice's studies

Now I should like to go back and look at some empirical efforts that seem to me to bear upon the whole issue of obviousness. I begin with what may be the first process-outcome study in the history of research on teaching. The results of this investigation were published by Joseph Mayer Rice (1897/1913) under the title "The Futility of the Spelling Grind." Rice reported, after studying tests on 33,000 school children, that there was no correlation worth noticing between amount of time devoted to spelling homework and classwork and competence in spelling.

Rice's evidence is still being cited in support of the argument that spelling competence results from "incidental" learning, rather than from any "systematic" teaching; that is, spelling is "caught" rather than "taught." So far as instructional time or "academic engaged time" is concerned, the issue does not appear to be the open-and-shut case implied by Phillips (1985) when he asked, "What kind of world would it be if achievement were not related to the time spent engaged on a topic?" (p. 311). As Rice (1897/1913) put it, "concerning the amount of time devoted to spelling . . . an increase of time . . . is not rewarded by better results. . . . The results obtained by forty or fifty minutes' daily instruction were not better than those obtained where not more than ten or fifteen minutes had been devoted to the subject" (pp. 86–87).

Apparently, showing a relationship between time on task and achievement was not as easy as falling off a log, as it should have been if the relationship between time-on-task and achievement were necessarily true, that is, a truism. At least in one subject matter, namely, spelling, the relationship between time-on-task and achievement was fragile, perhaps even nonexistent. So perhaps the relationship depended on the subject matter. Perhaps other factors also made a difference. Things may be more complicated than we should expect if the relationship were a truism.

Similarly, if smaller groups were always easier to control, a relationship that Phillips assumed to be a truism, then they should show higher time-on-task and thus higher achievement. However, the trickiness of the relationship between class size and achievement is by now well established. Reducing class size from 40 to 20 does not improve achievement with any consistency at all. Glass (1987) reported that it required an "exhaustive and quantitative integration of the research" to refute well-nigh unanimous older assessments (e.g., Goodlad, 1960) that class size made no difference in achievement, student attention, and discipline. Even then Glass found that the relationship of class size to achievement appeared only probabilistically (in 111 of 160 instances, or 69%) when classes of approximately 18 and 28 pupils were compared. Moreover, the duration of the instruction made a big difference: the relationship was stronger in studies of pupils taught for more than 100 hours. In addition, the class size had to be reduced dramatically to make a major improvement: "Bringing about even a 10 percentile rank improvement in the average pupil's achievement . . . may entail cutting class size (and, hence, increasing schooling costs) by a third to a half" (p. 544).

Alleging that a relationship (e.g., the size-of-group relationship to the ease of control) is a truism implies that it should always be found and that no exceptions should occur. Thus, all bachelors without exception are unmarried, all colored objects without exception are colored. By the same reasoning, if the group size-controllability relationship were a truism, all smaller groups should be easier to control than all larger groups. If the age-reasoning ability relationship were a truism, all older children should be capable of more abstract and valid reasoning than all younger children. But, of course, the last two examples are untrue. If a truism is "an undoubted or self-evident truth, especially one too obvious or unimportant for mention" (*Webster's New Collegiate Dictionary,* 1979), then these relationships are not truisms because they are not always "undoubted" or "self-evident."

Suppose we change the "truism" to a probabilistic statement (e.g., children *tend to* learn more, the more time they spend on a subject; time on task is positively but *imperfectly* correlated with achievement). Now the research aims to determine the strength of the tendency, or the magnitude of the positive correlation. Does the r equal .05, .25, .45, .65, or .85? It seems to be a truism that the size of the time on task versus achievement correlation depends on many factors: the reliability of the achievement measure, the variabilities of the two variables, perhaps the subject matter, and so on. Is the research to answer these important and specific practical questions still unnecessary?

Here may lie one key to the problem: To enhance the truism with the specifics that make it have value for theory and practice, the research does become necessary. Even if the broad generalization is a truism, the specifics of its actualization in human affairs – to determine the magnitude of the probability and the factors that affect that magnitude – require research. Even if "smaller groups tend to be more easily controlled" were a truism, we would ask, how much difference in group size is needed to produce a given difference in controllability? How do other factors – age and gender of group members, task difficulty, and the like – affect the difference in controllability resulting from changes in group size? Similar questions would apply to all the other seemingly truistic findings. Even if intelligent people could always (without any research) predict the direction (positive or negative) of a relationship between two variables, they could not predict its size and its contingencies without research-based knowledge.

Lazarsfeld's examples

Let us go back now to Lazarsfeld's examples of obvious results from the World War II studies of *The American Soldier*. Recall his examples of the "obvious" conclusions from that study: better educated men showed more psychoneurotic symptoms; men from rural backgrounds were usually in better spirits than those from cities; Southern soldiers were better able than Northerners to stand the climate in the South Sea Islands; White privates were more eager to become non-coms than Black privates were; Southern Negroes preferred Southern to Northern White officers; and men were more eager to be returned to the States during the fighting than they were after the Germans surrendered.

Lazarsfeld (1949) asked, "Why, since they are so obvious, is so much money given to establish such findings?" However, he then revealed that

> *Everyone of these statements is the direct opposite of what was actually found.* Poorly educated soldiers were more neurotic than those with high educations; Southerners showed no greater ability than Northerners to adjust to a tropical climate; Negroes were more eager for promotion than whites, and so on. . . . If we had mentioned the actual results of the investigation first, the reader would have labelled these "obvious" also. Obviously something is wrong with the entire argument of obviousness. It should really be turned on its head. Since every kind of human reaction is conceivable, it is of great importance to know which reactions actually occur most frequently and under what conditions . . . (p. 380)

Lazarsfeld's rhetorical ploy has always impressed me as fairly unsettling for those who make the allegations of obviousness, but its force depends on whether we are willing to grant him his assumption that we accepted the first version of the research results as valid, so that he could then startle us with his second presentation, which gave the true findings: the results that were actually obtained. It might be argued that Lazarsfeld's assumption was unwarranted and that most of us would not have believed that first set of statements that he later revealed were spurious.

The Mischels' study

So I took notice when I heard about investigations that made no assumptions of the kind that Lazarsfeld's exercise required. The first of these (Mischel, 1981; Mischel & Mischel, 1979) consisted of giving fourth- and sixth-grade children *(Ns* = 38 and 49, respectively) items presenting psychological principles stated in both their actual form and the opposite of the actual forms. For example, the first item dealt with the finding by Solomon Asch that college students would respond contrarily to the evidence of their senses about which of three lines had the same length as a comparison line when the students first heard four other students (confederates of the investigator) misidentify the same-length line. The second item concerned Harry Helson's finding that the same water temperature feels cooler on a hot day than on a cool day. In all, there were 17 such items, some of which were presented to only one of the two grade-level groups. The children circled the one of the two to four choices that they thought described what would happen in each situation.

Of the 29 opportunities for either the fourth graders or the sixth graders to select the actual research result to a statistically significant degree, the groups did so on 19, or 66%. One group or the other was wrong to a statistically significant degree on five opportunities, and there was no statistically significant correctness or incorrectness on 5 opportunities. Clearly, the children had substantial success, but far from the perfect record that would support the allegation of almost universal obviousness.

But these were only children. What about college students and adults? And what happens when the research results are presented as flat statements rather than as multiple-choice items requiring the selection of the actual result from two or more alternatives?

Baratz's study

Baratz (1983) selected 16 social research findings from various studies, and then did an experiment. She manipulated, for each of the findings, whether the statement concerning that finding was the true finding or the opposite of the true finding. She also presented each finding, either the true one or the opposite one, with or without an explanation of the finding. That second manipulation was intended to "explore the possibility that adding explanations to the findings may render the findings more obvious" (p. 20). Thus, each of her subjects – 85 male and female undergraduates enrolled in introductory psychology at Stanford University – evaluated 16 findings: four statements with a true finding plus explanation, four statements with the opposite finding plus explanation, four statements with a true finding without explanation, and four statements of an opposite finding without an explanation. Each finding was presented in the same format: first, the question addressed by the study, such as "a study sought to determine whether people spend a larger proportion of their income during *prosperous* times or during a *recession*." And for this study the reported finding was "In prosperous times people spend a larger proportion of their income than during a recession." The statement of the opposite finding differed from that of the true finding only in the order of the critical terms, and half of the findings were followed at the time by a short explanation, which was presented as the "explanation given by our subject."

Here are two sample pairs of the true and opposite findings used by Baratz in her experiment: "People who go to church regularly tend to have more children than people who go to church infrequently" versus "People who go to church infrequently tend to have more children than people who go to church regularly" and "Single women express more distress over their unmarried status than single men do" versus "Single men express more distress over their unmarried status than single women do."

For each of the 16 findings presented to each student, the students were asked how readily predictable or obvious the finding was and were instructed to choose one of the responses on the following four-point scale:

1. I am *certain* that I would have predicted the result obtained rather than the opposite result.
2. I *think* that I would have predicted the result obtained rather than the opposite result, but I am *not certain.*
3. I *think* that I would have predicted the opposite to the obtained result, but I am *not certain.*
4. I am *certain* that I would have predicted the *opposite* to the obtained result.

The subjects were asked to express their "initial impressions of the relevant findings, i.e., the kind of impression that you might form if you read a brief article about the research in your daily newspaper" (p. 25).

In a summary table, Baratz presented the mean percentage of subjects who marked either "I am *certain* that I would have predicted the reported outcome" or "I *think* I would have predicted the reported outcome" for pairs of opposite findings. When the reported outcome was "A," 80% of her students claimed they would have predicted that outcome. When the reported outcome was "B," 66% of her subjects claimed they would have predicted that outcome. Thus, as Baratz put it, "It is clear that findings that contradict each other were both retrospectively judged 'obvious'. . . . These results show clearly that reading a result made that result appear obvious. No matter which result was presented, the majority of the subjects thought that they would have predicted it" (p. 26).

I considered Baratz's experiment and her findings to be persuasive. They seemed to provide evidence against the argument that social research yields only obvious findings. Her results indicated that intelligent people, namely, Stanford undergraduates, tend to regard any result they read, whether it is the true one or the opposite of the true one, as obvious. This tendency to say results are obvious was, of course, only a tendency; not all of her subjects followed that tendency, but it was a majority tendency.

Wong's study

Baratz's research on obviousness dealt with results from a fairly wide range of the social sciences, but I had been focusing on research on teaching and particularly on one area within that field: process-outcome research. That kind of research seeks relationships between classroom processes (what teachers and students do or what goes on in the classroom) and outcomes (what students acquire by way of knowledge, understanding, attitude, appreciation, skill, etc.). Would such research results elicit obvious reactions similar to those obtained by Baratz?

A few years ago, Lily Wong, a Stanford graduate student from Singapore, replicated and extended Baratz's experiments, but with findings from process-outcome research on teaching. Wong chose her respondents from four different categories of persons who differed on the dimension of how much they might be expected to know about classroom teaching. At the low end of that dimension were undergraduates in engineering; next, undergraduates majoring in psychology; next, teacher trainees; and at the high end, experienced teachers. Each of these four groups of respondents was sampled both from Singaporeans and from Americans residing either at Stanford University or in the neighboring area. In total, Wong used 862 Singaporeans and 353 Americans. For the research findings, she used 12 statements based on results of process-outcome research carried out in the elementary grades, results that had been cited in the third edition of the *Handbook of Research on Teaching* (Wittrock, 1986) and in textbooks of educational psychology. Her items came from the results of research by Anderson, Evertson, and Brophy; Brophy and Evertson; Good and Grouws; Soar and Soar; and Stallings and Kaskowitz. Here is the first of her 12 items: "When first-grade teachers work on reading with a small group of children, some attend closely to just the children in the small group, whereas others monitor children's activities throughout the classroom. The class's reading achievement is higher *when teachers monitor the entire classroom*" versus ". . . *when teachers attend to just the children in the small group.*" Here is the second item: "When first-grade teachers work on reading with a small group of children, some call on the children in a fixed order, whereas others call on children in a random order. Reading achievement is higher *when children are called on in a fixed order*" versus ". . . *when children are called on in a random order.*"

Wong had five forms of questionnaires: Form A, Forms B_1 and B_2, and Forms C_1 and C_2. Subjects completing Form A had to select in each item the true finding between two options – one stating an actual finding of research on teaching at the primary-grade level and the other stating the opposite of the actual finding. The subject then rated the chosen statement on a 4-point scale from 1, "extremely obvious" to 4, "extremely unobvious."

Subjects completing Forms B_1 or Form B_2 were required to rate the obviousness of each of 12 single statements presented as actual research findings. In fact, 6 were true findings and 6 were the opposite of true findings. Each of the 24 statements from Form A thus appeared in either Form B_1 or Form B_2.

Form C subjects were given the same purported findings as Form B subjects, but in Form C, each statement was accompanied by a possible explanation. Subjects in Form C had to rate not only the obviousness of the findings but also the clarity of the explanations.

Wong's results on Form A showed that her respondents chose both actual findings and opposite findings. On 4 of the 12 items, her subjects chose the actual finding more often (see p. 37), but on the other 8, they chose the false finding more often. The r between percentage choosing a finding and the mean obviousness rating of the finding was .66. The respondents to Forms B and C rated about half of the opposite findings as obvious. Wong concluded that

> Judging by the smaller proportions of respondents choosing the actual findings as the real findings, and the mean rating of obviousness on the presented (both actual and opposite) finding statements, we can say reasonably that people can not distinguish true findings from their opposites. (p. 86)

The Singaporeans rated most of the items as more obvious than the American subjects did in all conditions. There were few gender differences in the average responses to the various forms. Teachers were no more accurate, on the average, than the other groups in the selection of true findings: "In the rating of obviousness of items, knowledge and experience [in teaching] were found to have some significant effect on several items. This does not mean that teachers and trainees rated true findings more obvious or opposite findings less obvious than the psychology undergraduates and the engineering undergraduates" (Wong, 1987, p. 87).

Wong concluded that her results "clearly confirmed the idea that knowledge of outcome increases the feeling of obviousness. Thus, when people claim to have known it all along when an event is reported to them, their claim is often not warranted" (p. 88).

WHERE THE ISSUE STANDS

From the work of Baratz and Wong we can conclude that the feeling that a research result is obvious is untrustworthy. People tend to regard as obvious almost any reasonable statement made about human behavior. A recent example comes from the *Arizona Daily Star* of March 8, 1988, in an article about the booklet entitled *What Works,* compiled by the U.S. Department of Education. The booklet contains brief discussions, with references to the research, of 41 research findings considered potentially helpful to schools and teachers. The headline read, "Restating the Obvious."

My most recent example comes from the June 1990 issue of *The Atlantic* (Murphy, 1990): "A recent survey (by me) of recent social-science findings . . . turned up no ideas or conclusions that can't be found in Bartlett's or any other encyclopedia of quotations" (p. 22).

As suggested by an anonymous referee for this article, the results of Baratz and Wong are consistent with the conclusions of Nisbett and Wilson (1977): "[There may be little or no direct introspective access to higher order cognitive processes" (p. 231). Thus the cognitive processes that lead one to regard a research result as obvious are probably non-veridical unless, as Ericsson and Simon (1980) argued, the response is based on (a) short-term memory leading to verbalization of information that (b) would have been attended to even without the instructions given. It is questionable whether judging the obviousness of research results always meets these requirements.

The same reviewer also suggested that these results do not belie the fact that most adults' generalizations about human interactions are at least functional. I agree; otherwise human society would be impossible.

Another issue arose in a conversation between Robert D. Hess and me. Upon being apprised of judges' tendency to regard as obvious both actual research results and their opposites, Hess asked about the frequency with which the results had been confirmed through replications. His question calls for research in which the "obviousness" of research results frequently confirmed with high consistency would be compared with that of research relationships frequently studied with results of only low consistency. Examples of both high-consistency and low-consistency results can be found in the synthesis of results of research on teaching by Walberg (1986). His Table 7.2 (pp. 218–219) contains results whose "percentage positive" across replications ranges from very low (where 50% is completely inconsistent) to very high (where 0% and 100% are completely consistent).

An investigator could administer questionnaires similar to those of Baratz (1983) and Wong (1987), but using items representing both (a) frequently studied with highly consistent results and (b) frequently studied with highly inconsistent results. It would then be possible to determine the difference, if any, in the mean obviousness rating of these two types of research results. It may turn out that only items of Type b would be rated obvious in both their actual and opposite forms. A frequently replicated and highly consistent result – for example, the "result" that auto drivers in England stay to the left side of the road whereas auto drivers in the United States stay to the right side of the road – will almost certainly be rated highly obvious in its actual form and highly *non*obvious in its opposite form. Here the requisite knowledge is widely possessed, and the "obvious" reaction will not occur. Much depends on the relationship between the content of the research result and the background knowledge of the judge of the result's obviousness. Both Baratz and Wong may have studied results whose relationship to their judges' background knowledge was tenuous. Even Wong's experienced teachers, who probably had never thought about or encountered the phenomena dealt with in the research results used by Wong, had too little background knowledge to be able to detect the nonobviousness of the opposite-to-actual results.

Thus, the obvious reaction may be hypothesized to occur only when the judge's background knowledge in relation to the judged research result is weak. If the hypothesis is borne out, the question might be raised, How does a representative sample of social and educational research results fare, as to their obviousness in actual and opposite forms, when presented to a representative sample of the persons who might be expected to encounter or be concerned with those results? That is, research on obviousness now needs to be aimed at maximal external validity, or the degree to which the obviousness research is relevant to real life.

The issue joined by Schlesinger when he attacked students of human affairs who use scientific methods has its roots in the old controversy that C.P. Snow (1964) examined later in *The Two Cultures: And a Second Look*. Snow was concerned with the mutual disregard and disrespect of natural scientists and scholars in the humanities. Snow regretted this condition, but it still exists. Schlesinger's denunciation of social research reflected what Karl Popper called the antinaturalist position: the position that the scientific method useful for studying the natural world is inappropriate for the study of human affairs. The response of Paul Lazarsfeld reflects the position, held by Karl Popper and many others, that scientific method *is* appropriate for the study of human affairs.

Scientific method need not be used, in my opinion, only for the construction of a social science – where such a science is defined as a network of laws that will hold over whole eras and in many different cultural contexts, just as the laws of mechanics hold in different historical periods and in contexts as different as planetary motion and the motion of a pendulum. Rather, scientific method can be used for what Popper called "piecemeal social engineering," a more modest enterprise aimed at improving human affairs by applying scientific methods to the development and evaluation of new "treatments" – in education, in social welfare projects, or in fighting against drugs.

I have speculated (Gage, 1989) that people gravitate toward one or the other of Snow's two cultures – toward science (natural or social) or toward humanistic insight and sensibility – because their upbringing and intellectual experience have inclined them toward one or the other. The wars between the several paradigms in social and educational research may result from temperamentally different (i.e., not entirely rational) intellectual predilections, often developed during the secondary school years. If so, improved education may someday produce scholars and educational researchers who experience no conflict between their scientific and humanistic orientations.

In any case, the allegation of obviousness may now be countered with the research result that people tend to regard even contradictory research results as obvious. Perhaps even that result will henceforth be regarded as obvious.

NOTES

This article is based in part on the Maycie K. Southall lecture at George Peabody College, Vanderbilt University, on February 27, 1990.

I am grateful to my daughter, Sarah Gage, for calling the Murphy (1990) article to my attention.

REFERENCES

Baratz, D. (1983). How justified is the "obvious" reaction. *Dissertation Abstracts International, 44/02B*, 644B. (University Microfilms No. DA 8314435.)

Conant, J. B. (1963). *The education of American teachers.* New York: McGraw-Hill.

Ericsson, K. A., & Simon, H. A. (1980). Verbal reports as data. *Psychological Review, 87,* 215–251.

Gage, N. L. (1989). The paradigm wars and their aftermath: A "historical" sketch of research on teaching since 1989. *Teachers College Record, 91,* 135–150.

Glass, G. V. (1987). Class size. In M. J. Dunkin (Ed.), *The international encyclopedia of teaching and teacher education* (pp. 540–545). Oxford: Pergamon.

Goodlad, J. I. (1960). Classroom organization. In C. W. Harris (Ed.), *Encyclopedia of educational research* (3rd ed., p. 224). New York: Macmillan.

Keppel, F. (1962). The education of teachers. In H. Chauncey (Ed.), *Talks on American education: A series of broadcasts to foreign audiences by American scholars* (pp. 83–94). New York: Bureau of Publications, Teachers College, Columbia University.

Lazarsfeld, P. F. (1949). *The American soldier* – an expository review. *Public Opinion Quarterly, 13,* 377–404.

Mischel, W. (1981). Metacognition and the rules of delay. In J. H. Flavell & L. Ross (Eds.), *Social cognitive development: Frontiers and possible futures.* New York: Cambridge University Press.

Mischel, W., & Mischel, H. (1979). *Children's knowledge of psychological principles.* Unpublished manuscript.

Murphy, C. (1990). New findings: Hold on to your hat. *The Atlantic, 265*(6), 22–23.

Nisbett, R. E., & Wilson, T. D. (1977). Telling more than we can know: Verbal reports on mental processes. *Psychological Review, 84,* 231–259.

Phillips, D. C. (1985) The uses and abuses of truisms. In C. W. Fisher & D. C. Berliner (Eds.), *Perspectives on instructional time* (pp. 309–316). New York: Longman.

Rice, J. M. (1913). *Scientific management in education.* New York: Hinds, Noble & Eldredge. (Original work published 1897)

Schlesinger, Jr., A. (1949). The statistical soldier. *Partisan Review, 16,* 852–856.

Snow, C. P. (1964). *The two cultures: And a second look.* New York: Cambridge University Press.

Walberg, H. J. (1986). Syntheses of research on teaching. In M. C. Wittrock (Ed.), *Handbook of research on teaching* (3rd ed., pp. 214–229). New York: Macmillan.

Wittrock, M. C. (Ed.). (1986). *Handbook of research on teaching* (3rd ed.). New York: Macmillan.

Wong, L. (1987). Reaction to research findings: Is the feeling of obviousness warranted? *Dissertation Abstracts International, 48/12,* 3709B. (University Microfilms No. DA 8801059.)

INDEX